CHINA'S 40 YEARS OF REFORM AND DEVELOPMENT

1978–2018

Other titles in the China Update Book Series include:

1999 China: Twenty Years of Economic Reform
2002 China: WTO Entry and World Recession
2003 China: New Engine of World Growth
2004 China: Is Rapid Growth Sustainable?
2005 The China Boom and its Discontents
2006 China: The Turning Point in China's Economic Development
2007 China: Linking Markets for Growth
2008 China's Dilemma: Economic Growth, the Environment and Climate Change
2009 China's New Place in a World of Crisis
2010 China: The Next Twenty Years of Reform and Development
2011 Rising China: Global Challenges and Opportunities
2012 Rebalancing and Sustaining Growth in China
2013 China: A New Model for Growth and Development
2014 Deepening Reform for China's Long-Term Growth and Development
2015 China's Domestic Transformation in a Global Context
2016 China's New Sources of Economic Growth: Vol. 1
2017 China's New Sources of Economic Growth: Vol. 2

The titles are available online at press.anu.edu.au/publications/series/china-update-series

CHINA'S 40 YEARS OF REFORM AND DEVELOPMENT
1978–2018

Edited by Ross Garnaut,
Ligang Song and Cai Fang

Australian National University
PRESS

社会科学文献出版社
SOCIAL SCIENCES ACADEMIC PRESS (CHINA)

Published by ANU Press
The Australian National University
Acton ACT 2601, Australia
Email: anupress@anu.edu.au

Available to download for free at press.anu.edu.au

ISBN (print): 9781760462246
ISBN (online): 9781760462253

WorldCat (print): 1042816554
WorldCat (online): 1042816575

DOI: 10.22459/CYRD.07.2018

Cover design and layout by ANU Press

Contents

Part V: Trade, investment and global integration

Figures

Tables

Contributors

Chunlai Chen, The Australian National University

Gregory C. Chow, Princeton University

David Dollar, The Brookings Institution

Peter Drysdale, The Australian National University

Cai Fang, Chinese Academy of Social Sciences

Fan Gang, National Economy Research Institute

Kailin Gao, Peking University

Ross Garnaut, University of Melbourne

Bob Gregory, The Australian National University

Samuel Hardwick, The Australian National University

Bert Hofman, World Bank

Biliang Hu, Beijing Normal University

Jikun Huang, Peking University

Yiping Huang, Peking University

Wei Jiang, Southwestern University of Finance and Economics

Zhang Jun, Fudan University

Gerard Kelly, Reserve Bank of Australia

Nicholas Lardy, Peterson Institute for International Economics

Kunwang Li, Nankai University

Justin Yifu Lin, Peking University

Shouying Liu, Renmin University of China

Wei Liu, Renmin University of China

Guangrong Ma, Renmin University of China

Guonan Ma, University of Macau

Xin Meng, The Australian National University

Barry Naughton, University of California (San Diego)

Jiahua Pan, Chinese Academy of Social Sciences

Dwight H. Perkins, Harvard University

Ivan Roberts, Reserve Bank of Australia

Scott Rozelle, Stanford University

Zhongkai Shen, Peking University

Ligang Song, The Australian National University

Bijun Wang, Chinese Academy of Social Sciences

Xiaolu Wang, National Economy Research Institute

Xun Wang, Peking University

Christine Wong, University of Melbourne

Wing Thye Woo, University of California (Davis)

Yang Yao, Peking University

Yongding Yu, Chinese Academy of Social Sciences

Kunling Zhang, Beijing Normal University

ZhongXiang Zhang, Tianjin University

Acknowledgements

The China Economy Program (CEP) at the Crawford School of Public Policy of The Australian National University (ANU) acknowledges the financial support for the China Update 2018 provided by the ANU China initiative. We thank the program support and editing assistance provided by Dr Elizabeth Buchanan and our colleagues from the East Asia Forum at The Australian National University. The China Update 2018 marks 40 years of China's economic reform and 20 years of CEP research. We sincerely thank our contributors around the world for their valuable contributions to the book series and update events throughout these years. Thanks also to the ANU Press, notably Emily Hazlewood, and copyeditor Jan Borrie for their expeditious publication of the book series. We thank the Social Sciences Academic Press (China) of the Chinese Academy of Social Sciences in Beijing for translating and publishing the Chinese version of the book each year—making this valuable research available to a wider readership.

Abbreviations

ABC	Agricultural Bank of China
AIIB	Asian Infrastructure Investment Bank
AMC	asset management company
APEC	Asia-Pacific Economic Cooperation
AREAER	*Annual Report on Exchange Rate Arrangements and Exchange Restrictions*
ASEAN	Association of Southeast Asian Nations
ASEAN+3	Association of Southeast Asian Nations Plus Three
BIS	Bank for International Settlements
BOC	Bank of China
BRI	Belt and Road Initiative
CA	current account
CAP	collective action plan
CASS	Chinese Academy of Social Sciences
CBIRC	China Banking and Insurance Regulatory Commission
CBRC	China Banking Regulatory Commission
CCB	China Construction Bank (People's Construction Bank of China)
CCCP	Central Committee of the Communist Party
CEO	chief executive officer
CFETS	China Foreign Exchange Trade System
CFIUS	Committee on Foreign Investment in the United States
CIRC	China Insurance Regulatory Commission
CMA	China Meteorological Administration
Comecon	Council for Mutual Economic Assistance
CoVaR	conditional value-at-risk
CPC	Communist Party of China
CPI	consumer price index
CPTPP	Comprehensive and Progressive Agreement for Trans-Pacific Partnership
CSRC	China Securities Regulatory Commission
DRC	Development Research Center

EBRD	European Bank for Reconstruction and Development
ESOP	Employee stock ownership program
FDI	foreign direct investment
FGD	flue-gas desulfurisation
FPA	farmers professional association
FSDC	Financial Stability and Development Committee
FTA	free trade agreement
FTAAP	Free Trade Area of Asia and the Pacific
FTC	foreign trade corporation
GATS	General Agreement on Trade in Services
GATT	General Agreement on Tariffs and Trade
GCF	gross capital formation
GDP	gross domestic product
GFC	Global Financial Crisis
GFRS	government financial reporting system
GFS	Government Financial Statistics
GIO	gross industrial output
GNI	gross national income
GNP	gross national product
GW	gigawatt
HCS	household contract system
HMT	Hong Kong, Macau and Taiwan
HRS	household responsibility system
HSR	high-speed rail
hukou	household registration system
IAP	individual action plan
ICBC	Industrial and Commercial Bank of China
ICOR	incremental capital–output ratio
IECFR	Index of Effectiveness of China's Financial Regulation
ILO	International Labour Organization
IMF	International Monetary Fund
IPO	initial public offering
IPSAS	International Public Sector Accounting Standards
IRENA	International Renewable Energy Agency

ISFRC	Index of Systemic Financial Risk in China
KA	capital account
KORUS FTA	United States–Korea Free Trade Agreement
kWh	kilowatt hour
LGFV	local government financial vehicle
LLC	limited liability company
LNG	liquefied natural gas
LSG	Leadership Small Group
M&A	merger and acquisition
M2	money supply
MC-25	'Made in China 2025'
MES	marginal expected loss
MFN	most favoured nation
MIIT	Ministry of Industry and Information Technology
MOF	Ministry of Finance
MOFCOM	Ministry of Commerce
MW	megawatt
NAO	National Audit Office
NBS	National Bureau of Statistics
NDRC	National Development and Reform Commission
NPC	National People's Congress
NPL	nonperforming loan
NUI	New Urbanisation Index
ODI	outward direct investment
OECD	Organisation for Economic Co-operation and Development
OLI	'ownership advantage, location advantage and internalisation advantage'
PBC	People's Bank of China
PFM	public financial management
PICC	People's Insurance Company of China
PLA	People's Liberation Army
PPP	purchasing power parity
PRC	People's Republic of China
QR	quantitative restriction

R&D	research and development
RCEP	Regional Comprehensive Economic Partnership
ROA	returns on assets
ROE	returns on equity
ROFA	returns on fixed assets
RUMiC	Rural–Urban Migration in China survey
S&T	science and technology
SAFE	State Administration of Foreign Exchange
SASAC	State-owned Assets Supervision and Administration Commission
SCE	state-controlled enterprise
SCIO	state capital investment and operations company
SDR	Special Drawing Rights
SEZ	special economic zone
SME	small and medium-sized enterprise
SNA	System of National Accounts
SOB	state-owned bank
SOE	state-owned enterprise
SOME	stated-owned mining enterprise
SRC	Systems Reform Commission
SSSR	supply-side structural reform
STEM	science, technology, engineering and mathematics
TFP	total factor productivity
TFR	total fertility rate
THAAD	Terminal High Altitude Area Defense
TI	Transparency International
TISA	Trade in Services Agreement
TPP	Trans-Pacific Partnership
TRIM	Agreement on Trade-Related Investment Measures
TRIPS	Agreement on Trade-Related Aspects of Intellectual Property Rights
TSP	temporary storage program
TTIP	Transatlantic Trade and Investment Partnership
TVE	township and village enterprise
UDIC	urban development and infrastructure company

UN	United Nations
UNCED	UN Conference on Environment and Development
UNCTAD	United Nations Conference on Trade and Development
UNFCCC	United Nations Framework Convention on Climate Change
US	United States
USTR	United States Trade Representative
VAT	value-added tax
WTO	World Trade Organization

Introduction

To mark 40 years of reform and development in China (1978–2018), this book brings together the work of many of the world's leading scholars on the Chinese economy. In 31 separate contributions, they reflect and present views on policy reform, economic growth and structural change over four fateful decades. These were years in which China moved from being a poor, backward country to achieving living standards above the world average and now approaching those of the high-income countries. Over these four decades, China moved from near economic isolation to be the world's largest trading economy.

China's economic reform and opening to the international economy began with the decisions of the third plenary meeting of the eleventh Central Committee of the Communist Party of China (CPC) in 1978. To mark the twentieth anniversary of reform, two of the authors (Ross Garnaut and Ligang Song) organised a conference at The Australian National University, the papers from which were published in 1999 by Asia Pacific Press as *China: Twenty years of economic reform.*

There was great interest in the conference and the book, and we repeated the proceedings two years later, and then every year thereafter. We adopted the bracing practice of having the book published by ANU Press each year for release on the eve of the conference. This meant it could be discussed in a timely way when we were all together. From 2007, we were joined in the enterprise by the Chinese Academy of Social Sciences, with a Chinese-language version of the book published by China's Social Sciences Academic Press (SSAP) and released in a separate seminar in China every year since then. ANU Press jointly published the Update books with the Brookings Institution Press and launched the books in Washington for three years in 2008, 2009 and 2010. Since 2010, the University of Melbourne has joined in a three-way collaboration, and we have added a Melbourne conference to the schedule each year. We thank other colleagues who joined us in co-editing the Update books throughout these years. They are Wing Thye Woo (2008 and 2009), Jane Golley (2010 and 2011), Huw McKay (2012) and Lauren Johnston (2015, 2016 and 2017). ANU Press has been a pioneer of online publications, and the China Update book series has reached wide readership globally through its open-access system.

So, a Chinese and international network of scholars of the Chinese economy has been examining closely and publishing on Chinese economic reform, development and structural change for 20 years.

Over the two decades, we have published important contributions drawn from the latest authoritative research from leading economists in China, Australia, the United States and other countries. Many of these authors have joined us in this fortieth anniversary issue of the book.

The contributors to this volume discuss, from differing perspectives, the origins, content, consequences and future of reform. The 31 chapters explore what has happened in the transformation of the Chinese economy and how that has affected the world economy. They discuss an unfinished agenda for reform. They draw lessons for the future from the experience of the four preceding decades. They begin to sketch what the world can expect in China's fifth decade of reform and development.

Part one contains eight chapters providing general interpretations of the reform experience by deeply experienced and well-known scholars who have been closely engaged in analysing, interpreting and explaining the Chinese experience of reform for all of its 40 years (Gregory C. Chow, Dwight H. Perkins, Ross Garnaut), for most of those years (Cai Fang, Ligang Song, Liu Wei, Yang Yao and Justin Yifu Lin and Zhongkai Shen) or through periods as a senior World Bank official in China (David Dollar and Bert Hofman). Each looks at the history through a personal lens. Inevitably, there is some overlap in the matters covered. We think the different interpretations of similar issues enrich the whole. For example, on the most fundamental of historical questions, Chow presents reasons why China's circumstances made reform inevitable in 1978, while Garnaut emphasises the role of human agency—the decisions taken by leaders at critical times that shaped subsequent developments.

Part two contains 11 chapters on reform and development relating to major economic issues, policy instruments or institutions. Each of the authors is an authority on the issues covered—Xiaolu Wang on macroeconomic development, Guonan Ma, Ivan Roberts and Gerard Kelly on growth and restructuring, Zhang Jun on price system reform, Fan Gang, Guangrong Ma and Xiaolu Wang on the process of marketisation, Christine Wong on the fiscal system, Cai Fang on demographic change, Yiping Huang and Xun Wang on banking reform, Yongding Yu on foreign exchange reform, Nicholas Lardy on private sector development, Ligang Song on the experience of state-owned enterprise (SOE) reform and Barry Naughton on the remaining agenda for SOE reform.

Part three contains four chapters on how the relationship between rural (at first mainly agricultural) and urban China has developed through the reform period, by scholars who are recognised for their work over several decades on the subject: Bob Gregory and Xin Meng on migration, Shouying Liu on land reform, Biliang Hu and Kunling Zhang on urbanisation and Jikun Huang and Scott Rozelle on agriculture.

Part four contains two chapters describing the most evident and perhaps most consequential changes from China's new model of growth, adopted and partially implemented in the fourth decade of reform: ZhongXiang Zhang on energy, highlighting the transition to low-carbon technologies, and Jiahua Pan on climate change.

Part five presents five chapters on different aspects of China's deepening interaction with the global economy over the past four decades: Peter Drysdale and Samuel Hardwick broadly on integration into the international economy, Kunwang Li and Wei Jiang on trade, Chunlai Chen on inbound investment and Bijun Wang and Kailin Gao on outbound investment, and Wing Thye Woo on the evolving China's external economic disputes with the United States and possible solutions.

We are aware that the whole is an eclectic treatment of the complex reality of Chinese reform and development over the past 40 years. Most readers will want to dip into chapters covering matters in which they are particularly interested rather than reading the whole volume from cover to cover. We are confident there is much of interest to people everywhere who are interested in the whole human experience of modern economic development, as well as in the remarkable manifestation of the phenomenon over the past four decades in the world's most populous country.

Ross Garnaut, University of Melbourne
Ligang Song, The Australian National University
Cai Fang, The Chinese Academy of Social Sciences

Melbourne, Canberra and Beijing, 19 July 2018

1. 40 years of China's reform and development: How reform captured China's demographic dividend

Cai Fang, Ross Garnaut and Ligang Song[1]

China's reform, opening-up and resultant economic growth in the past 40 years provide a new constellation of experience we can study to understand the nature of modern economic growth. This chapter describes the process of reform and opening-up of the economy, and its nexus to accelerated economic growth. It describes and provides some data on the experience of trade and growth over the past 40 years. It sketches some of the main elements of reform, changes in incentives that have driven economic growth, changes in economic structure that have followed and the rising role of China in the global economy. It highlights new challenges that China faces after 40 years of reform.

Introduction

The eleventh Central Committee of the Communist Party of China (CPC) held its third plenum from 18 to 22 December 1978. This meeting reestablished an older CPC ideological line of 'seeking truth from facts'. It decided to shift the focus from political movement to economic development. This laid the foundation for reform and opening-up.

In the winter of the same year, Xiaogang, one of the poorest villages in Fengyang county in Anhui province, abandoned its collective brigade production structure and became the pioneer for contracting collectively owned land to households. Such a practice—later known as the household responsibility system (HRS)—spread nationwide in the early 1980s and replaced the people's commune system that had existed for a quarter of a century. This was the first break in the planned economy.

China initiated the change from central planning to mainly market exchange simultaneously with opening up to international trade and investment. Domestic economic development and participation in economic globalisation have marched forward hand in hand.[2]

1 We thank Xiaoying Wang for her help in assembling the data for most of the figures used in this chapter.

2 The International Monetary Fund (IMF 2006: 4) considered 1979 the start year for China's economic take-off.

Deng Xiaoping was a source of, sponsor within the party for and, for two decades, the protector of China's reform and opening-up policy. In July 1979, under Deng's influence, the central government decided to establish 'special export zones', later called special economic zones (SEZs), in Shenzhen, Zhuhai and Shantou in Guangdong province and Xiamen in Fujian province. This signalled the start of China's opening to the outside world.

This experiment was extended to 14 large cities in coastal areas in 1984, the newly established province of Hainan in 1988, and a host of cities along the Yangtze River and interior border cities in the early 1990s. These domestic steps to open to the international economy were extended to global institutions with China's application to resume the status of a contracting party to the General Agreement on Tariffs and Trade (GATT) in 1986 and its accession to the World Trade Organization (WTO) in 2001.

China's reforms are 40 years old. The Master said: 'At 40, I perceived truth and doubts ceased.'[3] A wealth of empirical materials accumulated over 40 years confirms the wisdom of internationally oriented market reform and helps us to draw theory from experience to guide future reform.

China's reform and opening-up is in the process of delivering to 1.4 billion Chinese people the fruits of the most consequential socioeconomic change and institutional innovation in human history. If it is able to maintain momentum in reform at a more challenging time, it is likely to deliver high-income status to the Chinese people by the early 2020s—more than doubling the number of people living in countries with that status (Figures 1.1 and 1.2).

China's reform and opening-up has both universal and unique features.

This chapter seeks to answer the following questions: How and why did China miss the opportunity of catching up with the developed countries during its planned economy era? How was China's economic growth enhanced by removal of institutional constraints, factor accumulation and improvements in resource allocation? At the current stage of China's development, with upper-middle incomes, what new approaches are required for China's growth engine to gain new momentum, and to drive China into the ranks of the high-income countries?

3 This is an oft-recounted quotation in *Confucian Analects*; the English translation is quoted from Jin (2005: 4).

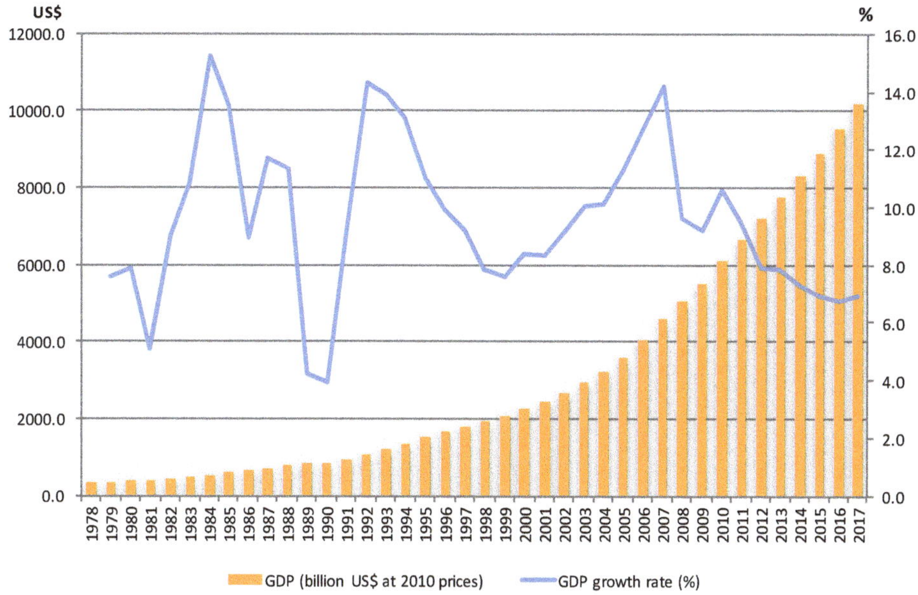

Figure 1.1 China's GDP (LHS) and growth rate (RHS), 1978–2017

Sources: UNCTAD Statistics (unctadstat.unctad.org/EN/).

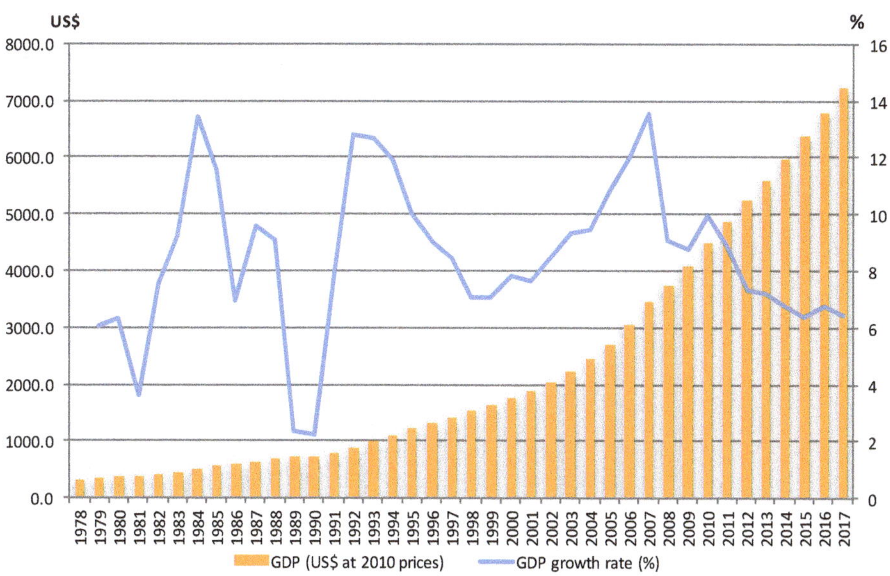

Figure 1.2 China's GDP per capita (LHS) and growth rate (RHS), 1978–2017

Sources: UNCTAD Statistics (unctadstat.unctad.org/EN/).

Missed opportunity of convergence in the planning era

In 1980, China ranked near the lowest in the world in gross national income per capita. It ranked much higher in terms of major human capital indices, and about the middle for average years of schooling for the population aged 25 and older and for life expectancy at birth (Cai 2015a: 40).

Although per capita income was very low, the capital stock and rate of capital accumulation were much higher, and China had demonstrated strong capacity to mobilise capital. In the period 1953–78, the average investment rate was 29.5 per cent—significantly higher than the world average and most developing economies (Lin et al. 2003: 71–4).

The planned economy lacked the necessary institutional conditions for efficient resource allocation and work incentives. Cross-nation studies and China's experience show that rejection of the market mechanism under planning causes inefficiency in resource allocation. Lack of autonomy in business decisions and lack of incentives depress work effort.

Through the planning period, high rates of capital accumulation and rapid increases in the labour force did not lead to commensurate rates of economic growth because productivity performance was low. Resource misallocation distorted the industrial structure. Appropriate technology was not applied in economic activity.

Through the early years of the People's Republic of China and the planning system, beginning in the early 1950s, China moved from the demographic combination of a high birth rate, high mortality rate and low population growth to one of a high birth rate, low mortality rate and high population growth. The latter state, with rapid growth of the population and labour force, has often been part of a process of economic involution.[4] The result has been a dual economy characterised by a labour surplus in agriculture (Lewis 1954).

In the late 1960s, fertility began to decline, bringing down population growth. Population conditions more conducive to economic growth—with a potential demographic dividend—emerged. The accumulated labour surplus provided potential comparative advantage in the production of labour-intensive goods and services. The demographic dividend would magnify the benefits. Linked with open international trade, this could have spurred high-speed economic growth.

4 Economic history shows that near the end of the Malthusian poverty trap as a stage of development, many countries began to experience a process of economic involution characterised by accumulation of massive surplus labour in agriculture, followed by entry to the stage of dual-economy development conceptualised by Lewis (1954).

This opportunity was not taken, because a comparative advantage–defying rather than a comparative advantage–following strategy was adopted.[5]

China sought to promote industrialisation and to catch up with the advanced countries by mobilising resources and allocating them through central planning without international trade.

China's planned system had three elements: the macropolicy environment, planned resource allocation and micromanagement institutions (Lin et al. 2003). The development strategy gave impetus to industrialisation, but the economic system that emerged had severe defects.

The macropolicy environment gave priority to heavy industry in the hope of speeding up capital accumulation and industrialisation. The industrial structure deviated far from China's comparative advantage and a disproportionate part of output was allocated to investment rather than to consumption.

The highly centralised planning system denied a role for markets. It was suitable for implementing the economic plan, but led to an imbalance between the supply of and demand for products and a failure to allocate resources to their most valuable uses. Total factor productivity (TFP) declined and dragged down economic growth.

Micromanagement institutions characterised by nationalisation of industry and collectivisation of agriculture were arranged to carry out the national plan and match the planning system. Lacking operational autonomy and work incentives, the production units—state-owned enterprises (SOEs) and people's communes—operated extremely inefficiently. This contributed to the decline in TFP.

The Chinese economy in the planning period was almost completely isolated from the world economy. In 1978, the share of exports plus imports in gross domestic product (GDP) was only 9.7 per cent. Primary products (agricultural products and raw materials) contributed more than half of the low level of exports. There was no direct investment. Maddison (2007: 102) estimates the annual average growth rate of GDP in the period 1952–78 was 4.4 per cent in purchasing power parity (PPP) terms. This was below the average for developing countries.

Spence (2011: Pt 1) argues that the global economy started an era of convergence about 1950. Since the 1950s, a number of initially poor economies have caught up with the developed countries. Maddison's data show that in the period 1952–78, the annual GDP growth rate was 4.3 per cent in the rich countries, 4.9 per cent in 'others' and 4.6 per cent for the world average.

5 For the definition of the two contrasting strategies, see Lin and Wang (2010); for analysis of the adoption of the Chinese strategy in the late 1950s, see Lin et al. (2003).

China's relative performance was worse in per capita terms, because its population growth was higher. In 1952, China's per capita GDP was US$538 in 1990 prices. This was 8.7 per cent of the average of the rich countries, 46.5 per cent of the 'others' and 23.8 per cent of the world average. By 1978, China's per capita GDP (US$978 at constant price) had fallen as a percentage of each of those three groups, to 6.8 per cent, 42.1 per cent and 22.1 per cent, respectively.

We can conclude that in the first three decades of the People's Republic, China not only missed the chance to catch up with the developed countries, but also fell further behind the rest of the world.

Let us examine how the planned economy led to inefficient resource allocation.

In 1952, 82.5 per cent of the labour force worked in agriculture. That was potentially a source of surplus labour for modern economic development.

In the mid-1960s, the population dependency ratio—the ratio of the working aged to the dependent population—began to fall, overwhelmingly from the decline in the proportion of people younger than working age. From this time, China enjoyed a demographic dividend that theoretically could have been translated into accelerated economic growth.

The Lewis model and its application to developing countries (Lewis 1954; Cai 2016) show that an abundant labour force not only delivers labour supply, but also helps to maintain a high savings rate, avoids diminishing returns to capital and raises allocative efficiency as labour is transferred from agriculture to other sectors. The planning model stopped China from enjoying all these benefits. The share of agricultural labour was still 74.5 per cent in 1977.

Zhu (2012) has developed a lower estimate than Maddison of average GDP growth: 2.97 per cent in the period 1952–78. The labour force grew at 3.63 per cent, and increases in capital stock and human capital made large positive contributions. The decline in TFP dragged growth down by 72 per cent from what it would otherwise have been.

The 'Great Leap Forward' and the Cultural Revolution were the most disastrous episodes during the planning period. We can presume that losses during these catastrophes contributed much of the underperformance of the planning period, although the extent of the contribution is difficult to estimate. Kwan and Chow (1996) attempt an estimate.

Impact of reform and opening-up

Adequate capital accumulation and efficient allocation of physical and human capital are prerequisites for successful economic development. Reform of a planned economic system to provide these prerequisites requires at least three conditions to be met. First, the reform should bring benefits to at least one major group of participants, to provide political support. Second, these benefits cannot be at the expense of any other substantial groups in society—that is, the reform has to deliver a 'Pareto improvement'. Third, the reform should start in a key area to transmit its momentum to other areas of the system.

The early reforms in rural China characterised by the introduction of the HRS and the abolition of the people's communes met these conditions rather perfectly. The HRS was at first accepted for individual cases and, as early as the late 1970s, was piloted in some poor, remote areas and eventually encouraged nationwide by the central government. By the end of 1984, all production brigades and 98 per cent of households in rural China had adopted the HRS. The people's commune system was officially abolished at this time. This reform immediately improved incentives for agricultural production by granting farmers autonomy over operations and rights to profits from more efficient use of their land and labour, which gave them incentives to raise productivity.

In the period 1978–84—the years of transition from the people's communes to the HRS—grain yield per unit area increased by 42.8 per cent, total output of grain increased by 33.6 per cent and real agricultural value added increased by 52.6 per cent. Lin (1992) shows that 46.9 per cent of the increase in agricultural output can be attributed to the HRS. The jump in agricultural production mitigated the shortage of urban supply and gradually laid the foundations for the abolition of the rationing system in the early 1990s.

In the same period, the nominal average income of farm households increased by 166 per cent. The number of rural residents living in absolute poverty dropped from 250 million to 128 million, with the poverty line rising from RMB100 to RMB200 (Cai 2015a: 4).

Figure 1.3 presents the data as to how the share of the population in poverty has been falling consistently through the reform period.

Similar reforms on a different timetable and with greater difficulty were implemented in urban areas. A system of bonuses for employees was introduced in SOEs in 1978, which aimed to align incentives for employees with enterprise performance. This was followed by the state granting autonomy to and sharing profits with enterprises.

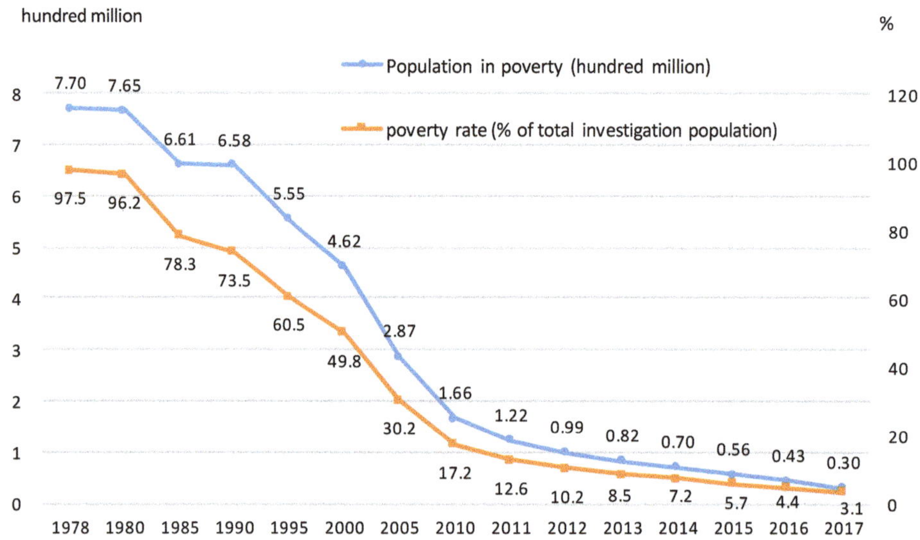

Figure 1.3 China's poverty population (hundred million), 1978–2017

Sources: State Council Information Office (2016); National Bureau of Statistics (NBS various years).

SOE reform as the core of urban reform has had several threads (Garnaut et al. 2006). One related to making SOEs viable market players, and began with the expansion of enterprises' autonomy, building up to corporatisation. Granting autonomy to enterprises began with pilot programs in some cities in the late 1970s. It was quickly extended to more regions, and then to the whole country in the early 1980s. Simplification of government controls on enterprises and delegation of authority followed through the 1980s. SOEs achieved management autonomy on setting wages and bonuses, hiring and firing workers, purchasing and selling goods and services, pricing products and utilising their own cash flows for investment.

Experiments were conducted with a variety of management forms, including managers' responsibility, enterprise contracts, asset leasing and shareholding systems. In the late 1990s, a more radical measure was introduced: 'grasping the large, letting go of the small'. This involved corporatising large SOEs based on modern enterprise management principles and privatising small and medium-sized enterprises.

A second thread involved redefining the relationship between SOEs and government. Early reform in this area featured the state sharing profits with enterprises through a host of measures aimed at introducing market discipline and accountability.

In 1988, the State Council established the State-owned Assets Administration Bureau, which was renamed the State-owned Assets Supervision and Administration Commission (SASAC) in 2003. SASAC, on behalf of the state, is responsible for supervising the central government's nonfinancial state enterprises. Similar organisations were established at the local level to supervise state assets owned by local governments.

The third thread was the introduction and then encouragement of nonstate enterprises (Garnaut et al. 2001). Property rights and governance structures were reformed to allow a wider range of nonstate enterprises. Competition between enterprises with different kinds of ownership and the introduction of mixed ownership of enterprises helped to increase the efficiency of SOEs.

There is now considerable competition between enterprises with different forms of ownership. In 2015, of the revenue from businesses with annual revenue of RMB20 million or more, only 4.1 per cent was generated by those registered as SOEs. The rest was generated by enterprises with 29 other kinds of ownership, including private individuals and partnerships, limited liability corporations, foreign-funded enterprises and joint ventures between Chinese and foreign enterprises.

The gradual introduction of profit-based incentives for business units in and outside agriculture has increased the importance of getting prices right. Having prices reflect true economic value is necessary for efficient resource allocation in a market economy. Enterprise reform therefore requires effective markets for setting prices for factors of production, goods and services. Transitions in markets for capital, labour, goods and services were all achieved through a 'double-track approach'. For a while, market and state-determined prices existed alongside each other. Over time, the role of market prices expanded and that of planned prices declined.

Reforms in other areas have been, by and large, carried out around these main threads. Problems arising from the process of reform and development have been dealt with pragmatically as they have arisen.

The overall direction is for the roles of central and local governments to be gradually transformed from direct involvement in economic activities to promoting equity and broadly based development through providing basic public services. Around this general direction of change, there has been a tendency for local governments to compete fervidly with one another in pursuing growth of GDP and public revenue.

This last characteristic of entrepreneurial government, while running against the general objectives of reform, has provided powerful impetus to economic growth. It has also led to overinvolvement of government in directly allocating resources, which has impeded the role of market forces (Chu and Song 2015). Since the beginning of the second decade of the twenty-first century, the Chinese Government has asserted a stronger commitment to providing public goods, including basic education, social protection, market regulations and macroeconomic policies, rather than directly participating in business activity.

China's opening up to the international economy has proceeded in parallel with domestic reform. China has benefited in many ways from expanding imports and exports (Figure 1.4), attracting foreign investment, investing overseas and participating in global governance. Interaction with the international economy has helped Chinese enterprises to adopt advanced technologies and management and, more generally, to become more competitive through exposure to world-class competition. It has allowed China to translate the demographic dividend into massive gains from trade.

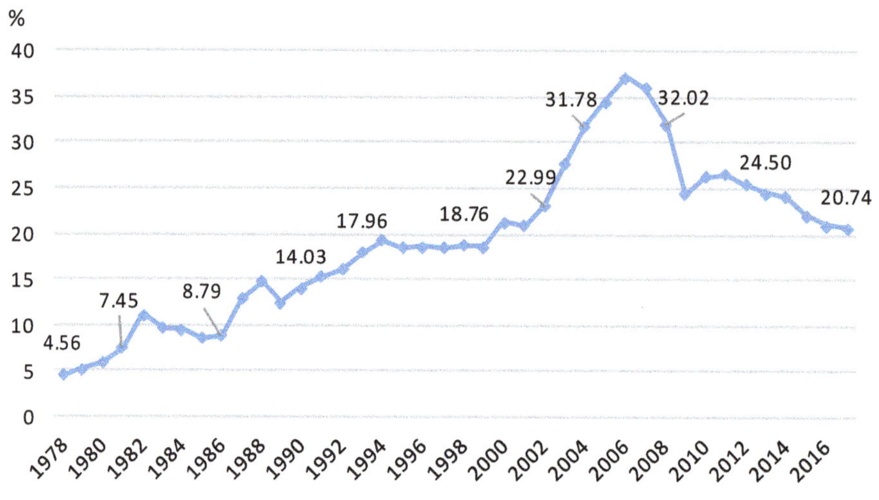

Figure 1.4 China's export share of GDP, 1978–2017
Source: IMF (2018).

Impact of demographic dividend

The demographic dividend emerges when growth in the working-age population exceeds that of the dependent population. Figure 1.5 shows that, in China, the population window of opportunity coincided with the first three-and-a-half decades of reform and opening-up. The demographic dividend began to withdraw a few years ago.

The low and declining dependency ratio, while it persisted, contributed to China's distinctive high growth rate beyond the direct influence of a high rate of growth in the labour force. It also contributed to the high savings rate. The abundant supply of labour from the countryside delays the onset of diminishing returns to capital and, by so doing, makes capital accumulation a main engine of economic growth.

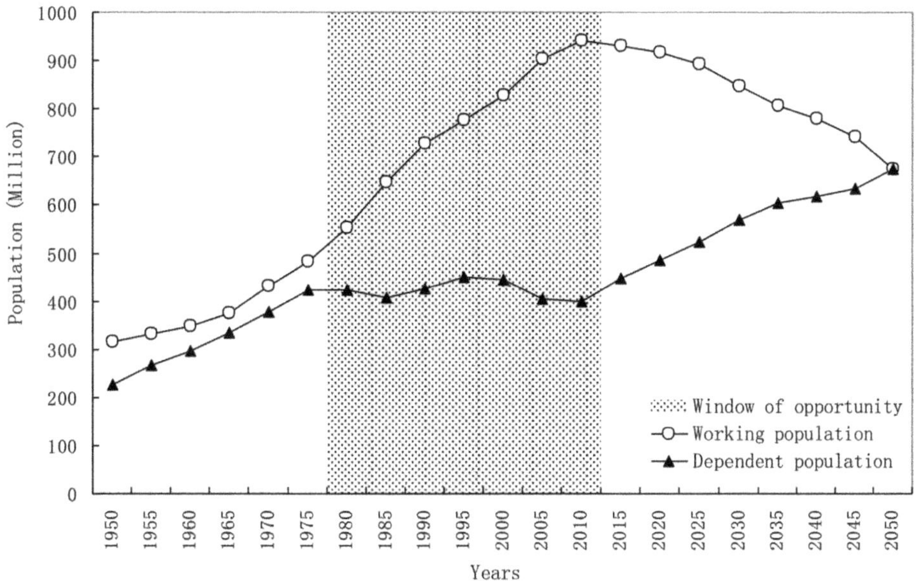

Figure 1.5 Changing trend of age structure and population window of opportunity

Source: UN DESA (2015).

Through most of China's reform period, returns to capital remained extraordinarily high (Bai et al. 2006). After the Lewis turning point characterised by labour shortage and wage inflation,[6] returns to capital have rapidly diminished (Lewis 1954; Bai and Zhang 2014).

An abundant supply of labour has been widely recognised as a favourable factor for rapid growth of a developing country when it is catching up with the global frontiers. Less well understood is that improvement of human capital in the less-developed countries is greatly assisted by a favourable age structure of the population. This increases the availability of education—expressed as years of schooling—for the average new entrant to the labour market (see Cai et al. 2016).

The World Bank (1998) estimated the contribution of labour inputs to GDP growth—measured in terms of both quantity and quality—to be 17 per cent. Cai and Zhao (2012) estimated the labour contribution to be 8 per cent and human capital 4 per cent. Whalley and Zhao (2010) estimated the direct and indirect contribution of human capital to be as high as 38 per cent.

Labour mobility from lower to higher productivity uses—between rural and urban areas, among sectors and among regions—contributes significantly to TFP growth by increasing allocative efficiency. Cai (2017) found that labour productivity

6 For discussions on China's arrival at the Lewis turning point, see Cai (2015b).

growth in the period 1978–2015 can be decomposed into 55.1 per cent from improved performance within each sector (primary, secondary and tertiary), with the balance from intersectoral movement of labour.

The World Bank (1998) divided TFP growth in China into increased intersectoral efficiency and a residual. It found that the former—namely, productivity growth resulting from labour movement from lower productivity sectors (agriculture and SOEs) to higher productivity sectors (nonagricultural sectors and newly established enterprises)—contributed 16 per cent of the GDP growth in the period 1978–95. Cai and Wang (1999) found that the labour transfer from agricultural to nonagricultural sectors constituted the majority of TFP growth and 21 per cent of per capita GDP growth in the period 1978–98 (Figure 1.6).

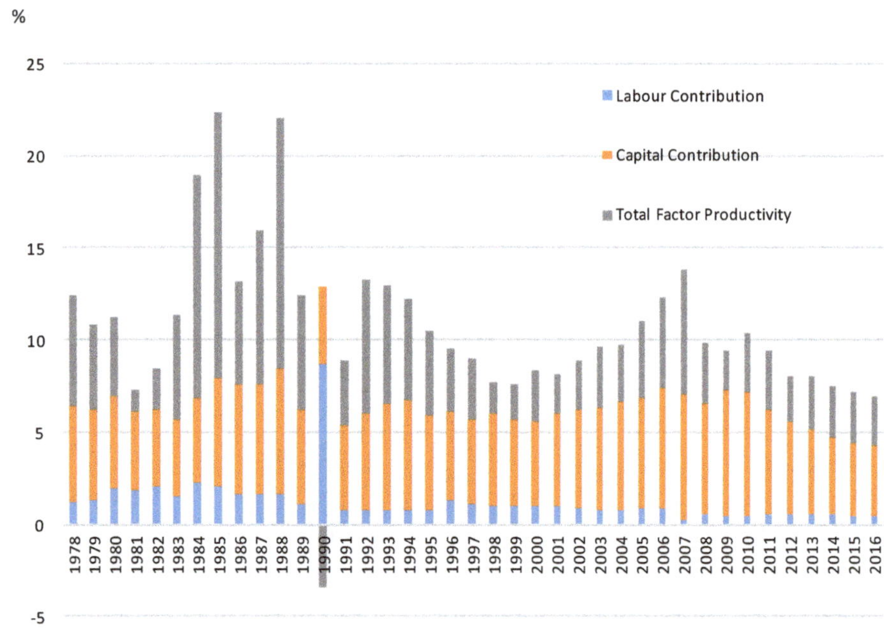

Figure 1.6 China's GDP growth decomposition, 1978–2017
Source: The Conference Board (2018).

Some scholars have taken the dependency ratio as a proxy variable to estimate the demographic dividend's contribution to China's economic growth. Wang and Mason (2008) estimated the dependency ratio contributed 15 per cent of economic growth in the period 1982–2000, while Cai and Zhao (2012) estimated it contributed 27 per cent in the same period.

These empirical findings suggest that the outstanding performance of the Chinese economy has been the result of reform and opening-up cashing in on advantageous demographic and other underlying conditions. Cai and Lu (2013) estimated that the potential GDP growth rate was 9.7 per cent in the period 1979–95 and 10.4 per cent in 1997–2010.

Cai (2017) estimated that while total employment in rural and urban areas increased from 402 million in 1978 to 775 million in 2015, the share of agricultural labour dropped from 69.6 per cent to 18.3 per cent.

Strong employment growth spreads the improvement in living standards. Despite a widening income gap in most of the reform period, three effects have helped to disperse the results of reform, opening-up and growth, and so helped to win the legitimacy of that reform and opening-up.

First is the increase in employment. The expansion of labour-intensive industries created numerous jobs outside agriculture. In the period 1978–2015, while GDP and per capita GDP in real terms increased by 29 and 20 times, respectively, real consumption of rural and urban Chinese households, on average, increased by 16 times. For many years, the improvement of people's living standards owed more to increased nonagricultural employment than to higher wages.

For example, Cai et al. (2009: 220) estimate that in the period 1997–2004 the number of migrant workers—defined as rural labourers who worked in cities for six months or longer—increased from less than 40 million to over 100 million. While there was no significant increase in the real wage rate, total wages grew at an annual rate of 14.9 per cent in real terms. As a result, the share of wages in rural households' income increased from 24.6 per cent to 34 per cent.

Second is the more recent increase in the wage rate (Garnaut and Huang 2006). Since the Chinese economy entered the Lewis turning point, or period,[7] some time from 2004, the wages of ordinary workers have increased rapidly. In the period 2003–16, the average wage of migrant workers in real terms grew at a rate of 10.1 per cent. As a consequence, after 2009, the Gini coefficient of residents' income and the income gap between rural and urban households both fell steadily.

Third is the effect of redistribution policy. Coinciding with the arrival of the Lewis turning point, China's central and local governments have intensified redistributive policies. These include strengthening the poverty alleviation program in rural areas, expanding the coverage and equalising the provision of public services, raising mandatory minimum wages and relaxing household registration control over population migration (Cai 2016).

7 Garnaut (2013) has noted that in China, as a large and differentiated country, the Lewis turning point would not come at a single point in time, but emerge through the economy over a period.

New development stage and unfinished tasks

In the past 40 years, China has gone a long way towards two important systemic transitions—from a planned to a market economy, and from a dual economy to neoclassical growth. China has also undergone a rapid demographic transition, from high to low fertility.

Economic reform and opening-up to the world economy have created an institutional environment in which a demographic dividend has been translated into extraordinary economic growth (Table 1.1). Reforms of incentive mechanisms, enterprise governance, price determination, resource allocation systems, foreign trade and investment and the macropolicy environment have contributed differently at each stage of development.

Table 1.1 Summary of growth sources and their trends

Growth factors	How they worked	Features and implications
Capital accumulation	Low dependency ratio conducive to high savings; unlimited supply of labour prevents diminishing return on capital	Unsustainable; as labour becomes scarce, return on capital begins diminishing
Quantity of labour	Population structure guarantees labour supply, which turns into comparative advantage in labour-intensive manufacturing	Unsustainable; demographic dividend disappears as economy passes Lewis turning point
Human capital	Education expansion and mass labour entry improves quality of stock of workers	Education expansion eventually slows, calling for enhancing its quality and equality
TFP	Increase from improvement of incentives and resource allocation system	Increasingly challenging and important to sustain growth; requires new sources of increase
TFP, of which: resource reallocation	Reallocative efficiency of resources through labour mobility from agriculture to industrial sectors	Dominant in early stage of development; diminishes after Lewis turning point
TFP, of which: technology	Utilisation of advantage of backwardness through absorbing foreign technology and management	As gap narrows, technological progress increasingly relies on independent innovation
Population factor	Widely defined demographic dividend is manifested in all factors driving rapid growth	Diminishes as China ages; second dividend available from removing remaining barriers to movement

Source: Authors' summary.

For a certain period, investment and net exports rather than consumption contributed disproportionately to economic growth in China (Figure 1.7). Sustaining strong growth now requires consumption to play a more important role in driving expansion of the economy. Progress has been made in recent years: increases in total household and government consumption now exceed increases in investment (Figure 1.8).

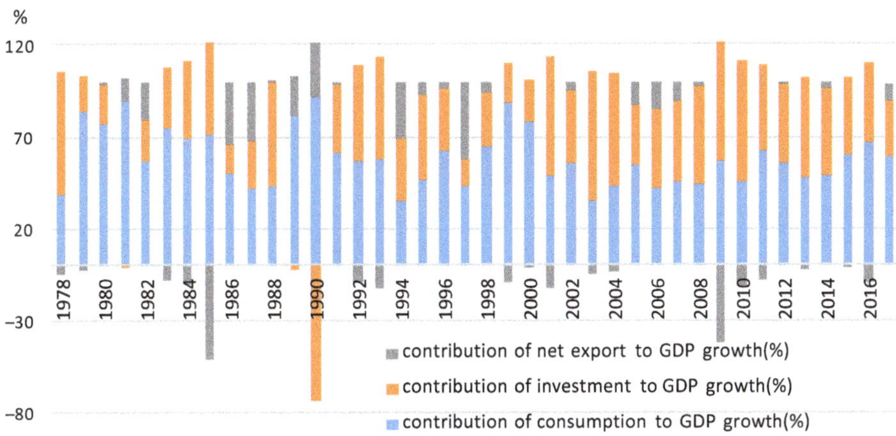

Figure 1.7 Contribution of consumption, investment and exports to China's GDP growth, 1978–2017

Source: NBS (various years).

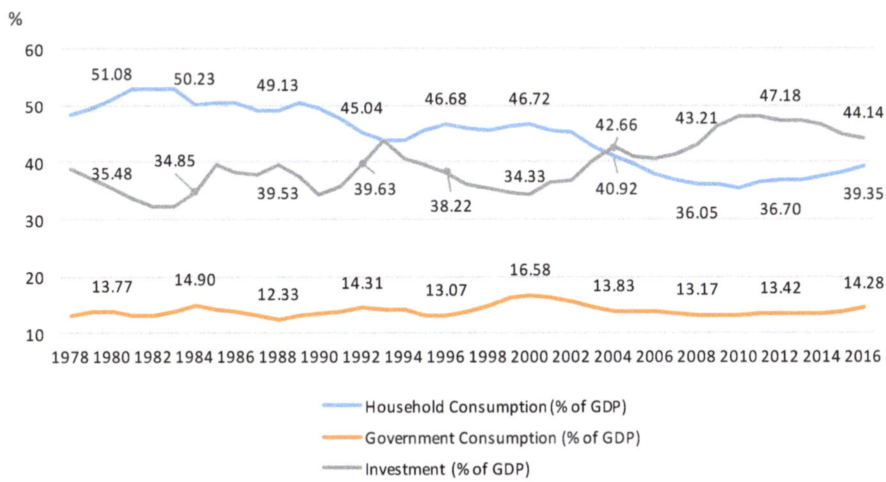

Figure 1.8 China's consumption and investment share of GDP, 1978–2017

Source: NBS (various years).

If China is to graduate from upper–middle-income to high-income status, its growth needs to shift from reliance on increases in labour and capital supply to reliance on productivity enhancement. This requires more effective markets—and reforms that are inherently difficult.

As summarised in Table 1.1, after the Chinese economy entered the Lewis turning point—characterised by a labour shortage and rising wages—the demographic dividend diminished rapidly. All of the elements that drove rapid growth in the first quarter-century of reform became weaker. The potential growth rate was bound to decline. A labour shortage means that wages grow faster than productivity. The rapid increase in the capital–labour ratio leads to a sharp decline in return to investment. The shrinkage of new entrants to the labour market slows the improvement of human capital. The deceleration of labour movement from agriculture to other sectors removes a source of rapid improvement in allocative efficiency, leading to a sharp fall in TFP growth.

All of these considerations lower China's potential growth rate by a considerable amount.

Cai and Lu (2013) estimate that China's potential growth rate has fallen from about 10 per cent per annum prior to 2010 to 7.6 per cent in the period of the twelfth five-year plan (2011–15) and 6.2 per cent in the thirteenth five-year-plan period (2016–20). Nevertheless, Cai and Lu (2016) suggest that the decline of China's potential growth rate will be smooth and slow and, until 2050, will remain higher than 3 per cent. The slowdown in the actual growth rate has so far followed this trajectory.

Growth theories and the lessons of experience show us that growth slows in the transition from dual-economy development with potential for catching-up with advanced economies to neoclassical growth at the global technological frontier (Eichengreen et al. 2013; Barro 2016). However, the pace at which potential growth falls and the extent to which it deviates from the potential growth rate differ across countries (Eichengreen et al. 2011).

China will not be exempt from the iron law of regression to the mean in the long run (Pritchett and Summers 2014). However, by deepening reform and upgrading its industrial structure, China can prevent its potential growth rate from falling too fast, find its way out of the 'middle-income trap' and accomplish its goal of modernisation.

Deeper reform is essential to spur on future economic growth. The difference between reform and status quo outcomes is dramatically large (Cheremukhim et al. 2015).

One reason the maintenance of productivity growth through deeper reform is now more difficult than in earlier decades is that it is now harder to find improvements that benefit one substantial group in society without hurting others. It is harder now to find Pareto improvements of the kind associated with the introduction of the HRS.

This raises new challenges. First, reform now faces resistance and interference from vested interests. Second, in the course of the 'creative destruction' necessary for tapping new sources of growth, some workers will lose established jobs and some enterprises will disappear. There will be perceptions of a public interest case for slowing reform—the product of what Corden (1974) called the conservative social welfare function. To meet those challenges, the reform dividend—the added economic value from new reform measures—should be made available to the losers of reform. This converts a Pareto improvement into a Kaldor–Hicks improvement (Scitovsky 1941).[8]

Successful reform to maintain growth in these circumstances requires political wisdom and determination. The required policy measures include redefining fiscal expenditure responsibilities between central and local governments, strengthening social protection for unemployed workers and disadvantaged families and more generally compensating the losers from reform.

There is some opportunity for allocative gains from moving people from agricultural and other rural employment into employment with higher productivity in the towns, through removing artificial barriers to relocation. This, too, faces resistance from established urban residents. Again, wisdom and determination from government are required to unlock a reform dividend.

Future TFP growth will have to come, to a considerable extent, from innovation, involving Schumpeterian 'creative destruction'. Studies suggest that in developed countries, allocative efficiency relating to the entry, expansion, contraction and exit of firms within narrowly defined sectors can contribute one-third to one-half of national productivity growth (Foster et al. 2008). To make such a mechanism work in China requires deepening reforms to increase competition, break monopolies, encourage entrepreneurial activities and strengthen social protection.

The road ahead will be harder in some important respects than the road already travelled. The difference between continuing along the road and staying still is the difference between China joining the ranks of the high-income countries and being caught in a middle-income trap (Armstrong and Westland 2016).

References

Armstrong, S. and Westland, T. (2016), Escaping the middle income trap: Trade, investment and innovation, in F. Hutchinson and S. Basu Das (eds), *Asia and the Middle Income Trap*, Oxford: Routledge.

Bai, C.-E. and Zhang, Q. (2014), The rates of return to capital and the analysis of the determinants, *The World Economy* (10): 3–30.

8 A 'Kaldor improvement' refers to a change in which the total gains outweigh the total losses so that it is possible for beneficiaries—perhaps through government—to compensate nonbeneficiaries for the losses they suffer. As a result, no one suffers in the end. See Kaldor (1939).

Bai, C.-E., Hsieh, C.-T. and Qian, Y. (2006), *The return to capital in China*, NBER Working Paper No. 12755, Cambridge, MA: National Bureau of Economic Research.

Barro, R. J. (2016), *Economic growth and convergence, applied especially to China*, NBER Working Paper No. 21872, Cambridge, MA: National Bureau of Economic Research.

Brandt, L., Ma, D. and Rawski, T. G. (2014), From divergence to convergence: Reevaluating the history behind China's economic boom, *Journal of Economic Literature* 52(1): 45–123. doi.org/10.1257/jel.52.1.45.

Cai, F. (ed.) (2010), *Transforming the Chinese Economy, 1978–2008*, Leiden: Brill.

Cai, F. (2015a), *Demystifying China's Economic Development*, Beijing and Berlin: China Social Sciences Press and Springer-Verlag. doi.org/10.1007/978-3-662-46103-7.

Cai, F. (2015b), The making of dual economy as a stage of economic development, *Economic Research Journal* (7): 4–15.

Cai, F. (2016), *China's Economic Growth Prospects: From demographic dividend to reform dividend*, Cheltenham, UK: Edward Elgar.

Cai, F. (2017), Reform effects in China: A perspective of labor reallocation, *Economic Research Journal* (7): 4–17.

Cai, F. and Lu, Y. (2013), The end of China's demographic dividend: The perspective of potential GDP growth, in R. Garnaut, F. Cai and L. Song (eds), *China: A new model for growth and development*, Canberra: ANU E Press.

Cai, F. and Lu, Y. (2016), Take-off, persistence, and sustainability: The demographic factor in Chinese growth, *Asia & the Pacific Policy Studies* 3(2): 203–25. doi.org/10.1002/app5.139.

Cai, F. and Wang, D. (1999), The sustainability of economic growth and the labor contribution, *Economic Research Journal* (10): 62–8.

Cai, F. and Zhao, W. (2012), When demographic dividend disappears: Growth sustainability of China, in M. Aoki and J. Wu (eds), *The Chinese Economy: A new transition*, Basingstoke, UK: Palgrave Macmillan.

Cai, F., Du, Y., Gao, W. and Wang, M. (2009), *Labor Economics: Theories and Chinese experiences*, Beijing: Beijing Normal University Publishing Group.

Cai, F., Guo, Z. and Wang, M. (2016), New urbanisation as a driver of China's growth, in L. Song, R. Garnaut, F. Cai and L. Johnston (eds), *China's New Sources of Economic Growth. Volume 1: Reform, resources and climate change*, Canberra: ANU Press. doi.org/10.22459/CNSEG.07.2016.03.

Cheremukhim, A., Golosov, M., Guriev, S. and Tsyvinski, A. (2015), *The economy of People's Republic of China from 1953*, NBER Working Paper No. 21397, Cambridge, MA: National Bureau of Economic Research.

Chu, S. N. and Song, L. (2015), Promoting private entrepreneurship for deepening market reform in China: A resource allocation perspective, *China & World Economy* 23(1): 47–77. doi.org/10.1111/cwe.12099.

The Conference Board (2018), *Total Economy Database*, April, New York: The Conference Board. Available from: www.conference-board.org/data/economydatabase/.

Corden, W. M. (1974), *Trade and Welfare*, Oxford: Oxford University Press.

Eichengreen, B., Park, D. and Shin, K. (2011), *When fast growing economies slow down: International evidence and implications for China*, NBER Working Paper No. 16919, Cambridge, MA: National Bureau of Economic Research.

Eichengreen, B., Park, D. and Shin, K. (2013), *Growth slowdowns redux: New evidence on the middle-income trap*, NBER Working Paper No. 18673, Cambridge, MA: National Bureau of Economic Research.

Foster, L., Haltiwanger, J. and Syverson, C. (2008), Reallocation, firm turnover, and efficiency: Selection on productivity or profitability?, *American Economic Review* 98(1): 394–425. doi.org/10.1257/aer.98.1.394.

Garnaut, R. (2013), Macro-economic implications of the turning point, in Y. Huang and F. Cai (eds), *Debating the Lewis Turning Point in China*, Routledge: London.

Garnaut, R. and Huang, Y. (2006), Continued rapid economic growth and the turning point in economic development, in R. Garnaut and L. Song (eds), *The Turning Point in China's Economic Development*, Canberra: Asia Pacific Press. doi.org/10.26530/OAPEN_459745.

Garnaut, R. and Song, L. (eds) (2006), *The Turning Point in China's Economic Development*, Canberra: Asia Pacific Press. doi.org/10.26530/OAPEN_459745.

Garnaut, R., Song, L. and Yao, Y. (2006), Impact and significance of state-owned enterprise restructuring in China, *The China Journal* (55): 35–63.

Garnaut, R., Song, L., Yao Y. and Wang, X. (2001), *Private Enterprise in China*, Canberra: Asia Pacific Press.

International Monetary Fund (IMF) (2006), Asia rising: Patterns of economic development and growth, in *World Economic Outlook*, September, Washington, DC: IMF.

International Monetary Fund (IMF) (2018), Global economic outlook 2018 dataset. Available from: www.imf.org/external/datamapper/NGDP_RPCH@WEO/OEMDC/ADVEC/WEOWORLD.

Jin, P. (ed.) (2005), *The Quotations by Confucius*, Beijing: China Federation of Literary and Art Circles Publishing House.

Kaldor, N. (1939), Welfare propositions of economics and interpersonal comparisons of utility, *Economic Journal* 49(September): 549–51. doi.org/10.2307/2224835.

Kwan, Y. and Chow, G. (1996), Estimating economic effects of political movements in China, *Journal of Comparative Economics* 23(2): 192–208. doi.org/10.1006/jcec.1996.0054.

Lewis, A. (1954), Economic development with unlimited supplies of labor, *The Manchester School* 22(2): 139–91. doi.org/10.1111/j.1467-9957.1954.tb00021.x.

Lin, J. Y. (1992), Rural reforms and agricultural growth in China, *American Economic Review* 82(1): 34–51.

Lin, J. Y., Cai, F. and Li, Z. (2003), *The China Miracle: Development strategy and economic reform*, rev. edn, Hong Kong: The Chinese University Press.

Lin, J. Y. and Wang, Y. (2010), China's integration with the world: Development as a process of learning and industrial upgrading, in F. Cai (ed.), *Transforming the Chinese Economy, 1978–2008*, Leiden and Boston: Brill.

Maddison, A. (2007), *Chinese Economic Performance in the Long Run, 960–2030 AD*, 2nd edn, Paris: OECD Publishing.

National Bureau of Statistics (NBS) (various years), *China Statistical Yearbook*, Beijing: China Statistics Press.

Pritchett, L. and Summers, L. H. (2014), *Asiaphoria meets regression to the mean*, NBER Working Paper No. 20573, Cambridge, MA: National Bureau of Economic Research.

Scitovsky, T. (1941), A note on welfare proposition in economics, *The Review of Economic Studies* 9(1): 77–88. doi.org/10.2307/2967640.

Spence, M. (2011), *The Next Convergence: The future of economic growth in a multispeed world*, New York: Farrar, Straus and Giroux.

State Council Information Office (2016), *China's progress in poverty reduction and human rights development*, [in Chinese], White Paper, 17 October, Beijing: State Council Information Office. Available from: www.scio.gov.cn/tt/zdgz/Document/1494216/1494216.htm.

United Nations Department of Economic and Social Affairs (UN DESA) (2015), *World Population Prospects: The 2015 revision*, DVD edn, New York: Population Division, UN DESA.

Wang, F. and Mason, A. (2008), The demographic factor in China's transition, in L. Brandt and T. G. Rawski (eds), *China's Great Economic Transformation*, Cambridge: Cambridge University Press.

Whalley, J. and Zhao, X. (2010), *The contribution of human capital to China's economic growth*, NBER Working Paper No. 16592, Cambridge, MA: National Bureau of Economic Research.

World Bank (1998), *China 2020: Development challenges in the new century*, Oxford: Oxford University Press.

Zhu, X. (2012), Understanding China's growth: Past, present, and future, *Journal of Economic Perspectives* 26(4): 103–24. doi.org/10.1257/jep.26.4.103.

Part I: The Chinese economic transformation

2. 40 years of Chinese economic reform and development and the challenge of 50

Ross Garnaut

On 22 December 1978, the eleventh Central Committee of the Communist Party of China (CPC) completed its third plenary meeting.

There was no contemporary recognition in the West of its significance. The twentieth, thirtieth and now fortieth anniversaries have received far more attention. In the intervening years, China and its relations with the international community have been transformed.

We published the first of this series of books about the Chinese reforms and economy on the twentieth anniversary, 20 years ago. China's economy had expanded by five times over the intervening two decades, and its foreign trade by 12 times. Consumption levels had greatly increased for nearly half of the world's people in poverty. From being an isolated, autarchic economy, China through the 1990s absorbed about half of the foreign direct investment (FDI) flows to developing economies. From having no trade or investment ties with Taiwan and South Korea, by the 1990s, China was the first or second largest export destination of one and the third largest of the other.

Even greater had been the transformation of the Chinese mind. Tens of millions of Chinese were by then part of an international community of ideas and information. With the expanded role of the market had come a substantial widening in the sphere of personal freedom—to travel and to communicate with others.

Changes of this dimension and at this extraordinary speed are unsettling and potentially destabilising. Yet for all the disruption of change, and the many new problems it had generated, most Chinese welcomed the transformation over the first two decades. Certainly, the large increase in living standards was appreciated enough to provide a base for continuity in political leadership and institutions despite the immense stress and dislocation.

The pace of change has been maintained over the second 20 years of the reform period. The economy in 2017 was 5.3 times larger than in 1998, and international trade 12.6 times. The information networks in which ordinary citizens participate within and beyond China have expanded beyond the wildest imagination of 20 years ago. This is partly the march of global technology and partly the movement of Chinese people to the global frontiers of knowledge and technology—somewhat constrained by the authorities' restrictions on the use of those new technologies. More than 140 million Chinese now have passports for travel abroad and 751 million communicate with each other and outsiders through the internet.

The tensions over growing income and wealth inequality at the first and second decadal anniversaries have continued, and have been joined by concerns about deteriorating environmental conditions affecting the health of many people across the country. The abuse of office for personal enrichment has been a continuing and increasing source of resentment, eventually growing into a threat to the stability of Communist Party rule. The correction of growing inequality, environmental deterioration and corruption has become a central policy objective. The elimination of poverty is now a policy goal. Rapidly rising living standards for ordinary people as labour became scarce and state policy focused on distributional issues provided a salve to social tensions from the later years of the third decade of reform.

Now, approaching the fortieth anniversary, China has become such a large economy that changes in the rate or character of its growth affect people everywhere, generating tensions in China's external relations and feeding back into domestic political and economic realities in complex ways. China is now large enough to be consequential to the developed countries' ways of relating to each other and the developing world, and to ideas and norms relating to domestic political organisation everywhere.

Ideas and policy in the first 20 years

When Deng Xiaoping and his supporters took decisive control of the Central Committee of the CPC 40 years ago, they brought to an end what Deng himself once described to former Australian prime minister Bob Hawke in my presence as two years of indecisive economic strategy and policy after the death of Mao Zedong in 1976. During those two years, policies embodying pragmatic acceptance of a large role for domestic and international market exchange were in contest with Maoist commitments to local and national autarchy, central planning, state-owned enterprises (SOEs) in the cities and people's communes in the countryside.

Deng and his supporters were victims of the Cultural Revolution. The reaction against the anarchy of that decade was their political launching pad. They had been the managers of the early periods of Communist Party success, in the 1950s before the 'Great Leap Forward' and in the brief interlude between the recognition of failure of that first lethal experiment in unworldly application of Maoist theory and the anarchy of the second. They harked back to earlier success, when markets had been allowed to play substantial roles at least in the countryside, within a system in which central planning was supported by a firm administrative order.

The reformist leaders of December 1978 were aware that the world had changed from the earlier days of partial success. They were aware of China's military vulnerability, as an economically weak and technologically backward society. They were deeply conscious that China shared the world's longest border with an apparently economically successful, technologically advanced and politically expansionist authoritarian state, the world's second military superpower. Some of them were aware as well that their rivals from the Chinese civil war across the Taiwan Strait, their compatriots in colonial Hong Kong and their Cold War enemies in South Korea were enjoying sustained economic success that raised deeply challenging questions about China's own continuing backwardness.

It was China's strategic vulnerability that had caused and allowed premier Zhou Enlai to champion the modernisation of industry, agriculture, science and technology and national defence in the early 1970s, after the armed clashes along the border with Russia in Heilongjiang. The intensification of the Sino–Soviet conflict and China's 'four modernisations' provided the context for diplomatic rapprochement with the United States and for Deng Xiaoping's temporary rehabilitation as vice-premier in the early 1970s. China's national policy lurched dangerously as competing ideas and political forces struggled to take control of the tiller of state. The ultimate directions were strongly influenced by the arrest by the People's Liberation Army (PLA) of the 'Gang of Four' after the death of Mao.

Important steps were taken to create a base for future growth in this period of indecisive policy. The awesome denial of formal education during the Cultural Revolution ended, with the return of competitive entry into the great universities in 1977. China's state enterprises experimented with the purchase of productive new technologies from abroad, but there were crosscurrents and countercurrents, continued ideological contests over high policy and uncertainty as subordinate leaders watched for the emergence of a clear national direction.

Since December 1978 there has been no turning back.

It is not that Deng and his colleagues obtained endorsement for an elaborate, comprehensive new economic policy or plan. There was no blueprint for China's economic reform and internationalisation—even less than there had been in Taiwan and South Korea at the beginning of their sustained, rapid growth 15 years earlier.

But after the 1978 plenum, there was acceptance in China that domestic and international exchange through markets was a necessary and acceptable component of a national development strategy. There was pragmatic acceptance that institutions and policies that raised national economic output had a valid place in China—summed up in Deng's rehabilitation of an early Maoist exhortation to 'seek truth from facts'.

The new political environment after 1978 saw foreign trade, FDI and the utilisation of external technological cooperation and capital in all forms become acceptable elements of national policy. Local experiments with new forms of organisation of agricultural production were allowed, leading, within a few years, to the virtually complete replacement of the people's communes with the immensely more productive household responsibility system (HRS). Markets became important for exchange for the rapidly expanding agricultural output.

The strands were drawn together in the 1987 CPC congress's acceptance of general secretary Zhao Ziyang's characterisation of China as a backward country in the 'primary stage of socialism', in which the first national objective had to be the strengthening of the national economy.

The absence of a comprehensive reform strategy, the eclecticism of economic policy and the gradualism of change were heavily criticised by foreign observers through the first two decades—and sometimes still are today. But the absence of a blueprint was an inevitable consequence of China's circumstances, and in practice a virtue.

This was because there was no conceptual basis for a market-oriented economy. A few leaders, and a few intellectuals around the edges of policy, had absorbed some understanding of internationally oriented growth in Japan, South Korea, Taiwan, Hong Kong and Singapore. But the main understanding grew out of experience with the new patterns of economic development themselves, through observations of the operation of markets within China and increasing contact with foreign experience and ideas.

Nor was there an ideological basis in the early years for articulation of a model of development based on the operation of markets, deeply integrated into the international economy. Deng Xiaoping's political control of the CPC and the PLA was strong but not unconditional. It was built partly on others' confidence that he stood firmly for continued Communist Party political dominance and commitment to some undefined minimum core of socialist principles and objectives.

The absence of a blueprint was a virtue because any theoretical model of reform of the centrally planned economy in China would have been deeply flawed. The rapid unwinding of a centrally planned economy, dominated by SOEs in the cities and communes in the countryside, is fraught with risk of massive dislocation—a reality that was imperfectly understood before the unhappy later experience of Eastern Europe and the former Soviet Union. Some of the great strengths of the Chinese economy in the era of reform came as a surprise to Chinese and foreign observers alike and would have been given an inadequate place in a development blueprint built on the received theory and experience of others. First among the surprises was the extraordinary dynamism of industrial production in the township and village enterprises (TVEs) that grew from the remnants of the disintegrating people's communes.

Deng used to describe economic reform in China as 'crossing the river by feeling the stones' at each step. Hu Yaobang described reform in a letter to Bob Hawke as an experiment without precedent. In the uncertain months following the dismissal of Hu from the office of general secretary of the CPC in January 1987, Deng alluded uncharacteristically to the Chinese classics in a conversation with the secretary general of Japan's Liberal Democratic Party, Noboru Takeshita. He compared the path of reform with the mission of Guan Yu, who had to cross five passes and cut down six generals to achieve his noble objective.[1]

These metaphors contain important insights. Chinese reform required transformations in ideology, in ideas about economic development and policy, in law and regulatory systems and in economic institutions. Above all, it required the accumulation of new knowledge and wisdom in a billion Chinese minds, as people learned to do new things in an economic and social world that was fundamentally changed.

These transformations in ideology, ideas, policy, law, institutions, knowledge and experience occurred concurrently, reinforcing each other, and each created problems for others when it ran into trouble.

It took great courage and faith in some abstract and thinly formed ideas for the Chinese collective leadership to wade into the river of reform—and a clear understanding that the maintenance of the status quo in centrally planned China in the aftermath of the Cultural Revolution meant continued backwardness, vulnerability and eventually instability in a rapidly developing East Asia and changing world.

On establishing his preeminence in the exercise of political power, Deng identified two effective agents for reform: Hu as general secretary, for reform of the CPC, and Zhao as premier, for reform of state institutions and policy. As general secretary, Hu led the task of replacing the huge cadre of beneficiaries of the Cultural Revolution with people able to lead and support reform. Zhao was the leader of the practical business of policy reform. Each made extraordinary contributions of leadership and intellect, managing change on a scale and at a pace that were unique in human experience. Each was informed by experience to the view that successful economic reform and development would require a widening of the scope for open discussion of policy, for dissent within the limits set by the imperatives of continued undisputed Communist Party rule and for reform of the political system to make policy somewhat more open to pressures from the rapidly changing society beyond the central leadership. Deng eventually came to doubt the will and the capacity

1 When Takeshita visited The Australian National University in November 1998, I reminded him of the 1987 conversation, which was reported at the time in the Chinese press. He remembered it more for Deng Xiaoping's imprecision in the numbers and details of economic policy than for his classical allusion!

of each to secure and enforce the authority of the CPC, causing the dismissal of Hu in January 1987 after student demonstrations in Shanghai and of Zhao, then CPC general secretary, in the crisis over the management of unrest in Beijing in May 1989.

General secretary Jiang Zemin and other successors to Hu and Zhao after the leadership crisis of 1987–89—selected by Deng and, until his death in 1997, sustained by him—placed a higher premium on stability. They defined and narrowed the boundaries of discussion of political system change—in the end, without diminishing commitment to internationally oriented market reform. Deng's legacy of both internationally oriented economic reform and strong state political control has persisted and gathered stronger support under other leaders in the two decades since his death—the latter most decisively under General Secretary Xi Jinping since 2012.

In the early years of reform, courage and faith, and a clear view of the futility of standing still, were required in the leadership of all state institutions. In the great universities, ageing professors—some with pre-revolutionary experience of academic institutions in the West—were called back from the disgrace of the Cultural Revolution to the massive and depressing replacement of half a generation lost to disciplined education. Some leaders of pre-revolutionary business who had opted to make their lives in the mainland, and who had mostly been rewarded by humiliation in the years before reform, accepted invitations to lead market-oriented new state businesses as examples for the huge and cumbersome enterprises that had grown within the framework of central planning.

In one of the boldest of early reform decisions, in the first decade, many tens of thousands of young people were sent or allowed to go abroad as students—to America, Australia, Japan, Europe and Hong Kong. They became channels for information and agents of change when they returned to live and work or, more commonly, when they returned to visit or simply kept in touch with home. They were later overwhelmed numerically by private students going abroad. Student exchanges have educated large numbers of Chinese and foreigners about their shared and differentiated human experience.

The conceptual gap that had to be bridged in the course of reform was immense, extending into every corner of economic policy.

To take one corner, the idea that a country can maximise the value of its production and incomes through open trade, relying on imports for goods and services in which the economy has comparative disadvantage, is not intuitively obvious to Chinese any more than to anyone else. Even where policymakers accept the logic of comparative advantage, its full reflection in policy is resisted by vested interests which expect to be damaged by it. In China, the usual resistance to specialisation according to comparative advantage was reinforced by the heavy emphasis on autarchy in communist central planning, by the special Maoist exhortation to 'self-reliance' and by the overlay of security concerns about dependence on foreign trade. Inside and outside China there were doubts about the capacity and willingness of the rest of the world to adjust to much higher levels of Chinese exports.

The acceptance of the idea that there are gains in specialisation according to comparative advantage came slowly, and each major sector of the economy became a battleground over acceptance. The idea gained enough ground for policy change to allow the beginnings of rapid expansion of exports of labour-intensive manufactures alongside rapid growth in imports of a range of capital-intensive and technologically sophisticated manufactured goods and of industrial raw materials. The gains from trade then made their own eloquent case for going further. An important milestone was Zhao Ziyang's articulation of a coastal economic strategy in early 1988, under which coastal China would expand its export-oriented manufacturing base, building on its relative abundance of labour and drawing raw materials from international markets.

The understanding of comparative advantage and the gains from trade was assimilated into Chinese development policy so thoroughly that official and academic China at the fourth decadal anniversary of reform have become sources of education on Ricardian theory and practice. As US President Donald Trump denies the advantages of international specialisation according to comparative advantage, President Xi, at Davos in early 2017 and at Boao in early 2018, explains the shared interest in open trade. Professor Lin Yifu's Center for New Structural Economics at Peking University has become a source of knowledge on comparative advantage, influencing development planning to good effect in some African countries (Lin and Wang 2017).

Reform in the first decade was constrained by the legacy of CPC ideology—specifically, the elements of ideology associated variously with Marx, Lenin, Stalin and Mao. The ideological legacy of Mao turned out to be the least constraining for economic reform, once the CPC had delivered its verdict that Mao was 70 per cent right and 30 per cent wrong. On the legacy of Marx, the theoretical distance of classical Marxism from the practical decisions of state, and its denial of the possibility of socialism in a backward country, weakened the constraint it placed on reform. Some intellectual gymnastics were required in the mid-1980s to render the operation of a labour market consistent with the labour theory of value. What then remained was a commitment to avoid the extremes of income inequality that the Chinese leadership associated with capitalist developing countries, and a view that the state should continue to own the largest enterprises in key economic sectors and guide development elsewhere to some extent. The Leninist legacy of firm Communist Party control through 'democratic centralism' remained a cardinal principle of Deng's. It has never been successfully challenged. It remains a premise of the leadership at the fortieth anniversary. The Stalinist legacy of central planning had little continuing ideological resonance after the early 1990s.

Beyond ideology and policy, there were immense problems of a highly practical kind, especially in reforming the system of central planning. The practical challenge was how to build the regulatory system, the institutions and the human knowledge and skills to implement reform policy and to make the partially reformed system work. Among the most difficult tasks was the building of an institutional framework to implement monetary policy and therefore macroeconomic stabilisation indirectly, as is necessary in a market economy. Through the first 15 years of reform, weaknesses in this area had generated a cycle of growth, inflation and balance of payments pressure that seemed to be widening over time (Garnaut and Ma 1993). The apparent 'soft landing' after the inflationary boom of 1993–95 was suggestive of progress that has since been sustained—with the large role of costly direct controls on investment during that episode a feature of subsequent stabilisation crisis management as well.

By the mid-1990s, it was clear to the Chinese Government that sustained, stable growth required fundamental reform of SOEs. Partial success in this allowed stronger enforcement of hard budget constraints after the Asian Financial Crisis.

The decadal crises

Reform in China has not and could never have been a smooth process. There have been challenges at every step, some bumps in the road, detours and dead ends. Through an accident of numbers, the challenges reached a climax at the first three decadal anniversaries. While the fortieth anniversary approaches with apparent relative stability in domestic economic and political conditions, the growing challenge of China's relations with the developed countries, especially the United States, may make these times the most difficult of all.

At the tenth anniversary, acute problems of managing demand in the partially reformed economy and the inefficiencies and arbitrage opportunities of dual pricing manifested as elite and popular anxiety about inflation, corruption and the directions of economic reform. Bob Hawke and Chinese premier Li Peng met in Canberra late in 1988. I was one of a few people present at a small dinner at Hawke's residence. The two leaders discussed the itinerary for a reciprocal visit in the new year. Hawke, seeking ground for cordial interpersonal communication, expressed his pleasure in anticipation of playing tennis with former vice-premier Wan Li and golf with general secretary Zhao. 'Why would you want to spend time with them?' Premier Li responded, alerting us to the high political temperature.

The political cauldron boiled over as huge numbers of students and others poured into Tiananmen Square in Beijing to express their grief at the death of former general secretary Hu Yaobang in April 1989, lingered in increasing numbers and attracted others to their weakly bounded discussion of China's political landscape. The upper echelons of the CPC divided over the appropriate response. Division was resolved by Deng reaching from outside the formal structures to secure military action.

The unrest within the community and division within the party leadership had economic consequences as well as economic origins. Economic growth in 1989 and 1990 was by far the slowest in the reform era, contributing to a Western Pacific recession in 1990 and 1991. As Chinese rates of growth soared from 1991, the effect on others' recovery from recession was emphatic.

The two years after the political crisis of 1989 saw profound uncertainty over the direction of reform—the only time in 40 years in which it was possible that the increasing use of markets and deepening integration into the international economy might be reversed. Uncertainty was brought to an end by Deng's tour of southern China in 1992 and his exhortation to deepen reform and interaction with global markets.

The next half-dozen years saw rapid expansion of the role of the nonstate and especially the private sectors (Garnaut et al. 2001), massive increases in foreign trade and investment and the establishment of mechanisms for monetary and fiscal management that, with deft application, moderated what had been dangerous cyclical variations in demand and economic activity.

It is a sign of the greatly expanded role of international trade and payments that crises at the twentieth and thirtieth anniversaries mainly involved China's interaction with the external economy rather than domestic tensions.

The twentieth anniversary saw China grappling with the consequences of the Asian Financial Crisis. The crisis began in July 1987 with immense speculative capital outflow from, and then currency depreciation in, Thailand. It quickly spread into deep recession and currency depreciation across all of South-East Asia and South Korea, with a slump in activity and large yen depreciation in Japan (McLeod and Garnaut 1998).

China experienced a sharp downturn in exports and speculation that it would join its neighbours in currency depreciation. Its response had two parts. One was to defy the regional trend and fix the renminbi exchange rate against the US dollar. The second was to offset the downward pressure on domestic employment and incomes with the largest Keynesian fiscal and monetary expansion the world had ever known. The response was motivated mainly by imperatives of domestic stability but was also seen at home and abroad as being helpful to stabilisation of activity and exchange rates elsewhere in East Asia. It was a risky strategy: net exports fell sharply, the trade and current accounts went into deficit and there was speculation against the renminbi and Hong Kong dollar. The fiscal expansion, fixed exchange rate and consequent increase in the current account deficit could not have been sustained indefinitely. In the event, the strategy was validated before it had reached its time limit by recovery in the rest of the East Asian economy, to which Chinese strategy made a substantial contribution.

The Chinese macroeconomic response to the Asian Financial Crisis was brilliantly successful, but it left a deeply problematic legacy of structural change. Monetary and fiscal expansion was administered through public institutions—SOEs and national, provincial and municipal governments. This cut across the rapid expansion of the relative role of private enterprise and, more generally, the increase in market-directed relative to state-directed activity, which had accumulated great momentum through the 1990s.

The restoration of a larger state role was one of two sculptors of a new pattern of growth through the first decade of the twenty-first century. The other was Chinese membership of the World Trade Organization (WTO). The long and sometimes tortuous path to Chinese membership had commenced in 1986 with a request for Australian technical support for the Ministry of Foreign Trade and Technical Cooperation. Momentum was broken by international reaction to the political conflagration of 1989. Discussion of China's WTO entry was mired in controversy through the 1990s as the developed countries felt their way through their own responses to China becoming a major player in the global economic system (Garnaut and Huang 2001).

The strands finally came together at the Asia-Pacific Economic Cooperation (APEC) leaders' meeting in Shanghai that preceded the WTO ministerial meeting in Doha in late 2001. Asia-Pacific heads of government saw the admission to the WTO of what was soon to be the world's second largest economy and the launching of a new round of multilateral trade negotiations as acts of international solidarity in the immediate aftermath of the 11 September 2001 terrorist attacks in the United States.

The entry of China was the most important development in the life of the newly formed WTO. Inside China, it locked in commitment to deep integration into the global trading system and the domestic institutional changes that were necessary to that end. Externally, it constrained the clamour for arbitrary protectionist responses to China's emergence through the early twenty-first century as the world's largest trading economy. The other product of late 2001 solidarity, the Doha Round, on the other hand, was bound in shallows and miseries.

The expanded role of the state and deeper integration into the international trading system framed a remarkable period of Chinese growth led by investment and exports. The investment share of economic activity—disproportionately and increasingly concentrated in infrastructure and heavy industry—rose to the highest ever, anywhere. Alongside infrastructure, much investment was concentrated in an increasingly diverse and sophisticated export sector. An even larger savings share supported high investment, so that the trade surplus rose to one-tenth of gross domestic product (GDP) in 2007.

Double-digit economic growth was supported by large-scale migration of labour from the countryside and wages that grew more slowly than total economic output. Rapid economic growth and slower increases in wages raised the profit share of economic activity. This supported the increasing savings, which, in turn, underpinned extraordinary levels of investment.

This remarkable period of investment and export-led growth made China, by late in the twenty-first century's first decade, the world's largest exporter and trader, the second largest economy by any method of measurement and by far the world's largest source of surplus savings for international investment. The flow of surplus Chinese savings into US Government securities supported imbalances of historic dimension in the US economy—massive budget, trade and current account deficits funded by capital inflow. They allowed the US Government to pursue for a while reductions in tax rates and increases in military expenditure without large increases in domestic interest rates. There is a sense in which the availability of Chinese savings to support US deficits enabled the persistence and increase in imbalances that helped to make the US vulnerable to financial crisis.

The strong growth of the early twenty-first century had its downside. Rapid increases in lending from and to SOEs led to deterioration in credit quality and manifold risks in the financial sector. Growing inequality within China sparked political disquiet. The unprecedentedly rapid expansion of coal-based heavy industry made China the consumer of half the world's coal and overwhelmingly the largest global emitter of greenhouse gases driving climate change. There was growing awareness of the costs for Chinese health and longevity of deterioration of air and other environmental quality (Chen et al. 2013).

Rising Chinese exports and trade surpluses were accepted in the developed countries with adjustment costs and some pressures for restriction, but ultimately with relative ease through the debt-funded expansion to 2008. The political context changed with the economic conditions after the Global Financial Crisis (GFC) of 2008. Protectionist pressures strengthened and resistance weakened, most importantly in the United States.

The financial risks after the response to the Asian Financial Crisis attracted urgent attention. Refinancing of the banks—successfully and at considerable budgetary expense—was a strong focus of premier Zhu Rongji's in the first years of the new century.

From early in the twenty-first century, there were calls from some economists for a new approach to economic growth. This was reflected in new official statements on development strategy, led by president Hu Jintao and premier Wen Jiabao. The new approach would be built on higher growth in consumption and lower growth in savings and investment, an expanded role for services in expenditure and output, greater reliance on domestic relative to export demand, reduced inequality in incomes and wealth and reduced pressure on the domestic and global environment. An early expression of the new goals was the introduction of a broadly based expansion of social security, education and health programs to raise living standards for rural and low-income urban residents (see Wong, this volume).

About the same time, a historic turning point in the real economy began to exert immense pressure in many of the directions required for the suggested new approach to development. In 2005, there were signs in some coastal cities that easy availability of surplus labour from the countryside at low wages was coming to an end (Garnaut and Huang 2006). The 2006 book in this series was entitled *The Turning Point in China's Economic Development* (Garnaut and Song 2006). It made the call that China was approaching a Lewisian turning point, in which continued strong growth in the modern sector of the economy would lead to rapidly rising real wages in both the towns and the countryside. This was followed by productive research into the implications of the end of surplus labour at the Chinese Academy of Social Sciences and Peking University (Cai and Huang 2013), and gradual incorporation of understanding of the importance of these labour market developments into a new model of growth. Growth in wages and the labour share of income during and beyond the turning period would contribute to reduced income inequality, higher consumption relative to savings and investment, lower export growth and trade surpluses and a lower rate of growth of polluting emissions. Discussion of and innovations in policy emphasised changes in taxation and government expenditure to support reduced inequality. There was also focus on upgrading of skills and innovation to build a more sophisticated economy as labour-intensive activities became less competitive. There was discussion of market and direct interventions to reduce the negative impact of Chinese growth on domestic and international environmental amenity.

The thirtieth anniversary of reform came as the world grappled with the GFC in 2008. In the months that followed the collapse of Lehman Brothers in the United States in September 2008, Chinese manufactured exports to North America and Europe fell sharply. Twenty million migrant workers in coastal cities were sent back to the countryside well in advance of the normal exodus for the Chinese Spring Festival. China was again vulnerable to a downward spiral in economic activity and exports (Garnaut with Llewellyn-Smith 2009: 109–10).

The G20 heads of government meeting in Washington, DC, in November 2008 agreed on concerted implementation of expansionary policies. The Chinese response to the onset of the GFC had been immediate and immense, and was extended after the G20 summit. Keynesian monetary and fiscal expansion was implemented on a much larger scale than during the Asian Financial Crisis a decade earlier. By late 2009, the downward spiral in activity at home had been reversed and rapid growth in Chinese imports was supporting recovery in the rest of the world.

As in the aftermath of the Asian Financial Crisis, the macroeconomic response to external financial crisis was prompt, large and brilliantly successful. For a few years from 2009, investment and output increased as rapidly on average as in the early twenty-first century. The return of strong economic growth restored labour scarcity and pressure for increased wages. Again, there was another side—similar to that of the stimulus in response to the Asian Financial Crisis a decade before. Again, the manner of implementing monetary and fiscal expansion reinforced the roles of state institutions and put on hold policy innovation to build a new model of growth.

By 2011, confidence in restored growth allowed resumption of focus on structural change. The party and the state returned to implementation of the new model of economic growth that had been forming in economists' and leaders' minds in the years before the GFC. The new leadership around Xi Jinping that took office in 2012 declared commitment to greater equity in income and wealth distribution, domestic and international environmental amenity and a more flexible and market-oriented economic system.

The 2013 book in this series announced the arrival of a 'new model for growth and development' (Garnaut et al. 2013). Subsequent books have reviewed progress so far. The early scorecard shows much reorientation of demand from exports to domestic expenditure. It reveals some modest progress in shifting demand from investment to domestic consumption and reversing the increase in inequality. Net exports and the current account surplus fell quickly and by large amounts. The scorecard shows considerable progress on changing the relationship between economic growth and pressure on the global environment; since 2013, more than the whole of the increase in electricity use has come from generation with zero greenhouse gas emissions. There has been some progress in changing the relationship between economic growth and pressure on the domestic environment, especially in Beijing and the great cities of coastal China. Progress so far on institutional reform to support higher productivity through the transition from an upper–middle to a high-income country is harder to find.

China's progress with the new model of growth will be tested by international developments. The interaction of increasing trade tensions with the political and geostrategic consequences of China's rapid growth and concurrent weakness in the US political system could, in extreme circumstances, build mutually reinforcing pressures for withdrawal from open trade into a fourth decadal crisis. It is likely, and not an extreme circumstance, that rising geopolitical and geostrategic tensions will introduce potential for conflict to disrupt economic development over the fifth decade of reform.

The immediate risk is from protectionism in developed countries and China's and other countries' responses to it. The scale and speed of China's trade expansion inevitably places pressure on the economic structure in other countries. Chinese export growth forces contraction in directly competing industries abroad. This kind of adjustment pressure accounts for much of the growing contemporary negative commentary on China's participation in international trade.

Resistance to structural change can take the form of political demands for restrictions on trade with a large, rapidly growing partner. Political systems are especially vulnerable to such pressures in times of high unemployment or low income growth—the circumstances of the developed democracies since the GFC.

These demands in the developed countries for protection against growing Chinese exports have had to be managed alongside declining support for 'globalisation' more generally. This, too, is a response to stagnation in the incomes of ordinary citizens—apparent in the United States since the eclipse, from the 1970s and early 1980s, of the dominant and successful post-1932 New Deal social-democratic approach to economic policy. The stagnation of workers' incomes was exacerbated in the United States and extended through most of the developed world by the GFC.

The reaction against globalisation is not directed specifically against China, but provides fertile ground for protectionist reaction against Chinese trade expansion.

Here, the most important case is the United States since the election of Donald Trump to the presidency.

As Corden and Garnaut (forthcoming) have set out in a recent paper, the Trump administration has implemented two major initiatives in economic policy: expanding the budget deficit to pay for cuts in corporate and personal income tax and increasing (or threatening to increase) barriers against imports (with the threats greatest against countries with which the United States has bilateral trade deficits—first of all, China). These initiatives are meant to do two main things: to increase growth in the US economy as a whole, and especially to increase employment and the incomes of manufacturing workers in rust-belt states, which swung towards

Trump in the 2016 presidential elections; and to reduce US trade deficits with the world as a whole, and especially with countries, first of all China, with which the US has large bilateral deficits.

Trump's policy changes come at a time of near full employment, after a long, slow but reasonably steady increase in US economic activity and employment after expansionary policies were adopted to offset the effects of the GFC.

The Trump policies are unlikely to achieve their objectives, and may have perverse effects. For good or ill, the economy operates within reasonably well understood laws that are not changed by forceful political assertion of a contrary reality.

The two policy initiatives together are likely to increase the US trade deficit in total and with each major trading partner. They are unlikely to increase total employment. They may (or may not) increase employment and incomes in industries specifically earmarked for increased protection. They are certain to reduce employment and incomes in other industries producing tradable goods and services—such as manufacturing beyond the industries receiving increases in protection.

It may be a dangerous time when the President sees the evidence of increase rather than reduction in the trade deficit, and the disappointing outcomes on employment in manufacturing and other export- and import-competing industries taken a whole.

Partner countries are adversely affected by an increase in American protection. Corden and Garnaut (forthcoming) have worked through the implications of their various possible responses. Foreign governments may choose not to react. They may choose to reduce their own trade barriers, either to persuade President Trump that he should now desist from his increases in protection or to increase gains from trade to offset losses from the change in US policy. They may retaliate by raising their own trade barriers, in the hope of forcing a reversal of American policy—or simply to persuade domestic political constituencies that they are 'standing up' to American pressure.

If other countries reduce their own protection, they will offset—perhaps more than offset—the losses from the increase in US protection. If their reactions persuade the Trump administration to desist, so much the better. This is the best response to the change in US policy from the point of view of economic welfare in China and other partner countries, and obviously for welfare in the United States and the world as a whole.

Doing nothing is second best. At least the costs of increased US protection will not be compounded by reduced gains from trade as a result of one's own decisions.

The worst outcome for the partner countries, the United States and the world as a whole is retaliation that leads to an increase in protection. This compounds the loss from the American action—in the retaliating countries and in the United States and the world as a whole.

Whatever the response of other countries, the outcomes from President Trump's policies may cause him to take the failed policies further. There is potential for large problems.

China handled the second and third decadal crises in ways that avoided long-term destabilisation of its development effort and helped to avoid unnecessary exacerbation of instability in the rest of the world. It has an opportunity to avoid destabilisation at the fourth decadal anniversary as well. The best way to minimise the chances of destabilisation is to avoid retaliation for any increase in US protection. China will do well if it gives substance to the rhetoric of President Xi at Davos in early 2017 and more explicitly at Boao in early 2018, and of Prime Minister Li Keqiang in Jakarta in May 2018, and takes this opportunity for accelerated liberalisation of trade at home and leadership of a new round of liberalisation in Asia.

Where is growth going and when will it end?

The experience of East Asia since the middle of the twentieth century, of China in 40 years of reform and of other countries in the past few decades tells us that sustained, rapid economic growth is no 'miracle'. Rather, it is a normal part of the human condition in a poor country that meets a number of conditions for growth.

Rapid growth is easier to sustain in its early decades than to initiate, until successful development has taken a country into upper-middle incomes where China is now—the threshold of entry into high-income status. The period immediately after the turning point of economic development in a densely populated country—when labour becomes scarce and wages rise rapidly—is a harvest time of political support for outward-looking growth: rising incomes are more effective in allaying doubts and undermining resistance to change when they are a current reality rather than a hope and a promise. Continued growth in incomes becomes more challenging after upper-middle incomes have been reached, requiring greater sophistication in economic institutions including markets, and making stronger demands on high levels of education, information and innovation (Armstrong and Westland 2016).

Nevertheless, the new experiences of East Asia and the older experience of industrialisation in the West tell us that growth and modernisation do not proceed in logarithmic straight lines. However, there is a strong tendency for them to continue until the world's economic frontiers are approached. At any level of development, but especially from upper-middle incomes, growth momentum can be broken temporarily or permanently by adverse developments of several kinds.

Booms and manias, followed by economic collapse, are ever-present risks of market economies and sometimes result in major lurches in policy that block a return to growth. The risk of financial crisis following a boom and bust in asset prices in China grows with diversification of financial intermediation away from large state institutions and the expansion of new kinds of financial intermediation that may be imperfectly understood by the regulatory authorities.

Poor policy, resulting from weakness in economic analysis or political manifestations of resistance to change, can block the continual reallocation of resources to more productive uses.

A failure of economic and political institutions to adjust to the changing structure and aspirations of the community as incomes rise can undermine social and political cohesion around the objective of growth.

Noting these risks to the continuation of strong growth, I said in my contribution to the book that marked 20 years of reform that it was more likely than not that ideas about policy, policy itself, institutions and the knowledge of Chinese people would evolve with the experience of rapid growth in ways that would sustain it (Garnaut 1999). The rapid growth that was concentrated among a few hundred million people in the coastal provinces would spread inland as regulatory and infrastructural barriers to internal trade were removed. It was unlikely, I said, and at odds with the experience of others, that there would be no setback to rapid growth—no recessionary end to a market mania, no large misjudgement of macroeconomic policy, no failure of leadership nerve or judgement on continued market or necessary political reform.

But the experience of the reform period suggested, I wrote, that it is more likely than not that the average growth of the first two decades would be sustained for several decades more. Output would double and double again over the next two decades. By the fortieth anniversary, I said, the several hundred million people in the dynamic coastal provinces would enjoy living standards broadly at the level of Taiwan at the end of the twentieth century.

Economic growth in China would not end in global famine, as had been famously contended (Brown 2000). Global markets could handle the growing demand for food that rising incomes in China would generate.

It would not end in national environmental catastrophe. Rising incomes would bring both the will and the economic capacity to do something about the environmental degeneration that was associated with urbanisation and industrialisation in China. China's sustained, rapid growth raised larger, global environmental issues, but not just for China.

In two decades, I said 20 years ago, China would face a huge challenge of demographic transition, when the one-child family was entering middle age and the number of young workers was shrinking. This would be much on the minds of leaders in the nineteenth CPC congress in 2017, as a threat to the longer-term dynamism of Chinese society and the economy.

But, I wrote, 2018 would be an unlikely end point for the growth process that began with reform. The modernisation of the vast inland of China would be in its early years. It was more likely that Chinese society—aware as never before of the pain and costs of growth—would choose to push ahead. It would be a natural and in no way miraculous outcome if the growth of China's first two decades of reform continued until most of China's people enjoyed living standards and productivity levels close to those in the world's most advanced economies.

Now, at the fortieth anniversary, we can see that what seemed most likely 20 years ago has come to pass.

What is most likely for the next decade?

Economic growth cannot be taken for granted, but it seems to me that the conventional economic threats to growth are less daunting now than at any of the first three decadal anniversaries.

Protectionism in the developed countries is an immediate threat, but, as we have seen, the avoidance of the most damaging outcomes can be influenced, if not completely secured, by China's choice.

The biggest risks for the decade ahead lie in the possibility of mismanagement by China and other major states of adjustment to China's emergence as the world's largest economy and, by many measures, its most powerful state.

We are not yet accustomed to China assuming the relative weight in the world economy that will emerge over the next decade or so.

The most recent data from the International Monetary Fund (IMF 2018) calculate China's share of global GDP measured in purchasing power at 18.7 per cent, compared with 15.1 per cent for the United States. The differential between Chinese and American growth has narrowed in recent years. A reasonable assessment might suggest a differential between Chinese and US growth rates averaging near 3 percentage points on average from now through the 2020s. The realisation of such an outcome would take Chinese purchasing power to roughly double that of the United States by 2030. There are downside risks to both US and Chinese growth, which would widen or narrow the differential if realised for one but not the other.

While purchasing power measures provide more realistic comparisons of the size of economies, for some purposes, especially related to influence in the international economy, conventional national accounts data converted at current exchange rates provide a more useful measure. This is a more volatile measure—for example, causing the size of the US economy to rise in the circumstances immediately ahead of us, with loose budgets, high interest rates and a strong US dollar. The size of the US economy by the national accounts measure would go into reverse in the period of dollar weakness that is likely to follow the debt-funded expansion.

By the national accounts measure, the World Bank (2017) estimates that the US economy was two-thirds larger than China's in 2016. Mechanical application of the 3 percentage point differential in growth rates would see the Chinese economy reach the size of the United States' around the fifth decadal anniversary.

This national accounts calculation does not consider one important additional factor. Purchasing power estimates of output systematically exceed national accounts calculations in developing countries for a good reason: wages are lower in the developing country, so the same nontradable goods and services are valued more highly in the developed country with higher wages. Once a developing country has passed the Lewisian turning point in economic development, labour incomes rise more rapidly than GDP. This leads to the reduction and eventually removal of the difference between comparisons based respectively on purchasing power and national accounts measurements. The national accounts measures of relative size converge over time towards the purchasing power estimates.

The result is that a developing country's GDP measured by national accounts catches up with a developed country's more rapidly than you would expect from mechanical application of a specified growth rate differential to current measures of relative size. China has passed the labour market turning point. Over the past 15 years, a substantial part of the difference between national accounts and purchasing power measures of GDP has disappeared. Purchasing power measures valued, on average, each unit of Chinese output five times higher than national accounts measures in the early 1990s. Today, purchasing power measures value each unit of Chinese output only two times higher. The difference between purchasing power and national accounts measures will continue to shrink as Chinese wages increase more rapidly than GDP. There will be convergence towards the purchasing power measures as Chinese incomes converge towards the levels of the developed countries. By the fifth decadal anniversary of reform, the continuation of the supposed differential between US and Chinese growth rates will see the Chinese economy about twice as large as the United States' by purchasing power, and moving towards twice as large when differences are measured by national accounts data.

The rise of Chinese average incomes into the range of the developed countries takes us into unknown territory in relation to the capacity of established Chinese domestic political institutions to manage the stresses of structural change.

Virtually all of the one-seventh of humanity living in countries with high average incomes now live within representative and competitive democratic political systems. Is this because there are powerful social forces requiring democratic political systems for effective management of high-income societies? Or is it a product of a particular history of development, which leaves open the possibility of stable economic and political management by the government of a one-party state after the country has entered the ranks of high-income countries?

China's average incomes are more likely than not to enter the range of the high-income countries by the standard definitions of the World Bank in the early 2020s. If there were no large change in the Chinese system of government, this would fundamentally change what had seemed to many to be an immutable association between high-income countries and competitive democratic political systems. A majority of the people living within high-income countries would then be governed by the Communist Party of China.

China's social and economic change over the past four decades has led to many political changes, although not a fundamental change in the Leninist political superstructure. Going forward, the great relative size of China means there will inevitably be a new and different type of interaction and competition between the Chinese and other political systems. There will be argument about whether government for the people is possible without representative government by the people. There will be more searching questions asked about the quality of government delivered by established competitive democratic political systems.

There is a positive element to this: competition for hearts and minds can strengthen focus on governing for the people in competitive democracies and communist party systems alike. But, without careful structuring of the terms of competition, it is likely to lead to suspicion and disruption, causing a failure of international cooperation at a time when it is essential for global peace and development.

My own view is that domestic order, good government and sustained development in China and the competitive democracies alike require explicit understanding of the terms of competitive engagement. They require mutual acceptance of differences in political systems. They require acceptance in each country that others will seek to insulate their own political systems from external political influence across national borders. They require acceptance that the competition between political systems may lead to different structures across high-income countries. Disruption is likely unless there is broadly based acceptance that the outcomes from contests over political systems in each country are to be determined by domestic processes within each.

Success in China and in the high-income countries as China moves towards the fifth decadal anniversary requires an explicit or implicit twenty-first-century grand understanding of these issues.

The contemporary international system has been built around the reality that the United States has been overwhelmingly the dominant global power since World War II.

China's economic weight will not be so overwhelming that it can exercise hegemonic power over the whole of the rest of the world even if it is twice the economic size of the United States. There will be other great centres of economic, political and strategic influence—most obviously, the European Union and India. Members of another tier outside the big four will be important, eventually with Indonesia having large influence, and with Russia, Japan and the post-Brexit United Kingdom as older powers in decline but retaining influence for some time. The second tier of powers will have more leverage in the emerging multipolar world than in the bipolar world after World War II or the unipolar decade immediately after the collapse of the Soviet Union.

The emerging structure of power in the international system has large implications for the political culture of international cooperation. International cooperation will be difficult, so we will need to economise on its use. Decisions will be better located at the regional and national levels except where there are strong reasons for effective action to require global agreement. Providing reasons for countries to act in ways that are consistent with the international interest will become increasingly important for effective international cooperation. Defining and measuring shared interests and sharing knowledge of the compatibility of national and global interests will be crucial. Concerted unilateral action in support of shared goals will be an increasingly important means to global ends, including on trade, climate change, global macroeconomic stability and global development.

Explicit agreement among the great powers will continue to be crucial for peace.

Will Chinese economic growth continue through to and beyond the fiftieth anniversary of reform? That will be determined by the answer to two other questions. Will the Chinese political system change enough to provide effective domestic political management when its citizens have joined the world's high-income people? Will the international community find ways to make the international system work cooperatively when China is overwhelmingly the world's largest economy?

References

Armstrong, S. and Westland, T. (2016), Escaping the middle-income trap: Trade, investment and innovation, in F. E. Hutchinson and S. Basu Das (eds), *Asia and the Middle-Income Trap*. New York: Routledge.

Brown, E. M. (2000), *The Rise of China*, Cambridge, MA: MIT Press.

Cai, F. and Huang, Y. (2013), Macro-economic implications of the turning point, in Y. Huang and F. Cai (eds), *Debating the Lewis Turning Point in China*, London: Routledge.

Cai, F., Garnaut, R. and Song, L. (eds) (2013), *China: A new model for growth and development*, Canberra: ANU Press.

Chen, Y., Ebenstein, A., Greenstone, M. and Li, H. (2013), Evidence on the impact of sustained exposure to air pollution on life expectancy from China's Huai River policy, *Proceedings of the National Academy of Sciences*, 110(32): 12936–41. doi.org/10.1073/pnas.1300018110.

Corden, M. and Garnaut, R. (forthcoming), The economic consequences of Mr Trump, *Australian Economic Review*.

Garnaut, R. (1999), Twenty years of economic reform and structural change in the Chinese economy, in R. Garnaut and L. Song (eds), *China: Twenty years of reform*, Canberra: Asia Pacific Press.

Garnaut, R. and Huang, Y. (2001), China's integration into the world economy, in R. Garnaut and Y. Huang (eds), *Growth Without Miracles*, Oxford: Oxford University Press.

Garnaut, R. and Huang, Y. (2006), Continued rapid growth and the turning point in China's development, in R. Garnaut and L. Song (eds), *The Turning Point in China's Economic Development*, Canberra: Asia Pacific Press. doi.org/10.26530/OAPEN_459745.

Garnaut, R. with Llewellyn-Smith, D. (2009), *The Great Crash of 2008*, Melbourne: Melbourne University Publishing.

Garnaut, R. and Ma, G. (1993), Economic growth and stability in China, *Journal of Asian Economics* 4(1): 5–24. doi.org/10.1016/1049-0078(93)90003-U.

Garnaut, R. and Song, L. (eds) (2006), *The Turning Point in China's Economic Development*, Canberra: Asia Pacific Press. doi.org/10.26530/OAPEN_459745.

Garnaut, R., Cai, F. and Song, L. (eds) (2013), *China: A new model for growth and development*, Canberra: ANU E Press.

Garnaut, R., Song, L., Yao, Y. and Wang, X. (2001), *Private Enterprise in China*, Canberra: Asia Pacific Press.

International Monetary Fund (IMF) (2018), *World Economic Outlook*, Washington, DC: IMF. Available from: www.imf.org/external/ns/cs.aspx?id=29.

Lin, J. and Wang, Y. (2017), *Going Beyond Aid: Development cooperation for structural transformation*, Cambridge: Cambridge University Press. doi.org/10.1017/9781316597354.

McLeod, R. H. and Garnaut, R. (eds) (1998), *East Asia in Crisis: From being a miracle to needing one?*, London: Routledge. doi.org/10.4324/9780203258675.

World Bank (2017), *World Development Report*, Washington, DC: The World Bank. Available from: openknowledge.worldbank.org/handle/10986/2121.

3. Reflections on 40 years of China's reforms

Bert Hofman[1]

In December 2018, it will be 40 years since Deng Xiaoping kicked off China's reforms with his famous speech calling on citizens to 'Emancipate the mind, seek the truth from facts and unite as one in looking to the future', which concluded the 1978 Central Economic Work Conference and set the stage for the third plenum of the eleventh Central Committee of the Communist Party of China (CPC). The speech brilliantly used Mao Zedong's own thoughts to depart from Maoism, rejected the 'two whatevers' of Mao's successor, Hua Guofeng ('Whatever Mao said, whatever Mao did'), and triggered decades of reforms that would bring China to where it is now—the second-largest economy in the world and one of the few that will soon[2] have made the journey from low-income to high-income country.

This fortieth anniversary is a good time to reflect on China's reforms. Understanding China's reforms is important first and foremost for getting the historical record right, and this record is still shifting despite the many volumes that have already been devoted to the topic. Understanding China's past reforms and, with them, the basis for China's success is also important for China's future reforms; understanding the path travelled, the circumstances under which historical decisions were made and what their effects were on the course of China's economy will inform decision-makers on where to go next. Third, reflections on China's reforms are increasingly important for the rest of the world. Because of China's economic success, more and more countries see China as an example to emulate, a model of development that could help them move from rags to riches within a generation.

With the nineteenth National Congress of the CPC last October, for the first time, as far as I know, China now also sees itself as such an example. One excerpt from General Secretary Xi Jinping's speech in particular signifies a departure from China's past ambitions and aspirations. In discussing the success of China, and by implication the Communist Party, Xi stated:

> It means that the path, the theory, the system, and the culture of socialism with Chinese characteristics have kept developing, blazing a new trail for other developing countries to achieve modernization. It offers a new option for other countries and

1 This chapter reflects the personal opinions of the author and should in no way be attributed to the World Bank, its executive board or its member countries. An earlier version of this chapter was presented at Fudan University.

2 By about 2024, in our estimates, or even sooner, if the renminbi appreciates more rapidly in real terms than anticipated.

> nations who want to speed up their development while preserving their independence; and it offers Chinese wisdom and a Chinese approach to solving the problems facing mankind. (Xi 2017)

In some ways, China's reforms followed many of the prescriptions mainstream economists would recommend (Figure 3.1). The country opened up for trade and foreign investment, gradually liberalised prices, diversified ownership, strengthened property rights and kept inflation under control. Continued (relative) macroeconomic stability allowed high savings to be turned into high investment and rapid urbanisation, which in turn triggered rapid structural transformation and productivity growth. But this simplifies and obfuscates the essence of China's reforms: it was the unique way in which China went about reforming its system that makes the country's reform experience of interest.

China's gradual, experimental method of reform of its economic system, especially in the early days, was in sharp contrast with the reforms in Eastern Europe and the former Soviet Union. Although they were often compared, China and other transitional countries were simply too different in terms of their initial economic conditions, political development and external environment to make comparison of much use. Similarly, comparison with much of the Latin American reforms seems out of place; the likes of Brazil, Mexico and Argentina were far closer to a market-based system than China in 1978, and their reforms—liberalisation and macroeconomic stability—were of a different order of complexity to China's. The policy prescription for Latin America was therefore focused on these issues, and the 'Washington consensus', which summarised the policy prescription for those countries, was never meant to be a growth or development model. Contrasting China's development approach with that of the Washington consensus therefore makes little sense.

At the onset of reforms, China was among the poorest nations on earth and a predominantly rural, agricultural country. China had barely 25 years of history of central planning, which had been marred by the failure of the Great Leap Forward and the political disruptions during the Cultural Revolution. The country was neither integrated into the world economy nor a member of the Council for Mutual Economic Assistance (Comecon). Internally—in part due to Mao's 'Third Front', which required individual regions to be able to survive economic isolation in case of a war—industry was inefficient, but also far less concentrated than in Eastern Europe and the former Soviet Union. When central planning was relaxed, competition among regions and their enterprises became possible, and economic oligarchy was avoided. Gradual reforms meant that the physical and human capital built under socialism did not become obsolete as a consequence of a transition shock. Perhaps most importantly, although major political reforms of the party and state were implemented over time, the state and the ruling party remained intact throughout, so China could focus on its economic and social transitions.

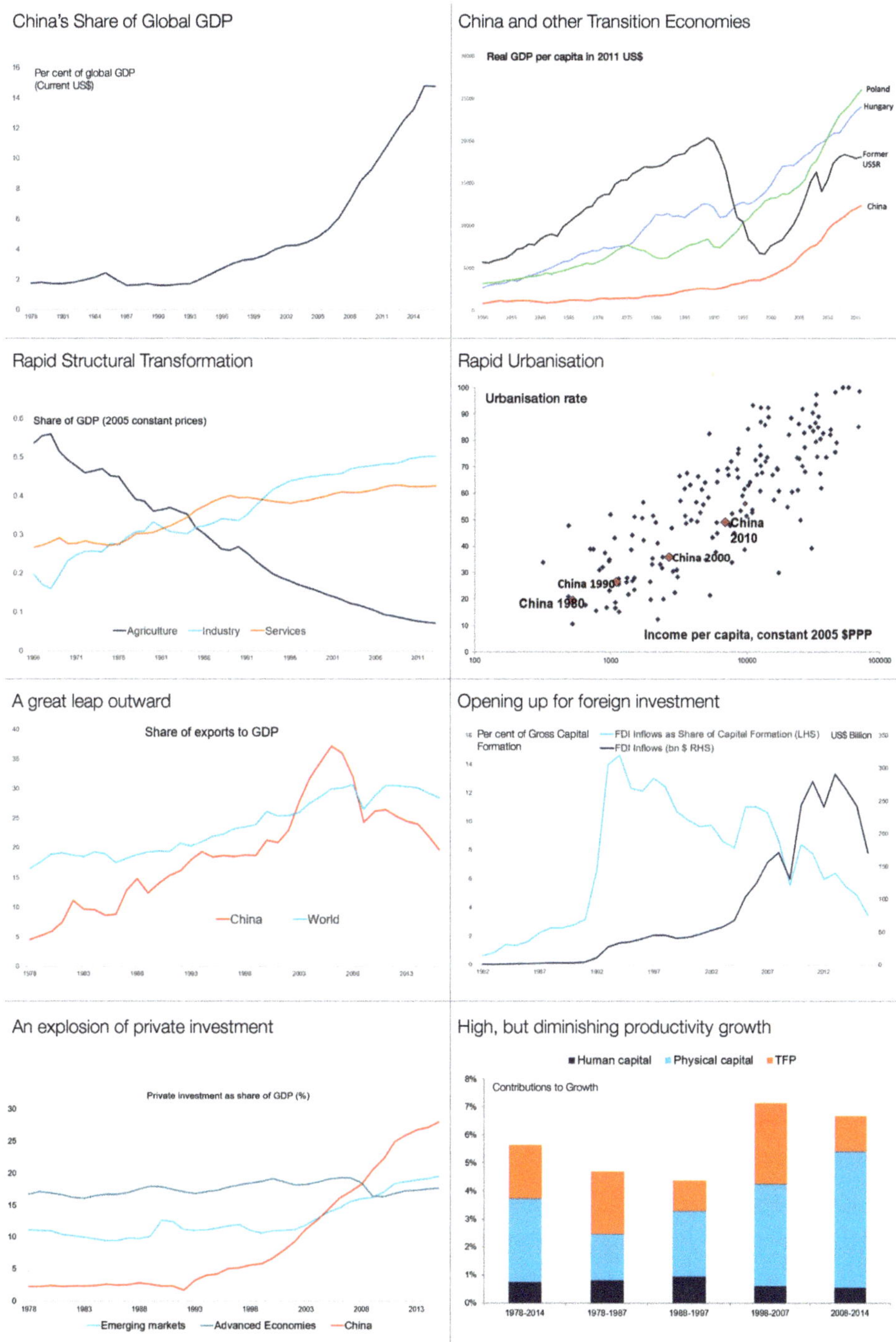

Figure 3.1 China's economic development, 1978–2016

Sources: World Bank (2018); Bolt et al. (2018).

In contrast, most other transitional countries were middle-income, highly urbanised and industrialised and had experienced more than 40 years and sometimes 70 years of collectivisation and state planning. They were highly specialised in production structure and integrated into the Comecon, with heavy concentration of industry in often monopolistic enterprises. The gradual reforms initiated in the system—first in Hungary and later in the Soviet Union—had met with only limited success, especially in the latter. Reforms started under conditions of large macroeconomic imbalances and a large monetary overhang, so price liberalisation led to an almost immediate and disruptive jump in inflation, which eroded people's savings.

The biggest difference with China was undoubtedly the collapse of political systems throughout much of the former Soviet Union and Eastern Europe. This collapse made a gradual transition of the economic system virtually impossible for most. For some, notably countries in Eastern Europe, a new institutional framework was swiftly found in the form of the European Union, to which most have now acceded. This adoption of a ready-made economic system eliminated the need for a search for institutions that would fit the individual country. Though perhaps less than fully suited for the middle-income transitional countries, the EU framework offered stability and a clearly specified reform path. As a result, the transitional recession for those that aspired to accede to the European Union was short, and most are now thriving high-income countries.

How did China reform?

Gradual reforms

Reforms in China developed only gradually, starting in rural areas with the household responsibility system and township and village enterprises (TVEs) and some initial steps to open up the economy to foreign trade and investment, which only started to play a significant role in the 1990s (Table 3.1). Gradual also were the moves on the financial sector and state-owned enterprise (SOE) reform, which were much discussed throughout the 1980s, but gained momentum only in the mid-1990s. 'Crossing the river by feeling the stones' became China's mode of economic reform, implementing partial reforms in an experimental manner, often starting in a few regions and expanding them on proven success. Only with the 1993 'Decisions of the CPC Central Committee on Some Issues Concerning the Establishment of a Socialist Market Economic Structure' did a broader overall strategy emerge. Yet, this, too, was implemented gradually and experimentally rather than comprehensively.

Table 3.1 Major reform steps in China, 1978–2017

Year	Reform step
1978	Deng Xiaoping's speech at the Central Party Work Conference, 'Emancipate the mind, seek the truth from facts and unite as one in looking to the future'
1978	Communiqué of the third Central Committee of the CPC, eleventh National Congress of the CPC, confirming 'four modernisations' as the major goal for reforms
1979	'Open door' policy initiated; foreign trade and investment reforms begin; law on joint venture companies passed
1979	Limited official encouragement of the household responsibility system informally initiated in 1976
1979	Three specialised banks separated from the People's Bank (the central bank)
1980	First four special economic zones created
1980	'Eating from separate kitchens' reforms in intergovernmental fiscal relations
1984	Socialist commodity economy endorsed at the third plenum of the twelfth National Congress of the CPC
1984	Individual enterprises with fewer than eight employees officially allowed
1984	Tax-for-profit reforms for SOEs
1986	Provisional bankruptcy law passed for SOEs
1986	CPC approves comprehensive 'Economic System Reform Implementation Plan'
1987	Contract responsibility system introduced to SOEs
1989	Retrenchment policy; halt on reforms
1990	Stock exchanges open in Shenzhen and Shanghai
1992	Deng Xiaoping's 'tour through the south' reignites reforms
1993	16-point program introduced to fight inflation
1993	Decision of the third plenum of the fourteenth National Congress of the CPC to establish a 'socialist market economy', paving the way for fiscal, financial and SOE reforms
1994	Renminbi convertible for current account transactions announced
1994	Tax-sharing system reforms introduced
1994	Policy banks established; commercialisation of banking system announced
1995	Central Bank Law, Banking Law and Budget Law enacted
1995	Fifth plenum of the thirteenth National Congress of the CPC confirms SOE reform plans to 'grasp the big, let go of the small'
1996	China in compliance with International Monetary Fund Article VIII (current account convertibility)
1999	Urban housing reforms initiated; almost all housing stock privatised
1999	Government reforms consolidate industry-related ministries and institutes
2001	China accedes to World Trade Organization
2001	Tenth five-year plan emphasises efficiency, structural change and industrial upgrading
2003	State Commission for the Restructuring of the Economic System merged with the State Planning Commission to create the National Development and Reform Commission (NDRC)
2003	Third plenum of the sixteenth National Congress of the CPC decision to 'perfect' the socialist market economy
2004	Chinese constitution amended to guarantee private property rights

Year	Reform step
2005	Construction Bank and Bank of China initial public offerings
2006	Sixth plenum of the sixteenth National Congress of the CPC establishes the goal of creating a 'harmonious society'
2006	Medium-term plan for science and technology approved
2008	Stimulus program launched in reaction to the bankruptcy of Lehman Brothers and the Global Financial Crisis (GFC)
2013	Twelfth five-year plan launched, emphasising rebalancing and avoiding the middle-income trap
2014	Third plenum of the eighteenth National Congress of the CPC decides on 'Decisive Role of the Market in Resource Allocation, Adherence to the Basis Economic System (Dominance of SOEs)'
2015	Fourth plenum of the eighteenth National Congress of the CPC decides on rule of law with Chinese characteristics
2016	Thirteenth five-year plan launched, emphasising innovation and productivity as drivers of growth
2017	Nineteenth National Congress of the CPC defines 'new era' and China's long-term goals for socialist modernisation

Sources: Hofman and Wu (2009); Gewirtz (2017); Bottelier (2018); Government of China official documents and publications.

There were several reasons for this gradual approach. First, gradualism was a means to circumvent political resistance to reform (Wu 2005). While the Cultural Revolution's political ideology of class struggle had been put to rest after Mao's death, many in the Communist Party retained a deep suspicion of the market and instead trusted the 'administrative' system (including the party) more. Gewirtz (2017) provides a lively account of these ideological battles in the early days of reform and how foreign advisors (including from the World Bank) played a role in this. Second, gradual, experimental reform was a pragmatic approach in a heavily distorted environment in which 'first best' solutions were unlikely to apply. Experimental reforms, confined to specific regions or sectors, allowed the authorities to gather information on the effects of reforms that could not be anticipated. They were also necessary to develop and test the administrative procedures and complementary policies needed to implement the reforms. With proven success, the experiment could be expanded to other regions and sectors. Third, experimental reform may have suited the Chinese culture well as a means to avoid loss of face; if something did not work, it could be abandoned as an experiment, rather than considered a policy failure. China's gradual strategy reinforced the credibility of reform over time. By undertaking reforms one step at a time, and starting with those most likely to deliver results, the government built up its reputation for delivering on reform. With every successful reform, the likelihood that the next one would also be a success undoubtedly increased. It also gradually built up the experience and skills for the design and implementation of reforms. Thus, by gradually reforming, China built up its 'reform' capital.

Decentralisation and incentives

Decentralisation to local government became a powerful tool for progress within the confines of central political guidance. Provincial and local governments received increasing authority over investment approvals and fiscal resources and policies. Provinces, municipalities and counties were allowed, and even encouraged, to experiment with reforms in specific areas, and successful experiments then became official policy and were quickly adopted throughout the country. In a way, by decentralising, China turned the country into a laboratory for reforms. The fiscal system and the political organisation within the CPC were key in aligning subnational government incentives with those of the centre. The fiscal reforms introduced in 1980, which became known as 'eating from separate kitchens', formed a de facto tax contracting system, with high revenue retention rates for local governments—in particular, for those that were set for growth. For instance, Guangdong province only had to pay a lump sum in revenues to the central government and could retain 100 per cent of the rest. This distributed the benefits of reforms to a large part of the population as well as to local government and party officials, who therefore had strong incentives to pursue growth and promote a market economy (Qian and Weingast 1997). Competition among local governments also served as an effective check on government power, even in the absence of formal controls of such powers.

Within the Communist Party, the personnel promotion system was based largely on achieving growth. The dominant criteria for promotion were growth itself, creation of employment, attraction of foreign direct investment (FDI), control of social unrest and achievement of birth control targets. Four of these five were closely aligned with GDP growth. Experience in the regions also counted heavily in the promotion to higher-level party posts, which provided the most talented with the incentives to gain that experience and to demonstrate their capacity to reform and spur growth. The entrepreneurial role of local government officials also compensated for the lack of the formal institutions of a market economy and ensured the alignment of investors' and local officials' interests. Taken together, this environment provided a strong incentive for growth. A disadvantage was imperfect macroeconomic control and repeated bouts of inflation driven by local government loosening of investment and credit controls. Further, these conditions gave rise to local protectionism, which threatened to undermine China's unified market and competition among domestic firms. It also encouraged corruption among officials as the dividing line between official roles and private interests became increasingly vague. While in the first decades of reforms corruption was controlled by harsh punishment, in the decade leading up to Xi Jinping's anticorruption campaign, corruption became a major political and economic challenge.

Pragmatism and transitional institutions

China's approach to reform provided room for the country's own particular institutions to emerge, which suited the country's purposes well at any given point on its reform path. The 'dual track' system for growing out of the planned economy was preeminent among all transitional institutions. It allowed a continuation of the planning system at planned prices, which avoided a collapse in production, but at the margin, the system allowed an unplanned economy to emerge. This also provided the information needed to gradually reform planned prices in such a way that, by the time of the abolition of most material planning in the mid-1990s, prices within and outside the plan had been largely aligned. Similarly, the de facto fiscal contracting system installed after 1980 gave subnational governments strong incentives for growth by leaving much of the incremental revenue in the provinces. Local officials' growing control over resources provided them with the incentives to pursue reforms and attract the investments needed to promote growth. The price, however, was a growing loss of macroeconomic control and, when inflation became the dominant concern in the early 1990s, the system was replaced with a more mainstream tax-sharing system, although not without a considerable political struggle led by then vice-premier Zhu Rongji.

Perhaps the most successful example of a transitional institution was the TVE—an enterprise form that operated outside the plan, but was owned and to some extent managed by local governments across rural China. Born out of the collective production brigades, these enterprises were highly successful in expanding production and creating employment, even though their ownership form was far from the private ownership that standard theory predicted would work best. However, as argued by Qian and Wu (2005), in an environment where private property was in many circles frowned on and barely protected by law, creating an ownership form that aligned the interests of local government with those of the enterprise was crucial for its development and survival. Although perhaps not the most efficient ownership form imaginable, it was a feasible one—one that was more efficient than the prevailing SOEs—and as such it increased the efficiency of the economy as a whole. As protection of property rights improved, the success of the TVEs started to falter and, in the past two decades, they have been overtaken by private and foreign-invested companies as the main source of growth and job creation.

China used its distinctive land policies to accelerate the country's development. Since the 1950s, land has been owned by the state in urban areas and by collectives in rural areas. Decentralising user rights to households in rural areas triggered sharp productivity increases in agriculture, which made rapid industrialisation possible. In urban areas, land value increases and conversion of rural to urban land played an important role in financing rapid urbanisation and infrastructure construction. By the early 1990s, lack of infrastructure had become a bottleneck for growth. Starting in large cities, urban development and infrastructure companies (UDICs) became part of the solution. Often capitalised by land user rights from local governments, UDICs were able to borrow funds to develop the infrastructure needed to expand cities for industrial and residential use. The increase in value of the land thus unlocked accrued to the UDICs, and they could use it to pay off their debt. UDICs were a practical means to allow local governments to borrow—something that had been banned in the 1995 Budget Law. By the second decade of this century, this mechanism of land-based finance had run out of steam and the disadvantages of the system started to outweigh the advantages. Local governments' overreliance on land revenue had led to excessive land conversion, inefficient city design, debt accumulation and social unrest among those communities whose land had been expropriated. Thus, the 2014 revision of the Budget Law opened up formal channels for local government borrowing, while gradually closing the off–balance sheet route.

Institutionalisation of reforms

The study and formulation of reforms and new policies—which is of importance to other countries that aspire to reform—was itself institutionalised in China. Starting with the China Academy of Social Sciences in the early days of reform—the only place in which the study of 'Western' economics had continued throughout the Cultural Revolution—a variety of think tanks sprang up to study and promote reform. Among the most influential was the Development Research Center (DRC) of the State Council, a policy research organisation directly under the Cabinet, which provided a continuing stream of inputs for reforms. In recent years, the DRC has been a partner of the World Bank, among others, in the *China 2030* (2013) and *Urban China* (2014) studies. Today, the Center for Knowledge for International Development under the DRC, founded in 2017, is tasked with studying China's reform experience to make it accessible and digestible for other countries. Another highly influential body was the Systems Reform Commission (SRC) (formally, the State Commission for the Reform of the Economic System), whose task was to propose reforms in the system. The DRC and SRC, while government organisations, were set up to provide China's leadership with options for reforms in the economic system and in economic policy. Not burdened by institutional interests like many traditional government departments, these organisations became the source of many of the reforms undertaken in the 1980s and 1990s.

Where next?

It is helpful to analytically distinguish three phases of reforms: market-*seeking* reforms, roughly from 1978 to 1993; market-*building* reforms, from 1993 to about 2003; and market-*enhancing* reforms, from about 2003 onwards (Figure 3.2). This division is to some extent arbitrary, and the timing of the phases is not exact. Nevertheless, such a division captures the distinct policy directions taken in each of the phases.

In the first phase, there was a genuine search for the right economic institutions for China. As argued above, in part driven by politics, experimentation and decentralised initiatives, China was searching for ways to allow more of the market into its system. Informed by reforms in Eastern Europe under communism, China's reforms concentrated largely on microeconomics, to some extent with a neglect of macroeconomics—and the highly volatile growth rate in the 1980s bears witness to that. After the retrenchment policy, Deng Xiaoping's tour through southern China made it clear that market reforms were there to stay.

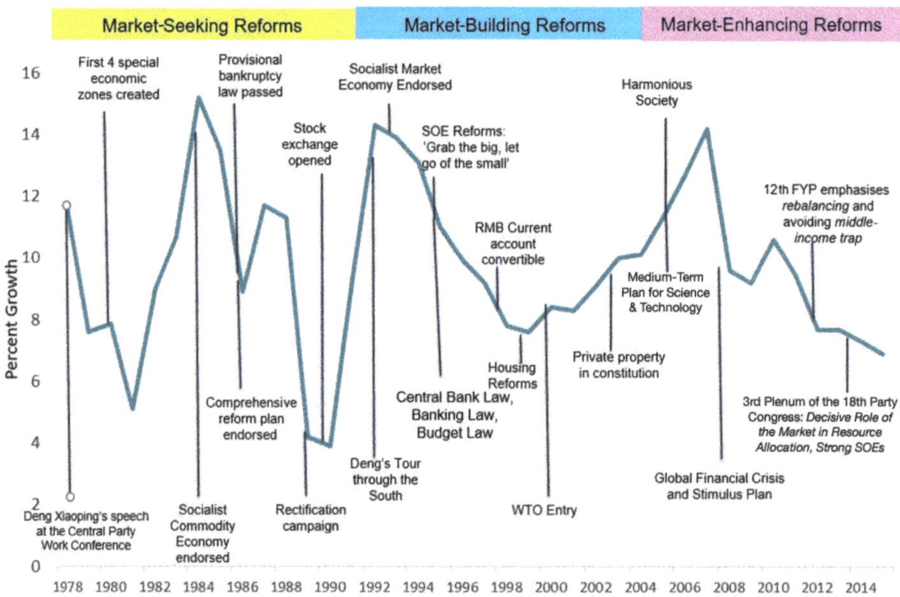

Figure 3.2 Phases of reform

Sources: Wind Database; Hofman and Wu (2009); Gewirtz (2017); Bottelier (2018); various official documents and publications of the Chinese Government.

The decisions of the third plenum of the fourteenth National Congress of the CPC in 1993 triggered the second phase by laying out a comprehensive plan to build the institutions for a market-driven economy, including a modern tax system, enterprise reforms and a financial system that separated policy banks from commercial banking. The start of serious SOE reforms in the mid-1990s allowed those commercial banks to become commercial, the credit plan was abolished in 1995 and housing and (urban) social security reforms followed. Entry to the World Trade Organization (WTO) in 2001 not only served as a lever for domestic reforms, but also ensured much greater competition on the goods market. The slashing of import tariffs made China far more competitive in exports, as well as a viable platform for final assembly of much of the Asia-based exports hitherto produced elsewhere. The unification of the exchange rate at highly competitive levels in 1995 helped boost China's 'great leap outward' and its emergence as a major exporting power.

The inclusion of private property rights in the Chinese constitution in 2004 concluded the market-building phase. This phase—the Zhu Rongji years, if you will—can be seen as one in which the state retreated and left increasing room for the market. Perhaps the best indicator of this was the explosion of private investment, which increased its share in the economy from less than 2 per cent in 1992 to some 15 per cent by 2003 (although some of this was due to a reclassification of collective enterprises as private). The share of private enterprises in industrial production rose from less than one-third in 1995 to 72 per cent in 2003 (Hofman and Wu 2009: Table 2; Lardy 2014: Ch. 3). In 1999, the Chinese Government also consolidated all industry-related ministries into the Ministry of Commerce and the Ministry of Industry and Information Technology.

Since then, reforms have focused on *enhancing* the market. The first of the two main ingredients of this is a gradual expansion of the social safety net (pensions, health care, welfare)—notably, after the 'harmonious society' became the goal of state policy in 2006. Second, we have seen a return of industrial policy, as noted by Ling and Naughton (2016). As these authors argued, 'techno-industrial policy' never left, but had been on the defensive after 1978, only to reemerge after Zhu Rongji left office. Perhaps to signify a new phase, the SRC, which played a key role in the reforms shifting from plan to market, was merged with the State Development Planning Commission in 2003 to form the National Development and Reform Commission (NDRC).

With the publication of the 'Medium-Term Plan for Science and Technology' and initiation of the '16 megaprojects' (both in 2006), industrial policy has returned to the forefront of the government's agenda. This has since been amplified with the fifth plenum of the fourteenth National Congress (on productivity and innovation), the thirteenth five-year plan and the 'Made in China 2025' strategy (in 2015). This return to prominence for industrial policy was supercharged by the GFC, which China countered with a large domestic stimulus, and which provided ample resources for central and local governments to pursue those policies. State banks and SOEs were called on to serve as instruments to implement this policy. Although the third plenum of the eighteenth National Congress in 2014 declared the market should play a 'decisive role' in the allocation of production factors, it also pledged adherence to the 'basic economic system', with public ownership playing a dominant role in the economy.

The new era

The nineteenth National Congress and President Xi's report confirm these policy directions: market-based allocation, a dominant role for public ownership and a strong emphasis on industrial policy and science and technology to achieve the goals of the 'first phase of the new era' (2020–35)—namely, socialist modernisation.

Interestingly, socialist modernisation was also what Deng Xiaoping envisioned when he set out on his reform program in 1978. Deng spoke of the 'four modernisations' of industry, agriculture, national defence and science and technology, the idea of which went back to Zhou Enlai, who first formulated this concept in the 1950s; it became policy in 1963, but was disrupted by the Cultural Revolution.

With 'socialism with Chinese characteristics for the new era', China seems to have found its own distinctive economic system, with markets and state ownership existing side by side and with industrial policy guiding the market. No doubt, the GFC contributed to the idea that a Western-style market economy was not the panacea for China's economic development, and that China had to develop its own economic system. China's current economic system has its own complexities and issues—both internal to China and in the international arena.

Domestically, there is tension between the central government's vision and industrial policies and their decentralised implementation. Once an engine of growth and institutional innovation, decentralised policy implementation has increasingly led to waste and overcapacity, as local governments pursue their own industrial policies and support their own enterprises at the expense of others—foreign and domestic alike. The government reorganisation announced at the 2018 National Congress promises increased central control over government policies and more limited space for local governments to pursue their own course, and is an attempt to resolve this tension. Changes in competition and budget policies further limit this space, while the government's anticorruption policies have reduced incentives for local officials to pursue their traditional entrepreneurial role. At the same time, the government's 'mass entrepreneurship' policies shift that entrepreneurial role further to the market—with a stronger role for the CPC in private enterprises to balance this.

Internationally, China's mixed system encounters increasing resistance. Aside from geopolitical considerations, recent trade tensions reflect the unease of many Organisation for Economic Co-operation and Development (OECD) countries with China's model. They see China's state-led and state-supported enterprises as unfair competition for their enterprises in trade and investment. Aside from trade measures, these countries increasingly call for reciprocity in investment restrictions, and are enhancing their restrictions on acquisition by foreign interests of enterprises with key technologies. These measures could undermine the international system that has much benefited China in the past, and which China's leaders have strongly supported in recent years against a rising tide of protectionism.

It is too early to tell how well 'socialism with Chinese characteristics for the new era' will serve China in achieving its two centennial goals, how the balance between the state and the market will shape up in the years to come and how China's industrial policies will remain compatible with the existing international economic system.

Irrespective of the outcomes, those who believed that by 'crossing the river' China would reach a familiar bank on the other side—a market economy not that different from the many varieties found in OECD countries—need to think again.

References

Bolt, J., Inklaar, R., de Jong, H. and Luiten van Zanden, J. (2018), Maddison Project Working Paper, no. 10. Available at: www.rug.nl/ggdc/historicaldevelopment/maddison/releases/maddison-project-database-2018.

Bottelier, P. (2018), *Economic Policy Making in China (1949–2016): The role of economists*, London: Routledge.

Development Research Center (DRC) of the State Council and World Bank (2013), *China 2030, Building a Modern, Harmonious, and Creative Society*, Washington DC.

Development Research Center (DRC) of the State Council and World Bank (2014), *Urban China, Towards Efficient, Inclusive and Sustainable Urbanization*, Washington, DC.

Gewirtz, J. (2017), *Unlikely Partners: Chinese reformers, Western economists, and the making of global China*, Cambridge, MA: Harvard University Press. doi.org/10.4159/9780674973459.

Hofman, B. and Wu, J. (2009), *Explaining China's development and reforms*, Working Paper No. 50, Washington, DC: Commission on Growth and Development.

Lardy, N. (2014), *Markets over Mao: The rise of private business in China*, Washington, DC: Peterson Institute of International Economics.

Ling, C. and Naughton, B. (2016), An institutionalized policy-making mechanism: China's return to techno-industrial policy, *Research Policy* 45: 2138–52. doi.org/10.1016/j.respol.2016.09.014.

Naughton, B. (1995), *Growing out of the Plan: Chinese economic reforms 1978–1993*, Cambridge: Cambridge University Press. doi.org/10.1017/CBO9780511664335.

Naughton, B. (2006), *The Chinese Economy: Transitions and growth*, Cambridge, MA: MIT Press.

Qian, Y. and Weingast, B. (1997), Federalism as a commitment to preserving market incentives, *Journal of Economic Perspectives* 11(4): 83–92. doi.org/10.1257/jep.11.4.83.

Qian, Y. and Wu, J. (2005), Transformation in China, Paper presented at 14th World Congress of the International Economic Association, Marrakesh, Morocco, August.

World Bank (2018), *World Development Indicators*. Available at: datacatalog.worldbank.org/dataset/world-development-indicators.

Wu, J. (2005), Understanding and Interpreting Chinese Economic Reforms, Singapore: Texere Press, Thomson–South Western.

Xi J. (2017), Secure a decisive victory in building a moderately prosperous society in all respects and strive for the great success of socialism with Chinese characteristics for a new era, Speech delivered at the 19th National Congress of the Communist Party of China, October, Beijing.

4. GDP and the new concept of development: Understanding China's changing concept of development in regards to GDP after the reform and opening-up

Wei Liu

Over the past 40 years of China's reform and opening-up, understanding of development has continued to deepen, with more scientific measures incorporated. China's transformative understanding of gross domestic product (GDP) is reflective of the change in views and concepts of development.

Introduction of GDP and China's original GDP denial

GDP is the most important indicator for the scale and growth of the economy of a country or region. It is a comprehensive measure of the value of the flow and stock of national economic activities.

Before World War II, measuring growth was a challenge. After the war, statistical measurement and empirical analysis of economic activities grew rapidly. The compilation of national economic statistics evolved into a national economic accounting system that comprehensively measured the flow and stock of aggregate national economic activity. GDP is the core measure in this system. The well-known United Nations System of National Accounts (SNA) has become the international standard for measuring economic activity. Keynesian and subsequent macroeconomics and economic growth theories were developed through its application.[1]

Before its reform and opening-up, China had long followed the theory and practice of the former Soviet Union. Despite significant differences between the conditions in China and the Soviet Union after Stalin in the late 1950s, China's

1 From the 1920s, Simon Kuznets' research on the measurement of national income and economic growth, and research on the national economic accounts system chaired by Richard Stone in the 1940s, promoted the development of traditional statistical research into the national income accounting system. As a result, Kuznets won the Nobel Prize for Economics in 1971 and Stone won in 1984.

understanding of 'industry' and its national economic accounting still followed the Soviet system. China established an accounting system that was different from the West's GDP accounting system, and was instead built on Soviet theorists' traditional understanding of Marx's labour theory of value and reproduction theory. It did not recognise nonmaterial output in the service and tertiary sectors. As the representative of economic theory in the former Soviet Union, Wassily Leontief's early chessboard balance sheet research was later developed into the famous input industry table, as well as analytical methodology.[2]

China had adopted a Soviet-style statistical accounting system based on gross industrial and agricultural production and other material products. Additional reasons for negating the value and significance of GDP were more deeply rooted. During the decade of the Cultural Revolution, when 'productivity theory' was criticised and class struggle was preeminent, China ignored the development of its economy, leading to the estrangement from the concept of GDP. When China ignored the importance of economic development gauged by the importance of national income statistics and resource allocation accounting, it was only natural that the significance of economic growth and economic development would be downplayed. The denial of GDP and the national accounting system was essentially a reflection of the off-centre ideology that neglected productivity and development. During China's long economic closure to the rest of the world, there was little access to economic growth comparisons with other nations and measuring its own economic activities with the internationally accepted national accounting system was difficult. The deeper systematic reason for the denial of GDP was that the GDP accounting system reflected market-based resource allocation. It was neither possible nor necessary to adopt the GDP accounting system for a centrally planned economy.

Recognition of GDP as an economic measure amid sustained rapid growth of the Chinese economy

At the beginning of China's reform and opening-up, the most pronounced developmental challenge the country faced was the elimination of poverty. With the deepening of China's understanding of the primary stage of socialism and the clarification of the Communist Party's position, consensus was reached to promote development and lift China out of poverty.

2 Leontief won the Nobel Prize for Economics in 1973.

On 4 October 1979, the chief architect of China's reform and opening-up, Deng Xiaoping, for the first time used the gross national product (GNP) indicator to define China's economic growth target, in a speech at the meeting of the first secretaries of the Communist Party of China (CPC) from all levels of government. Deng asked: 'Can we reach GNP per capita of over $1,000 [US dollars] by the end of this century?' He continued:

> Not long ago, I said that when our per capita GNP reached that figure, we will be in a much better position and able to provide more support to the poor countries of the Third World. We cannot do so now. China's per capita GNP is probably below [US]$300, so it is hard for us to increase it even 200 or 300 per cent. We shall have to work as hard as we did before. Even lowering the previous goal and fulfilling the lower targets, we shall still spare no effort to promote economic development and we will do every aspect of our work effectively. (Deng 1984)

This was the first time in the 30 years since the founding of the People's Republic of China that Chinese leaders used GNP indicators to set out development goals.[3]

Japanese prime minister Masahiro Ohira later asked Deng how China perceived its future modernisation targets. Deng used GNP as the basic measure in his reply, saying that from the end of the 1970s to 2000, China's total economic output should quadruple, with GNP per capita reaching US$800–1,000. He emphasised the hard work it would take to achieve this.[4] This opened up a grand plan for growth and development with GDP (GNP) as the core growth indicator and a goal of quadrupling GDP in China over 20 years (Liu and Cai 2006). From the national development and growth plan to the economic plans for all provinces and cities, GDP growth became the core planning and assessment indicator. The Chinese Government made plans to expedite the economic growth rate, and local governments began to compete with each other to achieve higher GDP growth. In practice, China met the target of quadrupling GDP at constant prices compared with 1980 three years ahead of schedule, in 1997. The government then proposed quadrupling GDP again, by 2020 from 2000, and achieved its goal of doubling 2000 GDP three years ahead of schedule, in 2007. From 2010 to the end of 2017, GDP increased at an average rate of 9.5 per cent per annum. China's share of global GDP increased from 1.8 per cent to about 15 per cent, ranking it second in the world. In 2017, China contributed more than 30 per cent of global economic growth. China's GDP per capita has jumped from more than US$250 to more

3 GDP and GNP are essentially the same accounting systems. As statistical indicators, the gap between the two comes mainly from the 'income of foreign factors': GDP is calculated based on the 'national boundary principle' and GNP is calculated on the 'national principle'. In the West, the use of GNP has a long history. Following the publication by the United Nations of the SNA in 1968, which used GDP, Western countries replaced GNP with GDP. However, since GNP placed greater emphasis on income, the World Bank still used GNP to measure the income level of various countries, but it was renamed gross national income (GNI).

4 Deng later said that, when I mentioned this matter, I was thinking of Mr Masahiro Ohira, who inspired us to set the growth target of quadrupling the GDP by the end of this century.

than US$8,800. According to the World Bank's country classifications by income level, China went from a low-income country to a lower–middle-income country (GNI per capita of US$1,026–4,035 in 2015 prices) in 1998, and to an upper–middle-income country (GNI per capita of US$4,036–12,476 in 2015 prices) in 2010. It is clear that during this process of sustained rapid growth, the core growth indicators and the corresponding economic growth plans are both centred on GDP.

There are several reasons why understanding of GDP in China has gone through such a transformation.

First, the clarification of the CPC's position on economic development during the primary stage of socialism has been developed and enforced. This process included Deng Xiaoping's view that development is the absolute first principle (Deng 2014), general secretary Jiang Zemin's 'Three Represents' theory (Jiang n.d.), Hu Jintao's 'scientific outlook on development' (Hu 2010) and Xi Jinping's 'thoughts on socialism with Chinese characteristics for a new era' (Hou 2017). China has always insisted on a dialectical historical materialist understanding of emancipating and developing productive forces. It has planned economic growth and development goals with GDP as the core indicator and promotes the doubling of GDP growth to catch up with leading economies.

The second reason for the transformation is the profound institutional change resulting from the reform and opening-up. The cultivation of a market mechanism has provided the economic basis for the use of GDP for national statistics and accounting, as GDP is a reflection of market economic activities. In addition, China's modernisation process has been combined with its globalisation. Both China's national economic accounting and its development targets must be compatible with international rules and standards, which propels the use of GDP.

Procedurally, China's acceptance of GDP has emerged from a fierce theoretical debate. Until the mid-1980s—during the transition from the planned to a market economy—China gradually unified and adopted the United Nations' SNA. This began first as pilot projects in a few provinces and cities (for example, Shanxi province, beginning in 1985). China then transitioned into using two sets of parallel accounting systems—one based on material production and one based on GDP. Finally, the SNA was fully adopted after 1987.

The GDP accounting system has its own limitations. First, exaggerated use of GDP to measure and explain economic and social development can lead to distortion of the economic growth model. We need to understand that we cannot use GDP to account for the totality of China's modernisation. GDP as a dominant measure is more effective in the primary stage of economic development. The limitations of GDP become more prevalent after severe economic shortages and long-term poverty have been eliminated and when an economy has moved beyond the Malthusian trap. Without changing the development model led by GDP growth, it is difficult to avoid the 'middle-income trap'.

Limitations of GDP and proposal of a new concept of development

The GDP accounting system is rooted in science. The emergence and continuous improvement of this system have greatly enhanced the allocation and accounting of economic resources. From the starting point (production) to the end point (demand) of national economic activities, the system comprehensively reflects all segments in the national economy in production, allocation, exchange and consumption, as well as the economy as a whole. Over a long period, this GDP-based economic system matures and becomes difficult to replace. Economists Samuelson and Nordhaus (1995) claimed that GDP was the greatest invention by humankind in the twentieth century. However, if GDP is used exclusively to guide the development of a national economy without considering its limitations, it will inevitably cause serious problems.

First, GDP emphasises quantity and does not directly reflect differences in the underlying economic structure. The largest national economy in terms of GDP may be based on an extremely backward economic structure, thus distorting the relationship between economic growth and the quality of economic development. It may reflect a large amount of economic expansion with no qualitative structural upgrading or growth fuelled by the quantity of factor inputs with no increase in total factor productivity. Economic growth refers to scale expansion or growth of GDP. Development refers to structural upgrading. Structural optimisation is the essence of economic development. The real difficulty in economic development is overcoming structural conflicts.[5] GDP expansion can be achieved at a rapid rate by over-relying on the expansion of factor inputs. Its easy achievement makes it handy as a short-term policy target, but this may aggravate deep structural imbalances in economic development, which in turn exacerbate short-term macroeconomic imbalances and severely limit long-term sustainable development.

5 For example, in the first half of the nineteenth century, China's GDP accounted for more than 30 per cent of the global total, ranking the country first in the world. The reason it declined rapidly after 1840 was, among other things, because the structural quality was backward, the industrial structure was still dominated by traditional agriculture and the organisational structure of social production was still dominated by small family production. Compared with the industrial structure supported by the Industrial Revolution in Europe and the United States, the production social organisational structure is based on the modern capitalist enterprise system. There is a qualitative difference. For example, in contemporary high-income oil-exporting countries, the GDP level leads in both total and per capita terms. However, such an economy is deformed, and thus strictly speaking belongs to the group of high-income countries but does not belong to truly modern countries. When it comes to categories, such a state is often called not a 'developed country', but an 'oil-exporting country'.

Second, GDP as an accounting system reflects the flow of economic activities during a certain period (one year), while national wealth is the accumulation of the stock of economic activities over the long term. When using the GDP method, ignoring the characteristics of the economic flows will cause serious damage to the national economy, especially if the goals for economic activity are short term and wealth accumulation and sustainability are underappreciated.[6]

Third, the GDP accounting system reflects the market's economic behaviour measured in prices. Economic activities that do not pass through market transactions and have no market prices are difficult to include in the GDP accounting system, yet markets do not account for all economic activities. For example, services provided by the military, police and governmental departments use economic resources and generate output, but cannot be allocated through market mechanisms. Another example is domestic work. In principle, a considerable part of domestic work does not go through market transactions. Therefore, it is difficult to incorporate into the national economic accounting system. Further, if pursuit of GDP growth becomes the overarching objective, a great deal of economic activity and resource allocation not based on market mechanisms will be excluded from the system of national accounts and thus ignored; these areas may require development, but are excluded from the GDP-based system.[7]

Fourth, if one-sided economic growth and development only are emphasised, and comprehensive social development is ignored, there will inevitably be distortion of the modernisation process. Accounting and evaluation of modernisation should encompass other measures of social development, such as the impact of economic development on ecological protection, holistic development of human society and the relationship between economic development and the level of people's happiness.

In response to these realities, proposals have been put forward for indices such as 'green GDP', the Human Development Index and the 'Happiness Index' to supplement the GDP indicator system and provide a better guide for comprehensive societal development.[8]

---

6 All the relevant economic activities of the investment project will be counted in the GDP of the current year, but all the economic activities for demolishing the project in the second year will also be counted in the GDP for the second year, but the accumulation of the accumulated wealth (stock) is zero, and at the same time during the process (flow forming) a large amount of economic resources are consumed, impairing the potential for sustainable development in the future.

7 Since the beginning of its reform and opening-up, China has carried out three economic censuses. In its census data, the component of GDP that has not been fully counted is 'services'.

8 'Green GDP', also known as the System of Environmental-Economic Accounting (SEEA), incorporates resources and environmental factors based on the existing national economic accounting. This is a very modern and advanced concept, but also very complicated. At present, no country in the world has established a sound and practical system of green accounting. The Human Development Index (HDI) reflects the level of human development in a country according to living conditions, educational level and level of affluence, measured by the three variables of life expectancy, years of education and per capita GDP. The 'Happiness Index' is published by the World Value Survey, which investigates political, economic, social, family, religious and many other issues, and ultimately comes down to the question: 'Are you happy?' This index is calculated by statistical processing of the respondents' answers (Liu 2005: Ch. 17, ss. 2–3).

The practical limitations of GDP as an accounting system are increasingly being recognised; its value is being questioned and improvements are being made.[9] In the early period of China's reform and opening-up, its socioeconomic development was in an extremely backward state. Reducing poverty was the overarching agenda. Doubling the national economy in terms of GDP was an objective historical necessity. Surpassing the 'poverty trap' requires rapid economic growth. Under the prevailing economic development conditions, environmental protection and wider social developmental issues were secondary. The conflicts between these goals and economic development were still not very sharp. Therefore, under Deng Xiaoping's advocacy, GDP value indicators were used to plan the long-term development goals for the first time after the twelfth National Congress of the CPC in 1984. Formulating growth and development guidelines based on GDP was considered relevant and feasible.[10] Overcoming the 'poverty trap' through GDP growth was consistent with the CPC's position of focusing on economic construction and prioritising development. The dialectical materialist conception of history was the basic supporting concept. The resulting sustained, high-speed economic growth profoundly changed China and brought about the concept of socialism with Chinese characteristics for a new era.

The constraints on China's social development in the new era have fundamentally changed, and these changes have brought new opportunities and challenges. China's development has come close to achieving the goal of 'national rejuvenation' while overcoming the middle-income trap, and it is now on its way to realising the government's stated goals of basic modernisation by 2035 and becoming a modern socialist country by 2050.

Old growth models cannot sustain balanced and coordinated development. On the supply side, the costs of labour, natural resources, environmental services and technological services have risen dramatically. Previous absolute comparative advantages have gradually disappeared. On the demand side, there is weakness in purchasing power and overcapacity. Therefore, management of stable and balanced growth, cost-induced inflation, adequate employment, long-term sustainable development and comprehensive social growth all require a fundamental transformation of the development model. China must shift from high-speed growth that has depended mainly on the expansion of factor inputs to high-quality

9 For example, US presidential candidate Robert Kennedy pointed out in the early 1960s: ' Yet the gross national product does not allow for the health of our children, the quality of their education or the joy of their play. It does not include the beauty of our poetry or the strength of our marriages, the intelligence of our public debate or the integrity of our public officials' (quoted in Rogers 2012).

10 The twelfth National Congress of the CPC continued to propose a target of quadrupling total economic output in the last 20 years of the twentieth century measured by gross industrial and agricultural output values, and later switched to the goal of quadrupling GNP proposed by Deng. In the end, the party clearly stated that, in accordance with international practice, the GDP approach to planning had been adopted (Liu and Cai 2006: Ch. 1).

growth that depends mainly on efficiency. There is a need for a new development philosophy that will define the path and guide the practice for a new economic development framework, culminating in a new concept of development.

References

Deng, X. (1984), *Selected Works of Deng Xiaoping. Volume 2, 1975–1982*, Beijing: Foreign Languages Press.

Deng, X. (2014), Development is still priority, *China Daily USA*, 22 August. Available from: usa.chinadaily.com.cn/opinion/2014-08/22/content_18468120.htm.

Hou, Q. (2017), CPC creates Xi Jinping thought on socialism with Chinese characteristics for a new era, *Xinhuanet*, 19 October. Available from: www.xinhuanet.com/english/2017-10/19/c_136689808.htm.

Hu, J. (2010), Scientific outlook on development, *China Daily*, 8 September. Available from: www.chinadaily.com.cn/china/cpc2011/2010-09/08/content_12474310.htm.

Jiang, Z. (n.d.), What is 'Three Represents' CPC theory?, *China.org*. Available from: www.china.org.cn/english/zhuanti/3represents/68735.htm.

Liu, W. (ed.) (2005), *Economics*, 2nd edn, Beijing: Peking University Press.

Liu, W. and Cai, Z. (2006), *GDP Going Down from the Altar: From economic growth to sustainable development*, Beijing: China CITIC Press.

Rogers, S. (2012), Bobby Kennedy on GDP: 'measures everything except that which is worthwhile', *Guardian*, 24 May. Available from: www.theguardian.com/news/datablog/2012/may/24/robert-kennedy-gdp.

Samuelson, P. and Nordhaus, W. (1995), *Economics*, 15th edn, New York: McGraw-Hill.

Xi, J. (2017a), *Discourse on Socialist Economic Construction*, Beijing: Literature Research Office of the Central Committee of the Communist Party of China.

Xi, J. (2017b), Secure a decisive victory in building a moderately prosperous society in all respects and strive for the great success of socialism with Chinese characteristics for a new era, Presented to Nineteenth National Congress of the Communist Party of China, Beijing.

Xi, J. (2018), Speech at the meeting of the Political Bureau of the CPC Central Committee on Learning the Modern Economic System, 30 January, *People's Daily*, 1 February.

5. The political economy causes of China's economic success

Yang Yao

China's economic growth since 1978 has been nothing short of a miracle, lifting most people out of poverty and the country to the rank of higher-middle income. Its citizens have witnessed a quantum leap in their standard of living, and the nation's wealth now rivals the greatest countries in the world. It is no exaggeration to say that China's rapid economic take-off has been *the* most significant economic event in the world in the past four decades. For economists, studying China's economic success is exciting. However, most studies to date have focused on its 'technical' aspects—that is, pointing out what China has done right in terms of economic policy and institutional reform—rather than on the 'principle' aspects, investigating the fundamental causes of China adopting good economic policies and implementing institutional reforms. The quest for these causes is a major new undertaking in political economy analysis. This chapter aims to contribute to this endeavour by offering three political economy explanations for China's economic success. First, an autonomous government—one that neither represents a specific social class nor is captured by a specific social group—enables the central government to adopt highly inclusive economic policies that favour long-term economic growth of the whole society. Second, economic decentralisation gives local governments strong fiscal motivation to develop the local economy. And third, a meritocratic promotion system gives local officials strong positive incentives and counters the negative consequences of decentralisation. This chapter analyses the inadequacies of previous studies, and then discusses these three causes.

Inadequacies in existing explanations

Comparing the growth of China over the past four decades with that of East Asia's successful economies shows that China shares common elements of their success, such as high rates of savings and investment, deep industrialisation, exports driven primarily by manufacturing products and an emphasis on education. Thus, from a purely economic perspective, China's galloping economy is nothing special, and has not exceeded the expectations of neoclassical economics. This does not mean that market forces alone drove China's success without any input from the government. On the contrary, the government has played a crucial role in the nation's economic success. While most scholars agree that government action has been important, academic opinion is divided over the exact role the government has played. A number of theories have been popular over the past few decades.

The institutional view

The reform launched in 1978 was the key that unlocked China's high rates of economic growth, and institutional reform was at its core. Price reform, state-owned enterprise (SOE) reform, granting market access to the private sector and opening up to the world were the most significant elements. Price reform was indispensable as the nation made the transition from a planned to a market economy. China adopted a gradual approach and completed its price reform over a 10-year period, between 1984 and 1994. SOE reform came next; this proved much harder than price reform because it triggered massive unemployment of millions of workers. China took 10 years to complete the transformation of 80 per cent of its SOEs from government-owned entities to market players. The private sector emerged during this time and became an economic pillar of significance equal to the SOEs, greatly enhancing China's economic vitality. The 1990s saw China's economic reform advancing at its fastest pace, creating a firm foundation for the exponential growth in the decade after China's 2001 accession to the World Trade Organization (WTO). Opening to the international economy, which began in 1980 with the establishment of four special economic zones (SEZs), also helped spur rapid growth after the WTO accession. If pre-WTO opening was concerned primarily with bringing in foreign investment, post-WTO opening was driven by the concept of 'going abroad'. From 2001 to 2008, China's export growth averaged 29 per cent per annum—more than quadrupling its total amount over the seven-year period.

A longitudinal comparison shows that economic reform was undoubtedly the engine driving China's rapid economic growth over the past four decades. This proposition, however, faces two challenges. First, what was the role of the industrial, technological and social development in the 30 years prior to China's reform? Although many mistakes were made in that period, its achievements cannot be disputed. As of 1978, a comparison of developing countries that were on a par with China in their stage of development and income levels (such as India) would reveal that China had a higher degree of industrialisation, a more comprehensive industrial system, stronger technological strength, greater coverage of basic education and longer life expectancy (Yao 2014). These achievements helped create a firm foundation for economic dynamism after the reform. Second, is the institutional thesis still valid when one compares China with other developing countries? Among the more than 140 developing countries (regions) in the world, most have adopted a market economy and are open to foreign investment, but only a handful has succeeded in substantially raising their income. If 45 per cent of US per capita income is adopted as the threshold for a high-income nation, only 11 countries (regions) have moved from the rank of middle-income nation to high-income nation since 1960. Therefore, establishing a market economy and opening to the world, while prerequisites, are not sufficient conditions for economic growth.

The development strategy view

Lin et al. (1996) proposed that the change in development strategy was the key to China's different economic performance in the pre-reform and post-reform periods. They distinguished between two types of development strategy—namely, catching-up and comparative advantage. The former refers to the government's approach to developing industries that defy the comparative advantages of the nation, while the latter refers to the government's approach to developing industries that conform to the nation's comparative advantages. Lin et al. (1996) believed that the planned economy failed because China initially adopted the catch-up strategy, and it has succeeded since economic reform because it has abandoned the catch-up strategy and adopted the comparative advantage strategy. As China's labour force was long the source of its comparative advantage, the comparative advantage strategy required development of labour-intensive industries. In subsequent works, Lin (2014) further emphasised the importance of upgrading the industrial structure when a nation's capital–labour endowment structure is upgraded. He believed this was in line with dynamic comparative advantage. At the same time, he also highlighted the crucial role the government can play in selecting which industries to support. The 'new structural economics' Lin has advocated has generally been considered representative of the 'facilitating state' theory.

Based on the history of China's industrial upgrading, the conclusions drawn by Lin and his co-authors about the role of comparative advantage are undoubtedly correct. The question is how can we explain the mechanism behind this relationship? According to the theory of new structural economics, this is the outcome of a deliberate choice by the government. However, this theory fails to explain why the market is unable to automatically select the industries that fit with a country's comparative advantage. Under the assumption of a complete market, we would never arrive at a conclusion in which the enterprises in that market would not select an industry with comparative advantage. Lin (2014) emphasised that the market is incomplete. However, this significantly weakens his theory because its crux is no longer comparative advantage (because comparative advantage would lead to spontaneous selection by enterprises in a complete market), but whether the government is necessary. This has been the subject of much discussion and study since the socialist debate between Oskar Lange and the Austrian School (notably Hayek) in the 1930s.

Meanwhile, the comparative advantage theory also needs to address the three decades preceding China's reform. All backward countries are trying to catch up with developed countries; they are aiming to attain the latter's standard of living within a relatively short period—much shorter than that taken by developed countries. Catching up comes in myriad forms and follows many paths. The path China has taken is to build a relatively comprehensive industrial base and accumulate robust technological strength at the expense of a generation, and then join international economic exchange to release its potential. This may not have been the optimal path. On the other hand, it may have been a productive path: developing heavy industry might have been the best choice at the time,[1] and, indeed, much was achieved by that strategy. It is contrary to say the least to deny there were any benefits from a development strategy based on heavy industry.[2]

The China model view

The 'China model' is often known as the 'Beijing consensus'. For the purposes of this chapter, the Beijing consensus refers to a new economic model that stands in contrast to the 'Washington consensus', which initially was a set of structural adjustment policies responding to the Latin American sovereign debt crisis in the 1980s (Williamson 2004), but which has since become synonymous with neoliberal economic doctrines. As such, the Beijing consensus has emerged as the antithesis of neoliberalism, although the specifics are a matter of debate. One view equates the Beijing consensus with socialism with Chinese characteristics, and places specific emphasis on the role played by state-owned economic components. For instance, the state-owned land system has meant that local governments can rapidly improve a city's infrastructure by way of land finance and SOEs can carry out national strategic goals. These assertions are credible to a certain extent, but do not necessarily go far enough to capture the key impetus of China's rapid economic growth. Clearly, if the state-owned components are that important, why did the country underperform during the central planning era when compared with the post-reform era? 'State capitalism' may be an answer to this question and may serve to generalise the Beijing consensus. State capitalism negates both economic planning and laissez-faire capitalism, and instead advocates a kind of socialism marked by strong government intervention, which, to a certain extent, accurately describes China's reality. The question is: does

1 Implementation of the import substitution strategy and the development of domestic heavy industries were the major policy recommendations of the World Bank, as well as the consensus of most Chinese academics at the time. A 1948 survey of Chinese students studying in the United States revealed that 51.5 per cent of the respondents believed the development of China's heavy industry should be advanced by way of nationalisation (Pepper 2017: 79).

2 Yao and Zheng (2008) constructed a dynamic general equilibrium model to comprehensively evaluate the heavy industry development strategy during the era of the planned economy. Their simulation found that by producing positive externalities, the strategy facilitated China's economic growth. However, the duration of this strategy was too long (the optimal duration is 12 years) and the subsidies received by heavy industry were too high.

it really capture the essence of China's economic success? In the past 20 years, the private sector has been the key driver of economic growth. Using state capitalism to generalise the Beijing consensus lends support to the views that discredit China's growth as being 'anti-people'. A consequence of state capitalism is the suppression of the welfare of ordinary people, which is contrary to the aim of economic growth, and precisely what has been used by some international observers to attack China's development path. Attributing China's success to state capitalism defeats one's own attempt to distil any merits from China's growth experience.

Another view is that the Beijing consensus is more flexible than state capitalism. This view holds that the most significant characteristic of the Beijing consensus is the flexible application of the prescriptions of neoclassical economics. As previously mentioned, from a purely economic perspective, China's economic success has not exceeded the expectations of neoclassical economics. However, China's government has conscientiously screened these prescriptions and their process of implementation has been gradual. A typical example is exchange rate management. In the planning era, the renminbi was grossly overvalued and became the key reason for China's hunger for foreign exchange. After the reform, the government became aware of this problem and began to adopt a dual-track exchange rate system. The official exchange rate was still overvalued and was used primarily to control imports. The market exchange rate was generally market driven and was used to encourage exports. This was a classic case of mercantilism; it was a flexible application of neoclassical economic theory. The two exchange rates were unified in 1994, and the currency was pegged at RMB8.25 to US$1 until 2005. Subsequently, the renminbi entered a managed floating regime, but exchange rate stability remained the fundamental goal. Fixed exchange rates helped drive China's exports significantly, accelerating industrialisation, but holding back workers' wages (Mao et al. 2017). Other examples include the dual-track price system, SOE reform and industrial policies. However, selectively applying the neoclassical economic prescription is not unique to China, but is a common feature among East Asian economies. Thus, using it to define the Beijing consensus is inappropriate. In reality, the task of scholars is not to find the unique characteristic(s) of a nation, but to discover the universal attributes of many nations. It is poor analysis to use the Beijing consensus to explain China's success.

The cultural view

To explain a country's success, culture is one factor that comes easily to mind. For instance, Weber's *The Protestant Ethics and the Spirit of Capitalism* explained the success of capitalism from the perspective of Protestant culture. In East Asia, neo-Confucians have attempted to use Confucian culture to explain East Asia's economic success, but serious economic analyses are rare. Zhu (2016) is an exception. After rejecting other explanations, Zhu pointed out that the culture of savings and education was a crucial factor in China's economic success. A high saving rate and a relatively high level of education are the key drivers of China's rapid economic growth, and Chinese culture contains elements that value both. One also has reason to believe these cultural factors have a positive effect to raise saving rates and levels of education. However, from an academic perspective, China has provided only one sample point; deriving a conclusion from this may not have universal significance. In fact, the biggest problem with using culture to explain economic success is that when researchers argue that a particular culture spurs economic growth, they are unable to exclude the possibility that other cultures can also promote economic growth. For instance, Weber placed the Protestant culture on a very high pedestal. As far as Protestantism is concerned, his arguments would have been just fine—Protestantism did encourage discipline, frugality and hard work—but they could not explain why the economy of Prussia, which was predominantly Protestant, took off later than that of France, which was predominantly Catholic. Certainly, he would not have been able to predict that Confucian culture would have an effect similar to Protestantism in the later part of the twentieth century. One of the challenges of the cultural explanation for the post-reform economic miracle is that Chinese culture has existed since ancient times. Why did it only begin to spur economic growth after the reform? Culture is a slow (long-term) variable, while post-reform economic growth has been a rapid (short-term) variable. We know that a slow variable cannot explain a fast variable. Culture may be important, but it needs another 'trigger variable' to become effective.

To summarise, the four popular views have all touched some truths of China's miraculous growth, but they are incomplete. In particular, they have focused on the 'technical' aspects of China's growth, exploring what China has done right in terms of economic policy and institutional reform, rather than on the 'principles'—the 'why' and 'how' China has done right. Organisations and individuals formulate policies and institutions. In the case of China, this is the government and its officials. The issue of 'principle' would then become: what factors have made the Chinese Government adopt policies and institutions that favour economic growth? What factors would incentivise officials to implement these government policies and adopt the right institutions? This chapter's answer to the first question is that the Chinese Government is an autonomous government. The answer to the second is that promotion is the strongest incentive, and economic decentralisation provides the platform for merit-based promotion.

The autonomous government

An autonomous government contrasts with a biased government (Yao 2009). A biased government is one that represents the interests of a minority in society. In most cases, it is a product of patron–client politics. The patrons are powerful characters who monopolise political and economic resources and hand them to their clients in exchange for political support and material benefits. Politics thus becomes a transaction between individuals, rather than political competition for the purpose of a common goal. In a country dominated by patron–client politics, the status of the ruler depends on the depth of his or her personal political networks as well as the amount of political and economic benefits he or she can offer to the clients in the networks. In this case, he or she must therefore succumb to the interests and welfare of this minority, thus ignoring the rest of society. Fukuyama (2014) has thus viewed patron–client politics as the greatest threat to liberal democracy.[3] In this context, the autonomous government becomes all the more meaningful. An autonomous government is one that does not form an alliance with, and is not captured by, any interest group in society. It is impartial towards different segments of society, but may have its own interests and agendas. Because it is unfettered by the claims of any interest group, an autonomous government has advantages over biased governments in terms of economic growth. Its economic policies are more inclusive and misallocation of resources is less common. Hence, it can advance economic growth better than a biased government (Yao 2009).

Whether a society can produce an autonomous government depends on that society's political structure and the political power (or state capacity) possessed by the government. A politically more equal society can produce an autonomous government more easily because the ruler does not have to worry about any group or an alliance of groups overthrowing his or her rule. Should a rebellion occur, he or she would be able to form an alliance with groups of equal strength to defeat the rebels. The higher the political power of the government itself, the less it should be concerned with rebellions by social groups. Thus, even if the political structure is less equal, the government is able to remain autonomous. Figure 5.1 illustrates this with an example of two social groups.

Figure 5.1 assumes there are two groups in society. Each has a certain amount of political power (the ability to mobilise or organise to defeat other groups), denoted by v_i, $i = 1, 2$. The government also has a certain amount of political power (mobilisation, suppression and other such abilities), denoted by v. Under what circumstances would an autonomous government emerge? If one of the two groups has stronger political power than the government, this group is able to replace the government. At this time, only if the government and the second group form an alliance, and the political power of this alliance is equal to or greater than that of the first group, can the government be protected from being replaced. This would require Equation 5.1.

3 The Philippines is a classic case of client politics. See Yao (2018: Ch. 15).

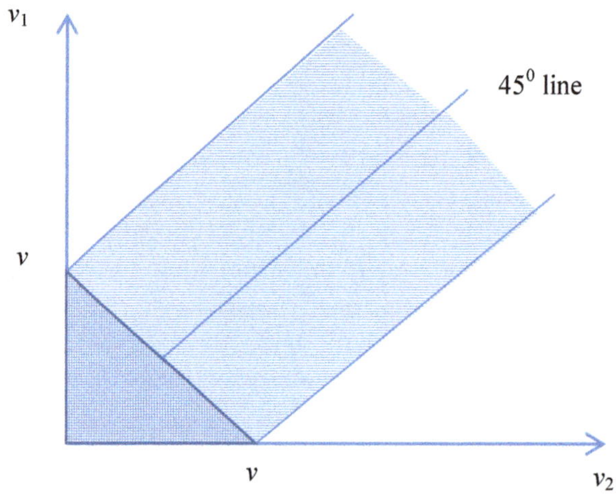

Figure 5.1 Political structure and the autonomous government
Source: Yao (2018).

Equation 5.1

$$v \geq | v_1 - v_2 |$$

However, the government cannot be so powerful that an alliance between the two groups is unable to check it. Thus, we also require Equation 5.2.

Equation 5.2

$$v \leq v_1 + v_2$$

Only when both conditions are met would the government choose to be autonomous. In Figure 5.1, the lightly shadowed area is where the autonomous government exists. The heavily shadowed area fulfils the condition in Equation 5.1, but not in Equation 5.2; here, the government can do as it pleases. The area in which the autonomous government exists is a tube along the 45° line in which the gap between v_1 and v_2 is modest—that is, society features a certain degree of equality in political power. Meanwhile, the width of the tube depends on the strength of the government's political power. A government with greater power can accommodate a more unequal political structure. These conclusions are also valid when more than two groups exist (see Yao 2018).

If we apply the above analysis to China, we see that, in the first two decades of its reform, China's relatively egalitarian social structure and the encompassing nature of the Communist Party of China (CPC) helped produce an autonomous government. In the early years of the People's Republic of China (PRC), the socialist revolution shattered the old social class structure and forged a new society that was almost completely egalitarian; and, in the next three decades, this social structure continued to be more equal than it would otherwise have been. Although this process was accompanied by pain and failures (particularly during the Cultural Revolution), a solid social foundation had been laid for economic reform. The CPC itself underwent enormous changes during the reform process. Starting with the 'truth debate' in 1978 and ending with the 'three representations' at the sixteenth CPC congress in 2002, the Communist Party completed its transition from a revolutionary party with an emphasis on class struggle to a ruling party representing the interests of the country. To use Olson's (1982) thesis, the CPC became an encompassing organisation—that is, its own interests significantly overlapped with the interests of society. With this transformation, the CPC brought capable people into the party, turning societal conflicts into internal party discussions. It formulated the party's fundamental policies through democratic centralism. In this process, the ruling status of the party was also enhanced. Thus, although Chinese society began to polarise dramatically in the 1990s, the CPC was able to remain autonomous.

As it remained relatively impartial towards different sections of society, the party-led government was able to adopt economic policies that benefited the entire society without restraint. In the early stages, reforms (such as rural reform) often resulted in Pareto improvement. Very quickly, however, most reforms and economic policies would fail to generate explicit Pareto improvement; only potential Pareto improvement could be achieved. Hence, locally and over the short term, the pro-growth policies that an autonomous government adopts may well be partial. The most well-known example of this is the SEZ. Clearly, over the short term, SEZs benefited only a minority, but over the longer term, SEZs have played an irreplaceable part in China's opening up to foreign investment. SOE reform and accession to the WTO are similar examples. A recent example would be the stimulus plans adopted after the Global Financial Crisis. When the crisis struck, expanding domestic consumption was the correct measure. What other countries did was disburse cash directly to encourage consumption. In China, all levels of government started a new investment boom and expanded production capacity. The reason China's government was able to do this was that its policy is not dictated by public sentiment, so it can be guided by a longer-term vision.

Nonetheless, along with the rapid accumulation of wealth and dramatic social polarisation, business interest groups have also sprung up quietly, and began to corrupt senior party and government cadres to form political–business alliances. After the eighteenth CPC congress, General Party Secretary Xi Jinping led a high-profile anticorruption campaign, not merely to root out the cancer of corruption and to purify the party, but also to eradicate these political–business alliances and to build a new relationship between the government and the business community. Over the longer term, the anticorruption campaign was an indispensable means of allowing the party and the government to return to their core roles, and to continue to remain relatively impartial towards different sections of society, thus consolidating the ruling status of the party. It also offered political assurance to the nation about maintaining a relatively high rate of economic growth over the longer term.

Economic decentralisation

An autonomous government can explain why the central government is willing to adopt pro-growth economic policies over the longer term, but does not adequately explain how these policies are thoroughly implemented in a country with a vast territory such as China. Economic decentralisation and a meritocratic promotion system for government officials are strong supplementary elements in the Chinese system. Decentralisation motivates local governments and officials to take the initiative to develop the local economy, while a meritocratic promotion system overcomes the negative effects of decentralisation, such as regionalism and corruption. This section discusses decentralisation, and the next the meritocratic promotion system.

China has been a unitary state since ancient times. After the Qing dynasty was overthrown, the Republic of China and then the People's Republic of China inherited this system. In a unitary state, how to balance local initiatives and national unification has always been a core issue of concern for the central government. Since Qin Shi Huang, the first emperor of unified China, established provinces and counties, China has created a rigorous bureaucracy and has governed its vast territory via a competent bureaucracy rather than a feudal system. From the perspective of preserving national unity and advancing the will of the state, this system has been, without a doubt, very successful, and was commended by Fukuyama (2014). However, this system suppressed local initiatives and hindered social and economic improvement.[4] After the founding of the PRC, the central government also had to face the issue of balancing central planning and local initiatives. During the first five-year plan period, the fiscal system was highly centralised. While the accelerated development of a number of heavy industrial projects was a positive result, it suppressed local initiatives. Mao Zedong was aware of this problem and specifically discussed the issue of incentivising both central and local authorities in his famous speech 'On the Ten Major Relationships'. However, decentralisation during the 'Great Leap Forward' in 1958 led to economic chaos. Subsequently, the fiscal relationship between central and local authorities wavered between decentralisation and centralisation until 1977, when a pilot system of local fiscal contracting was launched, and 1980, when the fiscal contracting system was officially established. In the next 14 years, the central government entered into different contracting agreements with the provinces, the content of which was adjusted according to prevailing circumstances, resulting in economic decentralisation.

---

4 For instance, the overly centralised tax system in the Song dynasty curbed the initiative of local officials to protect the local economy (Li 1999). As such, the seeds of capitalism in the Southern Song did not bloom into a capitalist economy.

Fiscal decentralisation was carried out hand-in-hand with China's overall economic decentralisation. In the 1980s, township and village enterprises (TVEs) emerged and prospered, becoming engines of China's industrial growth. Local governments played a crucial role in advancing the development of TVEs. At the time, private enterprises were not officially recognised. Entrepreneurs who wanted to start enterprises had to tie up with the local government, resulting in the emergence of a large number of so-called red-cap enterprises. The local government provided a political umbrella for these enterprises, helping them find production materials and sales channels. Hence, the local government erected a protective firewall between the central government and enterprises and played a positive part in market development and reform. Qian and Weingast (2011) believe that, in this regard, fiscal decentralisation is a type of fiscal federalism that protects the market. Fiscal decentralisation significantly motivated local governments to take the initiative to develop the local economy, which became an important force in propelling China's economic growth in the 1980s and 1990s.

The fiscal contracting system created many problems, one of which was the decline in the central government's share of the national budget. By the early 1990s, budgetary revenue figures alone showed that the central government's share of total government revenue had fallen to less than 20 per cent (Wang and Hu 1993). Local governments also had large amounts of extra-budget revenue. The central government's fiscal capacity fell significantly while local governments' influence was significantly enhanced. The implementation of the tax-sharing system in 1994 was intended to resolve this problem. This reform borrowed elements of the federal system such as that in the United States. It classified taxes into central, local and shared taxes, and established the value-added tax (VAT) at a uniform rate of 17 per cent, of which the central government took 75 per cent while local governments took 25 per cent. As the VAT was the largest tax after the tax-sharing reform, the share of the central government's budgetary revenue rose significantly, to more than 50 per cent. As such, this reform institutionalised fiscal decentralisation and strengthened the central government's revenue capacity. With this capacity, the central government was able to use fiscal tools to regulate and control local governments, the primary means of which were fiscal transfers back to the provinces. In the 1990s, fiscal transfers were based primarily on tax rebates and projects, which attended to the interests of developed provinces, but had no fiscal equalisation effect on a nationwide basis. In the new millennium, particularly after 2006, general transfers intensified and interprovincial fiscal gaps began to narrow. To date, transfer payments from the central government to the provinces are equivalent to 80 per cent of central fiscal revenue, achieving fiscal equalisation, on the one hand, and bolstering the central government's authority over local governments, on the other.

An international comparison would reveal that not all countries that implement fiscal decentralisation have been successful. In countries such as Russia and Indonesia, decentralisation actually increased opportunities for corruption among local officials (Blanchard and Shleifer 2001). Undeniably, this is also present in China. In addition, decentralisation has led to local protectionism, excessive competition and myopic behaviour among officials. Why, then, has China's economic performance been better than that of other countries? In recent years, some foreign observers believed that corruption among officials could well be the key to explaining China's economic success. The deceleration of China's economic growth in 2012–15 coincided with its anticorruption campaign, and has been used as proof for this assertion. The existing literature has put forward two theories supporting the idea that corruption promotes economic growth. The first is the 'greasing the wheels' theory, which holds that many government regulations in developing countries hinder economic growth. Thus, bribing officials helps to 'grease the wheels' for enterprises to circumvent unreasonable rules and regulations. The second is the rent-creation theory, which holds that to achieve economic growth, superiors deliberately retain some rents for subordinates in exchange for their efforts. Both these theories, however, fail the test of empirical evidence. In regards to the first, if the 'greased' official did not offer equal services to all players in the market, corruption would distort resource allocation and lower economic efficiency. Based on the anticorruption experience over the past few years, the 'large tigers' who have been arrested have generally exchanged interests with very few businesspeople. The additional services they offered were not universal. For instance, former railways minister Liu Zhijun took bribes from only one businesswoman, who gained enormous illegal profits by monopolising freight transport. There are even more problems with regards to the rent-creation theory—for instance, it is unable to explain why superiors have to resort to corruption rather than other means to motivate their subordinates. Nor can it explain why superior–subordinate exchanges occur in the first place. Most importantly, it has misinterpreted the operation of the CPC and failed to understand the effect of loyalty, discipline and institutions therein. The CPC is a highly institutionalised political party. The actions of an individual are subject to party discipline and the laws of the country. The party has a rectification mechanism and remains on high alert for misconduct. Although misconduct and corruption will emerge in the short term, in the long term, the rectification mechanism will play its role. The current round of anticorruption measures is a case in point.

Blanchard and Shleifer (2001) have long held that decentralisation has played a positive role in China because the country has a strong central government, which curbs the negative consequences of decentralisation. The central government has, on the one hand, guided and regulated local investment and other behaviour through various directives and transfer payment measures, and, on the other, has controlled local officials via its power to appoint and dismiss those officials. This has unified the goals of local government with those of the central government. The central government's power to appoint and dismiss local officials is a characteristic of a unitary state, and China has had significant historical experience creating an effective meritocratic promotion system for government officials. This is the topic of the next section.

A merit-based promotion system

China's system for selection and promotion of government officials can be traced back to the recommendation system (*jian-ju-zhi*) of the Western Han dynasty. Local officials were responsible for recommending young people to join the administrative system and for supplying talent to the state. At the same time, the imperial court implemented the appraisal system (*kao-ke-zhi*). Specially appointed officials were dispatched around the country to appraise the performance of local officials. Those who received good performance appraisals were promoted and those who performed poorly were punished (Deng 1987). However, cronyism and nepotism could easily pervade the recommendation system. Indeed, by the time of the Eastern Han dynasty, this had become a system of hereditary aristocracy. By the time of the Sui dynasty, China had developed *ke-ju*, or the imperial examination system, and selected talent based on exam results. This was more objective than the recommendation system and was less easily manipulated by individuals. Thus, China was the first country to invent the civil service system, and created a national governance structure in the modern sense based on this system (Fukuyama 2011). China's contemporary selection and promotion system for government officials has promoted the positive parts of the imperial examination system, and abandoned the unreasonable parts. On the one hand, young people can enter the administrative system by taking the civil service exam; on the other, the promotion of officials depends on their ability and performance. The Communist Party began to establish a selection and promotion system for leading party and government cadres in the 1980s, and introduced the 'Rules for the Appointment of Cadres' in 2002. These were revised in January 2014 and renamed the 'Rules for the Selection and Appointment of Leading Party and Government Cadres' (hereinafter, the rules),[5] which provided guidance on the appraisal as well as selection and promotion procedures for leading party and government cadres at every level of government.

The rules establish the 'principle of the party's authority of managing the cadre system'. To guide the selection and promotion process, the rules list a series of principles to be applied, including seeking talent from a large pool of candidates; valuing virtue and talent, but virtue first; publicly acknowledging performance; a democratic, open and competitive selection process; democratic centralism; and acting according to the law. The party committee at each level is responsible for

5 For the full text, see Xinhua News Agency (2014).

the selection and promotion procedures, with detailed guidelines provided by the rules. The rules also allow young officials to become 'reserve' officials for higher-level positions, and describe the appraisal procedures in detail. Reserve officials are normally arranged to rotate through different posts at the same administrative level. In addition to the conventional selection and promotion system, public selection is also used for selecting leading cadres, providing a channel for people working in non-government sectors to enter the civil service sector.

There is debate about the role that meritocratic promotion plays in the process of selecting officials. Some studies have found that officials who perform better during their term of office are promoted more easily (Li and Zhou 2005; Yao and Zhang 2015), but others have found that officials' personal connections with their superiors also have an impact (Shih et al. 2012; Jia et al. 2015). Unlike research that studied officials at only one level, Landry et al. (forthcoming) studied officials at the county, municipal and provincial levels, and found that economic performance had a larger impact on promotion among lower-level officials. Just as in a large firm, in government, ability and quality are highly valued when officials are first recruited. The higher the post, the less ability is taken into consideration, while other factors, including personal ties, become more valuable. Landry et al.'s study is able to unify the research conclusions relevant to economic performance and personal ties.

Current research, however, is focused on economic performance. Few are concerned with officials' abilities in other areas, although, in practice, the party's organisational department conducts appraisals on an integrated and comprehensive basis. Rather than focusing solely on their ability to develop the economy, the department also looks at officials' performance in advancing people's livelihoods, environmental protection and implementing central government polices. Wang and Liu's (2018) research is an exception. They studied the impact of establishing healthy cities on the promotion of officials and found that officials who have successfully established healthy cities have more opportunities for promotion.

On the whole, China's selection and promotion system possesses the attributes of openness, competitiveness and meritocracy. It is open to all who aspire to become administrative talent for the state; however, it does not offer shortcuts like those in democracies, but instead requires that a person enter the system when he or she is young and be prepared to be trained and improved within the system. It is competitive because the number of positions available is always smaller than the number of candidates. If one aspires to be promoted, he or she must compete with others. Last but not the least, empirical evidence shows that officials' ability plays a crucial role in their promotion—hence, the selection and promotion system reflects the value of meritocracy. Promotion is an important goal to which an official aspires. Driven by merit-based promotion, officials are motivated to work hard and to turn in an excellent report card. This, to a very large extent, curbs the negative consequences brought about by decentralisation, including corruption. Based on information revealed by the anticorruption campaign over the past few years, many of the 'large tigers' caught up in corruption had at the same time also been working diligently for local economic and social development; their incentive, to a very large extent, was the prospect of promotion. China's unique selection and promotion system explains why economic decentralisation has been so successful there.

Conclusion

This chapter has offered a political economy explanation for China's economic success. The rationale behind this explanation is that an autonomous government can adopt long-term pro-growth institutions and policies to benefit the economy; economic decentralisation strongly motivates local officials to take the initiative and a meritocratic promotion system guides these initiatives towards the development of the entire nation. China's experience offers useful lessons for other developing countries in at least the following three areas.

First, curbing patron–client politics so the government has sufficient room to pursue the interests of the entire society is the top priority of political transformation in developing countries. Most developing countries adopted electoral politics without a social revolution, so the existing unequal social and political structures survive and often lead to patron–client politics. The fundamental means of rooting out patron–client politics is to revamp these existing structures. However, this process will take a long time under the electoral politics system. What China has done offers useful lessons for the political transformation of other developing countries, but each will have to explore the specific means by which the transformation will take place.

Second, appropriate fiscal decentralisation can motivate local officials to take the initiative to develop the economy. Fiscal revenues in most developing countries are highly centralised with the central government while local governments frequently have rights only over expenditure. In these circumstances, local officials clearly lack incentives to develop the local economy. Granting local governments the right over revenue is a key feature of China's fiscal decentralisation and one reason it is successful. Decentralisation may be even more important for resource-rich countries, where government revenues are highly dependent on exports of natural resources. These countries are constantly troubled by the 'resource curse'. If the central government continues to control resource exports but practices decentralisation at the same time, local governments will look for opportunities to develop other types of economic activities because they have no control over resources, thus putting an end to the resource curse.

Third, giving officials positive incentives is as important as regulating their conduct. Western scholarship begins with the premise that human nature is evil, so restricting the conduct of officials is often thought to be the key to good governance. However, restrictions are only one aspect of good governance. In reality, officials also have to be positively incentivised to motivate them to do things that are good for society. In China, promotion is a strong positive incentive. Because most developing countries operate under electoral politics, a direct adoption of China's practice is impracticable. A substitute would be to strengthen political parties and give play to their advantages in terms of the selection and promotion of leaders. In this regard, a parliamentary system would be more advantageous than a presidential system. In countries with a parliamentary system, the public elects not just an individual politician, but also that politician's party. In addition, the future of the politician is highly correlated to his or her political party. If a party intends to rule over the long term, it must nurture qualified talent within the party.

The contemporary CPC system is both a product of the socialist revolution and a legacy of Chinese cultural traditions. It is the responsibility of contemporary Chinese philosophers and social scientists to summarise the experience of the past few decades and construct a new theory in language understood by the world. China is about to achieve its first 100-year goal—to become a well-off society. Next, it will set out to achieve its second 100-year goal—to become a modern and high-income country. In between, China needs to enhance its soft power. New theories summarising what China has done right will not only strengthen the country's soft power, but also contribute to the advancement of social sciences globally.

References

Blanchard, O. and Shleifer, A. (2001), Federalism with and without political centralization: China versus Russia, *IMF Economic Review* 48(1): 171–9.

Deng, X. (1987), A preliminary probe into the *kao-ke* system in West Han, *Peking University Journal (Philosophy and Social Sciences)* (2): 22–7, 33.

Fukuyama, F. (2011), *The Origin of Political Order: From prehuman times to the French Revolution*, New York: Farrar, Strauss & Giroux.

Fukuyama, F. (2014), *Political Order and Political Decay: From industrial revolution to democratic globalization*, New York: Farrar, Strauss & Giroux.

Jia, R., Kudamatsu, M. and Seim, D. (2015), Political selection in China: The complementary roles of connections and performance, *Journal of the European Economic Association* 13(4): 631–68. doi.org/10.1111/jeea.12124.

Landry, P., Lü, X. and Duan, H. (2017), Does performance matter? Evaluating political selection along the Chinese administrative ladder, *American Political Science Review* 51(8): 1074–105.

Li, H. (1999), A Study of the Industrial and Commercial Taxes in Song Dynasty, *Zhongguo Jingjishi Yanjiu (Journal of Chinese Economic History)*, 1999(2): 61–9.

Li, H. and Zhou, L. (2005), Political turnover and economic performance: The incentive role of personnel control in China, *Journal of Public Economics* 89(9–10): 1743–62. doi.org/10.1016/j.jpubeco.2004.06.009.

Lin, J. (2014), *The China Miracle Demystified*, Beijing: Peking University Press.

Lin, J., Cai, F. and Li, Z. (1996), *The China Miracle*, Hong Kong: The Chinese University of Hong Kong Press.

Mao, R., Yao, Y. and Zou, J. (2017), *Productivity Growth, Fixed Exchange rates and Export-led Growth*, CCER Working Paper 2017002, Beijing: China Center for Economic Research.

Olson, M. (1982), *The Rise and Decline of Nations*, New Haven, CT: Yale University Press.

Pepper, S. (2017), *Civil War in China*, Beijing: Contemporary China Publishing House.

Qian, Y. and Weingast, B. (2011), China's transition to markets: Market-preserving federalism, Chinese style, *Journal of Policy Reform* 1(2): 149–85. doi.org/10.1080/13841289608523361.

Shih, V., Adolph, C. and Liu, M. (2012), Getting ahead in the Communist Party: Explaining the advancement of central committee members in China, *American Political Science Review* 106(1): 166–87. doi.org/10.1017/S0003055411000566.

Wang, H. and Liu, S. (2018), Healthy cities and promotion, Unpublished ms.

Wang, S. and Hu, A. (1993), *A Report of China's State Capacity*, Shenyang: Liaoning Renmin Press.

Weber, M. (2002), *The Protestant Ethic and the Spirit of Capitalism*, Penguin Classics.

Williamson, J. (2004), The strange history of the Washington consensus, *Journal of Post Keynesian Economics* 27(2): 195–206.

Xinhua News Agency (2014), Party and government leading cadres selecting and appointing work regulations, 15 January, Beijing: Central Government Portal. Available from: www.gov.cn/jrzg/2014-01/15/content_2567800.htm.

Yao, Y. (2009), The disinterested government: An explanation of China's economic success in the transitional period, *Economic Review* (3): 5–13.

Yao, Y. (2014), The Chinese growth miracle, in S. Durlauf and P. Aghion (eds), *Handbook of Economic Growth. Volume 2B*, Amsterdam: North Holland. doi.org/10.1016/B978-0-444-53540-5.00007-0.

Yao, Y. (2018), *Political equality, coalition formation and economic growth in autocracies*, CCER Working Paper E2018004, Beijing: China Center for Economic Research.

Yao, Y. and Zhang, M. (2015), Subnational leaders and economic growth: Evidence from Chinese cities, *Journal of Economic Growth* 20: 405–36. doi.org/10.1007/s10887-015-9116-1.

Yao, Y. and Zheng, D. (2008), Heavy industry and economic development: The Chinese planning economy revisited, *Economic Research Journal* 43(4): 26–40.

Zhu, T. (2016), *The Chinese Growth Puzzle*, Beijing: China CITIC Press.

6. China's economic transformation[1]

Gregory C. Chow

Why economic reform started in 1978

Deng Xiaoping took over control of the Communist Party of China (CPC) in 1978. He was responsible for initiating reform of the planned economy to move towards a more market-oriented economy. In a sense, the change in policy can be interpreted partially as a continuation of the 'four modernisations' (of agriculture, industry, defence, and science and technology) announced by premier Zhou Enlai in 1964, but interrupted by the Cultural Revolution. This explanation was suggested to me by a former vice-premier of the People's Republic of China (PRC). On the other hand, a former premier once told me: 'The Cultural Revolution did great harm to China, but it freed us from certain ideological constraints.' These statements indicate that the Cultural Revolution did affect the thinking of top party leaders and thus the course of China's economic development. Taking these statements into account, together with other considerations, I offer the following explanation for the initiation of economic reform.

There were four reasons the time was ripe for reform. First, the Cultural Revolution was very unpopular, and the party and the government had to distance themselves from the old regime and make changes to win the support of the people. Second, after years of experience in economic planning, government officials understood the shortcomings of the planned system and the need for change. Third, successful economic development in other parts of Asia—including Taiwan, Hong Kong, Singapore and South Korea, known as the 'Four Tigers'—demonstrated to Chinese government officials and the Chinese people that a market economy works better than a planned one. This lesson was reinforced by the different rates of economic development in North and South Korea, and among countries in Eastern and Western Europe. Fourth, for the reasons stated above, the Chinese people were ready for, and ready to support, economic reform.

Given these four reasons, was economic reform in 1978 inevitable? My answer is yes. The first two reasons alone were sufficient to motivate the government to initiate reform. The urgency of the case was such that it had to occur as soon as the political leadership was ready after Chairman Mao Zedong's death. The Chinese

1 This chapter is an amalgamation of Chapters 3 and 4 in *China's Economic Transformation* by the author, published by Wiley Blackwell in 2015 (3rd edn). The author thanks Kunling Zhang for his help with amalgamating the chapters, and with adaptation and changes made to suit this publication. Permission is given by the publisher to reproduce the two chapters in this reduced form here.

economic reforms of 1978 are an instance of the possibility of predicting major social change by examining the prevailing conditions. As an introduction to our discussion of economic reform, it is useful to point out that the reform process has been spurred by a combination of the efforts of the central government and the natural desire of the Chinese people and lower-level government units to improve economic institutions for their own benefit. The role of the central government has been a gradual and experimental one and has proceeded in steps. It will be useful to keep this general picture in mind when studying China's reform process.

Agriculture

Reform of Chinese agriculture under the commune system initially occurred in 1978 and 1979, when commune leaders in some regions discovered through examples initiated by farmers that they could fulfil their output quotas by reorganising the commune internally. In essence, each farm household was assigned a piece of land and was held responsible for delivering a given quantity of a specified product so the commune could satisfy its procurement requirement. After fulfilling the delivery quota, the farm household was free to keep the remaining output for its own consumption or for sale in the market. This 'household responsibility system' (HRS) has the economic characteristics of private farming in a market economy. It amounted to each farm household leasing a piece of land and paying a fixed rent in the form of the output quota. The Fourth Plenum of the Eleventh Central Committee of the Communist Party (CCCP) officially adopted the HRS in September 1979. The subsequent rapid increases in agricultural output and farmers' incomes provided support for this system.

After 1978, rural markets began to reopen. Farmers were allowed to raise pigs, chickens and ducks, the farming of which had been banned during the Cultural Revolution as capitalist activities. They also engaged in sideline activities such as handicraft production that were previously the preserve of the communes. China's farm economy in essence returned to the private economy that had existed in the early 1950s before the organisation of cooperatives and the establishment of communes. One difference pertained to the ownership of land. Strictly speaking, ownership of land was and still is collective; it belongs to the commune or the village. The right of use belongs to the farmer who is assigned the land. Eventually, the right to use assigned land was guaranteed on a permanent basis and became transferable—hence, the difference between this right to use and ownership is moot. Reform therefore succeeded in allowing private farming to return to the agricultural sector.

During the first six years of reform (1978–84), the annual growth rate of the gross value of agricultural output nearly tripled, to 7.1 per cent. The HRS deals only with the production component of the market. Market reform in agriculture includes four other components, as pointed out by Huang and Rozelle (2014), on which much of the discussion in this section is based.

The second component is marketing and distribution. After the output is produced, it can be sold to government procurement agencies. Allowing the products to be sold in local markets is the second component of market institutions. Although agricultural commodity markets were allowed to emerge during the 1980s, their number and size were small. In 1984, the state procurement network still purchased more than 95 per cent of marketed grain and more than 99 per cent of marketed cotton. Later extension of the market included the sale of products abroad through private export companies. In the past decade, food exports have been growing faster than imports, but, in 2010, China was still largely self-sufficient (97 per cent) in food (including processed food).

The third component is the pricing of products. Instead of the government determining the prices of agricultural products, a market institution requires that the forces of demand and supply determine prices. Price changes had a positive impact on output during the first years of transition. This simply reflected the increase in supply as prices increased.

The fourth component is the development of financial institutions to support the development of agriculture. Credit institutions allowed farmers to borrow money to finance production and investment. Most farmers were able to carry on their production with little outside financing, as China's agricultural output and input markets were dominated by cash transactions. Where it was needed, liquidity was supplied by off-farm remittances and zero-interest loans. Insurance was provided by diversification, multiple cropping, high levels of irrigation and off-farm earnings.

The fifth component is the role of the government. First, there has been little effort by the government to organise small farms into larger cooperative organisations. Only about 20 per cent of China's villages had farmers professional associations (FPAs) in 2008 and only 10 per cent of farmers belonged to one—far below the levels in almost all other East Asian nations and many Western nations. Second, the government has provided research and development (R&D) in agriculture by developing technology for farmers. Such efforts have been controlled by the state agricultural research system, mainly to produce higher yields, and, after 2000, to improve quality. Only a small share of agricultural R&D in China is performed by the private sector, partly due to a 'crowding out' effect from the government programs.

Given the above market institutions, there is strong competition among millions of small farmers and traders, the levels of which have produced agricultural commodity markets that are highly integrated and efficient. Unlike the incomplete market reform in Chinese industry, agricultural market reform is almost complete. When we measure the extent to which China has become a market economy by the percentage of national output produced by financially independent and profit-motivated production units, we can include almost all agricultural output in this percentage.

While market reform of the agricultural sector has been successful, agricultural productivity and incomes did not increase as rapidly as in the early 1980s, creating serious problems of rural poverty. This problem will be discussed in terms of three components.

The first is the income gap between urban and rural residents. Rural poverty is not a result of the low income levels of the rural population. It is true that the gap in per capita income between urban and rural residents has widened, but the rate of increase for the latter has been so rapid that the rural population, on average, is much better off economically than before (see Chow 2000). If one insists on using income as the chief measure of rural poverty, the problem has to be viewed as either: 1) the deterioration of the relative income of rural residents in spite of the rapid increase in absolute income; or 2) discontent among the rural population created by the improvement in income itself (i.e. increasing expectations). Since neither of these two interpretations appears to be sufficient to explain the seriousness of the current problem, one has to seek other explanations.

The second component is the central government's unfavourable treatment of rural residents compared with urban residents. It has spent less on infrastructure investment in rural areas than in urban areas, and only a limited amount to improve agricultural productivity. It has provided fewer welfare benefits, including healthcare and education subsidies, to rural residents and, although labour mobility allowed farmers to move to urban areas to find work, those migrating workers did not have residence permits in the cities and could not receive services such as health care and schooling for their children. Although the commune system was abolished, procurement of farm products by government agencies has continued, but the procurement prices are often set below market prices. In addition, farmers were not allowed to sell their products to private traders, as private trading and transportation of grain were prohibited. The market economy therefore does not function for the benefit of farmers in the distribution and pricing of grain.

The third—and perhaps most important—component of the rural poverty problem is that farmers' rights can be violated by the illegal activities of local government officials. The most disconcerting example is the confiscation of land from farmers for urban development, for which farmers receive arbitrary compensation well below the market price. Many farmers and other rural residents are not paid what they are entitled for public work or for teaching in public schools. Farmers are also subject to illegal levies, including taxes on acreage that is not actually used, a special tax for growing commercial crops rather than grain and livestock, and fees for schools, road construction and other services provided by local governments. Through much of Chinese history, local government officials have considered themselves privileged, with the authority to rule over peasants. The abuse of power under the PRC is worse than previously because officials are given greater levels of power. Well-publicised stories of the abuse of power by local party and government officials are documented in Chen and Wu (2005). The abuse of power by local officials is known to be fairly widespread, as evidenced by the large number of protests by farmers reported in the media (see Han 2003; Zhang 2006: 19–20).

Enterprises

Enterprises are the second important production unit. The Chinese People's Congress adopted elements of reform for state enterprises in September 1980. At the opening of that session, vice-premier Yao Yilin, chairman of the State Planning Commission, announced that experiments giving state enterprises more autonomy and market competition would be greatly expanded. Industrial reform began in late 1978 with six pilot enterprises in Sichuan province; by the end of 1981, some 80 per cent of state-owned industrial enterprises were involved in the reform experiment. The major elements of industrial reform in the early years included some autonomy regarding the use of retained profits, production planning, sales of output, experimentation with new products and capital investment; adoption of an 'economic responsibility system' by assigning identifiable tasks to low-level units within an enterprise and paying them according to productivity; increasing the role of markets; streamlining the administrative system at the local level for state enterprises under local control; and encouragement of collectively owned enterprises.

The main difference between the reform of state-owned industrial enterprises and that of agriculture is that privatisation was not adopted for state-owned enterprises. Reform of state-owned enterprises turned out to be more difficult than that for agricultural production. In ideological terms, members of the Communist Party believed in the ownership and control of the major means of production by the state. Politically, government bureaucrats were unwilling to give up their power and vested interests by allowing state enterprises to operate independently. Economically, unlike small farms that are self-sufficient, large industrial enterprises were dependent on factors outside their control, including the supply of equipment and material inputs produced by other enterprises. In administrative terms, most state-owned enterprise managers did not have sufficient knowledge and experience to run a modern enterprise as an independent entity because they had been trained to obey production targets. Even with additional training, managers were reluctant to give up their old habits of dependence on the economic ministries.

Observing the limited success of the reform of state enterprises and the need to overhaul the entire economic system, the twelfth CCCP adopted a major decision relating to economic reform, on 20 October 1984. Individual state enterprises would be given autonomy in decisions regarding production, supply, marketing, pricing, investment and personnel to function as profit-seeking economic units. The scope of central planning was reduced—except in the case of certain major products—and the method changed from mandatory to guidance planning. Market forces rather than central control determined the prices of more products, while a macroeconomic control mechanism was developed through the use of taxes, interest rates and monetary policy under an improved banking and financial system. Various forms of economic responsibility systems were established within individual enterprises to promote efficiency, with differential wage rates instituted for different kinds of work and levels of productivity. The development of individual and collective enterprises was fostered to supplement state enterprises; foreign trade and investment were expanded and technological exchanges with foreign countries promoted. These steps were revolutionary, given the institutional and ideological tradition up to that point, but were limited in scope, because it was not possible to go further at that time.

In 1987, the 'contract responsibility system' was introduced to all state enterprises, with each signing a contract with the level of government that had control over it. Under the contract, the enterprise committed itself to pay the government a fixed annual tax and could retain any remaining profit. In practice, it was up to the enterprise to distribute any profit to workers and managers as bonuses, but managers' compensation was limited by social pressure. The incentive for management to improve efficiency and take risks was therefore limited. Profits were distributed to workers mainly to increase the popularity of and support for management. A second reason for the limited success of the contract responsibility system was that, in practice, when the profit of a state enterprise increased, its supervisory government authority demanded a higher tax than originally agreed on. In reality, the tax depended on profit and no longer had the desired incentive effects of a fixed levy.

While the reform of state enterprises was not entirely successful, the collective and private sectors were dynamic and expanding. As well as state enterprises, there are three other types of enterprise in China: collective, individual and overseas-funded—the last established under the country's open-door policy.

Township and village enterprises were established as rural collective enterprises with the support of local governments wanting to increase revenue. Unemployed labour could be used for nonagricultural production. Local governments had the land, capital and human resources to establish these enterprises, and they had the connections to cut through the red tape required to set up and run them. The ownership rights of these enterprises were often unclear, and yet they seemed to function well and were profitable. Their success provides a puzzle for economists.

The collective and private sectors grew much more rapidly than the state sector. From Table 6.1, we can see that, in 1978, individual and other types of industrial enterprises were nonexistent and state enterprises produced 77.6 per cent of total gross industrial output value. This was reduced to only 28 per cent in 1996, compared with the 39 per cent contributed by collective enterprises. One important conclusion to be drawn from these data is that even if state enterprises are not increasing their productivity, China's economy can continue to grow rapidly if the nonstate sectors remain vibrant, because the state sector accounts for only a small share of total output.

Table 6.1 China: Gross industrial output value by ownership (RMB billion in current prices)

	State-owned	Collective-owned	Individually owned	Other types	Total
1978	328.9	94.8			423.7
1985	630.2	311.7	18.0	11.7	971.6
1996	2,836.1	3,923.2	1,542.0	1,658.2	9,959.5

Source: NBS (1997: 413).

The inefficiency of state enterprises has been considered a major problem in the Chinese economy, but the seriousness of this is exaggerated on two counts. First, the productivity of state enterprises has been steadily increasing in the past two decades, although at a slower rate than that of the collective and private sectors. Second, the relative importance of state enterprises has been declining and the effect of the state sector's performance on the growth of the entire economy is less important than before. State enterprises remain, however, a significant burden for the government and the economy. They require government subsidies, while the entitlements of workers are a drain on government budgets and economic resources. In addition, such entitlements include more than just wages; the entire support system—including schools for their children, health care for their families and retirement benefits—is very costly. Reducing the size of enterprises creates an unemployment problem.

Several factors affect the economic efficiency of state-owned enterprises. There is a shortage of competent and well-trained managers and staff to operate a modern enterprise, along with a tendency to make management decisions based on personal relations and for personal gain at the expense of the enterprise. The system does not provide managers with appropriate incentives to work for the benefit of the enterprise; they are on a much lower pay scale than managers in similar collective enterprises. Nor is there a suitable governance system. Many workers still subscribe to the concept of the 'iron rice bowl'—that is, relying on the state to guarantee their job security. In addition, the equipment and technology of some state enterprises need to be updated. One important condition favourable to the reform of state enterprises is the high degree of competition from collective and foreign enterprises in both domestic and foreign markets.

The main avenue for continued reform of state enterprises is to restructure them to shareholding companies. In late 1998, when the East Asian Financial Crisis was affecting the Chinese economy, the privatisation of state enterprises was slowed for fear that sale prices might dip too low, to the benefit of corrupt officials under insufficient government supervision. In March 1998, premier Zhu Rongji announced that state enterprise restructuring should be completed in three years. His main objectives were to make profitable the majority of the 50 largest state enterprises, which were operating at a loss, and to restructure most small and medium-sized state enterprises into shareholding companies. The government reported that two-thirds of the 6,600 largest state-owned enterprises had surrendered to the state net profits in the year 2000 totalling RMB230 billion, although some might have falsified their accounts under pressure, as the government acknowledged.

To appraise the prospects of success of state enterprise restructuring in China, the following observations can be made. First, restructuring efforts in the early 2000s were a continuation of a series of attempts beginning in 1979 to reform state enterprises and make them financially independent, efficient and profitable. This is an evolutionary process, so dramatic results should not be expected in a short time. Second, there is a tendency for managers of state-owned enterprises to hold on to their power and resist change. Third, the success of an enterprise depends on many more factors than just the ownership and governance structure. Other important factors are the ability and resourcefulness of its managers and workers, the particular industry it is in, the degree of competition and so on. Fourth, on the positive side, the problems with state enterprises are not so urgent that they require immediate solutions. The government is proceeding at a deliberate speed. It is making sure not too many workers are laid off in any period. Fifth, and also on the positive side, with the introduction of foreign capital, management and technology through joint ventures and even buyouts of failing state enterprises, the performance of many has been and will be improved.

Price reform

An important component of the CCCP's October 1984 decision on economic reform was reform of the price system. The main objective was to decontrol administratively determined prices gradually, and allow prices to be determined by market forces, which would help state enterprises receive the correct signals for their economic calculations in the choice of inputs and the planning of outputs.

However, administered prices cannot be decontrolled immediately. First, there is the problem of equity. Allowing the prices of basic consumer goods to increase would affect the welfare of consumers, who have been subsidised. Second, production in the state-owned enterprises—which were supplied with low-priced inputs under the planned economy—would be disrupted. A compromise solution was to introduce a two-tier price system: one set of prices remained the same as before, while the market determined a second set for the same goods. State enterprises could still purchase their allotted amounts of inputs and sell given amounts of outputs at the administered prices. In addition, each enterprise could purchase additional inputs and sell above-quota outputs at prices determined by the market.

The two-tier price system provides incentives for enterprises to economise on inputs and increase outputs for profit. As practised in China in the 1980s, this system was therefore an economically efficient one. A possible economic inefficiency could result—in terms of the functioning of a market economy—if certain enterprises are operating at a loss without government subsidies and discontinue operation. As time went on, administered prices were gradually changed to match market prices and, by the 1990s, when the majority of products in China were sold at market prices, the two-tier price system was no longer needed.

Price reform was a gradual process beginning in the mid-1980s. How rapidly prices should be decontrolled was an important issue discussed at the top level of the Commission for Reconstructing the Economic System. The major concern with rapid deregulation was the adjustment producers and consumers would have to absorb. Once the government provided subsidies to producers in the form of low input prices and monopolistically protected output prices—and to consumers in the form of low prices for food, clothing and housing—an attitude of entitlement was formed. It would be politically difficult to change this without social protest. In the case of producers, the two-tier price system enabled them to keep their entitlements while allowing market incentives to operate at the margin. In the case of consumers, the prices of food items did not increase rapidly after decontrol because of the rapid increase in food supply resulting from the successful reforms in agriculture.

The banking system

To exercise macroeconomic control as practised in a market economy in lieu of central planning, a modern banking system had to be established. The People's Bank of China (PBC) was a mono-bank that had branches to accept deposits from the public. Its other functions were to issue currency and to extend loans to state enterprises according to the need specified by the planning authority. The PBC had no authority to decide on these loans. Commercial banks did not exist in the sense of being able to extend credit to enterprises according to the criterion of profitability. Reform of the banking system to serve the market economy progressed gradually in the late 1980s and early 1990s. In 1983, the PBC was nominally transformed into a central bank. Specialised banks—including the Industrial and Commercial Bank of China, the Agricultural Bank of China (ABC) and the People's Construction Bank of China—were established and given some autonomy to extend credit to state enterprises, but were also subject to central government direction. They were under local political pressure to extend credit for regional economic development. As a result, excessive expansion of credit led to inflation in 1985, 1988 and 1993. The chief tool to stop credit expansion was the imposition of credit quotas. In November 1993, the third plenum of the fourteenth CCCP decided to accelerate reform of the financial sector by giving more independence to the PBC as a central bank and transforming the specialised banks into commercial banks. In 1995, the People's Congress passed the Law on the PBC and the Commercial Bank Law, modernising the PBC as a central bank and the specialised banks as commercial banks—in principle, though not in practice.

To relieve the four state banks (including the PBC) of political pressure to extend credit, three 'policy banks' were created in 1994 to provide loans to state enterprises for the purpose of carrying out particular economic development policies: the State Development Bank, the Agricultural Development Bank and the Import and Export Bank. By early 1998, these policy banks accounted for only about 6 per cent of the loans of the big four banks. Since the early 1990s, new commercial banks have also appeared on the scene, taking the form of corporations with shareholders and boards of directors. In the late 1990s, these banks accounted for 15–20 per cent of loans and 8–10 per cent of deposits. These new banks have greater flexibility in decision-making and function slightly more like modern commercial banks. Their ownership structure has prevented them from operating more efficiently, and bank managers still behave like bureaucrats, holding on to their economic power. There is still political pressure and economic temptation to extend credit to state-owned enterprises at higher risk than cost–benefit calculations warrant. Managers and staff need more training and experience before they can operate as modern commercial bankers.

Furthermore, of their loan totals, the four state banks are coping with 20–25 per cent nonperforming loans—some US$200 billion out of a total of nearly US$1 trillion—as a result of past obligations to finance state enterprises. About 80 per cent of all the loans of the four state banks consist of loans to state enterprises. To solve these problems, a number of measures were taken in the late 1990s. Local bank managers were appointed by the bank's headquarters—rather than being subject to local government approval—freeing the four state banks from local government interference in their credit policy. The PBC was required to behave like the US Federal Reserve system, providing closer supervision of the behaviour of the commercial banks.

Is the Chinese banking system in crisis? The answer appears to be no, in spite of these shortcomings. In a market economy with a modern banking system, a banking crisis occurs when many loans become nonperforming. This was an essential characteristic of the finance sectors of the countries that experienced the 1997–99 East Asian Financial Crisis. The Chinese situation, however, is different. First, speculative investments in China—though they exist in the real estate market and in the production of consumer goods—are less serious and are subject to strict government supervision. In countries such as Thailand, Malaysia and Indonesia, much larger percentages of foreign investment were portfolio or financial in nature; foreign investors could, and did, withdraw their money quickly when investment opportunities appeared unfavourable. Second, governments in Thailand and Indonesia maintained exchange rates that overvalued their own currencies before the crisis occurred. The central bank of Thailand covered up the loss of a large amount of foreign reserves to support the Thai currency by selling dollars in the futures market. Once investors recognised the loss of foreign reserves and the overvaluation of the Thai baht, the risk to their investments became apparent and they withdrew their money swiftly, leading to a sharp devaluation of the baht. The Chinese currency was not overvalued. More importantly, people have confidence in the value of their deposits in the banks because they believe that the government owns the banks and implicitly guarantees their deposits. The fact that 20–25 per cent of total bank loans are bad has not affected this confidence and is not likely to lead to large withdrawals of deposits. Given the high savings rate of the Chinese people and the limited alternatives for their savings, in the 1990s, the ratio of savings deposits to gross domestic product (GDP) in China was rising.

To deal with the large amounts of bad debt on the balance sheets of the four large state-owned commercial banks, the Chinese Government in 1999 set up four asset management companies, each serving to restructure the bad debts of one large bank. The method of restructuring is for the asset management company to take over the bad debts of the bank it serves in exchange for its own debt, to strengthen the structure of the bank's balance sheet. The asset management company in turn tries to collect from the state enterprises part or all of the debt in its possession. It has the power to supervise and monitor the financial position of the state enterprises as their creditor. It can also sell the debts in the market, possibly at a price below book value. As long as the bad debts do not increase rapidly and Chinese people keep making deposits, the commercial banks will continue to function.

Banking reform is only one aspect of the reform process and shares some of the characteristics of reform in other state sectors. In spite of its present shortcomings, the Chinese banking system appears to be serving some basic functions of financial intermediation, although not efficiently. The banking system can be expected to improve in time, but only slowly.

Foreign trade and investment

China's economy was essentially a closed one before its economic reform. In 1978, the total volume of its foreign trade—or the sum of the values of its exports and imports—amounted to only 7 per cent of its national income. Deng Xiaoping's open-door policy encouraged the opening of China to foreign imports and the promotion of exports. By 1987, the volume of foreign trade had increased to 25 per cent of GDP and, by 1998, to 37 per cent. As a component of aggregate demand, exports weakened as a result of the currency devaluations in, and the reduced demand from, several Asian countries including Japan during the East Asian Financial Crisis. While some of the state-owned companies engaged in foreign trade were not doing well, private and foreign companies were taking an active role in promoting Chinese exports of a variety of consumer goods to the world market. Even when the rate of increase in the volume of exports was smaller in 1998, the rate of growth in GDP was affected only moderately because exports account for only 20 per cent of GDP. (Note that in 1996, China's GDP grew by 9.6 per cent while its exports grew by only 1.5 per cent.) In the meantime, the government adopted a variety of measures to stimulate exports, including the lowering of export duties and refunding taxes on raw materials used to produce exports.

Foreign investment—the second component of the open-door policy—was promoted through the opening of different regions of China. In 1982, the now well-known Shenzhen economic zone bordering Hong Kong was created. Foreign investors could set up factories there to take advantage of inexpensive skilled labour and pay them at market-determined wage rates, unlike the rates prevailing in other parts of China. Investors also received special tax breaks. In less than a decade, Shenzhen developed from a piece of farmland to a modern city. Soon other economic zones and special areas were created for the convenience of foreign investors. Foreign investment increased from an annual rate of less than US$1 billion in 1978 to nearly US$30 billion in 1998.

In 1997, the flow of foreign direct investment (FDI) continued to be strong—10.1 per cent higher than in 1996. In the first five months of 1998, FDI fell by 1.49 per cent compared with the same period in 1997. The trade surplus and the surplus in the capital account helped increase the amount of foreign reserves in China, from US$2.3 billion in 1977 to US$142.8 billion by the end of 1997. As China continued to record a trade surplus during the first few months of 1998, and foreign investment continued to flow in (although at a slower rate), foreign exchange reserves should have been accumulating accordingly; in fact, they increased much more slowly.

As well as the inflow of foreign reserves from a trade surplus and foreign investment, the value of the Chinese currency was supported by large foreign reserves and by its strong purchasing power. China's currency was strong compared with the US dollar, at an exchange rate of RMB8.3 per dollar, because China had a lower inflation rate than the United States. Retail prices in China in March 1998 were 1.2 per cent lower than in the same period in 1997, and remained nearly constant until the middle of 1998. These factors provided strong fundamentals for the value of the Chinese currency and made devaluation unnecessary. Even if the trade surplus had fallen because of competition in world markets from Asian countries, which had devalued their currencies, the economic fundamentals and the political will of the Chinese leadership were strong enough to prevent a devaluation of the Chinese currency. If neighbouring countries had retaliated by further devaluing their currencies, this would have diminished any possible gain from a Chinese devaluation. From a political perspective, the government tried to maintain the value of the renminbi because it was attempting to play a positive role in contributing to the stability of Asian financial markets.

Institutional infrastructure

Since the beginning of its economic reform, China's education system has been improving and returning to its pre–Cultural Revolution state. Universities were opened, and students were given opportunities to take examinations to enter universities and graduate schools. Intellectuals who had been criticised and mistreated were restored to their previous status and given due respect. The population as a whole wanted to absorb new ideas and knowledge from other countries, having been deprived of such knowledge when China was closed to the outside world. From 1985 to 1998, the Ministry of Education sponsored cooperative programs with foreign educational institutions to improve education in China. At the same time, individual universities were given the freedom to invite foreign scholars to lecture. Students were permitted to go abroad to study. Modern textbooks were adopted in university courses. As time went on, skills in modern languages, especially English, improved rapidly, and texts in English began to be adopted. Privately initiated and funded educational institutions were encouraged in the late 1990s and have since flourished. Schools from the primary level to colleges and professional schools have received support from overseas Chinese.

The government has made a serious effort to modernise the legal system, motivated by the overarching national modernisation agenda and the need to engage with the international business community, especially foreign investors. The Ministry of Education in the early 1980s began to set up programs for legal education, training many lawyers. There was also a need to set a modern legal framework for domestic social order. The People's Congress has created many laws governing individual and corporate behaviour, with a system of courts set up to enforce them. On paper, today's Chinese laws are comprehensive and modern in content, but their enactment has not greatly changed the behaviour of the Chinese people.

Reform policies similar to those of Taiwan

It is interesting to note that several economic policies adopted by the leadership of mainland China during its reform process are similar to those adopted by the Government of Taiwan more than two decades earlier.

The growth of both economies is the result of a reduction in government intervention and the encouragement of private initiative. In both economies, to initiate the development process, the government had a set of general policy guidelines; and, in each case, the government reduced its intervention and allowed more private initiatives. Essentially, by providing citizens with freedom and economic opportunities—however incomplete—both governments succeeded in developing their economies. The second common feature is the importance of the agricultural sector in the early stage of growth. In both Taiwan and mainland China, the increase in agricultural productivity was achieved mainly by redistributing land to farmers. Third, the promotion of exports is an important component of both countries' development strategy, with the prosperity of the export sector a major source of rapid economic growth. The fourth commonality is the government emphasis on the stability of the general price level. Both governments learned from the bitter experience of hyperinflation in China before the establishment of the People's Republic in 1949. The fifth common element is the gradual lifting of restrictions on imports and the setting of an official exchange rate close to the free-market level.

There are also differences in the degrees to which market forces are allowed to operate in the two economies. Suffice to say the bureaucratic behaviour of mainland China's economic officials interferes with the working of free enterprise to a larger extent than that of their counterparts in Taiwan. In the 1960s and 1970s, foreign investors in Taiwan also experienced corruption, but not to the extent that occurred in mainland China in the 1980s and 1990s. The reason is China's planned economy and the Cultural Revolution had made its bureaucrats very hungry for money. As economic conditions and government administration improve, corruption and disruptive bureaucratic behaviour will decrease. Another difference between the two countries is the role of state enterprises, which have more influence in mainland China, with its socialist economy. Nevertheless, there are certain instances in which the mainland Chinese Government is more open to the outside world, including permitting foreign investors to participate in the building of economic infrastructure, such as superhighways, and permitting imports of foreign automobiles—neither of which was allowed in Taiwan. One common policy has been to restrict foreign commercial banks from entering the domestic market to compete with domestic banks.

Reasons for the success of China's economic reform

Since economic reform started, China's real output as measured by GDP in constant prices has grown at a remarkable average rate of 9.6 per cent per annum. There is no question that China has experienced a rapid rate of economic development, but what explains the success of its reforms?

First, Chinese leaders are pragmatic and not subject to ideological restraints. Of course, some policies were not proposed because Communist Party members were not ready to accept them at the time. On the subject of pragmatism, Deng Xiaoping said that one should not care whether a cat is black or white as long as it catches mice.

Second, there was no blueprint for the economic institutions and policies that were adopted through experimentation. This is a process of learning by doing or, as Deng put it, of 'crossing the river while feeling the stones'. There are two advantages of such experiments: they identify what works and, when successful, they introduce the old guard to new ways, convincing them to give their support to the reform program. This process has been characterised as 'gradualism', in contrast with the 'shock therapy' adopted by some Eastern European countries, which attempted to change to a market economy almost immediately.

Third, the reforms had the support of the Chinese people and government officials who had experienced the failure of the planned economy. They desired a new system after the excesses of the Cultural Revolution.

Fourth, there was political stability while the reforms took place; the Communist Party remained in power and was able to exercise leadership.

Fifth, much credit must be given to the Chinese leaders themselves. Deng, in particular, should be given most of the credit for working behind the scenes to oversee the general direction of the reforms. He advocated pragmatism and experimentation. Some top leaders were not willing to let China deviate from its traditional course, and there was a difficult political balancing act at the top level of the Communist Party. Zhao Ziyang was a brilliant economic thinker who served as premier and later party general secretary, and who designed and carried out economic reform; and Hu Yaobang was the humane and highly respected party secretary. The subsequent premier, Zhu Rongji, was also very skilful in managing the economy, while general secretary Jiang Zemin kept the country and the party in order. There have been numerous capable officials in the Chinese Government whose contributions cannot be enumerated here.

Given the pragmatic attitude and the ability of Chinese leaders and government officials, as well as the willingness to experiment and the support of the people, there was no way China's move towards a market economy could fail—unless a market economy does not work better than a planned economy (which no economist believes). Why did almost no one in 1979 forecast the rapid transformation and growth of the Chinese economy that was to come? Very few people at the time understood that there were sufficient conditions for the success of the economic reforms. The high degree of success of the reform process was partly due to the accompanying rapid growth of GDP, to which able Chinese labourers and entrepreneurs contributed. At a given stage of reform, the human capital of the Chinese people (though this is difficult to measure) allowed the economy to grow rapidly, and the rapid growth itself pushed the reforms forward. In addition to domestic human capital, both human capital and financial capital were supplied by thousands of overseas Chinese—in Hong Kong and elsewhere—and by foreign investors. Not many people in 1979 recognised the quality of China's human capital and its role in promoting economic reform indirectly through increasing China's national output. Without high-quality human capital, economic institutions and market incentives alone cannot produce rapid economic growth.

The above positive features of China's economic reform process need to be balanced with some qualifications. Political stability and the government's ability to manage the economy were not perfect. Inflation and corruption in the late 1980s created much discontent among the urban population. Student demonstrations started in April 1989 at the memorial of the death of party secretary Hu Yaobang and lasted until June. Failing to end the demonstration by other means, Deng Xiaoping sent in tanks to disperse the protesting students in Tiananmen Square. Hundreds of people were killed, including citizens of Beijing who tried to stop the tanks and members of the Chinese Red Army.

All over the world, there was an immediate critical reaction to this incident—to an extent probably unexpected by Deng. Government officials and businesspeople from many foreign countries refused to go to China. Foreign investment and tourism declined. The government suffered a big shock from internal disagreements about how to handle the demonstrations, and from the negative reaction in many parts of the world. However, the reform policy continued—contrary to the expectations of some foreign observers. In February 1992, during his visit to Shenzhen, Deng took the opportunity to reaffirm and, in fact to further push, domestic economic liberalisation and the open-door policy. Later that year, the party congress declared China's economy a socialist market economy. By the end of 1992, China had resumed its rapid growth path after the disruption of the Tiananmen incident. The incident served as a test of the stability of China's political system and the able leadership of Deng, who managed to regain support after so much external and internal criticism.

The degree of institutional reform achieved can be measured by the contributions of the market institutions to national output at the beginning of the twenty-first century. The *China Statistical Yearbook* (NBS 1997: 42) provides the following breakdown of GDP from 1996 of RMB6,859.4 billion: primary industry, RMB1,388.4 billion; secondary industry, RMB3,361.3 billion; and tertiary industry, RMB2,109.7 billion. If all primary industries (namely, agriculture), 75 per cent of secondary industry (since state enterprises account for less than 30 per cent of gross industrial output and some are profit-oriented) and 50 per cent of tertiary industry (since much retail trade is private) are considered as the output of profit-maximising producers, a total of RMB4,964.3 billion of the GDP of RMB6,859.4 billion is so produced. This amounts to 72.4 per cent of the Chinese economy being market-driven, and is a good indicator of the stage reached by market economic reforms. This 72 per cent of market-driven GDP happens to coincide with the 28 per cent of gross industrial output value produced by state-owned enterprises, reported at the end of section three of this chapter.

The impact of WTO membership

At the turn of the twenty-first century, China was in the process of joining the World Trade Organization (WTO). To meet the conditions to enter the WTO, China agreed to gradually lower its tariffs on agricultural and industrial products and open its service and manufacturing industries. The lowering of tariffs would lead to an increase in imports of both agricultural and industrial products for consumers. The prices of these products were expected to decline and the quality of the products would improve—both to the benefit of Chinese consumers. Foreign manufacturers operating in China would also provide competition, with China's low-cost labour and savings on the cost of transporting final products into the country. Financial and telecommunication firms in China would have to upgrade their products to survive foreign competition.

WTO membership will also affect China's economic structure. Structural changes include changes in the relative importance of different industrial sectors and of state versus nonstate sectors. Tertiary industry is expected to increase its share of GDP partly as a result of China's entry into the WTO. The stimulus to the domestic service industry provided by foreign competition and expected foreign investment will lead to more rapid growth than would otherwise have occurred. The high-technology component of the manufacturing sector will increase in importance partly because of the expected increase in foreign investment. The domestic manufacture of consumer durables—especially automobiles—will suffer from the increase in imports, while increased foreign investment in the automobile industry will help increase domestic production. The expected growth in both the service and the manufacturing sectors will lead to a further decline in the share of agriculture, but this would take place even without entry into the WTO. The relative decline in the agriculture sector will be hastened by foreign competition as a result of the lowering of tariffs on agricultural products. The total effect of WTO entry on China's industrial composition is, however, limited.

Premier Zhu Rongji's main motivation for promoting China's entry into the WTO was to use foreign competition to speed up economic reform in both the industrial and the service sectors. In the late 1990s, reform in both sectors was slow because of the vested interests of a group of managers appointed under a previous administration who were determined to hold on to their positions. Simply changing state enterprises to shareholding companies did not lead to the replacement of incumbent managers or to the adoption of new ways of doing things. Foreign competition provides a more powerful force to combat such inertia. How successful such outside pressure will be depends on how strong the inertia is. In addition, for fear of creating too much social instability, the government cannot and will not allow competition to come in too rapidly. The slow speed of entry to China's market is codified in a schedule that lowers tariffs gradually and permits foreign firms to enter the financial and telecommunications industries step by step. Informally, there is red tape and other means to delay foreign competition, which can be exercised by central, provincial and local government officials.

Li et al. (1999) applied a dynamic computational general equilibrium model of the Chinese economy to study the impact of WTO membership. Four aspects of WTO membership are discussed: 1) tariff reduction; 2) stepwise abolition of nontariff barriers to industrial products; 3) increased import quotas on agricultural products and eventual abolition of all import quotas; and 4) phasing out of quotas on China's exports of textiles and clothing to developed economies. The impact of WTO membership on economic growth comes from two sources: specialisation through international trade and an increase in efficiency within each industrial sector through competition. The study estimated that China's real GDP in 2005 would be 1.5 per cent higher from the first source due to the above policies. This increase is derived from increased specialisation in trade according to China's comparative advantage, as WTO entry allows more agricultural imports and textile and clothing exports, in particular. If the gain in total factor productivity is incorporated, the average annual growth rate in GDP from 1997 to 2010 will be 1 per cent higher after entry into the WTO. Bear in mind that the annual growth rate projected for this period is approximately 7.5 per cent; I believe it might serve as an upper bound on the effect of WTO entry. There will be inertia to inhibit the forces that promote both sources of output growth. In fact, these forces were already operating in the 1990s, and are expected to continue even without WTO membership.

One should also consider the impact of WTO membership in hastening the modernisation of China's legal system as it is forced to deal with more and more foreign firms. The impact on legal institutions will include changes in formal institutions and laws and, to some extent, in the legal behaviour of the Chinese people. Since the mid-1990s, many new commercial laws have been enacted governing corporate behaviour, bankruptcy and the behaviour of banks and other financial institutions. Furthermore, the Chinese judicial system has been modernised and improved. The practice of litigation is now more widespread and the number of lawyers has increased dramatically. There were also signs at the beginning of the 2000s that, as the country becomes wealthier and the government makes greater efforts to enforce the law, Chinese citizens have tended to become more law-abiding. One important role of the WTO is to settle disputes on matters related to world trade between countries; this will help promote order in international business activities.

WTO membership will also have an effect on China's political system. Membership could increase both the demand for and the supply of democratic government. On the demand side, the further economic development and modernisation made possible under WTO membership will increase people's interest in democratic government and their ability to participate in it. On the supply side, the outlook of government leaders will become more global and modern. Such effects will be positive, but one cannot expect them to occur very rapidly. There are inhibitions derived from the historical, social and bureaucratic traditions of China.

In summary, I have suggested reasons WTO membership could have positive impacts on China's institutions. The impacts are small, because the provisions of membership are limited in scope. The effects are expected to be gradual, not only because the terms of membership are to be introduced in steps, but also because economic, legal and political institutions are difficult to change. In addition to the formal provisions to open China's economy gradually, the central government is monitoring the speed of changes to avoid social instability. At the same time, local governments and bureaucrats will seek to stall the changes with red tape if they find them too threatening to local economic institutions. Slow changes in China's institutions may be desirable. Some observers consider the social changes in China since 1978 have been as rapid as the Chinese people can absorb.

As well as the substantive provisions for entry, WTO membership has symbolic significance: China's position in the world economic community is recognised. The conditions for entry to the WTO will serve as a blueprint for China's institutional changes for at least a decade, even if the provisions agreed to do not take effect as early as the formal statements claim. In the meantime, helping Chinese leaders project a better image of themselves in the world community will improve their own confidence to govern and the confidence of the Chinese people in their leaders. The psychological effects of WTO membership may make Chinese leaders more willing to adopt democratic reforms and Chinese citizens more patient in following their leaders as they guide the gradual political change in China towards more democratic government. I make this positive concluding statement under two assumptions. First, the most important objective of all political leaders—including the Chinese—

is to secure their political power. Second, if their political power is assured—and notwithstanding the bureaucratic inertia underlying one-party rule in China—Chinese political leaders are likely to try their best to modernise China and fulfil the dream of generations of Chinese since the Opium War of 1840.

Prospects for reform

There are three sets of forces affecting the Chinese reform process in the early twenty-first century, which should be kept in mind when we examine the prospects for future evolution of China's economic institutions. First is the role of the government, which is by and large positive in initiating reform in various sectors. For economists who believe in limiting the role of government in a market economy, the experience in China confirms the important role of the government in carrying out institutional reform and implementing economic policies to deal with crisis situations—the latter in developed economies as well. To the extent that government actions are required, the competence of government officials is an important factor determining the success of economic reform and economic policies. China has selected some very competent people to serve as government officials, the prevalence of corruption notwithstanding. The Chinese Government also has the will to modernise the economy, as evidenced by its efforts at reform since 1978.

Second, there are market forces pushing reforms forward, two important components of which are private enterprise and foreign investment. Joining the WTO will add impetus in that direction. The third set of forces, however, is institutional inertia, which could slow the process, including government bureaucracy and vested interests in state enterprises and the banking system. There is a lack of trained and competent personnel to run modern enterprises and commercial banks, and the development of human capital is a time-consuming process.

For almost two decades, continued economic growth and reform have been the two most important characteristics of the Chinese economy. These characteristics persisted during the East Asian Financial Crisis and continued in the first decade of the twenty-first century. Reform of the banking system and of state enterprises remains one of the most important tasks facing the Chinese Government. The East Asian Financial Crisis had both positive and negative impacts on economic reform. On the negative side, the speed of reform was somewhat reduced, as evidenced by the introduction of restrictive policies on foreign exchange transactions and on the privatisation of state enterprises. On the positive side, the crisis provided new experience for policymakers, and new observations for economists, of the nature of desirable institutional changes. In any case, the East Asian Financial Crisis led to a reexamination of existing economic institutions and will benefit the outcome of reform in the long run. When the crisis receded, economic reform resumed its speed in China, as it had after the political shock of the events in Tiananmen Square in 1989. The Chinese Government seems determined.

I hope to have conveyed to the reader the following major characteristics of the Chinese economy.

First, although China was once a planned economy, by the turn of the century, it had become essentially a market economy. As a first approximation, one should treat China's economy as a market economy.

Second, and related to the first, is that the economic ideology of traditional communism has almost disappeared. To anticipate and assess the future economic policies of the Chinese Government, one should understand its officials as pragmatic and, by and large, intelligent decision-makers whose objective is to improve China's market economy. Such an understanding avoids the mistakes of many Western observers in predicting a return to central planning after the Tiananmen incident and in predicting a devaluation of the renminbi, a banking crisis and serious unemployment during the East Asian Financial Crisis.

Third, as a qualification of the first point, the Chinese market economy has many shortcomings and economic reforms are not complete. In spite of this, the economy has grown and will continue to grow rapidly in the next decade or two because of the resourcefulness of the Chinese people and because it is not necessary to have a perfect economic system to sustain a fairly high rate of growth.

Fourth, further reform of China's economic institutions will be a slow process because the institutional changes that could be made easily were made in the first two decades of reform, leaving the difficult ones still ahead. These characteristics of the Chinese economy should remain essentially valid for the first one or two decades of the twenty-first century.

Fifth, to understand the nature of the inertia preventing further reform, one must examine Chinese traditions before the establishment of the People's Republic. For example, tradition has led and will continue to lead to bureaucratic behaviour in the management of state enterprises and will restrict the freedom of private enterprise to enter the market and function as effectively as in an open market economy. Reform of formal legal institutions alone cannot change the legal and bureaucratic behaviour of the Chinese population.

Sixth, one can expect both the nationalism aroused after China's defeat in the Opium War of 1840 and the strong urge for modernisation and economic development to affect China's economic and diplomatic relations with other nations.

In summary, one might call the Chinese economy a 'bureaucratic market economy' (its official designation is 'socialist market economy'). It is bureaucratic in two senses. First, state-owned institutions, including the commercial banks and state enterprises, are controlled and run by bureaucrats. Second, nonstate enterprises—both domestic and foreign—have to deal with bureaucrats in the central government and sometimes also in the state sector to conduct their business. Both institutional characteristics hamper the growth of the Chinese economy and are unlikely to change in the near future.

The directions of economic reform have remained the same. According to an article in *The New York Times* on 25 May 2013, China's Prime Minister, Li Keqiang, announced that the central government would reduce the state's role in economic matters to unleash the creative energies of the nation. This includes giving private businesses a bigger role in investment decisions and setting prices. According to a directive issued on the Chinese Government's website, the broad proposals include taking gradual steps to allow market forces to determine bank interest rates and to promote the entry of private capital into finance, energy, railways, telecommunications and other areas. Foreign investors will be given more opportunities to invest in banking, finance, logistics, heath care and other sectors. Furthermore, the decision of the CCCP on economic reform released on 20 October 1984 already listed most of the directions for reform announced by Li Keqiang in 2013. Another important characteristic in the process of economic reform and policy formulation is that the implementation of an announced policy may be slow or may not even be completed as a result of various obstacles.

References

Chen, G. and Wu, C. (2005), Chinese Farmers Survey, Taipei: Ta-Ti Publishing.

Chow, G. C. (1988), *Market socialism and economic development in China*, Research Memorandum 340, Princeton: Princeton University Econometric Research Program.

Chow, G. C. (1993), Capital formation and economic growth in China, *Quarterly Journal of Economics* 108(August): 809–42. doi.org/10.2307/2118409.

Chow, G. C. (1994), *Understanding China's Economy: Part I*, Singapore: World Scientific Publishing Company. doi.org/10.1142/2430.

Chow, G. C. (2000), China's economic policy in the context of the Asian Financial Crisis, *Pacific Economic Review* 5(February): 97–108. doi.org/10.1111/1468-0106.00092.

Directorate General of Budget, Accounting and Statistics (various years), *Statistical Yearbook of the Republic of China*, Taipei: Directorate General of Budget, Accounting and Statistics.

Han, J. (2003), Chinese collective land ownership into shareholder ownership, *China Economic Times*, 11 November.

Huang, J. and Rozelle, S. (2014), China's agriculture: Past failures, present successes and enabling policies, in G. C. Chow and D. H. Perkins (eds), *Routledge Handbook of the Chinese Economy*, London: Routledge Taylor & Francis Group.

Ishihara, K. (1993), *China's Conversion to a Market Economy*, Tokyo: Institute of Development Economies.

Lau, C.-m. and Shen, J. (2000), *China Review 2000*, Hong Kong: Chinese University Press.

Li, S., Wang, Z., Huo, F. and Xu, L. (1999), *WTO: China and the world*, [in Chinese], Beijing: China Development Publishing Co.

Lin, J. Y. (1988), The household responsibility system in China's agricultural reform: A theoretical and empirical study, *Economic Development and Cultural Change* 37(April): S199–224. doi.org/10.1086/edcc.36.s3.1566543.

Lin, J. Y., Cai, F. and Li, Z. (1996), *The China Miracle: Development strategy and economic reform*, Hong Kong: Chinese University Press.

National Bureau of Statistics (NBS) (1997), *China Statistical Yearbook*, Beijing: China Statistics Press.

Perkins, D. (1988), Reforming China's economic system, *Journal of Economic Literature* 26(June): 601–5.

Reynolds, B. L. (1988), *Chinese Economic Reform: How far, how fast?*, San Diego: Academic Press.

Vogel, E. (1989), *One Step Ahead in China: Guangdong under reform*, Cambridge, MA: Harvard University Press.

Woo, W. T., Sachs, J. and Schwab, K. (2000), *The Asian Financial Crisis: Lessons for a resilient Asia*, Cambridge, MA: MIT Press.

World Bank (1997), *China 2020*, Washington, DC: The World Bank.

Zhang, X. (2006), *Asymmetric property rights in China's economic growth*, DSGD Discussion Paper No. 28, January, Washington, DC: International Food Research Institute, Development Strategy and Government Division.

7. Reform and development strategy

Justin Yifu Lin and Zhongkai Shen

China is this year celebrating the fortieth anniversary of its reform and opening-up, marking the transition from a planned to a market economy. China's astonishing growth since 1978 is unprecedented in human history. In the first section of this chapter, we will review China's growth performance in the past four decades and the accompanying problems. In section two, we will analyse how it was possible for China to achieve such growth performance during but not before the transition, as well as why other transitional economies have not achieved a similar performance. Section three will analyse the causes of problems accompanying China's growth miracle and ways to overcome them. Section four will discuss China's growth potential and future outlook, while section five concludes the chapter with a discussion of the implications of China's growth miracle for other developing countries and for economics more generally.

The growth miracle and its problems

China has achieved remarkable success in the 40 years since its reform and opening-up began in 1978. Before its transition from a planned to a market economy, China was one of the poorest countries in the world. Its per capita gross domestic product (GDP) in 1978 was just US$156—less than one-third of the average for sub-Saharan African countries, which was US$490 in the same year. However, since then, dramatic changes have occurred in China. The annual GDP growth rate averaged 9.5 per cent from 1978 to 2017.[1] China is now an upper–middle-income country, with a per capita GDP of US$8,640 in 2017 measured by market exchange rates. In 1978, China accounted for only 4.9 per cent of the global economy—measured by purchasing power parity (PPP)—while this number increased to 18.6 per cent in 2016. Such a high rate of growth for such a long period has not occurred before in human history. Moreover, China has made a great contribution to the global fight against poverty. In 1978, about 81 per cent of people living in rural areas and 84 per cent of people with a living standard below the international poverty line of US$1.25 per day. During the past 40 years, more than 700 million people in China have been lifted out of poverty. As is well known, to help developing countries grow and reduce poverty, many multilateral and bilateral development institutions were

1 Unless otherwise indicated, the statistics for the Chinese economy reported here come from the National Bureau of Statistics' *China Statistical Abstract 2017*, *China Compendium of Statistics 1949–2008* and various editions of the *China Statistics Yearbook*, all published by China Statistics Press.

set up after World War II. And yet, by 2000, if the number of people lifted out of poverty in China were subtracted from the world total, the number of poor people in the world increased rather than decreased.

Like other low-income countries before 1979, China was inward-looking. At that time, exports accounted for 4.1 per cent of China's GDP and imports for 5.6 per cent. In other words, about 90 per cent of Chinese GDP was not related to the global economy. However, from 1978 to 2016, the average annual growth rate of trade was 14.8 per cent. China's trade dependency ratio (trade to GDP) reached 32.7 per cent in 2016. With such dramatic growth performance, in 2009, China overtook Japan to become the second-largest economy in the world. In 2010, it overtook Germany to become the largest exporting country in the world. In 2013, it overtook the United States to become the largest trading country in the world; the total volume of Chinese exports and imports was larger than that of the United States. In 2014, China overtook the United States to become the largest economy in the world, measured by PPP.

Poverty, disease and illiteracy are usually considered fundamental issues for a developing country. With such great economic progress, the wellbeing of people in China has been significantly improved. Average life expectancy increased from 67.8 years in 1982 to 74.83 years in 2010. In 1982, more than one in five Chinese were illiterate and only 6.78 per cent had received education to senior high school or middle special school level and above. By 2010, China's illiteracy rate was reduced to 4.08 per cent and more than 14 per cent of citizens had been educated to senior high or middle special school level and above.

China's dynamic growth has also contributed to global growth and stability. During the Asian Financial Crisis in 1997, China maintained the stability of its exchange rate and dynamic growth of its economy and helped the East Asian economies' quick recovery. By 2000, only three years after the crisis, East Asia was once again the fastest growing region in the world. China was the first country to recover from the 2008 Global Financial Crisis (GFC), in the first quarter of 2009, and has contributed more than 30 per cent of global growth annually since then.

China's influence in global governance has increased with its economic growth, and it is now the third largest shareholder of the World Bank and the International Monetary Fund (IMF). China has also championed its ambitious Belt and Road Initiative (BRI), which proposes to build infrastructure to connect markets in Asia, Europe and Africa. Despite open opposition from the United States at its inception, the Asian Infrastructure Investment Bank (AIIB)—proposed by China as a vehicle for the BRI—has 77 member countries today, making it one of the largest multilateral development institutions in the world. In 2015, the renminbi was listed as one of five currencies in the IMF's Special Drawing Rights (SDR) basket, alongside the American dollar, the Japanese yen, the euro and the British pound. This designation moved the renminbi one step closer to becoming an international reserve currency.

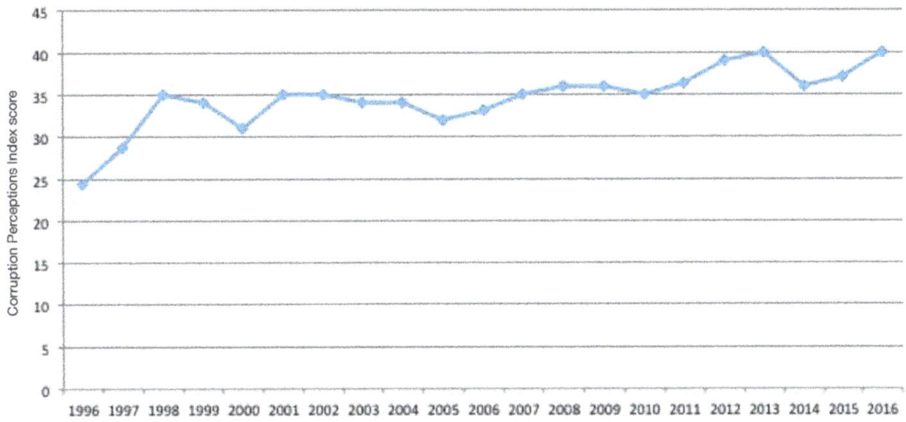

Figure 7.1 China's score on the Corruption Perceptions Index, 1996–2016

Note: The Corruption Perceptions Index ranges from 0 to 100. The lower the score in a country is, the higher is the perception of corruption in the country.

Source: Transparency International (2017).

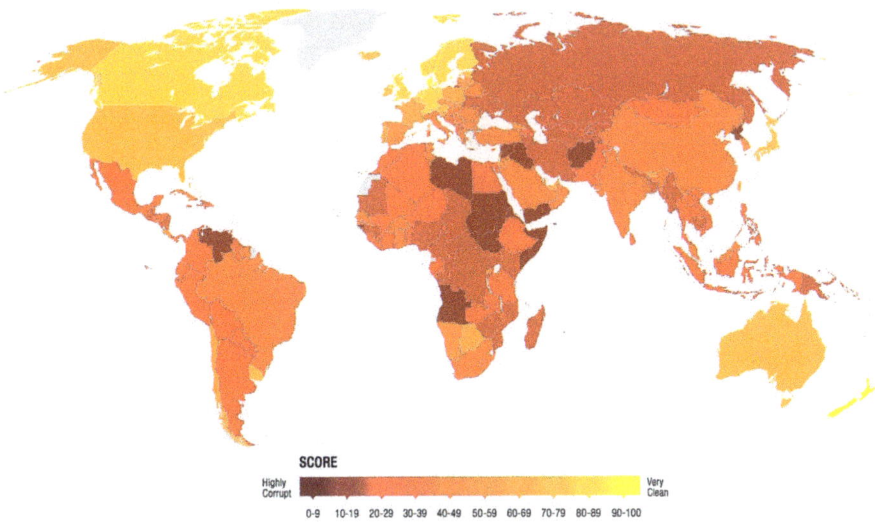

Figure 7.2 Corruption Perceptions Index scores of 176 countries/territories in 2016

Source: Transparency International (2017).

China's extraordinary growth has, however, come at a considerable cost. In addition to environmental degradation and food safety issues—the result of rapid industrialisation and lack of appropriate regulations—China's Gini coefficient, a commonly used measure of inequality, reached 0.465 in 2016, which is above the international warning line of 0.45. Closely related to income inequality is corruption. Transparency International (TI) has published its Corruption Perceptions Index annually since 1996, ranking countries by their perceived levels of corruption, as determined by expert assessments and opinion surveys. The index currently ranks 176 countries on a scale from 100 (very clean) to 0 (highly corrupt). According to TI data, China's average annual score on the Corruption Perceptions Index was 34.6 from 1996 to 2016, indicating a relatively high degree of corruption (Figure 7.1). China was ranked 79 of the 176 countries or territories in the index (Figure 7.2).

China's miracle in historical and international perspective

Why was China able to achieve such extraordinary growth during its transition?

Why was China able to grow so dynamically during the reform period? Our answer is simple: the latecomer advantage.

Rapid and sustained growth in per capita income is a modern phenomenon. Based on the studies of Maddison (2001), average annual per capita income growth in the West was only 0.05 per cent before the eighteenth century, rising to about 1 per cent in the nineteenth century and reaching about 2 per cent in the twentieth century. Therefore, to understand how China was able to grow so rapidly during the past four decades, one needs to understand the nature of modern economic growth.

As mentioned, China's per capita GDP increased continuously, from US$155 in 1978 to US$8,600 in 2016. Achieving this kind of continuous growth requires a continuously rising level of productivity, the foundations of which are technological innovation and industrial upgrading. Technological innovation in existing industries will improve their level of productivity, while industrial upgrading allows the reallocation of resources from low to higher value-added sectors. This process of innovation and upgrading is the foundation of continuous productivity and income growth in any nation—developed and developing. Furthermore, to realise the potential of new technologies and industries, improvements in both hard infrastructure, such as power and road networks, and soft infrastructure, including legal frameworks and financial institutions, are required to reduce transaction costs and share risks.

In advanced high-income countries, technological innovation and industrial upgrading require costly and risky investments in research and development (R&D) as their technologies and industries are already at the global frontier. To upgrade, therefore, they have to invent new technologies and industries to move these frontiers forward. Moreover, the institutional innovation required to realise the potential of new technology and industry often follows a costly trial-and-error, path-dependent evolutionary process (Fei and Ranis 1997). From the end of the nineteenth century until now, the average annual growth rate of per capita GDP and per capita labour productivity in high-income countries was about 2 per cent per year.

Developing countries, however, can acquire, imitate or borrow technologies, industries and institutions from the advanced high-income countries during the catch-up process. In this way, technological innovation and industrial upgrading in developing countries involve lower costs and fewer risks than in high-income countries. This is the so-called latecomer advantage. If developing countries are able to fully exploit this advantage, they can achieve higher rates of technological innovation and industrial upgrading than the advanced high-income countries. Thus, it is possible for them to grow at an annual rate several times that of high-income countries for decades before closing the income gap.

In the postwar period, only 13 of the world's economies achieved continuous annual GDP growth rates of 7 per cent or more for 25 years or more (World Bank 2008). The Commission on Growth and Development, headed by Nobel Laureate Michael Spence, found the first of five common features of these 13 economies was their ability to tap the potential of the latecomer advantage—that is, they 'imported what the rest of the world knew and exported what it wanted' (World Bank 2008: 22).

China adopted its opening-up strategy and tapped the latecomer advantage in 1978, joining this group of 13 economies. Effectively exploiting the latecomer advantage has allowed China to emerge as the world's workshop and achieve sustained rapid economic growth for a long period.

Why was China unable to attain similar success before its transition started?

If the latecomer advantage was the reason for China's extraordinary growth performance after 1978, the same advantages should have existed for centuries before 1978, so why did China not benefit before the reform and opening-up? Again, our answer is simple: because China voluntarily gave up the latecomer advantage.

When the People's Republic of China (PRC) was established in 1949, China accounted for 4.2 per cent of the global economy, but this number increased to only 4.9 per cent by 1978. This came about because China adopted the wrong development strategy at that time and therefore failed to exploit the latecomer advantage.

As is well known, China was the largest economy and among the most advanced, powerful countries in the world before modern times (Maddison 2007). Like many other Chinese social and political elites, Mao Zedong and other first-generation revolutionary leaders were inspired by the dream of achieving rapid modernisation to make people rich and the nation as powerful as the developed countries. To achieve an income level as high as the developed countries required China to have the same advanced industries as high-income countries to reach the same level of labour productivity. Creating a system of national defence as strong as that in high-income countries required defence industries capable of producing equally sophisticated military equipment. Thus, the lack of industrialisation in China—especially of the large, advanced, capital-intensive heavy industries that were considered the foundation of high labour productivity and military strength—was regarded as the key reason for China's backwardness.

Starting in 1953, China adopted a series of ambitious five-year plans to accelerate the building of modern advanced industries, with the goal of overtaking the United Kingdom within 10 years and catching up with the United States within 15 years. These advanced industries were related to national defence, the knowhow for which was not freely available and, in fact, was embargoed for China. Faced with these challenges, China had to 'reinvent the wheel' and do its own research to acquire these technologies. In so doing, China voluntarily chose to forgo the potential of the latecomer advantage.

Moreover, China did not have comparative advantages in the priority industries at that time. In 1953, 83.5 per cent of the labour force was employed in the primary sector, and China's per capita GDP, measured by PPP, was only 4.8 per cent of that of the United States. Given China's endowment structures and income level, it did not possess a comparative advantage in these industries, which were extremely capital intensive. Firms in these industries therefore lacked viability in an open, competitive market. They could not develop spontaneously according to market forces. The only way to develop and sustain these industries was for the state to use administrative measures to mobilise and allocate resources to priority industries and give protection and subsidies to the nonviable firms by distorting the prices of capital and other inputs. Firms in the priority industries were also given a market monopoly and thus enjoyed monopoly prices.

These interventions and distortions enabled China to quickly build up modern advanced industries, test nuclear weapons in the 1960s and launch satellites in the 1970s. Undoubtedly, these were significant achievements. However, resources had been misallocated, the incentives were distorted and the labour-intensive sectors in which China had a comparative advantage were depressed. Thus, by the 1970s, although China had established most of the modern industries of the day, it remained a poor country with more than 80 per cent of its population employed in agriculture.

Only after 1978, with the reform and opening-up, did China start to develop the sectors in which it had comparative advantages—that is, labour-intensive light manufacturing. China's labour costs were low and so were competitive in domestic and international markets. Earning high profits in the light manufacturing sectors, China quickly accumulated capital, paving the way for its industrial upgrading.

In this process, China finally started to benefit from the latecomer advantage. This is why our explanation for China's failure to grow as rapidly before 1978 as it did after that time is so simple: the wrong development strategy deprived China of the ability to benefit from its long-existing potential for rapid growth.

Why did few other transitional economies perform equally well?

The attempt to build large-scale modern industries on an agrarian base occurred not only in China, but also in other socialist and nonsocialist countries after World War II. The development of modern advanced industries was considered the only way to achieve rapid economic take-off and eliminate poverty (Prebisch 1950). Development strategies oriented towards heavy industries and import substitution became popular after the 1950s among developing countries (Lal and Mynt 1996). To implement such development strategies, as China had, these countries introduced distortions and interventions, which caused economic inefficiency. As a result, after World War II, while high-income countries grew at about 2 per cent per year, the average annual per capita GDP growth rate of most developing countries was less than 2 per cent, and thus the income gap between high-income and developing countries increased rather than decreased (Maddison 2001).

While China embarked on its transition from a socialist planned to a market economy in 1978, many other countries embarked on transitions under the guidance of the World Bank and the IMF in the 1980s and 1990s. Compared with China's stable and continuous economic growth, other countries suffered from economic collapse, stagnation and frequent crises. It is natural to ask why most other transitional economies did not perform as well as China. Our answer to this is also simple: because other economies followed the wrong transition strategy.

When they began their transition, many countries followed the neoliberal 'Washington consensus', which was based on the argument that the misallocation of resources caused by excessive government intervention led to unsatisfactory economic performance. Based on this logic, to improve their economic performance, socialist and developing countries were advised to adopt a 'shock therapy' approach of privatisation, marketisation and stabilisation to immediately remove all distortions, end government intervention and allow markets to function freely. However, such distortions and interventions were endogenous to the needs of protecting nonviable firms in priority sectors. If these distortions were removed suddenly, these large-scale industries would go bankrupt, resulting in high unemployment and acute social disorder. Many such heavy industries formed the backbone of the military industry and national defence. After trying the Washington consensus shock therapy, many countries reintroduced subsidies and protection through the back door to preserve large-scale industries for the purpose of providing jobs and securing their national defence.

Compared with the distortions before transition, the newly introduced distortions were even more inappropriate and more inefficient. There is convincing evidence to support this argument. For example, in Russia today there are eight oligopolies in military-related heavy-industry sectors. After privatisation and all kinds of crises, these oligopolistic groups received greater subsidies and protection than they had under the former Soviet Union. Similar situations prevail in other Eastern European and in Latin American and African countries. This is because after privatisation managers of firms in priority sectors had greater incentive to ask for subsidies, which could be simply used to build their own personal wealth. In contrast, before privatisation, this would have amounted to corruption and would be punishable. Furthermore, because of soft budget constraints, managers would ask for even higher subsidies. As a result, reform led first to a certain degree of chaos followed by stagnation and frequent crises (Lin 2014).

China also embarked on a transition from this type of distorted economy, but it managed to maintain stability and dynamic economic growth. The main reason for this is that China adopted a pragmatic, gradual and dual-track approach: understanding that existing sectors could not survive without protection and subsidies, the government continued to provide them for as long as was required. Meanwhile, the Chinese Government also liberalised entry into new sectors, most of which were labour-intensive and small-scale traditional sectors. After lifting the repression of these sectors in 1979, Chinese and foreign firms were allowed to enter these industries. Indeed, the Chinese Government not only liberalised, but also actively facilitated and supported entry into, industries that were consistent with China's comparative advantage at that time as a labour-abundant country.

To turn the comparative advantage into competitive advantage, China also needed to provide adequate infrastructure and a good business environment. However, in 1979 and the 1980s, infrastructure in China was extremely poor, and a lack of financial resources meant it was impossible to improve infrastructure nationwide. Given the limited resources, the Chinese Government set up special economic zones (SEZs), industrial parks and export zones, improving infrastructure in a limited number of areas. Moreover, in SEZs and other economic zones, all distortions were removed, leading to a good business environment. In addition, a wide range of services—for example, comprehensive business services—were provided in the SEZs and industrial parks. As a result, new industries consistent with China's comparative advantage could utilise the infrastructure, business environment and services in these zones and make themselves competitive in international markets.

It was for these reasons that Chinese exports increased rapidly after 1978. A few other socialist economies, such as Poland, Slovenia and Vietnam, adopted a similar dual-track approach and achieved outstanding performance in their transitions. Thus, utilising a gradual, dual-track approach and the latecomer advantage during its transition, China accumulated capital quickly and Chinese industries gradually upgraded from labour-intensive to capital and technology-intensive in the dynamic economic growth process.

The causes of remaining problems and the way out

Reasons for the remaining problems

The gradual, dual-track approach to transition is, however, a double-edged sword. While it has enabled China to achieve stability and dynamic economic growth, it has also created a series of problems, especially corruption and disparities in income distribution.

The protections and subsidies within the dual-track transition were endogenous to the needs of protecting nonviable firms in priority capital-intensive industries, which went against China's comparative advantages. One of the most important costs for these industries was that of capital. While fiscal appropriation was provided before the start of the transition in 1979, the source of capital for these industries shifted to bank loans and the equity market. Four large state banks and a stock market were set up to meet the capital needs of large enterprises in the 1980s. Given that firms in these industries were nonviable, they required subsidies. As a result, interest rates and capital costs were artificially repressed. Therefore, whoever had access to banks' credit services or the stock markets would be subsidised. In 1979 and the 1980s, all firms in China were state owned. Gradually, success in new sectors saw some domestic firms grow to become large enterprises. These large firms could also receive subsidies by borrowing from the large state banks or by listing on the stock market. These subsidies were in fact paid for by households, farms and small and medium-sized industrial and service firms who put their money into the banking sector or the stock market and who were poorer than the owners of the enterprises they financed. The subsidisation of the operations of rich people's firms by poorer people was one of the most important drivers of increasing income disparities.

Moreover, this financial repression created economic rents accruing to whoever had access to financial services, resulting in rent-seeking, bribery and corruption.

Before 1979, in accordance with the provisions of the Chinese constitution, all natural resources were 'owned by the state—that is, by the whole people'. At that time, natural resources were managed free of charge by large-scale state-owned enterprises (SOEs) and were provided to those enterprises at very low prices. After 1979, the government allowed private firms to enter the mining sector and liberalised price controls, while maintaining low concession fees due to the state-owned mining enterprises' need to cover expenditure on redundant and retiring workers. Thus, the newly established private mining enterprises, which had no redundant or retired workers, could become rich overnight. In addition, monopoly rents existed in large service sectors, such as telecommunications and finance. These were another cause of inequality and corruption.

Another problem was environmental pollution, which worsened with the rapid development of manufacturing, which has high energy and emissions intensities compared with agriculture and services, and uses massive amounts of coal. Pollution in China is therefore related to its development stage, and can be mitigated by environmental regulation and supervision, and will be much improved when China becomes a high-income, service-dominated economy.

How to deepen reform?

The main reason for maintaining transitional distortions was the need to protect nonviable SOEs in comparative advantage–defying, capital-intensive industries. After 40 years of dynamic growth and capital accumulation, many of these industries are now consistent with rather than defying China's comparative advantages and firms in these industries have become viable in open, competitive markets—including internationally.

The reason for maintaining distortions has disappeared. It is time for China to complete its transition and remove all remaining distortions—specifically, by removing financial repression and allowing the development of small financial institutions and local banks to provide credit services for agricultural households and small and medium-size enterprises. Furthermore, it is necessary to remove the retired workers' pension burden from the stated-owned mining sector and impose taxes on the natural resource sector. It is also essential to encourage access to and competition in the service sectors where large monopoly rents remain, such as telecommunications and the energy and financial sectors.

Indeed, the above measures were among those in the reform agenda announced by the Chinese Government at the third plenary session of the eighteenth party congress. During his first five-year tenure as national leader, in 2012–17, President Xi Jinping engaged the assistance of his ally Wang Qishan in a sweeping anticorruption drive. He proposed allowing the market to play a decisive role in resource allocation by eliminating the remaining distortions in the dual-track reform system; and advocated for tight environmental regulation, which would balance high growth with 'green' growth. Hopefully, the implementation of a reform agenda of this kind and the removal of these distortions will eliminate the root causes of income inequality and corruption.

The new normal and China's economic outlook

China's annual GDP growth rate dropped from the average annual rate of 9.6 per cent in the period 1978–2016 to 6.7 per cent in 2016 (Figure 7.3). The reason for this slowdown is hotly debated in China and the debate is closely followed globally. To answer the question of whether China can maintain its dynamic economic growth in the coming years, one needs to know the size of China's growth potential and the reasons for the deceleration of growth since 2010.

Many economists thought the deceleration was due to the decline of growth potential after more than three decades of extraordinarily high growth as well as domestic structural problems.

We will first estimate China's growth potential and analyse the main cause of recent growth deceleration.

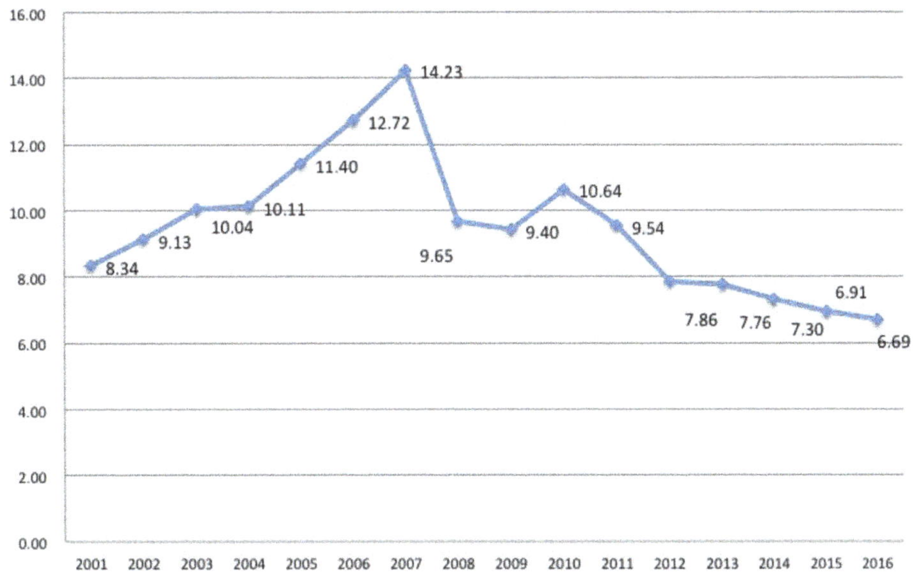

Figure 7.3 China's GDP growth rate, 2001–16 (constant 2010 US$)
Source: World Bank (2018).

How large is China's growth potential?

China's potential for rapid economic growth depends on the size of the latecomer advantage it still enjoys. To measure this, one should compare China's per capita GDP with the per capita GDP of high-income countries such as the United States, because per capita GDP is a proxy for a country's average labour productivity, which is a measure of the degree of technological advancement and industrial valued added.

Measured by PPP, in 2008, China's per capita GDP was 21 per cent of that of the United States (Maddison 2010). This status relative to the United States was similar to that of Japan in 1951, Singapore in 1967, Taiwan in 1975 and South Korea in 1977—all of which stood at 21 per cent.

In the following 20 years, Japan grew at an average annual rate of 9.2 per cent, Singapore grew at 8.6 per cent, Taiwan grew at 8.3 per cent and South Korea grew at 7.6 per cent. After 20 years of dynamic economic growth, Japan's per capita income, measured in PPP, was 65.5 per cent of that of the United States in 1971, while Singapore was 53.9 per cent in 1987, Taiwan was 54.2 per cent in 1995 and South Korea was 50.2 per cent in 1997. These four Asian economies were among the 13 referred to above as having tapped into the growth potential deriving from the latecomer advantage and as enjoying high growth rates of 7 per cent or more for 25 or more years.

Just as these economies were able to utilise the technology gap and exploit the latecomer advantage to grow for 20 years at between 7.6 per cent and 9.2 per cent per year, China has the potential to grow at 8 per cent per year for 20 years after 2008.

What were the reasons for the deceleration of China's growth to below its potential after 2010?

If China's potential growth rate was 8 per cent, why has that growth decelerated to below 8 per cent? The potential growth rate is estimated according to supply-side technology; however, moving from potential to its realisation depends also on demand-side conditions.

To answer this question, let us come back to the GDP accounting identity—that is, $GDP \equiv C + I + G + NX$. From a demand-side perspective, keeping government expenditure unchanged, there are three components of GDP: exports, investment and consumption. This shows that, from the demand side, the deceleration was the result mainly of declining growth rates of exports and investments due to external and cyclical factors.

First, high-income countries—including the United States, Western European countries and Japan (Figure 7.4)—have not yet recovered from the GFC of 2008; in these countries, the GDP growth rate was less than 3 per cent per year, which was the average level for high-income countries before the GFC. As a result, household income stagnated. In addition, households had large debt burdens before the GFC that they need to reduce. These factors contributed to stagnation of household consumption in these countries and depressed international trade, with a major negative impact on Chinese exports, as China is a major global supplier of consumption goods. From 1978 to 2016, China's average annual export growth was about 15.3 per cent; in 2016, it was about –7.7 per cent. This downturn was one of the reasons for the deceleration of Chinese growth.

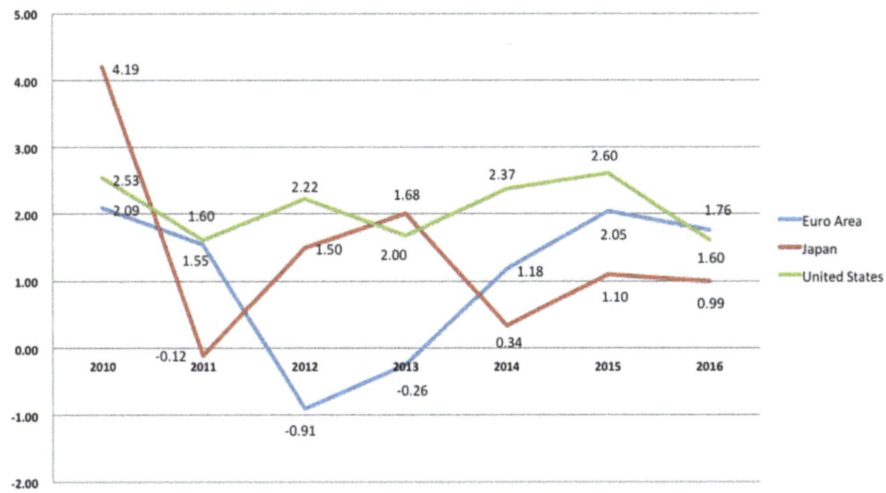

Figure 7.4 GDP growth rates of high-income countries, 2010–16 (constant 2010 US$)

Source: World Bank (2018).

The second reason for the deceleration was that, to deal with demand shock from the GFC, most countries adopted a countercyclical fiscal expansion to support investment. These projects were mostly completed; nevertheless, the global economy has not fully recovered. The private sector's incentives for investment remain low. Without a new round of stimulus programs, investment growth rates will drop.

As for consumption, since China maintains a high employment rate, household income has continued to grow rapidly, at about 8 per cent per year, with consumption growing at a similar rate. The growth of consumption is the reason the country has managed to maintain a growth rate of about 7 per cent per year.

The above two factors affected not only China, but also other countries, causing the other BRIC members (Brazil, Russia and India) (Figure 7.5) and export-oriented high-income/high-performance East Asian economies to experience a similar pattern of deceleration, as shown in Figure 7.6. As their household income and consumption did not grow as rapidly as China's, their growth deceleration was even sharper than China's.

In short, although China as a transitional economy has many internal structural problems, the deceleration since 2010 is due mainly to external and cyclical factors.

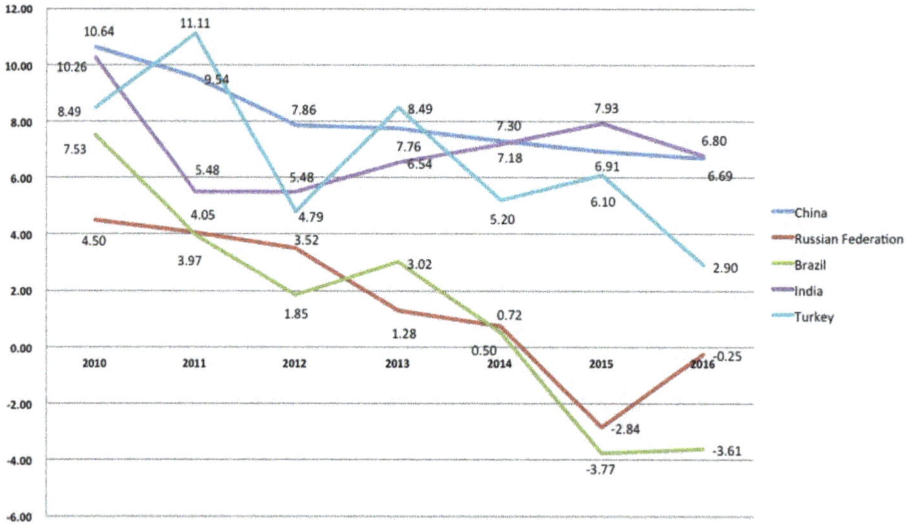

Figure 7.5 GDP growth rate in BRIC countries and Turkey, 2010–16 (constant 2010 US$)

Source: World Bank (2018).

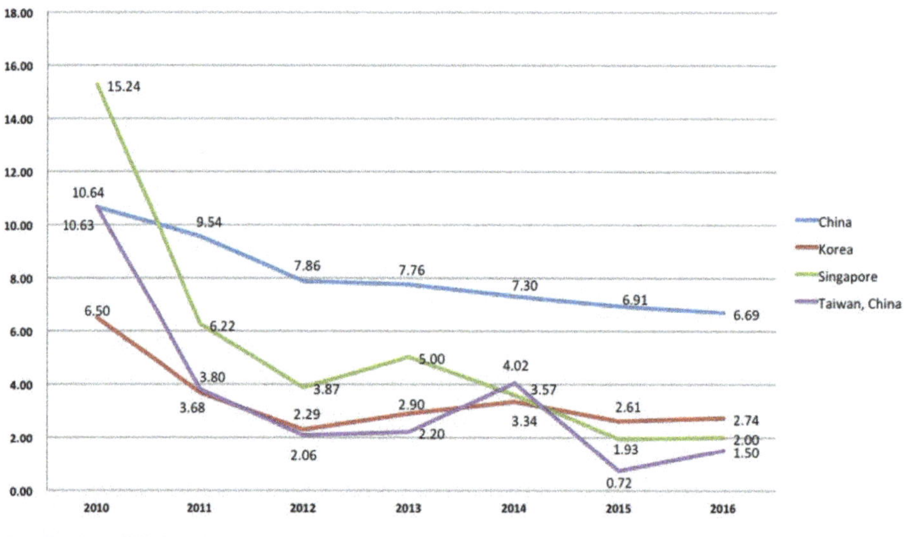

Figure 7.6 GDP growth rate in high-performance export-oriented countries, 2010–16 (constant 2010 US$)

Source: World Bank (2018).

China's economic outlook

So, how can China maintain a relatively high growth rate in coming years? Or, what are the advantages China can make use of to drive its dynamic growth? As is well known, due to a lack of fundamental structural reforms, Japan stagnated after the burst of its economic bubble in 1991. High-income countries are likely to suffer a similar fate—growing at less than the normal rate of 3 per cent per year and repressing global trade. Therefore, given sluggish external demand, China's growth will come mainly from domestic demand.

As a middle-income developing country, China still has plenty of good opportunities for investment in industrial upgrading, urban and interurban infrastructure and environmental protection, in spite of the excess capacity in many sectors. Another advantage is that China has a very sound fiscal position. In 2015, national, provincial and local government debt was less than 60 per cent of GDP—among the lowest in the world. In addition, China still has more than US$3 trillion in foreign exchange reserves—the largest in the world. With good investment opportunities and abundant financial resources, China will maintain a reasonable rate of investment growth, creating jobs and increasing household incomes and consumption. Under these conditions, there is no reason for China not to reach its annual growth target of 6.5 per cent or more in the coming years. If China does maintain such a growth rate, it is very likely that, by as early as 2020 or no later than 2022, its per capita GDP will reach or pass the threshold of US$12,700, making China a high-income country (Lin et al. 2016). By 2030, China will become the largest economy in the world, measured by market exchange rates. It is very likely China will be the third economy—following Taiwan and South Korea—among more than 200 developing economies to successfully develop from a low-income to a high-income economy since World War II.

What are the implications of China's growth miracle for other developing countries and for economics?

Are there useful lessons that can be drawn from China's experiences over the past 40 years? Absolutely.

First, as long as they know how to make full use of their comparative advantages in their industrial development and as long as they tap the latecomer advantage in technological innovation and industrial upgrading, all developing countries have the opportunity to grow at 8 per cent or more for several decades. For this to happen, a country needs to have an efficient market and a facilitating government. A well-functioning market is a precondition for the development of industries according to a country's comparative advantage, since only with such a market can relative prices reflect the relative scarcities of factors in the economy and guide entrepreneurs to adopt technologies and enter into industries consistent with the comparative advantages determined by the economy's factor endowments. A facilitating government is also essential to compensate the first movers' externalities and remove bottlenecks in hard infrastructure and soft institutions to reduce transaction costs in the process of technological innovation and industrial upgrading. Once entrepreneurs follow the comparative advantage to develop specific industries in a competitive market and the state plays a facilitating role to turn those industries to competitive advantage, capital accumulation will be rapid, comparative advantages will change rapidly and the economy can tap into the potential of the latecomer advantage and grow dynamically for several decades.

Second, every transitional country has a lot of distortions, which cause resource misallocation and rent-seeking. It is desirable to remove these distortions. Such distortions are, however, in economic terms, largely endogenous. Unless the causes of a distortion are dealt with, an attempt to remove it can do a lot of harm. If there is a distortion and the economy is in a 'second-best' situation, the removal of the distortion without the removal of the cause will very often make the situation worse. A country embarking on reform should therefore be pragmatically employing transitory protection, as China did in the past four decades.

A careful liberalisation of entry into new sectors consistent with a country's comparative advantages and government facilitation of growth in those sectors can permit it to grow dynamically and preserve stability while preparing the ground for the removal of distortions. A pragmatic approach to develop step by step according to a country's evolving comparative advantage is of great value for developing countries.

At the same time, pragmatism is required in the transition. The final goal is the establishment of a well-functioning market economy, but it should be a process managed by the government paying attention to the needs of all sectors and providing them with business opportunities. In this way, the World Bank's dream of a world free of poverty may be possible.

As for economics, the implication is that in the past most theories were developed for high-income countries. Developing countries use these theories in the hope they will become high-income countries. The intention was good, but the results were often disappointing, due to the differences in the preconditions between developed and developing countries. The applicability of economic theory depends on the preconditions. Policies based on theories generated from the experiences of high-income countries do not, therefore, achieve the intended results in developing countries. It is desirable to develop ideas and theories based on the experiences of developing countries themselves.

In 2018, China is celebrating the fortieth anniversary of its transition from a planned to a market economy. China's rise from poverty to a world power in the past four decades is a growth miracle unmatched in human history and a goldmine of new development ideas and theories.

References

Fei, J. and Ranis, G. (1997), *Growth and Development from an Evolutionary Perspective*, Malden, MA: Blackwell.

Lal, D. and Mynt, H. (1996), *The Political Economy of Poverty, Equity, and Growth: A comparative study*, Oxford: Clarendon Press.

Lin, J. Y. (1992), Rural reforms and agricultural growth in China, *American Economic Review* 82: 34–51.

Lin, J. Y. (1995), The Needham puzzle: Why the Industrial Revolution did not originate in China, *Economic Development and Cultural Change* 43: 269–92. doi.org/10.1086/452150.

Lin, J. Y. (2003), Development strategy, viability and economic convergence, *Economic Development and Cultural Change* 53: 277–308. doi.org/10.1086/367535.

Lin, J. Y. (2009), *Economic Development and Transition: Thought, strategy, and viability*, Cambridge: Cambridge University Press. doi.org/10.1017/CBO9780511805622.

Lin, J. Y. (2011), New structural economics: A framework for rethinking development, *World Bank Research Observer* 26: 193–221. doi.org/10.1093/wbro/lkr007.

Lin, J. Y. (2012a), *Demystifying the Chinese Economy*, Cambridge: Cambridge University Press.

Lin, J. Y. (2012b), *The Quest for Prosperity: How developing economies can take off*, Princeton, NJ: Princeton University Press.

Lin, J. Y. (2013), Demystifying the Chinese economy, *Australian Economic Review* 46(3): 259–68. doi.org/10.1111/j.1467-8462.2013.12035.x.

Lin, J. Y. (2014), The Washington consensus revisited: A new structural economics perspective, *Journal of Economic Policy Reform* 18(2): 96–113. doi.org/10.1080/17487870.2014.936439.

Lin, J. Y. (2017), The rise of China and its implications for economics and other developing countries, *Area Development and Policy*: 1–11.

Lin, J. Y. and Li, F. (2009), *Development strategy, viability, and economic distortions in developing countries*, World Bank Policy Research Working Paper No. 4906, Washington, DC: The World Bank.

Lin, J. Y. and Monga, C. (2012), *The Growth Report and New Structural Economics*, Washington, DC: The World Bank. doi.org/10.1596/978-0-8213-8955-3.

Lin, J. Y. and Tan, G. (1999), Policy burdens, accountability, and soft budget constraints, *American Economic Review: Papers and Proceedings* 89: 426–31. doi.org/10.1257/aer.89.2.426.

Lin, J. Y., Cai, F. and Li, Z. (2003), *The China Miracle: Development strategy and economic reform*, Hong Kong: Chinese University Press.

Lin, J. Y., Monga, C., te Velde, D. W., Tendulkar, S. D., Amsden, A., Amoako, K. Y., Pack, H. and Lim, W. (2011), DPR debate: Growth identification and facilitation—The role of the state in the dynamics of structural change, *Development Policy Review* 29: 259–310. doi.org/10.1111/j.1467-7679.2011.00534.x.

Lin, J. Y., Wan, G. and Morgan, P. J. (2016), Prospects for a re-acceleration of economic growth in the PRC, *Journal of Comparative Economics* 44(4): 842–53.

Maddison, A. (2001), *The World Economy: A millennial perspective*, Paris: OECD Development Centre. doi.org/10.1787/9789264189980-en.

Maddison, A. (2007), *Chinese Economic Performance in the Long Run*, 2nd edn, Paris: OECD Development Centre.

Maddison, A. (2010), *Maddison Historical Statistics*, Groningen: Groningen Growth and Development Centre, University of Groningen. Available from: www.ggdc.net/maddison/.

Prebisch, R. (1950), *The Economic Development of Latin America and its Principal Problems*, New York: United Nations.

Transparency International (2017), Corruption Perceptions Index 2017. Available at: www.transparency.org/news/feature/corruption_perceptions_index_2017.

World Bank (2008), *The Growth Report: Strategies for sustained growth and inclusive development*, Washington, DC: The World Bank for the Commission on Growth and Development.

World Bank (2018), *Global Economic Prospects*, Washington, DC: The World Bank.

8. The complex task of evaluating China's economic reforms

Dwight H. Perkins

Scholars, practitioners and many others regularly comment on the pace of China's economic reforms, but there is no consensus on what constitutes slow or fast, partial or complete economic reform, either in China or in any other country. Economists often include in equations used to explain gross domestic product (GDP) growth a variable that purports to measure reform. Often this variable is based on surveys of 'informed individuals' or businesspeople, most of whom cannot possibly have the ability to make comparative judgements of more than two or three countries, if that. Total factor productivity (TFP) in growth equations is also sometimes used to measure whether or not economic reform is having an impact, but TFP is a residual that is high or low for a variety of possible reasons. Alternatively, many analysts of China's economy base their assessment of the pace of reform on reform in one or another sector that they think is critical to overall reform. The pace at which state-owned enterprises are made to face full domestic and international competition or the pace at which they are being privatised are often used. Others, particularly foreign observers, focus on financial reforms, ranging from the degree to which capital markets are open to the degree to which banks are managed and regulated according to practices widely used in high-income countries. None of these partial explanations comes close to capturing the complexity of fundamentally changing an economy from one kind of system to another.

In this chapter, I will attempt to outline the main components of economic reform in China and will give my views—where I have some basis for judgement—on the pace of reform in these components. First, however, one must define what one means by economic reform. In the context of China and in this chapter, economic reform is defined as elimination of the institutions of a command economy and replacement of them with the institutions of a modern market economy similar to those in most of the high-income countries of the world. It is assumed that this transformation has had and continues to have a positive impact on GDP growth. This definition, however, does not include all institutions and policies that impact the rate of GDP growth. Growth can be, and often is, affected by investment strategies or by the level of research and development expenditure, for example, but that would be as true in a command as a market economy.

There are five distinct types of institutions that are fundamental to a well-functioning market economy, all of which are substantially different from the institutions of a centrally planned command economy: 1) markets on which all or most goods and services are bought and sold; 2) ownership and property rights that lead economic actors, particularly producers, to behave in a way consistent with the requirements of efficient markets; 3) legal and regulatory institutions that can protect property rights, solve disputes and correct for market failures in a way that is fair and efficient; 4) capital markets and a financial sector that are much like those found in high-income market economies; and 5) markets for labour and land that govern the allocation of these factor inputs and avoid major distortions such as those of the Chinese household registration (*hukou*) system. These five criteria are based on neoclassical economic theory. If the five criteria are carried out in rigorous accordance with this theory, the economic system will be efficient in the Pareto concept of efficiency. Most high-income market economies approximate these requirements to a substantial degree. China's experience in some of these five areas, however, differs from these criteria to a degree that raises the issue of whether the leadership of the country accepts all five criteria as a generally desired goal, even if the country deviates from them for practical political reasons. Or, whether instead China rejects some aspects of the five and substitutes something fundamentally different.

In what follows, we attempt to identify—within the limits of this author's knowledge—the degree to which China is implementing each of these five criteria in turn. In areas where the country—like all countries—falls short of the theoretical ideal, we ask whether this is because there are political barriers to overcome, because reform takes time or because China's socialist market economy with Chinese characteristics is substituting something fundamentally different.

Creating markets for goods and services

China largely completed the transformation from a centrally planned administrative allocation of goods and services to market allocation at market-set prices in the 1980s and 1990s. In rural areas, this happened quickly in 1979 and the early 1980s, with the freeing up of rural markets where farmers could trade with each other and with outsiders coming in to purchase local products. Prices for major crops were controlled for a time and continue to be monitored, but largely reflect market demand and supply. Urban markets and prices, particularly for industrial inputs, took much longer to make this transition. The dual price system—under which centrally planned and allocated goods were sold at state-set prices and production above planned quotas was sold on the market—continued into the 1990s.

Resistance from powerful state-owned enterprises, among others, made moving at the outset to a one-price system politically impossible. By the mid-1990s, however, the dual price system had largely disappeared. This change resulted mainly from the actions of producer enterprises, not from central government action. Producer incentives were changed by encouraging them to make profits and by rewarding them accordingly, and they preferred to sell their goods at the much higher market prices. Purchasing agents for user enterprises might prefer the lower state-set prices, but not if they found themselves facing long delays and shortages because of difficulty getting allocations at those prices. The replacement of the dual price system with a single price system was not the only area where reform in China proceeded from the grassroots up rather than from the central government down. The Communist Party of China (CPC) plenum of 1992 in essence recognised what was going on by redefining the ultimate goal as creating a 'socialist market economy'. Today, the government controls very few domestic prices, and most of the areas where such control does exist are in sectors where 'natural monopolies' lead most high-income countries to regulate prices.

The creation of markets and market prices in the 1980s and 1990s largely affected the allocation of domestically produced goods and services. The purchase and sale of imports and exports remained under central government control for longer. Initially, foreign trade was controlled by a few monopoly trading corporations, but, gradually, the number of organisations allowed to participate in international markets was expanded and producing enterprises could then buy inputs themselves and sell their output on the world market.

When China joined the World Trade Organization (WTO) in 2001 on terms that did not include the exceptions given to 'developing countries', China agreed, in principle at least, to allow its domestic markets to open to international goods at international prices (subject to some tariffs). There is an ongoing debate around the world about how faithfully China has implemented WTO rules and practices, and there are certainly some Chinese practices that involve subsidies to exports or restrictions on imports that are inconsistent with WTO rules, but any attempt to measure these distortions or to compare them with similar distortions in other East Asian or European economies is far beyond the scope of this short chapter. By any reasonable standard, Chinese goods and services are sold on markets at market prices that are broadly consistent with international prices for traded goods.

Enterprises in both the private and the public sectors face competition, although competition between public and private enterprises is often not on a level playing field. China's transition to a market economy in this area, therefore, is largely complete. It is not clear, however, whether the remaining unequal competition between some public and private enterprises is a desired outcome or simply an incomplete transition due to the political and personal interests of particular groups—something that exists in all countries. There is also in China still more government regulatory involvement in many markets than what is found in the most efficient market economies, but that is typical of many developing countries for a variety of reasons.

Ownership and property rights

Most scholars regard private ownership and property rights as having played a critical role in the development of Europe and North America, and privatisation was a central part of many of the reform programs in Eastern Europe and Russia in their transition from command to market economies. A broad privatisation effort, however, has never been a central part of China's post-1978 economic reforms. The role of the state sector in China has nevertheless fallen steadily, to be replaced with a kind of private enterprise. At the outset of reform, this was evident mainly in the agricultural sector. By the early 1980s, most rural communes had been replaced with individual household farms. The state, however, continued to hold ownership of the land and it was made available to farmers through long-term leases. The rules governing land leasing have gradually changed over time and farmers are generally allowed to sublease their land to others if, for example, they are working mainly in urban jobs. Subleasing, however, is subject to various rules that change from one region to the next. We will return to this issue later.

At the beginning of the reform period, all industry, most commerce and all financial institutions were either state-owned or collectively owned. That began to change after 1984, but only slowly. Rural and urban smaller-scale collective industries remained as collectives well into the 1990s before most began to be privatised. Rural collective enterprises in the past did have a kind of property right, but it was based on the practice of respecting the land farmed by a given commune or brigade as in some sense belonging to that commune or brigade. Land could be taken for major projects by the central government, but land was not commonly transferred from one commune to another. Collective enterprises under a commune or brigade also in a sense belonged to the unit where they were located and that carried over to the townships and villages that replaced the communes and brigades. Smaller state-owned enterprises were also gradually privatised as market forces became steadily more dominant. Successive party congresses increased their formal recognition of private enterprises and a version of private property rights.

Most current industrial data apply to enterprises with sales above a certain size (RMB5 million through to 2010 and RMB20 million thereafter). Most industrial enterprises smaller than this were, for the most part, run privately. The ownership data for the larger enterprises are presented in Table 8.1, and are arranged grouping together types of ownership that are mainly state-owned, collectively owned or privately owned. There are private shareholding companies, but a majority of those listed on the Shanghai and Shenzhen stock exchanges have majority state ownership and are in effect state-owned enterprises. The collective form of ownership is largely disappearing for larger enterprises. Foreign-funded enterprises are mostly private and their share is rising more rapidly than any other sector, including domestic private industrial enterprise ownership. The major uncertainty about ownership is with the category of limited liability companies (LLCs). Solely state-owned LLCs are listed separately, as are privately owned LLCs, but, then, what are the 'other' LLCs? They have average sales of RMB300 million, suggesting that many or even most may be independent of direct state control—but that is conjecture.

Table 8.1 Industrial enterprise revenue (RMB billion)

	2001	%	2015	%	2015/2001
	GVIO		GVIO		%
State enterprises	1,722.919		4,520.2		262.4
Shareholding	1,269.834		9,963.1		784.6
Sole state LLC	514.226		4,661.8		906.6
Joint	85.076		27.2		32.0
Subtotal	**3,592.055**	**37.6**	**1,9172.3**	**17.3**	**533.7**
Collective and cooperative	1,304.745	13.7	822.6	0.7	63.5
Private	876.089		38,639.5		441.0
Hong Kong, etc.	1,184.719		9,692.6		818.1
Foreign-funded	1,537.372		14,877.2		967.7
Subtotal	**3,598.180**	**37.5**	**63,209.3**	**57.0**	**1,756.7**
LLCs and other	1,049.716	11.0	27,781.1	25.0	2,646.5
Total	**9,544.696**	**100.0**	**110,985.3**	**100.0**	**1,162.8**

GVIO = gross value of industrial output.

Sources: NBS (2003: 459; 2016: Table 13.1).

Formal ownership in 2018 of the other urban and large-scale sectors of the economy varies considerably. The dominant enterprises in the banking sector are mostly state-owned, although there is some private and foreign ownership. Ownership in the insurance sector is somewhat murky, but there is clearly substantial state ownership in some major companies and all are highly regulated by the state. In commerce, state-owned enterprises control only 7 per cent of all sales, but LLCs, sole state-owned and other enterprises account for 43 per cent. The rest are mostly private. State-owned firms account for only 12 per cent of the gross value of construction activity in 2015 and only 10 per cent of the floor space under construction. In the transport sector, railroads are state-run, as are most (but not all) of the major airlines.

The 2013 third plenum reform list did not include a call for privatisation of state-controlled firms. It did suggest there could be an increase of 'mixed ownership', where private capital joined with public capital, but the main thrust of the reforms was to make both the state-controlled and the private-controlled sectors perform better by making them face market competition. In that context, enterprises with monopoly rights gained through government administrative directives would be eliminated, but this in no way implied that state-controlled enterprises would become just like private firms. A key difference was that top management in all state-controlled enterprises is and will continue to be selected by the CPC's Organisation Department, not by public or private shareholders. The Organisation Department does make a serious effort to find competent people to place in top enterprise and government management positions, but loyalty to the party remains the essential characteristic of these appointments. Many in top management are more like senior civil servants than private entrepreneurs; their career is in the party and the party moves them from one position to another, both in producing enterprises and in government. They will stress enterprise profits if that is what the party wants, but most of the time the party has diverse goals, many of which are not typically found in the objectives of private enterprise management.

One should also not overstate the independence of private-sector management. The government and party have substantially more control over the actions of private enterprises than is the case in most high-income market economies in Europe, Japan and North America. Business decisions in China are subject to myriad government regulations and approval processes. Even small-scale enterprises often have close ties with local governments, without which many would have trouble surviving. Private firms—except very small ones—have their own party committees. Those committees are not supposed to be involved in management, but they do have a role in ensuring that the firm adheres to the broad objectives of the party, and management ignores those objectives at their peril. To make that clear, the CPC and the government, just prior to the nineteenth party congress in October 2017, issued a statement respecting private sector rights and promising a favourable market environment for them—but in return for private entrepreneur patriotism and acceptance of stronger party guidance (MERICS 2017).

The private sector is clearly playing a steadily increasing role in the country's economy in large part because private-sector firms consistently outperform state-controlled firms. That said, the nineteenth party congress and Chairman Xi Jinping's three-hour speech made it clear that China, today at least, has no intention of moving all the way to having an enterprise leadership for whom maximising profits is the overarching objective. The much wider range of objectives of the party leadership in Beijing and the party committees in the enterprises—both public and private—will continue to play an important and possibly dominant role. Throughout much of the world, state-run enterprises with multiple government-set objectives have generally proved to be substantially less productive than their private-sector counterparts, which are able to set their own goals (in contrast with private-sector firms that are highly regulated by governments).

Is there any evidence of whether party and government leadership in China is providing a more or less favourable climate for enterprises over time? One set of quantitative data we have on that score are the annual *Doing Business* surveys of the World Bank (Table 8.2).

Table 8.2 China: *Doing Business* overall ranking

	2006	2007	2008	2009	2010	2011	2012	2013	2014	2015	2016
Overall ranking	93	83	83	89	79	91	91	96	90	84	78
Registering property	21	29	30	32	38	43	44	48	37	43	42
Resolving closing	75	57	62	65	68	75	82	78	54	55	53
Enforcing contracts	62	20	18	18	15	16	19	19	35	7	5
Minority interests	83	83	88	93	93	97	100	98	132	134	123
Trading across borders	38	43	48	44	50	60	68	74	98	96	96
Paying taxes	168	168	132	130	114	122	122	120	120	132	151
Getting credit	101	84	59	61	65	67	70	71	71	79	62

Sources: World Bank (various years).

As the data in Table 8.2 indicate, over the past decade, 'enforcing contracts'—a critical issue for businesses both private and public—has become significantly better. For the most part, however, China ranks far below most of the more successful developing economies. China's 2016 ranking at 78 puts it at a similar level as Turkey (69), South Africa (74) and Ukraine (80).

A better measure of whether the Chinese Government and the CPC's leadership over enterprises has been positive or negative for the economy would be a sector-by-sector, public and private study of productivity gains over time compared with similar data for other market economies at a similar stage of development and with less government or political party leadership. That exercise is far beyond what is possible here.

The legal system

Closely related to the property rights issue in judging China's economic reforms is the status of the country's legal system. In high-income countries in North America and Europe, the legal system is arguably the principal institution enforcing property rights. When either other individuals or the government threaten those rights, the property owner does not typically go to the highest government official as possible to ask for support. The individual or company threatened goes to court. In a similar vein, the parties to all manner of disputes—if they cannot resolve these disputes through direct discussions between the parties involved—may go to a mediator, but more often they go to court. The courts are the ones to apply and interpret the laws in economic or civil disputes. The judges who preside over these courts are highly educated in the law and, while they are appointed by politicians in most cases, once appointed, they act independently of the government, including the people who appointed them.

China's legal system in the economic sphere falls far short of the standard of the stronger legal systems in the West. That said, China's legal system has come a long way from where it was at the beginning of the economic reform period in 1978. During the Cultural Revolution, the legal system was effectively dismantled and the law profession abolished. Beginning in 1978, the legal system had to be rebuilt from scratch and the economic laws on the books—written for a Soviet-type command economy—had to be completely rewritten for what was to become a market economy. The creation of a modern legal system in the economic sphere had also to deal with the historical experience of Chinese businesses that rarely went to the formal legal system to settle disputes. Disputes going back centuries were settled directly by the parties involved or in accordance with guild rules or the rules of other kinds of associations, not by the local government magistrate who had the authority to try formal legal cases. This practice even applied in places such as Hong Kong, where there was and is a judicial system modelled after that in England.

A modern market-oriented judicial system in the Chinese mainland did not spring up overnight in the 1980s. Even rudimentary market-oriented economic laws, such as laws on corporate taxes or contract disputes, did not really exist in the 1980s. The decision to make foreign investment in China legal early in the 1980s attracted mainly Hong Kong and other overseas Chinese businesses that were experienced with working in societies where security—including security from state predation—was handled by establishing personal ties with local authorities. By the 1990s, however, many of the formal laws required in a market economy were in place and a judicial system capable of implementing that legal framework had begun to be created. The quality of that legal system initially, however, was low. Judges had little or no training in the law and the number of trained lawyers was still very small for a nation with millions of businesses and a population of more than 1 billion. That situation changed steadily as more and more judges received legal training and the law profession and law schools became accepted as essential parts of a modern market economy, at least in the economic sphere. By the beginning of the twenty-first century, more and more individuals and businesses were going to the courts to settle disputes, particularly in the economic sphere. The data for the continued rapid expansion of court cases in the economic sphere and in the number of lawyers are presented in Table 8.3.

Table 8.3 Judicial system—quantitative indicators

	2002	2010	2015
Cases accepted by courts			
Contract disputes	2,266,695	3,222,555	6,013,386
Economic rights disputes	869,013	1,444,887	2,325,392
Administrative	80,728	136,353	220,398
Number of lawyers	136,684	195,170	297,175

Sources: NBS (2003: 836; 2011: Tables 23.9, 23.30, 23.31; 2016: Tables 24.18, 24.19, 24.20).

During the first part of the twenty-first century, court cases in the economic sphere rose at 8 per cent a year, starting from an already substantial level in 2002. Clearly, an increasing number of businesses and individuals concluded that the courts were a logical place to go to settle disputes—something that would not have been the case through much of Chinese history and certainly not during the 1960s and 1970s. But why, as indicated in Table 8.3, were there so many fewer cases in the administrative sphere? These cases mainly involved individuals and businesses going to court over government actions in the economic sphere. It is likely that people and companies did not go to court in such cases because there was only a very small chance of success.

Quantitative studies have come up with some answers as to where the legal system is most used to settle disputes. This evidence can in turn be used indirectly to provide evidence of the changing quality of the judicial system. To begin with, there are far more cases and more lawyers per capita in the more advanced provinces on China's coast than in central and western China (with a few exceptions). There are also more pressures from foreign-owned firms (which are mostly on the coast) for judicial reform than from Chinese-owned firms (including those in Hong Kong), both private and public. The latter rely more on personal relations with officials through entertainment and outright bribery than the former, and thus feel less need for protection through the legal system. The smaller number of administrative cases, as noted above, in part reflects the fact that courts tend to be biased in favour of the government in such cases. The legal system has also been designed in part to limit disputes that could become serious challenges to political stability—notably, for example, with respect to labour disputes that could turn violent. These and other problems, of course, also exist within the criminal law and legal system and in political cases, but the focus in this chapter is on the economic system.[1]

1 For a much more in-depth discussion of these and related issues about the legal system, see Wang (2015), on which this short paragraph is largely based.

As in other areas, legal reform in China is progressing steadily but not through dramatic changes in the government's design or management of the system, rather through gradual professionalisation of the judiciary and legal fields. Progress is far greater in areas that are the most advanced in terms of other market-oriented reforms than in areas where state involvement in the economy is much greater and foreign investment is lower. Even in the most advanced areas, the legal system as it pertains to the economy has major biases and limitations. Put differently, there is no consideration of having a judiciary truly independent of the executive branch of the government. The role of the CPC—as defined both at the nineteenth party congress and on many previous occasions—makes clear that the long-term objective of legal reform does not include moving towards full judicial independence on the Western model. Nevertheless, the system is far more advanced towards a modern market-oriented legal system than was the case only one or two decades ago.

Capital markets, financial reform and macroeconomic policy

The financial system in a market economy is fundamentally different from that in a command economy, in terms of both structure and the main goals of the system. In a command economy, the financial sector's main role is as a backup to help implement plan targets. It also takes deposits from individuals and makes loans, but the loans are nearly automatic if required by the plan and are mainly for working capital, not investment. Investment decisions in China were made by central, provincial and local planners and much of the financing came directly from the government budget. The financial system in a market economy, in contrast, is central to the operation and performance of the system, as it mobilises the savings of millions and loans that money to investors. Getting the design and implementation of the financial system wrong in a market economy can lead to recessions, inflation, balance of payments crises and/or secular stagnation. There is, however, ongoing debate even in high-income countries about just how the financial system should be designed and managed. Failures—mainly in the financial systems and macroeconomic policies of several Asian countries—were responsible for the sharp recessions in many developing countries in 1997–98. Even more serious failures of the financial system in high-income countries, particularly the United States, caused the severe world recession of 2007–09.

In a sense, China in the early 1980s created a modern market-oriented financial system almost overnight, when the Soviet-style mono-bank system was abolished and replaced with four state-owned commercial banks and a central bank, the People's Bank of China (PBC). But that system continued to operate in key respects much like the old mono-banking system. When state-owned enterprises needed money, the commercial banks provided it to them whether or not they were credit-worthy. Savers could either hoard cash at home or put their money in one of these commercial banks and receive a modest rate of interest. Interest rates were fixed by government fiat for both savers and borrowers and done in a way to ensure the banks made a profit. This situation continued well into the 1990s. One result was periodic bouts of inflation as demand for investment funds by the state sector surged and the banks would accommodate and the money supply would rise. High-level authorities ended inflationary bouts by giving administrative orders to the banks to cut their lending.

The head of the central bank—similarly to the pre-reform command economy period—was little more than a civil servant carrying out the orders of higher-level authorities until then deputy prime minister Zhu Rongji was made head of the PBC in the early 1990s, with authority to wring inflation out of the system. The result of that change was a peaking in 1995 of the consumer price index, followed by a fall in the rate of price increases to the low single digits, where it has remained since (consumer prices rose by an average of 1.8 per cent per annum from the end of 1997 through to 2017). The methods for reining in inflation, however, were initially similar in some respects to those of the past: the banks were given lending quotas and those quotas were enforced. But, increasingly, the emphasis on lending quotas gave way to indirect controls over lending.

There was also a major problem by the 1990s of nonperforming loans in the banking system. Officially, in the mid-1990s, nonperforming loans constituted 25 per cent of the total assets of the banking system and, unofficially, many observers believe the true figure was much higher. An elaborate system of asset management companies was created to take over the nonperforming loans and the banks were made solvent by simply paying these companies the full value of the loans. In effect, the central bank printed the money and gave it to the banks.

By the late 1990s, the banking system had begun a process of changing the behaviour of those running the banks to make them behave more like commercial banks in a high-income market economy. Gradually, the banks began to make loans to private-sector enterprises and mortgages to consumers. They began to pursue profits and to establish systems for properly appraising the credit-worthiness of their borrowers. New credit instruments such as personal credit cards were introduced, along with a wide variety of modern banking practices from abroad. Many new smaller banks were founded and government policy banks were established as one of several steps to remove politics from bank lending. Modernising the banking system in China has been an ongoing process, not a one-stop radical reform. The process continues to this day, and astute participants in the system compare practices favourably with those in other market-oriented banking systems.[2] The dominant banks, it should

2 For a systematic micro-look at recent reform efforts in the banking system, see Stent (2016).

be noted, remain state enterprises and there is no plan to privatise them. The Organisation Department of the CPC selects the top managers and the banks still take into account the leadership of the party in their decisions. Wringing politics out of the system has meant efforts to get rid of local political interests in bank decision-making, not getting rid of national or central party political interests.

The Shanghai and Shenzhen stock exchanges were formally started in 1990, but in the 1990s were mainly vehicles for selling shares of state-owned enterprises to private interests. Over time, the stock exchanges have listed more and more firms, including private ones. The China Securities Regulatory Commission (CSRC) regulates the stock market. Its regulations—like those of the China Banking Regulatory Commission (CBRC)—are similar to those of high-income market economies. Having modern regulations adjusted for local conditions is one thing; enforcing them is another. This is the case for stock markets around the world, but particularly in developing countries, and China has a long way to go before predatory practices such as insider trading are reduced to an acceptable level. This is partly a learning process for the regulators, but it is also a learning process for the population at large, which participates in the market. That is still an ongoing process in the United States, and only the Hong Kong exchange comes close to reaching America's far from perfect level.

Furthermore, even in the United States and Europe, once one gets beyond such issues as preventing insider trading, the precise nature and amount of regulation required are fiercely debated and there is no consensus on an ideal middle ground. China today (2018) is still at the highly regulated end of this debate, largely because of ongoing direct state ownership of the largest financial enterprises. Given that China avoided the major recessions of 1997–98 and 2007–09, it has experienced only a few periods where there were balance of payments concerns but no major crises[3] and inflation has been negligible for the past two decades, it is hard to argue that China has the regulatory balance wrong. However, as one looks at some of the financial problems that have arisen in the past one or two decades and others that might arise, such a conclusion about China's design and regulation of the financial system is premature.

The problems of financial reform that have been the focus of attention in recent years are those created largely by incomplete market reform in the banks and partly by central government initiatives that were financed in ways that were not sustainable. These include the rapid expansion of 'shadow banking' and the increasing burden of local government debt. There is also a more general issue of whether China's

3 There were concerns, for example, that external influences from the East Asian Financial Crisis of 1997–98 might impact exchange rate policy negatively, and there was a sharp drop in foreign exchange reserves in 2015 and 2016, but nothing that required China to rein in growth.

periodic bailouts of nonperforming loans in the system have created a serious level of moral hazard that could lead to slower growth in the future than otherwise would have been the case.

The term shadow banking refers to a range of informal financial vehicles—often called wealth management products—the principal purpose of which is to attract savings funds that were seeking higher returns than could be achieved at the low state-fixed interest rates on deposits paid by the banking system. The commercial banks themselves initiated many of these products, but they were recorded separately from the banks' formal balance sheets and were unregulated by the CBRC. The central bank dealt with this in part by abolishing the state-set ceiling on deposit rates in 2015. In 2017, however, market interest rates in China as well as around the world remained very low, so wealth management products remained attractive. The solution was to regulate shadow banking, and that process was under way by 2017, but was only in the beginning stages. There are observers who suggest that shadow banking, given its large and growing size, could lead to a major financial crisis. That, however, seems unlikely given that virtually all of the money is lent and borrowed by domestic individuals and institutions and the government has always been both able and willing to bail out nonperforming assets of this kind in the past. The danger from continuing bailouts, if they become necessary, is less a financial crisis and more the possibility of increasingly risky and poor decision-making by lenders leading to slower long-term growth.

The local government debt problem similarly resulted from macroeconomic decisions by the central government. The central government, in a successful effort to avoid the 2007–09 world recession, instituted a large economic stimulus; however, less than one-quarter of the financing of that stimulus and other similar efforts later was provided by the central government itself. Instead, it instructed local governments to finance an even larger share, although all but the richest local governments lacked sufficient tax revenue to cover financing costs directly. Local governments—subject to restrictions on their ability to borrow—nevertheless were able to indirectly create financial vehicles to cover their investment obligations. The result was a steady rise in local government debt. Eventually, the total local government debt reached RMB24 trillion, at the end of 2014. The central government had to rescue many local governments from bankruptcy, turning RMB8 trillion of that debt into government bonds.

The local debt issue also illustrates how the central government since the third plenum of 2013 has begun to address shortcomings in its management of fiscal policy. One of the principal problems of the local government debt was that the central government had little knowledge of how fast that debt was rising. Only a few (three or four) people in the understaffed Ministry of Finance were responsible for overseeing this debt, local government records were minimal and reporting to the centre was often nonexistent. It took a special central government audit to get the 2014 figure. At the same time, the government passed a revised budget law that required local governments to keep detailed budget documents and to make those documents available online as well as to the Ministry of Finance. The revised budget law has now been implemented and local budgets are available online. That said, proper and accurate implementation of the revised budget law will require large numbers of financial officers with relevant training—probably in the tens of thousands—in local government and their affiliated organisations. It is unlikely the required numbers of financially skilled personnel are available as of 2018, but the change is nevertheless real.[4]

Another area of finance where reform has progressed is in the opening of the country's capital markets so that capital can to some degree move in and out of the country with increasing ease. Many of the controls over these capital flows, however, remain on the books and they were used to restrict openness in 2015 and early 2016 when capital outflows led foreign exchange reserves to fall by more than US$700 billion in less than a year, before levelling off later in 2016. That experience suggests that, at China's current stage of development, complete market-friendly reform should probably not include full opening of its capital markets. It may be in the interests of financial institutions in high-income countries for China to fully open its capital markets, but it is not in China's interests to have to deal with rapid short-term inflows and outflows of hundreds of billions of dollars on a monthly or daily basis. China needs time to reach a more long-term stable equilibrium in its international capital markets before lifting capital controls entirely. At a minimum, any prudent manager of the economy would want to have such tools in reserve for emergencies.

The issue of open capital markets illustrates another consideration that needs to be taken into account in assessing the state of financial reform in China: not all financial innovations in recent years in high-income countries have had a positive impact on those economies, as 2007–09 made clear. Even some of the innovations that were positive in high-income countries could easily prove to have negative consequences for a country at China's current state of development.

Financial reform is a complex topic, but there is no doubt that China has made major progress in creating a modern financial system suitable for a market economy. Some of the older financial institutions such as the banks are now quite sophisticated, while new institutions such as insurance companies and the stock exchanges are far short of where they need to be.

Progressing to an efficient financial system will take time, but, in most respects, the direction is clear and substantial progress has been made. One change that would make the financial systems of China more like those in most high-income

4 This discussion of local government debt is based mainly on work by Christine Wong. See, for example, Wong (2017).

countries, however, is not going to occur. The Chinese Government and the CPC and its Organisation Department are not going to substantially reduce their role in controlling and directing that system. High-income market economies generally remove government from direct control over the sector, relying in part on setting a regulatory framework designed to limit predatory behaviour and managing the sector mainly through the indirect controls of monetary and fiscal policy. China has, at least for the near future, decided to stop short of that goal.

Labour markets, land markets and rural–urban migration

In the pre-reform era, land and labour markets did not exist. Land was owned by the state ('by the whole people') and urban land use was allocated to units by the government and could be taken away by the government. In rural areas, use rights for land were held by rural communes, brigades and production teams, but not by households. The government could take away land use rights but generally did so only for major infrastructure projects, such as a dam that flooded farmland. Central planners also allocated urban skilled labour and the hiring of unskilled or semi-skilled workers was administratively distributed to individual enterprises by urban labour departments. Rural labourers, for the most part, stayed in the commune, brigade and team into which they had been born or married. Rural to urban migration was tightly controlled by a variety of mechanisms and these controls were largely responsible for China having an unusually low rate of urbanisation prior to 1978. One positive benefit of these controls was that women registered as urban residents became a much larger component of urban employment than in the past. This benefit disappeared, however, when migration from rural areas was no longer restricted; the share of women in the urban labour force fell substantially.[5]

The rapid development of industry after 1978 caused urban labour shortages that were initially dealt with in part by urban enterprises contracting with rural enterprises to produce key inputs. This approach, however, began to quickly give way in the 1980s to allowing increasing amounts of rural labour to migrate to urban jobs either through the labour bureaus or directly to the enterprises. The system of administrative allocation of skilled personnel gradually gave way to a system where urban skilled labour could change jobs and enterprises with increasing freedom. By the twenty-first century, China had a market-based labour system in its urban areas.

5 From 1965 to 1978, the number of women workers and staff in state-owned enterprises (all enterprises were either state or collectively owned) grew from 7.86 million to 21.26 million (NBS various years) and kept on rising in the 1980s and early 1990s (in all urban units), peaking at 58.9 million in 1995, before beginning to decline after 1997, to only 41.6 million in 2002 (NBS 2003: 139).

Urban land use changed in 1990 to a system whereby enterprises could lease (but not 'own') land for up to 70 years. This approach was often encumbered by the need of the enterprise to find alternative housing for those already on the land, for example, but that gave way to urban governments mostly leasing land at market prices. The privatisation of housing began slowly in the early 1990s, but became nationwide policy by the end of that decade. Housing that had been allocated by enterprises to their employees was sold to the employees at highly discounted prices and a private market for new housing was created. After the initial privatisation, virtually all urban housing is either leased or rented to households at market prices. The rapid expansion of private housing in turn led the banking system to make mortgages an increasing, and now quite large, portion of their loan portfolios.

Two major related distortions remain as of 2018—one in the labour market and the other with respect to rural land. The major labour market distortion is the *hukou* system that divides the population into rural and urban residents and makes it difficult to switch registration from rural to urban. Since much schooling and a variety of health and other welfare and insurance programs in urban areas are available only to registered urban residents, this has a major impact on the welfare of urban workers and their families who are registered as rural residents. There is an efficiency, as well as a welfare, loss from this practice. Children of migrants are often left behind with their grandparents in the villages, where they receive an education inferior to that of their urban counterparts. They also learn little about how to cope with urban life even though once they attain working age they will spend most of their life in cities.

Compounding this situation is the fact rural land use rights can sometimes be taken away if migrants succeed in changing to urban registration status. Migrant leasing of land use rights to others is allowed and restrictions on the practice have gradually been removed, but the system still falls well short of an unfettered market system. The announcement following the nineteenth party congress that rural land rights, including the right to lease land, would be strengthened could correct some of the imperfections in the system. Another major distortion that remains is the classification of land into arable land for agricultural use and land that can be used for local enterprises and buildings of various sorts. The price of the latter kind of land is much higher than that of agricultural land, but only local officials have the ability—legally or otherwise—to change land from one classification to the other. Among other problems, this is a major source of local corruption and related rural disputes.

The *hukou* system is widely criticised in China and it is gradually being phased out, particularly in cities where there is an effort to attract more migrants to fill local enterprise labour requirements. The system, however, is still very much in place in many other cities, including those like Beijing and Shanghai that have the highest incomes and the most job opportunities.

Conclusion

Clearly, China has made substantial progress over the past four decades in creating an economy governed increasingly by market forces. Progress on this score began slowly in the 1980s in large part because the objective of the leadership and most of the reformers in the early stages saw the market as one of several instruments—not the main instrument—for creating a better performing economic system. That changed by the mid-1990s to a consensus to create a socialist market economy, but much of the progress towards that goal came from actions starting at the bottom and working their way up to the leadership rather than from top-down government and party-led reforms. Both the gradual replacement of the two-price system with a one-price system and the rapid development of township and village enterprises reflected this bottom-up reform effort. Government control of this burgeoning market system was still often exercised through administrative controls rather than indirect market forces, particularly in the financial sphere.

By the late 1990s and at the beginning of the twenty-first century, however, market forces largely governed China's economy. Most goods and services were distributed at competitive market prices. Urban housing and land were increasingly governed by market forces, as were the urban labour market and rural to urban migration. Large distortions, however, remained in the rural areas, particularly with respect to land and, because of the *hukou* system, to labour. Elsewhere, the institutions of a modern market economy were steadily strengthening. That was true of the respect for property rights—in particular, private property rights—but also in the gradual strengthening of the legal system. At the national level, the central bank became more like a central bank in a high-income country and the financial institutions beyond the banks grew rapidly and became stronger. In some areas, such as the stock market, however, the financial system still falls far short of the high-income market economy standard. That is even more the case for the legal system as it applies to the economy. China today also retains many controls over capital flows in and out of the country. The reasons for the retention of these controls reflect the fact that the financial system—despite all of its technical sophistication—still has not settled into a stable equilibrium where such controls would not be needed.

The main area where the Chinese market economy differs in a major way from most high-income market economies is in the role of the government and the CPC. Government regulatory involvement in the economy is far greater than in most high-income market economies, and direct state ownership of controlling interests in the economy is also more pervasive. Perhaps of even greater significance, however, is the central role of the CPC and its Organisation Department in both selecting the personnel in the system—including in many of the enterprises—and strongly influencing the behaviour and objectives of those parts of the modern urban economy that it does not directly control. The nineteenth party congress made clear that that role for the party is not going to change and is, if anything, going to be strengthened.

That level of party involvement virtually guarantees that politics and other non-economic objectives will play a larger role in economic decision-making even at the micro level than is normally the case in high-income market economies. It is not that party and state influence by definition requires economic decision-makers to deviate from the market efficiency requirement that they maximise profits or, more realistically, that they not deviate from that goal more than in most relatively efficient market economies. Nearly a century ago, Abba Lerner (1944) and Oskar Lange (1936) demonstrated that enterprise management in socialist economies with widespread state ownership could simply order management to maximise profits. They could thereby achieve a closer approximation of what an efficient market required than was found in the actual behaviour of management in capitalist market economies. Few if anyone today, however, believes that state ownership and political party influence would in fact emphasise profit maximisation to the exclusion of other political and social objectives. The nineteenth party congress confirmed that the CPC's political goals will continue to play a major role in enterprises, both those directly owned or controlled by the state and those that are private.

What is less clear is how this greater role for politics in economic and enterprise decisions will affect the performance of the economy. The 2012–17 slowdown in economic growth and the falling rate of TFP growth could be due in part to this large role for politics.[6] A number of studies have shown that the productivity of state-owned enterprises is lower than that of the private sector. Many countries have attempted to make state-owned enterprises as efficient as those that are privately owned, usually with only limited success. The overall slowdown of China's GDP growth and TFP, however, can be explained in part by actions having little to do with whether or not the market is functioning well. All countries that have to date reached high–middle-income status have experienced a decline in their GDP growth rate. In China, in addition, the continued emphasis on infrastructure investment despite declining returns in that sector is another example, although the continued emphasis on infrastructure could also be considered the result of politics (Gatley 2018).

We do not yet, therefore, have a measure that can provide us with a quantitative assessment of the degree to which China has created an efficient market economy. Given the complex nature of moving from a centrally planned command economic system to a market economy, a simple economic measure of progress from one

6 My own estimates based on the methodology in my earlier essay with Thomas Rawski suggest that TFP has fallen from an average rate of 3 per cent per annum in 2006–11 to 1 per cent per annum in 2012–16 (Perkins and Rawksi 2006: 829–86).

system to the other may not be possible.[7] What this chapter has argued is that attempts to measure this progress by looking at one or another element of the process, such as financial reform or the number of state-owned enterprises, are not the answer. One must assess the complete complex picture, even if that requires qualitative judgement and/or multiple quantitative assessments.

References

Gatley, T. (2018), The working capital heist, *Gavekal Dragonomics*, 9 January.

Lange, O. (1936), On the economic theory of socialism, *The Review of Economic Studies* 4(1): 53–71.

Lerner, A. (1944), *The Economics of Control: Principles of Welfare Economics*, New York: MacMillan.

Mercator Institute for China Studies (MERICS) (2017), *China update: Loyalty to the party becomes top duty of private entrepreneurs*, 12 October, Berlin: MERICS.

National Bureau of Statistics (NBS) (various years), *China Labour Wage Statistics*, Beijing: China Statistics Press.

National Bureau of Statistics (NBS) (2003), *China Statistical Yearbook*, Beijing: China Statistics Press.

National Bureau of Statistics (NBS) (2011), *China Statistical Yearbook*, Beijing: China Statistics Press.

National Bureau of Statistics (NBS) (2016), *China Statistical Yearbook*, Beijing: China Statistics Press.

Perkins, D. H. and Rawksi, T. G. (2006), Forecasting China's economic growth to 2025, in L. Brandt and T. Rawski (eds), *China's Great Transformation*, Cambridge: Cambridge University Press.

Stent, J. (2016), *China's Banking Transformation*, Oxford: Oxford University Press.

Wang, Y. (2015), *Tying the Autocrat's Hands: The rise of the rule of law in China*, Cambridge: Cambridge University Press. doi.org/10.1017/CBO9781107785342.

7 The Kornai Index developed by Janos Kornai, which compares the ratio of input inventories with output inventories, measures in a single figure the degree to which a country has adopted a centrally planned command system; but we need a measure that captures the difference between two market systems that differ primarily in the degree of political involvement in the economy.

Wong, C. (2017), Rumbling of reform in China's fiscal foundations, *East Asia Forum*, 17 April. Available from: www.eastasiaforum.org/2017/04/17/rumbling-of-reform-in-chinas-fiscal-foundations/.

World Bank (various years), *Doing Business*, Washington, DC: The World Bank. Available from: www.doingbusines/reports/.

9. Decentralisation, local innovation and competition among cities

David Dollar

China's reform and opening (*gaige kaifang*) is best known for introducing elements of a market economy into what had previously been a rigidly planned system. Agricultural communes were broken up and farming returned to a family basis. Private foreign investment and trade were allowed—initially in a small number of special zones, but eventually throughout the whole country. A domestic private sector grew alongside the traditional state-owned enterprise sector. All of these were important and visible changes. But what is less well appreciated is that the reform also involved large-scale political decentralisation. Local governments were given much more autonomy than under the planned system. This produced two of the distinctive features of China's reform and development: first, it led to healthy competition among cities to create the best investment climates to attract, first, foreign investment and, then later, domestic investment; and second, it encouraged locales to seek innovative approaches to providing public goods. There are many examples of successful innovations in China being scaled up to benefit the whole country. Local innovation and competition were key factors in China's success.

Decentralisation and reform

Under the planned economy, China was largely cut off from global trade and investment. In the 1950s, it imported machinery and technology from the Soviet Union, but after the break between the two communist giants around 1960, China entered two decades of almost total isolation. The legacy of isolation and the Cultural Revolution was that China, at the end of the 1970s, was poorer by the standard official measures than sub-Saharan Africa, backwards technologically and in poor fiscal and financial condition.

After the death of Mao Zedong, a wide range of Communist Party officials, led by Deng Xiaoping, wanted to take the economy in a different direction. Deng believed that it was particularly important to open up the country to foreign ideas and technology. This notion was to a considerable extent still controversial, however, owing to the legacy of developed-country imperialism in China. Controversial new directions in Communist Party policy were often first tried on an experimental basis in a few locations, with good results then scaled up to the national level. In the case of opening up to foreign investment and trade, the party decided in 1979 to open four special economic zones that would be able to attract foreign investment and would have streamlined procedures for importing machinery and parts to be used in processing trade for export. Three of these zones were in cities in Guangdong and one in Fujian. Other cities quickly wanted to join the experiment. In 1984, another 14 cities were given the same opportunities as the special zones. In 1993, this was expanded to provincial capitals (more than 30) plus five inland cities along the Yangtze River and nine border cities (Eckaus 1997). Thus, within a relatively short time, dozens of Chinese cities had opened up to foreign trade and investment.

The implicit contract between the central government leaders and these local governments was clear: the government 'has no money. So we will give you a policy that allows you to charge ahead and cut through your own difficult road', Deng told party leaders at a policy meeting on the special zones in 1979 (Vogel 2011: 398). The central government did not have the resources to finance capital and technology imports, so local governments were encouraged to attract foreign investment. This policy set off intense competition among local governments to attract foreign investment. Foreign investors were interested in entering the Chinese market, and they had a large number of cities from which to choose. Investors were naturally attracted to cities that could streamline their local bureaucracy and centralise decision-making in a small number of government offices—the proverbial one-stop shop.

Deng's governing style encouraged this competition. According to Vogel (2011: 699–700):

> Deng pulled back on the governing structure that tried to penetrate everywhere. Instead of setting tight rules that local areas had to follow, he established a system in which governing teams, selected by the next higher level, were given considerable independence as long as they managed to bring rapid growth … In Deng's era and in the decades after Deng, those judgments [on local government performance] were based overwhelmingly on how much the team contributed to China's overall economic growth.

Cities such as Shenzhen, Dongguan, Foshan and Xiamen developed reputations for being hospitable to foreign investors and for having local officials who could help investors cut through bureaucratic problems. These successes naturally spread to other cities since local officials everywhere knew that much of the prospect for career advancement would depend on investment and growth. In the early 2000s, the World Bank surveyed more than 10,000 firms in 120 Chinese cities and found considerable variation in local investment climates as measured, for example, by the amount of time spent dealing with red tape, customs clearance times or the reliability of critical infrastructure such as power supply (World Bank 2004). Cities with better investment climates perform better on a range of economic dimensions, including involvement in global value chains.

Another key aspect of the local investment climate is infrastructure. China began its reform with very poor infrastructure and limited ability to address the gaps because of fiscal constraints. Some early policy decisions were key to resolving these bottlenecks. In the mid-1980s, the State Council allowed investments in the power sector to proceed on a cost-recovery basis. For a while, there was a dual pricing system in which 'old power' was very cheap, whereas 'new power' from recent investments was priced to cover the full cost of generation. New power spread quickly and eventually old power faded away, leaving China with a largely commercial power sector. The price of power has been higher in China than in many developing countries that subsidise it, but it is available and reliable. Similarly with roads: China has developed the largest system of toll roads in the world, with tolls that generally cover the cost of building and maintaining the network. This practical approach to infrastructure pricing enabled the key economic infrastructure—power, roads, seaports and airports—to expand quickly (Dollar 2008). Much of the financial responsibility for the infrastructure investment and management rests at the local level. Cities that could attract some initial foreign investment through better administration then had the capacity to finance investment in infrastructure, and the revenue stream from those investments spurred further expansion of the infrastructure network.

A final key issue in local industrial development was labour. Some of the locations that have risen to industrial prominence were little villages or towns with small populations at the beginning of the reform period. China began its reform with 80 per cent of its population in rural areas because the pre-reform system had maintained a rigorous household registration (*hukou*) system that prevented rural–urban migration. The *hukou* system continues to prevent permanent migration, but local officials found a way around this constraint through the use of migrant workers. Employers could recruit rural workers to come to work in factories, hotels and restaurants and construction activities. These migrants were typically young. They were not allowed to bring their families with them and they were not registered as urban residents, so they were not entitled to a full range of urban public services. This system was very supportive of rapid industrial development. Cities could attract workers, who lived in dormitories or on construction sites. There was no need for permanent housing, nor did the migrants make claims on the social services of the city government.

The number of migrant workers has risen from essentially zero at the beginning of reform to 282 million in 2016, according to official statistics. Migrants represent more than half the urban labour force and account for a majority of the increase in the urban labour force since the beginning of economic reform. The combination of competition among cities and the migrant worker system was extraordinarily powerful. Shenzhen went from basically nothing to a city of 20 million people. The fact that the locations with the best investment climates could attract so many workers so quickly gave a strong boost to the overall growth rate of the economy.

In trying to understand China's phenomenal growth record, a key reason has been this system in which local governments are given considerable autonomy, localities then compete intensely for investment and migrant workers and local officials are evaluated and promoted primarily on the basis of these economic results.

Local innovation and scaling up

The autonomy given to local governments also meant they could try out innovative approaches to providing public goods. Local governments everywhere face a host of challenges, from providing basic education to clean water and sanitation and protecting the natural environment. As the World Bank's country director based in Beijing from 2004 to 2009, I was fortunate to work with local governments all over China on their basic challenges in providing public goods. What struck me from that experience was that local governments often had clever innovations, and the ones that worked were quickly scaled up, either by other locales copying or by the success being codified in a national policy directive. I will illustrate this point with two examples in which the World Bank was involved. The point is not to exaggerate the role of the World Bank, which provided useful assistance in terms of introducing international experience. Rather, the point is to focus on the innovative role of local government. One example is from the urban arena and one from the rural.

The rural example involves the restoration of the Loess Plateau (World Bank 2007: 57). The plateau is an area of fine soil hundreds of kilometres west of Beijing covering parts of Shanxi, Shaanxi, Gansu, Ningxia and Inner Mongolia. By the 1980s, much of this area had been denuded through a combination of overexploitation by agriculture, grazing of sheep and goats and the removal of timber for use as fuel. It was this region that was the source of the sandstorms that plagued Beijing and other northern Chinese cities. Aside from the environmental problems, there were also tens of millions of people living in poverty because the lifestyle simply did not provide an adequate living.

During the period 1994–2005, two Loess Plateau watershed rehabilitation projects were carried out by local governments, with financial and technical support from the World Bank. The projects brought back the old idea of integrated rural development—something that has not worked well in most countries, often because local government does not have the capacity to implement a complex, cross-sectional project. The Loess Plateau projects were aimed at helping communities develop more sustainable lifestyles and offered a menu of options that could be tailored to suit by each community. A popular element was terracing of hilly terrain and planting of cash trees that do not require a lot of water. Some communities tried small-scale industrial activities, but these in general did not work well. Villages voted on what projects to implement and how to adjust in response to success or failure.

One of the key activities previously in the Loess Plateau had been raising sheep and goats. Their unrestricted grazing was a key reason any green thing that started to appear would immediately be eaten. Experts recommended a ban on grazing for large parts of the plateau. This was too controversial to be adopted on a large scale, but a few communities that had invested in cash trees established grazing bans covering significant areas. What everyone learned from this experience was that mother nature, left to her own devices, could recover very quickly. Vast brown areas became vast green areas. When other communities saw the effect of the grazing ban, they quickly followed suit.

While the grazing ban was key to the environmental restoration of the plateau, it did leave a hole in the income of communities. Many communities had eked out a subsistence living by raising sheep and goats even though there was little grass for their foraging. With those activities stopped, some communities responded by shifting to raising pigs, which does not require grazing and can be done using animal feed. A successful component of the project promoted pig-raising as follows: one woman from the village was chosen as the pilot, given training and provided with an initial stock of piglets. She repaid the 'loan' by training other women in the village and providing them with piglets as her stock expanded. Visiting Loess Plateau villages in the mid-2000s, I was impressed that the women were using mobile phones to track pork prices in nearby cities. It also helped that there was a good expressway connecting once remote parts of the area to the cities. The mobile phones and the expressways are a reminder of how complicated development is: the various interventions that enabled the restoration of the natural environment in the Loess Plateau would have been useful in isolation, but were much more powerful as a package that included integration of the region with the national economy. Many elements of the project spread beyond the project area and became standard policies throughout the Loess Plateau.

The urban example of innovation and scaling up involves water supply and wastewater treatment (World Bank 2007: 37). At the beginning of its reform, China was under-urbanised, with only 20 per cent of its population living in urban areas. One of the factors of economic dynamism noted above was the migration of hundreds of millions of people from the countryside to cities. The developing world is full of examples of cities that do not handle population growth well, unable to supply key urban services to the whole population. Even though China's urban population was small, only 50 per cent of it in 1990 was connected to the municipal water supply. More important, only 15 per cent had wastewater removal and treatment. Anyone who lived or travelled in China in the late 1980s or early 1990s will remember that rivers and lakes were fouled with untreated waste. This is a health hazard and an eyesore and nose-sore. The fact that the urban population roughly doubled between 1990 and 2005 greatly increased the scale of the challenge.

It was noted in the previous section that China early on took a practical approach to *economic* infrastructure. But this definitely did not apply to water supply and sanitation, which were considered public goods provided largely free of charge by the city government. Prices for water were nominal and pricing for wastewater treatment nonexistent. The lack of prices meant that demand was surging uncontrollably, while resources did not exist to expand supply. The World Bank's work in this sector started with the four megacities of Beijing, Chongqing, Shanghai and Tianjin, and later spread to dozens of cities around the country. Shanghai pioneered the key reforms. It corporatised the department responsible for water and sanitation and set it on a self-sustaining financial course. It was given a mandate to operate along commercial lines and generate sufficient user revenue to cover operating costs and service debt. To this end, in 1989, Shanghai introduced the first sewerage tariff in the country. It was controversial, since people were used to getting this service for free, but it was necessary to expand the required wastewater treatment plants and associated sewer network. Shanghai's initial success in cleaning up its rivers prompted other cities to move in the same direction. By 1999, Shanghai's approach was adopted as national policy through a multi-ministerial notice. Despite the surging urban population nationwide, the wastewater treatment rate climbed only steadily, from 15 per cent in 1990 to 60 per cent in 2010.

China's national policy goal is to move to full cost-recovery pricing, though it is not there yet. Still, the increased price of water has been significant and has had visible effects. Industrial use of water is down 30 per cent. And, despite rising per capita incomes, per capita water use in urban areas has been stable. The moves towards cost recovery have also made it possible to attract private investment into the sector, taking some of the fiscal burden off the state. There are now approximately 200 water or wastewater projects with private participation. Water and sanitation are a good example of national policy arising from local experimentation.

Downsides of decentralisation and local autonomy

While decentralisation and local autonomy have been very effective at generating investment and growth, the system does have some downsides and presents challenges for the future.

First, this model tends to put more value on growth than on other outcomes. The previous section highlighted some examples of how China is tackling various rural and urban environmental issues. Still, overall, China's development has taken a heavy toll on the environment. The country has many of the most air-polluted cities in the world and progress with cleaning up rivers and lakes has been greater in the south than in the north, where the water challenge is greater. If local officials are rewarded primarily for investment and growth during their typical five-year tenure in a position, they are not going to put sufficient weight on environmental considerations, especially ones whose main impact is long term. There has been much discussion within the party about broadening the criteria for evaluating local officials, but growth has remained the key evaluation criterion, along with political stability.

Second, the *hukou* system is a key factor behind the large rise in inequality that has occurred during China's reform. The average urban–rural income gap has risen above 3:1—one of the largest in the world. The *hukou* system puts labour at a disadvantage and locks the rural population out of better education and health services that are a foundation of human capital. There is ongoing discussion of reform of the *hukou* system, but local governments generally oppose this. Treating the vast migrant population as citizens would mean putting greater local fiscal resources into education, health, social security and housing.

Third, the negative effects of the *hukou* system are compounded by the extreme inequality in local government spending across Chinese jurisdictions. There is relatively little redistribution within China's fiscal system. This means that the more prosperous, faster-growing locales have large amounts of fiscal revenue, while poor, left-behind areas have few resources. From the point of view of *growth*, this is an efficient system in which the locales that can best use resources have the most resources; but the system is a problem from the point of view of *equity*. There are vast differences in the amounts spent on education and health in wealthy, coastal cities compared with the amounts spent in poor rural areas in the centre and west of the country. The children of migrants are literally 'left behind' in poor villages in which they receive poor-quality education. This is locking in inequality for the future. It will also eventually have a growth effect because these children will be the urban workforce of the future.

A fourth issue is that the current system skews incentives towards investment. China's overall investment rate has risen throughout the reform period and reached nearly 50 per cent of gross domestic product (GDP) in recent years. This raises questions about whether all this investment will in fact bear fruit in the future. For long-term growth, innovation and human capital accumulation are of central importance. But a local official trying to increase growth over a five-year period is not going to put much weight on those factors—they both take too long to pay off. The surest way to increase growth quickly would be new investment projects: constructing infrastructure and attracting factories to use it. Thus, the growth model does not put sufficient weight on human capital development and foundations of innovation such as intellectual property rights and a deep financial system. The old model worked exceptionally well as China grew from a low-income to a middle-income economy, but the next stage of development—from middle income to high income—relies less on factor accumulation and more on innovation. It is not clear whether China's mixed system of a large state sector and private initiative in some quarters will be able to generate sufficient innovation. The growth of total factor productivity in China's economy has slowed significantly in recent years, indicating that the investment-intensive model is running into diminishing returns, and that capital accumulation is not being replaced with innovation as a source of growth (Bai et al. 2016).

A final point is that the decentralised governance model in China favours results over rules. This approach creates a fertile environment for corruption. Corruption can deter investment and corrodes political order around a strong development objective. Certain types of corruption have flourished. All land in China is owned by the state. Farmers have use rights over agricultural land. But the government can take this land away with arbitrarily determined compensation. Many of the social and political disputes in China involve dispossessed farmers disgruntled at losing their land without compensation at full market value. Once local government has taken this land, it can auction it to developers and industrialists. If they pay the market price to use the land, this is a form of corruption that interferes little with the efficiency of investment, but rather is in the nature of a pure transfer from poor peasants to relatively well-off local officials. President Xi Jinping's anticorruption campaign has snared many 'tigers and flies'—that is, major and minor corrupt officials—but the only way to sustain reductions in corruption would involve institutional changes that provide more transparency and less discretion on the part of local officials.

In summary, local autonomy and the incentives to create good local investment climates and to innovate on public goods have all been important features of China's reform and its resulting success in achieving investment and growth. A lot of what has been successful in China's reform has bubbled up from below. At the same time, this system contributes to some of the key challenges that China now faces, including environmental degradation, rising inequality, overinvestment and government corruption.

References

Bai, C.-E., Hsieh, C.-T. and Song, Z. (2016), *The long shadow of a fiscal expansion*, Brookings Papers on Economic Activity, Washington, DC: Brookings Institution. doi.org/10.3386/w22801.

Dollar, D. (2008), *Lessons from China for Africa*, Policy Research Working Paper No. 4531, Washington, DC: The World Bank.

Eckaus, R. S. (1997), China, in P. Desai (ed.), *Going Global: Transition from plan to market in the world economy*, Cambridge, MA: MIT Press.

Vogel, E. F. (2011), *Deng Xiaoping and the Transformation of China*, Cambridge, MA: Harvard University Press. doi.org/10.4159/harvard.9780674062832.

World Bank (2004), *World Development Report: A better investment climate for everyone*, Washington, DC: The World Bank.

World Bank (2007), *China and the World Bank: A partnership for innovation*, Washington, DC: The World Bank. Available from: documents.worldbank.org/curated/en/339171468025448074/China-and-the-World-Bank-a-partnership-for-innovation.

Part II: Macroeconomic development and structural adjustments

10. China's macroeconomics in the 40 years of reform

Xiaolu Wang

China set out on the road of reform in 1978 and was gradually transformed from a centrally planned to a market economy. In the 40 years between 1978 and 2017, the economy maintained an average annual growth rate of 9.6 per cent. Per capita gross domestic product (GDP) increased from US$490 to US$7,795 in 2009 constant dollars.[1]

What led to the rapid economic growth in the past 40 years? What problems arose, and why? What will be the future trend of growth? This chapter will attempt to provide brief answers to these questions.

Why China embarked on the road to reform

By 1978, China's centrally planned economy had reached a dead end. After the devastating impact of the Cultural Revolution, the economy was on the brink of collapse.

China established a planned economy in the 1950s with reference to the Soviet model. Almost all enterprises were state-owned, producing goods according to the central plan. All profits were turned over to the government. Collectivisation took place in agriculture and the government purchased products at below-market prices.

At the beginning of the state-owned economy (1953–57, the first five-year plan period), there was strong momentum in development. The annual growth rate of GDP was 9.2 per cent and the growth rate of residents' per capita consumption was 4.5 per cent. However, in this period, the centrally planned economy was not fully formed. Private industry and commerce coexisted with the state-owned economy before 1956 and the free market had not been banned.

Comprehensive nationalisation took place in 1956. The private economy disappeared. Subsequently, the Great Leap Forward and communalisation, launched by Mao Zedong in 1958, and the Cultural Revolution, launched in 1966, led to

1 All data in this chapter are from the National Bureau of Statistics (NBS) unless otherwise indicated.

sharp economic contraction. GDP fell by 32 per cent between 1960 and 1962 and by 10 per cent during 1967–68. Growth was restored afterwards, although the energy has weakened significantly.

In the 25 years (1953–77) prior to reform, GDP grew at an average annual rate of 5.9 per cent—slightly higher than the global average over the same period. According to Angus Maddison's (2001) purchasing power parity (PPP) measure, China's average growth rate was 5 per cent during the period 1950–73, which was not significantly different from the global average of 4.9 per cent during the same period. During the subsequent four years, China's official GDP growth rate was only 4.2 per cent.

In the 25 years of the centrally planned economy, the government mobilised the country's resources for industrialisation, substantially boosted the investment rate and enabled preliminary industrialisation. From 1952 to 1977, the rate of capital formation increased from 22.2 per cent to 34.7 per cent and the rate of consumption dropped from 78.9 per cent to 65 per cent (both as a share of GDP). During this period, industrial value added increased by 11.3 per cent annually—much faster than GDP. The industrial share in GDP rose from 17 per cent to 43 per cent. There was considerable production capacity in various industrial sectors.

The whole society paid a huge price for the rapid industrialisation during this period. The development of agriculture and service sectors was slow and people's income and consumption growth was even slower. The government forced the acquisition of agricultural products at low prices to ensure urban supply and low industrial costs. Business profits were entirely turned over to the state—mainly for government investment in industry—with almost no increase in wage levels. From 1952 to 1977, the real growth rate of per capita consumption of rural and urban residents was 1.7 per cent and 3 per cent, respectively. These statistics are likely overstated, although they are significantly lower than the 5.9 per cent GDP growth rate and 3.8 per cent per capita GDP growth rate.

In 1977, the last year before reform, 250 million of China's 780 million rural residents were living in abject poverty. The living conditions of urban residents were better, although there was a serious lack of consumer goods. Food, clothing and other basic consumer goods were subject to supply rationing. In 1977, the national average per capita savings deposit was just RMB19 (US$11).

Industrialisation was accelerated at the expense of people's income and consumption, through administrative power and compulsion. Efficiency in this economic system gradually diminished—contrary to the original intention of catching up with developed countries. All economic activities were subject to government control, and people's enthusiasm for development and creativity were severely suppressed. Misallocation of resources and production inefficiencies were widespread. For the period 1952–77, economists estimated total factor productivity (TFP) was between 0 per cent and –1 per cent (see, for example, Chow 1993; Wang 2006). Despite the rapid expansion of industrial capacity and a few extraordinary technological achievements, such as the development of nuclear power and missile technology, technological progress was in general very limited.

China's per capita GDP in 1973, measured by PPP, was $839 (international dollars in 1990 prices)—only one-fifth of the global average at that time, less than half the average of 56 Asian countries and far below that of Japan, South Korea, Singapore, and China's Taiwan and Hong Kong (Maddison 2001). China's relative position in per capita GDP in the world was little changed from 1950. In this sense, China in the planned economy period failed to bring its people to prosperity or to narrow the huge gap with developed countries. Instead, growth gradually lost its energy in the long run.

These failures motivated China—after a decade of retrogression during the Cultural Revolution—to start the transition from a centrally planned to a market economy.

Economic growth accelerated rapidly from the beginning of the reform period, and has stayed high for nearly 40 years. Real GDP in 2017 was 39 times that of 1977, surpassing Russia, Canada, Italy, France, the United Kingdom, Germany and Japan to become the second-largest economy in the world.

During the 40 years of reform, urban and rural real income per capita increased annually by 7.3 per cent and 7.6 per cent, respectively. Per capita consumption of urban and rural residents increased annually by 6.4 per cent and 7.2 per cent, respectively—both of which were lower than the 8.5 per cent growth rate of per capita GDP, but much higher than in the pre-reform period. Measured by the official poverty line of RMB2,300 per annum (2010 constant price), the incidence of rural poverty fell from 97.5 per cent in 1978 to 7.4 per cent in 2016.

However, there have also been serious economic challenges. Income inequality widened, particularly in the past two decades. There has been serious corruption inside the Communist Party and the government. There is serious overinvestment and waste of public resources. The economic structure is imbalanced and TFP has been decreasing in recent years. There is excessive intervention by the government in the business sector, and the speed of economic growth is diminishing.

Initial battles to break the old system: 1978–84

In December 1978, the third plenum of the eleventh Central Committee of the Communist Party of China (CPC) repudiated the Cultural Revolution and decided to reform the economic administrative system. The plenum also decided to substantially increase the purchase prices for agricultural products (grain purchase prices were increased by 20–80 per cent). This meeting marks the beginning of the reform period.

Agricultural reform that feeds farmers

The first change was in the rural economy. The pre-reform system of people's communes had very low productivity and farmers generally remained poor. Mass production and an egalitarian system of income distribution, which replaced household production and household ownership, were economically inefficient. The government purchased grain at far below market prices and severely restricted farmers from selling products through the market. These arrangements dampened the production enthusiasm of farmers. In 1977, China's national grain output was 283 million tonnes and the average yield only 2,600 kg/ha of raw grain. After fulfilling the state requisition, many farmers were left hungry.

In 1978, farmers in Anhui and some other areas began a 'household contract system' to allow household production, in violation of official rules. This stimulated farmers' enthusiasm for production and significantly increased output. Some prefecture and provincial party and government leaders supported the change, which caused fierce ideological debate among senior leaders about socialism and capitalism, but eventually the reformers won. From 1979, the government allowed farmers to experiment with various modes of production and gradually liberalised the restriction on the household contract system (HCS). By 1984, the HCS (also known as the household responsibility system, or HRS) had spread throughout the country and the people's communes were abolished. Farmers were allowed to sell their products through the market.

From 1977 to 1984, national grain output rose from 283 million to 407 million tonnes. Output of cotton, oilseeds, fruits and some other agricultural products increased even more rapidly. The persistent problem of food shortage had been resolved. Substantial increases in output, increases in state purchase prices and the liberalisation of the agricultural product market together led to a 15.7 per cent real annual increase in farmers' incomes from 1978 to 1984. In the same period, agricultural value added grew at an annual rate of 6.8 per cent—up from 2 per cent in the period 1952–77. This lifted total annual real GDP growth by 1.5 percentage points over this period.

TVE development: Providing 50 million jobs

Agricultural reform raised labour productivity. With limited arable land, about half of China's rural labourers were no longer needed. Following the easing of policy restrictions, township and village enterprises (TVEs, formerly known as commune and brigade enterprises) that engaged in nonagricultural production developed rapidly in rural areas, and became important in accelerating economic growth. Urban reform had not yet started. State-owned enterprises (SOEs) were still chronically inefficient. TVE production responded to market demand, quickly making effective use of labour resources. TVEs became the frontline force in market-oriented reform.

TVE employment increased from 23 million in 1977 to 52 million (11 per cent of total Chinese employment) in 1984, and to 106 million in 1992. Initially, the government strictly limited the business scope of TVEs to farm machinery and tools and the processing of agricultural products. These restrictions were later relaxed and TVEs were allowed to enter most production fields. The ownership structure of TVEs also evolved, gradually expanding from collective enterprises to individuals and other forms of private enterprise. The share of nonagricultural TVEs in total national gross output value increased from 6.3 per cent in 1978 to 14.5 per cent in 1984. A rough estimate suggests that the annual growth rate of TVE value added at constant prices during this period was between 19 and 20 per cent, lifting the GDP growth rate by 1.2 percentage points (calculated from data in Ministry of Agriculture, Animal Husbandry and Fisheries 1986; NBS various years).

Initial SOE reform attempts and the SEZ experiment to embrace the market

During the same period, reform began in SOEs in the industrial and service sectors. In 1978, Sichuan province took the lead with an experiment to allow pilot SOEs to sell any production over the state quota through the market, and to retain a proportion of their profit to pay bonuses and employee benefits. This was the first attempt to introduce SOEs to market mechanisms, providing initial incentives in production and efficiency improvement. The experiment was a success, and the central government then extended the reform to the entire country in 1980, and SOEs began to partially participate in market competition.

Two other important reforms took place in 1979 and 1980. In the first, special economic zones (SEZs) were established in Shenzhen, Xiamen, Zhuhai and Shantou. Free-trade and preferential foreign investment policies were implemented in the SEZs. The second was preliminary fiscal reform. In 1980, the 'eating from separate kitchens' reform of the government budgetary system was introduced to give more autonomy to local governments to spur better local development. In 1983 and 1984, a two-stage taxation reform was introduced to replace the profit turnover system with an internationally common tax system. These steps established the necessary conditions for transition to a market economy.

What led to accelerated growth?

The reforms in 1978–84 mentioned above were not built on an explicit commitment to a market economy because there was huge resistance from those holding to traditional ideology, although all the reform measures were market-oriented.

During this period, the HCS and other agricultural reform and market-oriented TVEs provided initial impetus to the acceleration of economic growth. Introduction of market mechanisms into the SOE sector, establishment of SEZs and decentralisation of the fiscal system also contributed to growth. The GDP growth rate increased from an average of 5.9 per cent in the pre-reform period to an average of 9.6 per cent (Table 10.1).

Table 10.1 Contributing factors to growth acceleration, 1978–84

	Contribution to growth acceleration (percentage points)
GDP growth rate higher than pre-reform period	3.6
Contribution of agricultural reform	1.5
Contribution of TVEs	1.2
Initial SOE reform, SEZs and fiscal reform	0.9

Source: Author's calculations based on data from NBS (various years).

Moves towards the market: 1985–92

In October 1984, after clashes between reformists and conservative forces, the CPC Central Committee issued its 'Decisions on Economic System Reform', formally proposing to establish 'a commodity economy with plan'. At that time, the notion of a 'market economy' still had some negative connotations in mainstream ideology, while 'commodity economy' was considered a neutral alternative term for the market economy. This was an iconic shift from the planned economy assisted by market adjustment at the very beginning of reform to a market economy, although 'with plan' was not forgotten. Since then, reform has gradually expanded to all spheres of the Chinese economy.

The 1987 report of the thirteenth National Congress of the CPC set out clearly that reform was aiming to establish a 'socialist market economy'.

Through a 'double-track price system' to the market

Before the reform, the government purchased all enterprise products at fixed prices. The government set output levels, this resulted in serious shortages in some products, whereas others were in surplus. This rigid system made it impossible to bridge the gap between supply and demand, as prices could not be raised and production could not increase without changes in the central plan. Waste and shortages persisted for long periods.

The shift towards market prices was realised through the double-track price system reform. The experiment carried out by Sichuan province in 1978 to expand the autonomy of SOEs allowed the coexistence of planned and market prices. The experiment was later extended nationwide. In 1984, the Meganshan Young Economist Symposium put forward the idea of a combination of price adjustment and easing, which was adopted by the central government and later helped create a more complete 'double-track price' mentality. It meant that the planned price system remained in the short term to avoid major shocks, while prices were partially and gradually liberalised towards a market price system.

In practice, market prices emerged in the rapidly developing TVE and urban private enterprise sectors as well as partially in SOEs. TVEs and urban private enterprises had not been restricted by planned prices from the early stage of reform, which made market prices more widespread.

In 1988, the Chinese Government decided to conduct a 'price storm' to change to a market price system, but this failed because the time was not ripe. However, the price transition continued with the rapid development of the private economy. By the mid-1990s, market prices had gradually taken the place of planned prices. The double-track price system provided a path for smooth transition to a market economy. In contrast, Russia's 'shock therapy' price and other reforms triggered hyperinflation, major dislocation and loss of production.

Opening of coastal cities: Foreign investors

Following the establishment of four SEZs in 1979, the State Council decided in 1984 to extend the opening-up policy to 14 coastal cities, including Shanghai, Tianjin, Qingdao, Dalian and Guangzhou. This attracted a large number of foreign businesses and businesses from Hong Kong, Macau and Taiwan to invest in China's coastal areas, promoting trade growth. From 1984 to 1992, foreign direct investment (FDI) in China rose rapidly, from US$2.9 billion to US$58.1 billion. The total value of imports and exports rose from US$63.6 billion to US$165.5 billion. The ratio of total import and export value to GDP rose from 17 per cent to 34 per cent. A trade deficit of US$1.3 billion was replaced with a surplus of US$4.4 billion.

Foreign investment and trade expansion obviously contributed to economic growth. According to data from China's national industrial censuses, industrial enterprises invested in by foreign, Hong Kong, Macau and Taiwan businesses had a share of only 0.4 per cent of gross industrial output (GIO) in 1985, but this had risen to 13 per cent by 1995.

Development of nonstate enterprises

Before the reform, the industrial and service industries were dominated by SOEs. In 1977, SOEs had a 77 per cent share of GIO, with the remainder contributed by collectively owned enterprises, most of which were subordinate to local governments. After several years of vigorous development of TVEs and foreign-funded enterprises, the share of non-SOEs rose to 31 per cent, in 1984, and that of SOEs dropped to 69 per cent due to their slower growth.

After 1984, market-oriented TVEs continued to grow rapidly, while a large number of individual and private enterprises also emerged. Conservatives at the decision-making level repeatedly proposed a ban on private enterprises, but were not supported by the central government. In 1987, the thirteenth National Congress of CPC officially affirmed the positive role of the private economy. In 1988, the government promulgated provisional regulations for private enterprises and established their legal status. The development of TVEs and private enterprises was suspended as policies were tightened in 1989–91; however, it accelerated again from 1992 (see Garnaut et al. 2001). It is estimated that, during the period 1985–92, industrial output grew at an annual rate of 10.1 per cent in SOEs—up from the level in the initial stage of reform—and 17.3 per cent in non-SOEs (private, individual, collective and foreign-funded enterprises). The share of nonstate enterprises in GIO rose from 31 per cent in 1984 to 44 per cent in 1992.

Progress and stagnation of reform

Reform brought rapid economic growth in China, but a number of economic imbalances emerged. One was poor control over money and credit supply, which led to an inflation rate of 18 per cent in 1988–89. A second was rapidly expanding income inequality, caused by faster economic development in urban than in rural areas, in the eastern coastal than in the central and western areas and in social strata other than ordinary workers. A third imbalance arose because of ineffective monitoring of government power, leading to serious corruption and distortion of income distribution. These sparked strong dissatisfaction among the common people, leading to what was later known as the '1989 political disturbance'.

Generally speaking, this was caused by imbalances across various aspects of reform. First, the regulatory mechanism of the central bank was incomplete and could not effectively control money and credit supply. Second, there was a lag in establishing comprehensive social security and income redistribution systems along with the progress of marketisation to prevent excessive widening of imbalances in income distribution. Third—and even more crucially—political reform did not advance and there were inadequate supervisory and restraint mechanisms on government power, exacerbating corruption.

The need for reform in response to these problems was urgent, but policymakers were slow to act or in retreat. GDP growth fell to 4.2 per cent in 1989 and 3.9 per cent in 1990. Private sector development paused, and some reforms came to a standstill. There was an attempt to recentralise the authority that had been transferred to localities and enterprises. Some conservatives tried to reverse the direction of market-oriented reforms and return to the traditional centrally planned system. This generated widespread public dissatisfaction and boycotts by government officials at various levels in support of reform. Deng Xiaoping then turned the tide and delivered a warning speech during his 1992 tour of southern China, saying 'whoever wants to change the line, principles, and policies since the Third Plenary Session will be defeated by the people who do not agree' (Deng 1992). China returned to its reform path. In 1992, development of the nonstate sector accelerated and GDP growth returned to double-digit levels (Garnaut et al. 2001).

Who contributes the most to accelerated growth?

During the period 1985–92, GDP maintained a high annual growth rate of 9.6 per cent. Table 10.2 estimates the respective contributions to accelerated economic growth of the market-oriented non-SOE sector, the partially market-oriented SOE sector and the household-based agricultural sector. Nonstate enterprises enjoyed vigorous levels of development and were the major contributors to high economic growth during this period. The efficiency of SOEs rose, but institutional problems remained.

Table 10.2 Factors contributing to accelerated growth, 1984–92

	Growth rate (%)	Contribution to growth acceleration (percentage point)
GDP	9.6	3.6
Nonstate sector	17.3	2.2
SOEs	10.1	0.4
Agriculture	3.7	0.5
Other factors		0.5

Note: Due to lack of data for the service industry, we use the growth rates of industrial value added and the relative shares of SOEs and nonstate enterprises in industry to calculate their respective growth rates, and to approximate growth rates and the relative shares of the entire nonstate and SOE sectors, and their contribution to the acceleration of GDP growth. The contribution of agriculture is based on the extent to which its growth rate surpasses that of the pre-reform average of 2 per cent, weighted by its share of GDP.

Source: Author's calculations based on data from NBS (various years).

Promoting and complementing the market: 1993–2002

After 1992, in the new wave of reform and development following Deng's tour of southern China and the reaffirmation of the reform orientation by the fourteenth National Congress, the market-oriented nonstate sector continued to grow and flourish, with the total economy also growing rapidly. In addition, due to aggravation of some structural imbalances in the economy, several reforms were advanced.

Tax-sharing reform: Balancing distribution of government resources

In the initial stage of reform, the control of public resources was decentralised. Local governments and enterprises had autonomy over and incentives for using economic resources and promoting economic growth. However, the proportion of government revenue in GDP was decreasing year by year and the central government budget was increasingly hard-pressed. From 1978 to 1994, the ratio of budgetary revenue to GDP dropped from 31.1 per cent to 10.8 per cent. Total government revenue (including extra-budgetary revenue) declined from 40.6 per cent to 16.7 per cent of GDP. It was a challenge to fund the necessary public service functions of government. Moreover, central budgetary revenue in 1993 accounted for only 22 per cent of total government revenue and only 2.7 per cent of GDP.

In response, the so-called tax-sharing reform was carried out in 1994. The collection of central and local taxes was separated, to enable each tier of government to manage taxes in its own sphere. In addition, provision was made for the central government to transfer funds to the localities. This change caused central government revenue to rise substantially. The share of budgetary revenue in GDP rose year by year, to 15.7 per cent in 2002, while the share of total government revenue reached 24.8 per cent in that year. The central government's financing problem was solved.

However, a new problem emerged. The ratios of budgetary and total government revenue to GDP have continued to rise. By 2016, they reached 21.4 per cent and 35.2 per cent, respectively—close to the pre-reform levels. This increased the burden on business. In addition, public resources were increasingly concentrated with the central government and local government revenue declined. In some areas, public servants' salaries were not paid on time and expenditure on public services was affected. As compensation, the central government allowed local governments to charge land transfer fees. These fees were raised higher and higher, pushing up housing prices, especially in large cities.

SOE restructuring

Although a principle of SOEs having sole responsibility for profit and losses, based on market rules, has been applied for many years, there were problems in the operational mechanism. In practice, SOEs enjoy their profits but are seldom held responsible for their losses. Governments have sometimes intervened too much, draining enterprises of vitality, and sometimes too little, allowing managers to squander or steal public assets. This caused SOEs' losses to increase rapidly. However, some leaders bound by traditional ideology had been reluctant to push forward with further SOE reforms.

In 1995, most small and medium SOEs in industry suffered losses, and only large SOEs remained profitable. This encouraged the central government to adopt a policy known as 'grasp the large, let go of the small'. Most large SOEs were corporatised, while small ones were subject to restructuring, including through mergers, leases of assets, bankruptcy and sale.

This reform has led many poorly managed small SOEs into bankruptcy or privatisation. The number of SOEs and state-controlled shareholding companies (together called state-controlled enterprises, or SCEs) in the industrial sector decreased sharply, from 118,000 in 1995 to 41,000 in 2002. However, the total profit of these SCEs rose from RMB67 billion to RMB263 billion and the profit–cost ratio rose from 3 per cent to 7 per cent during the same period. Surveys found that many privatised former SOEs turned from loss to profit, and efficiency improved significantly.

SOE reform in the 1990s was generally successful. Without such drastic reforms, many badly managed SOEs would have become a heavy burden on development. However, there were problems. There was insufficient preparation for restructuring. Sometimes a lack of transparency led to loss of public assets and improper enrichment of a small number of people. Tardiness in establishing a social security system caused many laid-off workers to endure difficulties, despite an emergency relief payment.

One lesson from this is that future structural reforms will require adequate preparation and thoughtful programming to ensure a transparent process and fair results. Another is that a flexible labour market requires a sound social security system to protect workers.

Establishing a social security system

Social security in the centrally planned period was only available for public servants and SOE workers. Employment in the public sector was secured and payments to retirees and employees' medical expenses were borne by their employers.

Other urban and rural workers and residents had no such insurance. During the reform period, the lack of social security became an increasing problem and further increased income inequality.

The pace of establishing a social security system accelerated from the mid-1990s. In 1997–98, the State Council decided to establish the urban employees' basic pension insurance and basic medical insurance systems. In 1999, the unemployment insurance regulations were promulgated and coverage was expanded to the urban nonstate sectors. By 2002, 147 million urban workers (58 per cent of total urban workers) were covered by basic pension insurance, 102 million (40 per cent) were covered by unemployment insurance, 94 million (37 per cent) by basic medical insurance, 44 million (17 per cent) by injury insurance and 35 million (14 per cent) by maternity insurance. This was an important step forward, although coverage remains far from complete.

Accession to the WTO

China's accession to the World Trade Organization (WTO) in 2001 allowed it to become an equal participant in international trade. The process of accession involved domestic reform. Many existing domestic laws, regulations and traditional management methods were in conflict with international rules and had to be changed, which contributed to improvements in the business environment. After accession, China's export processing industry expanded rapidly. Abundant domestic labour resources were effectively utilised; employment opportunities and labourers' incomes increased rapidly. In 2001, the total volume of imports and exports was equivalent to 38.5 per cent of GDP, and reached a high of 64.2 per cent in 2006. This played a crucial role in promoting subsequent economic growth.

Further development of the private economy

From 1992 to 2002, non-SOEs maintained annual growth of 16.9 per cent—significantly higher than the annual growth rate of SOEs (and later SCEs) of 8.6 per cent in the same period. Nonstate enterprises' share in total sales revenue in the industrial sector increased from 44 per cent to 60.2 per cent during this period, surpassing that of SCEs. Of sales by nonstate enterprises, private firms contributed two-thirds, with the rest contributed by nonstate-dominated shareholding companies and limited liability companies, foreign funded enterprises and those from Hong Kong, Macau and Taiwan as well as collective and cooperative enterprises. Collective enterprises' share decreased to about 3 per cent of nonstate industrial sales by 2002. From that time, the nonstate enterprise sector can be regarded as the private sector.

During this period, private enterprise continued to lead China's rapid economic growth. Annual economic growth of 9.8 per cent was 3.9 percentage points higher than the average in the planned economy period. The private nonagricultural sector contributed 3.3 percentage points of the total, while the SCE sector made a negative contribution of –0.3 percentage points of the total.

In 1992, China's per capita GDP was only US$423 (converted at the going exchange rate). It reached US$1,148 in 2002. In 1998, China moved from a low to a middle-income country according to the World Bank's classification.

Market reform advances and political reform lags

During the period 1993–2002, tax reform and the establishment of a social security system provided the basic conditions for a modern market economy, while SOE reform and accession to the WTO promoted further marketisation. The great defect was that reform of the political system had been indefinitely delayed. In addition, the previously proposed reforms to separate the functions of government from those of the party, and to separate enterprise management from government administration were not followed through. Leaders at different levels of the CPC had monopoly power and were not open to public scrutiny. Some evolved into undisciplined overlords and became seriously corrupt. This was the main cause of the deterioration of government administration and market distortion.

A decade of hope and fear: 2003–12

After China's accession to the WTO, the economy became more outward-oriented. Its export-processing industry enjoyed rapid growth, with substantial increases in imports and exports. There was rapid urbanisation and economic growth; improvements in public services, social security and income redistribution systems; and major infrastructure developments. The first two advances were a result of increased marketisation. In the last two areas, the government played a positive and complementary role to the market in sustaining economic growth.

There were also serious negative changes: the first was the continued widening of income inequality; and the second was unprecedented corruption in the public sector. Macroeconomic policies also had excessively short horizons. Excessive government intervention in investment, land allocation and enterprise operation disrupted the role of markets in optimising resource allocation and led to structural imbalances.

Outward orientation, urbanisation and private sector growth

After China's WTO accession in 2001, trade and export-oriented processing industries flourished. In 2007, before the Global Financial Crisis (GFC), the share of import and export value in GDP reached 62 per cent—20 percentage points higher than in 2002. It decreased after the GFC, to 45 per cent in 2012.

During the period 2002–12, urbanisation accelerated for three reasons. First, exports supported a large number of new jobs in urban areas, attracting many rural–urban migrant workers to cities. Second, in 2001, the State Council revised urbanisation policy from 'strict controls on the scale of large cities and active development of small cities and towns' to a policy of 'coordinately developing large, medium and small cities and towns' in line with market trends. Third, the Sun Zhigang incident in 2003—in which migrant worker Sun Zhigang died in Guangzhou as a result of physical abuse he suffered while being detained under the custody and repatriation system—triggered a strong expression of public opinion, resulting in the State Council's abolition of restrictive and discriminative policy measures against rural migrant workers and liberalisation of the movement of people between urban and rural areas.

During the period 2003–12, the urbanisation rate increased from 39 per cent to 53 per cent, with an annual increase of 1.4 percentage points, which significantly exceeding previous periods.

The private sector continued to grow substantially faster than the SCE sector. Private enterprises' share in industrial output increased from 60 per cent to 76 per cent, and continued a 3.3 percentage point contribution to economic growth.

During this period, China rose from a lower–middle to upper–middle-income country according to the World Bank's classification. Together with RMB appreciation, GDP per capita at the exchange rate rose from US$1,148 in 2002 to US$6,338 in 2012.

Rural livelihoods, social security and infrastructure

Rural reforms in the 1980s played a crucial role in improving the agricultural sector. After several years' rapid growth, the energy released by reform was exhausted and agricultural production entered a period of slower growth. The income gap between urban and rural areas expanded again. The agricultural tax coupled with the local collection of miscellaneous fees imposed a big burden on farmers. In 2006, the State Council formally abolished the agricultural tax and related fees.

Important achievements between 2003 and 2012 included major increases in the coverage rate of basic social insurance for urban employees, from 37 per cent to 71 per cent. A basic pension insurance system for urban and rural nonworking residents and a basic medical insurance system for urban nonworking residents were established, covering 484 million and 272 million people, respectively, by 2012. In rural areas, the new rural cooperative medical system and the rural minimum living allowance system achieved full coverage.

During this period, infrastructure construction progressed rapidly. The total length of expressways increased from 25,100 km to 96,200 km. Railways increased from 71,900 km to 97,600 km, of which high-speed rail contributed 9,356 km by the end of 2012. Cargo volumes increased from 507 million tonne-kilometres to 1.738 billion tkm, while passenger turnover increased from 141 million to 334 million passenger kilometres.

Income disparity and corruption

Between 2003 and 2012, the income disparity of Chinese citizens expanded significantly. The Gini coefficient of income increased from 0.433 in 2002 to the highest on record of 0.491 in 2008. It then began to ease, to 0.474 in 2012. Widening income inequality as measured in official data relates to the urban–rural wage gap and regional disparities. However, a major part of widening income disparity in reality is caused by corruption and improper use of public resources and is missing from the official data.

The author's previous studies show that some urban residents in the past had large amounts of 'grey' income (income without a proven legitimate source) that was not included in official income statistics, and was concentrated mainly to the top 10 per cent of urban households. Grey income was estimated to be RMB2.4 trillion in 2005, RMB4.6 trillion in 2008 and RMB6.2 trillion in 2011—roughly equivalent to 12 per cent of GDP in 2011 (Wang and Woo 2011; Wang 2013). Grey income is mainly a result of corruption and institutional defects, including poor management of public funds in government investment, improper distribution of public resources and monopolistic benefits, lack of monitoring of government authorities, bureaucracy and corruption in the public services sector. These phenomena were found to be intensifying and seriously threatening social fairness and long-term economic development.

Macropolicy, government intervention and structural imbalance

Between 2003 and 2012, monetary policy continued to be loose. Growth of money supply (M2) in most years exceeded 16 per cent, significantly exceeding the rate of GDP growth. In 2009, in response to the GFC, it reached a high of 28 per cent. This led to severe bubbles in the capital and real estate markets, and the stock market indices plunged as the bubbles burst. Housing price increases in megacities such as Beijing, Shanghai and Shenzhen reached hundreds of times the annual income of wage earners, which seriously impacted ordinary workers.

During this period, the scale of government and SCE investment expanded considerably, with its share of GDP growing from 18.9 per cent in 2002 to 24.8 per cent in 2009, before decreasing slightly to 23.1 per cent in 2012. Beyond necessary investment in infrastructure and urban development, inefficient government investment is widespread. Investments by various levels of government were often associated with the pursuit of improper interests and it became common for officials with power over government investments to accept bribes.

In recent years, large-scale government investment and easy money supply have no longer generated high economic growth. From 2002 to 2012, the consumption rate dropped from 60.6 per cent to 50.1 per cent of GDP and the capital formation rate increased from 36.9 per cent to 47.2 per cent of GDP. Excessive capital formation led to severe overcapacity in industry and housing and a sharp decline in the rate of return on capital.

During the period 2003–12, the growth rate of the SCE industrial sector dropped to 6.9 per cent from 8.6 per cent in the previous period, reflecting a marked decline in productivity growth. However, private enterprise continued to maintain a high growth rate, at 14.4 per cent. As a result, its share in industry increased from 60.2 per cent to 76 per cent.

Government intervention in business has expanded with controlling power over resource allocation. The Index of Marketisation of China's provinces developed by the National Economic Research Institute (NERI) shows a significant deterioration in the period 2008–10 in the 'relationship between the government and the market' as well as in 'development of factor markets' (Wang et al. 2016).

It is crucial for future economic development to clarify the relationship between the government and the market.

Looking forward to continuing reform: 2013–17

After the eighteenth National Congress of the CPC in 2012, China's reform program took a new turn. The party engaged in a desperate fight against corruption and also sought to deal with the imbalances in economic structure and to revitalise the economy. In particular, it committed to continuing institutional reform.

Anticorruption measures and improved income distribution

According to incomplete statistics, from 2013 to 2017, more than 190 senior officials at the provincial governor and ministerial level, and many more at lower levels, were punished for corruption. The anticorruption campaign has had a strong deterrent effect on corrupt officials and applied a brake to the spread of corruption.

The anticorruption campaign reduced losses and improper distribution of public resources and improved income distribution. The official Gini coefficient decreased from 0.474 in 2012 to 0.465 in 2016—but this did not include grey income in either year. The decline in real inequality was probably greater than that indicated in the official data. Improvements in income distribution also raise household consumption, indirectly supporting economic growth.

Fighting corruption through judicial and administrative means may have only a short-run effect. Reform of the political and administrative systems is necessary for a fundamental solution.

Reform and structural rebalancing

The Chinese economy has encountered problems of structural imbalance in recent years. Industrial sectors suffered from serious overcapacity due to overinvestment. Nationwide, the leverage ratio reached 250 per cent—indicating high financial risks. GDP growth continued below 7 per cent after 2015, for the first time since 1978. TFP significantly decreased. Slower export growth in recent years has made a negative contribution to economic growth, although plenty of evidence indicates that major causes of this were accumulated problems due market interference such as continuing heavy government investment and loose monetary policy.

The eighteenth CPC Central Committee made a decision in 2013 to allow the market to play a decisive role in resource allocation, but, in practice, few major changes have been seen. The government's short-run priority is structural rebalancing. In the past year or two, there have been some achievements in this regard, as well as negative effects due to intensive use of administrative measures. For example, administrative measures to reduce excess capacity resulted in a sharp rebound of energy and raw materials prices, while many loss-making SOEs were still protected by local governments. There has been little improvement in productivity.

The macrolevel leverage ratio (the ratio of nonfinancial enterprises, government and household debt to GDP) has been increasing, although the growth rate of M2 slowed to 8.2 per cent in 2017 from 11–14 per cent in previous years. The leverage ratio may decline in the coming two or three years, although this is uncertain.

Getting rid of structural imbalances and reviving the economy depend on reform of the system. Of particular importance are the following measures.

First, government reform is needed to transform its functions from a focus on GDP to a focus on public services and maintaining a good market environment, so as to reduce its intervention in the economy.

Second, the government needs to promote fiscal and taxation reforms to improve the distribution and use of public resources, to reduce inefficient government investment and waste and to further strengthen education, medical services and the social security system. The household registration system needs reform to enable more than 200 million rural–urban migrants to settle in cities and enjoy equal access to social benefits.

Third, land reform and opening the land market is needed for better allocation of resources and to suppress real estate bubbles.

Fourth, it should maintain a neutral monetary policy to bring down the high leverage rate in the next few years for economic stability.

Most of these reform items have been included in the official reform plan, although implementation has been slow. A lesson may be learnt from previous reforms: reform is a need of the general public and cannot be achieved only by efforts at the decision-making level. Public support and participation are the key elements for success.

Economic growth

The average GDP growth rate in 2015–17 was 6.8 per cent—significantly lower than the average of 9.6 per cent during the past 40 years. The Chinese Government and most economists have accepted that the period of high growth has ended and future growth will be in a higher-medium range—likely meaning between 5 per cent and 7 per cent. However, slower growth is mainly the result of institutional problems, which will either become more serious or will be solved through reforms and policy adjustments. The future is therefore uncertain, but there is still great potential for future growth.

First, urbanisation has remained the engine of economic growth in past decades, with the urbanisation rate reaching only 58.5 per cent—significantly lower than that of developed countries. There is plenty of room for further urbanisation to drive economic growth, although some urbanisation policies and related institutional arrangements need adjustment, such as the urban household registration system.

Second, in the process of moving from a middle-income to high-income country, China's growth in household consumption will play a crucial role in sustaining economic growth. The current rate of consumption in China is too low (53.6 per cent in 2016). Adjustment of government policy to improve public services and social security could improve income distribution and household consumption.

Third, experience indicates that huge impetus for growth and technical innovation is stored in the private enterprise sector. The key to releasing this potential is to maintain a good business environment for fair market competition and the rule of law—in particular, reducing government intervention on markets, restricting monopolistic power and improving legal protection of intellectual property rights.

Analysis shows that, with the implementation of the reforms and policy adjustments mentioned above, future economic growth could be restored to above 7 per cent, and China could join the high-income–country club before 2030 (see Wang and Zhou 2016).

References

Chow, G. (1993), Capital formation and economic growth in China, *The Quarterly Journal of Economics* (August).

Deng, X. (1992), Deng Xiaoping's southern tour speech (1), *People's Web*, 18 January to 21 February (published online 14 October 2008), [in Chinese]. Available from: gd.people.com.cn/GB/123947/128569/133843/8171345.html.

Garnaut, R., Song, L., Yao, Y. and Wang, X. (2001), *Private Enterprises in China*, Canberra: Asia Pacific Press.

Maddison, A. (2001), *The World Economy: A millennial perspective*, Paris: OECD Publishing. doi.org/10.1787/9789264189980-en.

Ministry of Agriculture, Animal Husbandry and Fisheries (1986), *Township and Village Enterprise Statistical Data*, Beijing: China Statistics Press.

National Bureau of Statistics (NBS) (various years), *China Statistics Yearbook*, Beijing: China Statistics Press.

National Bureau of Statistics (NBS) (2009), *China Compendium of Statistics 1949–2008*, Beijing: China Statistics Press.

Wang, X. (2006), Growth accounting after statistical revisions, in R. Garnaut and L. Song (eds), *The Turning Point in China's Economic Development*, Canberra: ANU E Press.

Wang, X. (2013), Grey income and distribution of national income: 2013, [in Chinese], *Comparative Studies* (5): 1–50.

Wang, X. and Woo, W. (2011), The size and distribution of hidden income in China, *Asian Economic Papers* 10(1): 1–26. doi.org/10.1162/ASEP_a_00064.

Wang, X. and Zhou, Y. (2016), Forecasting China's economic growth by 2020 and 2030, in L. Song, R. Garnaut, F. Cai and L. Johnston (eds), *China's New Sources of Economic Growth. Volume 1*, Canberra: ANU Press. doi.org/10.22459/CNSEG.07.2016.04.

Wang, X., Fan, G. and Yu, J. (2016), *Marketization Index of China's Provinces: NERI report 2016*, [in Chinese], Beijing: Social Sciences Academy Press.

World Bank (various years), *World Development Indicators*, Washington, DC: The World Bank.

11. China's economic rebalancing: Drivers, outlook and the role of reform

Guonan Ma, Ivan Roberts and Gerard Kelly[1]

Reforms to transform China's centrally planned economy into a market-oriented one presented enormous challenges for macroeconomic management. In the first 15 years of reform, the main challenge appeared to be difficulties in maintaining short-term expenditure within the productive capacity of the economy, to avoid a pronounced tendency towards periodic bursts of excess demand, deficits in external current payments and inflation (Garnaut and Ma 1993; Raby 2001). Reforms in the financial and monetary systems, and the learning-by-doing of the People's Bank of China (PBC), led to relatively smooth management of the external balance problem from the mid-1990s, although there was a brief upsurge in the current account deficit at the height of the East Asian Financial Crisis in 1998 (Song 1998).

After the crisis, observers tended to view the macroeconomic problem as one of excessive savings (a tendency for incomes to exceed consumption by a large margin) and external payments surpluses (a tendency for domestic productive capacity to exceed domestic expenditure by a sizeable amount). At the same time, the composition of domestic expenditure exhibited a marked shift away from consumption spending towards domestic gross capital formation. Thus, in the second half of the first 40 years of reform, these expenditure imbalances—and the question of how they might be resolved—increasingly became a focus of concern for policymakers and academics alike.

This chapter examines the build-up and subsequent unwinding of China's expenditure imbalances in the past two decades of reform. It presents macroeconomic evidence that rebalancing from a lopsided investment and export-driven pattern of growth towards more consumption-driven growth is already occurring in China. It examines the reasons for the emergence of the expenditure imbalances—in particular, China's high national saving rate, positive impulses to growth arising from economic reforms and a prolonged boom in housing. It then considers the prospects for their resolution, focusing on the role of structural change, the resilience of household demand and a decline in the return to capital since 2011. In this context, it also discusses the role the government's current reform plans and macroeconomic policies can play in the rebalancing process.

1 The views expressed in this chapter are those of the authors and should not be attributed to the Reserve Bank of Australia. The authors appreciate the comments and suggestions provided by the book's editors, but are solely responsible for any errors.

China's unbalanced growth pattern, which features a high investment–GDP/low consumption–GDP ratio and a sustained current account surplus, has been a focus of international policy discussions since the mid-2000s (Bernanke 2007; Obstfeld and Rogoff 2009). Rebalancing the pattern of expenditure has also become a priority for the Chinese Government. Premier Li Keqiang recently reiterated this aspiration, observing that 'consumption is crucial for China's economy to grow and remain stable, and is the main engine for optimizing economic structure' (State Council 2017).

Several authors contend that China's imbalances are rooted in labour and capital market distortions that artificially lowered the cost of labour and capital, repressed consumption and suppressed the value of the renminbi (Lardy 2008; Huang and Tao 2011; Pettis 2013). They argue that the imbalances may be tackled by reducing these distortions. In contrast, Ma et al. (2013) argue that China's twin imbalances—domestic expenditure falling noticeably short of income and, within domestic expenditure, a rise in the investment share at the expense of the consumption share—can be understood as the products of large income windfalls spurred by reforms and other structural changes that were saved, giving rise to large external surpluses. An advantage of this explanation is that it reconciles strong consumption growth, even faster growth in investment and a modest consumption share with the rise of the external surplus during the early 2000s. Ma et al. (2013) predict that, as these windfalls fade, saving will fall and the imbalances will be reduced.

To clarify the reasons and prospects for rebalancing, we first review the literature and empirical evidence regarding the main factors behind the expenditure imbalances, emphasising the central role of a high and rising Chinese saving rate. Second, we highlight the extraordinary strength of Chinese household consumption growth in comparison with other economies. Even if consumption has been 'repressed' by factor price distortions, as argued by some analysts, such comparisons cast doubt on the likelihood that an acceleration of consumption will be the primary driver of further rebalancing of domestic expenditure. Any meaningful rebalancing is most likely to flow from a deceleration of investment.

Third, we present evidence from China's flow-of-funds accounts showing that conventional analysis understates the role of investment by households in supporting capital accumulation in recent years. While recent discussions stress the need to reform financial markets to foster rebalancing, we argue that, in the long run, rebalancing will probably happen anyway as a natural outcome of dwindling income windfalls arising from worsening demographics, fading positive productivity shocks and maturing housing markets—all of which helped drive the imbalances in the first place.

Fourth, using an approach similar to Bai et al. (2006), we show that returns to capital in China declined after 2011, driven by a rise in the capital–output ratio and a rise in the labour share of income. The fall in returns to capital occurred alongside an upward shift in the cost of debt funding, which reduced incentives for the corporate sector to invest. A continuation of this trend in the longer term would be expected to place further downward pressure on the growth of investment.

While structural forces are likely to continue to drive the rebalancing process that started early in the current decade, new reforms and government policies will affect how that process unfolds. We argue that success in meeting environmental and financial reform objectives may itself be endogenous to an ongoing shift to a less investment-intensive growth pattern. We also argue that some government policies adopted since 2015 could help lift corporate profitability and thus actually stimulate investment; nonetheless, if implemented effectively, they could also enhance investment efficiency and soften the impact of slower overall investment growth on national income and consumption. Reforms that improve social security and reduce households' incentives to save could support consumption in a period of slowing investment growth. Indeed, the national accounts identity implies that for rebalancing away from investment to occur without a rise in the external imbalance, the national saving rate must fall.[2] State-owned enterprise (SOE) reform—if it leads to a leaner and more efficient state-owned sector—could reduce wasteful investment and thereby facilitate rebalancing. In contrast, a cultivation of large 'national champion' SOEs could lead to a focus on size rather than efficiency, deterring competition from the private sector and slowing the rebalancing process.

Understanding China's expenditure imbalances

In the space of three decades, China's aggregate demand composition was transformed. From the 1980s to the end of the first decade of the 2000s, household consumption as a share of gross domestic product (GDP) fell from more than one-half to a little over one-third, while gross capital formation jumped from one-third to just below one-half (Figure 11.1). China's saving rate rose even faster than its investment rate, from 35 per cent of GDP in the early 1990s to above 50 per cent by 2007, widening the current account surplus from less than 2 per cent to 10 per cent of GDP in 2007. In short, China experienced a greater domestic expenditure imbalance *and* external imbalance during this period. It is worth noting that, by 'domestic expenditure imbalance', we are referring simply to high-investment/low-

2 The identity can be expressed as $S/Y - I/Y = (X - M)/Y$, where S, I, Y, X and M refer to saving, investment, GDP, exports and imports, respectively. China's trade balance has closely approximated the current account balance as a share of GDP in recent decades.

consumption shares of expenditure. This differs from the traditional concept of 'internal imbalance' seen in the international trade literature, which is a tendency towards unemployment or inflation (Meade 1951; Swan 1963; Corden 1960).

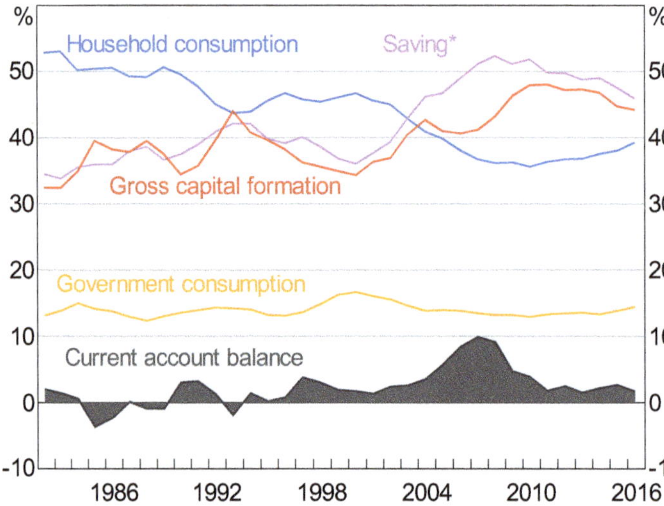

Figure 11.1 Aggregate demand and the current account: Share of nominal GDP

* Gross capital formation plus current account balance.

Sources: Authors' calculations; CEIC Data; NBS (2015).

In just a few years after 2007, the current account surplus shrank to below 3 per cent of GDP. This rapid external rebalancing was facilitated by both a currency appreciation and, initially, a sharp rise in the investment rate, which coincided with a peaking but still stubbornly high national saving rate (Ma et al. 2013). Put differently, China's domestic expenditure imbalance increased while its external imbalance eased. Since 2011, however, the expenditure imbalance has started to resolve, with a rising consumption share and a falling investment rate balancing each other to maintain a relatively low and stable current account balance that fell below 2 per cent of GDP in 2016. The trend decline in the national saving rate during the 2010s has been key to the process of rebalancing by supporting robust consumption growth in the face of slower investment growth while shrinking the external surplus.

Who saves and who invests in China?

At a more disaggregated level, an analysis of the Chinese flow-of-funds data available for 1992–2015 helps answer the question of who consumes, who saves and who invests—a core issue in any discussion of expenditure rebalancing. The flow-of-funds data are conceptually consistent with the national accounts on both an expenditure and an income basis, but they also reveal the breakdowns of these expenditure and income flows by household, corporate and government sectors.[3]

During these two decades, gross capital formation as a share of GDP rose by 10 percentage points, yet the national saving rate climbed even more—by 12 percentage points (Figure 11.2). The saving rate peaked at 52 per cent of GDP in 2008, declining thereafter. By contrast, the investment rate plateaued at 47 per cent in the early years of the current decade, partly owing to the large-scale government stimulus program in the wake of the Global Financial Crisis (GFC). The three sectors—household, corporate and government—all supported China's high and rising investment and saving rates during the period 1992–2015.

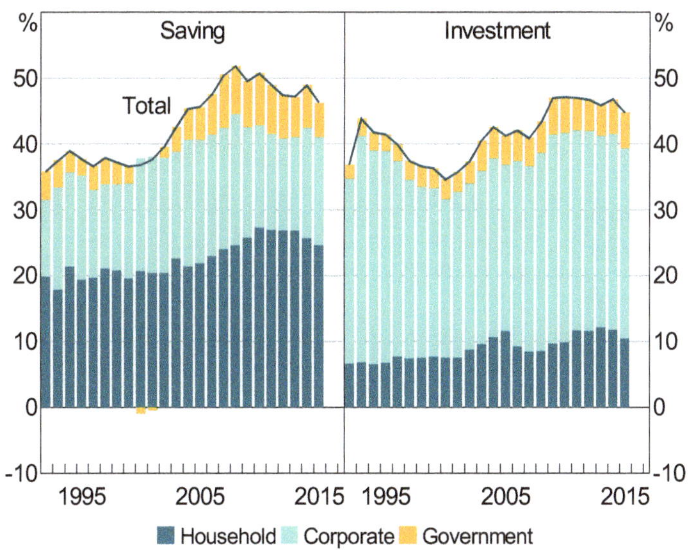

Figure 11.2 Saving and investment by sector: Flow of funds, share of GDP

Note: Adjusted for 'acquisition less disposal of other nonfinancial assets'.

Sources: Authors' calculations; CEIC Data.

The household sector has been the largest driver of gross domestic *saving*, accounting for around half in 2015 and generating two-thirds of the rise in the national saving rate during the two decades for which we have flow-of-funds data. The corporate and government sectors each contributed one-fifth of the increased saving. As a share of GDP, household saving increased steadily, starting in the early 2000s. After a brief period of dissaving in 2000–01, government saving surged, while corporate saving peaked in 2008 and has since fallen.

3 See Ma et al. (2016) for a more detailed discussion.

In contrast, the dominant—albeit most volatile—source of *investment* has been the corporate sector. In 2015, the corporate, household and government sectors represented 64 per cent, 24 per cent and 12 per cent, respectively, of investment. By comparison, government investment has risen steadily over time, particularly since the early 2000s, when government saving also began to increase, before easing off in 2011–15.

A little-noticed fact, however, is that within the space of a couple of decades, investment undertaken by *households* almost doubled, singlehandedly accounting for well over half of the 8 percentage point increase in China's investment share of GDP during this period.[4] In fact, if we plot total household and nonhousehold expenditure (that is, the sum of consumption *and* investment) as a share of GDP, we observe a compositional shift towards household expenditure starting as early as 2008, several years before the rebalancing towards consumption began (Figure 11.3). Indeed, if the rise in the investment share during the two decades is viewed as evidence of 'overinvestment', these data suggest that the household sector could be one principal culprit.

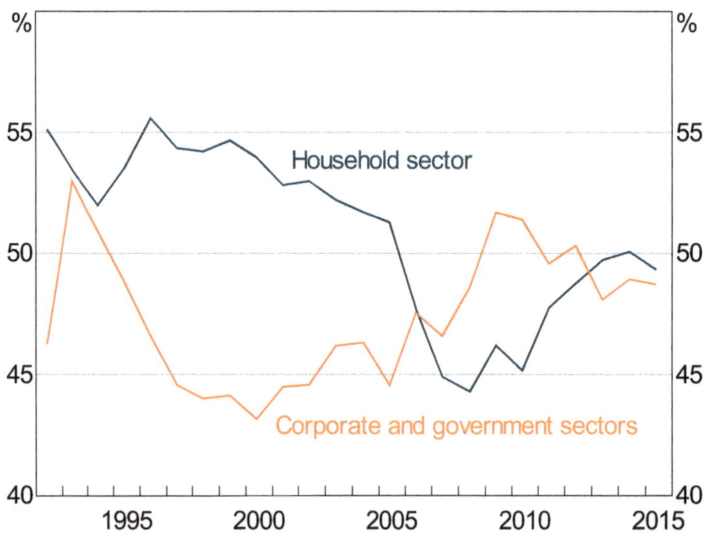

Figure 11.3 Household and nonhousehold expenditure: Flow of funds, share of GDP

Sources: Authors' calculations; CEIC Data.

There are a couple of reasons why we might observe a rising share of investment by households. The first is capital accumulation associated with self-employment. Between 1992 and 2015, rural and urban self-employment more than tripled as

4 This represents the continuation (and acceleration) of a trend first noticed by Kuijs (2005).

a share of total employment, rising to around 12 per cent. Investment by households is likely to have accelerated accordingly. Rising self-employment has been an important byproduct of China's growing private sector (Lardy 2014).

A second—probably more important—explanation is that housing-related investment by individuals has increased substantially since the early 1980s. Agricultural sector reforms in the 1980s prompted a burst of housing construction activity by farmers. Then, in the 1990s, the government initiated a wave of de facto state housing privatisation in urban areas that led to substantial renovation and upgrading of old state housing units. The 2000s witnessed a surge in the floor space of residential housing built by developers, but ultimately using funds supplied by the household sector, as well as considerable upgrading of apartments sold in rough 'shell' form by developers. These three waves of private housing construction and upgrading activity are likely to have contributed to growth in measured investment by the household sector.

The roles of income and the saving rate in household consumption

In contrast to its prominent role in driving the rising aggregate saving and investment rates, the household sector's share of gross national disposable income fell through the 2000s, while the shares of the corporate and government sectors saw corresponding increases (Figure 11.4). Since 2008, the household income share has started to recover—at the expense of the corporate income share—but, in net terms, the household income ratio has remained below the level of the 1990s. As a share of GDP, the decline in household income and a rise in household saving together imply a steep rise in the average propensity to save out of household disposable income.

Although the literature emphasises the declining household share of income as the main factor weighing down the household consumption share of GDP (Ma and Wang 2010; Perkins 2015), the flow-of-funds data suggest that households' rising average propensity to save has been more important in explaining the declining share of household consumption. Household consumption as a share of GDP can be decomposed as Equation 11.1.

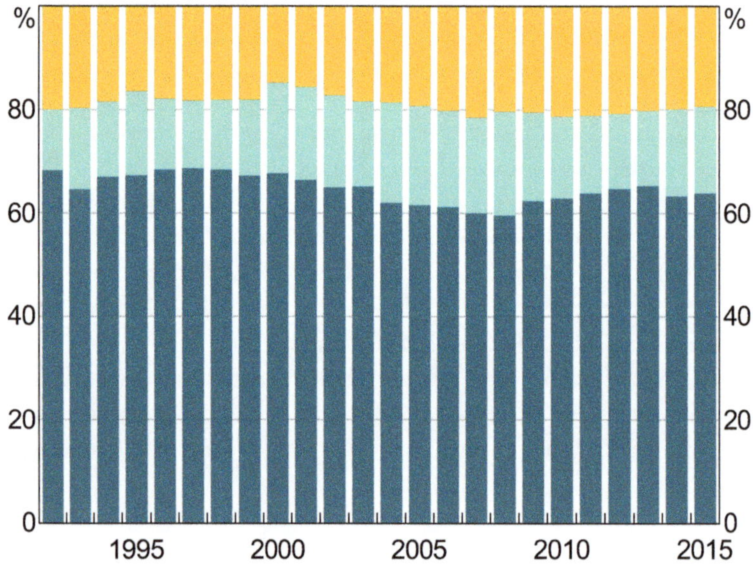

Figure 11.4 Income by sector: Flow of funds, share of gross domestic income

Note: Adjusted for 'acquisition less disposal of other nonfinancial assets'.

Sources: Authors' calculations; CEIC Data.

Equation 11.1

$$C^H/Y = (1 - S^H/Y^H).\ Y^H/Y$$

In Equation 11.1, C^H, S^H and Y^H refer to household consumption, saving and disposable income, respectively. Using this equation, we calculate that the decline in the household income share (Y^H/Y) and increase in the average propensity to save (S^H/Y^H) contributed one-third and two-thirds, respectively, of the fall in the household consumption share in GDP during the period 1992–2015.

Previous literature explains China's high and rising *average propensity to save* as arising from the increasing burden of private health and education expenses in a climate of underdeveloped financial markets, which increased self-insurance/precautionary saving motives (Blanchard and Giavazzi 2006; Chamon and Prasad 2010). Other explanations emphasise the interaction of a lifecycle of saving—dissaving in early life, positive saving in working years and dissaving in retirement—with China's rising working-age population (Modigliani and Cao 2004).

To these we can add a complementary (and simpler) explanation. Specifically, as a share of GDP, the increase in household investment can itself account for more than three-quarters of the rise in household saving and thus could explain more than half of the reported fall in the household consumption share during the period 1992–2015. Put differently, if we capped gross capital formation undertaken by the household sector at its 1992 level for all subsequent years and allocated the remaining investment to consumption, household consumption would have declined from 48 per cent of GDP to only 42 per cent, instead of the recorded 38 per cent in 2015. Similarly, household saving would have risen from 20 per cent of GDP to 21 per cent, instead of the observed 25 per cent (Figure 11.5).

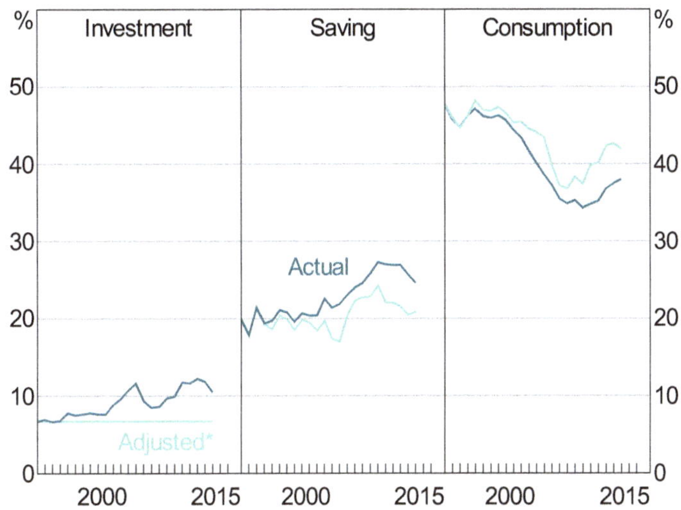

Figure 11.5 Household sector—actual and adjusted: Share of GDP

* Investment capped at 1992 level; remainder allocated to consumption.

Sources: Authors' calculations; CEIC Data.

The *household income share*, on the other hand, has primarily been weighed down by the falling share of labour compensation for most of this period. Falls in the shares of net current transfers, as social welfare programs have been withdrawn, and net property income (partly due to rising interest payments) also contributed to the fall in the early 2000s (Figure 11.6). The decline was partly offset by rising net income from sales of land use rights (reflected in 'net acquisition of nonfinancial assets') and net 'other factor income' associated with the rise in the ranks of the self-employed.

Some observers attribute the falling labour share to the relaxation of restrictions on internal migration under the *hukou* (household registration system) from the 1980s, which permitted a larger pool of incoming surplus rural labour and restrained urban wage growth despite a relaxation of wage controls (Perkins 2015). However, other researchers emphasise the effect of increased labour mobility across regions and industries, which led to a compositional shift from agriculture—where the labour share of income is very high—to industries where the labour share is lower (Bai and Qian 2010; Ma and Wang 2010).

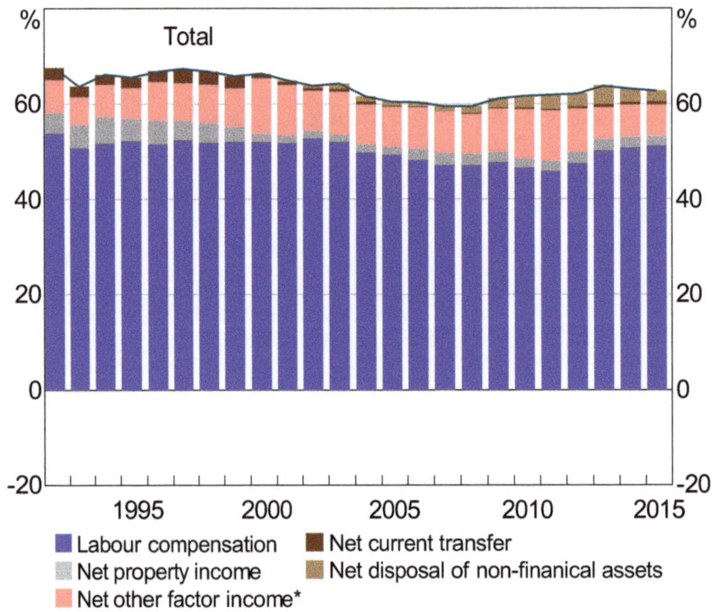

Figure 11.6 Household disposable income: Share of GDP

* Household sector value-added income less payments for labour compensation and production tax.

Note: Adjusted for 'acquisition less disposal of other nonfinancial assets'.

Sources: Authors' calculations; CEIC Data.

How unusual is China's pattern of investment and consumption?

Descriptions of China's consumption, investment and saving patterns as 'unbalanced' are usually made with reference to cross-country and historical comparisons. Indeed, until 2011, when the process of rebalancing began, China had domestic expenditure compositions that were unusual among major advanced and emerging market economies, featuring one of the highest investment rates and lowest household consumption rates (Figure 11.7). In contrast, China's external imbalance does not appear excessive when compared with a number of these other economies.

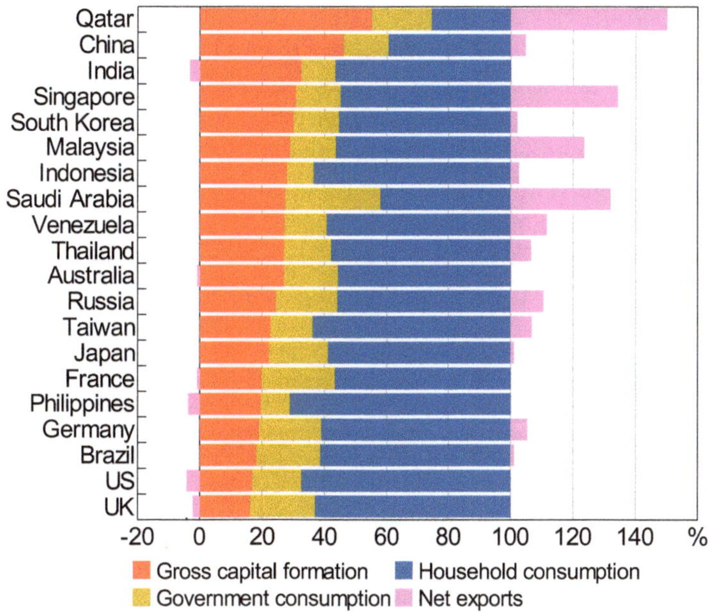

Figure 11.7 International comparison of expenditure composition: Share of gross national expenditure, 2001–11, cumulative

Sources: Ma et al. (2016, 2017).

The modest consumption share of GDP and its fall over recent decades raise the question of whether Chinese consumption has been 'weak' by international standards. On average, household consumption growth was the lowest among all the major domestic expenditure components during the period 1978–2016 (Table 11.1). However, growth has still averaged 9 per cent for more than three decades. The lopsided nature of China's growth pattern reflects the fact that investment had been expanding at an even faster, double-digit pace until 2010. Since 2011, rebalancing has clearly started: private consumption has grown faster than investment, while the current account surplus has eased.

Table 11.1 China: Growth of GDP expenditure components (1978 constant prices, compound annual growth rate, per cent)

	GDP	Consumption			Gross capital formation	
		Total	Private	Government	Total	Fixed
1978–2016	9.6	9.2	9.0	9.8	10.1	10.7
1978–2010	9.9	9.3	9.0	10.3	10.6	11.2
2011–16	7.3	7.7	8.4	6.1	7.0	7.7

Note: Private consumption data for 2014–16 are estimates.

Sources: Authors' calculations; CEIC Data; NBS (2015).

A simple international comparison also puts China's so-called investment-led and consumption-repressed growth pattern in perspective. Figure 11.8 displays 20-year windows for the maximum annualised growth rates for investment and private consumption for selected economies in the postwar era. While high relative to most economies, China's maximum speed of capital accumulation during this period is outstripped by the experiences of Taiwan, Japan and Korea. In contrast, at its peak, Chinese private consumption growth exceeded that of most major economies. China's pattern of domestic demand has certainly been unusual, but, on this metric, Chinese household consumption has been anything but 'anaemic'.

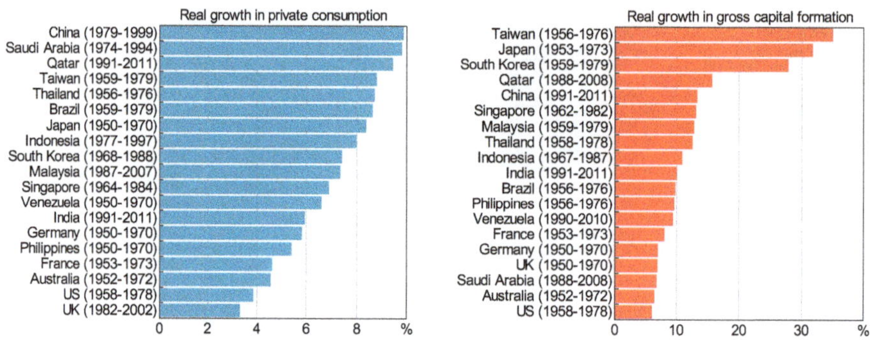

Figure 11.8 International comparison of consumption and investment growth: Maximum 20-year annualised rate

Sources: Ma et al. (2016, 2017).

Explaining the imbalances

Two competing—but also potentially complementary—hypotheses have been offered to explain the 'puzzle' of China's sustained surplus saving and unbalanced pattern of domestic demand. These emphasise, respectively, the role of factor price distortions and the role of structural change. The first view argues that policy distortions such as regulated interest rates, subsidised resource prices, currency undervaluation and 'artificially' low labour compensation due to *hukou* policies have all depressed household consumption, stimulated investment and boosted exports relative to an assumed counterfactual (Huang and Tao 2011).

However, the implications of such distortions are often more ambiguous than they appear at first glance. For example, low regulated benchmark deposit rates are sometimes thought to suppress household consumption in China (Lardy 2008), but the empirical evidence is sparse. Nabar's (2011) provincial panel estimation for the period 2006–09 finds a dominance of income over substitution effects due to 'target saving' behaviour by households. Time-series analysis by Berkelmans et al. (2016) finds that deposit demand does not respond positively to increases in deposit rates. Yet, the evidence relies heavily on the relationship between saving or deposits and inflation-adjusted regulated deposit rates. The de facto interest rate deregulation since the late 2000s via the issuance of wealth management products with market-based interest rates may have offset any effect of regulated interest rates in suppressing consumption.

Subsidised energy costs may support a higher rate of investment and production than would be possible at market prices, but they may also help explain China's rise as a big net energy importer, which, *ceteris paribus*, would tend to reduce the current account surplus. Similarly, while the *hukou* system impedes rural–urban migration, as discussed earlier, the relaxation of such policies may be partly responsible for driving the labour share of income *lower* in the 2000s.

The alternative view, of Ma et al. (2013), assigns a greater role to structural economic changes. Given the difficulty of identifying the net effect of factor price distortions on imbalances, this view emphasises the central role of China's high saving rate in understanding the twin imbalances. It holds that multiple large favourable demand and productivity shocks in the 1980s, 1990s and 2000s lifted potential growth, thereby giving rise to large income windfalls that were mostly saved while still boosting both consumption and investment spending.

The first two decades of the reform era witnessed at least two significant positive shocks to income growth: the successful rural household responsibility system in the 1980s and the large wave of employees leaving their state employers to create their own private businesses in the early 1990s. The forced restructuring of state firms reduced job security, improved efficiency, cleared room for expansion of private firms and lifted corporate earnings—all boosting private saving. Institutional changes in the pension system, private home ownership and the introduction of mortgages also strengthened incentives to save and fuelled a property investment boom. Finally, China's accession to the World Trade Organization (WTO) in 2001 prompted a wideranging market opening, facilitated technology transfers and secured access to a booming foreign market—all of which supported corporate cash flows.

The deregulation of housing markets deserves special emphasis. In 1988, the Chinese Constitution was amended to legalise transactions in land use rights, laying the foundation for private home ownership (Fang et al. 2016). Housing provided by SOEs to their employees was successively privatised at a discount to the replacement cost and mortgages were introduced, leading to a sharp increase in residential investment (Figure 11.9).[5] This housing boom stimulated capacity-building in both upstream and downstream industries, including steel, cement, glass, household

5 We use the estimates of nominal residential gross fixed capital formation from Koen et al. (2013), projected forward using data on real estate fixed-asset investment.

appliances and financial services. Using official data, Xu et al. (2015) estimate that, directly and indirectly, residential housing accounted for nearly one-third of GDP growth in 2013.

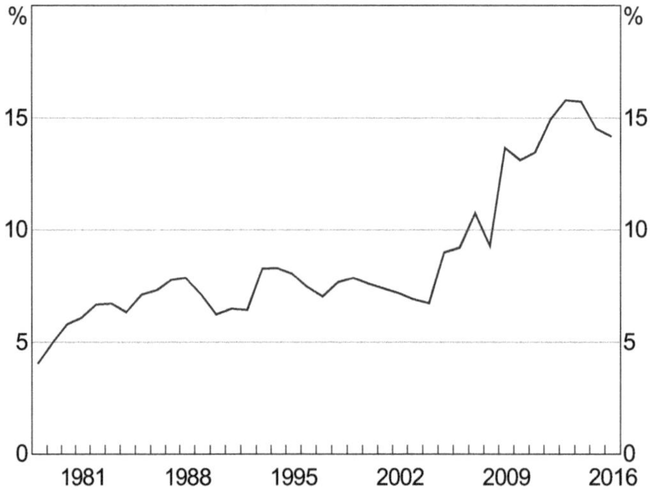

Figure 11.9 Residential investment: Share of nominal GDP
Sources: Authors' calculations; CEIC Data; Koen et al. (2013).

The rise of private home ownership in the late 1990s boosted incentives to save for households that were motivated to upgrade their housing and accumulate private assets, while generating higher investment. The property investment boom in the 2000s further boosted land sales proceeds accruing to local governments, helping to fund infrastructure investment. At the same time, increased mortgage borrowing drove larger gross interest payments and a corresponding fall in households' net property income, contributing to the decline in the household share of income in the 1990s and 2000s. In sum, the opening of the housing market can be viewed as a prolonged positive impulse to the economy, sustaining returns to capital, boosting investment and lifting both private and public savings (Ma et al. 2013; Xu et al. 2015).

Prospects for rebalancing domestic expenditure

It is commonly thought that a more balanced pattern of domestic demand in China would have local and global benefits. A higher consumption share could be directly welfare-enhancing if it is facilitated by reforms and policies that improve the income distribution and develop the social safety net. Some also argue that China's current account surplus underpinned global imbalances, which contributed to the GFC in 2008–09 (Obstfeld and Rogoff 2009). A further argument for rebalancing is that the high investment share has been sustained by sharply rising leverage. Rebalancing can therefore help address associated financial risks and reduce the likelihood of a financial crisis occurring (Pettis 2013).

Indeed, leverage has played an important role in China's unbalanced growth pattern, particularly since 2008. Prior to this, the foreign sector appeared to have accommodated China's big capacity build-up without much leverage, as the current account surplus surged (Figure 11.10). Despite the 1998–2008 investment boom, the nation's total credit to the private nonfinancial sector as a share of GDP rose modestly, from 106 per cent to 116 per cent. In part, this reflected rapid price inflation in the 2000s, which helped deflate the debt principal. However, from another perspective, it is likely rising Chinese investment was mostly 'funded' by a surge in retained earnings arising from a booming export market after China's WTO accession (Ma and Laurenceson 2017).

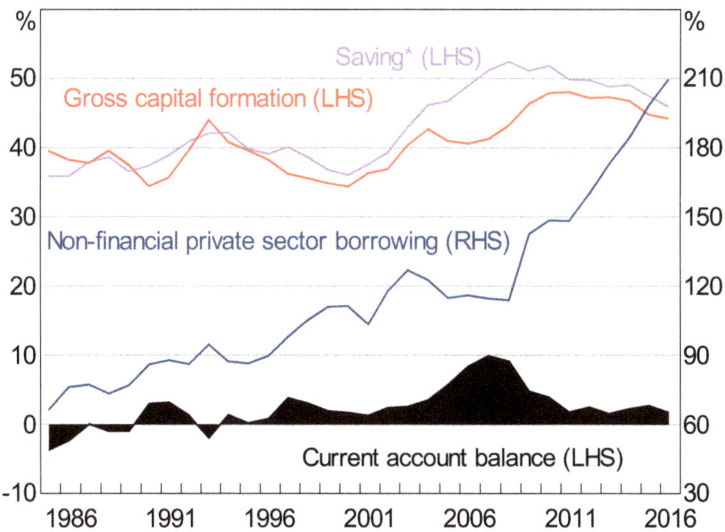

Figure 11.10 Saving, investment and leverage: Share of nominal GDP

* Gross capital formation plus current account balance.

Sources: Authors' calculations; CEIC Data; NBS (2015).

In contrast, the shrinking of China's current account surplus—from 10 per cent of GDP in 2007 to 2 per cent by 2014—coincided with a rapid 'leveraging up'. The surplus saving was reduced by a sharp increase in investment growth, as Chinese policymakers responded aggressively to the negative external demand shock due to the GFC through a combination of monetary and fiscal stimulus. Total credit to the nonfinancial private sector jumped from 116 per cent of GDP in 2008 to 210 per cent in 2016. Finally, externally oriented firms—pressured by weaker cash flows due to dwindling overseas sales—may have resorted to higher leverage to fund replacement investment. Thus, the rapid compression of China's external surplus, while reducing global imbalances, arguably came at the price of a steep rise in domestic leverage.

How might expenditure rebalancing play out in practice? The very high rate of consumption growth in recent years suggests that, realistically, any rebalancing to a higher consumption share is more likely to involve a deceleration of investment than an acceleration of consumption. The historical record supports this view. Ma et al. (2016, 2017) have shown that in a sample of 167 economies between 1950 and 2011, there are only 10 cases of expenditure rebalancing on this definition. In the majority of cases, household consumption growth in the period after such a 'rebalancing' was lower than in the previous period. The reasons behind historical rebalancing experiences are also diverse. In some cases (such as that of Angola in the 1990s and early 2000s), the timing corresponds to periods of political conflict and famine, while in others (such as Thailand and South Korea in the same period), a degree of rebalancing followed external crises.

Thus, the way in which rebalancing proceeds depends on the reasons for the imbalances. In China's case, it is likely that saved windfalls from positive shocks helped to drive the unbalanced expenditure pattern. The reversal of these shocks as the working-age population declines, the pace of urbanisation slows, the effects of earlier market-oriented reforms fade and housing markets mature is likely to foster rebalancing in the future.

The role of maturing housing markets may prove to be especially important. The housing sector has evolved from an initial undersupply 20 years ago to a more even supply–demand balance currently, even with some pockets of oversupply (Wu et al. 2015) where returns to new investment have fallen. The outlook for urbanisation and demographics suggests that in trend terms Chinese residential construction may already have peaked (Berkelmans and Wang 2012; Perkins 2015). The eventual withdrawal of this prolonged positive impulse to investment could be expected to propel the rebalancing process.

The return to capital: A mechanism for expenditure rebalancing

As slower investment growth—rather than even faster consumption growth—is the main channel through which expenditure rebalancing is likely to occur, we now consider a key mechanism: the decline in the return to capital relative to the cost of funding new corporate investment in China. To do so, we estimate the return to capital using an approach similar to that of Bai et al. (2006), based on Jorgenson's (1967) neoclassical theory of investment.[6]

The basic equation to obtain a real net rate of return for owners of capital is Equation 11.2.

Equation 11.2

$$R_t = i_t - \dot{P}_t^Y = \frac{\alpha_t(P_t^Y Y_t)}{P_t^K K_t} + \left[\dot{P}_t^K - \dot{P}_t^Y\right] - \delta_t$$

In Equation 11.2, i_t measures the nominal return to capital, P_t^Y is the GDP deflator, P_t^K is the price of capital (proxied by the investment deflator), α_t is the capital share of income, Y_t is total income, K_t is the capital stock and δ_t is the depreciation rate. In this formulation, the return to capital comprises three parts: an estimate of the marginal revenue product of capital, a 'capital gain' term (the change in the price of capital in terms of consumables) and a depreciation rate. When the prices of capital and output are the same, the return to capital equals the marginal physical product of capital ($\alpha_t Y_t / K_t$)—the product of the capital share and the inverse capital–output ratio—net of depreciation.

Our calculation uses the National Bureau of Statistics (NBS) expenditure-side estimate of GDP in constant 1978 prices and a corresponding deflator. We derive estimates of real gross capital formation (GCF) and the investment deflator using data on expenditure-side contributions published for the period 1978–2016. We use these data to construct an aggregate capital stock using the perpetual inventory method (for details, see Ma et al. 2016). We calculate the capital share, α_t, by estimating the labour share, $1 - \alpha_t$, using flow-of-funds labour compensation data. To extend the sample, we back-cast the pre-1992 labour share using provincial compensation data and project it to 2016 using (rescaled) household income data from the NBS household survey, which tracks the flow-of-funds labour compensation data closely.

Figure 11.11 shows our estimates of the capital–output ratio and the labour share of income. The capital–output ratio has grown rapidly in recent years, although it increased at a slowing pace through the late 1990s and early 2000s, even declining in 2007. Yet, coinciding with the government's macroeconomic stimulus in 2008–09, it began to increase sharply and has since maintained its upward trajectory.

6 For a more detailed discussion of our approach, see Ma et al. (2016).

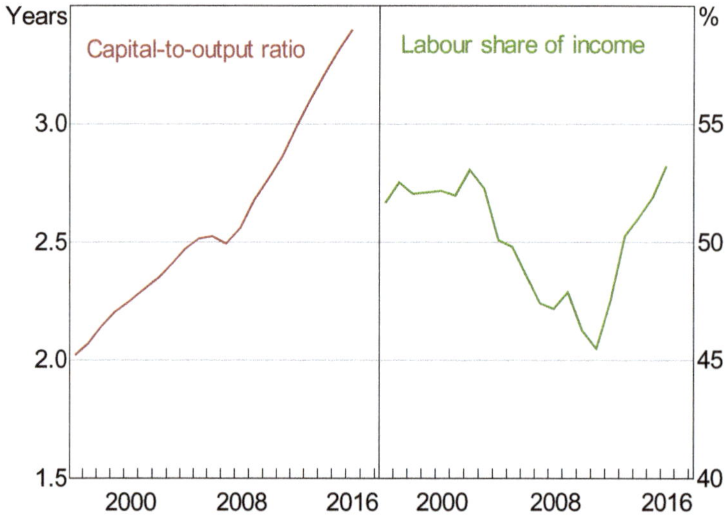

Figure 11.11 Components of the return to capital
Sources: Authors' calculations; CEIC Data; NBS.

The labour share of income fell from the mid-1990s onwards, contributing to China's high return to capital until the early 2010s; since 2011, however, the downward trend has reversed, weighing on the return to capital while supporting private consumption. This experience differs from that of many advanced economies that have seen the labour share of income continue a trend decline (Karabarbounis and Neiman 2014). One possible reason for the reversal is that China's working-age population has started to decline, weighing on growth in the labour supply. This may have been reinforced by slowing rural–urban migration, consistent with assessments that China has passed the 'Lewisian turning point' at which the quantity of 'surplus' labour in the countryside begins to decline, lifting unit labour costs (Garnaut and Song 2006; Cai 2011; Ma et al. 2013).[7] Industrial structure has also changed noticeably since the early 2000s, characterised by a shift from agriculture and capital-intensive heavy manufacturing towards services, which probably increased the labour share. While changes in future circumstances (such as a tendency towards increased automation or a more general revival in incentives to invest that raise capital intensity) could alter this trend, if the labour share continues to rise, it is likely to support further expenditure rebalancing in coming years.

Combining the above ingredients, we obtain an estimate of the return to capital (Figure 11.12). Our estimate suggests that the return to capital increased in the mid-2000s, but, since 2008, has experienced an oscillating decline. Mechanically, the decline can be accounted for largely by a resumption of the upward trend in the

7 See also the special issue, 'Debating the Lewis Turning Point in China', of the *China Economic Journal* (Vol. 3, No. 2, 2010).

capital–output ratio. More intuitively, it reflects a fall in the 'efficiency' of investment (a declining marginal increment to GDP growth from each unit of investment), consistent with slowing productivity growth, as well as more moderate growth in aggregate demand after the peak period of stimulus in the late 2000s. Until 2011, the falling labour share of income offset the deteriorating marginal product of capital, but the rebound in the labour share has reinforced it more recently.

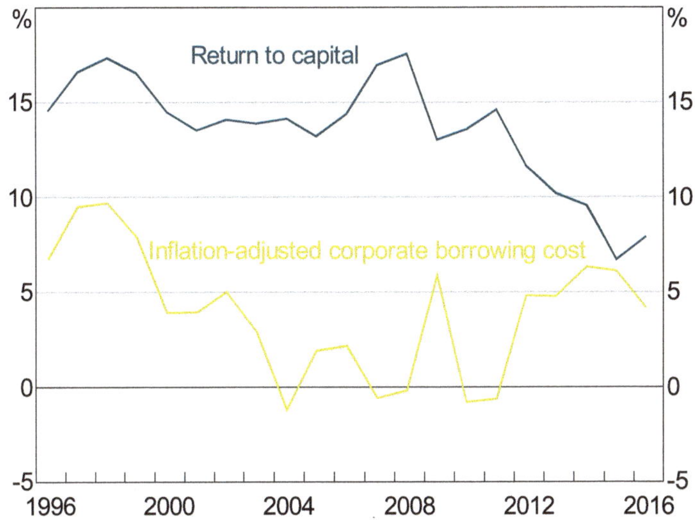

Figure 11.12 Return to capital and corporate borrowing cost

Sources: Authors' calculations; CEIC Data; NBS.

As business investment hinges on the gap between the prevailing corporate funding cost and the expected earnings from new projects, it is likely that the decline of the return to capital since 2008 has reduced incentives for new investment. To consider this trade-off, we compare the estimated return to capital with an estimate of inflation-adjusted corporate borrowing costs. We proxy the latter with a weighted average of selected bank, bond and 'shadow banking' interest rates, deflated using the implicit GDP deflator.[8]

The broad trends in our return to capital and financing cost indicators suggest that the gap has probably narrowed considerably in recent years. Combined with the easing of macroeconomic stimulus after 2010 and efforts by authorities to achieve a gradual slowing in broad credit growth, the narrowing gap may help account for the halving of the average pace of China's investment, from 15 per cent in the first decade of the 2000s to 7–8 per cent in the current decade.

8 See Ma et al. (2016) for a discussion of data sources and details of the calculations.

However, after several years of convergence, the return to capital and the corporate borrowing cost diverged modestly again in 2016.[9] Our calculations align with the observed pick-up in producer price inflation and industrial profits in 2016, both of which can plausibly be considered outcomes of the 'supply-side structural reform' policies adopted by the Chinese Government in late 2015, as discussed in the next section. This raises the broader question of how the mix of policies and reforms being pursued by the Chinese Government affects the incentives for investment, and whether they are likely to foster rebalancing away from investment or impede it in the future.

Implications of reforms and macroeconomic policies for rebalancing

While the fading of favourable demand and productivity shocks and the rise in the capital–output ratio have been instrumental in expenditure rebalancing to date, looking ahead, macroeconomic policy, economic reforms and institutional factors will also play important roles in shaping this process. However, as the timing and speed of their evolution may not be coordinated, the net implications for expenditure rebalancing are not straightforward. Furthermore, the links between reform and rebalancing are not unidirectional. Reform never proceeds in a vacuum: it is undertaken in response to socioeconomic developments and pressures that on their own may already be leading to a more balanced growth pattern. These points can be illustrated with reference to the three overlapping streams of reform-related initiatives announced since the start of China's current administration.

The first wave of reforms are those stemming from the third plenum of the eighteenth Central Committee of the Chinese Party (CCP) in 2013, at which the leadership pledged a 'decisive role' for the market in resource allocation. Subsequent initiatives included: a relaxation of the one-child policy; expanded funding for social security; value-added tax reform; efforts to support technological innovation; policies to strengthen the governance and efficiency of SOEs; and deregulation in parts of the financial sector (following efforts undertaken during previous administrations). A second wave of policies belong to the 'supply-side structural reform' (SSSR) package announced in 2015, which primarily sought to address rising leverage and excess capacity, and facilitate industrial upgrading. A third wave of announcements was made during and after the nineteenth national congress of the CCP in 2017, which, among other things, aim to control systemic financial risks and focus more on environmentally sustainable and higher 'quality' growth (potentially with less

9 Mechanically, the increase in the estimated return to capital (in both nominal and real terms) was due to a significant reversal of deflation in the price of capital (proxied by the investment deflator) in 2016. At the same time, a related pick-up in economy-wide inflation lowered the inflation-adjusted cost of borrowing.

emphasis on GDP growth targets). The multifaceted nature of these programs, the shifting emphasis placed on them by the government and the uncertainty surrounding their implementation undermine a simplistic equation of 'reform' with 'rebalancing'.

We can consider first the case of the SSSR policies, which seek to address a number of pressing economic challenges. The SSSR package comprises various interventions to reduce industrial excess capacity, evict unprofitable 'zombie enterprises', lower housing inventory, support technological innovation and slow the build-up of corporate leverage.[10] Such policies could, if implemented effectively, also enhance the *efficiency* of investment and facilitate domestic expenditure rebalancing by reducing the impact on national income and consumption of a given slowing in investment growth. Administrative restrictions on new investment into 'overcapacity' sectors could also help further slow overall investment growth. However, other components could help sustain an unbalanced pattern of growth for longer. In particular, lowering financing costs for businesses and introducing capacity/supply restrictions that raise output prices could boost the return to capital (as suggested by our estimates for 2016) and encourage stronger investment than might otherwise occur. Nonetheless, by increasing corporate profits and nominal GDP growth, these policies could also lift the ratio of capital expenditure that is funded internally by firms and slow the accumulation of corporate debt (Ma and Laurenceson 2017).

The recent drive to control financial risks is also relevant for rebalancing. The gradual deregulation of the financial system over the past decade has contributed to financial deepening but also to an expansion of nonbank finance and 'shadow banking' funding channels. Moreover, the surge in credit demand from local governments during the 2008–09 stimulus encouraged a proliferation of local financing vehicles to circumvent regulations prohibiting local government bond issuance. Rapid financial innovation, combined with fragmented oversight, probably slowed the process of expenditure rebalancing. The recent shift in policy emphasis towards tougher and better coordinated regulation of shadow finance has scope to dampen inefficient investment activities. However, initiatives to support deleveraging in the corporate sector are more likely to succeed, in practice, if the general growth pattern shifts to one that is less focused on rapid debt-financed capital accumulation. In other words, rebalancing away from investment may be as much a precondition for deleveraging as it is a consequence.

Similarly, plans to foster a more environmentally sustainable pattern of growth, featuring reduced carbon dioxide emissions and lower reliance on fossil fuels, may only be possible if investment in construction, plants and equipment—all of which tend to be energy-intensive—can grow at a more moderate pace. Related policies

10 The official description of these policies embodies five aspects: deleveraging, destocking, reducing excess capacity, reducing costs and addressing 'weak links' in the economy (Xinhua News Agency 2016).

include production cuts in heavily polluting regions to meet air quality targets and plans to build a nationwide emissions trading scheme. Yet, in a development sense, the shift to a less carbon-intensive, less polluting pattern of growth may be more a *consequence* of an expanding middle class and higher living standards than it is a cause. The need for reform is endogenous to rising pressure on policymakers from more affluent Chinese citizens with higher expectations of a clean environment. Indeed, the higher incomes, changing consumption behaviour and greater lifestyle-related expectations of these citizens are already supporting expenditure rebalancing. It is also worth noting that efforts to improve environmental sustainability may support faster investment in green energy, hybrid vehicles and recycling capacity, partly offsetting any slowing in less sustainable forms of investment.

If successful, endeavours to strengthen social security—especially measures to resolve funding gaps and to allow portability of welfare benefits across jurisdictions that are otherwise restricted by *hukou* policies—could have a range of effects, including increased labour mobility, faster urbanisation and reduced motives for precautionary household saving. The announcement in 2017 of a new round of equity injections from SOEs to supplement the national and regional pension funds signals some momentum in this direction. Reforms that facilitate a fall in the national saving rate are, ultimately, essential for domestic expenditure rebalancing to occur without a material rise in the external imbalance. However, despite the fact that better-funded and more universal social welfare coverage could help reduce households' propensity to save, policies that facilitate urbanisation could boost the labour supply in urban areas, thus tempering growth in wages and consumption, and may fuel public demands for improved or expanded urban infrastructure.

Finally, it is worth emphasising that a reduction in investment growth, for whatever reason, may only result in a more balanced expenditure pattern if it is accompanied by an increase in the *efficiency* of investment. Using a simple framework, Ma et al. (2017) illustrate how, mechanically, for an unchanged efficiency of investment (proxied by the inverse of the incremental capital–output ratio), the benefits for consumption growth of a faster rebalancing away from investment are cancelled by the negative overall effects on growth. Therefore, reforms that lower costs for businesses, lower barriers to entry in markets and create a more level playing field between the private sector and SOEs could enhance the efficiency of new investment so that less investment is required to generate a given amount of income (and consumption) growth. Reforms that aim to improve the efficiency of SOEs may also facilitate rebalancing, but this possibility is counterbalanced by the risk that contemporaneous efforts to create stronger 'national champions' could unintentionally give priority to size rather than efficiency and reduce competition from the private sector.

While the net implications of the government's multifaceted agenda are uncertain, and reform is not entirely exogenous vis-à-vis rebalancing, the importance of government policy for the pattern of growth cannot be underestimated. The reduced emphasis on headline growth targets apparent at the nineteenth party congress could facilitate a slowdown in investment growth. Moreover, aspirations to enhance investment efficiency, improve the social safety net and lower precautionary saving by households collectively have the potential to lend support to the rebalancing process in the longer term.

Conclusion

This chapter has considered the prospects for continued expenditure rebalancing in China—that is, a shift from a pattern of growth driven by investment to one driven by consumption—and the interplay with the government's reform plans. Our preferred explanation for the expenditure imbalance emphasises the role played by the opening up and deregulation of housing markets as one of multiple prolonged positive productivity and demand impulses to the Chinese economy over 40 years of reform that simultaneously boosted private and public saving, sustained returns to capital and lifted investment.

An analysis of the flow-of-funds accounts reveals that conventional analysis understates the role of the household sector in contributing to the high investment share of the economy by neglecting the effect on investment of households' housing purchases. We argue that the rebalancing to date has occurred, at least in part, as an outcome of dwindling income windfalls from worsening demographics, fading positive productivity shocks and maturing housing markets—all of which helped to drive the imbalances in the first place.

We also present estimates suggesting that the return to capital has been trending lower while the domestic cost of funding has been rising. Although the rebound in industrial inflation and profitability in 2016 at least temporarily slowed these trends, if they resume in the medium term, they are likely to place additional downward pressure on investment growth. The extraordinary resilience of Chinese consumption in recent years suggests that any rebalancing is likely to be driven by weaker growth of investment rather than even stronger consumption growth.

Finally, we argue that the mix of policies and reform plans now being pursued by the government will condition the speed and extent of future rebalancing. In some cases, such as environmental policies and financial risk reduction, the achievement of reform objectives will itself be contingent on a less investment-intensive pattern of growth. In many cases, the effects of government policies on the consumption and investment shares of GDP are ambiguous *ex ante*. Certainly, endeavours to strengthen and broaden the social safety net have scope to reduce household saving and support consumption growth. Likewise, policies that lift the efficiency of investment through deleveraging and greater market discipline could help ameliorate the negative effects of lower investment growth on household income and consumption. Yet the promise of these initiatives must be balanced against the possibility that other policies could help an unbalanced pattern of growth persist for longer, and the concern that cultivating bigger and stronger SOEs could inadvertently prioritise size over efficiency and reduce competition from the private sector.

References

Bai, C.-E. and Qian, Z. (2010), The factor income distribution in China: 1978–2007, *China Economic Review* 21(4): 650–70. doi.org/10.1016/j.chieco.2010.08.004.

Bai, C.-E., Hsieh, C.-T. and Qian, Y. (2006), The return to capital in China, *Brookings Papers on Economic Activity* 2(2006): 61–101.

Berkelmans, L. and Wang, H. (2012), *Chinese urban residential construction to 2040*, RBA Research Discussion Paper No. 2012-04, Sydney: Reserve Bank of Australia.

Berkelmans, L., Kelly, G. and Sadeghian, D. (2016), Chinese monetary policy and the banking system, *Journal of Asian Economics* 46: 38–55. doi.org/10.1016/j.asieco.2016.08.001.

Bernanke, B. (2007), Global imbalances: Recent developments and prospects, The Bundesbank Lecture, 11 September, Berlin.

Blanchard, O. and Giavazzi, F. (2006), Rebalancing growth in China: A three-handed approach, *China & World Economy* 14(4): 1–20. doi.org/10.1111/j.1749-124X.2006.00027.x.

Cai, F. (2011), *Beyond Demographic Dividends*, Series on Chinese Economics Research, vol. 5, Singapore: World Scientific Publishing.

Chamon, M. D. and Prasad, E. S. (2010), Why are saving rates of urban households in China rising?, *American Economic Journal: Macroeconomics* 2(1): 93–130. doi.org/10.1257/mac.2.1.93.

Corden, W. M. (1960), The geometric representation of policies to attain internal and external balance, *The Review of Economic Studies* 28(1): 1–22. doi.org/10.2307/2296244.

Fang, H., Gu, Q., Xiong, W. and Zhou, L.-A. (2016), Demystifying the Chinese housing boom, in M. Eichenbaum and J. Parker (eds), *NBER Macroeconomics Annual 2015. Volume 30*, Chicago: University of Chicago Press.

Garnaut, R. and Ma, G. (1993), 'Economic Growth and Stability in China', *Journal of Asian Economics* 4(1): 5–24. doi.org/10.1086/685953.

Garnaut, R. and Song, L. (eds) (2006), *The Turning Point in China's Development*, Canberra: ANU E Press and Asia Pacific Press. doi.org/10.26530/OAPEN_459745.

Huang, Y. and Tao, K. (2011), *Causes of and remedies for the People's Republic of China's external imbalances: The role of factor market distortions*, ADBI Working Paper No. 279, Tokyo: Asian Development Bank Institute.

Jorgenson, D. (1967), The theory of investment behavior, in R. Ferber (ed.), *Determinants of Investment Behavior*, New York: Columbia University Press.

Karabarbounis, L. and Neiman, B. (2014), The global decline of the labor share, *Quarterly Journal of Economics* 129(1): 61–103. doi.org/10.1093/qje/qjt032.

Koen, V., Herd, R., Wang, X. and Chalaux, T. (2013), *Policies for inclusive urbanisation in China*, OECD Economics Department Working Papers No. 1090, Paris: OECD Publishing.

Kuijs, L. (2005), *Investment and saving in China*, World Bank Policy Research Working Paper No. 3633, Washington, DC: The World Bank.

Lardy, N. R. (2008), *Financial repression in China*, PIIE Policy Brief No. PB08-8, Washington, DC: Peterson Institute for International Economics.

Lardy, N. R. (2014), *Markets over Mao: The rise of private business in China*, Washington, DC: Peterson Institute for International Economics.

Ma, G. and Laurenceson, J. (2017), China's debt challenge: Stylized facts, drivers and policy implications, *The Singapore Economic Review* 61(1): 1–23. doi.org/10.1142/S0217590817420103.

Ma, G. and Wang, Y. (2010), China's high saving rate: Myth and reality, *International Economics* 122: 5–39. doi.org/10.1016/S2110-7017(13)60028-1.

Ma, G., McCauley, R. and Lam, L. (2013), The roles of saving, investment and the renminbi in rebalancing the Chinese economy, *Review of International Economics* 21(1): 72–84. doi.org/10.1111/roie.12021.

Ma, G., Roberts, I. and Kelly, G. (2016), A rebalancing Chinese economy: Challenges and international implications, in I. Day and J. Simon (eds), *Structural Change in China: Implications for Australia and the world*, RBA Annual Conference Volume, Sydney: Reserve Bank of Australia. Available from: www.rba.gov.au/publications/confs/2016/pdf/rba-conference-volume-2016-ma-roberts-kelly.pdf.

Ma, G., Roberts, I. and Kelly, G. (2017), Rebalancing China's economy: Domestic and international implications, *China & World Economy* 25(1): 1–31. doi.org/10.1111/cwe.12184.

Meade, J. E. (1951), *The Theory of International Economic Policy. Volume I: The balance of payments*, London: Oxford University Press.

Modigliani, F. and Cao, S. L. (2004), The Chinese saving puzzle and the life-cycle hypothesis, *Journal of Economic Literature* 42(1): 145–70. doi.org/10.1257/002205104773558074.

Nabar, M. (2011), *Targets, interest rates, and household saving in urban China*, IMF Working Paper No. WP/11/223, Washington, DC: International Monetary Fund.

National Bureau of Statistics (NBS) (2015), *Expenditure-Side GDP Data for 2013 and Historical Revisions*, 3 June, Beijing: China Statistics Press. Available from: www.stats.gov.cn/tjsj/zxfb/201506/t20150603_1114905.html.

Obstfeld, M. and Rogoff, K. (2009), *Global imbalances and the financial crisis: Products of common causes*, CEPR Discussion Paper Series No. 7606, Washington, DC: Centre for Economic Policy Research.

Perkins, D. H. (2015), Understanding the slowing growth rate of the People's Republic of China, *Asian Development Review* 32(1): 1–30. doi.org/10.1162/ADEV_a_00040.

Pettis, M. (2013), *Avoiding the Fall: China's economic restructuring*, Washington, DC: Carnegie Endowment for International Peace.

Raby, G. (2001), The 'neither this nor that' economy, in R. Garnaut and Y. Huang (eds), *Growth Without Miracles*, London: Oxford University Press.

Song, L. (1998), China (and the Asian Financial Crisis), in R. McLeod and R. Garnaut (eds), *East Asia in Crisis: From being a miracle to needing one?*, London: Routledge.

State Council of the People's Republic of China (State Council) (2017), Consumption still key engine to drive economy: Premier Li, 11 November. Available from: english.gov.cn/premier/news/2017/11/11/content_281475938592094.htm.

Swan, T. W. (1963), Longer-run problems of the balance of payments, in H. W. Arndt and W. M. Corden (eds), *The Australian Economy: A volume of readings*, Melbourne: Cheshire.

Wu, J., Gyourko, J. and Deng, Y. (2015), *Evaluating the risk of Chinese housing markets: What we know and what we need to know*, NBER Working Paper No. 21346, Cambridge, MA: National Bureau of Economic Research.

Xinhua News Agency (2016), China headlines: Supply-side reform to keep Chinese economy fit, *Xinhua Net*, 4 January. Available from: news.xinhuanet.com/english/2016-01/04/c_134977011.htm.

Xu, X., Jia, H. and Li, J. (2015), On the role played by real estate in the growth of China's national economy, [in Chinese], *Social Sciences in China* 2015(1): 84–101.

12. China's price liberalisation and market reform: A historical perspective

Zhang Jun

China's old planned economy had many defects. The spontaneous partial changes in land contracting to households in rural areas in the early years of reform were fragmented and unsystematic, but they did not create the conditions for the meltdown of the planned economic system. Economic reform was put on the national agenda in 1984, when the third plenary session of the twelfth Central Committee of the Communist Party (CCCP) passed its 'Decision on the Reform of the Economic Structure'. This decision set the goal of establishing a 'socialist commodity economy'—an audacious innovation at the time. After that, China's economic strategy lifted its focus from the urban economy to comprehensive reform. This initial step towards market reform and deregulation in China was followed, 10 years later, at the third plenary session of the fourteenth CCCP, by enunciation of the goal to create a market economy with Chinese characteristics.

To establish a 'commodity' and then a market economy, China had to liberalise the planning mechanism for fixing prices, correct price distortions in outputs and inputs and 'get prices right'. The shift in the focus of reform from agriculture to the urban economy made the last goal more complicated. At that time, food and basic consumer products were rationed in cities. State-owned enterprises (SOEs) formed a significant part of the economy, controlling prices for the means of production. Even an adjustment in 1 cent for a box of matches would have to be discussed and approved by the State Council, and price changes involved many sectoral vested interests.

The key issue was finding the optimal way to implement price reform. Should it be letting go of price control in a single step or a gradual adjustment of planned prices to eliminate supply shortages? Was China in a position to ease price control in one go? Was it possible to realise the equilibrium price by gradually adjusting prices? How great would be the shock on the economy and society? Would price reform result in hyperinflation and consequently suffocate reform? These became hard issues in 1984 and beyond—not only for the leaders of reform, who were uncertain of which process to take, but also for Chinese economists.

By 1984, China already allowed the coexistence of two pricing systems for some agricultural products and several means of production. After 1984, Chinese economists started a focused discussion on the transition to price reform and a 'dual-track system'. A symposium in September 1984 was particularly important.

Moganshan symposium

The First Symposium of Young and Middle-Aged Economists was held from 3 to 10 September 1984 on Moganshan Mountain in Zhejiang province. The organisers called for papers early in March and received ardent responses from young economists from universities and research institutes and from the young and middle-aged in government departments.

More than 1,300 papers were received, of which 120 were formally accepted. The symposium was sponsored by the relevant central government departments and supported by local government. The secretary of Zhejiang's provincial party committee, the governor and other leaders delivered speeches, and seven task forces discussed papers, which were subsequently published.

Many participants in the Moganshan symposium were well nurtured in economic theories and sharp in expressing novel ideas. The discipline of the young participants earned the respect of their older comrades.

The symposium discussed eight topics:

1. strategies of price reform
2. self-financing for industrial enterprises
3. multipurpose issues concerning key cities
4. opening up to the outside world in 14 coastal cities
5. problems with financial system reform
6. the development and management of the stock-holding economy
7. changes in rural industrial structure
8. the current economic functions of the government.

The most fruitful theoretical and ideological discussion was on the strategic issues of price reform.

The symposium's first conclusion was that prices of industrial mining products should be raised. The second was to adjust the prices of and excessive subsidies for agricultural products. Two competing approaches were put forward on industrial price reform: combining adjustment with deregulation, while focusing on adjustment, and combining adjustment with deregulation and adjustment after deregulation. The supporters of these ideas were labelled the 'adjustment group' and the 'deregulation group'. A third approach gained support at the end of the meeting: dual-track pricing of the means of production, unifying the two prices by gradually reducing centrally planned prices and gradually increasing the scope of market regulation. Hua Sheng wrote a summary of the symposium entitled 'To smoothly implement price reform via an intended dual-track system' (see Huang 2005).

In 2005, Hua published an article titled 'The beginning and the end of the dual-track system' about the discussion of the 'dual-track system' at the Moganshan symposium:

> The controversy existed initially between people for adjustment and those for deregulation. At that time, the mainstream participants who favored adjustment, either major or minor, argued in detail the necessity and urgency of the price reform and the feasibility of the price adjustment plan. They also depicted the difficulties and risks of [a] one-step move towards a balanced market price. However, Zhang Weiying, a graduate student from China's Northwestern University and the representative of the deregulation school, advocated one-step or step-by-step deregulation of price control and the implementation of prices according to market supply and demand. The main argument against the deregulation school was that in the context of a planned economy, the one-step deregulation of price control was too unrealistic, and the market development also required a process of being nurtured. Since the market was not perfect, the equilibrium price of [the] market was difficult to realize, and such [a] price might not be optimized ... [A] group of postgraduates (Hua Sheng, He Jiacheng, Jiang Yue, Gao Liang and Zhang Shaojie) from the Chinese Academy of Social Sciences and Renmin University ... finally formed the idea of implementing the dual-track system with the combination of deregulation and adjustment; and entrusted me to participate in the listed debate and defense on behalf of all of us. (Hua 2005: 22–3)

The above has been verified by Gao Liang, who works for the National Development and Reform Commission in Beijing and who attended the Moganshan symposium as a postgraduate student of the Chinese Academy of Social Sciences (CASS). An interview with Gao was cited in Huang's (2005) article in the *Economic Observer*. Gao said the adjustment group could also have been labelled the 'price-calculating group'. At that time, the central government established a huge price model for computer analysis. Zhou Xiaochuan, Li Jiange, Lou Jiwei and other scholars from CASS and Tsinghua University also tested their models, hoping to estimate the equilibrium prices and deregulated prices in one go via the government's price adjustment. However, as price adjustment affected many vested interests, reform would encounter enormous resistance regardless of the approach. At the Moganshan symposium, a group of scholars represented by Tian Yuan, who had participated in policy research, focused on 'adjustment'. In contrast, the 'deregulation group'—represented by Zhang Weiying, a postgraduate student of China's Northwestern University—advocated gradual, step-by-step price control to bring about prices determined by market supply and demand (see Huang 2005).

The adjustment and deregulation groups actively published articles elucidating their views (representative articles include Lou and Zhou 1984; Guo 1985; Zhang 1985). The third group's suggestion of a dual-track transition with a combination of deregulation and adjustment immediately attracted the attention of State Council leaders. The CCCP's Decision on the Reform of the Economic System (October 1984), which was passed shortly after the Moganshan symposium, emphasised that reform of the price system would be the key to the success or failure of economic reform. In March 1985, the State Council officially abolished price control of above-quota producer goods. This decision was considered formal acceptance of dual-track reform. Hua et al. (1985) elaborated on the formation of the idea of the dual-track price system.

In 1988, on the 10th anniversary of the beginning of China's economic reform, Hua et al. (1988) published a long essay, referring to the Moganshan symposium and the process of formation of the idea of the dual-track price system. Their paper was immediately criticised, however, and their claims questioned by Shi Xiaomin and Liu Jirui (1989), who pointed out that the idea of a dual-track price system in China developed before 1984, and had been in use since 1979 for the reform of prices for agricultural products and other commodities. As for dual-track pricing of the means of production, Shi and Liu (1989) held that such a practice was clearly recognised in the 'Ten Articles on Power Expansion' promulgated by the State Council in May 1984—four months before the Moganshan symposium.

Twenty-three years later, Hua Sheng's memory of the Moganshan symposium was still quite fresh. He recalled in an interview with the *Southern Weekend*:

> At that time I was a representative of the price group and reported to Mr Zhang Jinfu, then General Secretary of the Leading Group of the CPC Central Financial and Economic Committee. I was particularly impressed by this event. Shortly after the Moganshan symposium, the Third Plenary Session of the 12th CPC Central Committee was held, and, as Deng Xiaoping said, this meeting rendered something new that had never been mentioned by the forefathers of CPC.[1] During that plenary session, the CPC Central Committee made a decision on the reform of the economic structure … [This] was the heyday of reform, when we were often invited to attend the meetings of the State Council, and to organize reform pilots around the country. (Southern Weekend 2007: D27)

1 Deng Xiaoping's comment on the CCCP's decision on economic system reform comes from his speech to the third plenary session of the Central Advisory Commission on 22 October 1984. The original reads: 'I said a few words when the Central Committee passed the decision the day before yesterday. I said that my impression was that a first draft of political economy has been written and that this is the political economy which has combined the basic principles of Marxism with the practices of Chinese socialism. I have this comment … This economic reform document is good, in the sense that has explained what is socialism, some sayings that have not [been] spoken by our CPC forefathers, some new words. I suppose that we have made it clear. In the past it was impossible for us to have composed such a document, and it is impossible to write such a document without a few years of practice.' See Deng (1993: 83–91).

The evolution of dual-track pricing

After 1984, the central government adopted dual-track pricing as the transition strategy for market reform, but would this eventually lead to a market-clearing system? In my book *Economics of Dual-Track System* (Zhang 1997), I pointed out that the dual-track pricing of some products before 1984 was related to the partial reform of incentive policies in the system of product distribution and increased autonomy for producers (decentralisation). After 1984, the dual-track pricing system was adopted as a planned strategy for transition to promote micro-reforms and the establishment of a market system.

The Great Leap Forward in 1957 and the Cultural Revolution in 1966 had greatly weakened the centralisation of the Chinese economy, causing deviation from the model of the former Soviet Union. In the Soviet Union, SOEs were vertically integrated across production, supply and marketing by the specialised departments (Chinese planning officials called these 'lines') of the central government. Administrative decentralisation made all levels of local government (commonly known as 'blocks') in China—from the provinces (cities) to the lower-level counties—responsible for the management of some SOEs. Qian and Xu (1993) compared the organisational structure of China's planned management system with a multidepartmental corporate governance structure—that is, a multidivisional-form company.

This combination of lines and blocks that evolved through administrative decentralisation affected economic decentralisation and partial marketisation reforms after 1978. However, as this was simply an administrative decentralisation between central and local governments and did not involve the delegation of power to the firm level, no production or sales could be transacted above the planned quotas, although physical barter or swaps often occurred among SOEs affiliated with different planning administrators.[2]

One of the effects of the delegation to local government of power over the product allocation system was to enhance their planning allocation powers (Huang 1987). The number of products under central and departmental administration fell far short of that in the Soviet system (see Table 12.1). The share of planned products allocated by local governments, however, was increasing, including even some first- and second-class materials previously under central or departmental administration; in addition, products of the 'five small industries' (farm machinery, iron and steel, coal, fertilisers and cement), developed during the Cultural Revolution, came under local government administration. Table 12.1 shows that, in 1965, the share of coal allocated by the central government rose to 75 per cent, with the other

2 The work of Pan Zhenming and Luo Shouchu in 1988 analyses the material exchange between enterprises under the planned economy (Pan and Luo 1988). For the differences between administrative decentralisation and economic decentralisation, see Liu (1988).

25 per cent allocated by local governments. In 1978, the local government share was 46 per cent. It was a similar story for cement: the local government share increased from 29 per cent in 1965 to 64 per cent in 1978, and to 70 per cent in 1979. The local government share of iron and steel soared to 42 per cent in 1979—an increase of 37 percentage points from 1965.

Table 12.1 Share of products under planned allocation by local government (per cent)

Product	1965	1978	1979
Coal	25	46	46
Iron and steel	5	20	42
Timber	37	19	18
Cement	29	64	70
Lathe	n.a.	65	n.a.
Automobile	n.a.	25	n.a.
Nonferrous metals	n.a.	n.a.	36

n.a. = not available.

Sources: Huang (1987); Granick (1990); Pan and Luo (1988).

Real economic decentralisation—that is, delegating decision-making power to producers—began in 1979. In July 1979, the State Council promulgated its Regulations on Enlarging the Autonomy of Business Administration, and first proposed that manufacturing enterprises should enjoy the right of marketing their own products. This was an important starting point for expanding the autonomy of SOEs and a crucial step in the reform of the planned allocation system. These regulations allowed producers to enjoy limited but important freedom of decision-making power over 'above-quota' output (Zhang 1997). According to these regulations, the products enterprises could sell themselves were limited to output above the production quota, products made from raw materials mainly obtained by the enterprises themselves, trial production of new products and old stock that the commercial and material sectors did not plan to purchase.

Chen and Qiao (1994) revealed that, even though there were strict limits on production beyond quotas, these expanded rapidly and, by 1984, covered virtually all the means of production under the centrally planned distribution system. The share of products sold by enterprises continued to increase.

In 1981, oil field operators were permitted to autonomously export crude oil above the base figure, at international market prices. In 1983, the state allowed the export of crude oil to substitute for imports refined with products sold on domestic markets at international prices. This generated dual prices for refined oil. To encourage increased coal production, in 1983, the government chartered a price increase of 25–50 per cent for above-quota production in 22 stated-owned mining enterprises (SOMEs), also known as *kuangwuju*. In 1984, the updated charter planned to include up to 37 SOMEs in the initial stage of the dual-track pricing system by the end of the twentieth century (Zhang 1992). The Decision on Further Expanding the Autonomy of State-Owned Enterprises in May 1984 increased the decentralisation of enterprises based on the State Council's Provisions for Business Management Autonomy Expansion, promulgated in July 1979.

The 1984 decision allowed all above-quota industrial production materials sold by the enterprises themselves to be priced within ±20 per cent of the state-determined price. In January 1985, instructions from the State Council, the National Price Bureau and the National Materials Administration removed the original price limit of 20 per cent above the state-determined price and allowed enterprises to sell above-quota products at market prices. At the same time, SOEs were entitled to receive the planned transfer of supplies before 1983, while the quotas for allocated means of production would still be supplied at the transfer price based on the 1983 transfer quota. Output in excess of this base could be purchased at market prices. It could be said that, by this time, in the industrial sector, the dual-track pricing system for the means of production had been legalised.

From February to November 1985, the China Economic System Reform Institute and the Beijing Institute of Young Economists conducted a survey on the dual-track pricing practices of 429 state-owned industrial enterprises. In 1984, the ratio of self-produced production to total sales of these enterprises was 30.1 per cent. From January to June 1985, the ratio had risen to 43.8 per cent.[3]

A research report by Diao Xinshen, based on this survey, offers a good analysis of how dual-track pricing affected the production decisions and behaviour of SOEs. Diao (1986: 47–8) wrote:

> The dual-track system implies that there are, at the same time, two kinds of prices for the outputs and inputs of an enterprise: the official price set according to the state administrative regulations and the floating market price formed by the market forces or determined by both parties of the transaction. The products produced and materials supplied as planned or under the quotas will be transferred, bought and sold, and allocated according to the official prices; for those above the quotas, they will be sold or bought at the market price … the market price, in fact, has played a decisive role for output and input of an enterprise at the margin. And via this marginal function, signals and impact have been formed to adjust the short-term supply and demand.

3 The product of this survey is a book titled *Reform: The challenges and options we face* (Diao 1986).

According to the survey by the China Institute of Economic Reform (Diao 1986), from 1982 to 1984, China saw an increase of 105.1 million tonnes in coal production, 55.9 million tonnes of which came from rural and township–owned mines (53.2 per cent), 22.6 million tonnes from local government–owned mines (21.5 per cent) and 26.6 million tonnes from central government–allocated mines (25.3 per cent) (see Table 12.2).

Table 12.2 Above-quota growth rate in coal production (per cent)

Year	Share of national coal production		
	Centrally allocated mines	Local government–owned mines	Non–state-owned mines
1978	55.3	29.1	15.6
1979	56.3	26.7	17.0
1980	55.5	26.2	18.3
1981	53.9	25.7	20.4
1982	52.5	25.6	21.9
1983	50.8	25.4	23.8
1984	48.3	25.0	26.2
Increase of 1984 over 1978	21.1	8.4	70.4
Increase of 1984 over 1982	7.7	13.3	38.3

Sources: Data for 1982 and 1984 from Diao (1986); for other years, from Byrd (1987).

The surge in coal production by local government–owned and rural and township–owned mines was mainly a result of new investment. In 1983, local governments raised RMB770 million chiefly by setting up or enlarging coalmines; more than 40,000 rural and township collectively owned mines were established within one year and the newly increased production capacity of the large collectively owned mines reached more than 10 million tonnes. Under the dual-track price system, profit-oriented enterprises tended to invest over the long term in products that would be regulated largely by the market; and, in turn, the share of market regulation expanded to gain above-quota growth.

Debate over the dual-track price system and the comprehensive reform initiative

In 1985, when the dual-track price system had been implemented in the industrial sector and for production materials, Chinese economists started a heated debate over the merits of this system. Guo Shuqing, Liu Jirui, Wu Jinglian, Lou Jiwei and Zhou Xiaochuan were the main economists opposed to dual-track pricing. They were also the main drafters and advocates of the 'comprehensive reform initiative'.

A large part of the controversy over dual-track pricing in 1985 stemmed from associated macroeconomic imbalances and rent-seeking activities during the early years of transition to the new system. Gradual liberalisation of above-quota production and price controls allowed speculation in buying and selling outside quotas, and rent-seeking emerged among planning authorities. In 1984–85, high inflation was driven by explosive consumption spending. China's economists argued over what macromanagement policies should be implemented.

Economists who opposed the dual-track price system believed it increased inflationary pressure. In addition, the use of arbitrage opportunities by officials and enterprise executives seriously damaged the fair distribution of income.[4]

At the beginning of 1985, four CASS graduate students—Guo Shuqing, Lou Jiwei, Liu Jirui and Qiu Shufang—submitted a report to the State Council (Guo et al. 1985), in which they claimed the dual-track price system was fundamentally flawed and would lead to chaos and failure of market reform. Then, with the support of some leaders of the State Council, the students started work on the design of comprehensive reforms (Guo et al. 1986). In this research report, they pointed out the 'eight major demerits' of the dual-track price system. They advocated the speedy abolition of dual-track pricing and the adoption of a comprehensive reform strategy with a view to solving the current macroeconomic imbalance and the spread of corruption (Guo et al. 1986).

In 1986, Wu Jinglian, Zhou Xiaochuan, Guo Shuqing and Li Jiange, who were at that time working in the State Council Economic System Reform Design Office, undertook a series of studies on the overall progress of economic reform (see Wu et al. 1988). They openly opposed the dual-track price system, claiming it was the equivalent of allowing left-hand and right-hand driving on the same road, which would inevitably lead to crashes and chaos. They noted the coexistence of two prices encouraged buying and selling within and outside economic plans as well as rent-seeking activities, resulting in rampant corruption. Zhang Zhuoyuan (1992) has noted that some economists advocated that more than 80 per cent of dual-track prices should be merged into the planned system as soon as possible. Only the limited, less important means of production, and those that supplied enough quantity to meet demand, would be traded in the market.

Criticism of the dual-track price system peaked at this time (see Zhang 1992).

In 1988, Wu Jinglian, an influential Chinese economist, held seminars in Beijing and Shanghai on the drawbacks of the dual-track system and compiled the results of discussions into a publication entitled *Corruption: Exchange between power and money* (Wu 1993).

4 Wu (2003: 66–70) also analysed the negative consequences of the dual-track price system and partial marketisation.

The most heated controversy took place between 1988 and 1989 in the *Economic Research Journal*. Hua et al. (1988) held that the dual-track system was the basis of China's market reform. In early 1989, Shi and Liu responded, criticising and disproving the view of Hua et al.

Other economists still supported the idea of using dual-track pricing in the transition to market pricing. One of these was Liu Guoguang, a senior Chinese economist. In 1985, he argued that the dual-track price system could provide effective incentives for producers, reinforce awareness of the need for cost-cutting and ease shortages of certain supplies—all of which formed a viable path for China to follow in carrying out market-oriented reforms (Liu 1985).

From 2 to 7 September 1985, the International Symposium on Macroeconomic Management (known as the Bashan Ship Symposium) was hosted by the China Society for the Reform of the Economic System (later the National Economic Restructuring Commission), CASS and the World Bank on the *Bashan*, a cruise ship on the Yangtze River. Participating economists discussed the issue of price reform in China. In the proceedings of this symposium (Office of Development, Institute of Economic Research, Chinese Academy of Social Sciences 1987), Liu Guoguang and others mentioned the vigorous discussion on the importance of market transition via dual-track pricing, referring in particular to the positive attitude of Polish economist Professor Wlodzimierz Brus:

> In China's dual-track system, the dual prices of products within and outside the plan are a typical embodiment of the dual planning system and the dual material distribution system. In the process of mode conversion, starting from the price reform with the combination of adjustment and deregulation, employing the intended changes of dual prices, and promoting the overall reform of the economic system, we can thus avoid a big shock that may be incurred by the reform. As Brus has stated, in a change from the rationing system to the commodity system, other socialist countries used to practice dual prices on consumer goods, but China has introduced dual prices into the means of production—this may be a positive creation: it serves as a bridge from the old system to the new system, allowing a smooth transition from direct control of the administration to indirect control through the market. (Office of Development, Institute of Economic Research, Chinese Academy of Social Sciences 1987: 10)

Should the reform of China's economic system proceed step by step or in a single move? Economists today talk about these two different strategic approaches as 'radical reform' and 'gradualist reform'. Chinese economists' discussion of these issues came 10 years before mainstream economists in the West began work on theoretical issues of reform.

The most dramatic change in the formation of China's economic reform strategy occurred in 1986. Economists were divided over strategies for and the sequence of price reforms: should reform of prices or reform of enterprise ownership come first?

From the third plenary session of the eleventh CCCP in December 1978 to the third plenary session of the twelfth CCCP in October 1984, China's reform focused on the liberalisation of agricultural production. The CCCP did not develop an approach to the overall reform of the economic system. The breakthrough Decision on the Reform of the Economic Structure was passed at the third plenary session of the twelfth CCCP, clearly setting out the goal of establishing a socialist commodity economy, and shifting the focus of comprehensive reform from rural to urban areas.

The 1985 CCCP passed its 'Proposal for Enacting the Seventh Five-Year Plan (1986–1990)', which included establishing, over five or more years, a basic economic system coordinated by the three systems of enterprise autonomy, market allocation and macro control. During that time, China's macroeconomic imbalances—external payments and inflationary pressures—were large. Reform of the economic system against such a macroeconomic background became the most important issue.

With economists disagreeing about the focus and sequence of reforms, Professor Li Yining of Peking University famously asserted that 'if China's reform fails, it may fail in price reform; and if China's reforms succeeds, it must be the result of the success of ownership reform' (quoted in Wu 2003: 73). Li believed China's economy was in an unbalanced state, and would stay that way a long time. In an unbalanced economy, it was not practical to improve the economy through price reform; therefore, China should focus on reform of enterprise ownership. Only through this could distorted price relations be corrected.

Other economists—such as Guo Shuqing (then studying in CASS's Graduate School), Lou Jiwei, Liu Jirui, Qiu Shufang, Wu Jinglian, Zhou Xiaochuan, Guo Shuqing and Li Jiange (who later worked in the State Council Economic Structural Reform Office)—formed the idea of a comprehensive reform package. Their earlier work must have influenced Zhao Ziyang, then premier of the State Council.

Between January and March 1986, Zhao delivered speeches at the National Economic Work Conference, the CPC Central Financial and Economic Leading Group Meeting and State Council executive meetings. He said that, in 1987–88, major steps should be taken to speed up the establishment of an institutional environment conducive to micro-competition:

> Specifically, the reform in the next year [1987] can be designed and studied from the following three aspects: the first is the price, the second is the tax, and the third is the finance. These three aspects of reform are interrelated … The key is the reform of the price system, and other reforms are carried out around the center of the price reform. (Quoted in Wu 2003: 72)

The steps identified in Premier Zhao's speech were quickly executed, followed by planning and design of reform programs. In his book *Contemporary China's Economic Reform*, Professor Wu Jinglian briefly reviewed this detail of his participation:

> In order to carry out the proposed complementary reforms, the State Council established in April 1986 the Office of Economic Reform Program Design. Under the direct leadership of the State Council and the CPC Central Financial Leading Group, the office formulated the plan of complementary reforms focusing on price, taxation, finance and trade, of which the price reform was to start in 1987 in the means of production. The reform approach was similar to the one introduced by Ota Sik as early as 1981 to his Chinese counterparts of the practice of reform in Czechoslovakia in the mid-1960s: 'Adjust first, then deregulate.' First, comprehensive adjustments of prices were made … and then controls on prices were totally lifted in one or two years, so as to fully achieve the unification of all prices. In terms of finance and taxation, the major steps were to convert the revenue-sharing system into the tax-sharing system and to introduce the value-added tax (VAT) and so on. (Wu 2003: 72–3)

Wu (2003) wrote of a dramatic and sudden change. An executive meeting of the State Council originally approved the design of the comprehensive reform package in August 1986; Deng Xiaoping himself supported this idea and rated it highly. However, in October, the leadership of the State Council suddenly changed its mind and decided to focus on reforming the ownership of SOEs, putting aside the proposed comprehensive and complementary reforms on prices, taxes and finance. In 1987 and 1988, with Li Peng now premier of the State Council (and Zhao Ziyang general secretary of the CCP), it decided to implement the contract system in SOEs. In other words, Li's thinking prevailed, replacing the focus on comprehensive reform.

In May 1988, when the State Council planned to carry out reform of prices and wages, the leadership finally rejected the idea of 'governance first, and then breakthrough' proposed by Wu Jinglian, Liu Guoguang and others, and instead adopted the view of Li Yining. This explains the following comment by Wu Jinglian published on the (now closed) China Academic Forum website:

> For several key moments, the policy proposals that later proved to be correct have been put forward to the center, and the basic idea of the economic reform and development strategy that he [Li] proposed, as well as many other policy proposals (such as the anti-inflation suggestion of 1984–1988) have now been proved correct by practice, although successive government leaders have often overlooked his views.

We do not have sufficient information to understand why the leaders of the State Council changed their minds in October 1986; however, there was a direct connection with the current macroeconomic situation. After the State Council adopted a policy of economic tightening during the inflation of 1984–85 and the People's Bank of China adopted a stringent monetary policy in the second half of 1985—raising interest rates twice in a row and tightening credit control—the economic growth rate declined sharply, to zero, in February 1986. In this sensitive period of economic downturn, it was very likely the State Council would consider easing monetary policy to stimulate production. The short-term effect of a comprehensive reform package centred on price reform was likely to be economic tightening. However, the focus was on reform of the enterprise and financial contract systems, decentralising power and helping to improve supply and restore prosperity.

The dual-track price system: A miracle or a myth?

It is now generally accepted that China's gradualist transition to a market economy has been relatively successful and has accelerated economic growth over the past 40 years. This chapter has shown that assessments of the dual-track price system in the early stage of China's market reform are mixed and controversial. There are different views on whether the time frame for the hybrid system of dual-track pricing to begin functioning was too short or too long. Either way, the hybrid system of a planned and market economy can be witnessed almost everywhere in post-reform China.

The idea of a dual-track price system and the coexistence of planning and the market in the Chinese economy have stirred great interest among mainstream economists.

William Byrd, an economist for the World Bank, made the dual-track price system the topic of his doctoral dissertation in economics. Papers based on the dissertation were published in the *Journal of Comparative Economics* (Byrd 1987, 1989). In his 1989 paper, Byrd defined a simple general equilibrium model in the hope of verifying the existence of equilibrium under the dual-track price system. If equilibrium exists, does this equilibrium satisfy the conditions of Pareto optimality?

His model was simple. Some of the key assumptions were: the existence of planned pricing and planned quotas, free markets not covered by the plan, planned targets lower than the productive capacity of the enterprise (so-called leftover plans) and SOEs pursuing profit maximisation.

As long as some strict conditions are realised, the efficiency of the coexisting planned and market tracks is actually equivalent to that of the market track alone. The existence of a planned track only changes the distribution of income, not the level of efficiency. This is much like the case when an economic agent within a typical market system is faced with a fixed amount of tax or subsidy.

Lau et al. (1997, 2000) later offered a simpler theoretical treatment of the dual-track price system, which they treat as a mechanism for the allocation of goods, demonstrating its allocative and Pareto efficiency in the first case:

> If the plan quantity is less than the fully liberalized market equilibrium quantity, then, independently of the initial conditions concerning the plan price and the degree of efficiency of rationed demand and planned supply, (1) the dual-track approach with either limited or full liberalization of the market track is Pareto-improving, and (2) the dual-track approach with full liberalization of the market track achieves efficiency. (Lau et al. 2000: 128)

They also consider the second case where the planned quantity is greater than the equilibrium quantity of a perfect market. This case applies to the overproduction of goods such as tanks and other low-quality unwanted goods or to the overemployment of labour. Their discussion shows that the results of Case II are quite similar to those of Case I.

Under partially liberalised market conditions, surplus demand and surplus supply could be balanced via the market track. Due to the large quantity of planned allocations (assignments), however, the total equilibrium quantity would be greater than the efficient equilibrium quantity, which is not efficient, although it is Pareto-improving.

Under fully liberalised market conditions, however, Lau et al. (2000) find that allocative efficiency can only be achieved when the rights and obligations in the plan can be exchanged on the market. They reach a different conclusion:

> If the plan quantity is greater than the fully liberalized market equilibrium quantity, then independently of the initial conditions concerning the plan prices and the degree of efficiency of rationed demand and planned supply, (1) the dual-track approach with limited or full liberalization is always Pareto-improving and (2) the dual-track approach with full liberalization achieves efficiency if the rights and obligations under the plan are enforced in terms of the rents. (Lau et al. 2000: 132)

This result reminds us of the famous 'Coase theorem'.[5] Because of Pareto improvement, a dual-track price system transitioning to a market price system creates no losers, and improves the lot of some people.

The above theoretical propositions are naturally conditional. To ensure the Pareto-improving nature of a dual-track price system, one needs to assume that the rights and obligations of the plan are fully guaranteed and fulfilled. For example, if the planned obligations are not implemented or there are violating behaviours between the planned track and the market, the dual-track system as a mechanism of transition

5 I have previously analysed and discussed the Coase theorem and its application in China's economic restructuring strategy (see Zhang 1997: 72–8).

will be greatly endangered. Under the dual-track system, the government should ensure the effective implementation of the rights and obligations in the plan, but this is not a given in many transitioning economies.

Murphy et al. (1992) find the reason the partial marketisation of the former Soviet Union (1985–91) was unsuccessful and did not lead to growth in production was probably due to the failure to achieve the planned distribution of some important means of production in certain SOEs. As a result, producers of these important means of production were free to choose to whom they would sell, while private firms were also free to buy their means of production at market prices, but the price controls were maintained by the state sector. Owing to the constraints of the existing planning system and price controls, SOEs were unable to compete with private enterprises in obtaining the means of production, and their production stalled. Large quantities of important means of production flew from SOEs to the weaker private sector.

Whether the fulfilment of the planned obligations of the original producers can be guaranteed is crucial to the smooth transition of production in the early stage of economic reform:

> China has pursued partial reforms of the sort described here, except that the central government maintained extremely strict enforcement of state quotas and allowed firms to sell only the units above the state quotas to private buyers. As a result, the government managed to contain the supply diversion problem. The Soviet government, in contrast, while nominally retaining delivery quotas for state enterprises, substantially relaxed plan enforcement. (Murphy et al. 1992: 899)

Therefore, for a Pareto improvement of the dual-track price system, it is imperative the reformers are capable of guaranteeing the implementation of the planned obligations during the period of market reform. This precondition obviously depends on the political climate. It is clear that China is pushing forward partial reforms within the existing political and administrative system, which maintains the authority of the central government and makes use of the existing political and organisational resources. During the period of partial reforms in the former Soviet Union, however, the authority of the ruling party and the government was greatly weakened, and the government was unable to maintain its original planned track. This is a significant difference. China has always been able to make full strategic use of its political and organisational resources for reform, which explains why its partial and gradual reforms have evolved smoothly.

All in all, when the dual-track price system was put forward as a reform idea at the Moganshan symposium in 1984, China had already been experiencing both planned and market systems in industrial production. The dual-track price system continued through the entire 1980s and into the first half of the 1990s. It generally did not cause violent friction or turmoil, and output grew. How did China maintain a dual-track system for so many years? Economists have become obsessed with this question. Some have associated the dual-track system with the ideal model of market socialism put forward more than half a century ago by Oskar Lange and Fred Taylor.

In the 'Great Socialist Debate' of the 1930s, Lange and Taylor developed their own thinking about the combination of planning and the market.[6] The model they conceived has a serious problem with incentives and cannot overcome the monopoly and bureaucratic problems of producers (SOEs). Australian economist Professor Clem Tisdell said of China's dual-track price system and the model of market socialism of Lange and Taylor:

> There are a number of differences and similarities between socialist and market systems such as those proposed by Lange and Taylor and China's two-tiered price system. Both systems aim at balancing market supply and demand. But the Lange and Taylor system requires the use of state marketing authorities. The two-tiered system only involves state authorities in exchange in relation to the portion of production subject to an official quota, and some products in China are not subject to any production quotas at all, so that the whole of supply and demand is subject to direct exchange between sellers and buyers in markets. Therefore, the Chinese system may be less costly in terms of market transaction costs than the Lange and Taylor scheme. Furthermore, it does not require the state to hold buffer stocks or to use equalisation funds to effect marketing, even though it makes prices more risky or uncertain for sellers than Lange's or Taylor's scheme. (Tisdell 1993: 148)

Conclusion

Over the past four decades, market reform of China's economy has secured unprecedented achievements in economic growth and structural change. The starting point of this marketisation was to relax and reform the centralised planning system. The key issue was how to transform planned prices into market-determined prices so as to correct distortions and resource misallocation. In 1984, the Communist Party maintained that reform of the price system would be the key to the success or failure of reform of the entire economic system. At the same time, it held that price system reform should proceed with caution since it was closely related to the overall state of the national economy and millions of households. Based on its development of production and the availability of financial resources, China could formulate a comprehensive plan and a step-by-step implementation to ensure that people's real income gradually grows.

6 For an explanation of these ideas, see Lange (1981) and Taylor (1987).

Unlike most transitioning economies, in China the stages of market-oriented reforms were carefully planned and gradually advanced. It is naive and risky to believe that the dismantling of planning control can automatically convert a planned economy into a market economy. In shifting from a planned to a market economy, China's reform leaders were very cautious and patient.

China's experience shows that one of the ways to carefully handle market reform is to employ an extensive process of trial and error: make full use of existing experience, use local pilot projects to determine the conditions that can be utilised and then, once the trials have rendered the expected results, shift the trials to a larger scale, making sure the entire process does not cause major shocks to the economy.

Before 1984, dual-track pricing already existed for some products, including agricultural produce and coal. After 1984, however, economists promoted the dual-track price system as a transition strategy to facilitate market reforms.

As illustrated by the formation of the idea of price reform, reformers and economists have forged a good relationship in the process of making reform easier and minimising its social cost—a relationship that has been absent in other transitional economies. This practice continues in China.

References

Byrd, W. (1987), The impact of the two-tier plan/market system in Chinese industry, *Journal of Comparative Economics* 11(3): 295–308. doi.org/10.1016/0147-5967(87)90056-4.

Byrd, W. (1989), Plan and market in the Chinese economy: A simple general equilibrium model, *Journal of Comparative Economics* 13(2): 177–204. doi.org/10.1016/0147-5967(89)90001-2.

Chen, G. and Qiao, G. (1994), Formation and price reform of the product market, [in Chinese], in F. Gang, L. Yang and Z. Zhenhua (eds), *Towards the Market: 1978–1993*, Shanghai: Shanghai People's Publishing House.

Deng, X. (1993), *Selected Works of Deng Xiaoping. Volume III*, [in Chinese], Beijing: People's Publishing House.

Diao, X. (1986), Price: The role of dual-track system and the direction of further reform, [in Chinese], in Survey Group of China Economic System Reform Institute (ed.), *Reform: The challenges and options we face,* Beijing: China Economic Publishing House.

Granick, D. (1990), *Chinese State Enterprises: A regional property rights analysis*, Chicago: University of Chicago Press.

Guo, S. (1985), On the targeted models of China's price system reform, [in Chinese], *Journal of Graduate School of Chinese Academy of Social Sciences* (3): 30–7.

Guo, S., Lou, J. and Liu, J. (1986), On the overall planning of system reform, [in Chinese], *Reference Materials of Economic Research* (35).

Guo, S., Lou, J. and Qiu, S. (1985), Comprehensive reform requires overall planning: A problem concerning the destiny of China's reform, [in Chinese], *Comparison of Economic and Social Institutions* (1): 21–6.

Hua, S. (2005), The beginning and the end of dual-track system, [Chinese trans.], *China's Reform* 1: 22–5.

Hua, S., He, J., Jiang, Y., Gao, L. and Zhang, S. (1985), On the road of price reform with Chinese characteristics, [in Chinese], *Economic Research Journal* (2): 27–32.

Hua, S., Zhang, X. and Luo, X. (1988), China's ten-year reform: Review, reflection, and prospects (Review), [in Chinese], *Economic Research Journal* (2): 13–37.

Huang, C. (1987), The role of local governments in planning and markets, [in Chinese], *Comparative Social and Economic Systems* (1): 14–19.

Huang, P. (2005), Hua Sheng: Dual-track system, *Economic Observer*, 4 July.

Lange, O. (1981), *The Theory of Socialist Economics*, [Chinese trans.], Beijing: China Social Sciences Press.

Lau, L., Qian, Y. and Roland, G. (1997), Pareto-improving economic reforms through dual-track liberalization, *Economic Letters* 55(2): 285–92. doi.org/10.1016/S0165-1765(97)00062-1.

Lau, L., Qian, Y. and Roland, G. (2000), Reform without losers: An interpretation of China's dual-track approach to transition, *Journal of Political Economy*, 108(1): 120–43. doi.org/10.1086/262113.

Liu, G. (1985), Economic system reform and macroeconomic management: Reviews on 'Macroeconomic Management International Symposium', *Economic Research* (12): 3–19.

Liu, J. (1988), On administrative decentralization and economic decentralization, [in Chinese], *Comparison of Economic and Social Institutions* (3): 8–14.

Lou, J. and Zhou, X. (1984), On the direction of China's price system reform and related models and methods, [in Chinese], *Economic Research Journal* (10): 13–20.

Murphy, K., Shleifer, A. and Vishny, R. (1992), The transition to a market economy: Pitfalls of partial reform, *The Quarterly Journal of Economics* 107(3): 887–906. doi.org/10.2307/2118367.

Office of Development, Institute of Economic Research, Chinese Academy of Social Sciences (1987), *Proceedings of China's Economic Reform: International Symposium on Macroeconomic Management on Bashan Ship*, [in Chinese], Beijing: China Economic Publishing House.

Pan, Z. and Luo, S. (1988), *Theory of Socialist Microeconomic Equilibrium*, [in Chinese], Shanghai: Shanghai Joint Publishing Corporation.

Qian, Y. and Xu, C. (1993), Why China's economic reforms differ: The M-form hierarchy and entry/expansion of the non-state sector, *Economics of Transition* 1(2): 135–70. doi.org/10.1111/j.1468-0351.1993.tb00077.x.

Shi, X. and Liu, J. (1989), Economists must first respect history and facts: Comments on 'Ten years of China's reform: Review, reflection, and prospects (Review)' by Hua Sheng et al., [in Chinese], *Economic Research Journal* (2): 12–34.

Southern Weekend (2007), Happiness is 'what the heart likes', [in Chinese], *Southern Weekend*, 17 May.

Taylor, F. (1987), The production guidance for socialist countries, [in Chinese], *Comparison of Economic and Social Systems* (3): 51–4.

Tisdell, C. (1993), *Economic Development in the Context of China: Policy issues and analysis*, London: Macmillan. doi.org/10.1057/9780230380189.

Wu, J. (ed.) (1993), *Corruption: Exchange between power and money*, [in Chinese], Beijing: China Economic Publishing House.

Wu, J. (2003), *Contemporary China's Economic Reform*, [in Chinese], Shanghai: Shanghai Far East Publishing House.

Wu, J., Zhou, X., Guo, S. and Li, J. (1988), *Overall Design of China's Economic Reform*, [in Chinese], Beijing: China Prospect Press.

Zhang, J. (1997), *Economics of Dual-Track System: China's economic reform (1978–1992)*, [in Chinese], Shanghai: Shanghai Joint Publishing Corporation and Shanghai People's Publishing House.

Zhang, W. (1985), On the idea of focusing on 'deregulation' in the price reform, *Reference Materials of Economic Research* (6).

Zhang, Z. (1992), Prospect of price reform in China in the 1990s, [in Chinese], in M. Xue, G. Liu, M. Wang, S. Sun, J. Wang, Z. Xiao, J. Tian, Y. Dai, T. Zhu, J. Li, J. Chen, H. Wang, L. Ji, S. Gao, J. Wang, S. Zhou, J. Wu, T. Mao, F. Dong, Z. Zhang, J. Chen, S. Zhou, Z. He, H. Zhao, S. Liu, C. Ji, L. Zhao, X. Zeng, X. Tian, S. Yang, Q. Zhu, S. Zhang, L. Di, C. Li, F. Huang and D. Yu, *China's Economic Development and Reform Exploration in the 1990s*, Beijing: Economic Science Press.

13. How has the Chinese economy capitalised on the demographic dividend during the reform period?

Cai Fang

Introduction

China's unprecedented economic growth during the period of reform that began in the late 1970s has been accompanied by a dramatic demographic transition—namely, a rapid decline in the fertility rate. In the period 1978–2015, China realised a real growth rate of gross national income (GNI) of 9.6 per cent—the fastest speed anywhere in the world in that period. On the other hand, according to the United Nations (UN 2015), China's total fertility rate (TFR) dropped from 2.5–3 in the late 1970s and early 1980s to a replacement level of 2 in the first half of the 1990s, and has remained constant at about 1.5 since the second half of the 1990s.

There has been debate among scholars and policymakers about the actual level of China's TFR. The results based directly on various censuses and 1 per cent population sampling surveys show an incredibly low TFR. For example, the rate was 1.22 according to the 2000 census, 1.34 according to a 2005 sampling survey, 1.19 in the 2010 census (Guo et al. 2014: 21) and 1.05 from a 2015 sampling survey (NBS 2016: 361). Even after data adjustment based on assumptions of statistical error, most scholars conclude that China's TFR remains at 1.4—a level lower than that published by the United Nations.[1] The TFR increased moderately only after relaxation of government policy allowed couples to have two children.

An unquestionable truth is that China's TFR has stayed at a level significantly lower than the replacement level for a quarter of a century. Before it eventually brought about population ageing supposedly unfavourable to economic growth, this rapid demographic transition had helped form a population pattern characterised by a rapid increase in the working-age population and a decrease in the dependency ratio (the ratio of dependants to the working-age population)—what economists call the 'demographic dividend'. The contribution of the demographic dividend to economic growth has been recognised and documented in the economics literature (for example, Williamson 1997).

1 Guo et al. (2014) presented ample evidence of a very low TFR in present-day China.

Researchers have examined the interplay between economic development and the demographic transition and estimated the contribution to growth of the population factor during China's reform period. For example, Wang and Mason (2008) find that the decline in the dependency ratio contributed 15 per cent to economic growth in the period 1982–2000, while Cai and Wang (2005) estimated the contribution of the dependency ratio was 26.8 per cent in the same period.

Let us consider a standard Cobb–Douglas production function (Equation 13.1).

Equation 13.1

$$Y = A * F(K,L) = K^{\alpha} * (AL)^{1-\alpha}$$

In Equation 13.1, Y denotes output (for example, gross domestic product: GDP) growth; K is physical capital input; L is human capital input, which can be divided into the amount of labour and its educational attainment; and A is total factor productivity (TFP), which can be decomposed into reallocative efficiency and a residual. In addition, some economists, acting as 'right-hand warriors' (Srinivasan and Bhagwati 1999), add into a growth regression dozens of explanatory variables that are considered both theoretically possible and statistically significant. The population dependency ratio as a proxy for the demographic dividend is one such variable.

Broadly defining the demographic dividend as a contributor to economic growth, however, requires looking into almost all variables in the right-hand side of a production function equation, while the contribution of the dependency ratio as a variable to economic growth is, at most, a residual of the demographic dividend.

Based on the experiences of China and other East Asian economies and drawing on the dual economy theory developed by Lewis (1954), we can extend the ability of the neoclassical theory of growth to explain broadly defined demographic dividend in economic growth. In what follows, I explain the relevance of growth factors to demographics and reveal broadly defined demographic dividends gained in China's transition, which can be supported by existing research.

First, the fact that a low and declining dependency ratio helps create a high savings rate, on the one hand, and that unlimited labour supply delays the phenomenon of diminishing returns to capital, on the other, makes capital accumulation the main engine of economic growth. In an early study of China, the World Bank (1998) found that capital accumulation accounted for 37 per cent of GDP growth in the period 1978–95. Covering a much longer period, Cai and Zhao (2012) estimated the contribution of capital accumulation to be double this amount. More recent research suggests that labour productivity enhancement was a significant driver of economic growth during the reform period (for example, IMF 2006; Zhu 2012), whereas, among the factors that increase labour productivity, capital deepening or the capital–labour ratio play a major, and increasing, role (IMF 2006; Kuijs 2010).

Some economists have criticised growth in which capital plays the overwhelming role, believing it is not much of a miracle and is not sustainable (for example, Young 2003; Krugman 2013). As the experiences of China and other East Asian economies show, however, in the Lewisian-type dual economy development stage, unlimited labour supply can prevent the phenomenon of a diminishing return to capital for a certain period. For example, research findings suggest that during most of China's reform period, the return to capital investment remained extraordinarily high (Bai et al. 2006) and, after the Lewis turning point—characterised by a labour shortage and wage inflation—returns to capital have rapidly diminished (Bai and Zhang 2014). This proves that the contribution of capital to growth is indeed part of the demographic dividend.

Second, advantageous population factors guarantee the size and quality of the labour force are sufficient to make a significant contribution to economic growth. Sufficient supply of labour has been widely recognised as a favourable factor in catch-up growth. What is often neglected is that the improvement of human capital in less-developed countries overwhelmingly relies on a favourable population age structure that ensures a steady flow of new entrants with increased years of schooling to the labour market.

According to the World Bank (1998), the estimated contribution to GDP growth of labour inputs, measured in terms of both quantity and quality, was 17 per cent, while Cai and Zhao (2012) estimated labour's contribution to be 8 per cent and that of human capital 4 per cent. By adding together the effects of the number of years of workers' schooling and the effects of education on productivity, Whalley and Zhao (2010) estimated the direct and indirect contribution of human capital to be as high as 38 per cent.

Third, labour mobility between rural and urban areas, among sectors and among regions following the direction from low to high productivity brings about an increase in the reallocative efficiency of resources, which is a significant part of TFP growth.

By decomposing sources of TFP growth in China into the reallocative efficiency of resources and a residual, the World Bank (1998) found that the former—namely, productivity growth as a result of labour mobility from low-productivity sectors (labour-surplus agriculture and labour-redundant state-owned enterprises (SOEs)) to high-productivity sectors (nonagricultural sectors and newly established enterprises)—contributed to 16 per cent of the growth in GDP in the period 1978–95. Cai and Wang (1999) found that labour transfers from agricultural to nonagricultural sectors were responsible for the overwhelming part of TFP growth and contributed 21 per cent to per capita GDP growth in the period 1978–98. In a more recent study, Zhu (2012) found that the sound performance of China's TFP in the period 1978–2007 can be attributed to the rapid expansion and productivity growth of nonstate enterprises.

Finally, for any country, increasing population size tends to intensify demand for and supply of innovation, which will fuel economic growth through speeding up technological progress and increasing TFP. This argument, put forward by growth theorists and economic historians, has been tested empirically (for example, Jones 2002). To my knowledge, however, there has not been any empirical study concerning modern China.

A population structure that is theoretically favourable for economic growth will not, however, be spontaneously translated into a demographic dividend—that is, a realistic driver of growth. In fact, the economic performance of many countries experiencing a similar demographic transition cannot rival that of China.

According to the World Bank and the International Monetary Fund (IMF) (2016: 268–73), countries with a TFR higher than a replacement level of 2.1 in 1985 and a working-age population that is declining or static in the period 2015–30 can be categorised as 'late-dividend economies', of which China is one of 54 such economies. In the period 1978–2015, China realised an annual growth rate of per capita GNI of 9.73 per cent, compared with the arithmetical average of 3.77 per cent in the 44 other economies with available data. Even taking into account a convergence effect—that is, observing the poorest countries in the late-dividend category that are supposed to have a potential similar to China's to grow faster—China stands out in terms of economic growth.

Generally speaking, reforms aimed at ameliorating key obstacles to economic growth could accelerate growth in the absence of conditions that are widely seen as essential for development.[2] For China in particular, its outstanding growth performance has been the result of its implementation of reform and opening-up, cashing in on the advantageous growth conditions. China has translated its demographic dividend into a high potential growth rate and ultimately realised unprecedented actual growth by improving incentive mechanisms in micro-management, getting prices right, developing factor markets, eliminating institutional barriers to mobility of production factors and embracing global markets, technology and competition.

The rest of this chapter is organised as follows. It first provides a retrospective of the formation of population policy, its impacts and the process of adjustment, showing that the demographic transition was a result of not only population

2 This proposition is credited to Hollis Chenery. See Brandt and Rawski (2008: 9).

policy, but also economic and social development. It then looks at how reforms in related areas released surplus labour from agriculture and expanded employment in nonagricultural sectors. It further empirically tests the effects of labour reallocation on labour productivity improvement and thus on economic growth. Finally, based on the prospect of future population change, it draws policy implications for further reform.

Population policy and the demographic transition

As early as the 1950s, China's top decision-makers began to note the country's mushrooming population, even though Professor Ma Yinchu's views on population and his proposals for birth control were severely criticised by his fellow scholars and political leaders (including chairman Mao Zedong). China's first population census was conducted in 1953; however, no decision was made on concrete policy measures at that time. It was only after the failure of the Great Leap Forward and the bitter experiences of the Great Famine in the late 1950s and early 1960s that Chinese leaders decided to take action to check the population boom.

By the end of 1962, the central government was advocating implementation of family planning to mitigate the momentum of population growth. In 1970, it officially incorporated the issue of population into the national economic development plan, but it was not until 1980 that the Chinese Government formally announced the one-child policy. Reading the official terms of the proposal publicised in 1988—that is, advocacy of late marriage and late childbearing, having fewer children and better child care and one child per couple—family planning did not appear to be compulsory. In reality, the word 'advocacy' here should be read to mean 'mandatory requirement'. In the 1990s, population regulations focusing on implementing the one-child policy had been successively approved by all provincial people's congresses (the local legislatures) and implemented by provincial governments.

It is not accurate, however, to regard the family planning policy in place in China for more than three decades as simply a 'one-child policy'. After a lengthy evolution, the structure of the policy package in 2010 could be described as comprising: 1) the one-child policy, which was applied to all urban and rural residents in six provinces, covering 35.9 per cent of China's total population; 2) the one-and-a-half child policy, under which rural couples whose first child is a girl were allowed to have a second child, and which covered rural residents in 19 provinces, accounting for 52.9 per cent of the total population; 3) the two-child policy, which was applicable to rural residents in five provinces and covered 9.6 per cent of the population; and 4) the three-child policy, which was applied to farmers and herdsmen of ethnic minorities in some areas and covered 1.6 per cent of the total population.

In addition, in the Tibetan Autonomous Region, urbanites were allowed to have two children and there were no restrictions on the number of children for farmers and herdsmen of Tibetan and other ethnic minorities with very small population size (see CDRF 2014: Ch. 4).

The strictness of the implementation of the family planning policy was not immutable. First, the policy was introduced at the same time as the initiation of China's market-oriented reforms and resulting economic growth. While adhering to the population control target, implementation has been directed more and more towards promotion of the economy, poverty alleviation, family development, social governance and economic incentives. Second, some provinces relaxed the restrictions quite some time ago—for example, permitting urban couples, both of whom were an only-child, and rural couples, one of whom was an only child, to have two children. More fundamental family planning reforms have been successively carried out—in 2014 allowing couples, one of whom was an only child, and, then in 2016, all couples to have two children.

In any country, economic growth and social development are the drivers of demographic transition. In China's case, its unique family planning policy is only an additional, and diminishing, driver. By examining three theoretical factors that are expected to have an effect on reducing the fertility rate—that is, implementation of population policy, increasing per capita GDP and human capital improvement—and regressing them as explanatory variables, Du (2005) found that all significantly contributed to lowering the fertility rate during the first decade of China's reforms, and that the effect of the policy variable disappeared, while that of the income and human capital variables remained in the second decade of reform.

To a reasonable extent, it is the outstanding performance of China's economic growth and social development that brought its TFR to below replacement level in the early 1990s, and kept it there since. As a result, natural population growth has dramatically slowed. In this, China has followed the universal law of demographic transition. What is unique about China's experience is that it took just 30 years or so for the country to complete its transition from a high-fertility to a low-fertility rate. In comparison, Western countries have taken more than twice as long to complete the transition. What is more, China entered its low-fertility phase much earlier than other developing countries with similar per capita income levels, which characterises it as a country that is 'growing old before getting rich'.

Figure 13.1 shows the changes in birth and mortality rates and their difference—namely, the natural population growth rate—since the founding of the People's Republic of China (PRC). If the abnormal decline in the birth rate, the rise in mortality and the subsequent enormous drop in the natural growth rate in the late 1950s and early 1960s are considered an external shock and their impacts on the overall, long-term trend are eliminated, one can conclude that China's population change in the past nearly seven decades has followed the general trajectory experienced in the pioneering countries.

Figure 13.1 Birth rate, death rate and natural growth rate of population in China

Sources: NBS (various years).

Before the mid-1960s, the sharp fall in the mortality rate and lagging response in the birth rate resulted in a rise of population growth. This 'baby-boom' aroused concerns in academic circles and among decision-makers, because no one at the time could foresee a fall in fertility.[3] During the 1970s, while the death rate continued to decline—although at a relatively slower pace—the birth rate also began to decline substantially, which brought about a sharp plunge in the natural population growth rate. Then came an era in which the mortality rate remained all but unchanged and, consequently, the birth rate and natural growth rate moved synchronously. They rebounded for a couple of years in the 1980s and then dropped again in the 1990s. China's natural population growth rate was always at a level of fewer than 10 per 1,000 after 1998 and has been lower than 6 per 1,000 since 2004.

As expected, such changes in fertility and population growth rates have altered the age structure of China's population. According to data released by the United Nations (2015), the Chinese working-age population (those aged between 15 and

3 It is commonly believed that Notestein (1945) coined the theory of demographic transition, as he was the first to provide a standard theoretical explanation for the decline in fertility being an inevitable stage of the demographic transition. There was no way for academics such as Ma Yinchu and decision-makers such as Mao Zedong to know such a theory stylised from global experiences.

59) increased from 373 million in 1965 to a peak of 941 million in 2010, while the dependency ratio calculated on this definition fell from 0.89 to a low of 0.43 in the same period.

That is, China enjoyed its most productive population structure in the period between the mid-1960s and 2010 and, within that, the period of economic reform—1978 to 2010—can be considered the population window of opportunity, or demographic dividend. The year 2010 is therefore an obvious turning point. As the working-age population declined and the dependency ratio increased after that time, the demographic dividend that spurred the high growth rate of the Chinese economy has been rapidly disappearing. If the population trend remains unchanged, it is predicted the working-age population will drop to 674 million and the dependency ratio will increase to nearly 1 by 2050 (UN 2015).

How has reform promoted employment?

In economic history, a situation in which a massive surplus of agricultural labour cannot be transferred to nonagricultural sectors through development of a dual economy (Lewis 1954) is sometimes called agricultural involution, which impedes labour productivity improvement in agriculture and delays industrialisation (see Huang 2002). In such a case, the advantageous population structure will not translate into a demographic dividend, and will instead become a population burden. The same goes with the 'iron rice bowl' and overstaffing in SOEs caused by planned assignment of jobs in urban areas depress efficiencies of enterprise management and resources allocation.

Given that full and efficient utilisation of abundant labour are preconditions for translating favourable population properties into factors that actually spur economic growth, it is necessary to examine how reform helped to promote employment and the reallocation of labour, to understand how China cashed in on the demographic dividend during the reform period.

Reforms that are conducive to the movement and reallocation of production factors in general, and of the labour force in particular, include many at both micro and macro levels. Overall, the economic growth spurred by reform has created plenty of jobs, and the elimination of institutional barriers through deregulation has motivated labourers—following market signals of employment opportunity and relative income—to leave low-productivity jobs, migrate among regions and sectors and take new high-productivity jobs. Therefore, by examining how migrant labourers have obtained rights of exit, mobility and entry, we can concisely document the processes of related reforms and their effects.

First, rural reforms released surplus labour. The introduction of the household responsibility system (HRS) was a critical reform that granted farmers the right to exit agricultural work with very low marginal labour productivity. Even before the system was officially implemented in 1978, the HRS was secretly piloted in some remote rural villages. After the third plenum of the eleventh Central Committee of the Communist Party (CCCP), which was convened in 1978, the government accepted, and eventually encouraged, the HRS, which became a symbol of the beginning of economic reform.

By the end of 1984, all production brigades and 98 per cent of households in rural China had adopted the HRS and the people's commune system was abolished. The original motive of the reform was to improve incentives for agricultural production by granting farmers autonomy of operation and rights of residual claimants. An unexpected outcome was that rural households have since obtained autonomy in owning and allocating factors of production.

Under the commune system, employment was confined to farming and, in many cases, solely to grain production; workplaces were restricted to production brigades in the home village and each brigade determined the hours of labour—all of which served to maintain patterns of resource misallocation. Under the HRS, once households had paid agricultural tax, met the state's procurement targets and turned over the collective retention, they had autonomy to decide which crops to plant and how to allocate their work time. With this autonomy, once the labour surplus became overt, farmers began to reallocate their labour and other factors of production.

Reforms also promoted labour mobility among sectors and between regions. Under the planned system, a troika of institutional arrangements—the commune system, the household registration (or *hukou*) system and the rationing of major agricultural products—had severely restricted labour mobility between sectors and regions. As incentives improved and labour efficiency increased, a labour surplus in agriculture appeared. One study (Taylor 1993) shows that, in the mid-1980s, surplus labour amounted to 100 to 150 million workers, accounting for 30 to 40 per cent of the total workforce. As institutional barriers were eliminated, surplus labourers began to move away from their previous areas of employment.

This labour transfer led successively to movement away from grain production alone to diversified farming; from farming to broadly defined agricultural sectors, including farming, forestry, animal husbandry, fishing and business sidelines; from agriculture to rural industries (township and village enterprises, or TVEs); and from rural nonagricultural work to urban employment.

There have been several breakthroughs in the reallocation of rural labour. First, with the abolition of the commune system and substantial enhancement of farm products, farmers were permitted to transport and sell their own farm products beyond their hometown—for the first time breaking the geographic restrictions on farmers' employment. Second, farmers were allowed to work in neighbouring towns (by providing their own rations), which, for the first time, broke the employment boundary between rural and urban sectors. In the early 1990s, with the abolition of the rationing system, there were no longer any practical obstacles to rural labourers working and living in cities.

Although the *hukou* system still segments the provision of public services according to residential identity—preventing migrant workers and their accompanying family members from equal access to compulsory education, basic social security programs, the minimum living guarantee program and subsidised housing—it no longer serves as an obstacle to labour mobility and population migration. In that sense, there has been a real breakthrough in reform of the *hukou* system.

Third, reforms break barriers deterring labour from entering high-productivity sectors. When the labour market was undeveloped and divided between rural and urban employment, labourers leaving agriculture could find only marginal jobs in nonagricultural sectors. For example, until the 1980s, TVEs absorbed the majority of labourers exiting agriculture. After 1992, the rapidly expanding labour-intensive manufacturing and nonpublic sectors in coastal regions began absorbing massive numbers of cross-regional migrant workers, creating the first wave of internal migration. In the late 1990s, radical reform of the employment system in SOEs began to link up rural and urban labour markets. As a result, barriers to labour mobility across regions and across sectors have been gradually eliminated.

Fourth, reforms create jobs and reallocate labour to urban sectors. The entry of new workers to the labour market and the relocation of those unemployed and laid-off in urban areas have followed a pattern similar to that of the transfer of surplus rural labour. Reforms carried out as early as the 1980s granted SOEs autonomy in hiring and firing—on paper. Managers, however, were not encouraged to use this autonomy, because the undeveloped labour market and imperfect social security system would have been unable to cope with the potential lay-offs. At the time, there was a lack of employment opportunities outside SOEs and no unemployment insurance system to protect any laid-off workers.

In the late 1990s, severe operational pressures in SOEs forced reform that was characterised by ending the longstanding concept of the 'iron rice bowl' and laying off redundant workers. This was the tipping point for reform of the urban employment system. First, to secure a basic living for laid-off workers, unemployment insurance and other social security programs were established. Second, workers were re-employed through the newly-developed labour market with the assistance of the government's proactive employment policy. Third, migrant workers were given more equal opportunities to compete with urban workers in the labour market, which activated an adjustment of labour stocks in urban sectors.

Finally, participation in the global division of labour expands aggregate employment. One of the important factors that allows China to cash in on its demographic dividend is the expansion of labour-intensive manufacturing, which has absorbed large numbers of migrant workers and gained a huge share of international commodity markets. This is what makes the Chinese experience so outstanding in the course of economic globalisation.

By analysing employment growth and its composition in the United States, Spence and Hlatshwayo (2011) show that, as a result of the massive transfer of manufacturing abroad, jobs in this sector were lost, with almost all of the new increment in employment coming from nontradable sectors in the period 1990–2008. They imply that offshoring destroyed the US economy. Taking the US case as a reference, we examine the expansion of China's nonagricultural employment.

Based on data from Chinese economic censuses conducted in 2004, 2008 and 2013, and using a similar categorisation method to Spence and Hlatshwayo (2011), we classify China's nonagricultural employment on the basis of corporate units in the censuses in the tradable and nontradable sectors, with a special focus on manufacturing and construction, which took the lion's share of employment in the two sectors, respectively. The total expansion and structural change of employment of those categories in the period examined are shown in Figure 13.2.

As shown in Figure 13.2, nonagricultural employment in urban and rural China expanded at an annual growth rate of 5.9 per cent in 2004–13, totalling 352 million workers in 2013. Growth in the tradable and nontradable sectors was also relatively balanced, with an annual growth rate of 6.9 per cent for the tradable sector and 4.7 per cent for the nontradable sector. As these levels are based on reporting from corporate units, real nonagricultural employment and its expansion in the period examined are likely greatly underreported. In what follows, by comparing different sources of statistics, we can examine the degree to which the actual level of employment differs from the census data.

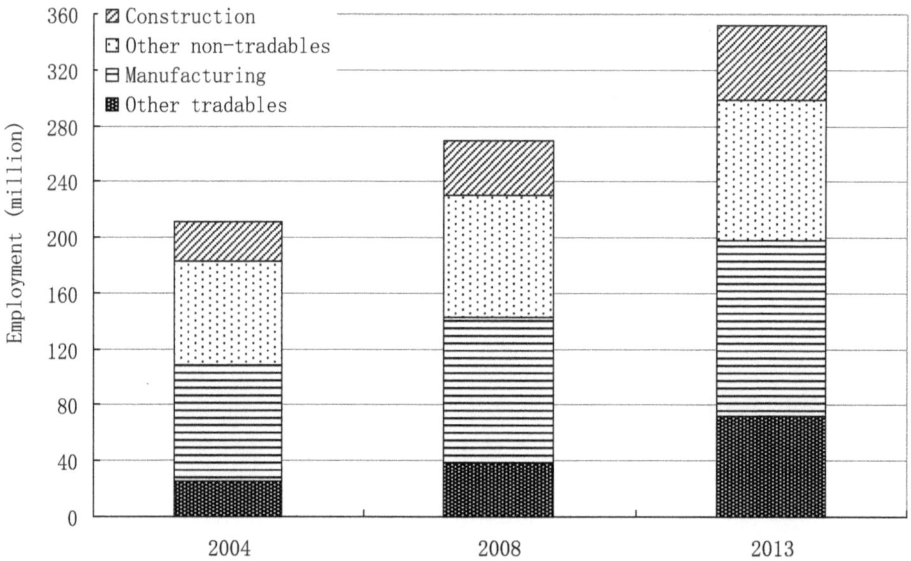

Figure 13.2 Expansion and composition of nonagricultural employment

Sources: Data from first, second and third economic censuses, NBS official website: www.stats.gov.cn.

The official statistics for urban employment collected yearly are based on 'establishments' rather than 'corporate units', generating a much greater amount of nonagricultural employment. According to these data, urban employment amounted to 178 million workers in 2015. By including employment in private enterprises and self-employment, the figure for urban employment increases to 368 million.

In addition, most temporary employees and dispatched labourers—many of whom are migrant workers—are not reported by enterprises and are therefore missing from the statistics. Therefore, the household-based survey conducted in accordance with the definitions of the International Labour Organization (ILO) shows an even larger number for urban employment, of 404 million. The difference between this survey data and the preceding data can be viewed as urban informal employment.

Even this number omits some migrant workers in urban sectors. A rough estimate shows that about 20 million migrant workers were excluded from the urban employment statistics (see Cai et al. 2016). If these migrant workers were also included in the statistics, total urban employment could be as high as 424 million in 2015.

Labour reallocation effects

As Kuznets (1957) points out, the essential aim of structural change is to reallocate factors of production (especially labour) from low-productivity sectors to high-productivity sectors, and therefore to increase the allocative efficiency of resources. Based on the experiences in East Asia (mainly China, Japan and Korea), Aoki (2012) identifies a unique stage of development led by structural transformation and called the K(uznets)-phase. Other researchers find that labour transfers to gain reallocative efficiency characterise the typical process of structural change in Asian economies (McMillan and Rodrik 2011), explain an important part of TFP, and thus labour productivity growth in China (Bosworth and Collins 2007), and contribute significantly to the growth of the Chinese economy as a whole (Du 2014).

In China, reforms have eliminated a host of institutional barriers to labour mobility and spurred labour reallocation from low-productivity sectors and regions to high-productivity sectors and regions. Such a Kuznets process has increased resource allocation efficiency, contributing to the improvement of TFP and supporting outstanding economic growth. That is, the demographic dividend has been embodied in both economic growth and structural changes in China during the reform period. The resource reallocation effects can be empirically examined as follows.

General experiences of economic development suggest that the agricultural share in output and employment declines over time as a result of an increase in a country's income level. After 40 years of economic development and demographic transition, total employment in China expanded from 402 million in 1978 to 775 million in 2015. Meanwhile, as a result of the large-scale transfer of agricultural labour, according to officially published data, the share of labour in the primary sector declined from 70.5 per cent to 28.3 per cent, while the share of labour increased from 17.3 per cent to 29.3 per cent in the secondary sector and from 12.2 per cent to 42.4 per cent in the tertiary sector.

As some researchers have argued, the official data likely overstate the size and share of agricultural labour (see Rawski and Mead 1998; Cai et al. 2013). Recalculations by Cai (2017) show the share of labour actually engaged in agriculture in 2015 is 18.3 per cent, and the corresponding share of labour in secondary and tertiary sectors is 33.4 per cent and 48.3 per cent, respectively. That is, the actual share of agricultural labour is at least 10 percentage points lower than indicated in the official data. Table 13.1 compares the shares of labour by sector between different data sources for China and the average levels of global and country groups by income level.

Table 13.1 International comparisons of labour distribution by sector (per cent)

Countries and regions	Primary sector	Secondary sector	Tertiary sector
China (official data)	28.3	29.3	42.4
China (adjusted data)	18.3	33.4	48.3
China (ILO data)	28.9	23.7	47.3
World average	29.5	21.5	48.9
Low-income countries	68.5	8.3	23.2
Low-middle-income countries	40.4	21.3	38.3
Upper-middle-income countries	23.9	24.0	52.1
High-income countries	3.1	22.5	74.3
High-income economies in East Asia	4.1	35.3	60.3

Note: The first line shows figures from official Chinese statistics, those in the second line are the author's estimates and the remainder are cited from ILO model estimations. Figures for the average levels of the world and economy groups are calculated as arithmetical means.

Sources: NBS (various years); ILO (2017); and author's estimations.

The official data suggest that China's labour distribution among sectors deviates from the international experience—in particular, through its larger share of agricultural labour and smaller share of service labour. The recalculated data are in line with what would be expected according to the economic growth and structural adjustment in China after three decades of reform. The share of agricultural labour, based on the recalculated data, is lower than the average level for upper–middle-income countries and substantially higher compared with the average levels for high-income economies.

China reached a per capita GNI of US$7,900 in 2015 and is approaching the transition from upper-middle- to high-income status. According to the World Bank's classifications, there are 13 countries that have relevance to China and for which data are available for comparative purposes. They range from Gabon, with per capita GNI of US$9,200 (similar to China's current level), to Croatia, with US$12,760 (close to the transitional threshold of US$12,600). In 2015, the arithmetical average share of agricultural labour of the 13 comparator countries was 12.8 per cent (ILO 2017)—that is, during the transition from its current status to high-income status, China will have to close the gap with those countries in terms of the sectoral distribution of labour.

We are now in a position to investigate the contribution of labour reallocation to labour productivity growth. In the period 1978–2015, according to calculations based on official data, China's labour productivity (GDP per worker in real terms) increased by 16.7 times: labour productivity in the primary sector increased by 5.5 times, in the secondary sector it increased by 13.5 times and in the tertiary sector, by 5.2 times. The calculations based on the adjusted data show a similar trend, but with a greater increase in labour productivity in the primary sector.

By adopting methods used to decompose sources of labour productivity growth proposed by Timmer and Szirmai (2000) and Bosworth and Collins (2007), Cai (2017) estimates the functional and structural factors contributing to labour productivity growth in China's reform period. The results are shown in Table 13.2.

Table 13.2 Labour productivity growth and contributing factors in China (per cent)

	Decomposition 1, based on Timmer and Szirmai (2000)				
	Total growth	Contribution of sectors	Structural effects	Of which: Static effect	Dynamic effect
1978–2015	1,671.3	55.1	44.9	4.6	40.2
	(1,671.3)	(56.0)	(44.0)	(5.5)	(38.6)
1978–1990	77.5	60.8	39.2	25.8	13.4
1991–2003	205.2	86.2	13.8	7.0	6.8
2004–2015	173.5	66.9	33.1	15.9	17.2

	Decomposition 2, based on Bosworth and Collins (2007)				
	Annual growth	Primary sector	Secondary sector	Tertiary sector	Sectoral reallocation
1978–2015	8.08	17.73	44.22	15.39	22.66
	(8.08)	(21.86)	(42.53)	(14.53)	(21.08)
1978–1990	4.90	15.65	34.46	16.57	33.32
1991–2003	9.75	7.44	61.30	16.71	14.55
2004–2015	9.58	6.68	48.69	20.27	24.36

Note: Figures in parentheses indicate results based on adjusted data.
Source: Cai (2017).

The decomposition results based on the method of Timmer and Szirmai (2000) show that, in the period 1978–2015, labour productivity growth in the Chinese economy as a whole can be attributed to sectoral contributions (55 per cent) and contributions from structural change (45 per cent). Of the latter, the contribution of the static shift effect, generated by a shift of labour towards sectors with a higher labour productivity level at the beginning of the period examined, was minor and the contribution of the dynamic effect, generated by a shift of labour towards sectors with higher labour productivity growth rates, dominated.

While the same decomposition is used to examine the periods 1978–90, 1991–2003 and 2004–15, the results show that structural effects were significant in the first and third periods, while sectoral contributions overwhelmingly dominated labour productivity growth in the second period. The static effect was significant in the second period, contributing 25.8 per cent to total labour productivity growth.

From the decomposition based on the method of Bosworth and Collins (2007), one can see that yearly growth in total labour productivity was relatively slow in the first period and then substantially accelerated in the second and third periods. Across the entire period, the contribution of the primary sector steadily decreased and the secondary sector served as a major contributor to total labour productivity growth. In the second period, the contribution of labour reallocation was relatively small.

Conclusion and future prospects

During most of its period of economic reform, China experienced a dual economy pattern of development similar to that described by Arthur Lewis (1954) in his monumental paper. In such a pattern, the elimination of institutional obstacles preventing sufficient accumulation and efficient allocation of factors of production translated the demographic dividend and thus potential growth into unprecedented economic growth. That is, a favourable population structure helped China create the necessary conditions for high potential growth characterised by a high savings rate, sufficient supply of labour, rapid improvement of human capital and radical resource reallocation through labour mobility.

As the demographic transition has entered a new stage, traditional sources of growth tend to be exhausted. First, the negative growth in the working-age and economically active populations has led to and is aggravating the labour shortage, weakening the comparative advantage of China's industry. Second, the rapid increase in the capital–labour ratio has resulted in diminishing returns to capital. Third, the slower growth in the number of new entrants to the labour market has slowed the rate of human capital improvement. Finally, ageing of the rural population has retarded urbanisation and thus diminished the momentum of labour reallocation in enhancing labour productivity.

All these changes point to the rapid disappearance of the demographic dividend, leading to a decline in the potential growth rate. The estimates of Cai and Lu (2013) show China's potential growth rate reduced from about 10 per cent in the period before 2010 to 7.6 per cent during the period of the twelfth Five-Year Plan (2011–15) and 6.2 per cent during the thirteenth Five-Year Plan (2016–20). The actual growth rate and the pace of its slowdown have so far followed this predicted trajectory.

As is predicted by the theory of growth and the experiences of other economies, in the transition from middle-income status to high-income status—an analogue to the transformation from a dual economy to the stage of neoclassical growth in most other cases—countries' growth rates inevitably and significantly slow (see Eichengreen et al. 2011; Barro 2016). The speed and degree of economic slowdown, however, vary from country to country, leading to different consequences in the long run (Eichengreen et al. 2013). For China, there are potentials it could tap into to help it avoid falling into the so-called middle-income trap.

The first is to maintain the traditional momentum of economic growth. There is still huge potential for China to narrow the gap with developed countries in its share of agricultural labour. Pushing through the unfinished reform of the *hukou* system—transforming migrants from guest workers to legitimate residents in urban areas—will greatly enhance labour participation in nonagricultural sectors and therefore resource reallocative efficiency. The gap in workers' levels of human capital between China and the developed countries can also be narrowed by reforming the system of education and training to extend the average years of schooling and improve the quality of education. Reforms in a series of areas will create a better policy environment for small and medium-sized enterprises and strengthen competition to prevent diminishing returns to capital.

Second is to tap into sustainable drivers of economic growth by improving TFP. As the capacity to reallocate resources between the agricultural and nonagricultural sectors reduces, the reallocation of resources among nonagricultural industries and enterprises within narrowly defined industries will provide a new source of reallocative efficiency—as long as there are differences in productivity among them. Reforms aimed at creating a level playing field and a mechanism for 'creative destruction'—for example, in the financial sector and among SOEs—could create sustained sources of long-term growth.

Liu Xiang, a scholar of the Western Han Dynasty (77–6 BC), said that 90 miles is only half of a hundred-mile journey. For the 'great rejuvenation' of the Chinese nation proposed by the eighteenth National Congress of the Communist Party of China in 2012—that is, becoming a modernised country by 2050—the past 40 years of reform indeed mark the halfway point to the final destination. Judging from past experiences and the potential of the reform dividend, reform and opening-up will remain immense sources of economic growth for China. The purpose of looking back at the past 40 years of reform is to push the remaining necessary reforms to a new level.

References

Aoki, M. (2012), The five phases of economic development and institutional evolution in China, Japan, and Korea, in M. Masahiko, T. Kuran and G. Roland (eds), *Institutions and Comparative Economic Development*, Basingstoke, UK: Palgrave Macmillan. doi.org/10.1057/9781137034014_2.

Bai, C.-E. and Zhang, Q. (2014), The rates of return to capital and the analysis of the determinants, *The World Economy* (10): 3–30.

Bai, C.-E., Hsieh, C.-T. and Qian, Y. (2006), *The return to capital in China*, NBER Working Papers No. 12755, Cambridge, MA: National Bureau of Economic Research.

Barro, R. J. (2016), *Economic growth and convergence, applied especially to China*, NBER Working Papers No. 21872, Cambridge, MA: National Bureau of Economic Research.

Bosworth, B. and Collins, S. (2007), *Accounting for growth: Comparing China and India*, NBER Working Papers No. 12943, Cambridge, MA: National Bureau of Economic Research.

Brandt, L. and Rawski, T. G. (2008), China's great economic transformation, in L. Brandt and T. G. Rawski (eds), *China's Great Economic Transformation*, Cambridge: Cambridge University Press.

Cai, F. (2017), Reform effects in China: A perspective of labor reallocation, *Economic Research Journal* (7): 4–17.

Cai, F. and Lu, Y. (2013), The end of China's demographic dividend: The perspective of potential GDP growth, in R. Garnaut, F. Cai and L. Song (eds), *China: A new model for growth and development*, Canberra: ANU E Press.

Cai, F. and Wang, D. (1999), The sustainability of economic growth and the labor contribution, *Economic Research Journal* (10): 62–8.

Cai, F. and Wang, D. (2005), China's demographic transition: Implications for growth, in R. Garnaut and L. Song (eds), *The China Boom and Its Discontents*, Canberra: Asia Pacific Press.

Cai, F. and Zhao, W. (2012), When demographic dividend disappears: Growth sustainability of China, in M. Aoki and J. Wu (eds), *The Chinese Economy: A new transition*, Basingstoke, UK: Palgrave Macmillan.

Cai, F., Du, Y. and Wang, M. (2013), Demystify the labor statistics in China, *China Economic Journal* 6(2–3): 123–33.

Cai, F., Guo, Z. and Wang, M. (2016), New urbanisation as a driver of China's growth, in L. Song, R. Garnaut, F. Cai and L. Johnston (eds), *China's New Sources of Economic Growth. Volume 1: Reform, resources, and climate change*, Canberra: ANU Press.

China Development Research Foundation (CDRF) (2014), *Demographic Developments in China*, London: Routledge.

Du, Y. (2005), The formation of low fertility and its impacts on long term economic growth in China, *World Economy* (12): 14–23.

Du, Y. (2014), Labor market changes and the new economic growth, *China Opening Journal* (3): 31–5.

Eichengreen, B., Park, D. and Shin, K. (2011), *When fast growing economies slow down: International evidence and implications for China*, NBER Working Papers No. 16919, Cambridge, MA: National Bureau of Economic Research.

Eichengreen, B., Park, D. and Shin, K. (2013), *Growth slowdowns redux: New evidence on the middle-income trap*, NBER Working Papers No. 18673, Cambridge, MA: National Bureau of Economic Research.

Guo, Z., Wang, F. and Cai, Y. (2014), *Low Fertility and Population Sustainable Development in China*, Beijing: China Social Sciences Press.

Huang, P. (2002), Development or involution? Eighteenth-century Britain and China: A review of Kenneth Pomeranz's 'The Great Divergence: China, Europe, and the making of the modern world economy', *Historical Research* (4): 149–76. doi.org/10.2307/2700299.

International Labour Organization (ILO) (2017), *Key Indicators of the Labour Market (KILM)*, Geneva: ILO. Available from: www.ilo.org/ilostat/.

International Monetary Fund (IMF) (2006), Asia rising: Patterns of economic development and growth, in *World Economic Outlook*, September, Washington, DC: IMF.

Jones, C. (2002), Sources of US economic growth in a world of ideas, *The American Economic Review* 92(1): 220–39. doi.org/10.1257/000282802760015685.

Krugman, P. (2013), Hitting China's wall, *The New York Times*, 18 July.

Kuijs, L. (2010), *China through 2020: A macroeconomic scenario*, World Bank China Research Working Paper No. 9, Washington, DC: The World Bank.

Kuznets, S. (1957), Quantitative aspects of the economic growth of nations II: Industrial distribution of national product and labor force, *Economic Development and Cultural Change* 5(Supplement): 3–110. doi.org/10.1086/449740.

Lewis, A. (1954), Economic development with unlimited supplies of labor, *The Manchester School* 22(2): 139–91. doi.org/10.1111/j.1467-9957.1954.tb00021.x.

McMillan, M. S. and Rodrik, D. (2011), *Globalization, structural change and productivity growth*, NBER Working Papers No. 17143, Cambridge, MA: National Bureau of Economic Research.

National Bureau of Statistics (NBS) (various years), *China Statistics Yearbook*, Beijing: China Statistics Press.

National Bureau of Statistics (NBS) (2016), *China: Tabulation of 1% population sampling survey data, 2015*, Beijing: China Statistics Press.

Notestein, F. W. (1945), Population: The long view, in T. W. Schultz (ed.), *Food for the World*, Chicago: University of Chicago Press.

Rawski, T. and Mead, R. (1998), On the trail of China's phantom farmers, *World Development* 26(5): 767–81. doi.org/10.1016/S0305-750X(98)00012-6.

Spence, M. and Hlatshwayo, S. (2011), *The evolving structure of the American economy and the employment challenge*, Working Paper, March, Maurice R. Greenberg Center for Geoeconomic Studies, New York: Council on Foreign Relations.

Srinivasan, T. N. and Bhagwati, J. (1999), *Outward-orientation and development: Are revisionists right?*, Economic Growth Center Discussion Papers No. 806, New Haven, CT: Yale University.

Taylor, J. R. (1993), Rural employment trends and the legacy of surplus labor, 1978–1989, in Y. Y. Kueh and R. F. Ash (eds), *Economic Trends in Chinese Agriculture: The impact of post-Mao reforms*, New York: Oxford University Press.

Timmer, M. P. and Szirmai, A. (2000), Productivity growth in Asian manufacturing: The structural bonus hypothesis examined, *Structural Change and Economic Dynamics* (11): 371–92. doi.org/10.1016/S0954-349X(00)00023-0.

United Nations (UN) (2015), *World Population Prospects: The 2015 revision*, DVD edn, New York: Department of Economic and Social Affairs, Population Division.

Wang, F. and Mason, A. (2008), The demographic factor in China's transition, in L. Brandt and T. G. Rawski (eds), *China's Great Economic Transformation*, Cambridge: Cambridge University Press.

Whalley, J. and Zhao, X. (2010), *The contribution of human capital to China's economic growth*, NBER Working Papers No. 16592, Cambridge, MA: National Bureau of Economic Research.

Williamson, J. (1997), *Growth, distribution and demography: Some lessons from history*, NBER Working Papers No. 6244, Cambridge, MA: National Bureau of Economic Research.

World Bank (1998), *China 2020: Development challenges in the new century*, Washington, DC: The World Bank.

World Bank and International Monetary Fund (IMF) (2016), *Global Monitoring Report 2015/2016: Development goals in an era of demographic change*, Washington, DC: The World Bank.

Young, A. (2003), Gold into base metals: Productivity growth in the People's Republic of China during the reform period, *Journal of Political Economy* 111(6): 1220–61. doi.org/10.1086/378532.

Zhu, X. (2012), Understanding China's growth: Past, present, and future, *Journal of Economic Perspectives* 26(4): 103–24. doi.org/10.1257/jep.26.4.103.

14. Marketisation in China from 1997 to 2014: Achievements and contribution to growth

Fan Gang, Guangrong Ma and Xiaolu Wang

China has persevered in its market-oriented economic reform for 40 years. Guided by a reform strategy of 'crossing the river by feeling the stones', China managed to avoid the major economic decline and crisis that occurred in other transitional economies such as Russia and others in Eastern Europe, and successfully transformed its centrally planned economy into a largely market-oriented economy. In the past 40 years, China has achieved average annual gross domestic product (GDP) growth of 9.5 percentage points, and overtook the United States to become the world's largest economy, measured by purchasing power parity (PPP), in 2014. Rapid economic growth has lifted millions of Chinese people out of poverty and improved their living standards.

To date, there is still a lack of quantitative studies of the contribution of marketisation to economic growth and the progress of productivity, due to the lack of a general indicator with which to measure the achievements of market-oriented reform.[1] Such reform is a systematic transformation of the country's overall economic, social and legal systems. This chapter employs the provincial level National Economic Research Institute (NERI) Index of Marketisation, developed by the NERI Reform Foundation, to account for the contribution to economic growth of market-oriented reform. The average marketisation score for China's 31 provinces increased substantially, from 4 to 8.4 in the period 1997–2014. However, during the period 2008–11, the marketisation process stagnated, probably because government intervention increased to cope with the Global Financial Crisis (GFC). Our findings indicate that, between 1997 and 2014, market-oriented reform contributed an average of 1.3 percentage points to the annual economic growth rate. The process of marketisation significantly improved resource allocation, which contributed to 35 per cent of the growth of total factor productivity (TFP).

The impact of market-oriented reforms on economic growth has been of great interest in transitional economics since the early 1990s (Roland 2000). Starting with the economic transitions in Eastern Europe and the former Soviet Union, economists began to study the impact of reform on economic growth in transitional

1 An exception is Fan et al. (2011), in which we examine the period 1997–2007. In this chapter, we extend the period to 1997–2014 by using the newly constructed marketisation index.

economies. The key to such research is to identify systematic indicators with which to measure the transition process. The annual *Transition Report* from the European Bank for Reconstruction and Development (EBRD) provides representative indices for various aspects of reform, such as price liberalisation, corporate reform, privatisation, foreign exchange and trade liberalisation, competition policy and reform of financial institutions, in 27 transitional economies. However, because of assessment difficulties, measurement problems, differences in research approaches, as well as the differences in countries' transition paths, previous studies have failed to reach consistent conclusions (Babetskii and Campos 2007). Some earlier studies, such as Havrylyshyn et al. (1998), using EBRD transition indices, and De Melo et al. (2001), using their own transition indices, concluded that market-oriented reform significantly contributed to economic development. However, these were not corroborated by subsequent studies. According to the results of empirical research by Falccetti et al. (2002), the effect of reform on economic growth is not robust and depends on the selection of sample countries and periods. Fidrmuc (2001) also found that, although economic transition had a positive effect on economic growth before 1995, the impact was insignificant for the period between 1996 and 2000.

As for the sample choice, all of the above studies were conducted on Eastern European and former Soviet countries. For a long time, mainstream international economists gave insufficient attention to China's different transitional path. Only in the past decade have China's economic achievements and transition experiences started to catch the attention of the international economics community. Nevertheless, research on the effect of China's marketisation on economic growth has been limited. In the NERI Index of Marketisation, we see marketisation as a systematic, and gradual, process of institutional development. We therefore measure the progress of marketisation from five aspects: the relationship between government and the market, development of the nonstate (private) sector, development of product markets, development of factor markets and the development of market intermediaries as well as a market-friendly legal environment. This system is constructed on the basis of objective statistics or survey data. We believe such a system can provide rich information on the process of marketisation. Furthermore, the NERI index provides panel datasets to catch regional differences over time, thus making cross-provincial comparison possible.

Part two of this chapter reviews the major achievements of marketisation in China between 1997 and 2014. Part three explains the econometric models and data we employed in our study. Part four presents the regression results and analysis, and calculates the contribution of marketisation to economic growth via growth accounting, while part five provides the conclusion.

China's achievements in marketisation

The NERI index is an assessment system for relative progress in marketisation for China's provinces using a comparative method. Marketisation is assessed in five fields by 23 basic indicators. Data are from both statistics and enterprise surveys. The NERI index is now available for the period 1997–2014. Five reports have been published (Fan and Wang 2001; Fan et al. 2003b, 2004, 2007, 2016).

In this index system, each of the 23 indicators is normalised into a basic index with a 0–10 relative score system for the base year. The best- and worst-performing provinces for a particular indicator are given scores of 10 and 0, respectively. Other provinces are rated in between, according to their performance in this indicator relative to the best and worst performed provinces. For a positively related indicator, for instance, the basic index score, *j*, for province *i*, noted as S_{ij}, is calculated with Equation 14.1.

Equation 14.1

$$S_{ij} = \frac{V_i - V_{\min}}{V_{\max} - V_{\min}} \times 10$$

After positive or negative variations over years, a basic index allows a province to have scores above 10 or below 0, so that its progress over time can be measured. For a certain field—for instance, development of the nonstate enterprise sector—a field index is constituted using a few basic indices. A total of five field indices constitutes the overall marketisation index. All field indices are weighted equally in the overall index, as are the basic indices in each field index.

The NERI marketisation index indicates the relative process of marketisation, but does not denote how far a province is from a pure market economy. So far, no economic theory can depict a full market economy—nor does such a thing exist in reality. However, the relative progress of marketisation is observable. The index is designed to compare the relative achievement of marketisation across provinces and measure their temporal changes. The multi-angle analysis and the horizontal and vertical comparability and measurement using objective indicators constitute the distinctive features of the NERI index. Another advantage of the index is that it avoids the subjective judgement that exists in other studies. A few of the indicators used in the NERI index are assessments collected from corporate executives, but the survey includes extensive samples, thus minimising the impact of random errors.

As indicated by the index, China has made significant achievements in marketisation. The average marketisation score for China's 31 provinces (including five autonomous minority ethnic regions and three municipalities directly under central administration) increased from 4 to 8.4 in the period 1997–2014 (see Figure 14.1).

However, the growth of the marketisation index is not steady. The marketisation process was slow between 1997 and 2000, during which time the average score increased by only 0.1 point each year. The marketisation pace accelerated between 2001 and 2008, with an average annual increase of 0.37 point, suggesting China's accession to the World Trade Organization (WTO) in 2001 might have played a positive role in promoting its marketisation. However, the marketisation process again slowed substantially, in the period 2008–11, probably because government intervention increased to cope with the GFC. In the period 2012–14, the process began to grow again.

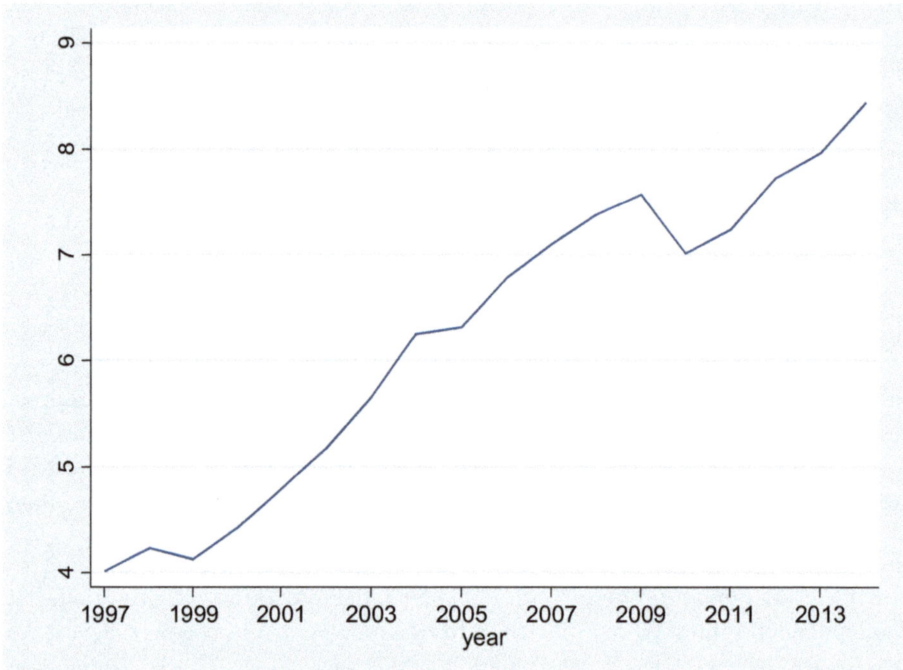

Figure 14.1 Average marketisation index score, 1997–2014

Source: Fan et al. (2016).

In terms of regional development, although all 31 provinces have made positive progress, the process of marketisation is uneven (see Figure 14.2). While the eastern coastal areas are more marketised, the level in some central and western provinces is relatively low. The standard deviation of provincial scores continued to widen after 1997, which indicates growing disparities in the interprovincial marketisation process (see Figure 14.3). Nevertheless, provinces with both high and low levels of marketisation all experienced appreciable progress in this period.

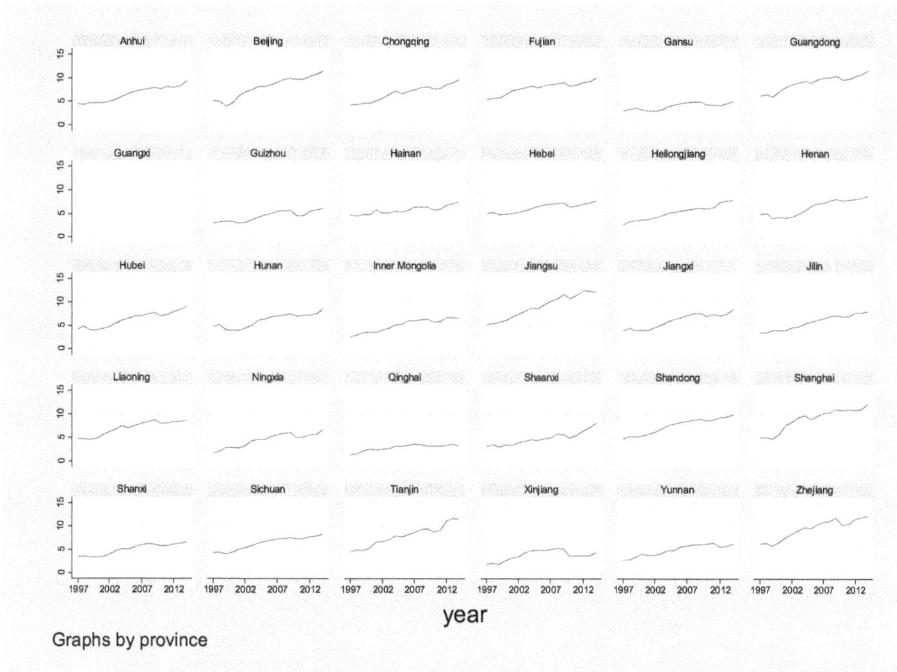

Figure 14.2 NERI index for progress in marketisation in Chinese provinces

Note: Due to limited data, we do not include Tibet, Taiwan, Hong Kong and Macau.

Source: Fan et al. (2016).

The five aspects of marketisation all improved between 1997 and 2014 (Figure 14.4). Rapid progress has been made in development of the private sector, market intermediaries and the legal environment, and the development of product markets. However, in terms of the government–market relationship, progress has stalled over the past few years. This indicates there is still too much unnecessary government intervention. The development of factor markets was slow between 2003 and 2010, but accelerated after 2011.

There are also bottlenecks in market-oriented transformation. Most importantly, institutional and legal frameworks are incomplete and, to some extent, conflict with the market mechanism. There are still unnecessary government interventions, unregulated financial collections and low administrative transparency. The size of government is increasing and the legal environment for the market is still undesirable, which indicates the need for further institutional change and public sector reform. At the sectoral level, the manufacturing sector is now nearly fully market-oriented, whereas marketisation in the financial sector is lagging. A few service sectors are still low in efficiency and lack market competition. Market intermediaries are underdeveloped.

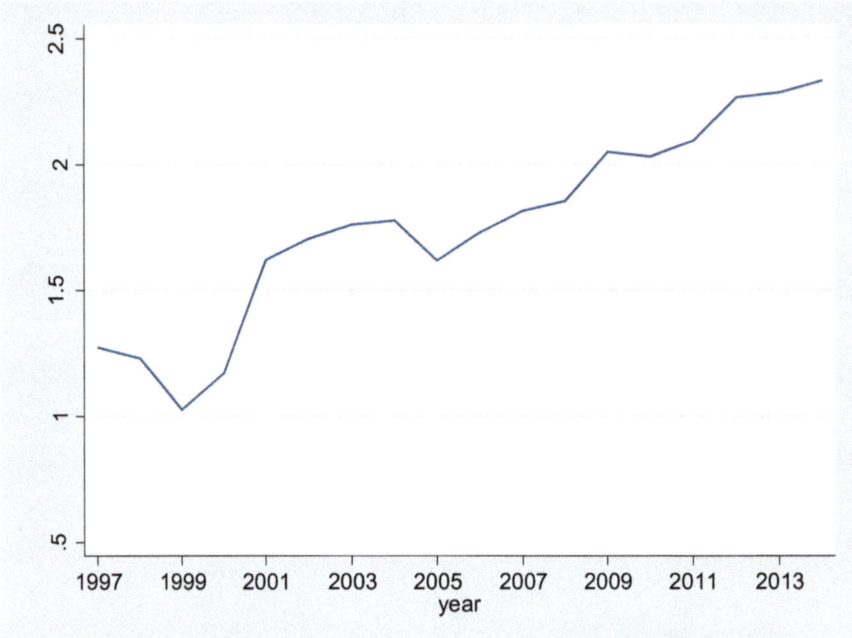

Figure 14.3 Standard deviation of marketisation index, 1997–2014
Source: Fan et al. (2016).

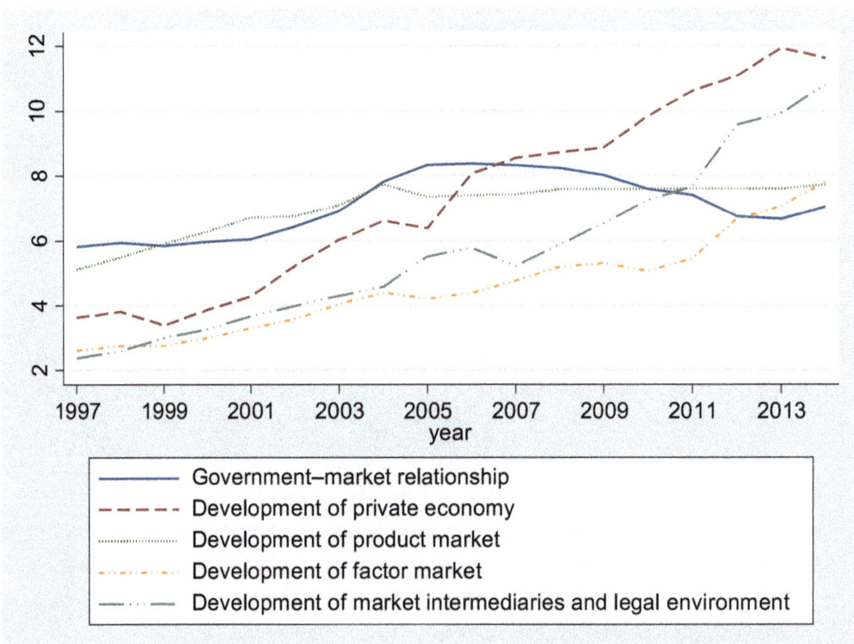

Figure 14.4. Scores for the five aspects of marketisation, 1997–2014
Source: Fan et al. (2016).

Model and data

A growth model for empirical study

For empirical study of economic growth, the Cobb–Douglas production function remains a commonly used functional form because of its analytical convenience. In Lucas's (1998) model, human capital, as an important production factor, is defined as effective labour determined by both the quantity and the educational level of the labour force—that is, the quality of labour. To distinguish the two effects, our study divides the Lucas-defined human capital into two variables—the size of the labour force and its educational level—in a Cobb–Douglas production function (Equation 14.2).

Equation 14.2

$$Y_{it}=A_{it}K_{it}^{\alpha}L_{it}^{\beta}E_{it}^{\gamma}$$

In Equation 14.2, Y_{it} denotes GDP; K_{it} is fixed capital stock; L_{it} is the labour force; and E_{it} is the average number of years of schooling for the labour force of province *i* in year *t*; α, β and γ are the output elasticities of physical capital, the labour force and years of schooling, respectively. A_{it} represents TFP, which comes from two main sources: technological progress and efficiency gains from both improvement in resource allocation and changes in the incentive mechanism at the firm level as a result of market-oriented reforms. Factors that have significant effects on TFP growth at the provincial level are technological progress, marketisation and improvements in infrastructure. Thus, TFP in this study is defined as Equation 14.3.

Equation 14.3

$$A_{it} = Ae^{(\rho MI_{it}+\delta \ln Tech_{it}+\theta Tran_{it}+\lambda_{i}+u_{it})}$$

In Equation 14.3, MI_{it} is the marketisation index of province *i* in year *t*; $lnTech_{it}$ is the stock of research capital in logarithmic form, which is an accumulation of research and development (R&D) inputs calculated using the perpetual inventory method; $Tran_{it}$ is the infrastructure condition in province *i* and is measured by the ratio of standard transport route length to the provincial population. Standard route length is converted from the length of railways and highways of different grades based on their transportation capacity. Meanwhile, λ_i denotes the fixed effect of provinces and is intended to capture province-specific productivity factors that do not change over time; and ε_i is the random disturbance term.

Substituting A_{it} in Equation 14.2 in Equation 14.3 and taking the logarithm on both sides, we arrive at the following econometric model (Equation 14.4).

Equation 14.4

$$\ln Y_{it} = \ln A + \alpha \ln K_{it} + \beta \ln L_{it} + \gamma \ln E_{it} + \rho M_{it} + \delta \ln Tech_{it} + \theta Tran_{it} + \lambda_i + \varepsilon_{it}$$

Description of variables and data

GDP

GDP statistics come from the *China Statistics Yearbook* (NBS various years [a]). They are adjusted to the 2000 constant price. The average annual GDP growth rate was 11.3 per cent in the period 1997–2014.

Years of schooling of labour force

This is calculated from the annual numbers of graduates from primary, secondary and tertiary educational institutions in the past 56 years and national census data. The numbers of years of schooling for graduates from the tertiary, senior secondary, junior secondary and primary levels were taken as 16 years, 12 years, nine years and six years, respectively.

Workers' years of schooling increased from 7.1 years in 1997 to 9.1 years in 2014.

Capital stock

Using the perpetual inventory method and taking 1952 as the base year, we calculated capital stock using fixed asset investment data for the past 56 years (data from the National Bureau of Statistics, NBS). The initial capital stock is assumed to be 10 times the value of fixed asset investment in 1952. The depreciation rate is set at 5 per cent for the period 1952–77 and is assumed to be under stable acceleration during the reform period (1978–2014) to ultimately reach 8 per cent. Because no statistics are available on the price deflator for fixed asset investment before 1991, this is replaced with the commodity retail price index. Between 1997 and 2014, China's fixed capital stock experienced an annual growth rate of 15.5 per cent—much higher than the GDP growth rate.

Research capital

We use the provincial stock of research capital to measure technological progress. This stock is an accumulated aggregation of spending on R&D, on imports of foreign technology and on domestic technology acquisition, using the perpetual inventory method. All statistics are taken from the *China Statistical Yearbook on Science and Technology* (NBS various years [b]). Due to incomplete statistics for years before 1996, we use 1996 as the base period. In keeping with the existing literature, we set the rate of research capital depreciation at 15 per cent. Between 1997 and 2014, provincial research capital stock increased, on average, by 14.7 times, indicating relatively rapid technological progress.

Infrastructure

Even though many types of infrastructure are involved, only limited statistics are available for some of them. The most important, and measurable, type of infrastructure is the length of highways and railways. To make the statistics comparable, we convert the route length of different grades of highways into a standard length, which is equivalent to grade-two highways according to their transportation capacity. We then combine railway length and standard highway length into standard route length using a conversion factor of 14.7. Between 1997 and 2014, China's standard route length per 10,000 people increased from 12.7 km to 31.7 km.

Results

Effects of marketisation on economic growth

Table 14.1 demonstrates the regression results of Equation 14.4. The first and second columns of Table 14.1 show the regression results for the fixed effect model. The third column shows the results from the random effects model. The Hausman test rejects the null hypothesis (random effect) and thus the fixed effect results are accepted. Based on results in column 2, the output elasticities of physical capital, labour and years of schooling are 0.39, 0.11 and 0.51, respectively. The coefficient of the marketisation index (MI) is 0.046, which shows that, with other conditions unchanged, an increase in the marketisation index score of 1 point leads to 4.6 per cent of GDP growth.

Table 14.1 Baseline results

	(1)	(2)	(3)
	ln (GDP)		
LnK	0.528***	0.387***	0.422***
	(0.011)	(0.015)	(0.015)
LnL	0.330***	0.108**	0.349***
	(0.044)	(0.044)	(0.029)
LnE	0.737***	0.512***	0.470***
	(0.088)	(0.079)	(0.082)
MI	0.057***	0.046***	0.042***
	(0.004)	(0.004)	(0.004)
Lntech		0.152***	0.118***
		(0.013)	(0.013)
Transport		0.006***	0.004***
		(0.001)	(0.001)

	(1)	(2)	(3)
		ln (GDP)	
Model	Fixed effect	Fixed effect	Random effect
Observations	540	540	540
R^2	0.996	0.997	

* significance level of 10 per cent

** significance level of 5 per cent

*** significance level of 1 per cent

Based on the regression results in the first column of Table 14.1, derived from growth accounting, Table 14.2 shows the decomposition of provincial economic growth between 1997 and 2014. It indicates that physical capital, labour quantity, educational level and TFP contributed 6.83, 0.37, 0.64 and 3.7 percentage points, respectively, to economic growth. Evidently, capital still plays an important role in economic growth. Among the factors that determine TFP, marketisation contributes 1.45 percentage points, technological progress contributes 1.08 percentage points and infrastructure contributes 0.4 percentage points to economic growth; the remaining unobservable factor contributes 0.77 percentage points. Market-oriented reform remains the most important factor in TFP growth.

Table 14.2 Growth accounting, 1997–2014

Factor	Contribution
GDP growth rate	**100%**
Factor contribution	**61.3%**
Material capital	52.3%
Quantity of labour	1.8%
Educational level	7.2%
TFP contribution	**38.7%**
Marketisation process	11.3%
Technology	19.9%
Infrastructure	6.2%
Nonobservable factor	1.3%

Effects of five aspects of marketisation on growth

To examine whether the various aspects of marketisation have different effects on economic growth, we replaced the general marketisation index in Equation 14.4 with five separate marketisation indices. Table 14.3 shows the regression results. All five aspect indices have a significant impact on economic growth. In terms of the magnitude of the coefficient, improvement of the government–market relationship has the strongest impact on economic growth.

Table 14.3 Five aspects of marketisation and economic growth

	(1)	(2)	(3)	(4)	(5)
			ln (GDP)		
LnK	0.435***	0.394***	0.412***	0.392***	0.413***
	(0.015)	(0.017)	(0.016)	(0.017)	(0.016)
LnL	0.246***	0.114**	0.188***	0.117**	0.102**
	(0.045)	(0.048)	(0.049)	(0.048)	(0.050)
LnE	0.508***	0.530***	0.489***	0.551***	0.504***
	(0.078)	(0.087)	(0.086)	(0.087)	(0.087)
Lntech	0.157***	0.197***	0.195***	0.206***	0.199***
	(0.013)	(0.014)	(0.014)	(0.013)	(0.014)
Transport	0.005***	0.005***	0.004***	0.005***	0.005***
	(0.001)	(0.001)	(0.001)	(0.001)	(0.001)
MI_1	0.029***				
Government–market relationship	(0.003)				
MI_2		0.008***			
Development of private sector		(0.003)			
MI_3			0.014***		
Development of product markets			(0.003)		
MI_4				0.009***	
Development of factor markets				(0.003)	
MI_5					0.004**
Development of market intermediaries and legal environment					(0.002)
Observations	540	539	540	540	540
R^2	0.997	0.996	0.996	0.996	0.996

* significance level of 10 per cent

** significance level of 5 per cent

*** significance level of 1 per cent

Note: All regressions use the fixed effect model.

Conclusions

Using the NERI Index of Marketisation, this chapter presents a quantitative analysis of the role of market-oriented reform in China's economic growth and TFP changes. Our results indicate that, for the period between 1997 and 2014, market-oriented reforms contributed an average of 1.3 percentage points to China's economic growth rate, accounting for 35 per cent of TFP growth. The contribution of marketisation may have been even greater because the acceleration of factor input growth, technology and infrastructure changes is also related to reform. This implies that China has embarked on the right path for transition from a planned to a market economy. Marketisation has been the primary cause of the acceleration of China's economic growth and TFP changes during the reform period.

Although there have been remarkable achievements, China's marketisation is not complete. Marketisation has made crucial progress in some parts of China—particularly in the eastern coastal areas—but in some less-developed areas, the market mechanism is still underdeveloped. In terms of the reform process in different fields, development of the product market has had major successes, but factor markets remain underdeveloped. The government–market relationship has seen limited improvement over the past few years and has even regressed in certain areas. Government sector reform has been lagging, and the size of government continues to expand. These problems may negatively affect future economic growth.

With consideration of the above, future reforms are recommended to focus on the following areas.

First, reform of the factor markets should be carried out to improve the institutional framework for capital and land markets. A market-based pricing mechanism should be established and transactions should be made transparent. The urban household registration system should also be reformed to promote rural–urban labour mobility and population migration.

Second, entry barriers to monopolistic sectors should be reduced, and both market competition and public monitoring mechanisms should be enhanced in those sectors. Resource taxes and SOE dividend distribution systems should be reformed to make better use of monopolistic profits.

Third, excessive government intervention should be further reduced and discriminatory policy treatment in terms of bank credit, interest rates and market access should be eliminated.

Last, government sector reform should be carried out to promote a transparent, noncorrupt and efficient government.

References

Babetskii, I. and Campos, N. (2007), *Does reform work? An econometric examination of the reform-growth puzzle*, Working Paper, Ann Arbor, MI: University of Michigan.

Caselli, F. and Gennaioli, N. (2003), *Dynastic management*, NBER Working Paper No. 9442, Cambridge, MA: National Bureau of Economic Research.

De Melo, M., Denizer, C., Gelb, A. and Tenev, S. (2001), Circumstance and choice: The role of initial conditions and policies in transition economies, *The World Bank Economic Review* 15(1): 1–31. doi.org/10.1093/wber/15.1.1.

Falcetti, E., Raiser, M. and Sanfey, P. (2002), Defying the odds: Initial conditions, reforms, and growth in the first decade of transition, *Journal of Comparative Economics* 30: 229–50. doi.org/10.1006/jcec.2002.1772.

Fan, G. and Wang, X. (2001), *NERI Index of Marketization of China by Province (2000)*, Beijing: Economic Science Press.

Fan, G., Wang, X. and Ma, G. (2011), The contribution of marketization to China's economic growth, [in Chinese], *Economic Research Journal* 9.

Fan, G., Wang, X. and Zhu, H. (2003a), Marketization index of China by regions, *Economic Research* 3: 9–19.

Fan, G., Wang, X. and Zhu, H. (2003b), *NERI Index of Marketization for China's Provinces: 2001 report*, [in Chinese], Beijing: Economic Science Press.

Fan, G., Wang, X. and Zhu, H. (2004), *NERI Index of Marketization for China's Provinces: 2004 report*, [in Chinese], Beijing: Economic Science Press.

Fan, G., Wang, X. and Zhu, H. (2007), *NERI Index of Marketization for China's Provinces: 2006 report*, [in Chinese], Beijing: Economic Science Press.

Fan, G., Wang, X. and Zhu, H. (2016), *NERI Index of Marketization for China's Provinces: 2016 report*, [in Chinese], Beijing: Economic Science Press.

Fidrmuc, J. (2001), Forecasting growth in transition economies: A reassessment, Mimeo.

Havrylyshyn, O., van Rooden, R. and Izvorski, I. (1998), *Recovery and growth in transition economies: A stylized regression analysis*, IMF Working Paper WP/98/141, Washington, DC: International Monetary Fund.

Lucas, R. E. (1988), On the mechanics of economic development, *Journal of Monetary Economics* 22: 3–42. doi.org/10.1016/0304-3932(88)90168-7.

National Bureau of Statistics (NBS) (various years [a]), *China Statistics Yearbook*, Beijing: China Statistics Press.

National Bureau of Statistics (NBS) (various years [b]), *China Statistical Yearbook on Science and Technology*, Beijing: China Statistics Press.

Roland, G. (2000), *Transition and Economics: Politics, markets and firms*, Cambridge, MA: MIT Press.

15. An update on fiscal reform

Christine Wong

In my chapter for the 2013 volume of the *China Update*, I described the evolution of China's system of public finance from the start of market transition, summarising progress to date and pointing to some of the remaining problems (Wong 2013b). It seems appropriate and timely for my chapter in this volume to focus on changes over the past five years—a period neatly bookended by the extensive reform package announced at the third plenum of the eighteenth Communist Party Congress in November 2013, and the latest reforms announced by the just-concluded nineteenth party congress. As it happens, these five years have been highly consequential in the reform of China's fiscal system and, although it is much too soon to know how the latest changes will play out, the direction of reform points to even more significant changes ahead, especially in central–local government relations.

One year after assuming the top leadership post in November 2012, Chinese President Xi Jinping rolled out a sweeping program of reform that was endorsed by the third plenum of the eighteenth party congress. The 60-point 'Decision on Several Major Questions about Deepening Reform' (Xi 2013) spells out an ambitious, comprehensive agenda of more than 300 reform initiatives that cover virtually every facet of China's economy, society and government, including reforms of the fiscal and financial sectors, state-owned enterprises (SOEs), land and property rights, liberalisation of factor prices, household registration, family planning and judicial and administrative reforms. In his 'explanatory notes' on these decisions, President Xi identified the reform of public finance as among the top three key issues to be addressed, noting that '[p]ublic finance is the foundation and important pillar of state governance' (Xi 2013).

Fiscal reforms were off to a rapid start under the energetic direction of then finance minister Lou Jiwei, who announced a comprehensive program that was to proceed in three phases. The first phase—to begin immediately—would focus on budget and public financial management reforms; phase two would begin in 2015 with a focus on reforms of the tax system; and phase three would begin in 2016 and focus on intergovernmental fiscal reform (Han et al. 2014).

Writing in the Communist Party journal *Qiushi*, Lou explained that China's fiscal system has not kept pace with the needs of its growing and increasingly complex economy:

> [T]he defects have become increasingly apparent: the budget management system is not standardized, transparent, or suited to the requirements of modern governance; the tax system ... is not conducive to supporting the shift to the new development paradigm,[1] social fairness, or market integration. The division of responsibilities between the central and local governments is unclear and unreasonable ... These problems ... affect not only the stability and sustainability of the fiscal system itself, they also [adversely] affect the national development strategy and the effectiveness of macroeconomic policy. (Lou 2014)

Lou (2014) argued that, 'in this round of reform, small patches and fixes will no longer suffice', and fundamental reform of the fiscal system was needed to build the foundation to support the modernisation of governance called for by the decisions of the third plenum.

Party and legislative support came swiftly. In June 2014, the Politburo approved the program for comprehensive deepening reform of the fiscal system. In August 2014, the Standing Committee of the National People's Congress approved the revised Budget Law, which mandates numerous changes and, for the first time, authorises local governments to borrow money for capital investments (NPC Standing Committee 2014). These were followed with numerous State Council directives providing detailed guidelines for implementation—for example, both Document 43 on local government debt issuance and Document 45 on deepening budget reform and shifting to medium-term budgets came in September 2014, and Document 63 on building an accrual-based financial management system and Document 71 on improving the structure of expenditures and cleaning up transfers came in December 2014.

After 2014, the momentum of reform appears to have slowed significantly, with few legislative achievements. Little progress was made in tax reform. Of the three areas identified by Lou Jiwei, only the replacement of the business tax with the value-added tax (VAT) was completed; few changes have been made to resource taxes, and the much-discussed property tax is still awaiting submission to the National People's Congress. As for intergovernmental reform, although preparatory work began in early 2014, when provinces were asked to prepare proposals for the revision of expenditure assignments,[2] no concrete measures had been put forward before Lou retired as finance minister in November 2016. With the loss of its most forceful and vocal advocate, the fate of deep fiscal reform appeared more tenuous as Xi Jinping's first term drew to a close.

1 As early as 2002, the government announced its goal of shifting to a development paradigm that promotes services and consumption in place of industry and investment (Wong 2010).

2 Fieldwork information, June 2014.

In this chapter, I trace the progress of reforms introduced since the third plenum (hereinafter referred to as the third plenum reforms) and argue that substantial progress has been made in building a framework for budget and public financial management that will provide strong support for the next phase, especially for intergovernmental reform. More importantly, the reforms have changed some incentives for local governments that have set in motion a new dynamic that should gradually clarify the boundary between the state and the market. However, some key aspects of the reform have to date been subverted—most notably, the effort to contain and manage local government debt, which was thwarted by a combination of political, institutional and economic factors.

Section two of this chapter provides a brief background of fiscal reforms over the past four decades and the problems leading up to the third plenum. Section three sets out the key measures of fiscal reform introduced since 2013, while section four assesses their implementation progress to date, focusing on changes in government financial reporting and transparency. Section five summarises and offers some concluding remarks on the prospects for fiscal reforms overall and on intergovernmental fiscal reform during Xi Jinping's second term.

Background to the third plenum fiscal reforms

In the course of transition over the past 40 years, China has had to completely rebuild the system of public finance and associated institutions—from the tax system to tax administration and budget management (Wong and Bird 2008; Wong 2013b). To date, the process has been incremental and reactive, aimed principally at 'putting out fires'. To stem the sharp fiscal decline caused by the dismantling of planning mechanisms that eroded state-owned enterprise profits—a primary source of government revenues in the old system—reforms focused first on rebuilding the government's revenue mechanism.[3] In 1994, a new system of taxes was put in place under the Tax Sharing System reform, which installed VAT, a business tax, a corporate income tax, a personal income tax and several taxes on the transactions of property and land. Though far from ideal, the tax system provides broad-based taxes and is highly income-elastic, and has produced buoyant revenues that grew at almost 1.5 times the rate of GDP through the first decade of this century.

With revenues recovering, the government turned in the late 1990s to financial management reform. A broad package was introduced that included new procedures for budget preparation and approval, and strengthened budget reporting to the National People's Congress. A new budget classification system was rolled out in

3 On the eve of reform, nearly 80 per cent of government revenue came from state-owned enterprises in industry (Wong 1993).

2006 to improve the tracking of expenditure by functional categories. Departmental budgets were introduced to clearly identify all resources and expenditures for each government department; the first step toward holding spending units accountable for the public monies they receive. Standardised procedures for government procurement were introduced, and a treasury single account was created to manage the government's cash receipts and payments. With these reforms, China had begun to put in place the basic infrastructure for a modern system of budget management.

A glaring omission in the reforms was the neglect of changes needed to repair intergovernmental fiscal relations, which had been eroded through the fiscal decline of the 1980s and decisively broken in 1994, when the Tax Sharing System abruptly recentralised the share of revenues without adjusting expenditure assignments. Since 1994, expenditure shares have continued to shift downward to local governments, who account for more than 85 per cent of total budget expenditures today while collecting only half the revenues, and are thus heavily dependent on central government transfers to finance the huge fiscal gap. The distortions created by this dysfunctional intergovernmental system have long been considered key sources of inefficiency in the Chinese economy (World Bank 2002, 2007; Wong passim).

Despite the urgency of intergovernmental fiscal reform though, its prerequisite is the completion of reform of public financial management begun in the late 1990s. This is highlighted by a brief review of the decade preceding the third plenum decisions. Hitting its stride after joining the World Trade Organization (WTO) and riding the wave of an exceptionally buoyant global economy up to the Great Crash of 2008, the Chinese economy grew at double-digit annual rates during the period 2000–12. Government revenues grew even faster, at an annual rate of 22 per cent, and growing revenues allowed for a robust expansion of government. Under the banner of creating a 'harmonious society', many new programs were introduced aimed at improving public services and expanding the social safety net to include rural citizens (Wong 2010, 2016). Many of these programs are huge: the move to provide free rural education covered some 150 million students at the outset in 2006, although the number had fallen steeply to fewer than 100 million by 2013 (MOE 2016). The rural cooperative medical scheme is even bigger—covering more than 830 million participants at its peak—and the basic pension scheme covers more than 500 million people. These programs have added enormous costs to the budgets of the counties and districts—the administrative level responsible for the provision of these services. As a result, the county-level (tier four) share of national budget expenditures jumped from 26 per cent in 2000 to 46 per cent in 2013.[4]

4 Author's calculations from Ministry of Finance (MOF) statistics.

Because these huge programs were rolled out without any significant adjustment to intergovernmental revenue-sharing arrangements, the added expenditure had to be met largely with transfers to county governments. Central government transfers to local governments grew from RMB246 billion in 2000 to RMB4.3 trillion in 2013. Of these, 74 per cent went to the county level, whose fiscal gap had grown to an aggregated total of RMB3.16 trillion![5]

This created several problems: first, the proliferation of programs led to an even greater proliferation of transfer programs, many of them earmarked. For example, there are at least half a dozen earmarked transfers for rural basic education, along with four to five categories of general transfers designed to support salary payments for teachers, calculated on various bases—and this is just at the central government level.[6] In China's fiscal system, these transfers have to be passed down through the administrative hierarchy level by level—from Beijing to the provinces, from the provinces to the municipalities and from the municipalities to the counties and districts. As they moved down through the hierarchy, earmarked grants were often divided further into finer categories as each administrative layer tried to target funds to where they were needed. By the time the funds reached the county level, there had sometimes been more than a dozen transfers just for basic education.[7] The earmarking was often ineffective (Liu et al. 2009), and the administrative burden of managing them created an extraordinary strain on the bureaucracy, far outstripping the capacities of the monitoring and supervisory systems (World Bank 2007).[8] While the new programs have expanded public services and brought many benefits, they have been marred by pervasive wastefulness, program capture, cost inflation and even the appearance of 'ghost teachers' and 'ghost schools'.[9]

The neglect of institutional reform was even more problematic in the cities, with the urban population growing from 191 million in 1980 to 731 million in 2013 (Wong 2013a, 2013b). Amid the steep fiscal decline in the 1980s through to the mid-1990s, the government had few resources to devote to urbanisation. To avoid hindering growth, political leaders tolerated and tacitly encouraged the use of informal, backdoor practices that enabled cities to obtain the resources needed for investment in infrastructure; China's municipalities grew and prospered by relying overwhelmingly on extra-budgetary resources—mainly land sales and off-budget borrowing (Wong 2009, 2013a). Even through the recent fiscal expansion, these practices continued and ratcheted up in intensity, operating largely beyond

5 Equal to 20 per cent of total expenditure in 2013.
6 MOF and fieldwork information.
7 Fieldwork information, 2006–07.
8 For the history of how systems of accountability were weakened by the dismantling of the planned economy and the subsequent long fiscal decline, see Wong (2009). For weaknesses of the systems of monitoring and evaluation, see Wong (2012, 2013a).
9 See World Bank (2007) and Fock and Wong (2008) for problems of rural public finance and service delivery, and Lin and Wong (2012) for examples of problems in the design and distribution of rural subsidies.

government financial oversight.[10] The easy access to money from land and borrowing, in an economy that was expanding at double-digit rates, led inexorably to excessive land takings, overdevelopment, urban sprawl and the creation of excess capacity in industry as cities competed for job-creating investment to raise land values. These activities also brought graft and corruption on an unprecedented scale, and left many cities with unsustainable levels of debt.

Many of the provisions in the fiscal reform package laid out in 2014 were aimed at correcting the problems just described: to build a more efficient framework for service delivery in a multilevel system and to rein in local government debt and extra-budgetary revenues and regain macroeconomic oversight over fiscal activities. Great emphasis was put on improving budget transparency and accountability by strengthening the legal foundations and giving the national and subnational people's congresses greater oversight authority. Intergovernmental reform aimed to clarify and realign revenue and expenditure assignments to reduce reliance on transfers, and tax reform aimed to reduce allocative distortions and make tax a more effective tool for supporting structural reforms of the economy and improving distributional outcomes.

Given the severity of the problems of local government debt and the extent of extra-budgetary financing, all efforts during the early phase of reform were focused on public financial management (PFM) reforms and regaining control over the budget and allocative processes, to establish the accountability mechanisms needed to support an improved intergovernmental fiscal system that would come later.

The third plenum reforms

By far the most important step in the fiscal reform package was the rollout of the revised Budget Law in August 2014, which laid the legal foundation for improving the budget process, codifying many aspects of central–local government responsibilities and building a robust system of PFM. Among its key provisions are stipulations for shifting to a medium-term budget framework to focus on expenditure planning and multiyear budget balancing, away from the rigidity of annual budget balancing and the associated pro-cyclical bias.

The law calls for budget reporting to be comprehensive, going beyond the traditional reporting of on-budget revenue and expenditure to include three additional components: the 'government fund budget', comprising the extra-budgetary and earmarked levies that were formerly called 'extra-budgetary revenues', the biggest piece of which is revenue from land sales; the 'state capital budget', comprising

10 For an early account of how the central government was kept largely in the dark on the development of local government financial vehicles (LGFVs) and the extent of local government borrowing, see Wong (2011).

remittances from SOEs; and the 'social security fund budget', comprising receipts and expenditures for pension and social insurance schemes. While the Budget Law requires the joint reporting of the four budgets, it stops short of calling for their consolidated management and allocation.

In a press conference held just after the Budget Law's passage, then finance minister Lou explained that budget transparency is paramount for combating corruption and stemming it at the source. The new Budget Law sets disclosure requirements for the scope, timing and content of comprehensive government financial reporting, not only for the four budgets, but also for selected key items, including transfer payments, government debt and departmental budgets for spending units. It also specifies legal liabilities for the breach of these budget disclosure norms (Article 92).

To ensure the accuracy and comprehensiveness of the information provided, the law specifies that budget reporting be based on accrual accounting to reflect the true operations, financial status and financial sustainability of government in the medium and long terms (Article 79). This mandate to adopt accrual accounting was endorsed by the State Council four months later, when it issued its 'Reform plan for building the comprehensive financial reporting system using accrual accounting' (Document 63) (State Council 2014b). Together, the Budget Law and Document 63 essentially committed the government to creating a new system of financial reporting. Indeed, Document 63 was ambitious in calling for the establishment by 2020 of the four systems: the government accounting system, the government financial reporting system, the system of auditing and disclosure mechanisms for government financial reports and the system for analysing and applying the information from government financial reporting to improve budget outcomes.

Another critical change under the Budget Law is the authorisation given to provincial governments to borrow through the issuance of provincial government bonds, with tight supervision by central and provincial people's congresses. Under the call to 'open the front door, lock the back door', the Budget Law stipulates that local governments must report on the amount and mode of debt and its purpose, as well as specifying the repayment sources, mechanisms of supervision and legal liabilities (Articles 35 and 94). Detailed guidelines for a debt management system are laid out in State Council Document 43, which ordered local governments to classify and report all outstanding debt by the end of 2014, and assigned to provinces the key role of registering and monitoring this debt (State Council 2014a). It prohibited local governments from borrowing through enterprises or local government financial vehicles (LGFVs) and required that existing LGFVs be separated from local government finance. In addition, the document laid out an ambitious plan to tackle the stock of existing debt by swapping existing bank loans with provincial government bonds.

Progress in implementation

It is not possible in this short chapter to provide a comprehensive review of implementation progress for the third plenum reforms. In this section, I will focus on three key areas: the process and pace of introducing the new system of government financial reporting, progress in increasing the transparency of reporting of government accounts and progress in building a system for managing and containing local government debt.

Government financial reporting

The purpose of accrual accounting is to provide more accurate and comprehensive information on government financial outcomes, including government assets, liabilities, revenue, expenses and cash flows. The new government financial reporting system (GFRS)[11] is expected to form an important part of the foundation for building a modern system of fiscal management that will promote sustainability and good governance. From the start, the Ministry of Finance (MOF) made clear that the new GFRS would be built on international standards modified to fit China's conditions.

Because the new GFRS will be so different from previous financial reporting practices, building this new system will be a complex project with many steps—from extending the scope of reporting to adopting accrual accounting standards, developing standardised accounting rules, building a balance sheet that includes all entities with claims on public resources and establishing an integrated information system linking all reporting entities. In many countries that have adopted accrual accounting, the process of building the system took up to a decade of sustained effort (Liu et al. 2015). In China, the size and difficulty of the project are magnified many times by the large size of the country and the highly decentralised fiscal system, where the GFRS has to be adopted by subnational governments down to the county and district levels—a group that includes more than 3,200 budgeting authorities with widely varying capacities.[12]

Identifying the reporting entities is among the first critical tasks in building the GFRS. According to the principle that government financial reporting must include all entities that have a material impact on the government's fiscal position, international standards call for the inclusion of all SOEs as well as LGFVs that meet

11 To distinguish this new system in China from the Government Financial Statistics (GFS) system widely adopted internationally, this chapter will refer to the Chinese system of government finance reporting as the GFRS.

12 Budgeting authorities include 31 provincial governments and five cities with 'line item' status (Shenzhen, Dalian, Qingdao, Ningbo and Xiamen), more than 300 prefectural level governments, 2,850 counties and districts and, of course, the central government itself.

the control criteria.[13] Given the large number and size of SOEs in China, including their impact on government finances will be an important corrective to what has long been a blind spot in budget reporting.

There are different ways of including the enterprises depending on the nature of their interaction with the budget. SOEs that are strictly market-oriented and have only an arm's-length relationship with government can be included as commercial enterprises. They must file an annual report with the government disclosing their operations and financial status, but their assets and liabilities need not be included in the government balance sheet. Enterprises that have close, recurrent financial interaction with government would be classified as government business corporations, and their accounts must be fully consolidated in the government financial statement. The differing reporting requirements for the two types of enterprises are briefly summarised in Table 15.1.

Table 15.1 Classification of SOEs and their reporting in the GFRS

SOEs	
Government business corporations ('Public benefit' SOEs)	Commercial SOEs
• Full disclosure. • Fully consolidated in government financial statements. • Included in government's statements of operations, cash flow and balance sheets.	• Full disclosure in a separate schedule in government financial report. • Assets and liabilities are not included in government balance sheet. • Net assets are recognised as government investment in government balance sheets.

The first big challenge for the GFRS reform is to collect financial information from SOEs as the basis for their classification as well as for recording. This is not as straightforward as it seems. Until now, enterprise information has been collected not by budget departments but by the State-owned Assets Supervision and Administration Commission (SASAC) and other supervisory agencies, with each agency using a different methodology for counting; there seems to be no agreed set of numbers. This is illustrated by the situation in Beijing Municipality. As shown in Table 15.2, data from four authoritative sources give significantly different statistics on the number of enterprises and their financial statistics.

13 This is true for both the International Monetary Fund's (IMF) GFS and the International Public Sector Accounting Standards (IPSAS). IPSAS determines that a government controls an entity if it meets the three criteria: 1) power over the entity (such as voting rights, the right to appoint senior management and to approve or veto the entity's business decisions); 2) exposure, or rights, to variable benefits (financial or nonfinancial) from its involvement with the entity; and 3) the ability to use its power over the entity to affect the nature or amount of the benefits from its involvement with the other entity.

Table 15.2 Differing counts of SOEs in Beijing Municipality, 2013 (RMB billion)

	Number of enterprises	Total assets	Total debt	Equity	Operating revenue	Profits
A	790	2,333.5	1,202.1	1,131.4	1,068.0	70.9
B	549	573.3	458.6	395.7	436.2	33.1
C	–	2,520.9	1,724.5	796.4	949.9	47.2
D	7,040	3,513.5	–	1,098.6	1,106.6	65.3

– no data

Sources: Row A from NBS (2014: Table 13-4); B: BMBS (2014: Table 11-8); C: Beijing Municipal SASAC (2015); D: MOF (2014: 605–6).

One reason for the differences may be that some of the data refer to all SOEs, while others refer only to SOEs above a specified minimum size; however, a more significant reason for the conflicting numbers may be the complex ownership and control structures that characterise many SOEs. To illustrate, in 2015, there were 46 SOEs that reported directly to the Beijing Municipal SASAC, but most of these were actually enterprise 'groups' comprising many subsidiary companies, so that the number of municipal-owned SOEs was many multiples of 46. For example, the Beijing Municipal Drainage Group (one of the 46) had 28 subsidiaries that engaged in different parts of the water business, from supplying fresh water to disposal of waste water and pipeline management—many of them independent legal entities.[14] For complex enterprises like this, the classification exercise will likely have to go to the subsidiary level.

To complicate matters further, many SOEs engage in some public goods provision alongside their market activities. For example, the Beijing Municipal Infrastructure Investment Corporation is responsible for the financing and construction of subways—a task that has clear characteristics of being a public good—but it also owns 11 subsidiary companies that engage in for-profit land and real estate development, and the extent to which these activities cross-subsidise one another is unrecorded.

Given the pervasive lack of a clear boundary between the public and the market, financial interactions between governments and SOEs are often fuzzy and complex. In these circumstances, a strict application of the International Public Sector Accounting Standards (IPSAS) and Government Financial Statistics (GFS) rules might require the full inclusion (with line-by-line consolidation of their financial status) of a huge portion of SOEs in the GFRS, which would impose an impossible task for quick adoption. In addition, there are some 660,000 public institutions, such as hospitals, universities, research institutes and so on, that provide public services at the behest of government but also have business incomes, and whose

14 Fieldwork information, June 2015.

financial relationship with government will require sorting through. To keep the task to manageable proportions, the interim solution—at least until 2015—has been for many local governments to classify all SOEs as commercial and focus on classifying their LGFVs.[15] In some localities the exercise morphed to simply classifying profitable enterprises as 'commercial' and unprofitable ones as 'public benefit' and putting the latter on the budget.[16]

Unresolved issues in classification notwithstanding, other preparatory work has been proceeding on the GFRS. In November 2015, the MOF issued a document on government financial reporting methodology that laid out plans for determining the scope of the trial effort. The plans called for the development of government financial information systems and training to be conducted in 2016, and, beginning in 2017, compilation of the pilot GFRS (MOF 2015b). In March 2018, the MOF officially launched a pilot program for compiling government financial reports for the 2017 fiscal year using accrual accounting. In this phase, the pilot involves 20 central government agencies and 20 provinces or line item cities, and focuses only on the budgets of the pilot agencies, rather than the whole government (MOF 2018b). Those involved in the pilot are to follow the 140-page trial 'Guidelines for the Preparation of Financial Reports for Government Departments' (MOF 2018a).

The work on construction of a government balance sheet also appears to be progressing. Led by the National Bureau of Statistics (NBS), working with 10 other agencies including the National Development and Reform Commission (NDRC), pilot work was conducted from May 2015 to the end of 2016 in 11 provinces. A draft 'Work Program for National and Local Balance Sheet Preparation' was circulated for comment and was signed off in April 2017 by 13 ministries and sent to the State Council. In June of that year, it was approved at the thirty-sixth meeting of the Central Leading Group for Deepening Reform, and formally issued by the State Council on 6 August 2017, launching the next phase of the work (Xinhua 2017a). However, this document has not been made publicly available. It has been widely reported that a trial national balance sheet was constructed for 2013 but has also not been published (see, for example, 21st Century Economic Herald 2017).

Budget transparency

While the progress of building the GFRS has been largely invisible to the general public, the remarkable progress in budget transparency has been much more visible and quantifiable. In just three years since the Budget Law laid down a mandate to release government financial reports to the public, every subnational government down to the county level has set up a website from which a trove of fiscal information

15 Fieldwork, June 2015.
16 Fieldwork, June 2016.

can be harvested by anyone with access to a computer or smartphone. This is in marked contrast with previous attempts to promote budget transparency—most notably in the earlier rounds of PFM reform in the late 1990s and mid-2000s, when there was little follow through and virtually no penetration to the subnational levels (Wong 2005; Liu 2017). Disclosure requirements are now codified and written into the Budget Law. Article 14 stipulates that governments at all levels must disclose their budgets to the public within 20 days of approval by the people's congress, and the disclosure 'shall explain important matters such as the receipt and uses of transfer payments and debt issuance'. Disclosure requirements are also applied to the budgets of government departments as well as to government procurement. The law also calls for budgets to be audited and for the audit reports on budget execution to also be made public (Article 73). Finally, Article 92 stipulates that failure to meet transparency requirements will trigger corrective action and an investigation into the administrative responsibilities of managers.

Monitoring and enforcement have followed. The MOF's Supervision Department issued a notification on 20 October 2015 announcing the first inspection would take place between 28 October and 20 November 2015. The stated purpose was to check compliance with the Budget Law's requirements for timeliness, completeness, level of detail and information disclosure (MOF 2015a). The inspection covered 258,296 budget units at the provincial, municipal and county levels, achieving 100 per cent coverage. It found compliance rates of 100 per cent at the provincial and municipal levels and 99 per cent at the county level for disclosures of both the 2015 budgets and the 2014 final accounts, but somewhat lower rates for disclosure of departmental budgets and provision of the required content (MOF 2016a).

On the basis of these findings, the MOF issued two documents in 2016 to provide further guidance on the scope of public disclosure. Document 123 stipulated that all local governments set up a unified online platform to disclose their budgetary information, and to include budget disclosure as an additional indicator in the performance evaluation of staff in local finance departments (MOF 2016b). Document 143 ('Operating Procedures for Local Government Budget Disclosures') provides more specific requirements: disclosures must cover all four budgets, with a minimum of six tables for the general budget, four tables for government funds and two each for the state capital budget and the social security fund budget (MOF 2016c). In 2016, an additional criterion was added to check for honesty, with inspectors urged to randomly select units and figures for verification, and to include their findings in the overall scoring.

Three rounds of nationwide inspections have been undertaken, including the third one concluded in December 2017 (Liu 2017). This monitoring effort and the change of incentives are clearly producing results. My own casual perusal of local budget reporting on government websites reveals a growing wealth of fiscal information that is now available online.

Local budget disclosures tend to follow the pace set by the MOF with some lag. For example, in 2009 the MOF provided 61 lines of detail in the final account of budget expenditures. In 2010, it moved to providing 1,020 lines of detail, and the number has since crept up to close to 1,100 lines. Many, but not all, local budget reports follow this template in providing detailed breakdowns of public expenditures running up to 1,000 lines or more. As required, they all contain information on transfers, both inflows and outflows, and all four budgets are provided and comply with the stipulated numbers of tables for each.

To date, these budget reports are still constructed under the old accounting system and on a cash basis. Detailed budgeting is quite advanced on the public finance budget (which used to be called in-budget), but less so on the government fund budget, and even less so on the state capital budget and the social security budget. As expected, the quality of reporting differs across regions, and is higher in the richer, more developed provinces than in the poorer, inland ones. At present, while the budgets are all available publicly, finding them is not always straightforward due to a lack of uniformity in where the information is placed, with budgets sometimes scattered across different websites or in different places within websites. The reporting format and content continue to differ across regions and administrative levels. With the increasingly stringent reporting requirements being implemented, these differences can be expected to shrink over time.

Indeed, this may already be changing. On 6 November 2017, Jiangsu officially launched the 'Jiangsu Budget and Final Accounts Open Access Platform', becoming the first province in China to provide a province-wide platform that includes all local government budget reporting. Developed and built by the provincial finance department and the government service office, the platform aims to provide a centralised portal from which all provincial-, municipal- and county-level budgets and final accounts information can be accessed by the public, and where all reports will use the same templates and uniform standards (Xinhua 2017b).

Managing and containing debt

The thrust of the reform effort in managing local government debt was to ameliorate the default risks from the large existing stock while moving local government borrowing from hidden, off-budget channels into the open, nudging local governments towards a more fiscally sustainable path.

Key provisions of the Budget Law were designed to put in place mechanisms for preventing unsupervised borrowing by local governments. For the first time, they are explicitly permitted to borrow, but under tight control. Article 35 stipulates that local governments can borrow only under quotas from the cap set by the National People's Congress and allocated by the State Council, and only for capital spending, with the use, repayment and assignment of responsibilities supervised by the local people's congresses. The borrowing must be done through bond issuance by the provinces, which are assigned responsibility for allocating and monitoring the debt. Local governments are prohibited from borrowing through any other means or organisations, and from providing guarantees for borrowing by state entities. Article 94 stipulates that any diversion or misuse of funds is punishable by dismissal of those responsible.

Under State Council Document 43, a plan was laid out to tackle the stock of existing debt and create a structure for managing it (State Council 2014a). Along with the Budget Law, this document prohibited LGFVs borrowing on behalf of local governments and ordered them to delink their finances from local government. All existing debt was to be classified as 'general', 'project' or 'enterprise' debt. All general and project debt would be moved to the government's accounts, and many LGFVs would be converted to SOEs. A national registry and an early warning system for local government debt would be built. A program was introduced in 2015 to swap government bonds for local government bank debt. By the end of 2017, RMB10.5 trillion in bonds had been swapped, significantly improving the term structure of local debt and reducing its servicing costs (NAO 2017).

Judging by the outcome of curtailing local government borrowing and keeping it within legal channels, these reform efforts have been a dismal failure. First, rather than fading into history, LGFVs have continued to flourish. World Bank staff estimated the total liabilities of LGFVs (in both bank credit and bonds) grew at more than 20 per cent per annum in both 2015 and 2016, surpassing the growth of overall corporate debt to see their share of outstanding debt in the nonfinancial corporate sector rise from 25 per cent in 2013 to 30 per cent in 2016 (World Bank 2017). In part, this was because the government temporarily lifted the restraint on LGFV borrowing in mid-2015 when economic growth slowed drastically. Ironically, because the debt reclassification exercise had removed a good deal of debt from the balance sheets of LGFVs, many were now in an improved position to borrow, and were unconstrained by the cap on government borrowing as their debt was, under the new Budget Law, not counted as government debt. One estimate has LGFV bonds reaching RMB47 trillion in June 2017—nearly three times the total local government debt recorded in the MOF monitoring system (Yu et al. 2018).

Second, local governments have continued to find hidden ways to borrow, including new ones such as public–private partnerships and service procurement contracts. Other methods are not so new: borrowing from SOEs, LGFVs and local banks and pushing fiscal expenditures on to them, non-payment of construction contracts, and so on (Yu et al. 2018). The numerous problems exposed by MOF inspections and by the National Audit Office (NAO) came to the top leadership's attention by mid-2016, culminating in the 'Plan for Emergency Response to Local Government Debt Risks', issued by the State Council in October 2016, which required all local governments to set up a Leading Group for Debt Management and assign responsibilities for strengthening monitoring and preparing emergency responses (State Council 2016). In April and May 2017, a package of decrees was issued jointly by the MOF, NDRC, People's Bank of China (PBC), China Banking Regulatory Commission (CBRC), China Securities Regulatory Commission (CSRC) and the Ministry of Justice, setting out further responsibilities of local governments for monitoring and assigning accountability not only for direct debt, but also for contingent debts, and again stressing that LGFVs must be delinked from government finances. The MOF issued several more directives in 2017 reiterating the prohibition of off-budget borrowing and the use of LGFVs for borrowing.

The one bright spot has been the growth and development of a market for government securities, including local government bonds. Over time, this may become a normal channel for local government borrowing. According to the MOF's accounts, 90 per cent of the local government debt currently reported is held in government bonds. While they are still not market-based, this may change over time.

Conclusion

The fiscal reforms initiated by then finance minister Lou Jiwei were comprehensive in scope and extremely far reaching. They set about building infrastructure for budget management that is better able to support the increasingly large and complex public sector in China, which rivals the size of the US Federal Government in annual spending. When completed, the new government financial reporting system will provide detailed information on the true size and operations of the public sector that will support more sophisticated whole-of-government analyses. Accompanied by stringent disclosure rules and improved accounting standards, the system will provide higher-level governments with the information base for designing improved intergovernmental arrangements—the ultimate goal of Lou's reform package.

In this review, I have identified significant progress towards installing the GFRS. More importantly, I believe the process of collecting and scrutinising the financial claims of all state-owned entities on the budget has also set in motion a new dynamic that will gradually lead to a clarification of the boundary between the state and the market, as local governments have greater incentive to loosen their ties to SOEs to reduce the administrative burden of reporting as well as to improve the government's balance sheet to make room for new debt. The remarkable increase in transparency in local government financial reporting will enhance the ability of higher levels to hold local governments accountable and reduce opportunities for the diversion of funds. Putting this information into the public sphere will also create greater potential for public participation in budgeting, whether intended or not.

These reforms are just starting, however, and their progress is fragile and could easily be reversed. The failure of debt containment provides a perfect illustration of the uselessness of building structures when rules can be circumvented or are not enforced. Even though a national registry of local government debt has been in operation since 2015—along with an early warning system for fiscal risks—to date, they are but empty shells, as they are unable to track hidden debt and do not count the contingent liabilities of LGFVs.

The experience of the past five years has confirmed the enormous difficulty of, and the long road ahead for, fiscal reform, which must compete with other macroeconomic concerns (such as the rate of growth) and powerful vested interests. The recent appointment of Liu Kun as finance minister signals that fiscal reform will continue in Xi Jinping's second term. With the focus turning to intergovernmental reform and doubling down on efforts to contain local government debt, Liu's experience in Guangdong should prove particularly useful since the province has been a leader in performance management and debt resolution.[17] While hoping for a supportive policy environment for fiscal reform, Minister Liu would do well to fast-track a program of capacity-building in the MOF and subnational finance bureaus. This new system is administratively far more demanding than the one being replaced, and will require higher-level skills.

References

21st Century Economic Herald (2017), The Central Leading Group for Comprehensively Deepening Reform approved the work plan to compile national and local balance sheets, [in Chinese], *21st Century Economic Herald*, 27 June. Available from: www.cb.com.cn/economy/2017_0627/1188687.html.

Beijing Municipal Bureau of Statistics (BMBS) (2014), *Beijing Statistical Yearbook 2014*, Beijing: China Statistics Press.

Beijing Municipal State-owned Assets Supervision and Administration Commission (SASAC) (2015), Website, [in Chinese]. Available from: www.bjgzw.gov.cn/qt/forepageview/gzhy/gzhy15.jsp.

Fock, A. and Wong, C. (2008), *Financing rural development for a harmonious society in China: Recent reforms in public finance and their prospects*, World Bank Policy Research Working Paper 4693, August, Washington, DC: The World Bank.

17 Liu headed the debt resolution in the bankruptcy of the Guangdong International Trust and Investment Corporation in the late 1990s (Times Weekly 2018).

Han, J., Li, G. and Yuxin, H. (2014), Deep changes that affect the modernization of the nation's governance system: Minister of finance Lou Jiwei explains the overall program for deepening reform of the fiscal system, *Xinhua*, 4 July.

International Monetary Fund (IMF) (2015), *Government Finance Statistics Manual 2014*, Washington, DC: IMF.

Lin, W. and Wong, C. (2012), Are Beijing's equalization policies reaching the poor? An analysis of direct subsidies under the 'three rurals' (Sannong), *China Journal* 67(January). doi.org/10.1086/665738.

Liu, L., Pradelli, J. and Zhao, M. (2015), *International experience on subnational financial reporting for managing fiscal risks*, World Bank Policy Note (Draft), Washington, DC: The World Bank.

Liu, M. (2017), An important promoter of 'transparent government': A special inspection of local budgets and final accounts open a 'window' for the public, *China Finance and Economics News*, 1 March. Available from: www.mof.gov.cn/zhengwuxinxi/caijingshidian/zgcjb/201703/t20170301_2544207.html.

Liu, M., Wang, J., Tao, R. and Murphy, R. (2009), The political economy of earmarked transfers in a state-designated poor county in western China: Central policies and local responses, *The China Quarterly* 200(December): 973–94. doi.org/10.1017/S0305741009990580.

Lou, J. (2014), Deepening reform of the fiscal and tax system to build a modern system of public finance, [in Chinese], *Qiushi* 20(13 October).

Ministry of Education (MOE) (2016), *Chinese Education Statistical Yearbook*, Beijing: China Statistics Press.

Ministry of Finance (MOF) (2014), *China Accounting Yearbook 2014*, Beijing: MOF.

Ministry of Finance (MOF) (2015a), *Notification on launching a special inspection of the situation of local budget disclosures*, [in Chinese], Doc. 84, Supervision and Inspection Bureau, 20 October, Beijing: MOF.

Ministry of Finance (MOF) (2015b), *Notification on the issuance of government financial reporting methodology (trial)*, MOF Doc. 212, 16 November, Beijing: MOF.

Ministry of Finance (MOF) (2016a), *Bulletin on inspection of local budget and final accounts and NEV subsidies*, [in Chinese], 8 September, Beijing: MOF Press Office. Available from: www.mof.gov.cn/zhengwuxinxi/bulinggonggao/tongzhitonggao/201609/t20160908_2413434.htm.

Ministry of Finance (MOF) (2016b), *Notice on conscientiously doing a good job on local government budget disclosures*, [in Chinese], MOF Doc. 123, Beijing: MOF. Available from: yss.mof.gov.cn/zhengwuxinxi/zhengceguizhang/201609/t20160924_2426035.html.

Ministry of Finance (MOF) (2016c), *Operating procedures for local government budget disclosures*, [in Chinese], MOF Doc. 143, Beijing: MOF. Available from: www.mof.gov.cn/gp/xxgkml/yss/201611/t20161121_2510868.html.

Ministry of Finance (MOF) (2018a), *Circular of the Ministry of Finance on revising and printing the 'guidelines for the preparation of financial reports for government departments (trial)'*, [in Chinese], MOF Doc. 29, 1 March, Beijing: MOF. Available from: www.weichicaiwu.com/law/4258.html.

Ministry of Finance (MOF) (2018b), *Notice of the Ministry of Finance on launching the pilot work of 2017 government financial report compilation*, [in Chinese], MOF Doc. 34, 12 March, Beijing: MOF. Available from: www.waizi.org.cn/doc/31883.html.

National Audit Office of China (NAO) (2017), Report of the Ministry of Finance on resolutely stopping local governments illegally raising debt, [in Chinese], 12 December, *Wall Street News*. Available from: wallstreetcn.com/articles/3051249.

National Bureau of Statistics (NBS) (2014), *China Statistical Yearbook 2014*, Beijing: China Statistics Press.

National People's Congress (NPC) Standing Committee (2014), *Decision on revising the 'People's Republic of China Budget Law'*, [in Chinese], 31 August, Beijing: NPC of the People's Republic of China. Available from: www.npc.gov.cn/npc/xinwen/2014-09/01/content_1877061.htm.

State Council (2014a), *Opinion on strengthening management of local government debt*, Doc. 43, 21 September, Beijing: State Council.

State Council (2014b), *Reform plan for building the comprehensive financial reporting system using accrual accounting*, [in Chinese], Doc. 63, 12 December, Beijing: State Council.

State Council (2016), *Plan for emergency response to local government debt risks*, [in Chinese], Office of the State Council Letter No. 88, 27 October, Beijing: State Council.

Times Weekly (2018), Finance Minister Liu Kun's past in Guangdong, [in Chinese], *Times Weekly*, 27 March. Available from: news.sina.com.cn/c/2018-03-27/doc-ifysrpxk6278916.shtml.

Wong, C. (1993), Public Finance and Economic Decentralization, in W. Galenson (ed.), *China's Economic Reform in the 1990s*, Ann Arbor: University of Michigan Press.

Wong, C. (2005), Public sector budgeting issues in China, in Organisation for Economic Co-operation and Development (OECD), *Governance in China*, Paris: OECD Publishing.

Wong, C. (2009), Rebuilding government for the 21st century: Can China incrementally reform the public sector?, *China Quarterly* 200(December). doi.org/10.1017/S0305741009990567.

Wong, C. (2010), Fiscal reform: Paying for the harmonious society, *China Economic Quarterly* 14(2): 22–7.

Wong, C. (2011), The fiscal stimulus program and problems of macroeconomic management in China, *OECD Journal on Budgeting* 11(3): 1–24. doi.org/10.1787/budget-11-5kg3nhljqrjl.

Wong, C. (2012), *Toward building performance-oriented management in China: The critical role of M&E and the long road ahead*, ECD Working Paper Series No. 27, September, Washington, DC: World Bank Independent Evaluation Group.

Wong, C. (2013a), Paying for urbanization: Challenges for China's municipal finance in the 21st century, in R. Bahl, J. Linn and D. Wetzel (eds), *Metropolitan Government Finances in Developing Countries*, Cambridge, MA: Lincoln Institute for Land Policy.

Wong, C. (2013b), Reforming China's public finances for long-term growth, in R. Garnaut, C. Fang and L. Song (eds), *China: A new model for growth and development*, Canberra: ANU E Press. doi.org/10.22459/CNMGD.07.2013.10.

Wong, C. (2016), Budget reform in China: Progress and prospects in the Xi Jinping era, *OECD Journal on Budgeting* 15(3): 27–36. doi.org/10.1787/budget-15-5jm0zbtm3pzn.

Wong, C. and Bird, R. (2008), China's Fiscal System: A Work in Progress, in L. Brandt and T. Rawski (eds), *China's Great Transformation: Origins, Mechanism and Consequences of the Post-Reform Economic Boom*, New York: Cambridge University Press.

World Bank (2002), *China: National Development and Sub-national Finance, a Review of Provincial Expenditures,* Report No. 22951-CHA, April, Washington, DC: World Bank.

World Bank (2007), *China: Public services for building the new socialist countryside*, Report No. 40221-CN, Washington, DC: The World Bank.

World Bank (2017), *China Economic Update—December 2017: Growth, resilience and reform momentum*, 19 December, Washington, DC: The World Bank.

Xi, J. (2013), An explanation of the Chinese Communist Party Central Committee decision on several major questions about deepening reform, [in Chinese], *Xinhua*, 15 November. Available from: news.xinhuanet.com/politics/2013-11/15/c_118164294.htm.

Xinhua (2017a), National Bureau of Statistics answers reporters' questions on the programme for national and local balance sheet preparation, [in Chinese], *Xinhua*, 31 October. Available from: www.xinhuanet.com/fortune/2017-10/31/c_129729861.htm.

Xinhua (2017b), Government finance reports can be checked and supervised in Jiangsu, *Xinhua Daily*, 11 November. Available from: news.sina.com.cn/o/2017-11-07/doc-ifynmnae2405315.shtml.

Yu, H., Wang, X. and Teng, J. X. (2018), China battles hidden local government debt, *Caixin Global*, 11 March. Available from: www.caixinglobal.com/2018-03-11/china-battles-hidden-local-government-debt-101219793.html.

Zhang, Y. S. and Barnett, S. (2014), *Fiscal vulnerabilities and risks from local government finance in China*, IMF Working Paper No. 14/4, January, Washington, DC: International Monetary Fund.

16. 'Strong on quantity, weak on quality': China's financial reform between 1978 and 2018

Yiping Huang and Xun Wang

Introduction

When China's economic reform began at the end of 1978, the country had only one formal financial institution, the People's Bank of China (PBC). This served as both the central bank and the commercial bank and accounted for 93 per cent of the country's total financial assets. In the following 40 years, the financial sector experienced major reform, opening and development. Today, China's 'big four' banks are regularly ranked among the 10 largest in the world. China's equity and bond markets have also joined the top ranks globally in recent years. China's currency, the renminbi (RMB), is part of the International Monetary Fund's Special Drawing Rights (SDR) basket, along with the US dollar, the euro, the British pound and the Japanese yen.

In this chapter, we take stock of China's past financial reform by asking five questions. What is unique in China's financial reform experience? What logic lay behind policy? How did the reform strategy contribute to China's economic growth and financial stability? Why did systemic financial risks escalate recently? And what further steps are required to establish an efficient and robust financial system, and contain systemic financial risks?

Our key findings can be summarised as follows. First, China's financial reform and development during the past four decades have been strong on quantity, but weak on quality. China has a large number of financial institutions and huge volumes of financial assets. Yet Chinese authorities maintain serious and extensive restrictions on financial markets, including on interest rates, exchange rates and funds allocation.

Second, this unique path derives from a much broader economic reform strategy—the dual-track approach between the state and the nonstate sectors. To support less efficient state-owned enterprises (SOEs), the government had to intervene in the allocation and pricing of production factors, which led to a dual-track approach to liberalisation in product and factor markets. Deep financial repression is a form of distortion. Repressive financial policies resulted in dual-track financial markets between the formal and informal sectors.

Third, this pattern of financial reform worked quite well initially, evidenced by strong economic growth, but it now creates risks. Empirical analyses confirmed that the positive 'Stiglitz effect' of financial repression on growth dominated in the 1980s and 1990s in China, while the negative 'McKinnon effect' dominated in the 2000s. Repressive financial policies also helped maintain financial stability, as they underpin investor confidence, although with increasing consequences of moral hazard over time.

Fourth, systemic financial risks increased dramatically over time, especially after the Global Financial Crisis (GFC). There were several causes. Persistently slower economic growth weakened micro-level balance sheets, with an increasing proportion of zombie firms. The combination of large money supply—from the bank-dominated financial system and the government's implicit guarantee policy—and the limited pool of investible assets expanded financial risks. Shrinking policy flexibility reduced investor confidence and increased market volatility.

Fifth, to complete the task of building an effective financial system, the government needs to take at least three further steps: create a level playing field, allow markets to work and improve financial regulation. Enforcing a stronger market will ultimately determine success or failure. Specifically, the government needs to end three dual-track systems—stopping protection for SOEs and state intervention in the financial market. The authorities will also need to make the regulatory system more independent, professional and authoritative.

China's unique financial reform strategy

About the turn of the twentieth century, China had a relatively strong financial sector. At that time, Shanghai was a major international financial centre. After the 1867 Paris International Monetary Conference, most Western countries shifted from the previous bimetallism (of gold and silver) to the sole gold standard. Even the traditional silver-bloc countries such as India and Japan also adopted the gold standard before 1900. As China was the only major country continuing with the silver standard, this shift in the international monetary system delivered a positive shock to the Chinese economy—increasing liquidity and devaluing the currency. Therefore, large parts of the economy prospered—particularly the textile industry, the property sector, the stock market and the banking industry. Such robust performance continued even as the Great Depression struck the Western world from 1929. The economic boom ended abruptly after the US Congress adopted the *Silver Purchase Act* in 1934.

The financial industry nearly collapsed during China's war against Japan in 1937–45 and the Chinese civil war in 1946–49. During the latter period, undisciplined money supply caused hyperinflation and macroeconomic instability, which in turn contributed to the fall of the National Party government. Soon after the Communist Party of China (CPC) took power in 1949, it started its socialist transformation. All financial institutions were nationalised after 1952 and then closed. All funds were collected and distributed through the central planning system, and there was little need for financial intermediation. At the beginning of economic reform in 1978, the PBC was the only financial institution operating, serving central and commercial banking functions.

In 1979, authorities quickly reestablished the Bank of China (BOC) and the People's Construction Bank of China (later renamed the China Construction Bank or CCB) and, in 1978, the Agricultural Bank of China (ABC). In 1984, the old PBC was split into two institutions, the Industrial and Commercial Bank of China (ICBC) and the new central PBC, and the People's Insurance Company of China (PICC) was reestablished. In 1991 and 1992, respectively, the government created the Shenzhen and Shanghai stock exchanges.

China's experience of financial reform exhibits a unique pattern. China was 'strong in establishing financial institutions and growing financial assets, but weak in liberalizing financial markets and improving corporate governance' (Huang et al. 2013: 44). China has large numbers of banking, insurance, securities and other financial institutions. In the banking sector, there are three policy banks, five large commercial banks, 12 national joint stock banks, 133 city commercial banks, five private banks and 859 rural commercial banks. In 2016, the 'big four' were all among the world's five largest banks and were identified by the Financial Stability Board as globally systemically important (Table 16.1). At the same time, Chinese financial markets and assets grew exponentially. Domestic credit provided to the private sector rose from 49 per cent of gross domestic product (GDP) in 1979 to 199 per cent in 2016. Broad money supply (M2) is already greater than in the United States and its proportion to GDP—208 per cent at the end of 2016—is among the highest in the world.

By the end of 2016, domestic stock exchanges had a total of 3,052 listed companies, and total market capitalisation reached RMB50.8 trillion (Table 16.2). China had the second largest market capitalisation in the world, accounting for 11.3 per cent of the global total. The market value of corporate and government bonds rose 151 times, from RMB418 billion in 1997 to RMB63.7 trillion in 2016. The proportion of debt finance in the country's total social financing also increased, from 5 per cent to 24 per cent. China is now the world's third largest debt market. China's insurance industry ranked third in the world at the end of 2016, with total insurance industry assets of RMB15.1 trillion and gross premium income of RMB3.1 trillion.

Table 16.1 Ranking of 10 largest banks in the world, 1996 and 2016 (US$ billion)

1996				2016			
	Bank	Country	Assets		Bank	Country	Assets
1	Deutsche Bank	Germany	503	1	ICBC	China	3,422
2	UFJ Bank	Japan	501	2	CCB	China	2,827
3	Sumitomo Bank	Japan	500	3	ABC	China	2,741
4	Dai-Ichi Kangyo Bank	Japan	499	4	Mitsubishi UFJ Financial	Japan	2,649
5	Fuji Bank	Japan	487	5	BOC	China	2,591
6	Sakura Bank	Japan	478	6	HSBC Holdings	UK	2,410
7	Bank of Tokyo-Mitsubishi	Japan	475	7	JP Morgan Chase	US	2,352
8	Norinchukin Bank	Japan	430	8	BNP Paribas	France	2,168
9	Crédit Agricole	France	386	9	Bank of America	US	2,147
10	ICBC	China	374	10	Credit Agricole	France	1,847

Source: The Financial Times Limited (2018).

Table 16.2 Summary information of China's capital market, 1990–2016

Equity markets						
Year	No. listed companies	Investor accounts ('000)	Market capitalisation (RMB billion)	Tradable volume (RMB billion)	Trading volume (RMB billion)	Funds raised (RMB billion)
1993	183	8,350	353	83	363	n.a.
1995	323	12,940	347	94	404	n.a.
2005	1,381	71,890	3,245	1,064	3,166	34
2010	2,063	133,910	26,542	19,311	54,563	895
2016	3,052	117,410	50,824	39,327	126,726	1,891
Debt markets						
Year	Debt issuance (RMB billion)	Year-end trusted value (RMB billion)	Government bond issuance (RMB billion)	Central bank notes (RMB billion)	Financial debt issuance (RMB billion)	Corporate bond issuance (RMB billion)
1990	32	n.a.	20	n.a.	n.a.	13
1995	181	n.a.	151	n.a.	n.a.	30
2005	4,218	7,340	704	2,788	716	205
2010	9,524	20,511	1,978	46,601	1,412	1,681
2016	18,564	63,700	9,109		5,242	8,224

n.a. = not available.

Sources: PBC (2016, 2017); Wind Database.

The state continues to intervene heavily in the operation of the financial system. The PBC regularly decides on base deposit and lending rates, although commercial banks' freedom in setting their own rates has increased over time. The central bank also frequently intervenes in foreign exchange rates, through the setting of central parity, defining daily trading bands and buying and selling foreign exchange. Chinese authorities have also adopted various ways of influencing the allocation of bank credit and initial public offerings (IPOs), through such means as loan quotas, industry policy and IPO approval. Most of the major financial institutions in the country have majority state ownership. According to one measure, China's degree of financial repression was higher than the average of both middle-income and low-income countries (Abiad et al. 2008). Among all 91 countries with available data, China ranked fourth for financial repression in 2005. These numbers are somewhat outdated, with progress in Chinese financial reform since then; however, China probably still lags behind many developing countries.

China's financial repression declined steadily over recent decades, but policy interventions remain common and frequent. One example is interest rate policy. From the late 1990s, the PBC gradually liberalised interest rates for both money and capital markets (Table 16.3). It also started to increase the flexibility for commercial banks to vary their deposit and lending rates around the base (the policy rates). In 2004, the PBC removed the ceiling on lending rates and the floor on deposit rates. In 2013, it removed the floor on lending rates and, in 2015, the ceiling on deposit rates. Unfortunately, these did not mark the end of policy intervention in bank interest rates. The PBC explained that further development in risk pricing capability and the interest rate transmission mechanism was required before commercial banks could be allowed to freely set their own deposit and lending rates.

Table 16.3 Key dates in interest rate liberalisation in China

Year	Key reform steps
1983	PBC granted the right to adjust the benchmark lending rate
1998–2004	Upper limit on lending rates gradually increased
1999	Interest rate liberalised in deposit wholesale market
2000	Foreign currency lending rates liberalised
2000	Foreign currency deposit rates for deposits over $3 million liberalised
2003	Floor on foreign currency deposit rates removed
2004	Ceiling on lending rates removed
2004	Floor on deposit rates removed
2012	Lower limit on lending rates increased
2012–15	Upper limit on deposit rates gradually increased
2013	Floor on lending rates removed
2014	Publication of 'Deposit insurance regulation (draft)', committed to secure deposits of less than RMB500,000
2015	Ceiling on deposit rates removed

Sources: Yi (2009); PBC website (www.pbc.gov.cn/zhengcehuobisi/125207/125213/125440/index.html).

The underlying logic of reform

Why did China pursue such a unique pattern of financial reform and development? To understand this, we need to go back to China's broad economic reform strategy. In retrospect, we can identify three dual-track reform strategies that the government adopted during the past 40 years. The first was between state and nonstate sectors. Protection of SOEs probably reflected political constraints. This led to the second dual-track liberalisation, between product and factor markets, as the government intervened in factor markets to support the less efficient SOEs. And financial repression being an important form of factor market distortion, this led to a dual track between formal and informal financial sectors.

The Chinese approach to reform, which Deng Xiaoping described as 'crossing the river by feeling the stones', is more gradual than the 'shock therapy' applied through suddenly privatising SOEs and dismantling central planning, as occurred in the former Soviet Union. At the core of China's approach is the dual-track strategy—continuing to protect SOEs while facilitating the rapid growth of other business forms (Fan 1994). The initial rationale for protecting SOEs is both political (SOEs are cornerstones of the socialist economy) and economic (to maintain employment levels). The dual-track reform strategy was therefore an inevitable rather than intentional choice.

This reform approach—once characterised by Naughton (1995) as 'growing out of the plan'—created a 'Pareto improvement'. As the private sector grew faster than the state sector under the dual-track strategy, the importance of the state sector in the overall economy declined over time and the transition to a market economy could be expected to be smooth. This approach delivered pretty impressive economic results, which Lin et al. (1995) called the 'China miracle'. Average growth was strong and there was no initial collapse of output or loss of jobs. SOEs' share in total industrial output declined steadily, from around 80 per cent in the late 1970s to around 20 per cent in the mid-2010s.

But this reform strategy worked only for a while, before some negative consequences rapidly emerged. In the late 1980s, arbitrage between the plan and the market became a major source of corruption. While SOEs' share in total industrial output dropped from 77.6 per cent in 1978 to 34 per cent in 1995, SOEs continued to cause major macroeconomic problems.

From the mid-1980s, various reform efforts, including responsibility systems, were directed towards improving SOEs' productivity and profitability. However, the state sector's financial performance deteriorated steadily. In about the mid-1990s, SOEs as a sector made a net loss (Huang 2001). To control the bleeding, the government had to adopt a dramatic reform program known as 'grasping the big and letting go of the small and medium', in September 1995. Government ownership was to focus on very large SOEs in strategic industries, releasing all small and medium-sized SOEs in competitive industries. In the following three years, about 30 million workers lost their jobs and more than half a million SOEs disappeared, through mergers and acquisitions, management buyouts and closures.

Deteriorating SOE performance caused a near-fiscal crisis in the early 1990s. The proportion of government revenues to GDP declined from 36 per cent in 1978 to a low of 11 per cent in 1992. This decline was partly a result of decentralisation. With declining profitability, SOEs contributed less revenue and also demanded more subsidies from the government. While the private sector was growing rapidly, it also tried hard to avoid paying taxes. Many local governments were unable to cover overheads in the early 1990s due to fiscal stress. To alleviate the problem, the central government in 1994 introduced a new tax-sharing system, dividing taxes into central (including value-added and consumption taxes), local (such as resource tax and stamp duty) and shared. The proportion of tax revenues to GDP gradually recovered, to 21–22 per cent.

Another consequence of deteriorating SOE performance was technical insolvency of the banks in the late 1990s. Abount 1998, China's average bad loan ratio probably reached 30–40 per cent (Bonin and Huang 2001). At that time, SOEs were the dominant borrowers from the banks. The government often instructed banks to make 'stability loans' to financially troubled SOEs. The Asian Financial Crisis pushed many Chinese banks to the edge of crisis, and the government had to introduce a series of measures to rescue the sector. In 1999, it established four asset management companies (AMCs), one for each of the 'big four' banks, to resolve the bad loans. In the first round, the AMCs transferred RMB1.4 trillion in bad loans from the banks at face value. In 2003, the authorities established the Central Huijin Company to inject capital into banks and other financial institutions. In 2005, the CCB introduced the Bank of America as its first foreign strategic investor. Other banks took the same steps in the following years. In 2006, the BOC and ICBC became publicly listed companies on the Hong Kong and Shanghai stock exchanges.

The banking problems in the late 1990s were a product of the second dual-track liberalisation strategy—between product and factor markets. Since the relatively less efficient SOEs continued to operate in increasingly open and competitive markets, they needed special support. As fiscal revenues declined rapidly relative to GDP throughout the 1980s, it became clear that the government would not have funding to support the SOEs. One alternative was state intervention in factor markets in favour of SOEs. If the government could influence the banks to continue to allocate large volumes of credit to SOEs, relatively cheaply, SOEs could survive even if their performance continued to deteriorate.

Asymmetric liberalisation of product and factor markets is an important feature of China's reform approach (Huang 2010). On the one hand, the government almost completely liberalised markets for agricultural, industrial and service products, for which prices are freely determined by demand and supply. This enables producers to identify market demand and profit opportunities. On the other hand, markets for production factors, including labour, capital, land and energy, remained heavily distorted, and the government continued to intervene in their allocation and pricing. Taking finance as an example, the authorities still play an important role in decisions on allocation of bank credit and IPO quotas, mostly in favour of SOEs. They also intervene in setting bank rates and exchange rates. These factor market distortions ensure that SOEs receive the necessary inputs at below-market prices (Huang 2010; World Bank 2012).

The beneficiaries of such subsidies included foreign joint ventures and large-scale private enterprises, as well as SOEs. At the beginning of China's economic reform, the government set up four special economic zones (SEZs) to attract foreign investors. Within the SEZs, companies were often exempted from tax payments for a fixed period and received free use of land and subsidised financial credit and energy. Later, many local governments offered such preferential policies to large numbers of enterprises in their own regions. In many cases, local governments competed with each other by offering more aggressive preferential policies. The essence of asymmetric liberalisation of product and factor markets is effective subsidy to enterprises by households (state-owned, foreign-invested and private enterprises; and producers, exporters and investors). Some estimates put the total of such 'subsidies' at 12 per cent of GDP immediately before the GFC (Huang and Tao 2010) (Table 16.4).

Table 16.4 Estimated cost distortions in China, 2000–09 (percentage of GDP)

	Labor	Capital	Land	Energy	Environment	Total
2000	0.1	4.1	0.5	0.0	3.8	8.5
2001	0.2	3.9	0.5	0.0	3.5	8.1
2002	0.8	3.9	0.4	0.0	3.3	8.4
2003	1.0	3.8	1.1	0.0	3.3	9.2
2004	2.0	3.1	0.9	0.6	3.0	9.5
2005	2.4	3.0	1.3	1.7	3.0	11.4
2006	2.7	3.1	2.0	1.6	2.8	12.2
2007	3.2	3.6	1.2	1.6	2.4	12.0
2008	3.6	3.4	1.0	0.7	1.9	10.6
2009	2.7	3.5	0.9	0.7	1.8	9.6

Note: The estimation of the labour component is based on the wage gap between migrant workers and urban employees. The repressed wage rates of migrant workers—due mainly to China's household registration and social security systems—significantly lower the production costs of labour-intensive private manufacturing enterprises, which indicates a kind of subsidy to enterprises by households.

Source: Adapted from Huang and Tao (2010).

Asymmetric liberalisation explains the coexistence of economic growth and worsening structural imbalances through the first three decades of China's reform. It also helps us understand why past financial reform was strong on building institutions and growing assets but weak on liberalising markets and improving governance.

Repressive financial policies led to the third dual-track system of financial markets, between the formal and the informal sectors. When financial policies protected SOEs, they discriminated against other enterprises. Therefore, although China already has large financial markets, undersupply of financial services is still common for small and medium-sized enterprises (SMEs) and low-income households. Gradually, informal sectors emerged, mainly in the form of a curb market and shadow banking. Recently, emerging digital finance may also be regarded as part of the informal market. The two sectors coexist; the formal sector serves mainly large companies and wealthy households with heavily distorted pricing and allocation of financial resources. The informal sector serves mainly SMEs and low-income households, with mainly market-driven pricing and allocation of financial resources. While the informal sector makes important contributions to financial intermediation, it is often unregulated, unstable and relatively small in size.

Preliminary assessment

What are the impacts of these dual-track systems on China's economic performance? A preliminary assessment suggests that, in the past, while creating inefficiencies and risks, they did not prevent the economy from growing rapidly. Although protection of SOEs caused some major problems in the 1990s, China's overall economic performance was remarkable. This is somewhat puzzling, as one would expect policy distortions to not only reduce the overall efficiency of resource allocation, but also increase financial and economic instability. Two important questions arise. Was China's economic miracle because of, or despite, repressive financial policies? And could China continue its past economic performance without significantly reducing financial repression?

In an earlier study, Huang and Wang (2011) tried to quantify the impact of financial repression on economic growth in China. They first constructed a financial repression composite index. Following Ang and McKibbin (2007), the index included the real deposit rate, interest rate control, capital account control, the reserve requirement ratio, state banks' share in total lending and the share of loans to SOEs. The index ranges from 0 to 1, with 1 indicating the highest level of financial repression.

Huang and Wang (2011) then estimated a growth equation, following the frameworks of Barro (1991) and Roubini and Sala-i-Martin (1992), using Chinese provincial data for the period 1979–2008. Their main estimation results are reproduced in

Table 16.5. They first looked at the whole period and then divided the sample period into 1979–99 and 2000–08. The coefficient estimate for the financial repression index was positive for the entire sample and the first subperiod, but turned negative in the second subperiod. These estimates suggest that, if there had been full financial liberalisation, real GDP growth would have been 0.55 percentage points lower in 1979–99 but 0.13 percentage points higher in 2000–08.

Table 16.5 Estimation of growth effects of financial repression in China

	Full sample		1979–99		2000–08	
Financial repression index	0.069***	0.167***	0.120***	0.356***	–0.136**	–0.132***
	(0.017)	(0.041)	(0.032)	(0.067)	(0.012)	(0.037)
Investment ratio	0.156***	0.133***	0.136***	0.083**	0.102***	0.100***
	(0.021)	(0.022)	(0.037)	(0.038)	(0.021)	(0.021)
Trade openness	0.013*	0.010	0.029**	0.026**	0.008	0.007
	(0.008)	(0.008)	(0.012)	(0.012)	(0.012)	(0.012)
Government consumption/GDP	–0.258***	–0.189***	–0.378***	–0.183***	–0.107***	–0.169**
	(0.049)	(0.055)	(0.070)	(0.085)	(0.073)	(0.083)
Share of SOEs in total output	0.027	0.039*	0.004	0.039	–0.054***	–0.039*
	(0.020)	(0.020)	(0.028)	(0.029)	(0.022)	(0.023)
Time trend		0.002***		0.003***		0.002
		(0.0008)		(0.002)		(0.014)
Observations	750	750	525	525	225	225
R^2	0.171	0.179	0.138	0.136	0.176	0.187

*** 1 per cent level of significance ** 5 per cent level of significance * 10 per cent level of significance

Notes: The dependent variable is the provincial real GDP growth rate. Estimation results for the primary school student enrolment rate are not reported since they are all insignificant. Numbers in parentheses are standard errors.

Source: Adapted from Huang and Wang (2011).

The positive effect discovered for the 1980s and 1990s was consistent with the reasoning of Stiglitz (1994, 2000). In the early stages of economic development, financial markets are often underdeveloped and might be unable to effectively channel savings to investments. Also, financial institutions are often immature and vulnerable to fluctuations in capital flows and financial stability. Repressive financial policies can actually promote economic growth through strong support to confidence and effective conversion of saving into investment. For instance, with an open capital account, the Chinese economy would have been more seriously damaged by the Asian and global financial crises.

The negative impact of financial repression on economic growth discovered for the 2000s was in line with analysis by McKinnon (1973) and Shaw (1973). State intervention in capital allocation might prevent funds from flowing to the most efficient uses. Protection of financial institutions and financial markets might also encourage excessive risk-taking due to moral hazard. Therefore, repressive financial policies would eventually hinder financial development, increase financial risks, reduce investment efficiency and slow economic growth. For instance, if the less efficient SOEs continue to take in more and more financial resources, the efficiency of the overall economy will decline steadily.

The negative 'McKinnon effect' and the positive 'Stiglitz effect' of repressive financial policies on economic growth probably exist simultaneously in any economy. The net outcome depends on the relative importance of these two effects (Huang and Wang 2011; Huang and Xu 2017). In the early stage of economic development and reform, the positive contribution of financial repression to economic growth through maintaining financial stability and converting saving into investment is greater than the negative effects on inefficiency and risk. We can call this the 'Stiglitz effect'. As the financial system matures, the negative impact of financial repression in terms of reduced capital efficiency and increased financial risks could outweigh its positive contribution; this is the 'McKinnon effect'.

The recent transition from the Stiglitz to the McKinnon effect in China suggests that repressive financial policies have become a drag on economic growth. After the GFC, China's GDP growth slowed steadily. Many factors contributed to this slowdown. Cyclical factors include sluggish global economic growth. Trend factors provide lower growth potential. In the meantime, financial repression favours less efficient SOEs in resource allocation and further impedes economic growth. Statistical analyses reveal that the share of SOEs in total industrial output already had a significant negative impact on growth in the 2000s, but an insignificant effect in the 1980s and 1990s.

Important evidence of growing systemic risk is the rapidly rising incremental capital–output ratio (ICOR) in recent years, which rose from 3.5 in 2007 to 6.3 in 2015 (Figure 16.1). ICOR describes the number of additional units of capital input needed to produce one unit of additional GDP. The rapidly rising ICOR points to sharply deteriorating capital efficiency and increasing difficulties in relying on stimulus policies to support growth. There are many reasons for the rising ICOR, including the effects of the big stimulus package adopted several years ago. Continued policy biases in favour of the state sector probably played an important part. In the post-GFC period, SOE efficiency deteriorated sharply because of massive overcapacity, but these companies continued to absorb large volumes of financial resources. The rising ICOR after the 2008 GFC coincides with the rising debt problem and divergence of leverage ratios between SOEs and SMEs. Rising leverage of SOEs and declining leverage of SMEs indicate that banking credit is allocated mainly to low-efficiency firms or even zombie firms, which worsens the investment efficiency of the economy and exacerbates the rising ICOR.

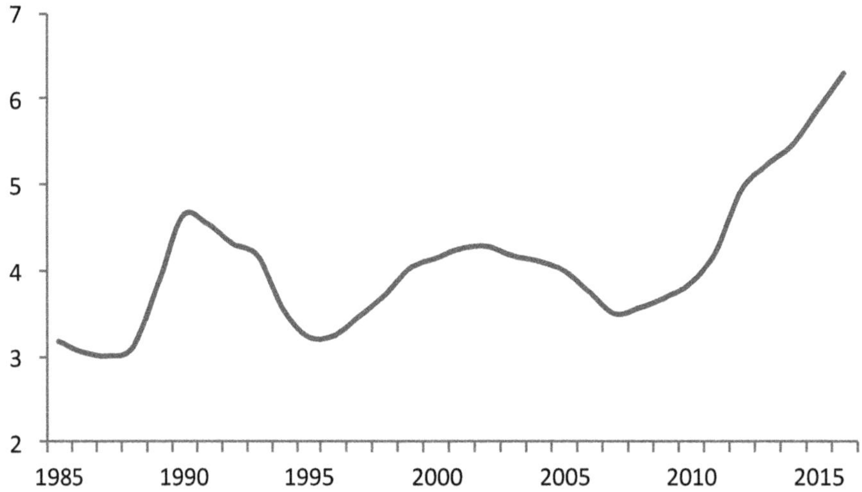

Figure 16.1 Incremental capital–output ratio in China, 1985–2016

Source: Authors' calculation based on data from Wind Database.

The banking sector's nonperforming loan (NPL) ratio also picked up quickly, rising from 0.94 per cent in June 2012 to 1.75 per cent in June 2016. Although the current official number is still quite small, there is widespread suspicion that the NPL ratio is significantly underestimated. One of the main reasons for the underestimation is the lifetime responsibility system, under which it is common for bank managers to try everything they can to hide NPLs. If we add 'special mentioned loans' to NPLs, the total ratio of problem loans was already 5.78 per cent in June 2016.

One of the international investor community's biggest worries about the Chinese economy is its high leverage ratio. The combined leverage of households, companies and the government is roughly 250 per cent of GDP (Figure 16.2). This aggregated number is not extraordinarily high; however, the nonfinancial corporate leverage, which is about 160 per cent of GDP, is unusually high. Over the past 10 years or so, when the state sector's leverage ratio has risen, the private sector's has declined. Using the large industrial enterprise dataset surveyed by the National Bureau of Statistics (NBS), Tan and Yin (2016) found that the average debt–asset ratio of SOEs (90th quantile) rose from 292 per cent in 2006 to 349 per cent in 2013, and that of non-SOEs (90th quantile) declined from 304 per cent to 206 per cent during the same period. Given that SOEs performed much worse than non-SOEs, on average, this rise in 'bad' leverage and fall in 'good' leverage are truly worrisome.

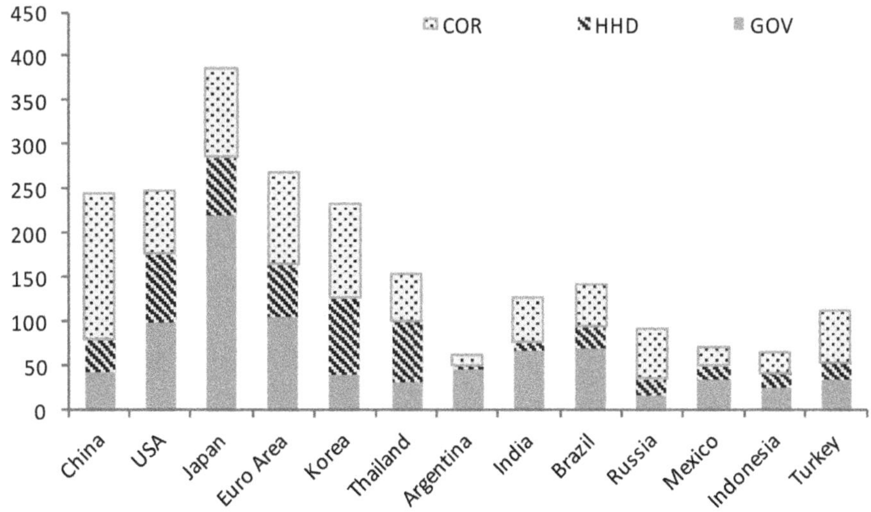

Figure 16.2 Composition of nonfinancial leverages, 2014 (percentage of GDP)

Source: Compiled using data from Tan and Yin (2016).

We attribute this latest divergence of state and nonstate corporate leverages to rising uncertainty about economic policy (Bachmann et al. 2013; Baker et al. 2016). This pattern is clear even among listed companies: as economic policy uncertainty increases, private companies become more cautious and postpone their investment and recruitment plans, while SOEs continue to expand (Wang et al. 2014). This explains why capital or financial efficiency declined significantly in recent years. The root cause of this deterioration is repressive financial policy or, more specifically, lack of market discipline for SOEs.

Growing systemic financial risks

Such increases in financial volatilities caused widespread concern about rising systemic financial risks in China. The latest *Financial System Stability Assessment* by the International Monetary Fund (IMF) and the World Bank, released at the end of 2017, drew attention to the rapid increase in credit and risky lending in less-regulated parts of the financial system (IMF and World Bank 2017). While the PBC disagreed with some of the report's assessments, the *Government Work Report* (NPC 2018), delivered by Premier Li Keqiang on 5 March 2018 at the National Congress of the CPC, identified three key economic policy battles in coming years. Guarding against systemic financial risks was listed as the top priority, ahead of alleviating poverty and strengthening environmental protection. Systemic financial risk is the risk of collapse of an entire financial system or market.

We construct the Index of Systemic Financial Risk in China (ISFRC) to provide a quantitative measure of the problem. By using data from 202 listed financial institutions and property developers between June 2007 and November 2017, we first calculated several indices by applying three different approaches for estimation—conditional value-at-risk (CoVaR), marginal expected loss (MES) and system risk—and then obtained an aggregate index using the weighted average method, after standardising the individual indices. The ISFRC shows that China's systemic financial risk escalated steadily after the GFC. After 2015, the aggregate index showed some moderation, but it has since remained at elevated levels, even as growth slowed marginally in 2017 (Figure 16.3).

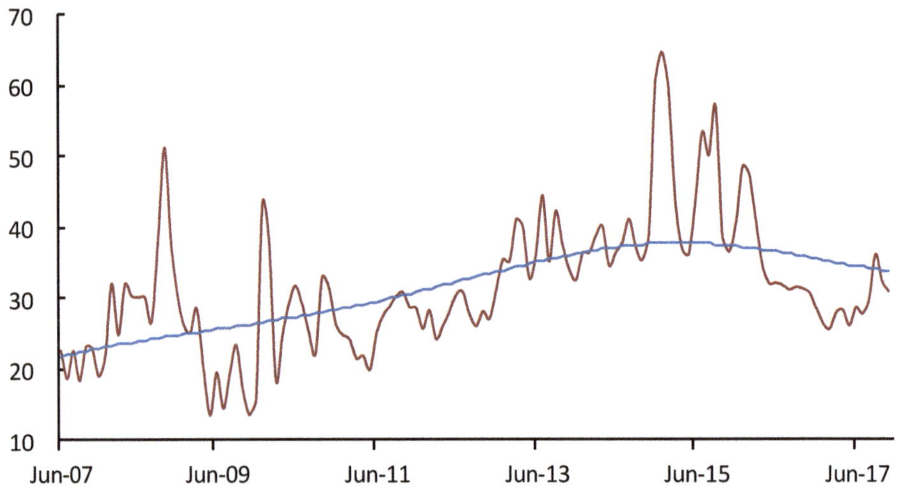

Figure 16.3 Index of China's systemic financial risk, 2007–17

Source: Huang and Wang (2017).

The steady rise in systemic financial risk is a new development. During the past 40 years, China was the only major emerging market economy that did not experience any serious financial crisis. In retrospect, China was able to maintain financial stability due to two important factors: rapid sustained economic growth and implicit government guarantees to financial institutions. Persistent strong growth helps absorb or even hide inefficiency. The government guarantee ensures no panic, even when the banks' bad loan ratios exceeded 25 per cent at the height of the Asian Financial Crisis. But both of these factors have now gradually given way to what the Bank for International Settlements describes as the 'risky trinity': rapidly climbing leverage ratios (as illustrated in Figure 16.2), declining productivity (as illustrated in Figure 16.1) and diminishing policy flexibility. This trinity could be highly correlated with a high probability of financial risk.

We think three factors contributed to the recent escalation of systemic financial risks. First, the continuous slowdown of economic growth—from above 10 per cent in 2010 to below 7 per cent in 2017—led to deterioration of corporate balance sheets and increases in financial risk. In contrast to previous episodes of slowing growth, this was the result of a battle between new and old industries. Many of the industries that supported Chinese economic growth during the past decades are no longer competitive due either to higher costs or to excess capacity. Bottoming of growth should be dependent on development of a large set of new industries. According to one study, the proportion of zombie firms—insolvent companies continuing to operate—in total industrial firms rose from about 3 per cent in 2011 to 16 per cent in 2013 (Tan and Yin 2016).

Second, the combination of excessive liquidity and limited investible assets could easily trigger asset bubbles and migration of financial risk. At the end of 2016, M2 reached 208 per cent of GDP—the third highest in the world. This could be explained partly by China's bank-dominated financial system, as most financial transactions in China are reflected in the expansion of M2. But China's monetary policy also has a built-in acceleration mechanism for M2: when the economy expands, M2 needs to accelerate to satisfy increased demand for liquidity; and when the economy shrinks, M2 needs to accelerate to stabilise the economy and markets. One consequence of abundant liquidity is that, when depositors are no longer happy with the interest rate returns they receive from the banks, they start to move their liquidity around the economy, searching for higher returns. This could easily inflate asset bubbles, which are often followed by painful corrections.

Third, the outdated regulatory framework also contributed to significant increases in financial risk. In the early 2000s, China established a segregated regulatory framework, with the PBC, the China Banking Regulatory Commission (CBRC), the China Securities Regulatory Commission (CSRC) and the China Insurance Regulatory Commission (CIRC) at its core. The principle of a division of labour among these regulatory bodies was that whoever issued licences should be responsible for regulation. This system worked reasonably well for quite a while—until recently. To gauge the effectiveness of financial regulation, we also construct the Index of Effectiveness of China's Financial Regulation (IECFR), which consists of three subindices: macroprudential (volatilities of purchasing power parity, or PPI; the consumer price index, CPI; stock prices and exchange rates); microprudential (the leverage ratio and NPL ratio of commercial banks); and consumer protection (ease of obtaining bank credit and protection of minority investors). The IECFR declines steadily after 2013 (Figure 16.4).

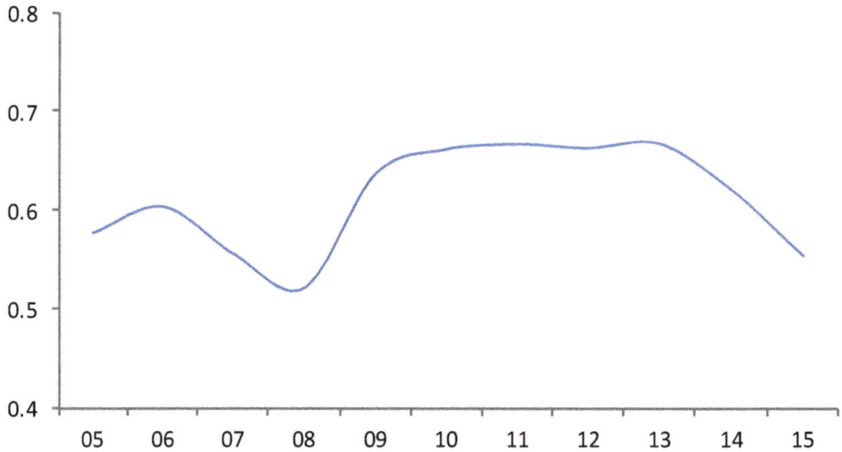

Figure 16.4 Index of effectiveness of China's financial regulation, 2005–15
Source: Huang and Wang (2016).

The main cause of the recent decline in the effectiveness of financial regulation was the increasing incompatibility between the institutional regulatory regime and the increasingly mixed operations of financial institutions. For instance, at the start of 2015, the CSRC was not aware of stock market investors' leveraging behaviour through the banking and trust sectors. Its regulatory policies focused on the institutions with licences, not the financial transactions. This left some important financial activities unregulated, especially shadow banking businesses and the fintech industry. This caused extremely volatile market sentiment in some areas (Figure 16.5). And, finally, the regulators were responsible for both financial stability and industry development, which often led to significant industrial expansion at the expense of financial stability.

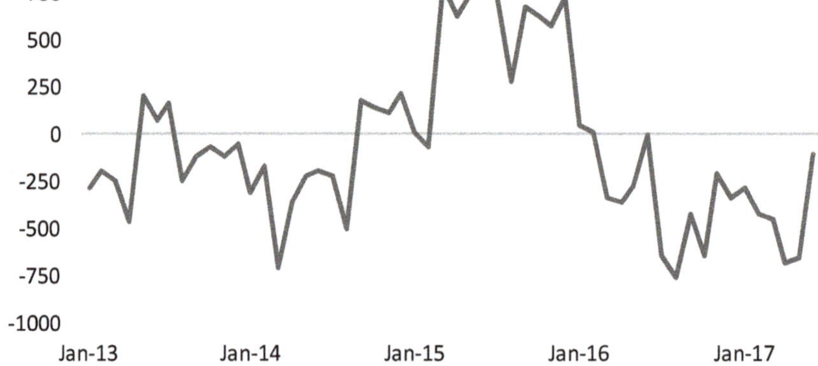

Figure 16.5 The sentiment index of China's fintech industry, 2013–17
Source: Wang and Dou (2017).

Required policy actions going forward

If the ultimate goal of China's financial reform is to build an efficient and robust financial system that can support economic growth in the long run, this task is, at most, only half-accomplished. After 40 years of financial reform, China has established a very comprehensive financial system, but market mechanisms are still constrained in many ways. The third plenum of the eighteenth National Congress of the CPC in late 2013 outlined a blueprint for financial reform, which covers three broad areas: lowering entry barriers, a free market mechanism and improving financial regulation (Table 16.6).

Table 16.6 Key measures of financial reform

Lowering entry barriers
1. Opening internally and externally; allowing financial institutions such as small and medium-sized private banks
2. Reforming financial institution policy
3. Developing multilayered capital markets; increasing shares of direct financing
4. Improving insurance and economic compensation systems
5. Fostering inclusive finance
6. Encouraging financial innovation; enriching layers and products of financial markets
Freeing market mechanisms
7. Improving interest and exchange rate mechanisms; forming a government bond yield curve
8. Promoting two-way opening of capital markets; accelerating capital account convertibility
Improving financial regulation
9. Fulfilling financial regulatory measures and prudential standards
10. Establishing a deposit insurance system; improving exit mechanisms
11. Strengthening construction of financial infrastructure; ensuring efficient operation and stability of the financial system

Source: Authors' compilation from NPC (2013).

Future financial reforms need to focus on three important tasks. The first is to continue market-oriented financial liberalisation. The key is to implement the principle decided at the third plenum of the eighteenth National Congress to let market mechanisms play a decisive role in the allocation of resources. This includes completing interest rate liberalisation, achieving a cleanly floating exchange rate and lowering entry barriers for both private and foreign financial institutions. Second is to restructure the financial system by increasing the importance of direct financing. China's financial system is still dominated by the banking sector, which is starting to have some negative effects, including high leverage ratios and weak capability for supporting industrial upgrading. Third is to recondition the regulatory system to maintain financial stability.

What will China's future financial system look like? Before the GFC, Chinese financial reform policies—intentionally or otherwise—were modelled on the financial systems in North America and Western Europe. Whether or not this implicit model is still the best choice for China needs to be seriously reconsidered. Many emerging market economies prematurely freed up market forces and suffered major financial instability. Even the model financial systems experienced serious financial crises in recent years. The critical test is not whether China should pursue further market-oriented reform; it is whether policymaking carefully balances improvement in efficiency with increases in risk. For example, China definitely should aim for greater openness of its capital account. But, at the same time, it should pay sufficient attention to adverse consequences, especially in relation to more volatile short-term cross-border capital flows.

For the immediate policy objective of containing systemic financial risks, the best strategy is systemic, focusing on opening the market, supporting innovation and strengthening policy coordination. The past approach of dealing with individual financial risks separately is no longer suitable, as such risks have increasingly become interconnected.

Specifically, we recommend Chinese authorities undertake policy actions in five areas:

1. Push ahead with market-oriented financial reforms and enforcing market discipline. While implicit government guarantees supported financial stability in the past, these are no longer sustainable. An effective market system should contain at least three key features: market-determined financial prices, including interest rates, exchange rates and bond yields; market-determined allocation of financial resources, including bank credit, IPOs and even cross-border capital flows; and a market-clearing mechanism, allowing defaults and bankruptcies. The PBC established the bank deposit insurance system in May 2015, but so far it has not played any role.
2. More effectively coordinate monetary, financial and other economic policies. In July 2017, the government established the new State Council Financial Stability and Development Committee (FSDC) to strengthen policy coordination. As the FSDC's office is located within the PBC and the PBC also took over the policymaking functions of the newly combined China Banking and Insurance Regulatory Commission (CBIRC), the central bank's role in the regulatory system has clearly been elevated. Yet the critical issue is still how to improve policy coordination and cooperation across different agencies. One possible way is to establish three committees with some overlapping members: a Monetary Policy Committee, Financial Stability Committee and Fair Trading Committee.
3. Adopt the 'twin-peak' regulatory model in China. While different regulatory models have different advantages, we favour for China the Australian or

US-type 'twin-peak' model, which separates the functions of prudential and macroeconomic regulation. The recent setup between the PBC and the CBIRC can be regarded as an important step towards a Chinese-style twin-peak model. Even more important is to change financial regulation, from institution-based to transaction-focused. Financial regulatory bodies need to be professional, independent and authoritative. For instance, it should be beneficial for the PBC to become an independent monetary policymaker.

4. Establish real-time monitoring mechanisms for financial risk. The pace of financial transactions picked up dramatically during the past decades, especially in areas involving digital technologies. The old-fashioned investigation methods are probably no longer appropriate. Macro and microprudential regulations should include effective working procedures analysing financial transactions and detecting potential financial risks. Currently, particular policy attention should be placed on shadow banking businesses, fintech activities, joint stock banks and some cross-sector financial transactions.
5. Carefully balance financial innovation and financial stability. In recent years, dynamic financial innovations created some new sources of financial risk, such as the subprime debt crisis in the United States. Some innovative transactions, such as those in fintech, actually make good economic contributions, by realising effective interest rate liberalisation and supporting the real economy. For those activities, the Chinese authorities could probably find ways to facilitate innovation within boundaries. The 'sandbox' framework popularly used in fintech is a good example. In the meantime, the authorities should also quickly contain those financial innovations that both increase risk and reduce transparency.

References

Abiad, A., Detragiache, E. and Tressel, T. (2008), *A new database of financial reforms*, Working Paper No. 2008-2266, Washington, DC: International Monetary Fund.

Ang, J. B. and McKibbin, W. J. (2007), Financial liberalization, financial sector development and growth: Evidence from Malaysia, *Journal of Development Economics* 84: 215–33. doi.org/10.1016/j.jdeveco.2006.11.006.

Bachmann, R., Elstner, S. and Sims, E. R. (2013), Uncertainty and economic activity: Evidence from business survey data, *American Economic Journal: Macroeconomics* 5(2): 217–49. doi.org/10.1257/mac.5.2.217.

Baker, S. R., Bloom, N. and Davis, S. J. (2016), Measuring economic policy uncertainty, *Quarterly Journal of Economics* 131(4): 1593–636. doi.org/10.1093/qje/qjw024.

Barro, R. (1991), Government spending in a simple model of endogenous growth, *Journal of Political Economy* 98: 103–26. doi.org/10.1086/261726.

Bonin, J. and Huang, Y. (2001), Dealing with the bad loans of the Chinese banks, *Journal of Asian Economics* 12(2): 197–214. doi.org/10.1016/S1049-0078(01)00082-3.

Fan, G. (1994), Incremental changes and dual track transition: Understanding the case of China, *Economic Policy* 19(Supp.)(December): 99–122.

The Financial Times Limited (2018), *The Banker Database*. Available from: www.thebankerdatabase.com.

Huang, Y. (2001), *Last Steps Across the River: Enterprise and banking reform in China*, Canberra: Asia Pacific Press.

Huang, Y. (2010), China's great ascendancy and structural risks: Consequences of asymmetric market liberalization, *Asian Pacific Economic Literature* 24(1): 65–85. doi.org/10.1111/j.1467-8411.2010.01250.x.

Huang, Y. and Tao, K. (2010), Factor market distortion and current account surplus in China, *Asian Economic Papers* 3(9): 1–36. doi.org/10.1162/ASEP_a_00020.

Huang, Y. and Wang, X. (2011), Does financial repression inhibit and facilitate economic growth: A case study of China's reform experience, *Oxford Bulletin of Economics and Statistics* 73(6): 833–55. doi.org/10.1111/j.1468-0084.2011.00677.x.

Huang, Y. and Wang, X. (2016), Reforming China's financial supervision system, Unpublished working paper, National School of Development, Peking University, Beijing.

Huang, Y. and Wang, X. (2017), Managing systemic financial risks in China, Unpublished working paper, National School of Development, Peking University, Beijing.

Huang, Y. and Wang, X. (2017), Building an efficient financial system in China: The need for market discipline, *Asian Economic Policy Review* 12(2): 188–205. doi.org/10.1111/aepr.12173.

Huang, Y., Gou, Q. and Wang, X. (2014), Financial liberalization and the middle-income trap: What can China learn from the cross-country experience?, *China Economic Review* 31: 426–40. doi.org/10.1016/j.chieco.2014.04.009.

Huang, Y., Wang, X., Wang, B. and Lin, N. (2013), Financial reform in China: Progresses and challenges, in Y. C. Park and H. Patrick (eds), *How Finance Is Shaping the Economies of China, Japan and Korea*. New York: Columbia University Press. doi.org/10.7312/columbia/9780231165266.003.0002.

International Monetary Fund (IMF) and World Bank (2017), *China: Financial system stability assessment*, Washington, DC: IMF.

Lin, J. Y., Cai, F. and Li, Z. (1995), *The China Miracle: Development strategy and economic reform*, Hong Kong: The Chinese University of Hong Kong Press.

McKinnon, R. I. (1973), *Money and Capital in Economic Development*, Washington, DC: The Brookings Institution.

National People's Congress (NPC) (2013), *Decision of the CPC Central Committee on Several Major Issues of Comprehensively Deepening Reform*, Beijing: NPC.

National People's Congress (NPC) (2018), *Government Work Report*, 5 March, Beijing: NPC.

Naughton, B. (1995), *Growing Out of the Plan: Chinese economic reform, 1978–1993*, Cambridge: Cambridge University Press. doi.org/10.1017/CBO9780511664335.

People's Bank of China (PBC) (2016), *China Financial Stability Report 2016*, Beijing: PBC.

People's Bank of China (PBC) (2017), *China Financial Stability Report 2017*, Beijing: PBC.

Roubini, N. and Sala-i-Martin, X. (1992), Financial repression and economic growth, *Journal of Development Economics* 39: 5–30. doi.org/10.1016/0304-3878(92)90055-E.

Shaw, A. S. (1973), *Financial Deepening in Economic Development*, New York: Oxford University Press.

Stiglitz, J. E. (1994), The role of the state in financial markets, in M. Bruno and B. Pleskovic (eds), *Proceedings of the World Bank Annual Conference on Development Economics, 1993: Supplement to the World Bank Economic Review and the World Bank Research Observer*, Washington, DC: The World Bank.

Stiglitz, J. E. (2000), Capital market liberalization, economic growth and instability, *World Development* 28: 1075–86. doi.org/10.1016/S0305-750X(00)00006-1.

Tan, X. and Yin, B. (2016), Non-financial corporate leverages, *China Foreign Exchanges* 11: 20–2.

Wang, Q. and Dou, X. (2017), *The sentiment index of China's fintech industry*, Working Paper, Beijing: Institute of Digital Finance, Peking University.

Wang, Y. Z., Chen, C. R. and Huang, Y. S. (2014), Economic policy uncertainty and corporate investment: Evidence from China, *Pacific Basin Finance Journal* 26: 227–43. doi.org/10.1016/j.pacfin.2013.12.008.

World Bank (2012), *World Development Indicators 2012*, Washington, DC: The World Bank Group.

Yi, G. (2009), *On the Financial Reform of China*, Beijing: The Commercial Press.

17. The reform of China's exchange rate regime

Yongding Yu

China has had an inflexible exchange rate regime for many decades. According to the International Monetary Fund (IMF), until 2015, China had a crawling-peg–like arrangement for its exchange rate regime. On 11 August 2015, the People's Bank of China (PBC) took a decisive step towards floating the renminbi (RMB) exchange rate. However, due to a misjudging of market sentiment at the time and bad luck, the reform experiment caused market panic and the renminbi quickly devalued. As a result, the PBC halted the experiment and introduced a new central parity rate–settling mechanism. According to the new rule, the RMB exchange rate with the US dollar was determined by the arithmetical average of the previous day's closing price and the current day's theoretical value of the renminbi's bilateral exchange rate against the dollar that can maintain the stability of the index of a given currency basket over the past 24 hours

This author has great reservations about this arrangement, which is intended to achieve both exchange rate stability and minimisation of the use of foreign exchange reserves. This is essentially mission impossible. In fact, only when devaluation pressure on the renminbi coincides with the falling dollar index can the RMB exchange rate move according to the rule, without the need to use a large volume of foreign exchange reserves.

The RMB exchange rate has started to stabilise since 2017. In the author's view, this stabilisation was a result of the combined affects of international and domestic factors, and cannot be attributed to the success of the new central parity price–setting rule—never mind that exchange rate stability should not be a policy objective of the PBC.

In recent quarters, the PBC has stopped its daily intervention in the foreign exchange market. This is a very positive development. Allowing the RMB exchange rate to float is the only solution for China to correct its external imbalances and allow the use of monetary policy to focus on promoting growth, prices and financial stability.

Exchange rate policy has been the focus of debates both within and outside China for the past 20 years. China's exchange rate policy is characterised by a fear of floating. When the renminbi is under appreciation pressure, authorities fear appreciation. When the renminbi is under depreciation pressure, they fear depreciation. For a long time, the renminbi was undervalued. While undervaluation is conducive to China's export drive and economic growth, it leads to cross-border misallocation of resources. As a poor developing country, China accumulated some US$4 trillion of foreign exchange reserves. When the renminbi is under devaluation pressure, the stability of the currency actually encourages the unwinding of hot money and facilitates capital flight. Within two years from 2014, China's foreign exchange reserves fell by an astronomical US$1 trillion.

The PBC has long tried to make the renminbi flexible. It embarked on a long march towards a floating exchange rate regime, in 1994, which was restarted in 2015 and reached an apogee on 11 August 2015. After retreating, the bank might now have taken the appropriate steps to finally unshackle the RMB exchange rate.

There is a large existing literature on China's exchange rate policy, but there has been little study of its evolution. Misconceptions about China's exchange rate regime since the 11 August 2015 ('8/11') reforms are prevalent. This chapter aims to clarify these misconceptions and explain how China's current exchange rate regime has been working. The thrust of the chapter is that China should stop designing any exchange regimes that need regular government intervention, which will lead to market distortion and national wealth losses regardless of how smart is the design. It is not worth the costs to continue an exchange rate regime that is not based on market demand and supply.

The chapter begins with a brief review of the long evolution of China's exchange rate regime. The second section deals with the 8/11 reforms and their aftermath. The third section is the focus of the chapter, and discusses in detail the RMB central parity rate–setting rule introduced in February 2016 and its role in stabilising the RMB exchange rate against large depreciation pressures. The fourth section introduces the most recent changes in China's exchange rate regime, while the final section provides some concluding remarks.

The evolution of China's exchange rate regime

According to the IMF's *Annual Report on Exchange Rate Arrangements and Exchange Restrictions* (*AREAER*) (IMF 2016), which provides information on the exchange rate arrangements of member countries, exchange rate arrangements can be divided into four broad categories: hard pegs, soft pegs, floating regimes and residuals. Within each broad category, there are different arrangements (Table 17.1).

Table 17.1 Classification of exchange rate arrangements

Type	Categories				
Hard pegs	Exchange arrangement with no separate legal tender	Currency board arrangement			
Soft pegs	Conventional pegged arrangement	Pegged exchange rate within horizontal bands	Stabilised arrangement	Crawling peg	Crawl-like arrangement
Floating regimes (market-determined rates)	Floating	Free floating			
Residual	Other managed arrangement				

Note: This methodology became effective on 2 February 2009 and reflects an attempt to provide greater consistency and objectivity in exchange rate classification across countries and to improve the transparency of the IMF's bilateral and multilateral surveillance in this area.

Source: IMF (2016).

Until 2015, China belonged in the country group with crawl-like arrangements. According to the IMF, for classification as a crawl-like arrangement, the exchange rate must remain within a narrow margin of 2 per cent relative to a statistically identified trend for six months, and there must be a minimum rate of change greater than that for a stabilised (peg-like) arrangement. In the *AREAER* for 2016, China's exchange rate regime was reclassified to 'Other managed arrangement', which is a residual category used when, for example, exchange rate arrangements shift frequently. Until 2016, there were 20 countries in this category: China, Algeria, Angola, Azerbaijan, Belarus, Cambodia, Egypt, Gambia, Guinea, Haiti, Kyrgyzstan, Liberia, Myanmar, Malaysia, Rwanda, Pakistan, South Sudan, Syria, Tajikistan and Vanuatu.

From 1949 until the late 1970s, the Chinese Government set China's official exchange rate at a greatly overvalued level, while setting internal exchange rates for different exports according to the 'costs for earning foreign exchanges' (Goldstein and Lardy 2009). In 1979, when the country began to pursue its reform and opening-up policies, it loosened foreign exchange controls and allowed exporters to retain a share of their foreign exchange earnings. This arrangement was called the 'foreign exchange retention system'. In October 1980, companies were allowed to sell to other companies foreign exchanges that they did not need for their own use. In January 1981, the government introduced an 'internal settlement rate' of RMB2.8 per US dollar, applicable to all trade transactions, alongside an official exchange rate of RMB1.5 per dollar for nontrade transactions. The official rate was pegged to a basket of currencies, while the internal settlement rate was pegged exclusively to the US dollar.

In the mid-1980s, the so-called foreign exchange swap centres were established, where companies traded foreign exchange and the exchange rate was determined on the basis of demand and supply. At the same time, the government gradually devalued the official exchange rate of the renminbi against the dollar. In early 1985, the government abolished the internal settlement rate and all international transactions were settled at the official exchange rate.

On 1 January 1994, the official and swap markets were merged. The official rate fell from RMB5.80 per US dollar to the prevailing swap market rate of RMB8.70 per dollar. Because four-fifths of all foreign exchange transactions were made in the swap market, the impact of the devaluation of the official exchange rate on China's trade was insignificant. The merging of these markets enabled the Chinese Government to proclaim that China's exchange rate regime was based on market demand and supply and 'unitary managed floating'. Use of the word unitary implied that the US dollar was the unit of value for the renminbi. By October 1997, the renminbi's exchange rate with the US dollar was 8.28.

Initially, China was happy with the managed floating arrangement and it had no problem allowing market demand and supply to determine the exchange rate. In fact, after the 1994 reform, the RMB exchange rate was on the rise, driven by the international balance of payments surplus. However, the East Asian Financial Crisis abruptly changed China's policy prospects. To prevent the renminbi from collapsing—as many other Asian currencies had—the Chinese Government, while tightening capital controls, adopted a policy of 'no devaluation', to calm market panic. China's exchange rate regime shifted from managed floating to a very hard de facto peg to the US dollar.

During the East Asian Financial Crisis, the consensus among Chinese economists was that, as soon as the large depreciation pressure on the renminbi disappeared, the currency should be de-pegged from the US dollar and return to a managed floating arrangement. However, after the crisis, this idea met with strong opposition from China's exporting sector, worried about the effect on the competitiveness of exports. The de facto peg persisted until 21 July 2005, when the PBC de-pegged the renminbi from the US dollar and revalued it, from RMB8.28 per dollar to RMB8.11 per dollar—an appreciation of 2.1 per cent. The PBC announced that the renminbi's closing rate against the US dollar at the end of each business day would be its central parity rate against the dollar the next day. The renminbi was allowed to fluctuate up to 0.3 per cent around the central parity rate. The PBC also said that determination of the renminbi's exchange rate would refer to a basket of currencies. It is worth noting the use of 'refer' rather than 'peg'. In fact, since then, the determination of the RMB exchange rate has rarely referred to a basket of currencies, let alone being pegged to the basket.

In responding to the Global Financial Crisis, China re-pegged the renminbi to the US dollar, from August 2008 to June 2010. According to the IMF, the exchange rate regime during this period fell into the 'stabilised arrangement' category. After June 2010, the IMF reclassified China's exchange rate system as a crawl-like arrangement. Since then, the renminbi has resumed its gradual appreciation, and the band of fluctuation eventually widened to ±2 per cent.

The '8/11' exchange rate reform and its aftermath

On 11 August 2015, the PBC introduced a new rule for setting the RMB central parity rate against the US dollar: the daily central parity quotes reported by primary dealers (major commercial banks) to the China Foreign Exchange Trade System (CFETS) before the market opens would be based on the previous day's closing rate of the interbank foreign exchange market, within a ±2 per cent band. This was a bold step towards a floating regime. If the closing rate today falls, tomorrow's RMB central parity rate will be set correspondingly lower. Hence, the official exchange rate (the RMB central parity rate set by the PBC) would move in response to changes in supply and demand in the foreign exchange market. If the exchange rate devaluation pressures were high, the exchange rate could devalue by a maximum 2 per cent in a day. It is not too far-fetched to imagine that if the devaluation pressures were very high, the RMB exchange rate could devalue by 20 per cent in 10 days.

The change in the rules of the game was too abrupt for the market to take, and the RMB exchange rate fell immediately. In the first two days of the '8/11' reform, the central bank was shocked to see the renminbi devalued by almost 3 per cent, especially given that before 11 August there were only moderate devaluation expectations in the market. The PBC feared the depreciation could spin out of control. On 13 August, it declared that it had no plan to reform China's exchange rate regime; this had been a one-time adjustment of the exchange rate and the 3 per cent adjustment so far achieved was enough to correct the overvaluation. Thus, the reform experiment was brought to an abrupt end.

With hindsight, we can say that if the central bank had not blinked after three days of the trial, and had waited for a week or two, the exchange rate might eventually have stabilised and the reform may have succeeded. The general direction of the 8/11 reform was correct, but unfortunately the PBC failed to carry it through. Expectations of the devaluation of the renminbi increased significantly, accompanied by a sudden surge of capital outflows. Stabilising the renminbi became the PBC's top priority. It intervened heavily in the foreign exchange market and, as a result, there was a huge fall in foreign exchange reserves—of hundreds of billions of dollars.

From 13 August 2015 to the Spring Festival in February 2016, no one was quite sure what was guiding the PBC in setting the RMB central parity rate. A discernable pattern was that whenever the market expected the renminbi to fall, it would instead rise. An obvious explanation for this is that the PBC was manipulating the exchange rate to move it in an unexpected fashion to punish those who were shorting the renminbi, hoping to break depreciation expectations by so doing. For many months after 13 August, despite the strong depreciation expectations, the renminbi actually appreciated.

This was a costly strategy. Because of the central bank's intervention in the midst of RMB devaluation pressure, China's foreign exchange reserves fell quickly. As soon as the market was no longer expecting a further weakening of the exchange rate, the PBC would stop its intervention and let the renminbi fall slightly. As soon as the market detected that the PBC had reduced its intervention, however, selling pressure returned and the central bank had to step in again to support the renminbi by selling more dollars.

The current RMB central parity rate–setting rule

The formula for the new RMB central parity rate–setting rule

In response to the rapid depletion of foreign exchange reserves and criticisms from the IMF and market participants about the lack of a transparent rule for setting the RMB exchange rate, a new approach was introduced in January 2016. It was based on the formula of 'the closing rate + the theoretical RMB exchange rate to keep the index of a currency basket unchanged over the previous 24 hours'. Although the central bank did not explicitly announce the rule, bank officials implicitly acknowledged its existence. In contrast with the 8/11 reform, instead of fixing the RMB central parity rate according to the previous day's closing rate, now the change in the RMB central parity rate on a trading day would be determined by the arithmetical average of two variables. The first variable is the difference between the previous trading day's closing rate and the previous trading day's central parity rate. The second is the difference between the 'theoretical' bilateral exchange rate of the renminbi against the dollar that can keep the index of a currency basket unchanged and the previous trading day's central parity rate.

Assuming that the previous day's RMB central parity rate is 6.1, the closing rate is 6.2, and the 'theoretical RMB exchange rate'—shorthand for 'the bilateral exchange rate between the renminbi and the dollar that makes the index of a currency basket unchanged over the past 24 hours'—is 6.15. According to the new rule, today's

RMB central parity rate is equal to 6.1 + [(6.2 – 6.1) + (6.15 – 6.1)]/2 = 6.175. This formula can be transformed into a second and simpler formula: the RMB central parity rate = [previous day's closing rate + the theoretical RMB exchange rate]/2 = [6.2 + 6.15]/2 = 6.175. The two formulas are equivalent. For the sake of simplicity, we will use the second formula in the discussion below.

The PBC uses the CFETS as its currency basket. According to the definition of the CFETS index, and with available data, anyone can calculate the RMB central parity rate against the dollar on a trading day before the market is open.

The 'theoretical RMB exchange rate'

The key to the formula is understanding the concept of the theoretical RMB exchange rate. A basket of currencies is a unit of value for measuring the value of goods, services and financial products (including currencies), and consists of a given set of currencies with a given number of units for each constituent currency. While a currency can be measured by the US dollar, it can also be measured by a basket of currencies. The Special Drawing Rights (SDR) is a typical basket of currencies, comprising 0.58 units of the US dollar, 0.39 units of the euro, 1.02 units of the renminbi, 11.9 units of the Japanese yen and 0.086 units of the pound sterling. Any currency can be measured by the SDR. For example, on 30 September 2016, the value of US$1 was SDR0.7164 or, equivalently, SDR1 was worth US$1.3958.

The value of the renminbi can be measured in dollars. For example, we can say that RMB1 = US$0.16129 (direct quotation) or, more commonly, US$1 = RMB6.2 (indirect quotation). To show how a basket of currencies can be used as a unit of value to measure the value of the renminbi, we assume that the US dollar/Japanese yen (USDYEN) is 100 and US dollar/Chinese renminbi (USDRMB) is 6.2. Since RMB6.2 = US$1 = US$0.6 + US$0.4 (0.6 and 0.4 are weights), we can substitute the yen for the dollar to achieve the relationship: RMB6.2 = US$0.6 + 0.4 × ¥100. If divided by 6.2, the equation becomes RMB1 = US$0.097 + ¥6.45.

Now we can say either RMB1 = US$0.16129 or RMB1 = US$0.097 + ¥6.45. In the first case, the renminbi is measured by US dollars. In the second, the renminbi is measured by a basket of two currencies, which consists of 0.997 unit of the US dollar and 6.45 units of the Japanese yen. It is worth emphasising that the two measurements are equivalent only on a given date—the base time when USDRMB = 6.2 and USDYEN = 100.

Pegging to a basket of currencies means that, in our example, whatever the bilateral exchange rate between the dollar and the yen, RMB1 should always be equal to US$0.097 + ¥6.45. RMB1 = US$0.16129 holds when USDRMB = 6.2 and USDYEN = 100. However, USDYEN changes over time. If USDYEN has become 140, and the renminbi is pegged to a basket of currencies consisting of 0.097 units of the US dollar and 6.45 units of the Japanese yen, the value of RMB1 should be US$0.1431. Equivalently, US$1 is now worth RMB6.99 instead of RMB6.2. This means that, due to the change in the US dollar/Japanese yen exchange rate—which is outside China's control—to maintain the peg of the renminbi to the basket of currencies, the RMB exchange rate against the dollar should also change.

Keeping a currency basket index unchanged means that no matter how the exchange rates between component currencies change, the currency basket index must always be equal to 1 (or 100). It can be shown that keeping the currency basket index unchanged (or pegging to the index of a currency basket) is equivalent to pegging to a basket of currencies. To illustrate, under a regime of 'pegging to a basket of currencies', the expression 'RMB1 = US$0.097 + ¥6.45' can be rewritten as Equation 17.1.

Equation 17.1

$$1 = 0.6\frac{\$/¥}{6.2} + 0.4\frac{yen/¥}{0.062}$$

In Equation 17.1, 6.2 is the US dollar/Chinese renminbi exchange rate and 0.062 is the Japanese yen/Chinese renminbi exchange rate in the base period. It can be verified that in the base period, when the US dollar/Japanese yen exchange rate was 100, we have Equation 17.2.

Equation 17.2

$$0.6\frac{\$/¥}{6.2} + 0.4\frac{yen/¥}{0.062} = 1$$

When the US dollar/Japanese yen exchange rate is no longer 100, to keep the index of the currency basket unchanged, the Chinese monetary authority has to change the US dollar/RMB exchange rate to offset the impact of the change in the dollar/yen exchange rate on the index of the currency basket. For example, if the US dollar has appreciated against the yen, from 100 to 140, to keep the index of the currency basket equal to 1, the renminbi must depreciate against the US dollar, from 6.2 to 6.99—a depreciation of 11.3 per cent. In this example, the theoretical RMB exchange rate is 6.99.

The CFETS index

The index of the currency basket to which the renminbi is supposed to be pegged is defined by the following formula (Equation 17.3).

Equation 17.3

$$CFETS = \frac{100.02}{0.2640\frac{\frac{\$}{¥}}{6.1190} + 0.2139\frac{\frac{Euro}{¥}}{7.4556} + \cdots\cdots}$$

In Equation 17.3, 0.2640 and 0.2139 are weights of the exchange rates of component currencies against the renminbi, which sum to 1.0002. The numbers 6.1190 and 7.4556 are the exchange rates of component currencies against the renminbi in the base period.

The CFETS index can be divided into approximately three components: the RMB exchange rate against the US dollar,[1] the dollar index and the index of the remaining currencies that are not included in the dollar index. Because currencies that are not included in the dollar index are not important in deciding the CFETS index, they are neglected in the discussion below. It is easy to see that if the dollar index is falling,[2] the RMB exchange rate against the dollar should rise. If the dollar index is rising, the RMB exchange rate against the dollar should fall. Hence, to peg to the CFETS index means that, in response to the fall in the dollar index, the RMB exchange rate should appreciate, and vice versa.

In the above discussion, movements in the RMB exchange rate and the dollar index are assumed to be independent. However, according to the new RMB central parity rate–setting rule, the RMB central parity rate on a trading day is jointly determined by the previous day's closing rate and the theoretical RMB exchange rate. In turn, the latter is calculated given the dollar index known when the market opens on the trading day as well as the CFETS index 24 hours previously. To illustrate, in the previous example, if the dollar index is falling, to keep the CFETS index stable, the RMB exchange rate should be 6.99. However, because the RMB central parity rate today is the arithmetical average of yesterday's closing rate and 6.99—the theoretical RMB exchange rate—unless the previous day's closing rate is also 6.99, the basket currency index today will be either higher or lower than 6.99. In other words, the central parity–setting rule has made the CFETS index a moving target, and pegging to a constant CFETS index is almost impossible. In contrast, pegging to a basket of currencies means the index of the currency basket should be kept unchanged within a narrow band for a long time—usually six months at least. Because China's central parity rate–setting rule requires that in determining the central parity rate the closing rate should also be taken into consideration, the CFETS index cannot be kept unchanged even within 24 hours. It is therefore incorrect to say China has adopted a currency basket peg regime.

1 The dollar index in the CFETS index is not exactly the same as the US dollar index that is published by US authorities, because the weights for currencies included in the former are not the same as those in the latter.

2 For the sake of simplicity, we do not discuss the index for the rest of the currencies.

The working of the new rule

If the renminbi is on a depreciation path while the dollar index is falling, according to the central parity rate–setting rule, today's RMB central parity rate must be higher than yesterday's closing rate, which in turn implies that sooner or later the central bank will probably have to 'lean against the wind' to artificially raise today's RMB closing rate to make sure it is kept within the 2 per cent band below today's central parity rate. It can be seen that the introduction of the peg element into the central parity rate–setting rule can slow the process of RMB depreciation, but it probably requires the central bank's constant intervention and the use of foreign exchange reserves.

If the renminbi is on a depreciation path while the dollar index is rising, according to the central parity rate–setting rule, today's RMB central parity rate falls, due to the fall in both today's theoretical RMB exchange rate and yesterday's closing rate—relative to yesterday's central parity rate. If the fall in the theoretical RMB exchange rate is less than yesterday's closing rate, today's RMB central parity rate will be higher than yesterday's closing rate. This means that if today's depreciation pressure is as large as yesterday's in terms of percentages per day, the PBC will have to intervene to keep today's closing rate within the 2 per cent band below today's central parity rate. But, compared with the case where the dollar index is falling, the intervention should be weaker.

If the theoretical RMB exchange rate falls below the previous day's closing rate, due to a persistent rise in the dollar index, the PBC may choose to avoid intervening but to allow the present day's closing rate to fall as long as it remains within the band so as to release the depreciation pressure on the renminbi. In this case, today's closing rate can be more or less equal to tomorrow's theoretical RMB exchange rate. As a result, while the renminbi is falling, the CFETS index can be quite stable.

Some argued that the depreciation of the renminbi between August 2016 and the end of that year was entirely attributable to the rise in the dollar index, and there was nothing wrong with the renminbi per se. In other words, there was no depreciation pressure in the foreign exchange market. Besides being factually incorrect—China ran an international balance of payments deficit for the whole of 2016, and the depletion of foreign exchange reserves continued until the second quarter of 2017—this argument ignores the role of the depreciation pressure on the renminbi in the determination of its central parity rate. If there were no depreciation pressures in the market, yesterday's closing rate would be equal to the RMB central parity rate set at yesterday's market opening. With a constant closing rate and a falling theoretical rate due to the fall in the dollar index, to maintain the stability of the CFETS index, today's RMB central parity rate should be set lower than yesterday's closing rate. However, to keep today's closing rate within the upper limit of the band, the PBC would have to buy the dollar and sell the renminbi in the foreign exchange market to pull down today's closing rate. This, in turn, would lead to an increase in foreign exchange reserves. This obviously was not the case.

It is worth noting that the most important entry point for intervention is the closing rate. Today's RMB central parity rate is determined by yesterday's closing rate and the dollar index that can be known only when the market is opening—but all these are historical and have already been decided. The only thing the PBC can do about today is influence today's closing rate. If the PBC reckons minimising the use of foreign exchange reserves is more important than stabilising the RMB exchange rate, it will allow the closing rate to fall until it hits the lower limit of the band. When the dollar index rises strongly and consistently, the PBC may significantly reduce its intervention to allow the closing rate to fall as much as possible to release depreciation pressure. In this case, the CFETS index may remain unchanged, while the renminbi is falling. The resulting stability of the CFETS index gives the market an impression that the PBC has adopted a peg to a currency basket and has stuck to it, and that the fall in the renminbi is a result of the rise in the dollar index rather than, for example, capital flight. This tactic seems quite successful.

The implementation of the new RMB central parity rate–setting rule

The trajectory of the RMB exchange rate against the US dollar and the CFETS index shows that the PBC has more or less followed the central parity rate rule (Figure 17.1). In the first four months of 2016 when the dollar index was falling—and hence the theoretical RMB exchange rate was rising—and faced with depreciation pressures on the renminbi, the PBC was reluctant to intervene forcefully for the sake of preserving foreign exchange reserves. Because the closing rate was constantly lower than the theoretical RMB exchange rate, the CFETS index fell materially alongside the fall in the RMB exchange rate.

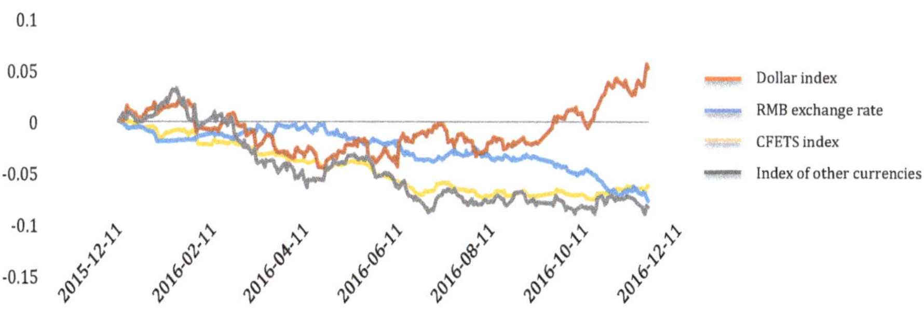

Figure 17.1 Behaviour pattern of CFETS index and its components

Source: Yu and Xiao (2017a).

From April to late July 2016, while the dollar index was on the rise, the PBC allowed the closing rate to fall substantially. As a result, the CFETS fell as well as the RMB central parity rate. From late August, the dollar index rose strongly. Hence, despite the closing rate and the RMB central parity rate continuing to fall, the CFETS index was rather stable.

Why was the new central parity rate–setting rule introduced?

It is clear that the central parity rate–setting rule makes it impossible for the renminbi to really be pegged to a basket of currencies because of the incorporation of the closing rate in the determination of the RMB central parity rate. What is the purpose of introducing such a rule? My guess is that the PBC hopes this mechanism will help stabilise the RMB exchange rate and gradually release depreciation pressures.

First, with the same depreciation pressure, the new rule can slow the pace of devaluation. For example, under the rule introduced during the 8/11 reform, if the RMB central parity rate depreciated by 2 per cent per day for 10 days, it would depreciate by 20 per cent. Under the new rule, however, if the closing rate is 2 per cent lower than the RMB central parity rate every day, the accumulated depreciation of the RMB central parity rate in 10 days could be as small as zero or even negative, because the determination of the next day's central parity rate will take into account changes in the dollar index. If the dollar index has fallen over the past 24 hours, the rise in the theoretical RMB exchange rate could more than fully offset the impact of the fall in the previous day's closing rate on today's RMB central parity rate. Of course, to ensure the actual RMB exchange rate in foreign exchange markets remains within the 2 per cent band, the PBC's intervention is unavoidable.

Second, for market participants, the uncertainty of the RMB central parity rate determination has increased significantly. No one can figure out tomorrow's RMB central parity rate until the opening of the market, when the theoretical RMB exchange rate can be calculated based on the information available on the dollar index. The central bank is pleased that the new mechanism brings uncertainty. Now the determination of the RMB central parity rate depends not only on the previous day's closing rate, but also on the dollar index, which is a result of interactions of all sorts of variables with global conditions. Market participants can only wait until tomorrow to know the dollar index, and there is no way for them to know in advance what tomorrow's RMB central parity rate will be. The uncertainty of the dollar index creates uncertainty in the RMB central parity rate. The increased uncertainty can to some extent curb the shorting activities and reduce depreciation pressure on the renminbi. However, this new pricing mechanism will not clear the market. The two-way fluctuations thus created are only partially market-driven, so cannot be sustained. More risks have been created for speculators, but more foreign exchange reserves have to be spent to achieve the central bank's preferred exchange rates.

The introduction of the 'countercyclical factor'

In 2016, and especially after the dollar index rose strongly in August, this mechanism was commonly regarded as quite good, because RMB depreciation expectations were receding and the fall in foreign exchange reserves was slowing. It is difficult to estimate how large is the contribution of the new RMB central parity rate–setting rule to the stabilisation of the renminbi. In fact, during this period, the exchange rates of all emerging market economies stabilised and rebounded, whatever their exchange rate regimes.

From the second quarter of 2017, China returned to an international balance of payments surplus. While the renminbi was on the rise, the dollar index started to fall. To follow the RMB central parity rate–setting rule, in such circumstances, both the theoretical RMB exchange rate and the closing rate, and hence the RMB central parity rate, should rise. Perhaps the rise in the theoretical RMB exchange rate was smaller than the closing rate and hence the rise in the RMB central parity rate failed to appreciate as strongly as the PBC would have liked.

In May 2017, the PBC introduced a 'countercyclical' factor in setting the RMB central parity rate. Now the RMB central parity rate will be determined by three factors: the bilateral exchange rate of the renminbi against the dollar, the theoretical RMB exchange rate and the countercyclical factor. Since 2017, the dollar index has been weakening and China's economic fundamentals have improved significantly. However, the appreciation of the RMB central parity rate has been just 1.07 per cent. According to the PBC, the irrational herd effect creates a procyclical tendency for the movement of the exchange rate. It seems the PBC believed the renminbi's closing rate failed to increase sufficiently to reflect the country's economic fundamentals. It is less clear why the closing rate would rise as a result of introducing the countercyclical factor. Perhaps it would send the market a signal that the PBC wants to see a larger appreciation of the renminbi, which in turn would help to strengthen RMB appreciation expectations and hence the RMB exchange rate. Or perhaps the introduction of the countercyclical factor just gave a freer hand to the PBC to prop up the closing rate of the renminbi and hence the RMB central parity rate, while still enabling the bank to insist it is acting in line with a preset rule.

The PBC has never been explicit about the calculation of the countercyclical factor and what weight it has been assigned in the formula for the RMB central parity rate. Neither is the logic in the justification for its introduction clear. Since the introduction of the countercyclical factor, appreciation of the RMB exchange rate against the dollar has strengthened, but it is not clear to what extent this can be attributed to the countercyclical factor.

On 9 January 2018, the PBC announced the suspension of the countercyclical factor in setting the RMB central parity rate. This led immediately to a fall of the RMB exchange rate in both the renminbi and offshore renminbi markets. The PBC provided no explanation of why it dumped the countercyclical factor. It is pretty clear, however, that the introduction of the countercyclical factor was not only a further step back from the direction embodied by the 8/11 reform, but also made the exchange rate–setting rule less transparent and verifiable. Furthermore, in the current domestic and international environments, any further strengthening of the renminbi is counterproductive for the Chinese economy. Neither the countercyclical factor nor the entirely central parity rate–setting rule is any longer needed. In fact, in late 2017, the head of the State Administration of Foreign Exchange (SAFE) announced that the PBC had stopped regular intervention in the foreign exchange market.

Concluding remarks

China's hands have been tied for more than a decade by the inflexibility of the exchange rate, which is one of the most important—if not the most important—prices. If the exchange rate does not reflect market supply and demand, misallocation of resources across countries and across generations is inevitable. As a result of the distortion, China has been importing 'dark matter'[3] for years. As one of the largest capital-exporting countries, holding more than US$2 trillion in foreign assets, China has run large investment deficits for many years. This is already very bad. Now China's foreign assets may have fallen significantly, while its foreign liabilities may have increased. This pattern in the international balance of payments will create serious problems in the future for an ageing China. A distorted exchange rate is a major contributor to this problem. I hope the Chinese authorities can make up their minds early to complete the drawn-out reform of the country's exchange rate regime as soon as possible.

References

Aghion, P., Bacchetta, P. and Banerjee, A. (2004), A corporate balance-sheet approach to currency crises, *Journal of Economic Theory* 119(1): 6–30. doi.org/10.1016/j.jet.2003.06.004.

Bergsten, C. F. and Williamson, J. (eds) (2004), *Dollar Adjustment: How Far? Against What?*, Washington, DC: Peterson Institute for International Economics.

3 Dark matter is a term coined by Ricardo Hausmann and Federico Sturzenegger (2006) to refer to the 'invisible' assets that explain why the United States is able to maintain investment income account surplus while running a huge current account deficit since 1982.

Bhalla, S. S. (2012), *Devaluing to Prosperity*, Washington, DC: Peterson Institute for International Economics.

Eichengreen, B. and Hausmann, R. (1999), *Exchange rates and financial fragility*, NBER Working Paper No. 7418, Cambridge, MA: National Bureau of Economic Research.

Eichengreen, B., Hausmann, R. and Panizza, U. (2007), Currency mismatches, debt intolerance, and the original sin: Why they are not the same and why it matters, in S. Edwards (ed.), *Capital Controls and Capital Flows in Emerging Economies: Policies, practices and consequences*, Chicago: University of Chicago Press. doi.org/10.7208/chicago/9780226184999.003.0004.

Gao, H. and Yu, Y. (2009), *Internationalisation of the renminbi*, Research Paper, Basel: Bank for International Settlements. Available from: www.bis.org/repofficepubl/arpresearch200903.05.pdf.

Goldstein, M. and Lardy, N. R. (2009), *The future of China's exchange rate policy*, Policy Analyses in International Economics No. 87, Washington, DC: Peterson Institute for International Economics.

Hausmann, R. and Sturzenegger, F. (2006), The implications of dark matter for assessing the US external imbalance. *CID Working Paper No. 137*. Available from: www.hks.harvard.edu/centers/cid/publications/faculty-working-papers/implications-dark-matter-assessing-us-external-imbalance.

International Monetary Fund (IMF) (2016), *Annual Report on Exchange Rate Arrangements and Exchange Restrictions 2016*, 11 October, Washington, DC: IMF. Available from: www.imf.org/en/Publications/Annual-Report-on-Exchange-Arrangements-and-Exchange-Restrictions/Issues/2017/01/25/Annual-Report-on-Exchange-Arrangements-and-Exchange-Restrictions-2016-43741.

Krugman, P. R. (1988), Target zones and exchange rate dynamics, *Quarterly Journal of Economics* 106(3): 669–82. doi.org/10.2307/2937922.

Liew, L. H. and Xu, H. X. (2007), *The Making of China's Exchange Rate Policy*, Cheltenham, UK: Edward Elgar.

Obstfeld, M. (2015), *Trilemmas and trade-offs: Living with financial globalisation*, BIS Working Paper No. 480, Basel: Bank for International Settlements. Available from: ssrn.com/abstract=2552572.

Rey, H. (2015), *Dilemma not trilemma: The global financial cycle and monetary policy independence*, NBER Working Paper No. 21162, Cambridge, MA: National Bureau of Economic Research.

Yu, Y. (1996), Macroeconomic management and capital inflows, [in Chinese], *World Economy* (October), Beijing: Institute of World Economics and Politics.

Yu, Y. (1997), Strategic thinking on the accumulation of foreign exchange reserves, [in Chinese], *World Economy* (October), Beijing: Institute of World Economics and Politics.

Yu, Y. (2003), Overcome the fear of RMB appreciation, [in Chinese], *Review of International Economics* (September–October), Beijing: Institute of World Economics and Politics.

Yu, Y. (2007), Global imbalances and China, *Australian Economic Review* 40(1): 1–21.

Yu, Y. (2011), Rebalancing the Chinese economy, *Economic and Political Weekly* 46(35)(27 August).

Yu, Y. (2012), Rebalancing the Chinese economy, *Oxford Review of Economic Policy* 28(3): 551–68. doi.org/10.1093/oxrep/grs025.

Yu, Y. (2014), *How far can renminbi internationalization go?*, ADBI Working Paper No. 46, February, Tokyo: Asian Development Bank Institute.

Yu, Y. and Xiao, L. (2017a), To accomplish the task of the unaccomplished '8.11 RMB Exchange rate reform', [in Chinese], *International Economic Review* 1: 23–41.

Yu, Y. and Xiao, L. (2017b), The direction of RMB exchange rate reform, [in Chinese], *Review of International Economics* (January–February), Beijing: Institute of World Economics and Politics.

Yu, Y. and Xiao, L. (2017c), China's capital flights explained, [in Chinese], *Review of International Economics* (September–October), Beijing: Institute of World Economics and Politics.

Yu, Y., Zhang, B. and Zhang, M. (2017), Renminbi exchange rate: Peg to a wide band currency basket, *China & World Economy* 25(1): 58–70. doi.org/10.1111/cwe.12186.

Zhang, B. (2012), Expectations, asset price, and aggregate demand: A simplified framework, [in Chinese], *China Economic Quarterly* 3: 893–908.

18. Private sector development

Nicholas Lardy

There is a widespread belief that the unprecedented pace and duration of China's economic growth is because China has developed a unique model of economic growth. This model is variously referred to as 'state capitalism', 'authoritarian capitalism', 'corporate Leninism' or 'regulatory capitalism' (McGregor 2012: 31). Those who believe that China has developed a unique economic model do not dispute the view that markets and private enterprise have come to play a substantially more important role since economic reform began in China in 1978. They acknowledge that reforms in the countryside in the first half of the 1980s effectively converted collective farming into private agriculture. They recognise that the state has largely abandoned its once pervasive control of prices in favour of market-determined prices for all but a few goods and services. And they concede that large parts of China's manufacturing industry, particularly consumer goods, are produced in private factories and distributed through wholesale and retail networks that are mostly privately owned and operated. And, of course, observation confirms that privately owned and operated hotels, restaurants and some other types of service firms have become pervasive in urban China.

But the proponents of the view that China has developed a unique economic model maintain that the state, through various mechanisms, retains control of what is sometimes referred to as the commanding heights of the economy. These mechanisms include continued dominant state ownership of critical industries, the widespread use of industrial policies developed by various state agencies, the proliferation of government funds designed to promote various government objectives and the continued state domination of the banking system, which also is used to promote various government policies. Some of these tools of government control are longstanding; others have emerged only in the past decade. These mechanisms have been noted in much academic writing (for example, Naughton 2016: 55–77) and the US Government pointed to these and other mechanisms as part of the basis for its refusal in 2017 to grant China market economy status (US Department of Commerce 2018).

While there have been some elements of economic policy in the past decade that reflect a resurgence of the state, this chapter argues that, in a 40-year perspective, the private sector has had a dominant role in China's economic transformation. The important caveat is that while the state sector has been drastically reduced in terms of its contribution to output and employment, its declining productivity since the Global Financial Crisis (GFC) combined with a growing claim on bank credit starting in 2013 mean that state-owned enterprises (SOEs) are a drag on China's economic growth.

The displacement of SOEs

The rise of private business in China since 1978 is largely the result of what might be called the displacement of SOEs. Unlike some other formerly centrally planned economies, in China, privatisation of SOEs has been only a minor contributor to the rise of private business. Rather, private firms have grown much more rapidly than SOEs. Displacement of SOEs in terms of output, investment and employment has been facilitated by three factors. First, the government and the Communist Party of China (CPC) very gradually opened the space in which private firms could operate. Second, private firms on average have been far more productive than SOEs, generating a high level of profits relative to their assets. Private entrepreneurs have reinvested these profits, leading to a pace of growth that SOEs ultimately could not match. Third, over time, private firms were able to borrow increasing amounts from banks and also were able to raise funds on the Shanghai and Shenzhen stock markets.

In the first decade or so of reform, government policy opened the economy to private economic activity only very slowly. As early as 1978, the National People's Congress adopted a constitutional amendment allowing 'individual labourers' to operate, but restricted the scope of these businesses by forbidding employment of more than seven nonfamily members. And, in 1982, the Chinese constitution was revised to include, for the first time, a provision protecting private property rights (Garnaut et al. 2005: 198). But not until 1988 did the government promulgate the Provisional Regulations on Private Enterprises, which for the first time provided a legal framework for private firms with eight or more nonfamily members.

In the mid-1990s, the implementation of the Company Law further boosted China's private sector. First, this law allowed private firms to organise as limited liability companies, meaning the personal wealth of an entrepreneur could be separated from the assets of the entrepreneur's business. Second, it facilitated the reregistration of more than a million collective firms as private companies—a process sometimes referred to as 'taking off the red hat'. In 2005 and again in 2010, the government lifted restrictions on the entry of private businesses into an increasing range of industries, such as civil aviation, which previously were reserved exclusively for SOEs. The government in 2008 began to provide special tax incentives for private companies—notably a lower corporate income tax rate and exemptions from the value-added and business taxes for firms with annual taxable income below certain thresholds (Lardy 2014: 89–93).

The attitude of the government and the CPC towards private firms also further evolved in important ways that supported the rise of the private sector. Initially, official documents did not even refer to the private sector but acknowledged the nonstate sector (which included collective firms) as an important component of the state-dominated economy. In 1999, in a constitutional amendment, the nonstate sector was upgraded to 'an essential component of a mixed economy' (Lardy 2014: 91). On the eightieth anniversary of the CPC in 2001, then general secretary Jiang Zemin invited private entrepreneurs to join the party, leading to a substantial change in the composition of party membership, away from workers and peasants towards wealthy private businesspeople (McGregor 2010: 31).

A second factor facilitating displacement of SOEs is that private firms have been far more efficient than SOEs, particularly as measured by return on assets. The dismal economic performance of SOEs in the 1980s and 1990s was made painfully clear by an accumulation of nonperforming loans (NPLs) in the banking system that was so large that, by 1997, China's largest state-owned banks, which lent predominantly to SOEs, were insolvent (Lardy 1998: 5). Premier Zhu Rongji led a two-pronged initiative to avoid a banking and financial crisis. The first prong was a substantial restructuring of the state sector. This led to the closure of thousands of mostly money-losing SOEs and the loss of tens of millions of jobs. The second component of Zhu's reforms was a massive write-off of NPLs by state-owned banks and their recapitalisation by the government. The most comprehensive estimate of the costs of restructuring China's banks from the late 1990s through to late 2005 is RMB4 trillion (Ma 2007: 31).

In the industrial sector, where we can measure the results of Zhu's reforms most accurately, the return on assets of SOEs rose rapidly from the late 1990s through to 2007, substantially reducing, though not eliminating, the underperformance of SOEs relative to private firms. However, since the GFC, the productivity gap between state and private industrial firms has widened significantly. As shown in Figure 18.1, by 2016, the returns of industrial SOEs had fallen by almost three-fifths from their high point in 2007, to only 3 per cent, while private industrial firms earned returns of 10.6 per cent—more than 1 percentage point higher than in 2007. As a result, the return on assets of registered private industrial firms in 2016 was three-and-a-half times that of SOEs—proportionately the largest gap in almost 20 years.

Figure 18.1 Return on assets of state and private industrial enterprises, 1998–2016 (per cent)

Source: NBS (2017: 424–5, 430–1); National Bureau of Statistics of China website (data.stats.gov.cn; accessed 5 September 2017).

The third factor facilitating the growth of private businesses was the increasing access of these firms to bank credit and funds raised through initial public offerings (IPOs) on the domestic stock markets and the sale of bonds. This process was very gradual; China's predominantly state-owned banking system initially directed almost all credit to SOEs. Flows of credit to private firms in the initial years of the reform process were miniscule, which is hardly surprising given official antipathy at the time towards private nonagricultural businesses and the state banks' lack of the credit skills needed to lend to small private companies. This began to change when China's central bank in the mid-1980s formally authorised the creation of urban credit cooperatives. This network grew rapidly and, by 1995, these cooperatives had become the principal source of formal credit for small private companies (Lardy 2014: 103). Eventually the large state banks, recognising that highly profitable private firms were on average more creditworthy than money-losing SOEs, directed a larger and larger share of their corporate lending to private firms. The story was similar in the equity market, where initially almost all IPOs were by SOEs. Over time, the mix changed. By 2017, 377 private firms went public, while only 31 SOEs did the same.[1]

1 In 2017, however, SOEs raised more money via the domestic stock markets because they dominated secondary offerings, which were much larger in terms of funds raised than IPOs (data from Wind).

These three factors—the opening of the economic space available to private firms, the superior financial performance of private firms and the increased access of these firms to funds from banks and the domestic stock markets—facilitated the process of displacement of state by private firms. This displacement in terms of output is easiest to analyse in China's industrial sector, which on the eve of reform accounted for more than two-fifths of gross domestic product (GDP) (NBS 2016a: 21–2). As shown in Figure 18.2, in 1978, SOEs accounted for almost four-fifths of industrial output (Lardy 2014: 75).[2] By 2015, this share had shrunk to one-fifth (NBS 2016b: 419, 427–8).[3] But, since China's industrial output in constant prices by 2015 was 47 times the level of 1978, the output of SOEs in 2015 was 12 times the level of 1978. Clearly, while industrial SOEs are shrinking rapidly in relative terms, they continue to expand in absolute terms.

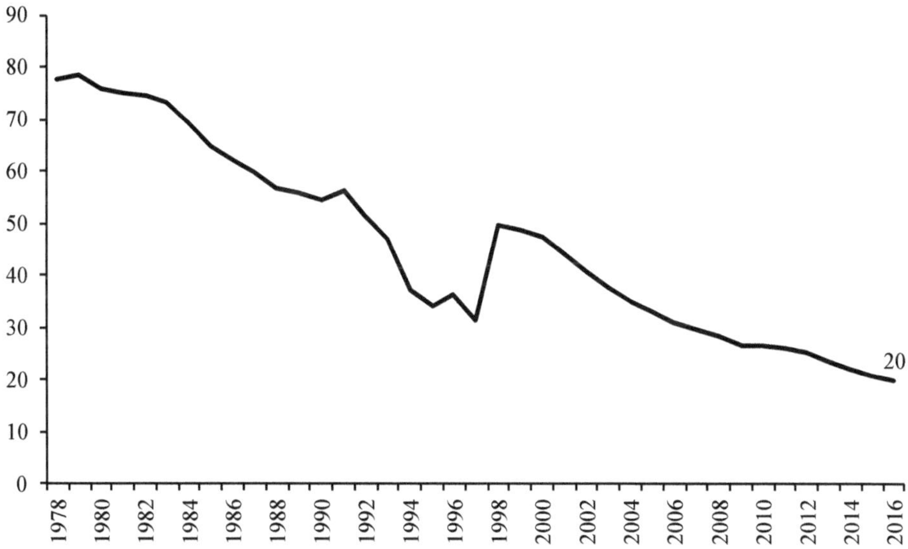

Figure 18.2 Gross industrial output of state enterprises, 1978–2016 (percentage of total gross industrial output)

Notes: Data include only above-scale firms, with sales greater than RMB5 million (1998–2011) and firms with sales greater than RMB20 million (beginning in 2011). This data series was discontinued after 2011, so in this figure data for 2012–16 are the state share of industrial sales value—a proxy for gross industrial output.

Source: Lardy (2014: 75); National Bureau of Statistics of China website (data.stats.gov.cn; accessed 12 June 2018).

2 The state share in 1978 is based on gross value of industrial output. Throughout this chapter, data on the share of state output and investment are inclusive of output and investment of traditional SOEs and traditional SOEs that have been transformed into limited liability and shareholding firms in which the state is in control because it is the sole, majority or dominant owner. For details, see Lardy (2016: 38).

3 Since gross value data disaggregated by ownership are no longer published, the state share in 2015 is based on revenue from principal business.

A major factor leading to the pattern of relative displacement of SOEs in terms of output was the diminished role of these companies in investment in industry. In the early years of reform, the majority of industrial investment was undertaken by SOEs and financed through the state budget. But budgetary financing of investment was gradually phased out by the mid-1990s. So, SOEs became increasingly dependent on retained earnings to finance investment. Because of the weakening financial performance of industrial SOEs by 2006, their share of all industrial investment had fallen to two-fifths and, by 2015, fell further to well under one-fifth (NBS 2007: 206–7; 2016b: 318–19).

While this transformation since 1978 has been dramatic, the pace of displacement of industrial SOEs in terms of both output and investment has an important limit. The reason is that industry, in Chinese statistical practice, consists of manufacturing, mining and utilities and these domains are not equally open to private firms. Most manufacturing is open to private firms and, by 2015, the SOEs' share of output had been reduced to 16 per cent. Mining and especially utilities, which accounted for 6 and 5 per cent of industrial output in 2015, respectively, are less open to private firms, so SOEs still accounted for 48 and 88 per cent of output in these two domains, respectively (NBS 2016b: 420–3, 426–9).

In contrast, in the service sector, the role of SOEs remains much more important than in industry. While comprehensive data on service sector output disaggregated by ownership are not published, the continued importance of SOEs is confirmed in investment data.

The last indicator of the displacement of SOEs is employment. In urban China in 1978, there were no private firms and individual businesses (sometimes referred to as self-employed) had only 150,000 workers—less than two-tenths of 1 per cent of urban employment. SOEs and government agencies employed 75 million workers and collective units—largely controlled and usually at least partially owned by local governments—employed another 20 million people. Employment in SOEs—that is, excluding those employed by government agencies—declined from about 59.8 million or 27 per cent of the urban workforce in 1999 to 46.9 million or 11 per cent of the workforce in 2016 (Lardy 2014: 139; NBS and Ministry of Human Resources and Social Security 2018: 262).

Mechanisms of state control

If private firms have displaced SOEs as measured by output, investment and employment, what are the potential mechanisms through which the state still exercises control and how important are these mechanisms?

One potentially important mechanism is continued dominant state ownership of critical industries. As already noted, the average share of state-controlled output across all industries has declined, but this may mask substantial variation, with the state continuing to dominate the most critical industries. Indeed, a 2006 policy document of the State-owned Assets Supervision and Administration Commission (SASAC) called for 'maintaining state ownership as the main element of the economy, concentrating state assets in important sectors' and what it called 'critical realms and strengthening the controlling power and leading role of the state economy' (Lardy 2014: 54). The document also specifically identified seven so-called strategic industries in which the state must maintain 'absolute controlling power' and nine so-called pillar industries in which the state must maintain 'relatively strong control' (SASAC 2006). The strategic industries include defence, electricity production and distribution, petroleum, telecommunications, coal, civil aviation and shipping.

It is not clear, however, whether state control in most of these strategic industries differentiates China from many other market-oriented economies. The defence industry is a special case in all major global powers and is not considered further in this chapter. State ownership or a high degree of regulation of electricity, petroleum, telecommunications and civil aviation is commonly observed in many economies. Electric power generation and distribution are a natural monopoly that means direct government ownership or heavy regulation is universal. Pemex in Mexico and Petrobras in Brazil are good examples of state monopolies in petroleum in market economies. Majority government ownership of Singapore Airlines and Thai Airways International does not lead us to believe that Singapore and Thailand are state-controlled economies.

Coal is a more interesting strategic industry because it is not a natural monopoly, and globally in recent decades there are few, if any, coal industries that are state owned or state controlled. But it does not appear that the Chinese Government has successfully exercised absolute controlling power of this industry. In 2005, just prior to the policy announcement on strategic industries, state coalmines produced 70 per cent of the industry's output. A decade later, the state share had fallen to less than 60 per cent (NBS 2006: 510–13, 520–3; 2016b: 420–3, 426–9).

A similar pattern prevails for steel—one of the nine pillar industries in which SASAC declared it would maintain relatively strong controlling power. In 2005, state steel companies were responsible for 49 per cent of the industry's output; by 2015, their share had declined to 28 per cent (NBS 2006: 510–13, 520–3; 2016b: 420–3, 426–9). The state may aspire to retain absolute power in the coal industry and relatively strong controlling power in the steel industry, but the evidence shows these industries are not an exception to the broad pattern in which SOEs are steadily losing market share to more efficient private firms.[4]

4 An exception is the tobacco industry, where the state, through its aptly named State Tobacco Monopoly Administration, continues to control 99.3 per cent of output in the industry.

Industrial policy is a second mechanism through which the Chinese Government seeks to exert continued economic control. The success of industrial policies everywhere is difficult to judge. What is the counterfactual—that is, what would have happened in the absence of such policies? Almost all the strategic and pillar industries identified in the government's 2006 industrial policy are in the manufacturing sector. It is not obvious whether the government has been able to maintain state ownership and concentrate state assets in the critical realms it has identified. As already noted, the share of manufacturing output accounted for by SOEs had fallen to just 16 per cent by 2015. The share of investment by SOEs in manufacturing fell from 22 per cent in 2006 to less than 8 per cent by 2015. Private firms account for more than three-quarters of investment in the manufacturing sector.[5] Even in narrowly defined strategic and pillar industries within manufacturing, such as coal and steel, the share of output produced in SOEs has fallen significantly since state ownership of these industries was first prioritised.

The most sustained industrial policy China has pursued is associated with SASAC. SASAC was established formally in 2003 when, at the central government level, it assumed oversight of about 200 of China's largest firms, including the three state oil companies, the three state telecommunications companies, most of the large state-owned power generating companies, the two state power distribution companies, the major state airlines, and so forth. All of these firms were large group companies or holding companies, each with numerous subsidiaries. Counting subsidiaries three levels down from the parent, these companies in 2010 controlled 23,738 firms—about one-fifth of all state nonfinancial companies.[6] Including 52,371 subsidiaries of group companies controlled by SASAC entities at the provincial level, SASAC controls three-fifths of all state nonfinancial companies. SASAC was charged with transforming these companies into so-called national champions.

While the creation of SASAC is certainly consistent with the view that the state has sought a more direct role in promoting economic development, it almost certainly should be judged a failure. Operationally, SASAC has focused on mergers of its firms within the same industry and capturing more funds for investment. As a result, central SASAC orchestrated dozens of mergers, in the process reducing the initial roughly 200 firms to less than 100 by mid-2017. Most of these mergers were of firms within the same industry. For example, SASAC merged China Ocean Shipping Group with China Shipping Group and merged the two rail car producers, CNR Corporation and CSR Corporation.

5 Private here includes registered private companies and limited liability and shareholding limited firms in which the sole, majority or dominant owner is private.

6 State ownership of most financial firms is vested in Central Huijin, a unit of the Chinese Investment Corporation—sometimes regarded as China's sovereign wealth fund.

SASAC firms were also showered with bank loans and were able to raise additional funds through initial and secondary public offerings on the Shanghai stock exchange and bond issuance. As a result, the assets controlled by SASAC firms soared from RMB10.6 trillion in 2005 to RMB54.54 trillion at the end of 2017. The increase of about RMB45 trillion is fully four times the after-tax profits these firms generated between 2005 and 2017.[7] Yet the return on assets of the universe of SASAC firms fell from 6 per cent in 2005 to only 2.4 per cent in 2015 and 2016, before recovering very slightly to 2.6 per cent in 2017.

Another potential mechanism of state control is government-run financing agencies that emerged starting in 2010. The earliest were technology funds—mostly established at the provincial level—to support long-term science and technology policy. More recently, the Chinese Government has established investment funds and state capital investment and operations funds that invest in priority growth areas. By the end of 2015, there were 780 investment funds, with RMB2.18 trillion in capital (Kennedy and Johnson 2016: 27). Since then, SASAC has established two additional large funds, the State-Owned Enterprise Structural Adjustment Fund and the China Reform Fund. By the end of 2016, government-run funds managed about RMB3.6 trillion (Mano and Stokoe 2017).

It is too soon to evaluate the success of these funds in promoting state economic policy. Several caveats are in order. First, although the reported cumulative magnitude of the funds seems large, it is not clear how quickly these funds are being invested. Firms raised only RMB1.1 trillion on the Shanghai and Shenzhen stock markets in 2017, so if these government funds are deployed quickly they could become more important than the domestic stock markets. Second, it is not clear the extent to which these funds will become a replacement for bank lending. The state may be more successful in promoting the development of the semiconductor industry through its National Integrated Circuit Investment Fund, financed in part by banks, than through uncoordinated bank lending in support of the industry.

The third mechanism of continuing state control is the state-dominated banking system. China remains a very bank-dominated financial system and almost the entire banking system is state controlled. Yes, China's largest state-owned banks have been listed on public markets, but typically only a minority of the shares of each bank have been sold to investors, meaning the banks remain state controlled. For China's largest state banks, this control is exercised by the central government and the Organisation Department of the CPC nominates the top leadership of each bank. For smaller institutions, such as joint stock banks and city commercial banks, some of which are also publicly listed, the controlling shareholder is a provincial or municipal government and presumably top managers of each bank are vetted by the

7 After-tax profits are estimated by applying the 25 per cent corporate tax rate to the reported pre-tax profits of SASAC firms.

CPC Organisation Department at the provincial or municipal level. There are only a handful of truly private banks—all quite small—and although there are numerous foreign banks, cumulatively, they control less than 2 per cent of bank assets.

Resurgence of the state?

In the northern autumn of 2013, a year into the leadership regime of President Xi Jinping and Premier Li Keqiang, the CPC endorsed a far-reaching economic reform program that, among other things, called for the market to play the dominant role in the allocation of resources (CPC Central Committee 2013). Five years later, however, most observers argue that little of this ambitious reform agenda has been implemented. Instead, China has announced a series of industrial policies that promote SOEs at the expense of private and foreign firms; the flow of bank lending to private firms has declined, not only as a share of the total flow of loans to corporate firms, but also in absolute terms; and President Xi in his first five-year term focused on his signature anticorruption campaign and consolidating his political power. This culminated in the northern spring of 2018 in a revision to the Chinese constitution that drops the clause limiting the term of office of China's president to two five-year terms.

Figure 18.3 Growth of state and private investment, 2007–16 (per cent, year over year)

Source: NBS (2017: 310–11); National Bureau of Statistics of China website (data.stats.gov.cn; accessed 5 September 2017).

The clearest empirical evidence of the resurgence of the state is in the investment realm. As reflected in Figure 18.3, from 2006 to 2011, the growth of private investment was quite strong—indeed, on average, it expanded at a pace about two and half times that of state investment. This pushed up the share of private investment from 36 per cent to 48 per cent. But from 2011, the pace of growth of private investment slowed dramatically, while the pace of state investment rose. By 2016, state investment grew at several times the pace of private investment.

The most plausible explanation of the waning of private investment is crowding out—an explanation supported by several pieces of evidence. First, the share of bank loans to nonfinancial corporations that went to private firms fell from 57 per cent in 2013 to only 19 per cent by 2015, while the share that went to SOEs almost doubled over the same period—from 35 per cent to 69 per cent. Second, financing of private firms through microfinance companies stalled after 2015. Lending by these companies grew rapidly from 2008, when the People's Bank of China and the China Securities Regulatory Commission first issued formal guidelines on microfinance companies. The volume of such lending levelled off at just less than RMB1 trillion in 2014, but has not grown since.[8]

Third, between 2011 and 2015, SOEs' profits rose by only RMB30 billion, or 1 percentage point, while the investment of these firms rose by almost RMB2 trillion, or more than 20 per cent. Much of the differential between the growth of investment and the growth of profits must have come from increased borrowing from banks.

Fourth, indirect evidence suggests that SOEs have borrowed increasing amounts of funds to cover their financial losses. In 2005, 50 per cent of all SOEs were lossmaking. By 2016, the share of lossmaking SOEs had declined slightly, to 45 per cent. Thus, roughly half of China's SOEs for more than a decade have been unable to fully cover their cost of capital. Moreover, the magnitude of losses generated by lossmaking firms increased sevenfold, from RMB243 billion in 2005 to RMB1.95 trillion in 2016. As a share of GDP, these losses doubled, from 1.3 per cent in 2006 to 2.6 per cent in 2016 (MOF 2015: 374; 2016: 369).

The rapid increase in the magnitude of SOE losses appears consistent with the decline in the return on assets of SOEs in this period. When the average return on assets falls persistently, the share of firms with negative returns and the magnitude of losses both naturally increase. Since very few firms go bankrupt or are taken over through merger and acquisition activity, it appears increased borrowing from banks covers a substantial portion of these financial losses. In the industrial sector, for example, the ratio of debt to equity or leverage ratio of SOEs increased from 132 per cent in 2005 to 163 per cent in 2015. When a large share of firms are lossmaking but they borrow money to finance investment, they are unable to fully cover their cost of loans and inevitably can stay in operation only by rolling over their loans—in

8 Data on microfinance lending are from Wind.

the process adding unpaid interest on the prior loans to the principal of the new loan. Inevitably, that means debt increases more rapidly than assets, equity falls and the ratio of debt to equity rises.

Private industrial firms also borrow to finance investment, but on average they earn returns that are three times those of SOEs and the incidence of lossmaking is only one-third that of SOEs, so, on average, they easily repay their loans. The borrowed funds are used to finance investment in plant and equipment, raising firms' assets. The subsequent repayment of the loans from profits reduces firms' liabilities. Thus equity (which equals assets minus liabilities) rises and the leverage ratio falls. The leverage ratio of private companies in 2005 was 147 per cent, but by 2015 it had fallen to 109 per cent.

Taken together, the evidence on investment and leverage suggests that, starting in 2012 and accelerating in 2016–17, SOEs have had an increasing claim on the loanable funds of the banking system. They have used these funds both to increase their share of investment and to offset the losses of the large fraction of SOEs that are lossmaking. Unfortunately, the returns on these investments continue to fall and the share of increased bank credit used to offset losses appears to be rising.

SOEs drag down China's growth

While private firms have been the dominant source of growth in output and employment over the past four decades, the resurgence of the state in the past five years has been inimical for China's growth for two reasons. First, President Xi has repeatedly called to make state firms larger and better. The former has certainly been achieved, largely due to mergers within the SASAC universe. No Chinese company was included in the Fortune Global 500 list when reform began. In 1996, two Chinese firms made the list, but by 2017 Chinese firms occupied 109 spots on the list, including three in the top 10. Virtually all of the Chinese firms on the Fortune 500 list are state controlled and many are group companies in the SASAC universe.

But the Fortune Global 500 is a ranking of companies by revenue; no consideration is given to any measure of efficiency, such as return on assets or return on equity. As Chinese SOEs have bulked up through mergers and additional investment, the number included on the Fortune Global 500 list has inevitably grown, but the efficiency of these firms has fallen. In 2015, for example, 12 of the 98 Chinese companies on the list were lossmaking. And, as previously noted, the return on assets of the large subset of state firms under the administration of central SASAC has fallen sharply since the GFC. The same is true of the broader SOE universe. The return on assets for SOEs in industry and construction fell from 5.5 per cent in 2007 to only 1.8 per cent in 2016; in services, the decline was from 4.1 per cent to 1.6 per cent (MOF 2015: 384, 388; 2017: 379, 383).

The second reason the resurgence of the state has been inimical for China's growth is that investment in the far more efficient private sector has been increasingly crowded out. This slowdown of private relative to state investment began in 2012 and became much more acute in 2016 when the growth of state investment surpassed the pace of private investment by a wide margin.

The central conclusion of this chapter is that China's economic growth in the reform era has been driven by the private sector operating in an increasingly market-oriented environment. In recent years, however, the state banks have allocated a growing share of their loans to SOEs. This is despite evidence that the performance of SOEs has declined precipitously in absolute terms and even more relative to private firms. Thus, a secondary conclusion of the chapter is that China's growth in recent years has been below potential.

China's growth in the first three-and-a-half decades of economic reform was largely due to an expanding role of markets and private firms. Since Xi Jinping came to power in 2012, there has been a new emphasis on state enterprises, industrial policy and the role of the party in the economy. This approach endures despite evidence that SOE performance continues to decline, both in absolute terms and even more relative to private firms.

Capturing China's potential for faster growth would require substantial additional economic reforms to raise the productivity of SOEs. First, China should suspend or even reverse the policy of creating ever larger SOEs through top-down, government-orchestrated mergers. The net effect of this program over more than a decade has been to reduce competition. These mergers have increased the market power of SOEs in many domains, inevitably reducing the incentive for innovation and cost reduction, leading to predictable declines in efficiency.

Second, the government should open up the portions of the economy where entry by private firms is still restricted—notably, in large parts of the service sector. Again, this would increase competitive pressure and perhaps lead to productivity improvements in SOEs.

Third, the government should encourage more market-driven merger and acquisition activity so that more efficient private firms could acquire the assets of state companies that remain underperforming, even in the more competitive environment envisioned above.

Fourth, Articles 4 and 41 of the Commercial Bank Law, promulgated more than two decades ago, should be strictly enforced (NPC Standing Committee 1995: 335–9). Article 4 states that commercial banks must 'operate on the principles of efficiency, safety, and liquidity; exercise independent operation; bear their own risks; assume exclusive responsibility for profits and losses'. Article 41 states that 'no unit or individual may compel a commercial bank to extend loans or provide guarantees'. Enforcement of these provisions would preclude local politicians from leaning on banks to extend loans to underperforming and money-losing companies that otherwise might have to suspend their operations. It would incentivise banks to direct more lending to more creditworthy, predominantly private firms, thus mitigating the crowding out that has undermined the expansion of the more productive private sector in recent years.

The conclusion that China's recent growth is below potential is contrary to the widely quoted view of Lant Pritchett and Larry Summers (2014), who argue that periods of super rapid economic growth are invariably followed by reversion to the mean. This approach led them to predict that China's growth between 2003 and 2033 might fall to as low as 2 per cent per capita. Their prediction, of course, could turn out to be correct. But, with appropriate further reforms, I believe China's growth would be somewhat more rapid than in recent years.

It is too early to make a definitive judgement on whether an enhanced role of the state and diminished role of the market in resource allocation can be the basis for successful, sustainable development in China. But the early evidence is not promising. China's most ambitious and longest-lived industrial policy to date, the program of investment and mergers orchestrated by SASAC, has certainly fallen short. And the reduction in the role of the market under President Xi has slowed China's economic growth.

References

Communist Party of China (CPC) Central Committee (2013), Decision on major issues concerning comprehensively deepening reforms, *China Daily*, 16 November. Available from: www.china.org.cn/china/third_plenary_session/2013-11/16/content_30620736.htm.

Garnaut, R., Song, S., Tenev, S. and Yao, Y. (2005), *China's Ownership Transformation: Process, outcomes, prospects*, Washington, DC: International Finance Corporation and International Bank for Reconstruction and Development.

Kennedy, S. and Johnson, C. K. (2016), *Perfecting China, Inc.: The 13th five-year plan*, Washington, DC: Center for Strategic and International Studies.

Lardy, N. R. (1998), *China's Unfinished Economic Revolution*, Washington, DC: Brookings Institution Press.

Lardy, N. R. (2014), *Markets over Mao: The rise of private business in China*, Washington, DC: Peterson Institute for International Economics.

Lardy, N. R. (2016), The changing role of the private sector in China, in *Structural Change in China: Implications for Australia and the world*, Sydney: Reserve Bank of Australia.

Ma, G. (2007), Who pays China's bank restructuring bill?, *Asian Economic Papers* 6(1): 31. doi.org/10.1162/asep.2007.6.1.46.

Mano, R. C. and Stokoe P. (2017), *Reassessing the Perimeter of Government Accounts in China,* IMF Working Paper WP/17/272, November, Washington, DC: International Monetary Fund.

McGregor, J. (2012), *No Ancient Wisdom, No Followers: The challenges of Chinese authoritarian capitalism*, Westport, CT: Prospecta Press.

McGregor, R. (2010), *The Party: The secret world of China's communist rulers*, New York: Harper Collins.

Ministry of Finance (MOF) (2015), *Finance Yearbook of China 2015*, Beijing: China Financial Magazine Publishing House.

Ministry of Finance (MOF) (2016), *Finance Yearbook of China 2016*, Beijing: China Financial Magazine Publishing House.

Ministry of Finance (MOF) (2017), *Finance Yearbook of China 2017*, Beijing: China Financial Magazine Publishing House.

National Bureau of Statistics (NBS) (2007), *China Statistical Yearbook 2007*, Beijing: China Statistics Press.

National Bureau of Statistics (NBS) (2016a), *China Statistical Abstract 2016*, Beijing: China Statistics Press.

National Bureau of Statistics (NBS) (2016b), *China Statistical Yearbook 2016*, Beijing: China Statistics Press.

National Bureau of Statistics of China (NBS) (2017), *China Statistical Yearbook 2017*, Beijing: China Statistics Press.

National Bureau of Statistics (NBS) and Ministry of Human Resources and Social Security (2018), *China Labour Statistical Yearbook 2017*, Beijing: China Statistics Press.

National People's Congress (NPC) Standing Committee (1995), Commercial Bank Law of the People's Republic of China, 10 May, in *Almanac of China's Finance and Banking*, Beijing: Financial Publishing House.

Naughton, B. (2016), Restructuring and reform, in *Structural Change in China: Implications for Australia and the world*, Sydney: Reserve Bank of Australia.

Prichett, L. and Summers, L. (2014), *Asiaphoria meets regression to the mean*, NBER Working Paper 20573, October, Cambridge, MA: National Bureau of Economic Research. Available from: www.nber.org/papers/w20573. doi.org/10.3386/w20573.

State-owned Assets Supervision and Administration Commission (SASAC) (2006), The state economy must guarantee absolute controlling power over seven sectors, *China Daily*, 19 December.

United States Department of Commerce (2017), A-570-053 Investigation, Public Document E&C VI: MJH/TB, Washington, DC: US Department of Commerce. Available from: enforcement.trade.gov/download/prc-nme-status/prc-nme-review-final-103017.pdf.

19. State-owned enterprise reform in China: Past, present and prospects

Ligang Song[1]

Reform of state-owned enterprises (SOEs) has been a core element of China's economic reform process over the past 40 years. SOEs formed the backbone of China's economy during the central planning era; their transformation is the most prominent among changes in China's enterprise system that have been taking place in tandem with other institutional and policy reforms in the course of the transition to a market-based economy. Market-oriented development has progressed with a reduction in the scope of the SOE sector in the economy. Unlike what has happened in the former socialist countries in Europe, in China, SOE reform did not involve rapid and widespread privatisation (Naughton 2007; Zhang 2009). China's reformers have been aware of the significant economic, social and political consequences of disruption caused by breaking up SOEs in a short time without creating the necessary conditions for change (McMillan and Naughton 1992). Therefore, China's economic transition is recognised for its gradualist and experimental approach to reform, with SOE reform a typical example. The primary goal of market-oriented reforms, as repeatedly reiterated by the Chinese Government, is to build a socialist market economy with the state-owned sector as a leading sector. This thinking and practice have had significant implications for the outcome of previous SOE reforms, as well as for the direction of future changes to the SOE sector.

SOE reforms have contributed to China's economic development in two ways: first, changes to SOEs have made room and created the necessary conditions for the emergence and flourishing of private enterprises and enterprises with other ownership forms. Second, such change has also helped to enhance the efficiency and competitiveness of SOEs, leading to the substantial growth of their output, which in turn enables SOEs, especially the large ones, to maintain their substantial share in the economy. Reforms have so far created a new generation of SOEs with diversified ownership types and a significant level of internationalisation. Now there are only a small number of SOEs that are purely state owned, with the majority of enterprises now state-controlled shareholding corporations.

1 I thank Son Ngoc Chu and Shenglang Yang for sourcing the background materials, including the data for the tables and figures.

This chapter begins with an analytical account of China's SOE reforms during the transition process. This section highlights the core issues of SOE operation, governance and performance that have been addressed across the different stages of reform. Issues include market competition and the soft budget constraint, ownership transformation, autonomy, enterprise monitoring and corporate governance and commercial objectives and policy functions of the SOEs. The chapter shows how these core issues have evolved and how China's gradualist and dual-track approach to market transition has taken place. Using a chronological approach and highlighting the consistency of SOE reforms within China's overall reform program, this chapter examines the SOE reform process in four stages: 1978–92, 1992–2003, 2003–13 and 2013 to the present. The chapter provides concluding remarks on the prospects of current SOE reform efforts.

The nature of SOEs and China's approach to SOE reforms in transition

SOEs were the main economic units in the enterprise system of nonagricultural sectors under the central planning system. The primary functions of SOEs were to fulfil the government's objectives for production and distribution of goods. The government played a crucial role in planning, coordination and resource allocation, while SOEs had little autonomy in determining what and how much to produce, adjusting the workforce or deciding on the use of surpluses or profits. Product prices did not function as the primary signal to guide an enterprise's production decisions, but instead were used by the government to channel resources between economic sectors, particularly the industrial sector for ambitious industrialisation plans (Naughton 2007: 60). Moreover, as government agents, SOEs were responsible for employees' welfare and that of their families, including housing, health care, education and retirement (Chow 2002: 69). The lack of market-based incentives and multiple functions of SOEs led to their low efficiency, contributing to the chronic problems of low output and shortages during the planned economy period. Because of these problems, SOE transformation is among the most significant areas of economic transition—namely, adopting a market mechanism for resource allocation and promoting efficiency with output expansion. In the literature on SOEs, the approach to reform and associated policy measures has focused on the following critical issues of enterprise performance.

Market competition and the soft budget constraint

Under central planning SOEs did not have to compete with each other or with enterprises of other ownership forms on the market to buy inputs and sell output. Instead, SOEs relied on the government agencies in their respective sectors for production needs and output distribution through 'material balance planning' (Naughton 2007: 61). It is, therefore, a primary step in SOE reform to expose the sector to market competition. Moreover, SOEs had few concerns about efficiency when making decisions on investment and production, other than meeting the output targets set by the government. They were financially dependent and supported by the government through different channels, including funding from state-owned banks and other fiscal sources from different government agencies, which Kornai (1986) in his seminal paper called 'The soft budget constraint'. Typically, subsidies, tax exemptions and soft credits are the key channels to help firms soften their budget constraint. As a result, they are less responsive to price signals and market rules and prone to losses and state assistance. SOEs' chronic soft budget constraint problem not only occurred under central planning, but also persisted into the market transition period (Kornai et al. 2003: 1095).

Ownership transformation

Given the dominant share of the SOE sector in the centrally planned economy, a key policy measure of China's SOE reforms is ownership change by reducing the government's holdings of SOE assets through partial or full privatisation of SOEs. This measure has the dual effects of reducing the government's cost burden from inefficient SOEs and creating opportunities for private firms to participate and expand (Garnaut et al. 2006). Ownership reform was, therefore, a cornerstone of the market reform program that began with the government's recognition of a multi-ownership economic system and private property rights (Chow 2002). The economy-wide ownership reform played a crucial role in the emergence of nonstate enterprises, significantly enhancing market competition in the early period of transition (Jefferson and Su 2006).

Autonomy, enterprise monitoring and corporate governance

The functioning of a market economy requires that the property rights of economic agents are clearly defined and enforced. In principle, SOEs are owned by the people and controlled by the government. The primary objective of SOE reform is to reduce government intervention in business operations and provide autonomy and delegate the use rights of SOE assets to managers. As a consequence, there is a separation between the owners and managers or ownership and control, giving rise to the principal–agent problem. The agency cost theory suggests that enterprise managers with the advantage of insider information may abuse their power to benefit themselves. The problem is usually more pervasive in SOEs due to the weak monitoring of assets caused by high costs of monitoring, as well as the lack of incentives created by the entrenched interests of supervisory agency officials (Milhaupt and Zheng 2015). This is why the issue of giving autonomy to and monitoring SOEs has been recurrent despite substantial changes in the scope of government and enterprise relations during different periods of reform. In the 1980s, enterprise autonomy was central among reform measures (Huang 1999). After 30 years, in the latest round of SOE reforms, increasing enterprises' independence is still a key objective of policymakers (Naughton 2016).

Commercial objectives and policy functions of SOEs and the sectoral dimension of SOE reform

Besides corporate governance, another crucial aspect of the complicated relationship between the government and SOEs in China is the dual nature of assigning functions to SOEs in the design of reform measures. On the one hand, supervisory agencies of central and local governments require SOEs to be profit oriented. On the other hand, SOEs are assigned to carry out government policy objectives. To some extent, the 'iron rice bowl' concept—a legacy of central planning—has maintained SOEs' substantial social welfare responsibilities for their employees, although this has been declining over time. It is, therefore, an expectation that SOEs will play an essential role in maintaining social stability by providing employment and protection of workers' welfare, especially when the social safety net is underdeveloped or when there are economic shocks. Over the past few decades, SOEs have played an essential role in developing large-scale infrastructure projects, carried out by governments at both central and local levels to support economic growth. SOEs have also been considered key instruments in promoting technological advances, securing strategic resources and advancing national interests. These government interests have been realised in selective industrial policies, which have a significant influence on the measures and practices of SOE reform, as seen in their sectoral distribution. There are specific government-directed works that were carried out by SOEs with public good properties. These policy functions have made it difficult to assess the performance of SOEs and the outcome of reforms. In presenting the multitask theory of SOEs, Bai et al. (2006) propose, and provide evidence of, how the low economic performance of SOEs is attributable to the multi-objective nature of their operation.

It is essential to consider these issues when reviewing the SOE reform process, as they are crucial aspects of SOEs' operation and development. Chronologically, the process of SOE reforms can be divided into four stages, marked by important policy documents and reform initiatives promulgated by the Communist Party of China (CPC) and the Chinese Government in line with their broad economic reform agenda.

Autonomy with the contract responsibility system and competition, 1978–92

At the beginning of the economic transition, state ownership of SOEs remained intact due to strong ideological and political perceptions of the need for the state to control all critical means of production (Chow 2002). Within that boundary, reform measures to improve the performance of SOEs were focused on granting autonomy to state enterprises and introducing a market mechanism.

In the early 1980s, an enterprise responsibility system was implemented based on the success of the household responsibility system, which had been introduced in the agricultural sector. The primary objective of the program was to increase SOEs' productivity, output and profitability. After fulfilling state plans and output quotas, enterprises were allowed to keep a share of total profits from production and make decisions about production plans, workforce adjustment and product marketing. In 1984, enterprise rights were extended to production planning, purchase of inputs, worker payment and recruitment, staffing and the use of retained profits. Under the contract system, each SOE was allowed to adopt a compulsory plan or market-oriented scheme. Under the compulsory scheme, the enterprise had to fulfil an output quota to be sold to the state at state-set prices, but it was supplied with material inputs at planned prices. Under the market-oriented scheme, the enterprise was allowed to sell on the market but had to buy material inputs at market prices (Chow 2002). As a result of providing greater autonomy and incentives, the program—initially trialled on 100 enterprises in Sichuan province—was quickly adopted and applied to 6,600 SOEs in 1980, to 42,000 in 1981 and almost the entire industrial sector in 1983 (Huang 1999: 99). In 1985, the contract responsibility system was introduced into the state industrial sector to create a formalised relationship between SOEs and the responsible government agency. The system was developed with greater emphasis on enterprises' responsibilities for profits and losses and more stable quotas on output and profits. By the end of 1988, the contract system had been applied to about 93 per cent of SOEs (Huang 1999: 102). At the same time, a two-tier price system was introduced (Chow 2002). The contract and two-tier price systems represent the typical dual-track and incremental approach to China's SOE reforms, with planning-based and market-based coordination mechanisms (Naughton 2007). These systems were gradually eliminated over time with the increasing introduction of market competition.

The contract responsibility system entailed the emergence of industrial product markets and competition among SOEs. At the same time, the government removed entry barriers to and encouraged the development of nonstate enterprises—mainly industrial collectives, and principally township and village enterprises (TVEs) and foreign-funded firms, especially those from Hong Kong, Macau and Taiwan (HMT). While there was no change in ownership within SOEs, this reform measure led to diversified ownership types in the whole industrial sector, creating significant competition in many industries (Jefferson and Su 2006). Another important reason for the rapid development of TVEs, mostly at the local level, was the decentralisation process in the mid-1980s that saw the delegation to local governments of more autonomy over budget revenue. This created incentives for local governments to support local businesses for greater revenue sources and a broader tax base.

Enterprise autonomy and market entry led to significant changes in the SOE sector that were conducive to China's industrial growth in the 1980s and early 1990s. Between 1978 and 1994, while the number of SOEs increased slightly, from 83,700 to 102,200, the number of collective enterprises, including TVEs, increased sharply, from 264,700 to 1.86 million units, and the number of individually owned and other enterprises reached 800,000. The total number of reported industrial enterprises surged from 300,000 to 10.02 million. Consequently, the SOEs' share in China's total gross industrial output declined from 78 per cent to 37.4 per cent. The percentage of collective enterprises grew to 37.7 per cent, surpassing that of SOEs (Jefferson 2016: 9). The trend of output share is consistent with that of output growth for industrial enterprises. In the period 1980–91, the annual output growth of SOEs was 7.8 per cent, while that of collectives was 18.6 per cent and of private enterprises, 140.6 per cent (Rawski 1994: 272). Despite slower growth, SOEs were an essential source for the growing emergence of collective and private enterprises' access to equipment, technical information, management skills and subcontracting opportunities (Rawski 1994). As a result of reform, industrial product markets were increasingly competitive, eliminating quasi-rents due to entry barriers, while the level of competition varied significantly across light and heavy industries (Jefferson and Rawski 1994). The main goal of dismantling the central planning system in the industrial sector as the first step of moving to a market mechanism was almost complete (Naughton 2007). Private sector growth occurred despite a lack of market-supporting institutions, especially clearly defined property rights.

The initial reform measures had significant effects on the performance of SOEs, which can be assessed using indicators of productivity, efficiency and financial performance.[2] Some studies found evidence that some of the SOEs surveyed had improved their labour and total factor productivity (TFP) through facing market competition (Jefferson and Rawski 1994; Huang 1999). However, SOEs recorded worsening financial performance throughout the reform period, especially after the mid-1980s. The SOE profit rate (returns on fixed assets, or ROFA) declined from 18 per cent in 1985 to below 6 per cent in the early 1990s, with an increasing number of lossmaking enterprises and substantial total losses (Song 2015: 184).

2 There is variation in efficiency and productivity estimates and their links with SOE reform measures among the empirical studies on Chinese industrial enterprises due to differences in sample selection, aggregation levels and methodologies, as documented by Huang (1999). This chapter is focused more on financial performance indicators, while some productivity performance measures are used selectively.

As a result, not only did SOEs' contribution to government revenue decline, but also there was a rising problem with soft budget constraints among SOEs, despite the government's efforts to cope with the problem. It was estimated that total fiscal and monetary subsidies to industrial SOEs grew from RMB6.3 billion (1.4 per cent of gross national product, or GNP) in 1980 to RMB268 billion (10 per cent of GNP) in 1992 (Huang 1999: 113).

While the increased market competition could be a leading cause of SOEs' worsening performance, other reasons emerged to do with underlying issues of SOE functions, management and monitoring. First, in the context of early transition, there was no social security system. SOEs had to bear policy burdens relating, in particular, to expenses for health care, housing and education for their workers, as a legacy of the central planning era, and also had to act as a social safety net maintaining employment for redundant workers (McMillan and Naughton 1992; Song 2015). Second, it appears the contract responsibility system was an initial step towards changing the enterprise–government relationship by replacing the government's direct control of enterprise operation with output–input contract control. However, enterprises claimed there was still significant government interference in their daily management. This gave rise to a problem with monitoring after enterprises were given autonomy, primarily caused by the separation of ownership and control (Song 2015). The lack of adequate monitoring was attributed to SOEs' poor performance (Huang 1999), and another consequence was that many managers abused their position for personal benefit such as through hiding profits (Chow 2002). This problem became more complicated in the later stages of SOE reform.

Ownership reform through 'grasping the large, letting go of the small', 1992–2003

The mounting losses of SOEs were a key factor leading to further reforms (Garnaut et al. 2006). Policymakers also saw a need to further develop an institutional base for the expanding market economy (Naughton 2007). The second stage of reform was characterised by ownership transformation (*gaizhi*), with a focus on the privatisation of SOEs, which began after Deng Xiaoping's tour of southern China in 1992. *Gaizhi* became an essential element in the government's grand strategy of building 'a modern Chinese enterprise system' for the 'socialist market economy', as set forth by the fourteenth National Congress of the CPC (Song 2015). In line with this target, priority reform steps were taken to develop an institutional framework for the modern enterprise system, based on the Western corporate model. The government issued the Company Law in 1993 and the Competition Law in 1994. The promulgation of specific laws and policies was a substantial step in establishing the regulatory framework for the growing multi-ownership enterprise sector and supervisory functions over SOEs (Mattlin 2007). Further, the *xiagang* ('laid-off') policy, which allowed a large number of workers to be laid-off in the process of ownership change, was carried out (Song 2015; Jefferson 2016). In 1997, the fifteenth National Congress set out the establishment of a social security system (Chow 2002). In the early 1990s, other complementary reforms were carried out, including to fiscal and trade policy. Fiscal system reforms were aimed at setting up a broad tax base and stable central–local government relations. Trade policy reforms unified exchange rates and liberalised the trade regime for enterprises of all ownership types. Moreover, stock markets were established and developed with the securities law enacted in 1999 to support the ownership transformation of SOEs (Naughton 2007). Trade reforms in the 1990s, aimed at China potentially joining the World Trade Organization (WTO), were another significant push factor for the SOE privatisation process (Jefferson 2016).

This process, promoted under the *gaizhi* policy for ideological and political reasons, took place at a large scale only after the central government adopted its policy of 'grasping the large, letting go of the small' (*zhuada fangxiao*) in 1995. This policy was formally approved at the fifteenth National Congress in 1997 (Song 2015). About 500 to 1,000 large SOEs were retained, while all other enterprises were restructured through sale or lease. The economic logic behind this policy was that the large firms performed much better than the smaller firms and had greater importance in the economy. While *gaizhi* served as a euphemism for privatisation, it was carried out in different forms, including through employee shareholding, public offerings (which did not change the state's control rights with internal restructuring measures such as debt–equity swaps), open sales, bankruptcy, leasing and joint ventures with foreign enterprises (Garnaut et al. 2006).

The *gaizhi* process, combined with related institutional changes, has resulted in the substantial transformation of the SOE sector and associated changes in the nonstate sector. In the period 1995–2003, the number of SOEs declined from 118,000 to about 34,000, and the SOE labour force fell by 44 million people (Song 2015: 191). In the period 1998–2003[3] alone, as shown in Figure 19.1, the number of SOEs decreased by about 23,600 units (Table A19.1), and their labour force dropped by 13 million people (Table A19.2). A group of state-controlled holding firms emerged in the SOE sector as a result of ownership reform. Importantly, *gaizhi* created an essential channel for transferring state production assets to the nonstate sector, which can be viewed as a reallocation of resources to more productive uses, which contributed to the rapid growth of this sector. In turn, the expansion of

3 Since 1998, China's National Bureau of Statistics (NBS) has reported statistics only for 'above-scale' industrial enterprises, which have annual sales revenue of at least RMB5 million, which is equivalent to about $600,000 at the 1998 exchange rate (Jefferson 2016). As a result, there was a sharp drop in the total number of all industrial firms. Therefore, the statistics reported in the tables and figures in this chapter cover the years 1998 to 2017 for the above-scale enterprises only.

nonstate enterprises supported the privatisation process by absorbing workers laid-off from the restructured SOEs. Moreover, ownership transformation helps both local and central governments to reduce the financial burden caused by poor-performing SOEs—a win–win situation (Garnaut et al. 2006). As a result, the relative importance of SOEs in total gross output and employment continued to decline, from about 52 per cent and 60 per cent, respectively, to about 44 per cent and 43 per cent between 1998 and 2002 (Figure 19.2). Overall, better resource allocation in the enterprise sector was one outcome of the ownership reform in this period.

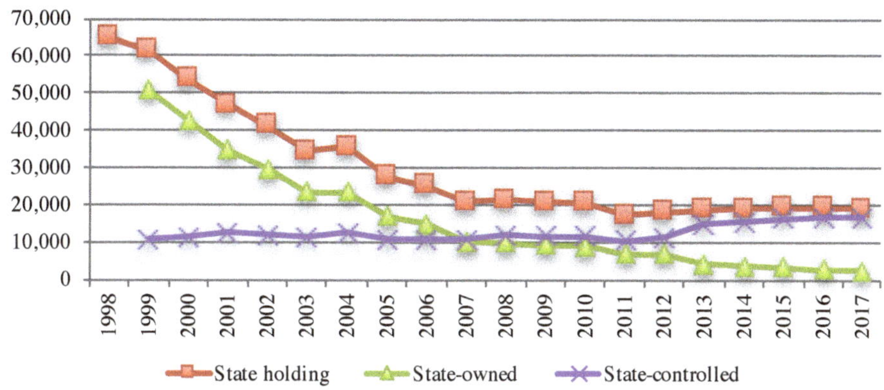

Figure 19.1 Number of state-holding enterprises, 1998–2017

Note: The state-holding enterprises include state-owned and state-controlled enterprises.

Source: CEIC China Database.

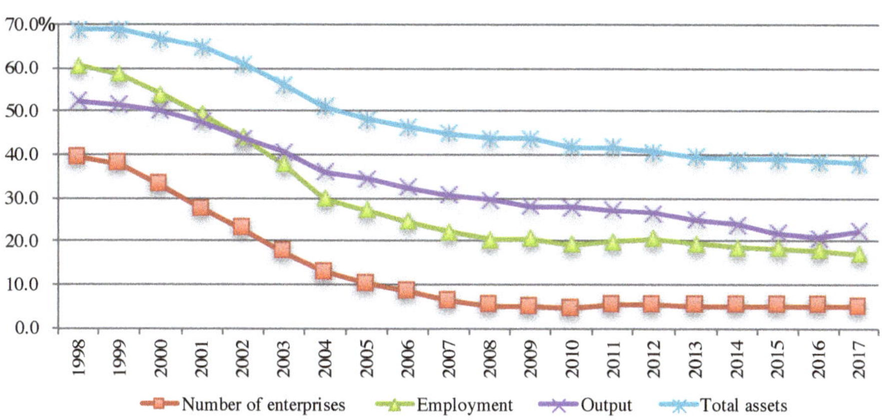

Figure 19.2 Changing relative position of state-holding enterprises, 1998–2017 (per cent)

Note: The state-holding enterprises include state-owned and state-controlled enterprises.

Source: CEIC China Database.

From the perspective of productivity, privatisation has been successful. Some studies find that ownership reform has improved the productivity of restructured enterprises. Sun and Tong (2003) find that early stage privatisation improved SOEs' earning ability and worker productivity. Garnaut et al. (2006) found evidence that those enterprises undertaking *gaizhi* improved their efficiency. Ownership transformation also had positive effects on SOEs in terms of financial performance. Song (2015) finds that SOEs' annual profit rate (ROFA) increased from a low of less than 2 per cent in 1997 to more than 6 per cent in 2002. Between 1998 and 2002 (Figures 19.3 and 19.4), the returns on total assets (ROA) and returns on equity (ROE) of the SOEs (including state-controlled shareholding firms) increased significantly and got close to those of private and other nonstate enterprises. As shown in Table A19.3, in the period 1998–2003, state-controlled shareholding enterprises (after *gaizhi*) appear to perform better as the share of lossmaking firms in this group is about 12 percentage points lower than that in the purely state-owned enterprises.

Although the performance of SOEs improved under extensive restructuring, they still lagged behind private enterprises. Between 1998 and 2003, the share of lossmaking firms in the SOE sector was still very high, at 35–39 per cent—about three to four times higher than that in the private sector (Table A19.3). Therefore, solving the bad debts of SOEs remained a challenging issue for reform. To deal with SOE debt and to support the development of the modern enterprise system, the government undertook banking reforms. Until the late 1990s, state-owned banks dominated China's banking sector. As financial subsidies were the main source of SOEs' losses, as shown above, SOEs dominated the state-owned banks' non-performing loans (NPLs). In 1995, the Law on the People's Bank of China and the Commercial Bank Law set out the main banking reform programs, providing a framework to impose hardening budget constraints on SOEs. Consequently, four asset management companies under the four largest commercial banks were set up in 1999 to deal with their NPLs to SOEs (Chow 2002).

The weaker financial performance of SOEs remained unresolved, so further reforms were needed. In addition to private and collective firms, the new shareholding enterprises, including the state-controlled ones, necessitated changes to the financial, fiscal and regulatory systems to address the government–enterprise relationship and, more broadly, to support the further development of the institutions of a sophisticated market economy with an open trade regime.

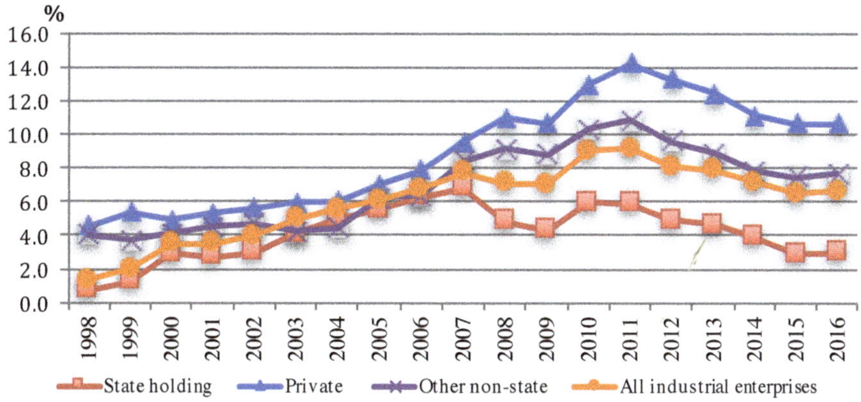

Figure 19.3 Returns on assets of industrial enterprises by ownership type, 1998–2017 (per cent)

Note: The state-holding enterprises include state-owned and state-controlled enterprises.

Source: CEIC China Database.

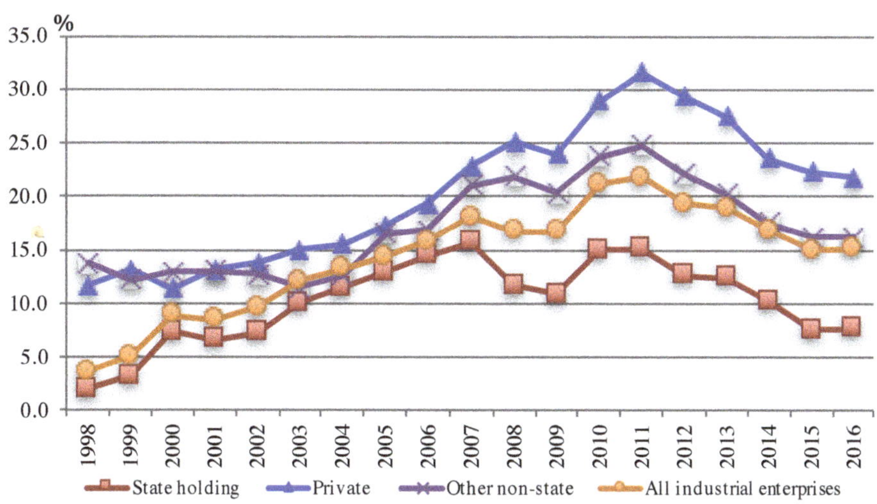

Figure 19.4 Returns on equity of industrial enterprises by ownership type, 1998–2017 (per cent)

Note: The state-holding enterprises include state-owned and state-controlled enterprises.

Source: CEIC China Database.

Restructuring large SOEs, corporatisation and going global, 2003–13

Keeping the large SOEs through *gaizhi* was the first step in building the modern enterprise system. Organisational change was another step in SOE reforms while SOE restructuring under *gaizhi* continued. With the release of the sixteenth National Congress's guiding principles on the consolidation and development of the publicly owned economy in line with the importance of developing the private economy (Yang 2015), the State-owned Assets Supervision and Administration Commission (SASAC) was established, in March 2003. SASAC itself is under the authority of the State Council. The national-level commission directly supervises central SOEs (*yang qi*), which are the largest in China's key industries, while indirectly overseeing local SOEs (*di fang guo qi*), which are under the direct supervision of local governments. The operations of SASAC as the central supervisory agency have had a significant impact on the outcomes of SOE reform.

SASAC's focus was on the preservation and increase of the state-owned assets of SOEs,[4] while continuing ownership reform to consolidate SOEs. The logic behind this is 'less is more … By controlling a small fraction of all SOEs, the state can maintain disproportionate control over profits, investments and the national economy' (Mattlin 2007: 45). As a result, the number of SOEs increased and they became huge corporations. From 2003 to 2006, the number of central SOEs under SASAC was reduced from 196 to 159 after consolidation and restructuring (Mattlin 2007). This number continued to fall, to 106, during 2015–16, with the largest enterprises in the industrial sector (Jefferson 2016: 3).

In line with the establishment of SASAC, the Chinese Government emphasised the control of strategic industries. The idea of this sectoral focus had already been put forward in the 'grasping the large, letting go of the small' policy. In September 1999, the fourth plenum of the fifteenth National Congress specified four groups of industries that were to retain SOE dominance: high technology, nonrenewable natural resources, public utilities and infrastructure services, and national security (Broadman 2002). In 2006, the State Council suggested a more specific list of industry groups and ownership goals, a detailed description of which is shown in Table 19.1.[5]

4 The supervision powers of SASAC are listed on its official website (en.sasac.gov.cn/n1408028/n1408521/index.html).

5 This list is a reference source as the industries and ownership goals included may vary over time due to different policy directions.

Table 19.1 Goals of ownership change by industry

Industry group	Industries included	Ownership goal
Strategic and key industries	Defence, power generation and distribution, oil and petrochemicals, telecommunication, coal, civil aviation, shipping	Maintaining 100 per cent state ownership or absolute control; increasing state-owned assets in these industries
Basic and pillar industries	Machinery, automobiles, IT, construction, steel, base metals, chemicals, land surveying, research and development	Absolute or conditional relative controlling stake; enhancing the influence of state ownership even as the ownership share is reduced, where appropriate
Other industries	Trading, investment, medicine, construction materials, geological exploration	Maintaining necessary influence by controlling stakes in key companies; in non-key companies, state ownership will be reduced

Source: Extracted from Mattlin (2007: Table 1, p. 16).

The government has used a variety of industrial policy measures to allocate resources, especially financial resources to SOEs in the strategic and pillar industries. The most common action is the use of administrative, technical or regulatory entry barriers (World Bank and DRC 2013). SOEs were also provided with preferential access to loans or credit through the banking sector, which is dominated by the state-owned banks (Song et al. 2011), and better access to land. These measures, in the context of marketisation, created substantial economic rents (Chu and Song 2015), which were accrued primarily to SOEs and provided them with a significant amount of earnings and savings with which to expand. Moreover, SASAC and other government agencies supported the expansion of SOEs through two additional avenues: public listings on domestic and international stock exchanges and international mergers and acquisitions (M&As). Notably, foreign M&As were a vital strategy adopted by SOEs to expand under the 'go global' policy put forward by the government in the early 2000s, with the primary objective of obtaining secure access to critical raw materials, resources and energy (Song et al. 2011). As a result, many SOEs had become among the largest corporations globally. In 2014, some 98 SOEs were on the Fortune Global 500 list, with their sales concentrated in energy, finance, telecommunication, engineering and construction and motor vehicle and parts industries (Jefferson 2016: 5).

Overall, the continuing SOE restructuring process under SASAC resulted in a substantial increase in the average size of SOEs. As shown in Table A19.1, the number of SOEs decreased significantly, from 34,280 in 2003 to 17,851 in 2012. A contributor to this drop in the state-holding enterprises was the reduction in the number of purely state-owned enterprises, as the number of state-controlled shareholding enterprises remained steady around 11,000 over the period 2003–12. This trend suggests that very few purely SOEs under restructuring were transformed into state-controlled shareholding enterprises. Moreover, between 2003 and 2012, the total asset value of purely SOEs and state-controlled enterprises increased substantially and consistently (Figure A19.1). Similarly, their revenue (output) value grew considerably, except during the Global Financial Crisis (GFC) in 2008–09 (Figure A19.2). These trends are consistent with SASAC's measures to restructure and consolidate SOEs, primarily through M&As. As a result, all became much larger in terms of total assets and sales output, as shown in Figures A19.3 and A19.4. The average size of SOEs in terms of total assets increased from RMB276 million in 2003 to RMB1.75 billion in 2012. Their average output value grew from RMB170 million to RMB1.37 billion[6] in 2012. The size of SOEs was increasing and they became much more significant than nonstate, foreign and HMT-funded enterprises over the period 2003–12. On average, the state-controlled shareholding enterprises were larger than the purely SOEs.

SOEs' contribution to the industrial sector continued to decrease. The state sector's share in the total number of firms drastically declined between 2003 and 2007, to a low level of about 5 per cent. Following a similar trend, SOEs' shares in total industrial employment and sales were still significant, at about 20 per cent and 25 per cent, respectively, in 2013. In contrast, in 2013, SOEs still held up to 40 per cent of total industrial assets, although this had declined from 56 per cent in 2003. The trend of SOEs' shares in the number of firms and total employment, sales and assets shows that substantial SOE restructuring took place between 2003 and 2007, and then slowed until 2013. However, this did not happen with the total value of assets, sales output and average firm size.

Several studies find that SOE restructuring continued to have significant positive effects on enterprise productivity in the period 2003–07 following SOE reforms in 1998–2003. Brandt and Zhu (2010) find that, in the period 1998–2007, SOEs' TFP growth was substantially higher than that in the period 1988–98, and even higher than that of nonstate enterprises. Hsieh and Song (2015) also find a significant increase in SOEs' TFP growth, resulting from restructuring during the period 1998–2007. In terms of financial performance, the SOE sector also improved substantially, and came close to private and other nonstate enterprises during the period 2003–07. As shown in Figures 19.3 and 19.4, the ROA of SOEs rose from about 4 per cent to 7 per cent, while the ROA of private enterprises increased from 6 per cent to 9.5 per cent—indicating a gap of 2–2.5 per cent. The ROE of SOEs grew from 11.5 per cent to 16 per cent, while the ROE of private enterprises increased from 15 per cent to 21 per cent—indicating a gap of 4–5 per cent.

6 Specific numbers were calculated using data obtained from the CEIC China Database.

SOEs' financial performance deteriorated noticeably during the period 2007–13, when there was rapid growth in the average size of assets and output. As shown in Figures 19.3 and 19.4, both the ROA and the ROE of SOEs dropped during 2008–09 and picked up again during 2010–11, before falling in 2012–13. This trend reflects the effects of the GFC and the impact of the government's stimulus policy. Private and other nonstate enterprises experienced a similar trend in their financial performance; however, the gap in financial performance between SOEs and private enterprises was increasingly larger. The gap in ROA and ROE increased to 5–8 per cent and 11–15 per cent, respectively. SOEs' productivity and financial performance would be lower than private enterprises if the economic rents generated by the government's market restrictions and control were separated from profits. This trend in the performance gap between SOEs and private enterprises is consistent with the difference in the percentage of lossmaking firms in the two groups. During the period 2003–13, the portion of lossmaking SOEs was in the range of 20–38 per cent, while that of private enterprises was between 6 and 15 per cent, as shown in Table A19.3.

The worsening performance of the whole SOE sector can be attributed to certain factors of SOEs' operation and governance. The first issue is the complex mix of policy and commercial objectives assigned to SOEs. There is a popular perception that, as well as commercial objectives, SOEs, as the backbone of the socialist market economy, have been designated to carry out public policy functions and obtain government objectives such as macroeconomic stabilisation, maintaining social stability and crisis response. For example, one public purpose of the SOEs can be seen in SASAC's guidelines on SOE corporate governance: SOEs are expected 'to promote the socialist harmonious society and … to thoroughly implement China's new ideas about economic development, social progress, and environmental protection' (Jefferson 2016: 5). Such activities are often not profitable, as their output is a public good. SOEs' lower returns also result from problems of overstaffing, particularly due to consolidation, as social security protection is a political and functional feature of the SOEs. SOEs internalise such losses in exchange for their privileged access to government-controlled resources, especially bank lending and land. Also, the government collected no dividends from profitable SOEs before 2007 (Mattlin 2007) and few dividends (5–15 per cent) after 2007 (Milhaupt and Zheng 2015). Those support measures have significantly exacerbated the SOEs' soft budget constraint problem. The soft budget constraint has been an ongoing problem, as is evident in the SOEs' NPL phenomenon. Jefferson (2016: 6) observes that there is a 'chronic tendency of China's political economy to replenish the diminished resources of the SOEs … through lending from the banking sector, primarily the four large commercial banks, which are themselves state-owned'.

The second issue is the weak oversight of SOE managers and weak corporate governance, mostly in the form of the principal–agent problem since autonomy was given to SOE managers under the contract responsibility system. With the policy of SOEs 'growing large and going global' after consolidation and restructuring, new dimensions of this issue emerged, with significant negative consequences on SOEs' performance. With authority delegated from the government, enterprise managers or corporate executives can make decisions on enterprise operation, investment, marketing, input supplies and contractor selection. However, there are challenges in monitoring the accountability of enterprise managers' business decisions for several reasons. First, despite the government's various personnel control measures, it is difficult and costly for it, and particularly SASAC, to keep senior SOE managers or executives in check due to their insider control and delegated authority (Milhaupt and Zheng 2015). Second, SOE managers possess significant personal power based on their party and administrative roles and personal social networks (Leutert 2016). And third, the boards of directors in state-controlled shareholding enterprises are influenced or dominated by the relevant government agency or SOE representatives, often including SOE managers themselves, while independent directors are a minority. As a result, SOE managers have been able to make business decisions for their benefit at the expense of their enterprises. The personal power of managers and the economic importance of large SOEs, especially central SOEs, have made them powerful interest groups holding sway over critical sectors of the economy, which can affect government policies (Zhang and Freestone 2013). The most evident result is rampant corruption and misconduct among SOE leaders. For example, *The Diplomat* reported in 2014 that the National Audit Office had uncovered 35 cases of bribery and embezzlement and managers in 11 inspected SOEs had spent company funds on luxury goods and entertainment (Hsu 2014). Another example is a report in the *South China Morning Post* that between November 2012 and April 2015, some 124 top officials in SOEs—most working in energy, infrastructure and telecoms—were facing corruption charges (Meng 2015).

Another consequence related to the SOE soft budget constraint is overinvestment, because as well as having easy access to funding sources, many SOEs also had considerable corporate savings from retained profits due to small dividend payments. Moreover, many local governments encouraged local SOEs to undertake large investment projects in pursuit of regional economic growth (Mattlin 2007). These have contributed to problems of overcapacity, large debts and 'zombie' firms, particularly in steel, coal and metal industries (Naughton 2016). At a sectoral level, lower efficiency and increased competitive pressures from private enterprises have seen SOEs' output share shrink while still holding a dominant share in some pillar and strategic industries. Such falls in output shares did not happen in national defence and other key sectors such as coal, ferrous metal, the production and supply of water and gas, metal ores, transport equipment, machinery and chemical products (Zhang and Freestone 2013). The imbalance between SOEs' output shares and their asset holdings suggests the removal of entry barriers, if any, and SOE ownership transformation would enhance the efficiency and output growth of these industries. Therefore, the issues with the performance of the SOEs discussed above are considered unfinished tasks of the most recent reform period.

Renewed mixed-ownership reform, corporate governance and challenges ahead, 2013 – present

The decision of the third plenum of the eighteenth National Congress in November 2013 marked the new wave of SOE reforms. The decision laid out important directions for reform to address the key issues of SOE governance and operation structure, including: 1) defining the functions of SOEs to determine levels of state ownership and control; 2) promoting mixed ownership; and 3) shifting from asset management to capital management and increasing dividend payments for social security funds (Yang 2015: 59). However, until 2015, substantial steps to implement the new SOE reform measures were carried out only after the guiding opinions and more than 10 regulations were issued (Naughton 2016: 65).

The State Council's initiative for developing mixed ownership in the guideline issued in September 2015 applied specific sectoral policies. For competitive sectors, the direction was to 'steadily promote the mixed ownership of SOEs and make sure both state capital and non-state capital engage in the operation of the relevant SOEs', while for strategic sectors, 'SOEs in the relevant sectors should remain state-controlled, but share-holdings of non-state parties are encouraged' (State Council 2015). A significant example is the share sale plan for China Unicom, China's second-largest telecom carrier. It was announced in August 2017 that it would sell US$11.7 billion in shares worth 35 per cent of its Shanghai-listed unit to a group of private and state investors, including tech giants Alibaba, Baidu, Tecent and JD.Com, and a sizeable state-owned insurance company, China Life Insurance Company. The telecommunications sector has long been a strategic sector under strict state control. This giant stride of partial privatisation will see the stake in the listed units held by Unicom's unlisted, wholly state-owned parent drop from 63 per cent to 37 per cent following the deal (Bloomberg News 2017). Private investors will also gain power over the daily operations of China Unicom, and will be able to appoint four members of the board of directors, which will also have six state shareholders and five independent members. Moreover, this initiative also encourages nonstate enterprises to enter parts of the strategic sectors that are unrelated to national security. For example, in November 2015, PetroChina restructured its natural gas division and planned to sell its stake in the natural gas network to China Reform Holdings, an agent of SASAC. The natural gas network would thus be established as an independent SOE to allow private and foreign capital to engage in the supply of natural gas (Hornby 2015).

It appears the Chinese Government has chosen the 'picking the winner' approach to mixed-ownership reform, with leading and large private companies that have emerged through market competition able to take a stake in large SOEs in previously restricted sectors. The process of partial privatisation has been carried out by a more market-determined process through stock markets, reducing concerns in previous stages of privatisation about corruption in selling state assets at low prices. It is a promising trend that more private capital is being allowed into strategic and pillar industries as more competition is introduced and private firms' technical, management and strategy expertise is utilised. At the same time, state-owned capital investment and operation companies under SASAC at the central and local levels have been set up to invest in both state and private enterprises. The focus of their investment are high-tech and new industries (for example, information technology, biopharmaceuticals, smart manufacturing, new energy and new materials) as part of the government's restructuring efforts to foster technological innovation for the productivity-driven growth model (Naughton 2016: 67).

In the 2015 guideline on deepening SOE reforms, for the first time, SOEs were divided into two categories: a public category (*gongyilei*) and a commercial category (*shangyelei*) (Central Committee of the CPC and State Council 2015). This classification creates a dual-track approach to evaluating the performance of SOEs. Specifically, this new guideline stipulates that public firms will be assessed by their cost control ability, the quality of their goods and services and the stability and efficiency of their operations. Political rather than market logic will, therefore, remain dominant in SOEs in the public class. In contrast, increasing market competition and improving financial performance will be the priorities for SOEs designated as commercial. While all this looks like a step towards a new round of marketisation in SOEs, these documents stress that SOEs should remain party controlled. SOEs will still serve political goals such as fostering indigenous innovation, supporting social stability and promoting economic initiatives abroad such as the Belt and Road Initiative (BRI), regardless of the category to which they belong. The stake in SOEs held by large private investors might not grant them real power to influence strategy for these enterprises. In practice, top SOE managers and chairpersons of boards of directors are appointed by SASAC and approved by the personnel bureau of the CPC, which means even though China Unicom has four private investors as board members, the Communist Party may still override their power. Nevertheless, the participation of private power on the boards of directors, at least partially, brings management experience and economic resources from the private sector, which may have potential benefits for the efficiency and financial performance of SOEs.

Another point of the 2015 guideline was the call for ongoing government-directed mergers to make SOEs larger and stronger, which has long been a stated goal. The logic behind government-directed mergers is to eliminate unprofitable SOEs without sacrificing employment, to end price wars among SOEs and embody the strategy of creating 'national champions' (Leutert 2016). However, the government-directed merger is a double-edged sword. Domestically, it does end price wars, overproduction of products and overlapping investment between SOEs in the same sector, but it also creates administrative monopolies that lead to stronger pricing powers and less external pressure to improve quality and services, which is an indirect subsidy to SOEs. Internationally, again, it does stop overseas price wars among SOEs and increases their international competitiveness in the short run, but the global competitiveness of SOEs might decline in the long term due to less pressure in the domestic market leading to fewer incentives to improve product quality and operational efficiency. The creation of overly large SOEs may also exaggerate the ills of these organisations—inefficient operations, communication gaps and weak oversight. Other potential problems include the creation of redundant staff and departments or duelling executive teams (Leutert 2016).

Nevertheless, to serve the BRI and 'going out' initiatives of SOEs, mergers to create large 'national champions' will help provide sufficient economic resources for overseas M&As and research and development (R&D). The mergers will also help avoid the loss of financial resources due to price wars among SOEs in the international market. One significant example in recent years is the merger of China CSR Corp and China CNR, the world's two largest manufacturers of rail rolling stock, with combined total assets of RMB299.7 billion (US$48.3 billion in 2014 prices), in 2015. Before 2000, CSR and CNR belonged to one company, China National Railway Locomotive & Rolling Stock Industry Corporation, and, in September 2000, the State Council approved the splitting of this company to promote domestic competition in locomotive and rolling stock manufacturing. However, in recent years, the revenue of these two large SOEs has relied more and more on the international market, and the price war between them has been a problem. In 2011, they fought a price war for a Turkish contract, which eventually went to a South Korean firm. In 2013, when they were competing for high-speed train contracts in Argentina, CSR proposed a quote that was far below that of CNR and far below the manufacturing costs. This led to the Argentines distrusting the quality of Chinese high-speed trains (Financial Times 2014) and the now-defunct Ministry of Railways openly criticising the incident. The merger put a full stop to the price war between CNR and CSR, which increased the competitiveness of Chinese high-speed trains in the global market. The Chinese Government has regarded the merger of CNR and CSR into China Railway Materials (CRM) as a successful case for the merger of other large SOEs. Many other large SOEs followed suit, such as the merger of Shanghai Baosteel Group and Wuhan Iron & Steel, which started in 2016, and other potential mergers within machine manufacturing, steel manufacturing, electricity and coal-related industries that undertake a substantial proportion of economic activities overseas.

The 2015 guideline also mentions personnel management reforms in SOEs. Traditionally, SOE managers are appointed by SASAC and enjoy a bureaucratic rank similar to government officials, which often leads to bureaucratism and low efficiency. The recent reform aims to establish a dual track for SOE personnel management. Managers belonging to the bureaucratic system enjoy lifelong job security but sacrifice a market-based salary, while managers outside the bureaucratic system enjoy market-based wages, but their jobs are contract-based with specific terms and subject to annual evaluation. This dual-track system still has a long way to go. The pilot program included only five SOEs in 2014, while in 2016 another three to five SOEs were to join this program (Ng 2016).

Following the 2015 guideline, a document issued by the State Council in April 2017 revealed some of the targets for recent SOE reforms, which aim to build a modern enterprise system while strengthening Communist Party control (State Council 2017). According to this document, a modern enterprise system was to be established in SOEs by the end of 2017. By the end of 2020, the role of the CPC in the corporate governance of SOEs should be strengthened, and company charters should exert a fundamental role over corporate governance. For wholly state-owned enterprises, external directors should be the majority on the boards of directors. Corporate governance should help entrepreneurs exert their full potential and nurture competent board chairpeople, professional managers and directors. Anticorruption measures will continue to be applied alongside reform, and management should be significantly improved as a result of changes to corporate governance. SOEs should operate independently following the laws of a market economy and enterprise development.

The renewed reform measures have had specific effects on the structure of the SOE sector. The number of purely SOEs continued to decline to 2017. In contrast, the number of state-controlled shareholding enterprises increased dramatically in the same period. These trends show that mixed-ownership reform measures have continued with the transformation of purely SOEs into state-controlled shareholding firms. In contrast with the shrinking number of firms, the size of purely SOEs increased sharply during the period 2015–17. This trend shows the significant impact of renewed ownership reform, with continued consolidation and new investment. State-controlled shareholding enterprises increased their total assets. However, the financial performance of SOEs in terms of ROA and ROE did not show any improvement, and their gap with private enterprises remained the same during 2013–16 (Figures A19.3 and A19.4). This situation suggests that while more radical reform measures have been taken recently, it will be some time before their impact on the overall performance of SOEs is evident.

Concluding remarks

After 40 years, market-oriented reforms have significantly transformed China's SOE sector. While now having a minor share in total numbers, employment and output, the SOE sector remains significant in the economy, accounting for nearly 40 per cent of total industrial assets in 2017, and has a dominant share in the banking and financial and other strategic sectors. The SOE sector has been transformed into a modern corporate sector with many large and globally operated corporations, diversified ownership and complex organisational and operational structures. The transformation of SOEs has been the key to the rise of the vibrant and rapidly growing nonstate enterprise sector. Under China's market-oriented transition, without a robust regulatory framework to capture and allocate economic rents, the use of SOEs in key industries and factor markets has helped the Chinese Government to mobilise resources for infrastructure investments to achieve the high growth rates seen in the reform period. SOEs have also played a vital role in meeting the government's policy objectives, such as macroeconomic and social stability and advancing national interests.

While reforms have led to improvements in the productivity and financial performance of many SOEs, the overall performance of the SOE sector has been declining and lagging behind private and other nonstate enterprises in the past 10 years. The current reforms have been targeted at the core issues of SOE operation and governance, including their function-based classification, ownership diversification, sectoral competition and entry barriers, autonomy and monitoring and corporate governance. With the most recent radical reform measures being implemented to address inherent problems in SOEs, their effects are yet to materialise and remain contingent on other market-oriented reforms.

It is time to reduce the number of lossmaking SOEs as their share in the state sector is still significantly higher than in the nonstate sector. This is consistent with the government's ongoing supply-side reforms to reduce excess capacity, deleverage and support industrial restructuring. Governments at both central and local levels have overseen the development of social security funds to help redundant workers. An essential source of funding could be the partial transfer of dividend payments from profitable SOEs, which may require additional institutional arrangements.

Further ownership reform of SOEs in pillar and strategic industries is conducive to efficiency and productivity, and state capital has also been invested in private firms in new industries. This demonstrates the growing role of the private sector in SOE-dominated and monopolistic industries. The definition of national interests has been changed to include leading private firms in strategic and new industries. It is reasonable to allow more private enterprise participation in providing public goods such as infrastructure development and services as long as transparent government procurement frameworks are adopted to ensure fair competition and avoid corrupt practices. With the increasing participation of private enterprise, it is also essential to strengthen the enforcement of tax laws and regulations on key inputs, resources and services markets to regulate economic rents for the public interest.

There is a need for the functions of current reforms to be focused more on the regulatory realm. Other market-supporting legal and regulatory changes should be reinforced in areas such as equal access to land and credit to reduce the soft budget constraint, transparent procedures for government funding for R&D and strengthening financial market regulations. With challenges to the reform of corporate governance in the largest SOEs, specific laws governing their operations and their relationships with government agencies are an option. This would help increase the transparency of their business activities in domestic as well as global markets. Caution needs to be exercised to avoid excessive party control, which could discourage the entry of private capital and interfere with enterprises' commercial operations.

China's SOEs continue to play a significant role in several strategic industries, including new sources of energy, telecommunications and information technology, automation, transport equipment (such as automobiles, aviation, shipbuilding and high-speed railways), new materials, space technologies, construction materials and infrastructure development. The government has also called on SOEs to play a critical role in achieving the goals of the 'Made in China 2025' policy, which aims to build high-end manufacturing industries across all key industrial sectors.

The new measures for market opening with further tariff reduction and market entry, announced by the Chinese Government in 2018, will accelerate the pace of SOE reform as the sector faces increased competition to make necessary adjustments. The success of SOE reform holds the key to deepening China's supply-side reform, which, if successful, will raise the prospect of more robust growth in China during the next phase of its development.

References

Bai, C. E., Lu, J. and Tao, Z. (2006), The multitask theory of state enterprise reform: Empirical evidence from China, *The American Economic Review* 96(2): 353–7. doi.org/10.1257/000282806777212125.

Bloomberg News (2017), Alibaba to China Life join Unicom's $11.7 billion stake sale, *Bloomberg News*, 16 August. Available from: www.bloomberg.com/news/articles/2017-08-16/unicom-to-raise-11-7-billion-via-stock-sale-to-alibaba-others.

Brandt, L. and Zhu, X. D. (2010), *Accounting for China's growth*, IZA Discussion Paper No. 4764, February, Bonn: Institute for the Study of Labor. Available from: ftp.iza.org/dp4764.pdf.

Broadman, G. (2002), The business(es) of the Chinese state, *The World Economy* 24(7): 849–75. doi.org/10.1111/1467-9701.00386.

Central Committee of the Communist Party of China (CPC) and State Council (2015), *Guideline on Deepening SOE Reform*, 24 August, Beijing: CPC Central Committee.

Chow, G. (2002), *China's Economic Transformation*, Malden, MA: Blackwell.

Chu, S. N. and Song, L. (2015), Promoting private entrepreneurship for deepening market reform in China: A resource allocation perspective, *China & World Economy* 23(1): 47–77. doi.org/10.1111/cwe.12099.

Financial Times (2014), The merger of CSR and CNR cannot solve the fundamental problem, [in Chinese], *Financial Times*, 26 December. Available from: www.ftchinese.com/story/001059858.

Garnaut, R., Song, L. and Yao, Y. (2006), Impact and significance of state-owned enterprise restructuring in China, *The China Journal* 55: 35–63.

Hornby, L. (2015), PetroChina restructures gas unit, *Financial Times*, 26 November.

Hsieh, C. and Song, Z. (2015), *Grasp the large, let go of the small: The transformation of the state sector in China*, NBER Working Paper No. 21006, Cambridge, MA: National Bureau of Economic Research.

Hsu, S. (2014), China's changing state-owned enterprise landscape: To maintain economic growth, SOE reform will need to be meaningful, *The Diplomat*, 25 June. Available from: thediplomat.com/2014/06/chinas-changing-state-owned-enterprise-landscape/.

Huang, Y. (1999), State-owned enterprise reform, in R. Garnaut and L. Song (eds), *China: Twenty years of reform*, Canberra: Asia Pacific Press.

Jefferson, G. (2016), *State-owned enterprise in China: Reform, performance, and prospects*, Working Paper No. 109R, Waltham, MA: Brandeis University, Department of Economics and International Business School.

Jefferson, G. and Rawski, T. G. (1994), How industrial reform worked in China: The role of innovation, competition and property rights, in *Proceedings of the World Bank Annual Conference on Development Economics*, Washington, DC: The World Bank. doi.org/10.1093/wber/8.suppl_1.129.

Jefferson, G. and Su, J. (2006), Privatisation and restructuring in China: Evidence from shareholding ownership, 1995–2001, *Journal of Comparative Economics* 34: 146–66.

Kornai, J. (1986), The soft-budget constraint, *Kyklos* 39(1): 3–30. doi.org/10.1111/j.1467-6435.1986.tb01252.x.

Kornai, J., Maskin, E. and Roland, G. (2003), Understanding the soft-budget constraint, *Journal of Economic Literature* XLI: 1095–136. doi.org/10.1257/jel.41.4.1095.

Leutert, W. (2016), Challenges ahead in China's reform of state-owned enterprises, *Asia Policy* (21)(January): 83–99.

Mattlin, M. (2007), *The Chinese Government's new approach to ownership and financial control of strategic state-owned enterprises*, BOFIT Discussion Paper No. 10/2007, 13 April, Helsinki: Bank of Finland Institute for Economies in Transition. Available from: ssrn.com/abstract=1001617.

McMillan, J. and Naughton, B. (1992), How to reform a planned economy: Lessons from China, *Oxford Review of Economic Policy* 8(1): 130–43. doi.org/10.1093/oxrep/8.1.130.

Meng, A. (2015), A quarter of Chinese SOE executives investigated for corruption work in energy sector, *South China Morning Post*, 28 April. Available from: www.scmp.com/news/china/policies-politics/article/1778702/quarter-chinese-soe-executives-investigated-corruption.

Milhaupt, C. J. and Zheng, W. (2015), Beyond ownership: State capitalism and the Chinese firm, *The Georgetown Law Journal* 103(665). Available from: scholarship.law.ufl.edu/facultypub/696.

Naughton, B. (2007), *The Chinese Economy: Transitions and growth*, Cambridge, MA: MIT Press.

Naughton, B. (2016), Restructuring and reform: China 2016, Paper presented at Structural Change in China: Implications for Australia and the World, Reserve Bank of Australia, Sydney.

Ng, J. (2016), China plans to expand the pilot program of market-based SOEs managers recruitment, [in Chinese], *Financial Times*, 4 July. Available from: www.ftchinese.com/story/001068296#adchannelID=2000.

Rawski, T. G. (1994), Chinese industrial reform: Accomplishments, prospects, and implications, *The American Economic Review* 84(2): 271–5.

Song, L. (2015), State and non-state in China's economic transition, in G. C. Chow and D. Perkins (eds), *Routledge Handbook of the Chinese Economy*, New York: Routledge.

Song, L., Yang, J. and Zhang, Y. (2011), State-owned enterprises' outward direct investment and the structural reform in China, *China & World Economy* 19(4): 38–53.

State Council (2015), *Guideline on Developing Mixed Ownership in SOEs*, Document No. 54, 24 September, Beijing: General Office of the State Council.

State Council (2017), *Instructions on Further Promoting Modern Corporate Governance in SOEs*, Document No. 36, Beijing: General Office of the State Council.

Sun, Q. and Tong, W. H. S. (2003), China share issue privatisation: The extent of its success, *Journal of Financial Economics* 70: 183–222. doi.org/10.1016/S0304-405X(03)00145-4.

World Bank and Development Research Center of the State Council (DRC) (2013), *China, 2030*, Washington, DC: The World Bank.

Yang, W. (2015), The new round of reform of state-owned enterprises, *Journal of Entrepreneurship in Emerging Economies* 7(1): 55–66. doi.org/10.1108/JEEE-10-2014-0036.

Zhang, D. and Freestone, O. (2013), China's unfinished state-owned enterprise reforms, *Economic Roundup No. 2*, 6 December, Canberra: The Treasury, Government of Australia. Available from: treasury.gov.au/publication/economic-roundup-issue-2-2013-2/.

Zhang, W. (2009), The 'China model' of SOE reform and its challenges, *China Economist* 4(2): 16. Available from: ssrn.com/abstract=1544336.

Appendix 19.1

Table A19.1 Number of enterprises by ownership type, 1998–2017 (unit)

Year	State-holding	State-owned	State-controlled	Private	Total
1998	64,737			10,667	165,080
1999	61,301	50,651	10,650	14,601	162,033
2000	53,489	42,426	11,063	22,128	162,885
2001	46,767	34,530	12,237	36,218	171,256
2002	41,125	29,449	11,676	49,176	181,557
2003	34,280	23,228	11,052	67,607	196,222
2004	35,597	23,417	12,180	119,357	276,474
2005	27,477	16,824	10,653	123,820	271,835
2006	24,961	14,555	10,406	149,736	301,961
2007	20,680	10,074	10,606	177,080	336,768
2008	21,313	9,682	11,631	245,850	426,113
2009	20,510	9,105	11,405	256,031	434,364
2010	20,253	8,726	11,527	273,259	452,872
2011	17,052	6,707	10,345	180,612	325,609
2012	17,851	6,770	11,081	189,289	343,769
2013	18,574	3,957	14,617	208,409	369,813
2014	18,808	3,450	15,358	213,789	377,888
2015	19,273	3,234	16,039	216,506	383,148
2016	19,022	2,459	16,563	214,309	378,599
2017	18,806	2,372	16,434	222,473	385,369

Note: The state-holding enterprises include state-owned and state-controlled enterprises.

Source: CEIC China Database.

Table A19.2 Industrial employment by ownership type, 1998–2017 (thousand people)

Year	State-holding	Private	Total industrial sector
1998	37,477.8	1,608.0	61,958.1
1999	33,945.8	2,290.6	58,050.5
2000	29,952.5	3,464.2	55,593.6
2001	26,751.1	5,415.2	54,408.4
2002	24,236.3	7,329.0	55,200.6
2003	21,628.7	10,276.1	57,485.7
2004	19,732.0	15,154.3	66,220.9
2005	18,748.5	16,920.6	68,959.6
2006	18,040.0	19,710.1	73,584.3
2007	17,429.9	22,529.1	78,752.0

Year	State-holding	Private	Total industrial sector
2008	17,941.0	28,718.9	88,376.3
2009	18,033.7	29,738.4	88,312.2
2010	18,363.4	33,120.6	95,447.1
2011	18,119.8	29,564.1	91,672.9
2012	18,927.7	31,213.0	92,729.4
2013	18,894.9	33,593.9	97,914.6
2014	18,426.7	35,053.2	99,772.1
2015	17,778.3	34,639.8	97,750.2
2016	16,959.3	33,977.6	94,755.7
2017	14,954.0	32,711.0	88,594.0

Note: The state-holding enterprises include state-owned and state-controlled enterprises.
Source: CEIC China Database.

Table A19.3 Share of lossmaking enterprises by ownership type, 1999–2017 (per cent)

Year	State-holding	State-owned	State-controlled	Private	Total
1999	39.2	41.1	29.9	7.9	27.3
2000	34.1	36.4	25.3	13.8	23.4
2001	36.0	39.0	27.7	13.4	23.0
2002	36.1	39.4	28.0	11.9	20.8
2003	35.2	39.2	26.9	10.9	18.6
2004	37.4	42.6	27.4	14.6	21.1
2005	35.5	41.0	26.9	11.9	17.8
2006	31.9	37.6	24.1	10.6	15.6
2007	25.8	30.3	21.6	9.2	13.6
2008	27.4	29.7	25.5	10.8	15.3
2009	26.3	29.2	24.0	9.8	13.8
2010	21.4	24.4	19.2	6.9	10.0
2011	20.6	22.2	19.6	6.0	9.4
2012	24.0	25.5	23.1	7.9	11.5
2013	24.7	26.4	24.2	7.8	11.3
2014	26.7	29.5	26.0	8.1	11.5
2015	28.9	28.4	29.0	9.1	12.6
2016	25.6	26.2	25.5	7.8	10.8
2017	24.7	26.9	24.4	9.0	11.8

Note: The state-holding enterprises include state-owned and state-controlled enterprises.
Source: CEIC China Database.

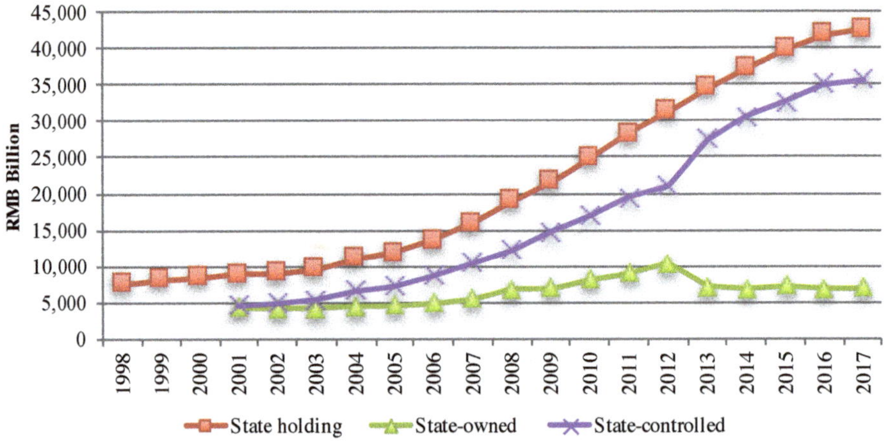

Figure A19.1 Total assets of state-owned and state-controlled enterprises, 1998–2017 (RMB billion, current price)

Note: The state-holding enterprises include state-owned and state-controlled enterprises.

Source: CEIC China Database.

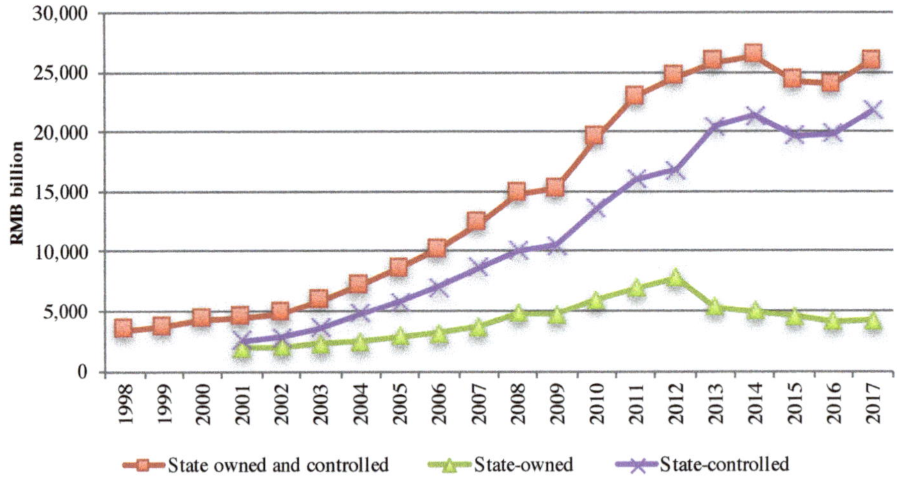

Figure A19.2 Output value of state-holding enterprises, 1998–2017 (RMB billion, current price)

Note: The state-holding enterprises include state-owned and state-controlled enterprises.

Source: CEIC China Database.

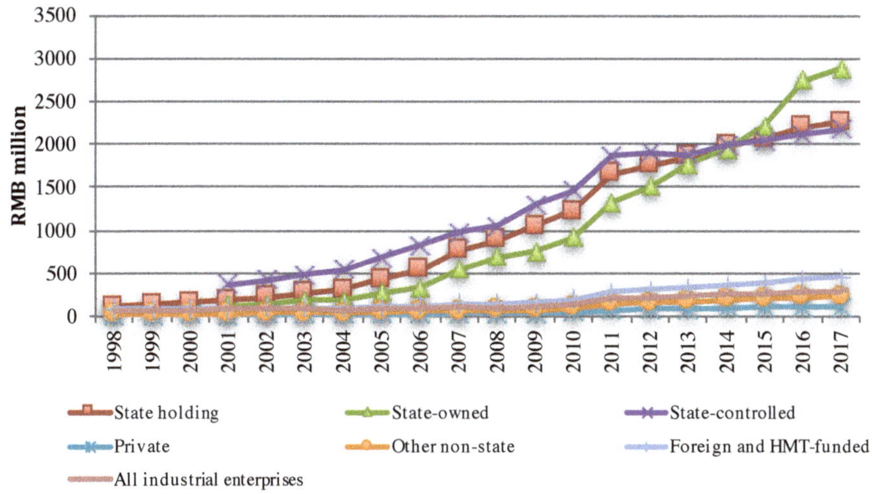

Figure A19.3 Average size of industrial enterprises by ownership type, 1998–2017 (total assets, RMB billion, current price)

Note: The state-holding enterprises include state-owned and state-controlled enterprises.

Source: CEIC China Database.

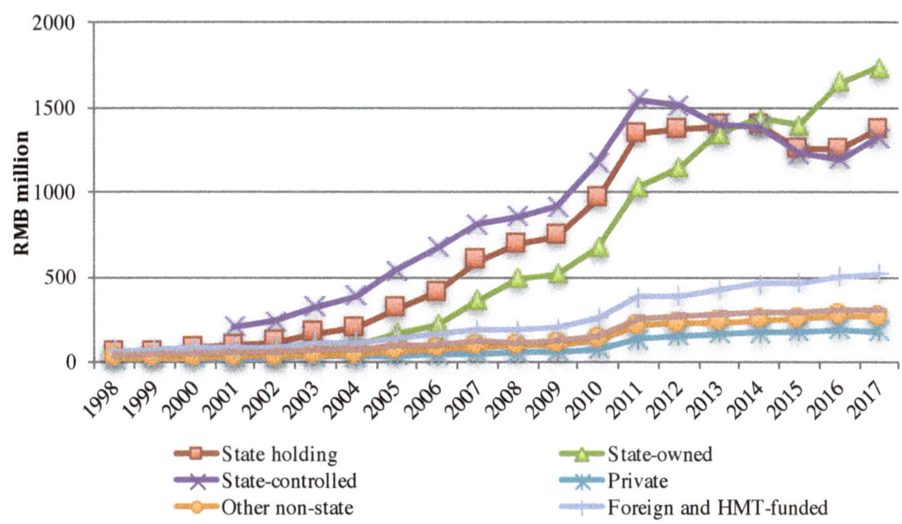

Figure A19.4 Average size of industrial enterprises by ownership type, 1998–2017 (sales output, RMB billion, current price)

Note: The state-holding enterprises include state-owned and state-controlled enterprises.

Source: CEIC China Database.

20. State enterprise reform today

Barry Naughton

For almost 30 years after 1978, state-owned enterprise (SOE) reform was one of the central initiatives of China's overall economic reform (see Song, this volume). But during the mid-2000s, the impetus behind SOE reform stalled and little was achieved for almost a decade. It was a surprise to many, then, when the November 2013 resolution of the third plenum of the National Congress of the Communist Party of China (CPC) listed SOE reform as first among its substantive sections, raising hopes for a renewal of SOE reform. After a false start in 2014, activity accelerated in 2016, and initiatives and pilot programs have proliferated since. As of mid-2018, what are we to make of the present reality of and future prospects for SOE reform in China?

This chapter argues that the new measures are significant and will make China's SOE sector more financialised, but also more politicised. Corporate governance reforms are moving ahead that will finally corporatise all SOEs, divide them into public service and commercial types, and allow the process of 'mixed ownership' to take a step forward. Firms will be financialised in the sense that SOEs will increasingly be controlled by ownership agencies with a clearer financial structure and interest; simultaneously, many SOEs will be allowed to acquire financial interests in a range of new subsidiaries (including formerly private firms). However, at the same time, SOEs will be subjected to much more intrusive oversight by Communist Party committees and the Communist Party will be embedded in the corporate governance structure. This embedding is associated with an accelerating effort to enlist SOEs in the party's developmental agenda, which implies giving SOEs more tasks and responsibilities designed to further national strategies. These complex changes will affect SOEs in conflicting and perhaps contradictory ways, which make it difficult to project the outcomes. This complexity also makes it worthwhile to begin with a brief general discussion of some of the dilemmas implicit in public ownership.

The impossible trinity

All corporate governance systems must confront the problem of aligning the interests of managers with those of owners. Managers have day-to-day control of the firm's assets and can use them in ways not intended by the owners—for personal aggrandisement, risky ventures or even corruption. In a private firm, the owners generally have a predominant interest in profit, so the corporate governance problem can generally be reduced to the question of how to align the interests of managers with long-term profit maximisation.

Publicly owned enterprises have these problems, but face an additional complication: the public owner may have objectives additional to long-term profit maximisation. After all, if the public demanded nothing more than profit maximisation, why have public ownership at all? Privatisation would ensure efficient and profitable operation, and the public financial interest could be achieved either by taxation or by retaining a purely financial interest in corporatised firms. Cross-national research on SOEs has commonly found that although there is an efficiency penalty to public ownership, it can be quite small when such enterprises are properly incentivised, and China's experience shows that it is not necessary to prioritise privatisation of SOEs during the transition to a market economy. Most of the efficiency gains can be achieved by allowing entry to and improving the incentive structure of SOEs, just as China did between 1978 and 2005. However, this observation suggests a paradox. On one hand, SOEs can be nearly as efficient as private firms if government keeps a hands-off attitude and rewards efficiency and profit maximisation. On the other hand, if SOEs are to behave exactly like private firms, why bother to have state-owned firms at all (Qian 1996)? Yet Chinese policymakers have consistently declared that public ownership was necessary.

Through most of China's reform history, the conflict between profitability and other government-imposed objectives remained in the background. Worries about the low efficiency and poor incentives of SOEs led, in the 1980s, to a focus on improving incentives for managers so they would be motivated to improve profitability. In the 1990s—an era dominated by increasing market competition—this effort became all the more urgent, as improving performance and profitability became a matter of life and death for most SOEs. When the State-owned Assets Supervision and Administration Commission (SASAC) was formed in 2003, an embryonic profit recovery of the surviving SOEs was underway, but it still felt tentative and SASAC's early agenda was focused on improving profitability and corporate governance more generally (Naughton 2010, 2015). To be sure, this focus on profitability did not entirely exclude other objectives for SOEs. For example, Lin et al. (1998) argued that SOEs were a cost-effective way to provide employment and social benefits, justifying a gradual reform strategy. And local government officials certainly enjoyed having SOEs under their control, to help with employment, roadbuilding and other local projects. But the central government was preoccupied with a reform program that would improve profitability and performance, and all of the other actors recognised that these central goals ultimately overrode all other objectives, because SOEs were in a critical condition. These priorities drove SOE reform well into the 2000s.

This state of affairs is no longer true today. SOEs became vastly more profitable in the 2000s, as restructuring, improved corporate governance and entry barriers created a more favourable operating environment. A psychological barrier was crossed in 2007, when central SASAC firms raked in RMB1 trillion in profits for the first time. The improvement in SOE profitability was not all efficiency gains—SOEs were increasingly concentrated in sectors where they retained some protection and they often had access to cheaper capital and inputs (especially land). However, careful studies of total factor productivity growth also show rapid rates of increase for incumbent state firms during this period (Brandt et al. 2012).

About this time, the central government became less concerned about profitability and began to ask SOEs to do other things as well. Especially when Wang Yong replaced founding head Li Rongrong as head of SASAC in 2010, the focus shifted to making SOEs 'big, strong' international champions and good public citizens. The fact that President Xi Jinping had, in 2009, at the fiftieth anniversary of the Daqing Oilfield, called SOEs 'an important foundation of Communist Party rule' also played a role in this shift (Xi 2009). When the Global Financial Crisis (GFC) hit at the end of 2008, policymakers were immediately concerned with using SOEs to boost domestic demand and lost any serious short-term interest in subjecting them to further financial discipline. With profitability no longer an urgent priority, SOE policy entered a period of drift, and the impetus for SOE reform faded noticeably between 2006 and 2009.

When SOE reform was resurrected in the third plenum resolution in November 2013, it was in a policy environment that was radically different to that in the 1980s and 1990s. Chinese policymakers have come face-to-face with the trade-off between better incentives, stronger oversight and the assignment of developmental and political goals to SOEs. The most recent reform packages seem designed to achieve more of all three of these objectives. Improved incentives are back on the agenda because the deterioration of SOE profitability has become a renewed concern. Profits of central SASAC firms dropped during the GFC and again in the (global) decline in commodity prices in 2015–16. Even after significant recovery in 2017, before-tax profits of central SASAC firms were only 2.6 per cent of gross capital—down from 6.7 per cent in 2007. But if policymakers now want SOEs to be more profitable, they also want to exercise much more effective oversight and political control over SOE. Slack oversight of SOE managers in the 2000s had certainly contributed to a number of cases of serious corruption and abuse of power. The most egregious of these was that of Zhou Yongkang, who had created a corrupt network at the China National Petroleum Company—the most profitable central SOE—and had then leveraged these resources into a personal political empire. Finally, the importance given to developmental and political goals for SOEs has also increased substantially. In particular, the importance of technology-oriented industrial policy has increased dramatically in recent years. While China has always had some kind of industrial policy, the recent effort is qualitatively different, because the scope, intensity and volume of resources involved is much higher than at any time in the past 40 years. Moreover, SOEs are supposed to play a big role in this policy. Thus, the current round of SOE reform differs from its forerunners in that policymakers hope to simultaneously achieve improvements in SOE incentives and governance, strengthened oversight and greater responsiveness to politically defined targets.

However, these objectives are at least partially contradictory and, to a certain extent, these three objectives should be thought of as an 'impossible trinity'. Policymakers can, in theory, achieve any two, but not all three. Profit incentives with strong oversight create a market environment governed by law and regulation. Multiple assigned objectives with strong oversight, on the other hand, leave little space for profit maximisation. Not only must managers scramble to meet multiple inconsistent targets; they must also use the trade-off among targets to deflect demands for rigorous profit maximisation. Multiple objectives are simply inconsistent with high-powered incentives (Holmstrom and Milgrom 1991). Finally, policymakers can assign multiple objectives and have weak oversight. This feasible—and commonly observed—outcome results in a kleptocratic state, as policymakers and SOE managers share the benefits of controlling public assets, allowing each to achieve their private objectives for as long as they serve the public. Clearly, Chinese policymakers today are not happy with any of these outcomes; they want to achieve more of all three objectives. In practice, that means trying to manage and minimise the trade-offs among the three, which is not an easy task.

The reform process

The difficulty of reconciling three competing policy objectives may explain the very uneven progress of SOE reform since the third plenum. During 2014, under the CPC's Leadership Small Group (LSG) on Comprehensively Deepening Reform, work on many aspects of SOE reform moved ahead quickly. There was intense debate and some occasional abrupt decisions, but the process seemed to be on track. Then, at the end of 2014, the process was suddenly put on hold and a new State Council LSG on SOE reform was set up, under the direction of state councillor Ma Kai. In September 2015, this LSG's general document on SOE reform was finally agreed to and ratified by the State Council and the central party (CPC and State Council 2015a). The document was couched in vague and occasionally contradictory terms, and it was understood from the beginning that multiple supplementary documents would also be required—a pattern the Chinese call '1 + N'. Within a year, 18 supplementary documents had been promulgated and, as a result, 2016 is often referred to as the first year of implementation for SOE reforms. Even so, most implementation in 2016 was described as 'pilot' or 'experimental'. The general approach was: as one pilot matures, complete it and move on to the next one.

Between early 2016 and the beginning of 2018, an overall approach to SOE reform finally emerged. By this time, of course, SOE reform has broadly come to be viewed as disappointing (Batson 2016). Many people think nothing is happening. The reality—as this chapter will argue—is that quite a lot has happened and some of it has important positive potential. But the overall process of SOE reform has been hobbled by the effort to achieve contradictory objectives. Improvement in corporate governance has been real and reverses the disappointments of almost a decade of stagnation (2006–16). However, efforts to subject SOEs to greater oversight, and particularly to increase direct Communist Party intervention in SOE management, have profoundly undermined this progress. At the same time, the increased desire to assign SOEs multiple objectives, emphasising their status as part of the 'national team', has enormously complicated the effort to strengthen SOEs' incentives to increase efficiency and profitability. The basic argument of this chapter is that the pursuit of contradictory objectives has hobbled the recent program of SOE reforms and will continue to obstruct progress in the future.

The next three sections describe recent SOE reforms in three groups, related to the main policy objectives they are designed to pursue. First, in order to improve incentives and efficiency, policymakers sought to reinvigorate the reform of corporate governance, to make SOE managers more effectively motivated to improve firm performance. Second, in order to improve oversight, policymakers have greatly strengthened the role of the Communist Party and other oversight bodies. Third, in order to more effectively assign new missions and tasks to SOEs, policymakers have created new ownership agencies that are taking over tasks from the former SASACs. Of course, all the measures taken do not fit neatly into three boxes, and contradictory policy impulses are evident in each area. Together, these initiatives will likely improve SOE performance in some respects, but undermine it in others. The prospect is a state sector that is simultaneously more financialised and more politicised.

Corporate governance reform

The foundation of Chinese SOE corporate governance reform was laid out with the 1995 Company Law, which envisaged the conversion of traditional SOEs into corporations (in the lingo of the day, the 'modern enterprise system'). As part of a gradualist process, SOEs were to be converted by their owners, as they were ready, into one of a variety of corporate forms—joint stock, wholly state-owned corporations, and so on. This process went quickly for one category of SOEs—that is, profitable firms that could be listed on domestic or international stock exchanges, thereby immediately raising money (sometimes vast sums) for their owners. However, it went very slowly for less profitable firms and, especially, for the rather opaque 'apex corporations' under the central SASAC. These 100-odd firms had retained some of the characteristics of the industrial ministries from which they evolved, and had often held on to money-losing subsidiaries to permit their more profitable counterparts to list smoothly on stock exchanges. They were much less transparent than listed firms and in a position to hoard and redistribute resources among subsidiaries. What little progress was made converting these apex firms came to a halt after 2006–08 and, in 2010, less than half had been corporatised.

In the current wave of SOE reform, a push was mounted to corporatise all central SASAC apex corporations by the end of 2017. In fact, victory was declared—only 22 years after the initial Company Law. Of the 97 central SASAC apex corporations, 87 are said to have established boards of directors and 83 of these have a majority of external directors (Yin 2018). Among provincial SOEs, it is claimed 92 per cent have established boards of directors. Although it is clear some of the conversions were last-minute and rushed, full corporatisation is a prerequisite to revitalising SOE corporate governance reform. The establishment of authoritative boards of directors in newly corporatised SOEs was one of the constituent components of the 1990s reform that stalled in the mid-2000s and has now been revived.

The importance of corporate governance reform in practice depends to a significant extent on the next step of governance reform, which is the classification of firms into distinct categories as public service or commercial. The initial classification is a straightforward differentiation between commercial and public service firms, with public service firms providing goods and services in a price-regulated environment and with government maintaining sole or controlling ownership. These firms are primarily local utilities. Far more fraught is the designation within commercial enterprises of two sub-types. Enterprises whose main business is in 'fully competitive' sectors should accelerate corporatisation; they may raise money from outside investors, even allowing state ownership to become a minority position, and they should list on stock markets. Commercial enterprises in 'less-than-fully competitive' sectors, by contrast, as those in natural monopoly sectors or in business 'relating to national security, or the commanding heights of the national economy or important sector or keypoint areas'. These less-than-fully competitive firms should be incentivised to 'better serve important national strategies and macroeconomic control' and, specifically, 'develop forward-looking strategic sectors as well as any specially assigned responsibilities' (SASAC et al. 2015). Since many big SOEs have scores or even hundreds of subsidiaries, it is not at all straightforward which firms should go into which type, and there has been considerable friction around the designation of firms. All the central SASAC firms were reportedly divided into types by the end of 2014, only to have the slate wiped clean and the effort restarted in 2016. After much activity in 2016 and 2017, SASAC declared the process complete in all its enterprises at the central level and all 31 provincial SASACs. Yet, in contrast to the situation at the end of 2014, there has been absolutely no information released about how many firms fall into each category or which firms they are. There is quite a lot at stake. Firms that are designated 'fully competitive' have essentially received the go-ahead to become more autonomous. They may bring in outside investors, even allowing the state share to fall below 50 per cent. (They may not sell off state shares to outside investors; dilution is allowed only through raising new investment.) When the state share falls below 50 per cent, mixed-ownership firms escape salary caps that were imposed on chief executive officers (CEOs) in 2014. These firms are eligible to adopt market-based selection of managers, in which open recruiting and flexible salaries are to be the main elements. Thus, among the category of fully competitive commercial enterprises, the next step of 'mixed ownership' has the potential to be significant.

Mixed ownership has been a high-profile element component of the current wave of SOE reforms since 2013, without ever having been clearly or consistently defined. To be clear, mixed ownership has been a feature of the Chinese state sector for a long time, ever since state firms began to list on the stock market in the 1990s. Now, strategic 'private' investors are to be attracted into previously monopolised state sectors, and public–private partnerships have been advocated as a way of diversifying funding for infrastructure investments. An example of the potential of mixed ownership reform is provided by a local pilot, Yunnan Baiyao. This provincially controlled healthcare and pharmaceutical firm, which developed from a century-old traditional Chinese medicine company, took on two private strategic investors as part of a dramatic restructuring and expansion. The state share declined to 49 per cent, giving the firm far greater autonomy (Chu et al. 2018).

However, much greater limitations are evident in the first, highly publicised case of a 'mixed-ownership reform' of a central SOE—that of Unicom, the number three telecom provider. In the summer of 2017, Unicom raised money from a consortium of 14 private sector investors, who injected RMB78 billion for a 35 per cent stake, potentially reducing the state's share to less than 50 per cent. However, the legitimacy of this restructuring was marred by suspicions that the investors had been herded into a compromise vehicle to provide Unicom with the prodigious sums necessary to roll out 5G telecom in the next few years. This rather clumsy process will only turn out to be a successful reform if the next steps of restructuring reveal a more dynamic and independent firm. In fact, these limitations are endemic in the current environment: truly private firms have been reluctant to participate in long-term contractual relations in which they have little bargaining power or legal protection. For example, most of the current public–private partnerships for which we have information are actually partnerships among different kinds of SOEs, not true private firms.

An interesting counterpart of private sector involvement in mixed ownership has been the determination to allocate 10 per cent of the existing state ownership to the Social Security Fund. Initiated in a few pilots in 2017, this program is to roll out for progressive implementation in all SOEs and financial institutions beginning in 2018 (State Council 2017). The significance of this for corporate governance is that it introduces a passive financial investor into the ownership structure who ought to have an interest purely in maximising share value. Another wrinkle in mixed ownership has been the enthusiasm displayed for employee stock ownership. Employee stock ownership programs (ESOPs) were begun in 2013–14, but then screeched to a halt at the end of 2014. Since 2016, 10 ESOP pilots have been moving forward again.

'Mixed ownership' also includes permission for SOEs to take stakes in private firms. Clearly, SOEs that have access to abundant cheap capital can use mixed ownership as a justification for expanding their control in the economy. The current wave of SOE reform clearly intends a strengthening of the state sector's effective presence in the economy. It does not countenance any privatisation or selling down of the state share. Of course, this is consistent with past policy, in which the CPC has insisted that public ownership should be the main body of the economy and state ownership should be the leading force, which must be consolidated and developed. But this attitude towards the state sector is being applied with much more consistency than in the past.

This discussion has made clear that the significance of corporate governance reform will depend significantly on what proportion of SOEs are placed in the 'fully competitive' type. For those placed in the 'less-than-fully competitive' type, their managerial autonomy will be significantly restricted. Once a firm is placed in this category, the government is supposed to maintain a controlling stake (CPC and State Council 2015a: Art. 5), and the managerial incentive contracts should be revised to reflect the special tasks and responsibilities assigned to the firm. Specifically:

> '[W]hile giving appropriate weight to profitability and increased asset value, these firms should increase the weight given to examining conditions relating to serving national strategies, guaranteeing national security and the operation of the national economy, or developing prospective strategic sectors. (SASAC et al. 2015: Art. 2.4)

In other words, SOE reform specifically includes creating a category of SOEs that will stay state controlled and that will increase the attention given to political objectives and reduce the importance of profitability. Conversely, the new powers given to 'fully competitive'–type firms are significant. If a large majority of SOEs are placed in this category, the current wave of reforms may have some positive effect. If not, it is likely any positive effects will be more than vitiated by the impact of policies seeking to increase oversight and assign additional tasks to SOEs.

Enhancing oversight

Efforts to improve oversight of SOEs have been a consistent theme of the past five years. President Xi's anticorruption campaign has, from the beginning, targeted SOEs as potential hotspots of corruption. The travelling inspection teams from the Central Discipline Inspection Commission have visited every central SOE, staying on site for several weeks to a few months, examining records and talking to a broad range of employees. In addition, new auditing mechanisms have been introduced and specific measures taken to guard against asset stripping and related party transactions.

By far the most important aspect of increased oversight has been the revived role for the Communist Party's leadership at every stage in the corporate governance mechanism. This new role is most clearly seen in the enterprise charter revisions that virtually every SOE carried out during 2017. Although these are not public documents, they circulate widely and their provisions are highly consistent, reflecting a set of top-down guidelines about the CPC's role in SOEs. These corporate charters incorporate the following provisions:

a. The CPC is formally embedded in the corporate governance system.
b. The chairperson of the board of directors should ordinarily be the first party secretary of the SOE.
c. Major strategic decisions of the SOE must be discussed *first* by the SOE CPC committee, and then passed on to the CEO. Both the board of directors and the firm management have an obligation to consult with the party committee before making important decisions.

These provisions reverse a fundamental tenet of Chinese SOE management that has been in place since the 1980s. Back then, the 'factory manager responsibility system' made clear that, in business matters, the factory manager (today's CEO), and not the party secretary, was the final decision-maker. That has been the predominant reality for the past 30 years. Now, the party secretary is once again the ultimate authority in SOEs. To be sure, there is a little ambiguity, due to the party secretary's dual role as chairperson of the board. The 'purpose', in a sense, of this arrangement is to prevent conflict between the chairperson of the board and the party secretary by uniting the roles in a single individual. Day-to-day management is still delegated to the CEO, who should maintain effective control of day-to-day decision-making. But obviously the scope for direct exercise of control rights by the party secretary is enormous. Moreover, the party secretary, by definition, is expected to execute CPC directives and national policies. His or her loyalty is to the party, rather than to the enterprise itself. This enhances oversight, but also creates new conflicts with managers, and makes it much easier for policymakers to assign multiple objectives to the firm. Indeed, the CPC is a special type of owner—one concerned with control rights only and with (usually) no claim on income streams. These missions are discussed in the next two sections.

Defining SOE missions

Over the past decade, Chinese policymakers have made more and more demands on state firms, which has led them to once again seek control rights. These demands are quite different from those in earlier years, and include using SOEs to spearhead China's development objectives. Today, these objectives include, most prominently:

1. Pioneering technological development. As Chinese development strategy shifts to innovation-led growth, SOEs have increasingly been called on to lead this process. More broadly, SOEs are expected to take a newly enhanced role in all industrial policies, from Strategic Emerging Industries to Made in China 2025.
2. Creating powerful national champions that will spread Chinese economic influence abroad. SASAC obsessively publicises the number of Chinese firms in the Fortune Global 500 list.
3. Maintaining macroeconomic stability by increasing investment when growth slows. Since 2009, when stimulus funds were channelled through SOEs to maintain aggregate demand, investment funding through SOEs has been a regular part of Chinese macroeconomic policy.
4. Leading sectoral and regional restructuring. In 2016, the promotion of supply-side structural reforms led to new responsibility being given to SOEs. The initial priority objective of this policy was to decommission excess heavy industrial capacity, and SOEs were asked to take the lead in organising capacity reduction cartels; now the policy has expanded into restructuring of other sectors, with SOEs still playing a prominent role. SOEs have also been asked to take the lead in the Belt and Road Initiative.

Chinese policymakers rarely display awareness of the importance of the competing objectives assigned to SOEs. Instead, with the revitalisation of the CPC under Xi Jinping, SOEs (like all state officials) are expected to be dynamic, bold leaders:

> As the core force of national economic development, SOEs should play the leading function in supply-side structural reforms. They should carry out every aspect of reform in a model way, and become the pioneers and main force of the reform. (Xinhuanet 2016)

Changing the objectives assigned to SOEs inevitably means exercising control through different means. The next section describes the institutional changes in the exercise of public ownership.

The institutional exercise of public ownership

A crucial part of the current wave of SOE reform since November 2013 has been the question of what type of institution should exercise public ownership rights. The current ownership agency, SASAC, is an evolutionary institution, established in 2004 to bring together previously dispersed ownership functions. SASAC has always struggled with limitations on its ownership rights and excessive regulatory mandates. The need to rationalise SASAC's complex bundle of income, control, supervision and regulatory powers has long been recognised. Since 2013, the proposed solution has been that of new state capital investment and operations companies (SCIOs). However, two competing conceptions of what these new investment companies should involve quickly emerged. The first was that the investment funds would operate as sovereign wealth funds, rather as they do in Singapore. It is easy to see that this approach is highly consistent with a view of state firms that sees maximising profit and improving efficiency as their predominant objectives. The owner focuses on residual income and the ownership agency is evaluated primarily on the financial performance of its portfolio. The Ministry of Finance proposed such investment companies in 2014, but their conception was discarded in favour of the creation of multiple investment funds with developmental objectives. That is, these funds would be expected to foster the creation of big competitive firms to develop emerging industries and to intervene in markets precisely to shape specific developments. This approach was developed in the proposals submitted by SASAC and was—not coincidentally—designed to be implemented by SASAC (at the national and provincial levels), which would gradually create SCIOs under its own auspices and transfer authority to them.[1]

This approach allowed SASAC to stay in control of the day-to-day creation and adaptation of new SCIOs. Eventually, SASAC's control rights may indeed pass to these SCIOs, but SASAC will directly manage this process. Multiple SOE reform documents—the '1 + N' process of specifying reform content—now refer to the role of these new ownership agencies. The SCIOs are explicitly instructed to exercise control functions more effectively, much more like an investment bank or a development fund than a wealth fund. The national funds are to have active restructuring roles:

1 This outcome is of course the result of the way the policy process was structured. The State Council LSG was headed by Ma Kai, a seasoned bureaucrat and former head of the erstwhile planning agency, the National Development and Reform Commission (NDRC), while its operational office was led by the head of SASAC. The top political leadership must have anticipated these outcomes when they created the LSG in this configuration (Chen and Naughton 2016). Xi Jinping and other top leaders must have consciously decided to endorse a conservative policy process in which existing agencies with a stake in exercising control rights would have the main voice in policy design.

> Push state capital into important industries and key sectors that affect national security, the commanding heights of the national economy and the people's livelihood; concentrate on keypoint infrastructure; concentrate on prospective strategic sectors; concentrate on outstanding enterprises with core competitive strength. Fully bring into play the SCIO companies to liquidate a batch of companies, reorganize a batch of companies, and innovate and develop a batch of companies … Fully bring into play the core and exemplary function of SOEs in realizing the strategy of innovation-driven development and become a manufacturing power; strengthen the predominant position of enterprises in technological innovation; attach great importance to training scientific personnel and highly skilled personnel. (CPC and State Council 2015a: Art. 14)

By 2017, SASAC had begun pilots with 10 SCIOs, each created by expanding the powers of an existing SASAC subordinate firm. Provincial SASACs have created 50–60 subordinate SCIOs. There is theoretically some differentiation between state capital investment companies, which were instructed to remake themselves into financially oriented holding companies with subordinate investment funds and operational companies, and state capital operations companies, which previously gained experience in restructuring distressed assets and reorganising orphaned state firms. However, in practice, the difference between the two has blurred and both forms will be referred to here as SCIOs. The pilots demonstrate that SASAC has chosen familiar subordinate firms to serve as SCIOs precisely because they have the experience to more effectively exercise control rights and are closely tied to SASAC itself.

An example can help clarify the situation. One of the central SASAC's apex firms is Guoxin (or China Reform Holdings). It has long had a special status among SASAC firms as a specialist in restructuring other firms, and has now been designated a state capital operations company. Its expanded responsibilities include raising an 'industrial guidance fund'. These funds, which are proliferating in the Chinese economy, are set up with a managing partner (in this case, provided by Guoxin itself), along with several limited partners providing financing only. Guoxin has set up an industrial guidance fund called China Venture Capital (Guofengtou). True to its name, China Venture Capital invests both in start-up firms and in acquisitions. It is the sole owner of a Silicon Valley–based venture capital firm called Canyon Bridge Capital Partners, which made an offer to buy the American Lattice Semiconductor in 2017.[2] Clearly, Guoxin has seized substantial financial autonomy and has used it in creative ways. Equally clearly, that autonomy is dependent on Guoxin serving as an effective instrument for government policy—in this case, the building of China's semiconductor industry. In pursuit of that objective, nearly any kind of activity is permitted. This case also shows a SCIO exercising developmental policy through fully financialised instruments. All of Guoxin's subsidiaries, including China

2 The acquisition was blocked by the Committee on Foreign Investment in the United States (CFIUS).

Venture Capital, are fully articulated corporate entities with clear incentives and responsibilities for the managing partner and the limited partners (although these are not on the public record). Indeed, even Guoxin itself is largely financialised, since it exercise a financial ownership stake in many firms without having the additional regulatory and command-and-control functions that SASAC had.

The creation of mission-oriented SCIOs is also apparent at the local government level. For example, Gansu province has incorporated most of its existing provincial plan into its new SOE reform program. Its new SCIOs are instructed to increase the amount of state capital in one of five named development zones, support provincial industrial policy and develop five strategic emerging industries: information technology, biopharmaceuticals, smart manufacturing, new energy and new materials. More than 80 per cent of the increase in state capital should be in 'strategic emerging industries, infrastructure, public services, and the externally oriented economy' (Gansu Provincial Department of Commerce 2016). Clearly, the SCIOs are expected to be developmental agencies.

The evolutionary and hybrid ownership institution SASAC is in the process of being replaced with new ownership institutions that can more aggressively and effectively exercise certain control rights. This rationalisation involves a sharper choice among alternative conceptions of the role of ownership agencies, and ends up supporting the focus on developmental objectives for SCIOs.

Conclusions

The current wave of SOE reform in China, while significant, is deeply troubled. To be sure, some of the inconsistencies in the current program simply reflect ordinary political compromises. Corporatisation with stronger boards of directors will give better transparency and clearer incentives, particularly in firms designated 'fully competitive'. This keeps reformers inside the politically enforced consensus and may provide them openings to push for better policies in the future. However, the overall program reflects the unmistakable victory of a political coalition that seeks to repurpose SOEs into developmental instruments. The choice of SCIO model reveals the preference of policymakers for a hands-on instrument that allows SOEs to be shaped into national champions and proactive shapers of development trajectories. This program is not likely to succeed. At the core of the problem is the 'impossible trinity'—the attempt to combine improved incentives, enhanced oversight and new missions for the SOEs.

First, SOEs are not likely to be effective instruments for the goals that policymakers are now assigning them. This is especially clear for the mission of becoming new technology pioneers. A large body of international experience demonstrates that entrenched incumbent corporations are bad at creating—and slow at adopting—

radical innovation. Few of China's SOEs are concentrated in high-tech sectors. For example, China's largest SOE coalminer is now developing a large and expensive program of alternative energy research, which will probably be a huge waste of resources. It is difficult enough to use a single instrument to achieve multiple objectives, and the inevitable trade-offs become much worse when the instruments are an inappropriate choice for one or more of those goals. This will likely turn into an expensive failure.

Second, assigning SOEs multiple objectives creates problems for the improvement of incentives. A basic result of modern principal–agent theory is that high-powered incentives are appropriate in a situation where there is a single objective, especially if it can be effectively monitored in the short run. However, if an agent is assigned multiple objectives, low-powered incentives and long-term career rewards are typically more effective (Holmstrom and Milgrom 1991). This is because higher rewards attached to one objective will draw effort away from the other objectives; therefore, an agent's judgement is needed to allocate effort and effectively juggle the trade-offs among objectives. China in the past gave quite high-powered incentives to managers and local government officials, because there was an overwhelming consensus on the importance of economic performance during the high-growth era (1978–2010). In the contemporary era, longer-term and lower-powered incentives may indeed be more appropriate to a more complex bundle of social goals, but it is unlikely this will be achieved by simply rewriting managerial compensation contracts. Stronger incentives are desired to reduce 'slack' and the pursuit of private benefits, but this is unlikely to be achieved by simply assigning rewards to different targets.

Third, with the assignment of multiple objectives to SOEs, oversight will likely deteriorate. This is because bargaining over the outcome of multiple performance indicators is virtually inevitable. SOE managers, who have to trade-off time and resources devoted to different outcomes, always have an argument for special treatment. If a company's profitability is below its peers, but it has done an outstanding job of subsidising one technology or another, should it not be given a pass on profitability? With multiple objectives, it is more difficult to reduce agency loss through heightened monitoring. Although the current vigorous anticorruption campaign can temporarily deter some private exploitation of control rights, the fundamental space for such exploitation increases with these multiple objectives.

However, these shortcomings should not blind us to the important changes taking place in China's SOE sector. At a minimum, the system appears to be creating more efficient instruments to carry out China's industrial policy objectives. The Guoxin example shows this. Moreover, as financialised 'mixed ownership' structures become larger and more complex, the additional oversight exercised by the CCP and new audit agencies may become more necessary. Thus, the goal of achieving a more efficient instrument that serves the state's developmental interests is partially achievable. Whether this is compatible with a profound restructuring and increased efficiency of the broader state sector depends on the evolution of reform from this point forward. In particular, the scope of the classification of fully competitive commercial enterprises will have particular importance.

While it is too early to determine whether these reforms will be 'successful', or whether they will turn out to be market-oriented, the emerging institutions are significantly different from the traditional system. Change has been introduced by fairly conservative interest groups—SASAC and the State Council SOE Leadership Small Group—which may indicate political limitations on the degree of expected change. Most important, there are important contradictions and tensions among the objectives of increasing oversight and giving firms more political and developmental missions, on the one hand, and improving their incentives, corporate governance, and financial flexibility on the other. Nevertheless, if local firms and ownership agencies are given sufficient leeway, and if the bulk of SOEs are reclassified as 'fully competitive commercial enterprises', these reform may lead to significant economic progress.

References

Batson, A. (2016), What not to expect from Chinese SOE reform, Blog, 21 September. Available from: andrewbatson.com/2016/09/21/what-not-to-expect-from-chinese-soe-reform/.

Brandt, L., Biesebroeck, J. V. and Zhang, Y. (2012), Creative accounting or creative destruction? Firm-level productivity growth in Chinese manufacturing, *Journal of Development Economics* 97(2): 339–51. doi.org/10.1016/j.jdeveco.2011.02.002.

Chen, L. and Naughton, B. (2016), An institutionalized policy-making mechanism: China's return to techno-industrial policy, *Research Policy* 45: 2138–52. doi.org/10.1016/j.respol.2016.09.014.

Chu, M., Kirby, W. C., Hua Dai, N. and Wang, Y. (2018), *Yunnan Baiyao: Transforming a Chinese state-owned enterprise*, Harvard Business School Case N2-318-078, rev. 20 March, Boston: Harvard Business School.

Communist Party of China (CPC) and State Council (2015a), Guiding opinions of the Central Committee of the Chinese Communist Party and the State Council on deepening the reform of state-owned enterprises, [in Chinese], *Xinhuanet*, 24 August. Available from: news.xinhuanet.com/politics/2015-09/13/c_1116547305.htm.

Communist Party of China and Central Office of the State Council (CPC and State Council) (2015b), Guiding opinions on promoting state-owned cultural enterprises to put social benefits first, and resolving social benefits and economic benefits together, [in Chinese], *Xinhuanet*, 14 September. Available from: news.xinhuanet.com/politics/2015-09/14/c_1116559409.htm.

Gansu Provincial Department of Commerce (2016), *Practical Views on Deepening State Enterprise Reform*, [in Chinese], 18 February, Lanzhou: Gansu Provincial Department of Commerce. Available from: gansu.mofcom.gov.cn/article/sjshangwudt/201602/20160201257319.shtml.

Holmstrom, B. and Milgrom, P. (1991), Multitask principal–agent analyses: Incentive contracts, asset ownership, and job design, *Journal of Law, Economics and Organization* 7(SI): 24–52.

Lin, J. Y., Cai, F. and Li, Z. (1998), Competition, policy burdens, and state-owned enterprise reform, *American Economic Review* 88(2): 422–7.

National Bureau of Statistics (NBS) (2013), *China Economic Census Yearbook*, Beijing: China Statistics Press.

National Bureau of Statistics (NBS) (2015), *Fixed Investment Statistical Yearbook*, Beijing: China Statistics Press.

National Bureau of Statistics (NBS) (2016), *China Statistics Yearbook*, Beijing: China Statistics Press.

Naughton, B. (2010), China's industrial capitalism: Is there a distinctive system? Can it be a model for others?, *Journal of Contemporary China* 19(65) (June). doi.org/10.1080/10670561003666079.

Naughton, B. (2015), The transformation of the state sector: SASAC, the market economy and the new national champions, in B. Naughton and K. S. Tsai (eds), *State Capitalism, Institutional Adaptation and the Chinese Miracle*, New York: Cambridge University Press. doi.org/10.1017/CBO9781139962858.003.

Qian, Y. (1996), Enterprise reform in China: Agency problems and political control, *Economics of Transition* 4(2)(October): 427–47. doi.org/10.1111/j.1468-0351.1996.tb00181.x.

State Council (2015), Several opinions of the State Council on reforming and perfecting the state-owned assets management system, [in Chinese], *Guofa* (63)(4 November). Available from: www.gov.cn/zhengce/content/2015-11/04/content_10266.htm.

State Council (2017), Notice of the State Council on printing and distributing the implementation plan of transferring some state-owned capital to enrich social security funds, [in Chinese], *Guofa* (49)(18 November). Available from: www.gov.cn/zhengce/content/2017-11/18/content_5240652.htm.

State-owned Assets Supervision and Administration Commission (SASAC) (2014), *SASAC Yearbook*, Beijing: SASAC.

State-owned Assets Supervision and Administration Commission (SASAC), Ministry of Finance and National Development and Reform Commission (2015), *Views on Demarcating and Classifying SOEs*, 29 December, Beijing: SASAC.

Xi, J. (2009), Speech at the 50th anniversary of the discovery of Daqing Oilfield, [in Chinese]. Available from: news.cnpc.com.cn/system/2009/09/23/001259157.shtml (site discontinued).

Xinhuanet (2016), SOE development is facing unprecedented difficulties, [in Chinese], *Xinhuanet*, 10 June. Available from: finance.ifeng.com/a/20160610/14475324_0.shtml.

Yin, Y. (2018), The new situation and new responsibilities of SOE reform, [in Chinese], *Xinlang Finance*, 26 May. Available from: finance.sina.com.cn/meeting/2018-05-26/doc-ihcaqueu4140308.shtml.

Part III: The development experiences

21. Rural-to-urban migration and migrants' labour market performance, 2008–16

Bob Gregory and Xin Meng

In 1978, the Chinese economy was segregated into two parts: the rural and the urban economies. Migration was forbidden. At that time, about 80 per cent of the population lived and worked in the rural sector. Economic reforms initiated in the agricultural sector in 1978 produced significant productivity increases and released a large portion of the rural workforce to move into the more productive nonagricultural sector to work. However, throughout the 1980s, rural-to-urban migration was still largely prohibited. Workers released from the agricultural sector, combined with the agricultural surplus and migration restrictions, created the conditions for the development of township and village enterprises (TVEs), which absorbed surplus labour and played a major role in generating growth during this period.

It was not until the early 1990s, when the open-door policy brought large-scale foreign direct investment (FDI) into Chinese cities and the demand for unskilled workers increased in locations away from the village, that the government gradually loosened rural–urban migration restrictions. This movement of migrant labour generated rapid economic growth associated with construction in cities and double-digit export growth. During this period, rural–urban migration increased, from 25 million in 1990 to 170 million in 2016 (see Figure 21.1). It is difficult to imagine how China could have grown so quickly for so long without this massive reallocation of labour.

Although labour could move to seek employment, there were still substantial restrictions in place to prevent permanent migration. As a result, most migration was temporary and many workers moved back and forth between villages and cities depending on their personal circumstances. There has been some weakening of these 'permanent' migration restrictions, but such reforms have been slight and longer city stays, which are increasingly occurring, are still largely confined to migrants with temporary status.

It now seems that the old growth model that has served China so well—built on increasing temporary migration to large cities—has come to an end. In the future, the relationship between rural–urban migration and economic growth will be very different, as the drivers of economic growth shift from manufacturing exports and construction in large cities to more diversified activities, primarily located in small cities. Large numbers of workers will continue to leave agricultural production, seeking higher incomes, but their employment destinations will change as they move to jobs much closer to home.

To a significant degree, the fundamental change in migration flows has already begun. Between 1998 and 2007, 100 million migrants augmented the large-city workforce. Between 2007 and 2016, the migrant addition was 20 million, but, between 2014 and 2017, there was almost no increase in migrant numbers in large cities.

The large shift in migration flows away from large cities towards small cities and rural towns has important implications for economic growth, economic policy and the balance of markets and government regulation as determinants of what happens to future large-scale labour reallocations. It is important therefore, as part of understanding this ongoing transition from one growth model to another, to map out and understand the nature of the migrant flows to the large cities and how economic outcomes in cities and villages have responded as the migration flows have changed. To begin to do this, we use data from the Rural–Urban Migration in China (RUMiC) survey that began collecting data in large cities and villages from 2008, just before the migration inflows to the large cities began to substantially moderate. The RUMiC survey extends to 2016, by which time significant net migration inflows to large cities had ceased.

The data reveal, to a large extent, what might be expected when migration inflows slow. We see, for example, substantial ageing of the migrant stock as the relative importance of young migrant inflows declines. Other migrant outcomes are also changing in expected ways, but only slowly, while others, to this point, seem little affected.

But one outcome of special interest to economists is not changing as expected. Large migrant inflows were encouraged by relaxation of government migration restrictions and the large wage gaps between the migrant wage in the city and what the migrant could earn at home. It might be expected therefore that large migrant inflows, increasing labour supply in the cities and reducing labour supply in hometowns, would gradually erode this income gap. As the gap narrows, net migration would be expected to slow as labour reallocation in China moved to a new equilibrium growth path. But this story does not seem to be fully consistent with the facts. As expected, the earnings gaps between the migrants' receiving cities and their hometowns are large at the beginning of the period, when migrant inflows are large, but what is not expected is that the income gaps are much the same at the end of the period, when there are very small additional net migration inflows. The migration flows seem to have stopped, but there is little evidence in our data of any obvious equalisation of relative labour market outcomes in the migration-sending rural hometowns and the migrant-receiving cities. So there are two puzzles here. First, why were the rapid and large migrant inflows ineffective in reducing the relative rewards for migration? Second, why has the net migration flow stopped when the relative rewards for migration are much the same as they were during the high migration period? These are important questions that we cannot fully answer here, but we make a start.

Consideration of these questions suggests that migration flows in China depend on the individual decisions of workers to move and government policies surrounding those decisions. The government has always played a large role in determining the geographic allocation of labour and it seems clear government policy has now changed. The new policy is directing immigrants away from large cities and towards small, more remote cities.

The economic implications of this new policy, and its interactions with decisions about where and whether to migrate, are particularly interesting. The old policy can be thought of as the government responding to economic forces pulling workers to cities and to excess rural labour; however, the new policies do not seem to be a response to the usual economic forces. The wage gap between cities and rural villages remains and hence the economic return to moving migrants to cities, at least measured by this metric, remains. It is not as though the absorption capacity of large cities, as measured by relative wages, has changed in any significant way. Hence, it appears the new policy is forgoing the economic gains that would come about by narrowing the wage gap between large cities and rural towns in pursuit of some other objective.

Given the availability of Chinese data, it is not a straightforward matter to disentangle the role of government policy on one hand and economic incentives on the other as determinants of the large changes in migrant flows. Hence we are forced to take a very indirect approach and this chapter is mainly descriptive, documenting what have been important migrant outcomes in large cities, what has changed and what has not. We see this as the laying of a firmer foundation on which to build an assessment of past migration impacts and to support various conjectures of what is likely to happen in the future. To some extent, the description updates the chapter by Meng (2013) for the 2013 *China Update*, but this chapter directs more attention to changing patterns of outcomes and how they might relate to changing migration flows.

The next section provides a general picture of the changing migrant flows. Section two examines the characteristics of the migrant stock in large cities. Section three documents the economic performance of migrants, while section four analyses the changing determinants of migrant earnings. Section five considers the changing pattern of migrants' wages across cities and conclusions are given in section six.

The changing flows of rural-to-urban migration

In Chinese statistics, there are two different definitions of rural-to-urban migrants (in Chinese, *Nong Min Gong*—literally, 'farmers turned workers'). The first definition refers to anyone with 'rural household registration' (*hukou*) who is not working in agriculture, including those who are working in a nonfarming job in their rural hometown. The second definition refers to those who become nonfarm workers by moving to cities—in other words, 'rural-to-urban migrants'. In recent years, the National Bureau of Statistics (NBS) has published the numbers for both definitions (see Figure 21.1).

In 1990, due to government restrictions, fewer than 25 million rural workers moved to the city to work, while a larger number worked at rural TVEs in their hometown. By the late 1990s, as China's 'open door' policy attracted more and more FDI, the demand in the cities for unskilled labour increased. As a result, rural-to-urban migration accelerated. The fastest period of migration growth was after China joined the World Trade Organization (WTO) and until the Global Financial Crisis (GFC). Immediately after the GFC, due to the reduction in global demand for Chinese exports, the increase in migration rates dropped sharply. Net migration appears to have increased little over the past three years. The demand for Chinese exports has not bounced back to pre-GFC levels and China's economic growth strategy has changed from export-driven to domestic demand–driven growth. As a result, most nonfarm job growth for rural *hukou* workers involves those who stay at home and work in nearby small towns.

To what extent the slowdown in migration to large cities is a response to market forces and to what extent it is the result of government policy is unclear. Our description of migrant outcomes will help us address this question. At this point, the data we examine suggest that policy shifts are the key determinants of the changing long-run pattern of migration flows and we note that the 'National New Urbanisation Plan 2014–2020' reinforces this judgement. The plan suggests the government had not let go of the fear of large or mega-city development and has become more determined to direct migrants towards small cities and to ignore the agglomeration advantages of further large-city development (see Meng 2014).[1] Despite economists' advocacy of the advantages to be gained from large or mega-city agglomeration effects in the economic development process, further migration to big cities seems to be a lost cause for now.

1 The 'National New Urbanisation Plan 2014–2020' emphasised the orderly building of small cities and towns to accommodate the future excess supply of agricultural workers (State Council 2014).

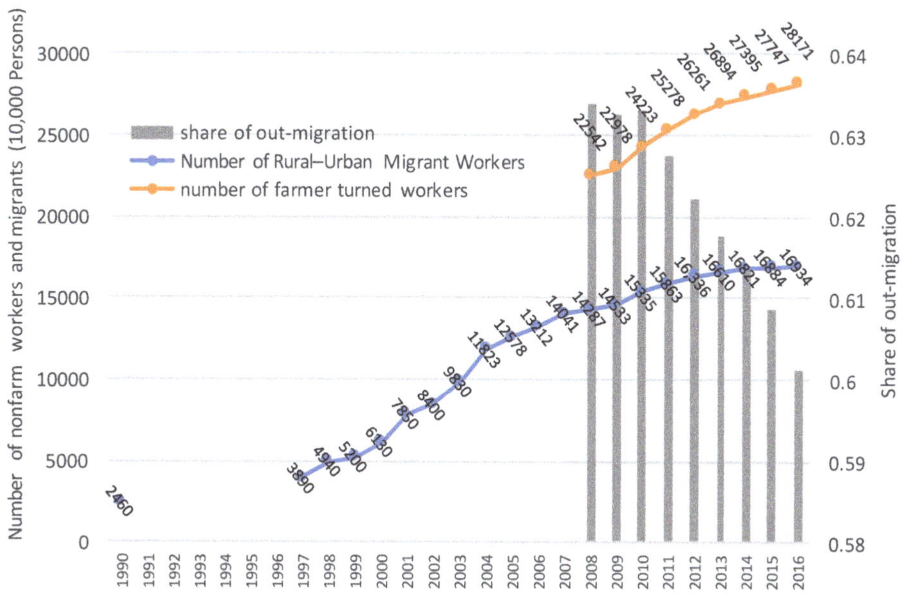

Figure 21.1 China's 'rural' workforce working in nonfarm jobs

Sources: The rural–urban migration data for 1990 are the authors' own calculation, using 1990 population census data; 1997 data are from World Bank (2009: Fig 2.41); data for 1998–2008 are from NBS (various years [b]) and thereafter from NBS (various years [a]).

The redirection of migrant inflows are impacted by policies at all levels of government. Local city restrictions on migrant access to social services and social insurance are one factor discouraging migration inflows to big cities, while large-scale central government investment in rural and small towns is a factor encouraging migration inflows to small cities. In many instances, such policies have an impact not only on migration inflows, but also directly on migrants who are already in large or mega-cities. In December 2017, for example, the Beijing city government heavy-handedly implemented a 40-day clean-up campaign to rid the city of unsafe buildings, in which about 8.2 million migrant workers had lived for decades. Many of these migrants subsequently left Beijing.

Characteristics of migrant workers

The RUMiC survey combines a longitudinal sample (panel old households) and a repeated cross-section sample (representative new households). The survey is randomly refreshed from each of the 15 cities in each survey year. Using these data, we present basic statistics to show the characteristics of the migrants and whether these have changed.

Table 21.1 Summary statistics of individual migrant characteristics

					Ever married		Opinion/attitude	
Year	Age	Male	Married	Years of schooling	Divorced/ remarried	No. of children	Stay in city perm-anently	Happy
	[1]	[2]	[3]	[4]	[5]	[6]	[7]	[8]
2008	31.02	0.61	0.62	9.11	0.029	1.33	0.60	0.89
2009	32.04	0.59	0.65	9.17	0.032	1.36	0.64	0.89
2010	32.34	0.59	0.64	9.28	0.028	1.39	0.62	n.a.
2011	33.01	0.56	0.68	9.23	0.034	1.40	0.62	0.89
2012	34.17	0.56	0.73	9.21	0.030	1.44	0.64	0.92
2013	35.20	0.55	0.75	9.21	0.036	1.48	0.67	0.93
2014	36.05	0.55	0.77	9.15	0.039	1.49	0.70	0.93
2015	36.36	0.55	0.77	9.23	0.040	1.52	0.64	0.93
2016	36.82	0.55	0.77	9.32	0.041	1.52	0.69	0.92
Panel (old households)								
2008	31.02	0.61	0.62	9.11	0.029	1.33	0.60	0.89
2009	33.08	0.58	0.73	9.01	0.036	1.39	0.69	0.88
2010	33.56	0.58	0.73	9.23	0.025	1.37	0.68	n.a.
2011	33.93	0.56	0.75	9.31	0.031	1.41	0.66	0.90
2012	34.95	0.56	0.76	9.19	0.032	1.44	0.69	0.93
2013	35.95	0.55	0.79	9.19	0.039	1.47	0.71	0.93
2014	36.59	0.55	0.80	9.23	0.037	1.51	0.71	0.93
2015	37.49	0.55	0.81	9.20	0.042	1.51	0.67	0.92
2016	37.78	0.55	0.81	9.28	0.041	1.52	0.71	0.93
Representative (new households)								
2008	31.02	0.61	0.62	9.11	0.029	1.33	0.60	0.89
2009	31.43	0.59	0.60	9.27	0.029	1.41	0.61	0.89
2010	31.12	0.60	0.55	9.32	0.033	1.34	0.56	n.a.
2011	31.62	0.56	0.59	9.12	0.040	1.43	0.55	0.87
2012	32.58	0.57	0.66	9.26	0.025	1.44	0.54	0.90
2013	33.53	0.56	0.66	9.25	0.029	1.45	0.60	0.94
2014	34.89	0.56	0.71	8.99	0.044	1.54	0.68	0.93
2015	33.98	0.54	0.69	9.31	0.036	1.48	0.58	0.93
2016	34.39	0.56	0.67	9.41	0.042	1.52	0.63	0.91

n.a. = not available

Table 21.1 presents the mean values of a selection of characteristics for those aged 15–64 years from each of our samples. Based on the representative sample, the average age of a migrant worker in our large cities has increased by three years over the nine years of data collection (from 31 to 34 years of age), there has been a slight increase in the number of women joining the migrant workforce (from 39 per cent to 45 per cent), more migrant workers are married (from 62 per cent to 68 per cent) and migrants' years of schooling have increased slightly (by 0.3 years). In addition, among ever-married migrants, the divorce rate (including those who have remarried) has increased (from 2.9 per cent to 4.2 per cent) and the number of children has increased, too (by 0.2 per family). These changes—particularly the increase in migrants' age, the marriage rate and the number of children—are to be expected when migration inflows substantially reduce. But they provide no obvious reasons for the fall in migration inflow rates.

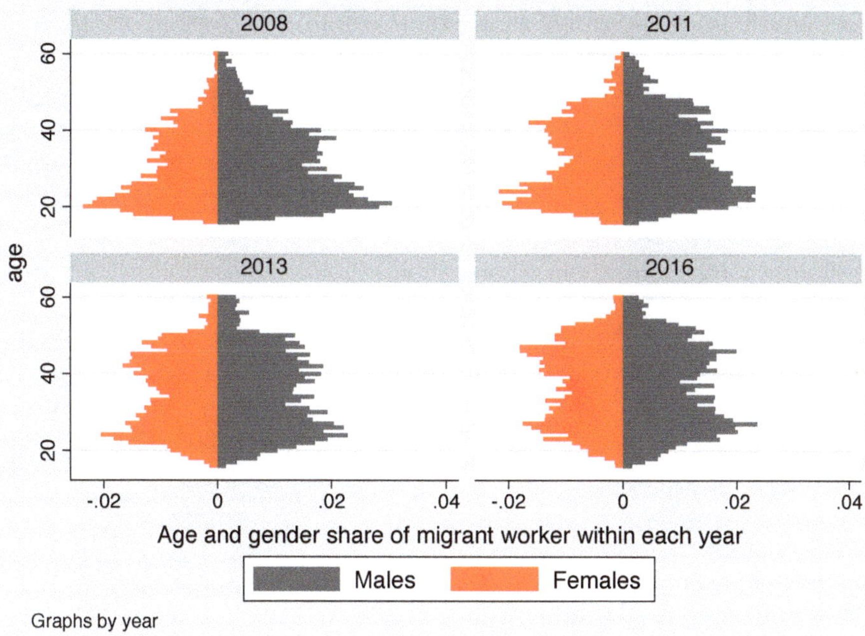

Figure 21.2 Age distribution of migrant workforce (full sample)

Source: Authors' own calculation from RUMiC data.

Averages often disguise important changes, so it may be worthwhile to look at changes in the distribution of some of these variables. Figure 21.2 indicates substantial changes in the migrant age distribution. In 2008, the dominant proportion of the migrant workforce was in the 16–35 year age group (65 per cent of men and 70 per cent of women). By 2016, the workforce was divided almost equally between those below 35 years of age and those above. The number of those above 35 years of age increased from 35 per cent for men and 30 per cent for women in 2008 to 40 per cent and 48 per cent, respectively, in 2016 based on a representative sample. The increase was largest for older women.

The question that naturally arises is whether the increase in older workers is the result of new older migrant inflows or a natural outcome of migrants staying longer in the cities. Changes in migrants' current job tenure may throw some light on this issue. If most of the older group comes from new inflows, we would expect their current job tenure to be relatively short.

Figure 21.3 shows that men and women over 35 years of age have been in their current job for quite a long time and the proportions of those in the long tenure categories have been increasing in recent years. In 2008, 40 per cent of women and 52 per cent of men aged over 35 years had five or more years of tenure in their current job. By 2016, the ratios had increased to 70 per cent for women and 72 per cent for men, suggesting a substantial part of the growth in the older age groups is being generated by migrants ageing in the city rather than by new inflows. These results are perhaps to be expected as the aggregate net migrant inflows have dropped dramatically.

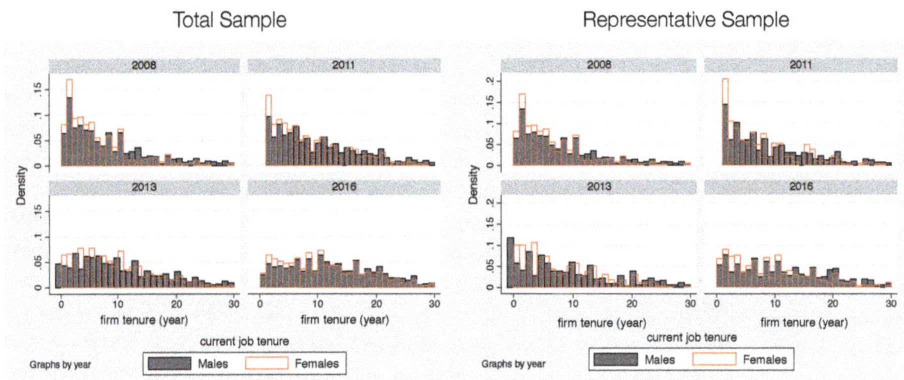

Figure 21.3 Current job tenure for workers aged 40 and above

Source: Authors' own calculation from RUMiC data.

The mean years of education have increased by 0.3 of a year. What can be said about the source of this increase? Figure 21.4 indicates that the marginal improvement in average education levels is generated mainly by a lift in the proportion of workers with a three-year college qualification, at the expense of junior and senior high school graduates. This is true for both men and women. A more striking observation from Figure 21.4, however, is that the proportion of women who are illiterate or have only primary school education has increased over time, from 16 per cent to 23 per cent, while the same pattern is not observed among men.

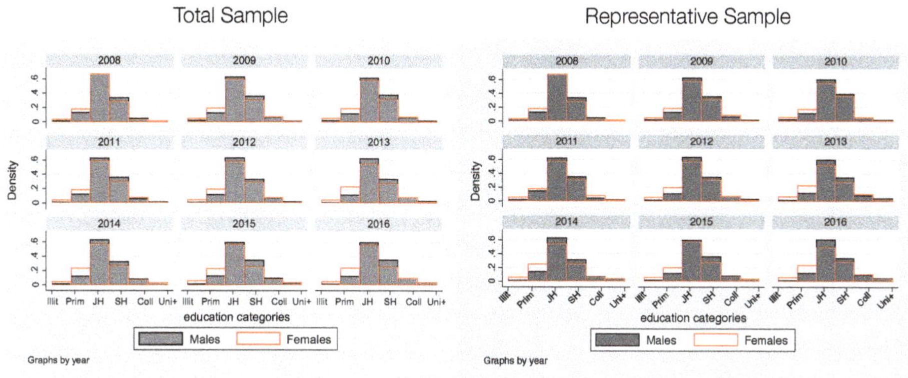

Figure 21.4 Education distribution by gender

Key: Illit = illiterate; Prim = primary school; JH = junior high school; SH = senior high school; Coll = three-year college; Uni+ = university.

Source: Authors' own calculation from RUMiC data.

Does this pattern suggest that the education level for rural women coming to the city has worsened or does it simply reflect the changing demographic structure of the current migrant female labour force—that is, a larger proportion of older women are now in the migrant workforce than before? To answer this question, we divide our sample into five different birth cohorts (1946–59, 1960–69, 1970–79, 1980–89 and 1990–99) to see whether those who were born in the 1980s and 1990s have a similar education distribution as those who were born earlier. If the young cohorts are better educated, the observed increase in the poorer educated must be due to the increase in the proportion of the older workforce in recent years. Figure 21.5 shows that women's educational attainment improved significantly in the recent birth cohorts. Thus, the older women who have remained in the city workforce have generated the increase in the proportion of poorer educated female workers.

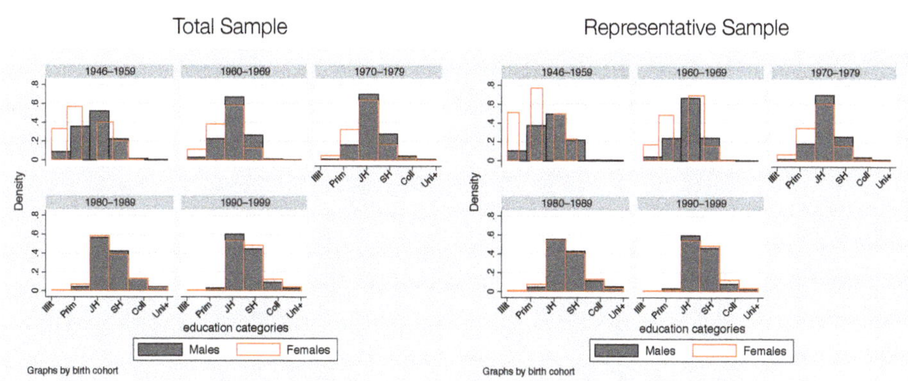

Figure 21.5 Education distribution by birth cohort and gender

Key: Illit = illiterate; Prim = primary school; JH = junior high school; SH = senior high school; Coll = three-year college; Uni+ = university.

Source: Authors' own calculation from RUMiC data.

To this point the changes in means and distributions of demographic variables seem slight, much as might be expected, and do not appear to provide any obvious answers for why net migration inflows have fallen so much.

The RUMiC survey also asks respondents a range of attitudinal questions, which might get more directly to the reasons for the slowdown of migration inflows. One question asked is: 'If policy allows, how long do you want to stay in the city?' The answers are particularly important. The majority of the sample, between 60 per cent and 70 per cent, wishes to stay in the city permanently, and this proportion has increased marginally over the data period (Column 7 of Table 21.1). Among migrants in cities there seems to be no attitudinal change that might explain why migration inflows have fallen. Indeed, preference for staying in the city is increasing.

RUMiC also asks migrants: 'Considering all aspects of your life, are you (1) very happy, (2) happy, (3) not very happy, or (4) very unhappy?' Table 21.1 presents the proportion who answer 'very happy' or 'happy'. More than 90 per cent of migrants fall into this category and, again, there has been no significant change that might explain the fall in migration inflows.[2]

The means of the data presented in Table 21.1, and their distributions, support two judgements: 1) demographic outcomes move in the expected direction when net migration inflows slow dramatically, and provide no obvious clues for why net migration inflows have fallen; and 2) attitudinal data also provide no significant evidence of increased dissatisfaction with city life.

Perhaps explanations for reduced migrant inflows can be found in the more direct measures of labour market outcomes, which may reflect large falls in the demand for migrant labour in large cities?

Migrants' labour market performance

Many migrants are drawn to cities by the large earnings gap between rural and urban areas. How has this gap changed over time and how does it relate to changing migration flows?

The RUMiC survey asked each worker: 'If you did not migrate, how much would you have earned per month at your rural hometown?' Based on these data, together with the migrants' reported monthly earnings in the city, we calculate the mean wage differential between the hometown and the city.

2 There has been a change in the proportion who answered 'very happy' and an increase in the proportion who answered 'happy', but our judgement at this stage is that this shift cannot explain the reduction of migrant inflows.

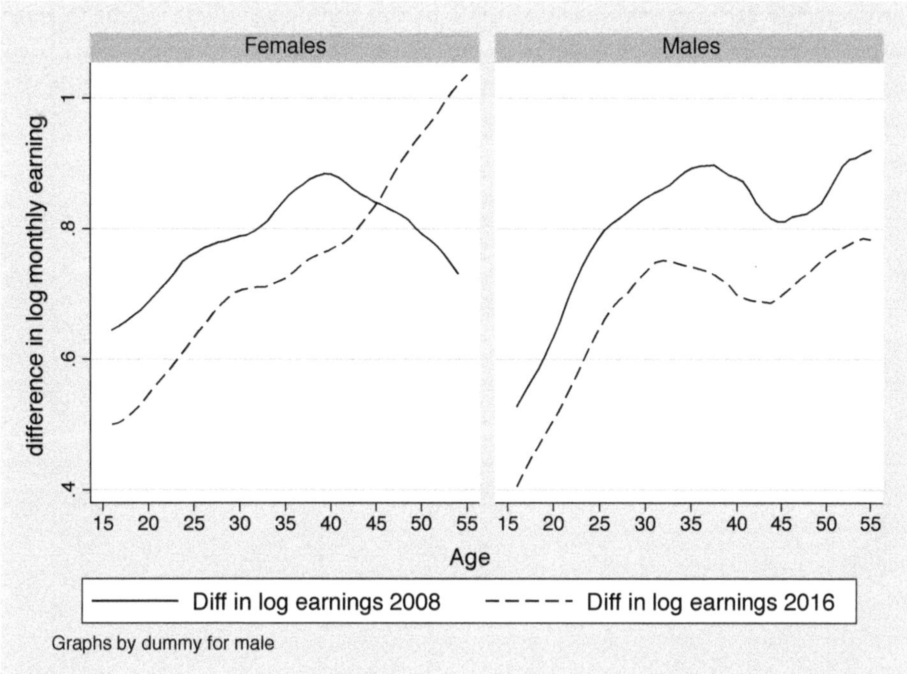

Figure 21.6 Log monthly earnings gap between city and rural hometown

Source: Authors' own calculation from RUMiC data.

In 2008—the year when net migration inflows were high—the difference in the average wages in the city and the hometown is 86 per cent (including for the self-employed). In 2016, when net migration inflows had ceased, the earning gap had reduced to 71 per cent. If only wage and salary earners are included, the gap in 2008 is 77 per cent and in 2016, 70 per cent. So earnings gaps have fallen, and the direction of change is as might be expected if this change were to reduce migration inflows. But is this fall in the earnings gap sufficient to cause net migration inflows to virtually cease? It seems unlikely and at this point our judgement is that a city premium of 70 per cent is still very high and the fall in the earnings gap seems slight and insufficient to explain such a large change in migration inflows.

Large earnings gaps and small falls through the period when migration inflows have fallen so much are found among all the groups we consider. Figure 21.6 presents the gaps by gender and age group for the first and last years of the survey. The failure of the earnings gap to narrow significantly by age and gender is yet another sign that the current trend for more rural workers to stay in their rural hometowns to work seems not to be a response to individual incentives, as is normally thought in market economies.

Although the earnings gap between the city and the home village seems to have narrowed slightly, real earnings in both the city and the home village have increased very considerably, and it seems probable that real and rapid income growth in the city is likely to validate the decision to migrate.

Figure 21.7 Log monthly real wages/income by gender and employment status

Source: Authors' own calculation from RUMiC data.

The left panel of Figure 21.7 shows that, in the past nine years, migrants' real wages increased by about 70 per cent for both male and female workers. The period of fastest growth was before 2013; thereafter the speed of increase slowed somewhat. Women have shared equally in this high growth rate, although they earn about 20 per cent less than men. Net income[3] for self-employed workers has also grown quickly, but not as fast as that for the wage/salary earners (Figure 21.7, right panel). Their net income increased by about 40 per cent over the nine years. Self-employed women were making about 20 per cent less than men at the beginning of the period, but the gap reduced somewhat at the end of the period, to about 15 per cent.

3 The self-employed reported their net income from the business divided by the number of owners of the business.

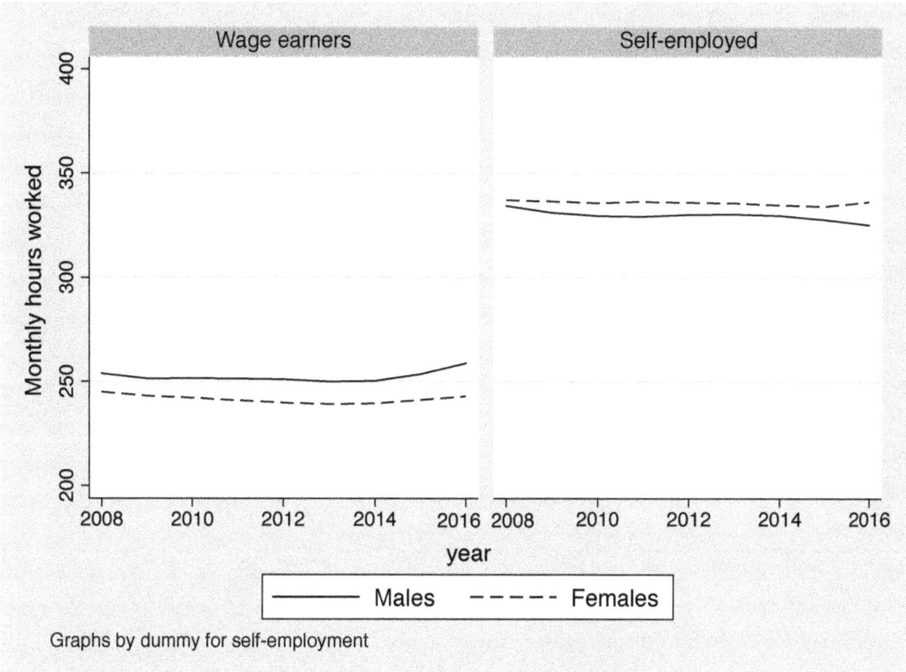

Figure 21.8 Monthly hours worked by employment status

Source: Authors' own calculation from RUMiC data.

Of course, earnings are not the only thing that matter, but also how much work needs to be done to receive these earnings. There have been limited changes in the long hours worked by wage earners and the self-employed (Figure 21.8). One could imagine an adverse reaction from migrants to these long hours worked and a demand for shorter hours as real incomes increase, but there is little evidence of any widespread dissatisfaction, as indicated by migrants' willingness to stay in the city permanently and their level of happiness (see the earlier discussion about the results from Table 21.1). Nevertheless, the long hours worked are striking.

If we assume for wage earners that an eight-hour day, six-day week are 'normal' then the normal monthly working hours should be no more than 207 hours. Both male and female migrant wage/salary earners report an average of 40 or more hours above this 'normal' monthly limit (more than 250 hours monthly), and there has been no noticeable change over our data period.

The self-employed also work very long hours—on average, close to 340 hours a month, or more than 11 hours a day for a seven-day week. How do these long work hours relate to income earned?

For the self-employed, average monthly net income levels have always been above the wage earner average, but their average hourly income has always been lower (Figure 21.9). In recent years, however, the relative position of the self-employed has improved. Between 2013 and 2016, the annual average real hourly earnings growth for wage and salary earners barely reached 1.5 per cent. For the self-employed, however, the growth was 11 per cent.

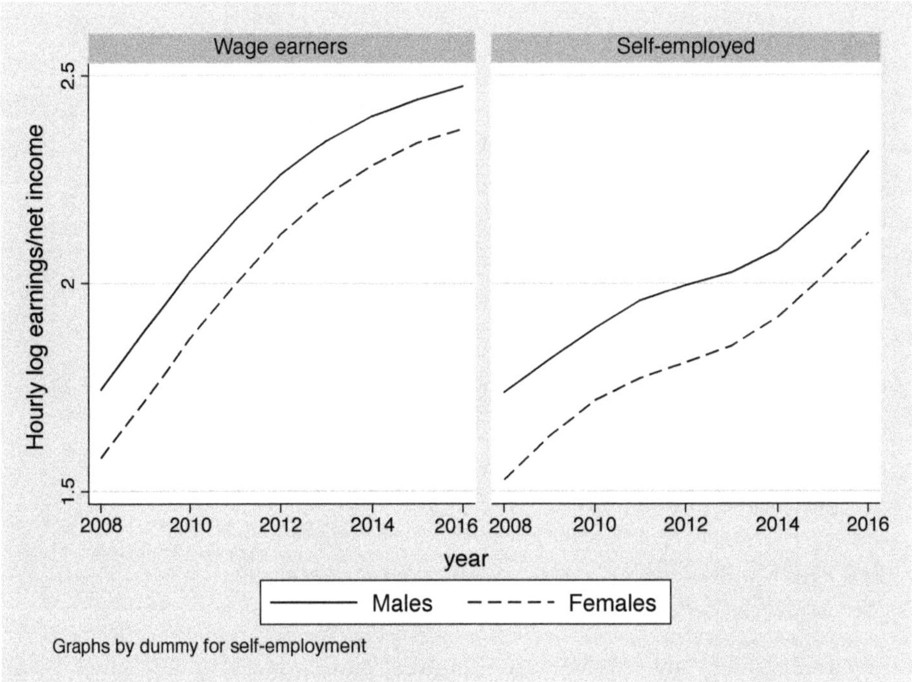

Figure 21.9 Hourly real log earnings/net income, by employment status

Source: Authors' own calculation from RUMiC data.

The stronger hourly income growth among the self-employed may be one reason their share among migrant workers has been increasing recently. For the representative sample, the proportion of migrant workers who were self-employed in 2008 was 24 per cent; by 2016, the ratio had increased to 29 per cent.

The change in the migration inflows should also impact on the length of stay in the city. Data in Figure 21.10 show that, on average, the number of years since first migrating to the city to work increased by four to five years between 2008 and 2016, and the increases occurred mainly after 2010 (post the GFC).[4] Self-employed migrant workers, on average, have been in cities for four to five years longer than wage and salary earners, and the increments over the past nine years are about the

4 Neither of these measures is the complete duration. The 'year since first migration' misses people who had a very short initial stay, left for their rural hometown and did not return during our data period; it ignores interrupted stays (many migrants move from their rural hometown to the city and back a few times); and it also does not take into account that the current length of stay does not represent the complete duration as many people will remain in the city for many years to come. Similarly, for current job tenure, short completed tenures are missed, and for current jobs, individuals will stay longer.

same as for their wage and salary counterparts. The lengthening of the average time since arrival in the city suggests the dramatic slowdown in net migration to the city has been generated primarily by reduced inflows of new workers rather than an increased exodus of workers who have been in the cities for a long time. This result is consistent with the ageing of the migrant stock.

There is no indication, however, that the slowdown of migrant inflows has impacted on job turnover. Migrant wage/salary earners have been in their current job for three to four years and this has not changed much over the past nine years. The current job duration for the self-employed—an average of six to seven years—is almost double that of the wage/salary earners, but it too has not significantly increased.

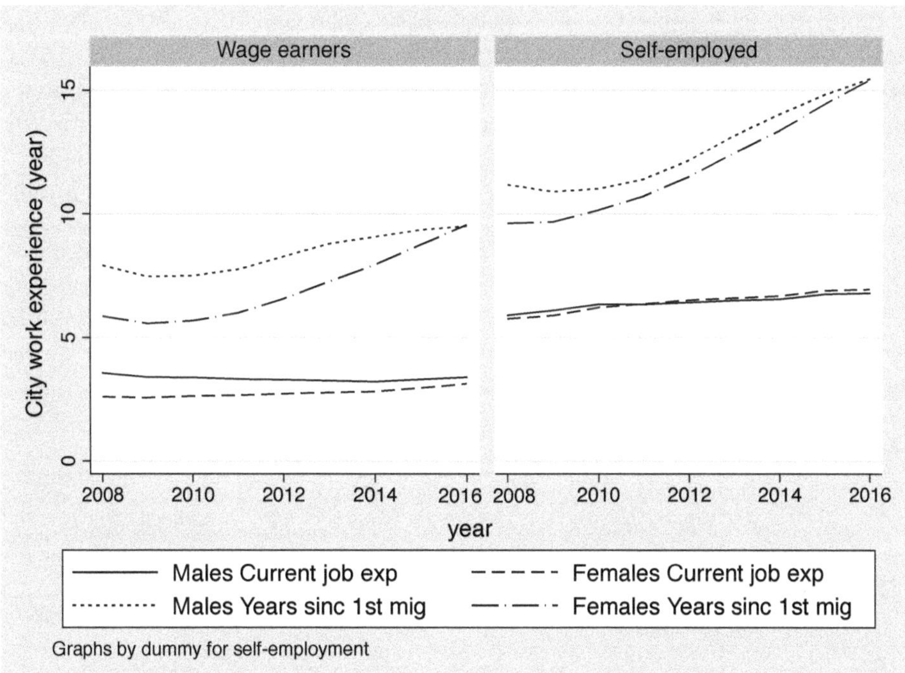

Figure 21.10 Years since first migration and current job experience

Source: Authors' own calculation from RUMiC data.

We also look at social insurance coverage and whether migrants have written contracts that legalise their employment position and protect their rights in case of disputes. Table 21.2 presents the social insurance coverage for all workers, for wage/salary earners and for self-employed workers, separately. Columns 1–3 present the total number of insurance types held by migrant workers. By law, employers must pay (jointly with employees) into five different insurance funds: health, unemployment, pension, workplace injury and housing. In 2008, the average migrant in the representative sample had 0.6 of the five types of insurance, with wage/salary earners having 0.8, while the self-employed had 0.04. Columns 4–6 and 7–9 list two of the most important insurance types for migrants: health and pension. For all workers, the incidence of these types of insurance has increased from 10 per cent and 17 per cent coverage in 2008, respectively, to 28 per cent for both in 2016. The most impressive improvement was made among wage/salary earners, rising from 13 per cent for health insurance and 21 per cent for pension insurance in 2008, to 39 per cent for both by 2016. These outcomes suggest an improving work environment for migrants. For self-employed workers, however, there is virtually no coverage.

From 2010, the RUMiC survey asked whether migrant wage/salary earners had signed a written contract with their employer. One important aim of 2008's New Labour Law was to ensure that workers have a written contract so any industrial relations dispute can be resolved through legal channels (Meng 2017). The law clearly states that if a written labour contract has not been signed with an employee within one year, the employer will be deemed to have signed an open-ended contract or will incur a penalty that requires the employer to double the salary paid to the employee (NPC 2007). The results from the RUMiC survey indicate that in 2010 about 49 per cent of wage/salary earners already had a written contract with their employer. The ratio did not change much. By 2016, about 53 per cent were covered by written contracts.

It seems the implementation of the New Labour Law has been more successful in achieving written contracts than in the provision of social insurance; however, over time, not much progress has been made.

Table 21.2 Social insurance coverage

	Number of social insurance funds			Percentage of health insurance coverage			Percentage of pension insurance coverage		
All workers	Panel sample	Rep. sample	Total	Panel sample	Rep. sample	Total	Panel sample	Rep. sample	Total
	[1]	[2]	[3]	[4]	[5]	[6]	[7]	[8]	[9]
2008	0.61	0.61	0.61	0.10	0.10	0.10	0.17	0.17	0.17
2009	0.59	0.62	0.61	0.12	0.10	0.11	0.16	0.17	0.17
2010	0.85	0.66	0.75	0.22	0.17	0.20	0.22	0.15	0.18
2011	0.84	0.76	0.81	0.19	0.16	0.17	0.21	0.20	0.21
2012	0.93	1.11	0.99	0.21	0.28	0.23	0.24	0.29	0.25
2013	1.11	1.02	1.08	0.27	0.24	0.26	0.28	0.24	0.26
2014	1.03	0.92	0.99	0.25	0.23	0.24	0.25	0.23	0.25
2015	1.06	1.07	1.06	0.26	0.25	0.25	0.25	0.25	0.25
2016	1.20	1.20	1.20	0.28	0.28	0.28	0.29	0.28	0.29
Wage/salary earners									
2008	0.78	0.78	0.78	0.13	0.13	0.13	0.21	0.21	0.21
2009	0.95	0.79	0.84	0.18	0.13	0.15	0.26	0.22	0.23

	Number of social insurance funds			Percentage of health insurance coverage			Percentage of pension insurance coverage		
All workers	Panel sample	Rep. sample	Total	Panel sample	Rep. sample	Total	Panel sample	Rep. sample	Total
	[1]	[2]	[3]	[4]	[5]	[6]	[7]	[8]	[9]
2010	1.29	0.84	1.05	0.33	0.22	0.27	0.33	0.20	0.26
2011	1.31	0.98	1.17	0.29	0.20	0.25	0.34	0.26	0.30
2012	1.50	1.45	1.48	0.34	0.36	0.35	0.38	0.37	0.38
2013	1.86	1.43	1.71	0.45	0.34	0.41	0.46	0.33	0.42
2014	1.77	1.31	1.60	0.43	0.32	0.39	0.43	0.33	0.40
2015	1.87	1.47	1.72	0.45	0.34	0.41	0.44	0.34	0.40
2016	2.07	1.68	1.94	0.49	0.39	0.46	0.50	0.39	0.46
Self-employed									
2008	0.04	0.04	0.04	0.02	0.02	0.02	0.01	0.01	0.01
2009	0.04	0.06	0.05	0.03	0.02	0.02	0.01	0.01	0.01
2010	0.05	0.03	0.05	0.02	0.01	0.02	0.01	0.01	0.01
2011	0.04	0.08	0.05	0.01	0.03	0.02	0.01	0.02	0.01
2012	0.04	0.07	0.05	0.01	0.02	0.01	0.01	0.02	0.01
2013	0.05	0.02	0.04	0.01	0.01	0.01	0.01	0.01	0.01
2014	0.05	0.09	0.06	0.02	0.01	0.01	0.02	0.03	0.02
2015	0.07	0.06	0.07	0.02	0.02	0.02	0.02	0.02	0.02
2016	0.03	0.04	0.03	0.01	0.01	0.01	0.01	0.01	0.01

To sum up, over the past nine years, migrants have made considerable progress with regard to labour market performance and conditions. In particular, migrant earnings have increased significantly. Hours worked have not changed much, while social welfare coverage has increased, although it is still at a very low level. Relative to what migrants would have earned in their rural hometown, city jobs were as attractive in 2016 as they were in 2008. It does not appear therefore that economic outcomes or labour conditions have deteriorated in cities and therefore the reason for reduced migration inflows must be found elsewhere.

Earnings determination

This section examines wage determination for migrant workers. Are there changes here that might impact on changing levels of migrant inflows?

Table 21.3 reports results from estimated log real monthly earning equations separately for all workers, for male and female workers and for wage/salary earners and the self-employed. The data are combined for all years and the equation specifications and the estimated results are similar to those reported for other countries and groups of workers.

The first column of Table 21.3 presents results for all workers, showing that age at arrival, years since first migration and current job experience all affect earnings. The younger the migrant is at the time of first arrival in the city, all other things being equal, the more likely it is they will receive higher earnings when employed. The return to years since first migration is positive and about the same as the return to current job experience, but earnings increase at a declining rate.

The next five coefficients present returns to different education levels relative to the omitted category of 'illiterate'. Junior high school graduates receive 14 per cent more earnings on average and senior high school graduates, 22 per cent more. Males earn about 16 per cent more than females, on average, and the self-employed earn about 16 per cent more than wage/salary earners—conditional on the number of hours worked. Standardising on other things, however, the more hours an individual worked in a month, the lower are the earnings/net incomes. The regressions also control for city and year fixed effects and all are statistically significant. Our model explains about 31 per cent of the variation in log monthly real wages, which is quite high relative to other cross-sectional wage regressions.

Table 21.3 also presents wage equations for males and females. As is usual, the pattern of coefficients is similar for both genders, but the combination of slightly different coefficients and slightly different endowments predicts that males earn more than females and the gap continues to widen for 25 years. Interestingly, self-employed women earn 21 per cent more than their wage earner counterparts, while this differential for men is only 13 per cent.

Table 21.3 Selected results from log monthly real earnings regressions

		By gender		By employment status	
	Total	Males	Females	Wage/salary earners	Self-employed
Age at time of arrival	–0.0085***	–0.0091***	–0.0079***	–0.0067***	–0.0139***
	[0.0003]	[0.0003]	[0.0004]	[0.0002]	[0.0006]
Years since first migration	0.0213***	0.0289***	0.0113***	0.0214***	0.0056**
	[0.0010]	[0.0014]	[0.0015]	[0.0010]	[0.0025]
Years since first migration²	–0.0008***	–0.0010***	–0.0006***	–0.0008***	–0.0004***
	[0.0000]	[0.0000]	[0.0001]	[0.0000]	[0.0001]
Current job experience	0.0156***	0.0159***	0.0151***	0.0203***	0.0072***
	[0.0010]	[0.0014]	[0.0016]	[0.0010]	[0.0023]
Current job experience²	–0.0005***	–0.0004***	–0.0006***	–0.0005***	–0.0003***
	[0.0000]	[0.0001]	[0.0001]	[0.0000]	[0.0001]
Primary	0.0603***	0.0588**	0.0591***	0.0374**	0.0834***
	[0.0143]	[0.0266]	[0.0162]	[0.0158]	[0.0266]
Junior high	0.1392***	0.1410***	0.1372***	0.1165***	0.1566***
	[0.0138]	[0.0258]	[0.0157]	[0.0152]	[0.0258]

		By gender		By employment status	
	Total	Males	Females	Wage/salary earners	Self-employed
Senior high	0.2201***	0.2119***	0.2351***	0.1951***	0.2625***
	[0.0141]	[0.0260]	[0.0167]	[0.0154]	[0.0273]
Three-year college	0.3818***	0.4027***	0.3550***	0.3534***	0.4409***
	[0.0159]	[0.0279]	[0.0196]	[0.0167]	[0.0360]
University and above	0.5299***	0.5202***	0.5430***	0.5019***	0.5833***
	[0.0204]	[0.0325]	[0.0275]	[0.0198]	[0.0603]
Hours worked	–0.0003***	–0.0004***	–0.0001***	0.0000	–0.0006***
	[0.0000]	[0.0000]	[0.0000]	[0.0000]	[0.0001]
Dummy for males	0.1573***			0.1655***	0.1177***
	[0.0040]			[0.0039]	[0.0088]
Dummy for self-employed	0.1573***	0.1279***	0.2067***		
	[0.0051]	[0.0069]	[0.0076]		
Dummy for representative sample	–0.0025	–0.0040	–0.0004	–0.0049	–0.0033
	[0.0045]	[0.0063]	[0.0065]	[0.0044]	[0.0107]
City fixed effects	Yes	Yes	Yes	Yes	Yes
Year fixed effects	Yes	Yes	Yes	Yes	Yes
Observations	61,334	35,068	26,266	41,102	20,232
R^2	0.31	0.28	0.34	0.44	0.19

*** $p<0.01$, ** $p<0.05$, * $p<0.1$

The pattern of coefficients for wage earners and the self-employed is also similar, but where there are differences they are larger than in the male–female comparison, especially in terms of the impact of labour market experience. Labour market experience delivers a significant positive return to wage and salary earners, but for the self-employed there is virtually no return on how long they stay in one job or how long they stay in the city.

We fitted separate earnings equations to each year to see whether there are any significant changes in wage determination patterns that might explain changing migration inflows (Table 21.4). There are some detectable changes through time, particularly between the returns on years of experience in the city, which seem to have increased, and the returns on years of experience in the current job, which seem to have declined. But we cannot find any strong patterns to explain why inflows to cities should fall or outflows increase.

Table 21.4 Earnings regressions for wage earners, 2008–16

	2008	2009	2010	2011	2012	2013	2014	2015	2016
Age at arrival	–0.0033***	–0.0063***	–0.0060***	–0.0076***	–0.0076***	–0.0069***	–0.0075***	–0.0087***	–0.0081***
	[0.0007]	[0.0007]	[0.0007]	[0.0007]	[0.0007]	[0.0009]	[0.0007]	[0.0009]	[0.0007]
Years since first migration	0.0226***	0.0162***	0.0154***	0.0129***	0.0294***	0.0173***	0.0259***	0.0244***	0.0300***
	[0.0030]	[0.0030]	[0.0031]	[0.0031]	[0.0029]	[0.0036]	[0.0029]	[0.0034]	[0.0026]
Years since first migration^2	–0.0008***	–0.0007***	–0.0006***	–0.0006***	–0.0010***	–0.0006***	–0.0010***	–0.0009***	–0.0010***
	[0.0001]	[0.0001]	[0.0001]	[0.0001]	[0.0001]	[0.0001]	[0.0001]	[0.0001]	[0.0001]
Current job experience	0.0313***	0.0341***	0.0328***	0.0171***	0.0117***	0.0207***	0.0133***	0.0140***	0.0121***
	[0.0034]	[0.0030]	[0.0033]	[0.0032]	[0.0029]	[0.0036]	[0.0029]	[0.0033]	[0.0025]
Current job experience^2	–0.0008***	–0.0008***	–0.0008***	–0.0004***	–0.0002	–0.0005***	–0.0001	–0.0003*	–0.0002**
	[0.0002]	[0.0001]	[0.0001]	[0.0001]	[0.0001]	[0.0002]	[0.0001]	[0.0001]	[0.0001]
Primary	0.0486	0.0129	-0.0661	-0.0042	0.0598	0.077	0.0986*	0.0403	0.0805*
	[0.0499]	[0.0401]	[0.0403]	[0.0483]	[0.0440]	[0.0549]	[0.0513]	[0.0537]	[0.0456]
Junior high	0.1123**	0.1026***	0.0242	0.0632	0.1313***	0.1514***	0.1980***	0.1213**	0.1457***
	[0.0485]	[0.0382]	[0.0381]	[0.0468]	[0.0419]	[0.0534]	[0.0500]	[0.0519]	[0.0440]
Senior high	0.2118***	0.1812***	0.0886**	0.1301***	0.2186***	0.2257***	0.2762***	0.1770***	0.2500***
	[0.0492]	[0.0388]	[0.0388]	[0.0475]	[0.0426]	[0.0542]	[0.0507]	[0.0528]	[0.0448]
Three-year college	0.3519***	0.3452***	0.2654***	0.2337***	0.4073***	0.3887***	0.4110***	0.3329***	0.4441***
	[0.0545]	[0.0433]	[0.0435]	[0.0512]	[0.0464]	[0.0579]	[0.0537]	[0.0562]	[0.0473]
University and above	0.5765***	0.4807***	0.3725***	0.3696***	0.4744***	0.5524***	0.6176***	0.5529***	0.5482***
	[0.0775]	[0.0635]	[0.0593]	[0.0613]	[0.0563]	[0.0658]	[0.0592]	[0.0630]	[0.0525]
Dummy for males	0.1547***	0.1846***	0.1822***	0.1934***	0.1612***	0.1515***	0.1552***	0.1348***	0.1570***
	[0.0107]	[0.0108]	[0.0111]	[0.0111]	[0.0111]	[0.0140]	[0.0119]	[0.0139]	[0.0110]

	2008	2009	2010	2011	2012	2013	2014	2015	2016
Dummy for representative sample		–0.0164	0.0207**	–0.0147	0.0036	0.0055	–0.0289**	–0.0367**	–0.0061
		[0.0115]	[0.0096]	[0.0115]	[0.0120]	[0.0156]	[0.0127]	[0.0148]	[0.0123]
Observations	4,969	4,874	4,849	4,917	4,651	4,130	3,984	4,359	4,352
R^2	0.31	0.33	0.30	0.26	0.26	0.20	0.27	0.22	0.32

*** p<0.01, ** p<0.05, * p<0.1

Table 21.5 Distribution of sector of employment, 2008–16

			Trades and services			
	Manufacturing	Other secondary industry	Total	Lower-end	Higher-end	Missing
	(1)	(2)	(3)	(4)	(5)	(6)
2008	23.85	16.33	58.86	52.60	6.26	0.97
2009	23.54	13.56	61.83	55.13	6.70	1.06
2010	22.14	13.34	63.16	55.30	7.86	1.36
2011	20.34	11.50	63.40	55.01	8.39	4.75
2012	21.59	12.53	63.95	54.77	9.18	1.93
2013	20.88	11.76	65.59	55.10	10.49	1.77
2014	20.04	10.26	68.61	59.63	8.98	1.08
2015	21.85	11.14	66.20	55.33	10.87	0.80
2016	22.42	9.65	66.98	52.94	14.04	0.94

There is, however, a shifting industry pattern of employed migrants, but not as much as might be expected in an economy that is changing so quickly. The share of total migrant labour employed in manufacturing has changed little. The large change is between the decline in construction (16.33 per cent to 9.65 per cent) and the increase in trades and services (58.86 per cent to 66.98 per cent) (see Table 21.5). The employment gains in the trades and services industry are in higher-end services, such as computer and internet services, financial market services, real estate, tourism, media and so on.

Figure 21.11 presents the returns to each level of education over the nine years. In general, education returns declined until 2010, but have now returned to 2008 levels.

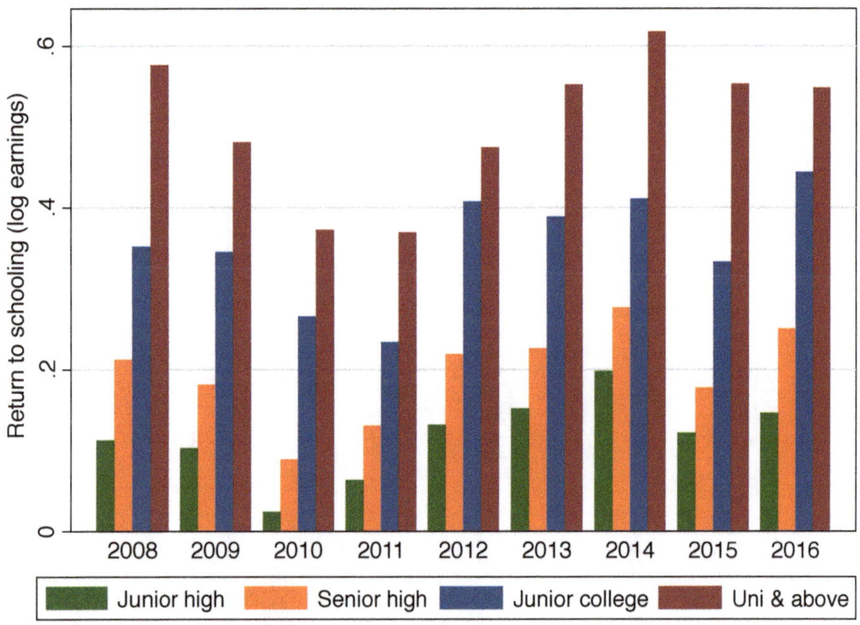

Figure 21.11 Returns to different levels of education, 2008–16

Source: Authors' own calculation from RUMiC data.

To sum up, there is evidence to suggest there was a structural change between 2010 and 2011 that may have impacted, at least for a while, on experience–earnings profiles and returns to education and, more permanently, on the industry sector of employment.

It is to be expected that the changing mix of jobs in cities will affect the demand for migrant workers, so it would be worthwhile examining this link in more detail. If, however, the changing mix of jobs reduced migration flows so dramatically, it is reasonable to think some evidence of this would be found in a large change in average wage relativities between the home village and the city, but on the basis of our evidence this appears not to be the case.

Wage variation across cities

One potential way to make progress in understanding the relationship between migrant flows and migrant outcomes is to analyse different outcomes across cities and ask why there is such a large variation in migrant earnings between cities and whether this variation has narrowed in response to migration. Do migrants move disproportionately to cities where earnings are highest? These questions are obviously related to the overarching question posed at the beginning of this chapter, which compared city wages with home village wages and asked whether these gaps can be related to changes in net migration to large cities.

In Figure 21.12, we present the earnings variation across our 15 survey cities. There are eight coastal cities (Guangzhou, Shenzhen, Dongguan, Shanghai, Nanjing, Wuxi, Hangzhou and Ningbo) and seven inland cities (Zhengzhou, Luoyang, Hefei, Bengbu, Chongqing, Chengdu and Wuhan). The cross-city earnings variation is calculated after allowing for the different characteristics of migrants in each city. This is done by including city dummy variables in the earnings equations described earlier, with Guangzhou used as the omitted category. Thus, each city's position is relative to Guangzhou. For example, real monthly earnings in Hefei in 2008—standardising for all personal migrant characteristics included in the regression for each city—were about 18 per cent below Guangzhou's real monthly earnings.

The data indicate there are large average earnings gaps for migrant workers in different cities, even after standardising for individual personal observable characteristics. The gap across these cities has not narrowed significantly over the past nine years. In 2008, the standard deviation of the city coefficients was about 0.19, while in 2016 it was 0.17. Between the top and bottom earning cities, the earnings gap in 2008 was 0.63 log points, and in 2016 it was 0.58 points.[5]

Figure 21.12 indicates that coastal cities have the highest incomes and inland cities the lowest, and the gap between the two does not seem to have narrowed. In general, cities also maintained their relative positions: Shenzhen and Shanghai maintained their higher incomes and Luoyang and Wuhan remained among the lower income group.

If migration flows are responsive to city wages, they will respond to real wages—that is, wages paid in the city need to be adjusted for city living costs. There are city-level consumer price index (CPI) changes available for each city to adjust for price changes over time, but no official special price indices with which to compare the cost-of-living differentials between cities. Urban economists, therefore, often turn to housing prices as a proxy to measure differing living costs. In addition, other costs

5 For inland cities, however, the variation has been reducing more significantly. In 2008, the gap between the top city (Hefei) and the bottom city (Luoyang) was almost 35 per cent. By 2016, the gap between the top-earning city (Wuhan) and the bottom earner (Luoyang) was only 16 per cent.

may generally be higher in large cities and rent levels do not adequately capture their effect. For example, the larger the city, the higher are the travel costs (both monetary and time) and these may not relate closely to average rent levels.

To explain migration flows, we should also consider the cost of travelling between the home village and the city. Long-distance migration may provide larger monetary gains on arrival, but may involve higher monetary and psychological costs of travel to the city, which may discourage many from migrating to higher-wage regions.

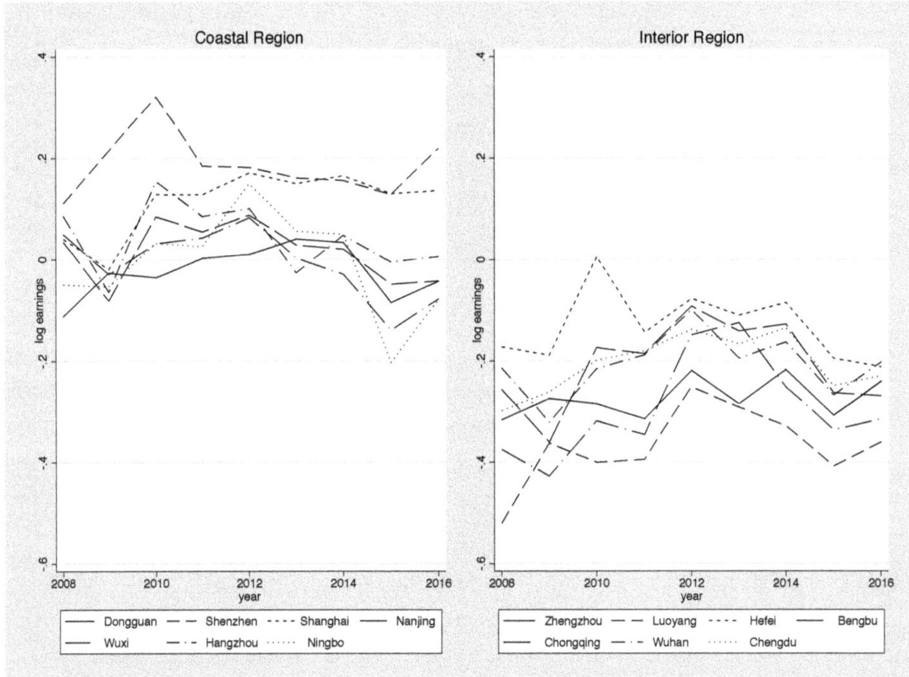

Figure 21.12 City earnings premium relative to Guangzhou, by coastal and inland regions, 2008–16

Source: Authors' own calculation from RUMiC data.

To gauge the extent to which differing living and mobility costs can explain wage variation across cities, we estimate city-level regressions using the city dummy variable coefficients extracted from estimating migrant earnings equations year by year as the dependent variable (i.e. the coefficients presented in Figure 21.12). We use annual city-level average rent paid by our sample migrants to measure the cost of rent, and use the population size of each city as a proxy for travel and other costs within the city. To explore the relationships between variations of costs of travel to the city and wages, we include in the regressions the proportion of migrants in each city from within the same province. We also include the number of provinces sending to a particular city, excluding the province in which the city is located (the larger the number of sending provinces, the higher is the level of mobility).

It is also possible that city-level wage variations follow government policy guidance. For example, cities where the local government wishes to push out low-profit, labour-intensive firms may set higher minimum wages. We use a direct measure of city-level minimum wages to capture this effect.

Finally, we also use city-level macroeconomic conditions to explain cross-city wage variations. These variables include log per capita gross domestic product (GDP), log per capita exports, the share of migrant workers employed in the manufacturing sector, the share of migrants working in the services sector, together with the city's secondary industry share in total GDP. Theoretically, if there is perfect labour mobility, city-level macroeconomic conditions should have little to do with city-level wage differentials.

We estimate the regression equation with one variable at a time to indicate associations with cross-city wage levels, and then include all variables in one regression (Table 21.6).

Column 1 in Table 21.6 includes only year dummy variables. Inspection of Figure 21.12 suggests there are no obvious important year-by-year variations of city wage effects and this is confirmed by the low r-squared of 1.3 per cent. The rest of the regressions, however, will control for these year dummy variables.

The next two columns (Columns 2 and 3) show the correlation between city wage variations and the log of city average rent and log of city population. Both variables exert a positive and statistically significant effect. The rent variable alone explains an additional 26.4 per cent of city-level wage variation. The log population explains 4 per cent.

The regression results in Columns 4 and 5 of Table 21.6 indicate that cities with a higher proportion of migrants from within their own province have lower wages, whereas cities with migrants from a larger number of sending provinces have higher wages (54 per cent and 63 per cent of wage variations are associated with variations in the percentage of migrants from the city's own province and the number of provinces that have sent migrants to the city, respectively). These results suggest migrants are responding to wage signals. High-income cities are attracting migrants from many outside provinces, whereas low-income cities have only migrants from nearby areas (higher intra-province migration).

Column 6 indicates that minimum wages set by local governments are also positively associated with wage variations across cities, explaining 55 per cent of these variations.

The variable that explains most wage variation (78 per cent) is log per capita exports (Column 7). Cities that export more per capita have higher migrant earnings. Log per capita GDP is important to a similar degree—associated with 60 per cent of the wage variations across cities. A city's industrial structure is also associated with wage variations, though to a much lower extent. The secondary industry share of city GDP within cities is negatively associated with city wages. The share of migrant workers in the manufacturing sector is positively associated while the share of service workers is negatively associated with city wages.

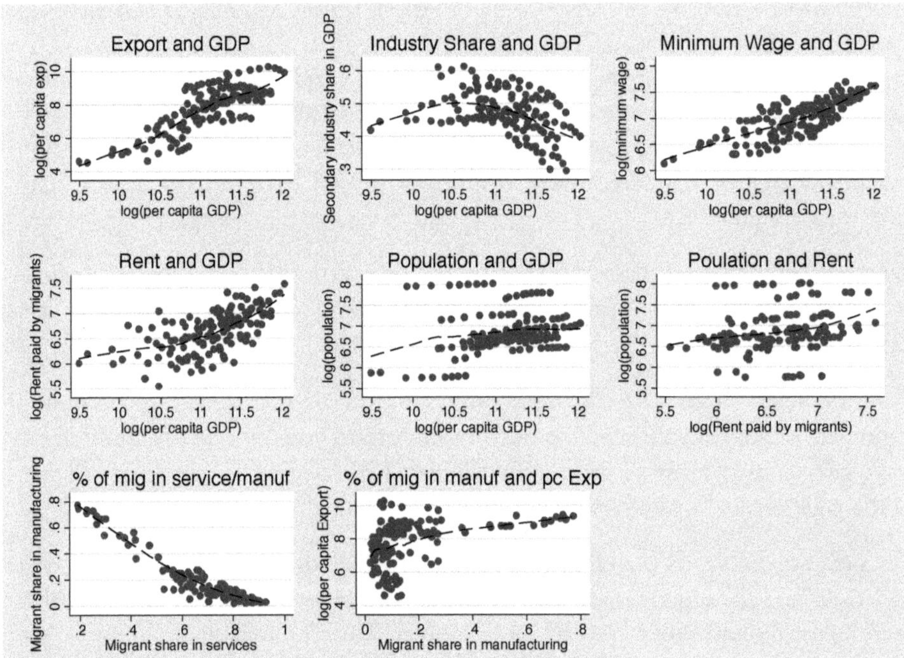

Figure 21.13 Correlations between city-level variables

Source: Authors' own calculation from RUMiC data.

It is important to understand that these regressions only examine the association between variables and do not estimate causal links between these variables and city-level wage variations. In addition, many right-hand side variables are highly correlated with each other; city per capita exports are highly correlated with city per capita GDP, as is city average rent paid by migrants and city population, and so on. Figure 21.13 presents these interrelationships. With so many multi-collinearities, it is not surprising that when all variables are included many coefficients switch sign and become statistically insignificant (Column 11 of Table 21.6). The dominant variables that remain statistically significant are per capita exports, rent paid by migrants, minimum wages, industry share of GDP, number of sending provinces for each city and migrant share in manufacturing or services. We keep these variables in the last column of Table 21.6.[6] The total variations in city wages that can be 'explained' by the association with these variables is 85 per cent, which is quite high. How, then, should we decide which of these factors dominates?

6 Due to high correlation between the migrant share in manufacturing and services, only one is included in the last column regression.

Following Dickens and Katz (1987), we derive a bounded range for the contribution of these variables. The lower bound is observed by examining the increase in explained variation by adding a particular variable of interest, whereas the upper bound is evaluated by using the variable of interest only in the regression. In our case, we use results in Columns 2–10 as the indication for the upper bound and obtain the lower bound for each variable by taking each variable or group of variables out of the regressions from Columns 11 and 12 to evaluate the difference each variable(s) made to the total adjusted r-squared. The lower bound contribution of the variables is listed in the two last rows of Table 21.6. This exercise shows the most important variable contributing to the variation in city residual wages is log per capita exports. The rest of the variables, despite their statistical significance, have trivial effects in explaining city wage variations.

To summarise the above descriptive analysis, the following points are important. First, although living costs can explain some of the cross-city residual wage variations, the power of explanation is rather small. Second, the signs of the correlation between city wage variation and that of the migrants' sending region composition seem to suggest that migrants are responsive to wage signals and the higher the wage, the higher is the proportion of migrants from afar. Third, despite the current level of mobility, which is quite high, wage variation across cities is still most strongly correlated with city macroeconomic variables—in particular, the per capita export level. These macroeconomic variables, to a large extent, capture city variations in productivity.

This last point leads us to conclude that although the current level of labour mobility is high, it is not high enough to eliminate the main part of cross-city wage variations. In fact, if only the cost of living variables are included (rent and population size), only 26 per cent of the cross-city residual wage variation can be explained.

Why are cross-city productivities so important? Why hasn't migration largely removed these macro effects? There could be two reasons for this. The first is that considerable policy-induced mobility restrictions remain, which stop more migrants from moving to higher-earnings cities and reduce relative wages. The second reason is that there are unobservable psychological costs of migration, which are much higher for those moving to higher-earnings cities than those moving to lower-earnings cities. Based on our current data, however, it is unlikely we can separately identify these two causes. In any case, the current policy—which encourages migrants to move to small hometown cities rather than large, more productive cities—should be part of the 'policy restrictions' we have in mind.

Table 21.6 City-level regressions

	(1)	(2)	(3)	(4)	(5)	(6)	(7)	(8)	(9)	(10)	(11)	(12)
	Year only	Rent	Population	Percentage of migrants within province	Number of source provinces	Minimum wage	Per capita exports	Per capita GDP	Industry share (services)	Industry share (manuf.)		
log(rent)		0.286***									0.098**	0.114***
		[0.043]									[0.037]	[0.034]
Log(popu)			0.070**								–0.013	
			[0.029]								[0.015]	
Percentage within province				–0.369***							0.007	
				[0.031]							[0.035]	
Number of source provinces					0.030***						0.005*	0.007***
					[0.002]						[0.003]	[0.003]
log(min_wage)						0.709***					0.164***	0.111**
						[0.058]					[0.059]	[0.056]
log(export_pc)							0.106***				0.059***	0.062***
							[0.005]				[0.010]	[0.009]
log(gdp_pc)								0.313***			0.020	
								[0.023]			[0.031]	
Secondary industry share									–1.524***	–1.477***	–0.368*	–0.128
									[0.234]	[0.237]	[0.210]	[0.155]
Percentage of migrants in service industry									–0.378***		–0.422***	
									[0.074]		[0.121]	

	(1)	(2)	(3)	(4)	(5)	(6)	(7)	(8)	(9)	(10)	(11)	(12)
	Year only	Rent	Population	Percentage of migrants within province	Number of source provinces	Minimum wage	Per capita exports	Per capita GDP	Industry share (services)	Industry share (manuf.)		
Percentage of migrants in manufacturing										0.326***	–0.267**	0.116**
										[0.070]	[0.110]	[0.051]
Year fixed effects	Yes	Yes	Yes	Yes	Yes	Yes	Yes	Yes	Yes	Yes	Yes	Yes
Observations	126	126	126	126	126	126	125	126	126	126	125	125
Adjusted R^2	0.0135	0.278	0.0531	0.549	0.621	0.562	0.787	0.614	0.337	0.315	0.864	0.852
Lower bound (11)		0.007	–0.001	–0.002	0.002	0.008	0.034	–0.001	0.014	0.006		
Lower bound (12)		0.013			0.009	0.004	0.054			0.006		

*** $p<0.01$, ** $p<0.05$, * $p<0.1$

Conclusions

The most important labour reallocation change in China is the slowing growth rate of rural *hukou* workers moving to large cities and the significant increase in rural *hukou* workers staying in their hometown to work in nonagricultural jobs. This redirection of labour reallocation does not appear to be a response to a narrowing of the earnings gap between the city and the rural hometown. In fact, the gap between migrant earnings in cities and what they would have earned had they stayed in their rural hometown to work in the nonagricultural sector in 2016 is almost as large as it was in 2008.

Furthermore, we find no evidence of increasing migrant dissatisfaction with life in the city. The proportion of migrants who are happy or very happy is much the same throughout the period. The proportion of migrants who would like to live in the city permanently is also unchanging. These facts lead us to conjecture that the large reduction in rural-to-urban migrants is primarily related to government policy. The economic return from allowing people to move to the city remains high, at least in terms of the wages they can earn.

Among rural-to-urban migrants over the past nine years there have been some large changes in age and gender composition in directions that might be anticipated when migrant inflows slow. It is to be expected that the migrant workforce would age. In 2008, only 23 per cent of men and 19 per cent of women in the workforce were aged 40 and above. By 2016, these ratios increased to 42 per cent for men and 45 per cent for women. Furthermore, a larger proportion of the older labour force comprises women who do not appear to be newcomers as they have been in their current job for more than five years.

As the inflow of new migrants has slowed, and the migrant workers have aged, it is to be expected that increases in the migrant stock's education would slow. The younger migrant generation is slightly better educated, but the increasing proportion of older migrant workers has low education levels, especially older women. Education improvement is slow. The average education level (measured in years of schooling) over the nine years has increased by less than 0.3 years.

The number of hours worked for both wage earners and the self-employed has not changed much despite the introduction of the New Labour Law, which stipulates that standard work hours should be no more than eight hours daily and no more than 40 hours a week. Work hours far exceed these standards. Wage earners, on average, worked 250 hours monthly and the self-employed worked 330 hours.

Real hourly earnings growth for migrant wage earners continues to grow strongly, although the growth has moderated since 2013, while the self-employed are doing better since 2013 in terms of hourly income. There is, however, no obvious link between these changes and reduced migration inflows.

So what might we expect looking forward? It seems fairly clear that the migration patterns of the post-GFC period will continue, partly because of the changing balance between export markets and internally stimulated growth, but mainly because it appears the slowdown in migration to large cities is primarily the result of policy. We cannot find significant evidence to suggest that the economic incentives for migrants to move to the large cities or their desire to stay in the large cities have declined. Rising agricultural productivity will continue to produce surplus farm labour that needs to find alternative jobs, but these other jobs will be located closer to home since the small city development strategy seems firmly in place.

References

Dickens, W. T. and Katz, L. F. (1987), Inter-industry wage differences and industry characteristics, in K. Lang and J. S. Leonard (eds), *Unemployment and the Structure of Labor Markets*, Oxford: Basil Blackwell.

Glaeser, E. L. and Gottlieb, J. D. (2008), The economics of place-making policies, *Brookings Papers on Economic Activity* (1): 155–253. doi.org/10.1353/eca.0.0005.

Glaeser, E. L. and Gottlieb, J. D. (2009), The wealth of cities: Agglomeration economies and spatial equilibrium in the United States, *Journal of Economic Literature* 47(4): 983–1028. doi.org/10.1257/jel.47.4.983.

Meng, X. (2013), Rural–urban migration, in R. Garnaut, C. Fang and L. Song (eds), *China: A new model for growth and development*, Canberra: ANU E Press. doi.org/10.22459/CNMGD.07.2013.09.

Meng, X. (2014), China's labour market tensions and future urbanisation challenges, in R. Garnaut, C. Fang and L. Song (eds), *Deepening Reform for China's Long-Term Growth and Development*, Canberra: ANU Press. doi.org/10.22459/DRCLTGD.07.2014.15.

Meng, X. (2017), The Labor Contract Law, macro conditions, self-selection, and labor market outcomes for migrants in China, *Asian Economic Policy Review* 12(1).

Moretti, E. (2011), Local labor markets, *Handbook of Labor Economics* 4: 1237–313. doi.org/10.1016/S0169-7218(11)02412-9.

National Bureau of Statistics (NBS) (various years [a]), *China Yearbook of Household Survey*, Beijing: China Statistics Press.

National Bureau of Statistics (NBS) (various years [b]), *China Rural Household Survey Yearbook*, Beijing: China Statistics Press.

National People's Congress (NPC) (2007), Labour Contract Law of the People's Republic of China, Beijing: NPC. Available from: english.mofcom.gov.cn/aarticle/policyrelease/internationalpolicy/200703/20070304475283.html.

State Council (2014), National New Urbanization Plan (2014–2020), *Xinhua News Agency*, 16 March. Available from: politics.people.com.cn/n/2014/0317/c1001-24649809.html.

World Bank (2009), *China—From Poor Areas to Poor People: China's Evolving Poverty Reduction Agenda, An Assessment of Poverty and Inequality*. World Bank. Available from: documents.worldbank.org/curated/en/816851468219918783/China-From-poor-areas-to-poor-people-Chinas-evolving-poverty-reduction-agenda-an-assessment-of-poverty-and-inequality.

22. The structure of and changes to China's land system

Shouying Liu

Institutional arrangements for landownership are fundamental to China's political and economic system. Landownership is a key and sensitive area of China's overall reform. China's unique land institutions and changes to them are central to the country's rapid economic growth and structural change.

Reform of the rural land system in the early 1980s marked the beginning of China's reform and opening-up, promoting its rural transformation and economic transition. Changes to the urban land system since the late 1990s have promoted China's historic shift from a rural country to an urban–rural society.

This chapter has five parts. The first briefly introduces the structural characteristics of China's land institutional arrangements. The second analyses the process of reform of the land system in the past 40 years and its path of change. The third discusses the historical contribution made by land institutional changes to China's rapid economic growth and structural change. The fourth gives a schedule of further land reform in the new development stage, while the final section concludes by providing some policy implications.

The structure of China's land institutions

The Chinese land system is a complete institutional structure, covering arrangements for farmland, land conversion and urban land use.

Farmland household contract system under collective ownership

Rural contracted land covers the largest share of total land and involves the largest proportion of the population. At the end of 2015, China had a total of 645.5 million hectares of agricultural land, 135 million hectares of which were farmland (Ministry of Land and Resources 2016). A total of 134.2 million hectares—accounting for 99.4 per cent of total farmland—were contracted to 23 million households (Qu 2015). The rural contracted land system was seen as a basic arrangement influencing agricultural performance, farmers' rights and social stability.

China's rural land system is unusual in the world and has thoroughly changed the countryside. In traditional rural China, farm households privately owned land, farming was undertaken mainly by self-employed family units and tenant farmers were the main operators of small farms. The ownership and management rights to the farmland were protected by law and contracts, while the cultivation rights, to a large extent, had the de facto attributions and functions of ownership (Fei and Liu 2007).

After the Communist Party of China (CPC) came to power, it installed socialism based on public ownership, promoting China's transition from a rural to an industrial economy (Mao 1991). For this purpose, the new regime created a series of state-led systems in rural areas (Du 2005), forming a unique collective rural landownership system, which had the following characteristics:

1. As a form of public ownership in rural areas, collective ownership was applied to rural land and the state implemented comprehensive political and economic control over rural areas through people's communes, production brigades and production teams.
2. The state exercised collective land property rights. Senior officials controlled the land use rights in production teams. Production teams were not entitled to select the land to be planted, and the right to revenue was truncated due to procurement by the state. Public investment and distribution to production team members were conditioned by the requirement to first complete tasks assigned by the state.
3. Agricultural economic activities and labour were arranged in a unified way by the production team, and production results were distributed in a uniform way based on work points (Zhou 1995).

The change in the political climate and recognition of the inefficiency of state-controlled collective ownership and unified operations saw China launch rural land reform in the late 1970s and early 1980s. Through grassroots innovations, official support and policy implementation (Rural Development Group 1984), a new rural land system acceptable to the relevant agents was formed. Rural land was to be owned by collectives and contracted to village households. The premise of the reform was collective landownership under a socialist system. At this point, the state produced numerous documents to declare collective ownership unchanged. First, land contracted to each household did not equate to private ownership (CPC Central Committee 1982). The collective ownership framework followed 'three levels of ownership, with the production team as the basic unit'. The relationship between peasants and the land was defined as a contractual one. Under collective ownership, rural land could not be bought or sold. Second, contracts were formed between the state, collectives and households. The initial contract arrangement was tacitly selected by farmers—something later regarded as a tripartite contract. The contract was meant to ensure the farm household was contributing adequately to the state, paying enough to the collectives and retaining any remaining production. After fulfilment of their national tasks and collective obligations, farmers could retain the residual claim of the collective land. Third, collective ownership was explicitly defined as ownership by all members, which differed from the 'commune members' in the collective farming period. Whereas commune members were provided with a certain income, the 'collective members' under the household responsibility system (HRS) could enjoy rights to all income from products grown on collective land. Collective ownership after the reform strengthened the identity of collective membership. Fourth, the clarification of property rights in the contracting of farmers on agricultural land separated collective ownership from the right of use, creating a real contracting right, strengthening the dominant position of farmers, improving farmers' right to use the contracted land and granting them rights to revenue and transfers. Fifth, as a result of the elimination of the farming system under which production teams organised production and distributed revenue, families replaced the production teams as the unit of agricultural production and in economic decision-making and income allocation. Farming households then became the operating entity of agricultural management. This was institutionalised by law.

Land conversion arrangements under dual ownership

In the past 40 years, China's high-speed economic growth has been accompanied by rapid industrialisation and urbanisation. From 2003 to 2015, 11.6 million hectares (Ministry of Land and Resources 2004, 2016) of agricultural land were converted to nonagricultural rural and urban construction land. The change of ownership was achieved both by conversion by the collective and by expropriation by the government.

From the beginning of rural reform until the revision of the Land Administration Law in 1998, the channel for the conversion of agricultural to collective construction land was open. In the early 1980s, a large number of surplus workers were released by agricultural reforms and the government encouraged farmers to use collective land to set up township and village enterprises (TVEs). As a result, the amount of rural construction land increased rapidly. Land utilised by TVEs in China was estimated to be 15,700 hectares in 1978 and about 56,300 hectares in 1985. From 1981 to 1985, an average of more than 600 million sq m per annum was used for new farmers' residences.

Until 1987, when the Land Administration Law was first implemented, there were three channels for converting rural land to nonagricultural construction land. First, as long as the construction conformed to the construction plan of the township (or village) and the county government's approval was obtained, rural residential construction, TVE construction, township (village) public facilities, public welfare construction and other township (village) construction could be carried out. Second, in the event that a collective agricultural economic organisation needed land to organise joint ventures with enterprises owned by the people, or collectively owned enterprises, it was allowed to requisition the land in accordance with the provisions of the state construction requisitions. The agricultural collective economic organisation could also, according to the contract, use the land use rights as its contribution to joint management. Third, residents with nonagricultural household registration (*hukou*) could use the collectively owned land for residential construction, with approval from the county government (Liu 2008a).

Land requisition was the main tool for conversion of agricultural land to nonagricultural use. In particular, after the channel for the conversion of collective construction land was closed, expropriation was the only legal path for land conversion. China's 1982 constitution backed the principles in the 1954 constitution in which the state may, in the interests of the public, conduct land requisition; however, it also put forward for the first time the idea that urban land would be owned by the state while collectives would own rural land. This established a dual landownership system.[1] The Land Administration Law promulgated in 1987 required that land conversion be based on the public interest. The definition of public interest was broad: the state could conduct land requisition for economic, cultural, national defence and social and public undertakings. Compensation was based on the principle of original use. The levels of compensation and resettlement subsidies were raised to no more than 20 times the average annual output of the three years prior to the requisition of the land. Employment and *hukou* status were provided to the peasants whose land was taken.[2]

Urban land use under state ownership

Before reform, China implemented a system of free and indefinite access to land. The Land Administration Law of 1987 stipulated two types of land use modes: administrative allocation and paid transfer. The institutions governing urban land use after conversion to state ownership not only provided land security for the rapid advancement of industrialisation and urbanisation, but also were an important source of capital for urban construction.

1 Refer to the *Constitution of the People's Republic of China*, adopted at the Fifth Session of the Fifth National People's Congress, 4 December 1982.

2 Refer to the *Law of the People's Republic of China on Land Administration*, Adopted at the Sixteenth Session of the Standing Committee of the Sixth National People's Congress, 25 June 1986.

Land institutional change in the reform era

Strengthening farmers' property rights

Legally clarifying collective ownership

China's Rural Land Contract Law and Property Law defined collective ownership as 'land collectively owned by peasants in rural areas that is fundamental to the basic rural operation system'[3] and 'the collective owner of collective land, in accordance with the law, is entitled to possess, utilize, dispose and obtain profits from the collective land'.[4] The 'peasant collective', as the subject of landownership, had three levels: the village peasant collective, the intravillage peasant collective and the township peasant collective (Wang and Zhou 2012).

Improving farmers' property rights for contracted land

Land contract rights are a special type of property usage right, and contracted land is the farmer's property (Liu 2002). Legislation clearly states that contracting farmers are entitled, in accordance with the relevant law, to use and obtain profits from the contracted land, to transfer the land contract rights and to organise production, operation and disposal of products. If contracted land is expropriated by law, the contractor has the right to receive appropriate compensation.[5] During the contract period, the collective cannot recover or adjust the contracted land so as to continuously extend the right to subcontract.[6] To restrict any infringement of farmers' land property rights, it is expressly stipulated that within the statutory period of the contract, no organisation or individual shall interfere in farmers' production and management autonomy, the contracted land shall not be unlawfully adjusted or claimed, the wishes of farmers shall not be contravened by forcing the transferral of the contracted land and farmers shall be protected from illegal encroachment on contracted land (State Council 2004).

Extending the land contract period for farmers

The initial land contract period of 15 years in 1984 (CPC Central Committee 1984) was extended to 30 years for the second contract period (CPC Central Committee 1993). The third plenary session of the fifteenth Central Committee of the CPC held in 1998 granted farmers long-term and guaranteed land use rights (CPC Central Committee 1998). During the third plenary session of the

3 Refer to the *Law of the People's Republic of China on Land Contracts in Rural Areas*, Adopted at the Twenty-Ninth Session of the Standing Committee of the Ninth National People's Congress, 29 August 2002.

4 ibid.

5 ibid.

6 ibid., s. 26.

seventeenth Central Committee, a proposal was made that contracting farmers' land rights could not be changed for a long time (CPC Central Committee 2008). The third plenary session of the eighteenth Central Committee reaffirmed this provision (CPC Central Committee 2013).

Redefining membership rights of collective ownership

The Central Rural Policy Research Office conducted a pilot experiment in Meitan county, Guizhou province, in the late 1980s, in which neither an increase nor a reduction in family members led to an increase or reduction in the land for that family. In 2002, the pilot results were written into the Rural Land Contract Law, which clearly says that the state will protect the long-term stability of the rural land contract and that within the contract period, the collective will not adjust the contracted land.

Changing the contract conditions

The government's obligations in relation to farmland were changed gradually. First, the amount of grain to be provided to the state by farmers was reduced. Initially, farmers were entitled to plant freely beyond their quota and to exchange food for currency. This reduced the linking of farmers' land to grain quotas. Second, the central government implemented grain marketing system reform, with the state buying grain in a market-oriented way. Grain quotas were terminated and the state provided farmers with grain subsidies. Collective obligations changed. In the 1990s, farmers had to contribute to a collective accumulation fund and a public welfare fund. The assessment burdens on contracting farmers were overwhelming. Subsequently, the 'one act, one discussion' method was adopted.[7] The farmer's obligation was not linked to the contracted land. Changes in state and collective obligations amplified the residual claim of farmers' land rights (Zhou and Liu 1997).

The family farming system as a constitutionally approved system

In 1991, the Chinese Government proposed that, for the first time:

> [T]he two-tier management system based on household contract management that combines unification and separation shall be stabilized in the long term, and constantly enriched and perfected as a basic system of the Chinese rural collective economic organization. (CPC Central Committee 2008)

7 An example of this is when a village decides to provide any item of public goods, each decision is made after a village consultation.

The Chinese constitution of 1999 explicitly states that 'rural collective economic organizations [must] implement the two-tier management system based on household contract management and combining unification and separation'. The Law on the Contracting of Rural Land in 2002 formally proposed the national implementation of the rural land contract management system. In 2008, the third plenary session of the seventeenth Central Committee of the CPC announced:

> [T]he two-tier management system based on household contract management combining unification and separation is suitable for the Socialist market economy, which is in line with the characteristics of the basic rural management system for agricultural production, constitutes the cornerstone of the party's rural policies, and must be unwaveringly adhered to. (CPC Central Committee 2008)

Local government monopolises land conversion

Since 1992, China has changed its policy on land conversion to cover collective construction activities. Rural land has to go through requisition and transfer as state-owned land when it is to be used for construction (CPC Central Committee 1992). The revised Land Administration Law, promulgated in 1998, legally restricted the conversion of agricultural land into collective nonagricultural construction land, excluding farmers from using collective land for nonagricultural construction, except for the

> use of land collectively owned by peasants of the collective economic organization approved in accordance with the law for the establishment of township and village enterprises and construction of residences by villagers, or use of land collectively owned by peasants approved in accordance with the law for the construction of village (township) public facilities.[8]

The law stipulated that 'the right to use of land collectively owned by peasants shall not be transferred, retransferred or leased for non-agricultural construction', and it retained the provision that 'rural collective economic organizations may jointly organize enterprises with other units and individuals in the form of equity participation of land use rights and joint operations'.[9]

The law followed the principle of land requisition for public use, the structure of urban and rural dual ownership and the original-use–based compensation principle, but the limit on land compensation and resettlement subsidies was raised to no more than 30 times the land's average annual output for the three years prior to the requisition of the land. This law also made two provisions that had a significant

8 Refer to the *Law of the People's Republic of China on Land Administration*, Revised and Adopted at the Fourth Session of the Standing Committee of the Ninth National People's Congress of the People's Republic of China, 29 August 1998.

9 ibid.

impact on land conversion, the first of which was the establishment of the 'land use control system', through which the government formulates a general plan for land use, stipulates use for land, controls the total amount of land used for construction and examines and approves annual quotas of construction land.[10] Second, if any unit or individual wishes to use land for construction, they must apply for the use of state-owned land in accordance with the law.[11]

China's problems with land requisition became more and more serious as the process of industrialisation and urbanisation accelerated. The Ministry of Land and Resources began a pilot reform of the land requisition system in 2001.[12] After 2003, the central government called for reform of the land expropriation system. The content and direction of the reform of land requisition were meant to safeguard the rights and interests of farmers, control the scale of land requisition, improve land requisition procedures and strictly define public and business uses. The third plenary session of the eighteenth Central Committee decided to make general reforms to the land system, including allowing rural collective construction land to be leased, transferred and to share profits of collective construction. This land then enters the market with prices and rights identical to those for state-owned land. To narrow the scope of land expropriation, land requisition procedures would be standardised and the safeguards for farmers whose land was requisitioned would be improved to be reasonable, standardised and multivariate. The range of paid uses of state-owned land would be expanded and the allocation of non–public-welfare land would be reduced; the secondary market for land leases, transfers and mortgages would be improved; and a reasonable mechanism would be established to adjust the price ratio of industrial land to residential land and raise the price of industrial land. A pilot program incorporating the above measures was carried out across the country (CPC Central Committee 2011). Reform of the rural land system officially began at the thirteenth session of the Standing Committee of the Twelfth National Congress of the CPC on 27 February 2015. This session adopted the State Council's decision to authorise the adjustment of legal provisions in 33 pilot counties (State Council 2015) and implemented the council's 'Opinions on Rural Land Expropriation' (State Council 2014).

10 ibid.

11 ibid.

12 Since 2000, Heilongjiang province has practised unified annual production for the main types of land requisition in each city and county. Hangzhou City in Zhejiang province and Nanjing City and Suzhou City in Jiangsu province no longer estimate compensation fees; rather, comprehensive consideration of land use, location, local economic development level, land supply and demand and other factors, combined with the level of social security of local urban residents, is used to determine land requisition compensation standards.

Capitalisation of urban land

On 1 December 1987, land use rights for 50 years for a lot of 8,588 sq m was publicly auctioned in Shenzhen—the first time land use rights had entered the market as an asset (Liu 2008b). Amendment of the Chinese constitution in April 1988 deleted the provision preventing land being rented and added a provision that allowed land use rights to be transferred in accordance with the provisions of the law. In May 1990, the State Council issued its interim regulations on the granting and transfer of rights to use state-owned land in cities and towns, which clearly stipulated that land use rights could be transferred in three ways—by agreement, bidding and auction.

The Land Administration Law of 1998 clearly stipulated that land use rights could be transferred in accordance with the law and the state would implement a system of paid use of state-owned land. The central government, as a representative of the landowner, would transfer state-owned land use rights within a certain period—by agreement, bidding or auction—to the land users, who would pay the government for those land use rights in accordance with the assignment contract. Since 1999, the paid land use system has been further reformed, reducing the proportion of allocated land and increasing the proportion of paid use land.

In May 2002, the Ministry of Land and Resources issued its 'Provisions on the Assignment of State-owned Land Use Rights', stipulating that land to be used for business, tourism, entertainment, commercial housing and so on must be transferred by bid tendering, auction or listing (Ministry of Land and Resources 2002). The total land area and value transferred by bid tendering, auction and listing increased from 6,600 hectares and RMB49.2 billion, respectively, in 2001, to 66,500 hectares and RMB549.2 billion in 2006 (Liu 2012). After the State Council's Document No. 28 of 2004 was issued—stipulating that the transfer of industrial land must be carried out by bidding, auction or listing—the proportion of state-owned construction land transferred by these means rose annually. In the period 2001–10, the proportion increased from 7.3 per cent to 88.3 per cent. Bidding, auction and listing accounted for 92.2 per cent of total revenue from land sales in 2010 (see Table 22.1).

Under the current land system, the government not only is the sole arbiter in the transformation of rural land into urban land, but also the only winner of the value-added income of the land in the process of land conversion. With land conversion, the government replaces the peasant collective as the owner and operator of the urban land. This has become the main tool for land development (Liu 2012).

Table 22.1 Total transferred land and the share of land transferred by bidding, auction and listing (BAL), 2001–15

	BAL				State-owned land transfer	
Year	Area (10,000 ha)	BAL percentage	Price (RMB billion)	BAL percentage	Area (10,000 ha)	Price (RMB billion)
2001	0.7	7.3	49.2	–	9.0	–
2002	1.8	15	96.9	–	12.0	–
2003	5.2	27.8	–	–	18.7	293.8
2004	5.2	29.2	325.4	55.2	17.9	589.4
2005	5.7	35.0	392.0	71.2	16.3	550.5
2006	6.6	28.6	549.2	71.5	23.2	767.7
2007	11.5	50.9	1,007.5	82.5	22.6	1,221.7
2008	13.4	81.9	952.9	92.9	16.3	1,026.0
2009	18.8	85.3	1,509.8	94.9	22.1	1,591.0
2010	25.7	88.3	2,600.0	95.9	29.1	2,710.0
2011	30.5	91.2	3,020.0	95.9	33.4	3,150.0
2012	29.3	90.8	2,550.0	94.8	32.3	2,690.0
2013	33.9	92.3	4,040.0	96.2	36.7	4,200.0
2014	25.1	92.5	3,180.0	95.2	27.2	3,340.0
2015	20.4	75.2	2,860.0	85.6	22.1	2,980.0

– no data available

Sources: Ministry of Land and Resources (2004, 2016).

Land system change and economic growth

Land system change has had a major impact on China's economic growth since 2008. Agricultural land reform has promoted the growth of agricultural production and released a large portion of the population from villages, providing a microfoundation for China's economic transformation. Although strict farmland protection has been implemented, the ample supply of land in regions with development opportunities has supported high economic growth. Local governments have used distorted industrial land prices and land supply to attract investment to provide industrial park infrastructure, which has contributed to rapid industrialisation and made China a world-class manufacturing factory. Land capitalisation and land financing have provided much of the enormous amount of capital for China's urban development and promoted rapid urbanisation.

Land is the engine that drives China's high economic growth

China's traditional development model relies on high growth and high investment. Because municipal and county governments are the real landowners, land has been the main tool for local governments to promote investment and growth. Over the past 40 years, land has had two roles: to safeguard national food security and to support high growth. To pursue growth in gross domestic product (GDP), an ample supply of land for expanding activities was required. During the period 2003–12, the total annual supply of state-owned construction land increased from 286,400 hectares to 690,400 hectares—an average annual increase of 10.3 per cent. The supply of land increases when economic growth slows (see Figure 22.1). Regional land supply policy underpins growth. Before the Global Financial Crisis (GFC), coastal regions with large demand for land experienced rapid growth in land supply in areas with rapid economic growth. Under the annual plan, scarce local construction land quotas were used mostly for the development of capital cities and major development zones. The flexible supply of construction land under strict farmland protections ensured high economic growth.

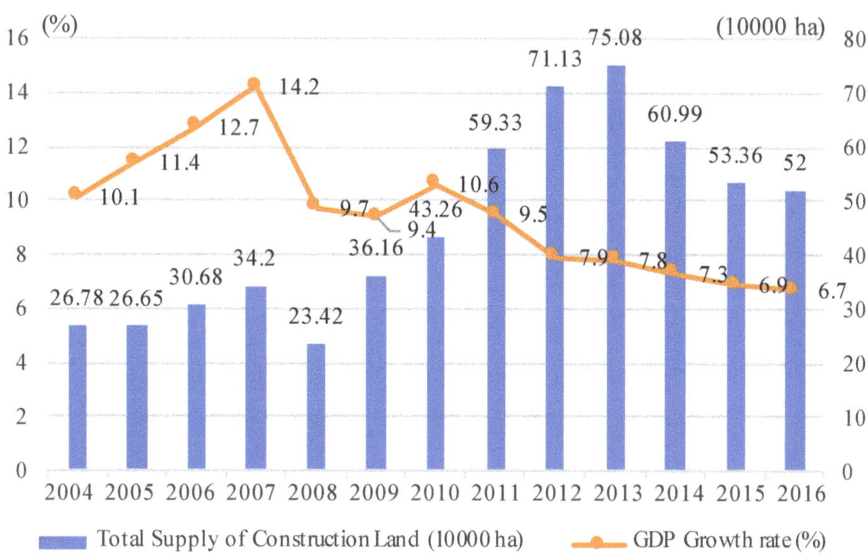

Figure 22.1 Supply of construction land versus GDP growth rate

Sources: Ministry of Land and Resources (2004, 2016); NBS (various years).

Farmland reform and agricultural transformation

A stable and efficient rural land institution was a prerequisite for overall reform and structural change in the past 40 years. Rural land reform improved land use efficiency in the direction of clarifying property rights, but also made it possible to launch structural change in rural areas.

First, the household responsibility system was established and persisted in agriculture, becoming the foundation of China's agricultural growth. This system was generalised from 1984. In 2016, despite the growth of new types of agricultural management, family contracted land still accounted for 99.4 per cent of all cultivated area. The production of food crops increased from 407.3 million tonnes in 1984 to 616.2 million tonnes in 2016, which can be attributed to the progress of agricultural technology, the increase of modern investment and the stability of the family management system.

Second, the reconstruction of human relationships with the land has promoted structural transformation. In traditional rural China, farmers were tied to the land. During the state industrialisation period, peasants were excluded from the process of industrialisation and were bound to collectively owned land. After implementation of the family contract system, peasants were able to participate in the local industrialisation of rural areas and subsequently to go out from their villages to participate in the industrialisation of other areas, becoming the main force to promote China's structural revolution.

Rural institutional reform and structural change promoted the transformation of the agricultural development model. The transfer of farmland increased, reaching 36 per cent in 2016. The balance of agricultural inputs shifted from labour to machinery. The focus of agricultural development has shifted from improvement of land productivity to improvement of labour productivity (see Table 22.2).

Table 22.2 Land system versus agricultural transformation

Year	2010	2011	2012	2013	2014	2015
Proportion of rural household contracting (%)	94.1	94.4	96.89	98.1	98.4	99.4
Farmland transfer rate (%)	14.7	17.8	21.25	25.7	30.3	33.3
Proportion of rural residents going out (%)	58.3	59.5	59.87	61.6	63.2	63.7
Proportion of agricultural net income (%)	29.1	27.2	26.6	26.5	25.7	25.1
Total power of agricultural machinery (million kWh)	927.8	977.3	1,025.6	1,039.1	1,080.6	1,117.3
Land productivity (kg/ha)	4,973.6	5,156.9	5,301.8	5,376.6	5,385.1	5,984.0
Labour productivity (kg/person)	1,960.1	2,075.2	2,168.0	2,260.9	2,316.9	2,410.3

Source: Ministry of Agriculture (various years).

Industrial land allocation and rapid industrialisation

After its reform and opening-up, China embarked a new path of industrialisation. This included industrialisation of collectively owned land in the countryside from the 1980s to the mid-1990s and the creation of industrial parks from the 1990s. This new pattern of industrialisation saw China become the world's factory, and its unique method of supplying industrial land played a significant role in this.

Surplus workers looking for employment after the agricultural land reforms drove rural industrialisation after the mid-1980s. The rigidities of the urban land system, and restrictions on the entry of rural labourers, meant the government could only permit peasants to build enterprises on collectively owned land. This required allowing collectively owned land to be entered into the nonfarming land market. Prior to the revision of the Land Administration Law of 1998, the two main forms of construction land use were in the countryside—peasants who built houses with their increased income following reform and those who built township enterprises on collectively owned land. Between 1993 and 1998, the amount of nonfarming construction land increased from 224,824 hectares to 367,854 hectares, while land for TVEs decreased from 13,943 hectares to 8,180 hectares (see Table 22.3). The advantage for peasants in developing enterprises on collectively owned land was that they did not have to pay for the land.

Rural enterprises solved the problem of land utilisation through land redistribution within the collective or by paying minimal rent for the use of collectively owned land. Rural industrialisation of collectively owned land radically changed the structure of national industrialisation. Until 1993, state-owned enterprises (SOEs), TVEs and foreign-owned enterprises each accounted for one-third of national gross output value (see Pei 2003).

Table 22.3 Statistics on the actual use of nonagricultural construction land (hectares)

Year	Nonagricultural construction land	Township collectively owned construction land	Township enterprise land
1993	224,824	30,183	13,943
1994	186,630	22,023	9,826
1995	190,376	19,909	11,621
1996	171,467	14,897	6,235
1998	367,854	16,558	8,180

Sources: Ministry of Land and Resources (2004, 2016).

After the mid-1990s, industrialisation on collectively owned rural land accounted for a large share of total cultivated land, caused environmental pollution and scattered industries. The Land Administration Law of 1998 brought into effect the institutional regulation of land use and gradually phased out the use of collectively owned land for nonagricultural construction. Industrial parks gradually replaced rural industrialisation as the main path to Chinese industrialisation and achieved particular success in eastern China and in parts of the central and western regions. The success of industrial parks was assisted by a distinctive land allocation pattern. First, the government used land to promote investment, providing land at low prices (and sometimes even for free or with negative rent). Second, local governments provided land for companies to carry out integrated development or to mortgage the land to a bank to fund construction. The industrial park would recoup value from revenue generated by the enterprises. Third, established enterprises in the park were provided with complete land use rights for 50 years. Enterprises could mortgage, sublease or transfer possession of the land, which stabilised their investment expectations and solved the financing demands for enterprise development.

Land is the secret to China's rapid industrialisation. If China had relied only on market allocation of land, the cost of industrial land would have been considerably higher than other land resources with better endowments, and rising land prices would have hindered industrialisation. Between 2000 and 2016, the national comprehensive land price increased at an average annual rate of 8.8 per cent, commercial services land prices increased by 9.6 per cent and residential land prices by 12.4 per cent. However, the average annual increase of industrial land prices has been only 3.5 per cent per annum (Table 22.4).

Table 22.4 Industrial land and industrial value added (per cent)

Index	Growth rate of industrial value added	Growth rate of land for industrial and mining warehouse space	Growth rate of industrial land price
2007	21.1	–8.34	15.7
2008	17.9	–34.4	4.8
2009	4.8	52.3	1.5
2010	19.6	7.0	5.4
2011	18.2	26.4	28.3
2012	7.1	8.3	–17.0
2013	6.4	3.0	4.5
2014	5.2	15.8	6.0
2015	1.1	–49.5	2.4
2016	4.8	–4.5	2.9

Sources: Ministry of Land and Resources (2004, 2016).

Land capitalisation and rapid urbanisation

After 2000, urbanisation in China accelerated. From 2000 to 2016, the urbanisation rate of the permanent resident population increased from 36.2 per cent to 57.4 per cent, growing at 2.9 per cent every year. Land capitalisation provided huge capital demand for urban construction. The linkage between local government maximisation of land profits and the rise in housing asset value was the major driving force for urbanisation.

First, the arrangement of bidding, auction and listing for commercial land increased the value of land capitalisation. Since 2003, the total area of land transacted by bidding, auction and listing in China is close to 4 million hectares, generating land revenue of RMB32 trillion. Land revenue in 2016 was 89 times as high as that in 2003.

Second, huge demand for housing caused by housing commercialisation and rapid urbanisation in this period has maximised land revenue for local governments. From 2003 to 2016, newly added housing stock in China reached 26 billion square metres. Real estate loans to developers and residential purchase loans increased by 6.8 times from 2003 to 2016, while housing prices increased by 2.9 times. Rising premiums on land encouraged local governments to further increase their land revenue through bidding, auction and listing for commercial land. In 2001, the area of land sold by bidding, auction and listing accounted for 7.3 per cent of total land sold; in 2014, it had reached 92 per cent. The increasing revenue from land sales has, on one hand, provided financial resources for local governments to engage in urban infrastructure construction; on the other, it has encouraged local governments to increase urban expansion to generate even more capital from land. From 2000 to 2015, the urban construction area in China increased by 1.4 times (see Table 22.5).

Table 22.5 Land capitalisation and urban expansion, 2003–15

Year	Urbanisation rate (%)	Urban construction area (sq m)	Government land sales revenue (RMB billion)	BAL area (%)	Land mortgage area (10,000 ha)	Land mortgage value (RMB billion)	Average sale price of commodity housing (RMB/sq m)
2003	40.5	28,308	542.1	27.8	–	–	2,359.0
2004	41.8	30,406	641.2	29.2	–	–	2,778.0
2005	43.0	32,521	588.4	35.1	–	–	3,167.7
2006	44.0	33,660	807.8	28.6	–	–	3,366.8
2007	44.9	35,470	1,221.7	50.9	–	–	3,864.0
2008	45.7	36,295	1,026.0	81.9	16.6	1,810.7	3,800.0
2009	46.6	38,107	1,591.0	85.3	21.7	2,585.6	4,681.0
2010	47.5	40,058	3,010.9	88.3	25.8	3,530.0	5,032.0
2011	51.3	43,603	3,150.0	91.3	30.1	4,800.0	5,357.1

Year	Urbanisation rate (%)	Urban construction area (sq m)	Government land sales revenue (RMB billion)	BAL area (%)	Land mortgage area (10,000 ha)	Land mortgage value (RMB billion)	Average sale price of commodity housing (RMB/sq m)
2012	52.6	45,566	2,690.0	90.8	34.9	5,950.0	5,791.0
2013	53.7	47,855	4,200.0	92.3	40.4	7,760.0	6,237.0
2014	54.8	49,773	4,294.0	92.5	45.1	9,510.0	6,324.0
2015	56.1	52,102	3,365.8	75.2	49.1	11,330.0	6,793.0

– no data available

Sources: CEINET Statistics database; Ministry of Land and Resources (2004, 2016).

Table 22.6 Land mortgage, cost and revenue, 2008–15

Year	Mortgaged land		Land cost		Land revenue	
	Area (10,000 ha)	Value (RMB billion)	Proportion of expenditure cost (%)	Cost proportion in land expropriation (%)	Actual input (RMB billion)	Net revenue (RMB billion)
2008	16.6	1,810.7	56.1	47.0	994.2	436.3
2009	21.7	2,585.6	53.8	44.5	1,424.1	658.3
2010	25.8	3,530.0	58.4	49.6	2,939.8	1,221.6
2011	30.1	4,800.0	71.8	57.5	3,347.7	942.3
2012	34.9	5,950.0	78.3	60.2	2,888.6	626.1
2013	40.4	7,760.0	81.7	60.9	4,125.0	755.1
2014	45.1	9,510.0	79.1	57.6	4,294.0	898.8
2015	49.1	11,330.0	79.8	60.3	3,365.8	681.3

Sources: NBS (various years); Ministry of Land and Resources (2004, 2016).

Third, land financing provided more capital for urban development. Especially after 2008, various levels of government established financing platforms, and land mortgages significantly increased. From 2008 to 2015, the area and value of mortgaged land increased from 166,000 hectares and RMB1.8 trillion, respectively, to 490,800 hectares and RMB11.3 trillion (Table 22.6).

Using land to drive development has supported China's rapid economic growth, but China has become increasingly reliant on this rapid growth. High economic growth is part of a cycle of increasing investment attracted by land, increasing taxes and population, expanding urban areas, increasing real estate prices and increasing revenue from land sales, mortgages and loans. While strong growth continues, the cycle can be sustained; however, when the economy suffers a downturn, certain sections of this cycle are negatively affected, which influences national economic performance. This is mainly manifested as follows.

First, the continuous increase in land supply no longer increases GDP. To deal with the GFC in 2008, China adopted looser fiscal and monetary policies, releasing land to prevent a possible economic downturn. Unfortunately, GDP growth reached a peak in 2009, and suffered a downturn thereafter. Although the loose supply in land lasted until 2013, the economic growth rate decreased from 10.6 per cent in 2009 to 7.8 per cent in 2013. After 2013, the economic downturn led to decreasing demand for land and a decreasing supply of construction land. The rapid economic growth rate of more than 10 per cent fell to a milder rate of 6–7 per cent, meaning that the mode in which economic growth will continue to be supported by loose land supply has gone forever (as shown in Figure 22.2).

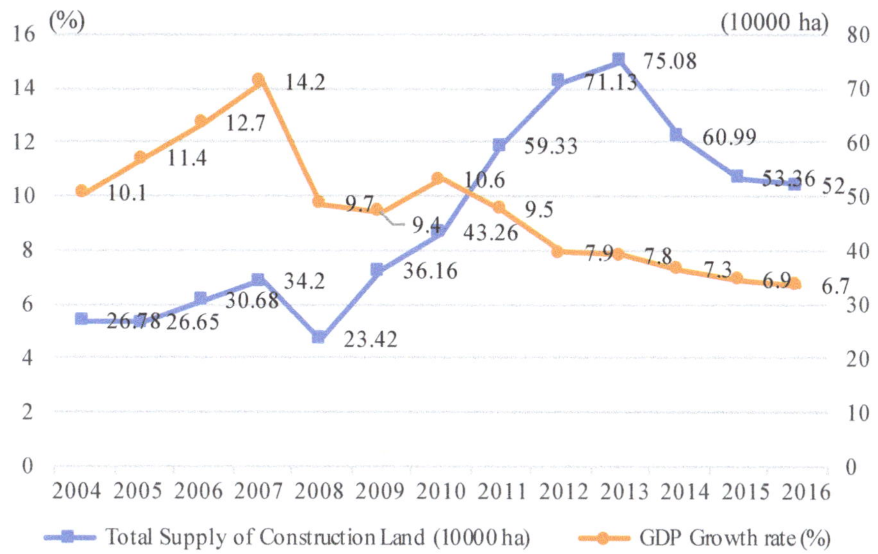

Figure 22.2 Relationship between land supply and GDP

Source: NBS (various years); Ministry of Land and Resources (2004, 2016).

Second, the efficiency of attracting investment through land is decreasing, and this mode of attracting investment for industrial parks started to change in 2004. This is manifested in the decreasing amount of industrial land in eastern China (see Figure 22.3). The main reason for this is that as enterprises in the eastern areas have been transformed through quality improvement and industrial upgrading, they no longer rely so much on low land costs and land mortgage financing to acquire loans. Although the industrial parks in central and western China have imitated those in the east by attracting investment through land and the provision of excellent infrastructure, the efficiency of investment attraction for industrial parks in these areas is not good. On the contrary, such efforts have brought high levels of government debt.

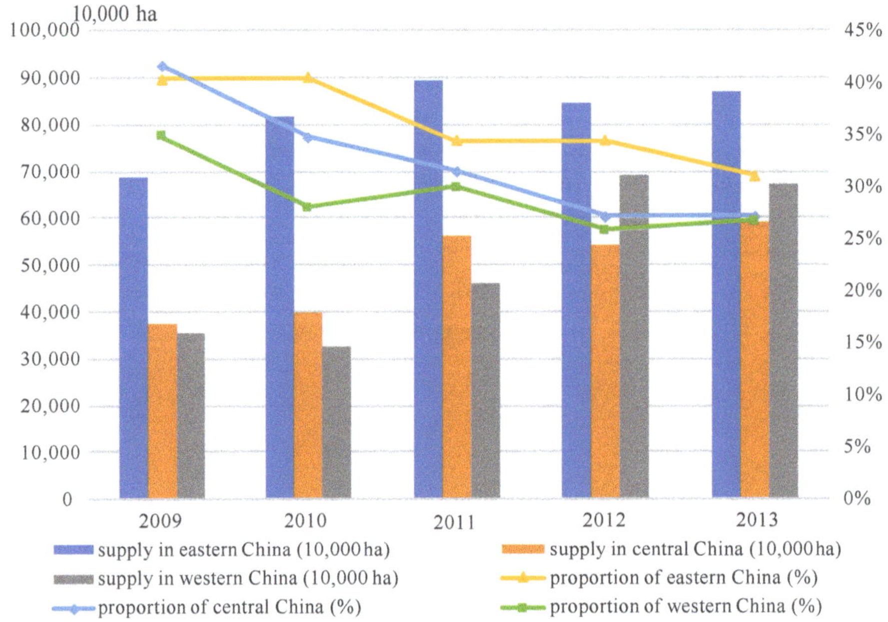

Figure 22.3 Supply structure of industrial land in different areas

Source: NBS (various years); Ministry of Land and Resources (2004, 2016).

Third, the land supply structure is seriously distorted, which works against structural reform. In fact, the imbalance in land structure is the most serious structural problem in China. A high proportion of land for industry and infrastructure and a low proportion for real estate makes land a tool for government to attract investment and maximise land revenue. Since 2011, the proportion of industrial land decreased from 32.8 per cent to 23.4 per cent, in 2016 (Figure 22.4). Meanwhile, the proportion of real estate land also decreased, from 28 per cent to 6.7 per cent, which shows that local governments have not changed the system used to protect land revenue by controlling real estate land supply. A more serious problem is that the proportion of infrastructure land in this period increased from 38.8 per cent to 55.9 per cent—matching the increase in infrastructure investment. The growth rate of infrastructure investment reached 28.6 per cent in 2016. In circumstances in which the real economy suffers a downturn and real estate investment reaches a turning point, governments can only rely on a larger supply of infrastructure land and increased infrastructure investment to maintain economic growth, but these short-term measures actually delay structural reforms.

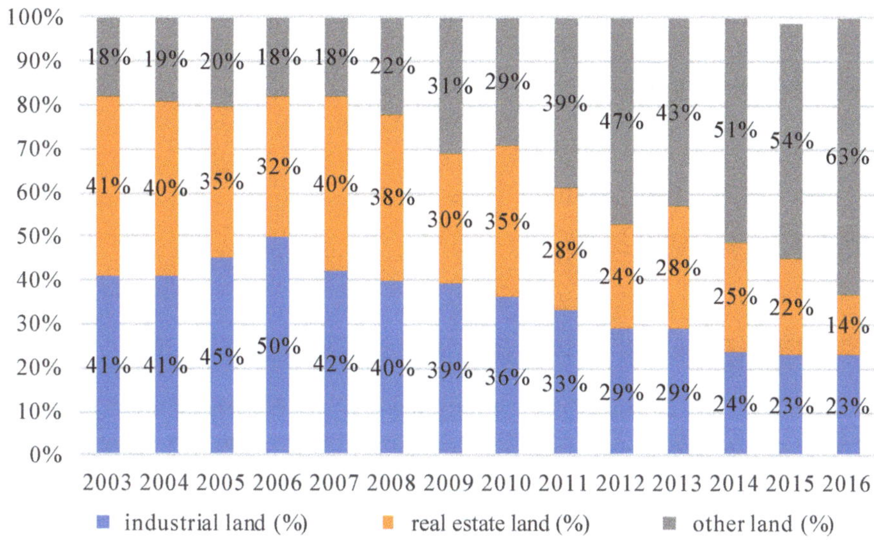

Figure 22.4 Supply structure of state-owned construction land

Source: Ministry of Land and Resources (2004, 2016).

Fourth, the sales cost of land has increased, net revenue from land has decreased and land mortgages have increased. Rapid urbanisation could be successfully completed in China. One important tool has been the low cost of land. The costs for the government to buy land have been low and most land revenue has been used for urban investment. But as land use in many cities has been transformed and farmers' awareness of their rights has awakened, land expropriation costs have substantially increased. Since 2008, the government's land sales cost has greatly increased, to above 50 per cent in many areas, and even above 60 per cent in others. The result is decreasing net land revenue for government, which was only 20 per cent in 2016. With decreasing net land revenue, the government is still increasing infrastructure investment and expanding construction of new areas in some cities. Government construction capital relies increasingly on land mortgages. From 2008, the area and value of mortgaged land increased from 166,000 hectares and RMB1.8 trillion, respectively, to 490,800 hectares and RMB11.3 trillion in 2016. The decrease in land revenue and increase in land mortgages mean higher financial debt risks.

Fifth, the government debt risk and bank finance risk have increased. First, the land mortgage value in many cities is evaluated when land prices are high. Once the economy suffers a downturn, demand for land will decrease and the gap between actual and estimated land values will be large. Second, from 2010 to 2015, the average proportion of land revenue in government debt reached 40 per cent. As land values are overestimated, local governments returned the debts after selling land for revenue. Third, there is excessive leverage. The nominal land leverage in midwestern

China is high, while the actual leverage for most provinces in the midwest is over two times. Here, the leverage ratio refers to the level of land mortgage financing to local government revenue.

Further land reform in the new development stage

Economic trends in the new development stage

China's new stage of economic transformation will no longer rely so much on land. International experience suggests China's economic growth will inevitably decline, slowing from its high of 10 per cent over the past 30 years. The economic structure will also undergo a series of profound changes. The service industry has surpassed secondary industry, internal demand plays a more significant role and economic growth increasingly relies on improvements in production forces and innovation. Quality and efficiency have been greatly increased (Perkins 2015; Liu 2015). In this new development stage, land will no longer play a key role as an engine of growth and will instead bring negative effects. Measures to protect economic growth through loose land supply will no longer be necessary, and will instead waste increasingly rare resources. The significance of improving the quality of economic growth by enhancing land allocation efficiency is far greater than that of promoting economic growth by increasing land supply. How supply and allocation of land will meet the changing demands of economic growth will be a major issue for relations between land and the national economy in the future.

Second, industrial transformation and upgrading means industrial development will no longer rely so heavily on the system suppressing the cost of land. China has become the world's factory largely because of its low land costs, supported by an independent land system; however, as the relative prices of other factors and system costs increase, it will not be able to maintain this status. In field investigations, some regions, cities, industries and enterprises stand out for their level of transformation and upgrading. After a new round of industrial competition and upgrading, new competitive manufacturing cities, industries, enterprises and products will appear in China, replacing the current manufacturing supported by industrial parks and low land costs. The most competitive manufacturing areas will no longer rely on low land costs and land mortgages to resolve their funding issues—and those who cannot compete and who rely on low land costs will not be able to escape their destiny of being phased out. Therefore, the next round of manufacturing development in China will be about how to revitalise the existing stock of land and optimise land use for competition rather than protecting land supply. Another feature of industrial evolution is deep integration between the manufacturing and service sectors and increasing the share of the service sector. In 2013, the service sector's share in the Chinese economy exceeded that of manufacturing. The shares of value added in the primary and secondary sectors with respect to GDP were 46.7 per cent and 44 per cent, respectively. Unlike the manufacturing industry, the service industry does not require much land; this change in the industrial structure will weaken the role of land in future industrial development. The major policy issues in the future will be around land use structure, construction optimisation, industrial land reallocation, industrial park transformation and changes in land supply.

Third, the land allocation mode changes from a single focus on urbanisation to interaction between urban and rural areas. The road to urbanisation in China has so far been one of rapid flows of population, land and capital from rural to urban areas, influenced by the large gaps between the two areas. The next stage of urbanisation will need to shift focus to the relationship between urban and rural areas and increasing their interaction. So far the interaction between the two has been based on population flows from rural to urban areas. The public policies of the cities in which the population is living or working are difficult to implement and farmers' relations with their homelands are hard to sever. Farmers will work in areas with the greatest economic opportunities, and city living will be the first choice for much of China's population. At the same time, as interaction between urban and rural areas increases, more and more of the urban population will come to rural areas to experience rural life. Population interaction and exchange between urban and rural areas will be enhanced. Second, Chinese villages have become highly differentiated; while many are in decline, others are undergoing revitalisation. The growth of some small towns will help connect urban and rural areas. Some cities will succeed because of their factor agglomeration, diffusion and innovative vigour. Allocation and connection between dynamic cities, towns and villages will be enhanced. Third, while those with capital explore investment opportunities in urban areas, as rural development opportunities increase, some will also look for opportunities in agriculture and villages. Fourth, changes in consumption and population flows will increase opportunities as well as demand for land for rural development. Interaction between urban and rural areas will therefore replace the single-focus urbanisation and the population will flow between urban and rural areas.

Fourth, agricultural evolution and rural transformation will require a review of the value of village space. The greatest changes in the next stage of China's development will be a revolution led by rural areas. As China has entered the ranks of well-off societies, national food demand will shift from quantity to quality, and the importance of agriculture for food production will decrease. The function and pattern of agriculture will undergo significant changes. Rather than simply providing basic food, agriculture will specialise to focus on offering quality, safe and 'green' products. Opportunities for profit from agriculture will be greatly enhanced. China will need to redefine agriculture and recognise its new role. In addition, differentiation and having children bring structural revolution. Another feature of the changes in the farmer group is generational differentiation. The basic track for first-generation farmers is leaving their home area and then returning, while the second generation is leaving and not coming back. The latter's relations with land, conceptions of agriculture and behavioural features have undergone fundamental change. Further, the features of rural industries have changed. With changes in urban demand, many rural industries have been revitalised and expanded, while technological and commercial innovations have expanded the market scope for many rural craftspeople and local specialties. As such, many villages have become differentiated. Traditionally, Chinese villages depended on farming; but, as people's relationship with the land and the mode of agricultural development have changed, villages are becoming greatly differentiated. Some villages are revitalising with vigour and have taken on new functions in the interaction between urban and rural areas, while others are in decline or decaying.

Land reform on the second half of the road to industrialisation

The function of land as a driver of development is changing and will soon end. The most complicated issue in Chinese economic transformation is how to move away from the development mode driven by land. This mode is like opium: highly addictive and difficult to quit. Moving on will depend on whether the a development mode can improve production efficiency and drive innovation. The difficulty is that, if the existing mode is useful and still works, it will not be replaced with a new one. And, when a new mode cannot be established, we will have to return to relying on the old mode. The disadvantages of the land-driven mode of development are becoming increasingly obvious, but I believe the economic downturn provides the opportunity to change this longstanding development mode. The general conclusion is that the costs and revenue structure of the land-based development mode will no longer be profitable.

We have several suggestions for how to truly say goodbye to the land-based development mode. First, the central government should make it clear that land is not to be used for development or for macroeconomic control (when the economy is turning down, land is released; when the economy is growing, land is controlled). Advantage should be taken of the decrease in land demand during the economic downturn to cancel the system of land control targets and transfer to a strict planning system. Second, land's role as a development engine should be changed to avoid deliberate economic growth. Local governments should be prevented from using low land costs to attract investment; and overcapacity and repeated construction should be reduced. The system of local government land sales for to generate benefits must be changed, and uncontrolled expansion of urbanisation must be reduced. Third, reform should be made to the land market pattern that gives local governments an exclusive monopoly, to allow landowners to participate in the land market under regulation. Fourth, the system by which local governments use land for financing should be reformed. Fifth, all land debts should be erased at once. The sixth suggestion is to build a national land operation company and ensure governments acquire a certain amount of revenue through its operation. Seventh, differentiated real estate taxes should be collected from land used for different functions.

Once the role of land as a driver of development ends, optimisation of the land structure will promote national economic structural reform. This can be done by reducing the supply of public land for infrastructure and the use of land to attract investment as a means of promoting economic growth. After nearly 30 years, the peak of massive investment in infrastructure in China is over. It is not right to increase infrastructure investment simply to protect the level of investment and growth, as this will cause further structural distortions. Expropriating large parcels of land for infrastructure will not only increase government expenditure, but also increase the conflict between governments and the farmers whose land is expropriated. The proportion of public land in urban areas is excessively high, and it is used for high-profile projects such as roads, public squares and large office buildings. This not only wastes large amounts of capital and land, it also causes the diversion of liveable and development sites in the cities.

Compared with international experience, China's land usage structure sees industrial land accounting for the highest proportion of land. Although this proportion has decreased in recent years, it is still excessively high. With economic structural optimisation and transformation and upgrading of the manufacturing industry, there is still much room to lower the proportion and supply of industrial land. This will be a major aspect of land allocation restructuring in the next period of reform. Instead of using low-cost land to attract investment to industrial parks, authorities should promote the transformation and upgrading of these parks. Industrial parks have made a significant contribution to China's development and helped it become the world's manufacturing plant. However, this has also distorted prices for industrial land. Enterprises occupy excessive amounts of land because of its low cost, and industrial parks speculate on land. Such drawbacks are becoming quite obvious in midwestern China. We must change the current method of attracting investment through low land costs and find a balance between investment and tax in the excessive infrastructure construction for industrial parks. We must then reduce the number of such parks, and merge those that are performing poorly.

Next, we should increase the proportion of land allocated for real estate, changing the supply of land for housing and restricting real estate market bubbles. Generally, we should increase the supply of land for housing and the proportion of housing land in total construction land. Different supply methods should be used for land for investment housing and for residential housing. The system of bidding, auction and listing should continue. Land and housing prices should be entirely allocated by the market, while the government allocates residential land. Affordable housing for residential use should be separated from that for investment purposes. A market for land for collective construction for villages or areas surrounding cities should be established, with farmers allowed to build and rent houses collectively using collective construction land. A benefit-sharing mechanism should be created for the structural optimisation of construction land.

So far, the relationship between urban and rural areas has been focused solely on urbanisation. The important supportive system is the land transfer system for urban and rural areas. Rural land can only become urban construction land through expropriation and nationalisation. Farmers and villages will lose land development rights. The loss of village development rights will cause rural labour migration, land allocation towards urban areas and fewer profit opportunities for capital in rural areas. To realise the interaction between production factors in urban areas and those in rural areas in China, we must reform urban and rural land allocation systems and allow farmers' collective land to enter the construction land market under regulation. We should realise the same rights for two kinds of collective land. This is the most important reform in terms of deciding whether China has truly become urbanised. It will play a decisive role in the sustainability of the Chinese development mode and the realisation of Chinese modernisation. Substantial reform consists of, first, reforming the land requisition system, and of improving the public interest in land management laws. This includes changing the original use principles for expropriated land, gradually implementing land market price compensation and implementing equitable prices and compensation rights for houses expropriated in urban and rural areas. Second is to implement the spirit of land reform raised in the third plenary session of the eighteenth National Congress, build an integrated market for construction land in urban and rural areas and establish construction land for collective operation that conforms to general land planning rules. Collective landowners should be allowed to transfer land by leasing, selling or becoming a shareholder. The use right for collective construction land can be used for transfers, rent and mortgages.

The promotion of farmland reform should centre on the separation of the three powers of collective ownership, contract rights and operation rights—clear definition of which will be key to innovation and farmland allocation. This is related to the method of restructuring the system of farming land rights and agricultural modernisation. First is to define collective ownership as ownership rights for collective farmers. Insist on collective farmers as the main body for collective land ownership. Village collective economic organisations or village committees, groups or farming collective organisations should only represent collective farmers to implement landownership. Second, the land contract right is the property right for collective members. Land contracts provide the legal rights for the possession and use of and income from contracted land, and can include transfers, swaps, renting (subcontracting), becoming a shareholder and winning profits. The contracting land operation right can be mortgaged, and contracted lands can be withdrawn voluntarily. Third, the land operation right is the farming right enjoyed by all kinds of agricultural management entities. The purpose of the land operation right is to provide holders with stable land use and investment expectations.

In the whole system of rural land reform, the most influential component for agriculture is land operations.

Conclusion

After 40 years of reforms and opening up, China has not only created a growth miracle unparalleled in human history, but also transformed itself from a rural to an urban society. Behind this great transformation is a systemic reform of land institutions. Rural land institutions moved from collective ownership to the household responsibility system, thereby protecting farmers' land rights. This process resulted in long-term sustainable growth in Chinese agriculture, massive rural–urban migration and unprecedented agricultural transformation. The conversion of agricultural land to nonagricultural uses and the introduction of market mechanisms made land a policy tool in driving high economic growth, industrialisation and urbanisation. However, we need to recognise that the role of land and its relationship with the economy will inevitably change as China's economy enters a new stage of medium–high-speed growth. With economic restructuring, low-cost industrial land will be less effective. Urbanisation is also shifting from rapid expansion to endogenous growth so that returns on land capitalisation will decrease and risks will increase. Therefore, China must abandon its land-dependent growth model through deepening land reforms and adapt a new pattern of economic development.

References

Central Committee of the Communist Party of China (CPC Central Committee) (1982), *Summary of the National Rural Work Conference*, 1 January, Beijing: General Office of the State Council.

Central Committee of the Communist Party of China (CPC Central Committee) (1984), *Circular of the Central Committee of the Communist Party of China on Rural Work in 1984*, 1 January, Beijing: General Office of the State Council.

Central Committee of the Communist Party of China (CPC Central Committee) (1992), Circular of the State Council on several issues concerning the development of real estate industry, *Guofa* (61)(4 October).

Central Committee of the Communist Party of China (CPC Central Committee) (1993), *A Number of Policy Measures Promulgated and Implemented by the Central Committee of the Communist Party of China and the State Council on the Current Agricultural and Rural Economic Development*, 5 November, Beijing: General Office of the State Council.

Central Committee of the Communist Party of China (CPC Central Committee) (1998), *Decision of the Central Committee of the Communist Party of China on Some Major Issues Concerning Agriculture and Rural Work*, 14 October, Beijing: General Office of the State Council.

Central Committee of the Communist Party of China (CPC Central Committee) (2008), *Decision of the Central Committee of the Communist Party of China on Some Major Issues Concerning Promoting Rural Reform and Development*, 12 October, Beijing: General Office of the State Council.

Central Committee of the Communist Party of China (CPC Central Committee) (2011), *Decision of the Central Committee of the Communist Party of China on Some Major Issues Concerning Comprehensively Deepening the Reform*, Beijing: People's Publishing House.

Central Committee of the Communist Party of China (CPC Central Committee) (2013), *Decision of the Central Committee of the Communist Party of China on Some Major Issues Concerning Comprehensively Deepening the Reform*, 12 November, Beijing: General Office of the State Council.

Du, R. (2005), *An Account by Du Runsheng: A record of significant decisions on the reform of Chinese rural institutions*, Beijing: People's Publishing House.

Fei, X. and Liu, H. (2007), *From the Soil*, Shanghai: Shanghai People's Publishing House.

Liu, S. (2002), Statement concerning the Law of the People's Republic of China on Land Contract in Rural Areas, [draft], 26 June 2001, Twenty-Second Session of the Standing Committee of the Ninth National People's Congress, Beijing.

Liu, S. (2008a), China's dualistic land rights system and land market incompleteness: Review and comment on current policy, law and local innovation, *Review of Economic Research* (31): 2–12.

Liu, S. (2008b), Collective land capitalization and rural urbanization: A Survey of Zheng Ge Zhuang village in Beijing, *Journal of Peking University (Philosophy and Social Sciences Edition)* (6): 123–32.

Liu, S. (2012), Risks and reform of land-based development model, *International Economic Review* (2): 92–109.

Liu, S. (2015), *Ten Years' Outlook for Chinese Economic Growth 2015–2024*, Beijing: China CITIC Press.

Mao, Z. (1961), *Report on the Second Plenary Session of the Seventh Central Committee of the Communist Party of China*, Beijing: Foreign Languages Press.

Ministry of Agriculture (various years), *Agricultural Statistics of the People's Republic of China*, Beijing: Chinese Agricultural Press.

Ministry of Land and Resources (2002), *Provisions on the Assignment of State-owned Land Use Rights by Means of Bid Tendering, Auction and Listing*, Decree No. 11, Beijing: Chinese Agricultural Press.

Ministry of Land and Resources (2004), *China Land and Resources Bulletin 2004*, Beijing: Chinese Agricultural Press.

Ministry of Land and Resources (2016), *China Land and Resources Bulletin 2016*, Beijing: Chinese Agricultural Press.

National Bureau of Statistics (NBS) (various years), *China Statistical Yearbook*, Beijing: China Statistics Press.

Pei, X. (2003), The contribution of collectively-owned land ownership to economic transition in China and countryside industrialization: An explanation of a resource allocation model, in H. Zongzhi (ed.), *Study on Chinese Countryside. Series 1*, Beijing: The Commercial Press.

Perkins, D. (2015), *East Asian Development: Foundations and strategies*, Beijing: China CITIC Press.

Qu, D. (2015), *China Agriculture Statistical Report*, Beijing: Chinese Agricultural Press.

Rural Development Group (1984), *Systematic Review of Rural Economic System Reform in China*, Chinese Social Sciences Press: Beijing.

State Council (2004), *Urgent circular of the General Affairs Office of the State Council on properly solving the current rural land contract disputes*, Telegram No. 21, 30 April, Beijing: General Office of the State Council.

State Council (2014), Opinions on rural land expropriation, putting collective-owned operational construction land into market, homestead system reform pilot work, *Zhongbanfa* (71).

State Council (2015), *Decision to Authorize the State Council to Temporarily Adjust the Relevant Legal Provisions in the Administrative Areas of the 33 Pilot Counties (Cities and Districts) in Daxing District, Beijing*, NPC Regular Session No. 1, Beijing: General Office of the State Council.

Wang, L. and Zhou, Y. (2012), On the perfection of rural land property rights system in China, *China Legal Science* (1): 45–54.

Zhou, Q. (1995), Reform in China's countryside: Changes to the relationship between the state and ownership (second part)—A review of the history of economic system change, *Management World* (4).

Zhou, Q. and Liu, S. (1997), Meitan: Land tenure change in a traditional agricultural county, in *Land System Construction, Experimentation, Monitoring and Evaluation*, Guiyang: CPC Guizhou Provincial Committee Policy Research Office and Guizhou's Meitan County Committee of the CPC.

23. New urbanisation in China: A multidimensional perspective—Empirical analysis of 289 prefecture and higher-level cities

Biliang Hu and Kunling Zhang

Since the first city came into being, the study of cities has been incessant. With the deepening of social divisions of labour and the expansion of industrialisation, urbanisation has become the dominant trend of the times and its study has become increasingly contested. The main stimulus of China's traditional urbanisation process is industrialisation, which is reflected in its export and investment-oriented economic growth model. However, in the process of promoting urbanisation, the mode of extensive industrial production caused a series of economic and social problems, including serious resource waste and environmental pollution. The deepening trend of population ageing has led to a declining demographic dividend—a dilemma for the export-oriented manufacturing industry, in which cheap labour is the main competitive advantage. Government-led large-scale infrastructure and investment in fixed assets are unsustainable, leading to a much faster rate of land urbanisation than that of population. In addition, the household registration (*hukou*) system disadvantages migrant workers in urban areas, resulting in unequal distribution of public services between urban residents and rural and regional migrant workers. Therefore, China's traditional pattern of urbanisation has reached a turning point in its development and faces a crucial transformation. Working out how to break through the dilemma of the traditional mode of urbanisation and embark on a path of new urbanisation with Chinese characteristics—a sustainable and people-centred model of urbanisation—have become important tasks for China in the new era.

From traditional urbanisation to new urbanisation

The traditional model of urbanisation—simply pursuing urban population growth and scale expansion—is unsustainable, and has created many social and economic problems. This has led to a search for a pattern of sustainable urbanisation—the idea of 'new urbanisation'.

New urbanisation with effective resource utilisation and environmental protection

The extensive development model of high consumption and high pollution is unsustainable, meaning the primary task of new urbanisation is to transform from a high-carbon to a low-carbon economy. Therefore, this new type of urbanisation must provide effective resource utilisation and protect the environment. The difficulties inherent in the traditional model of urbanisation are as follows.

High energy consumption

In 2015, China's gross domestic product (GDP) accounted for 15 per cent of the global total, however, its primary energy consumption accounted for about 22.9 per cent. Most of China's energy consumption occurred in its cities. At present, China faces a double disadvantage of high energy consumption and low utilisation efficiency. Urban energy consumption will grow year by year with increasing urbanisation. The International Energy Agency (IEA) predicted that, in 2015, China would account for 79 per cent of city energy consumption—nearly 23 per cent higher than the urbanisation rate of 56.1 per cent in that year—and will soar to 83 per cent by 2030.

High water consumption

China has serious water shortage and pollution problems. Rapid urbanisation has seen urban water use shift from industrial demand to household use. The efficiency of urban water usage directly determines the quality of urbanisation. According to China's Ministry of Water Resources, nearly 400 of 661 cities are in a water deficit, and among those more than 100 cities are experiencing a serious water shortage.

High land consumption

Urban sprawl is a common occurrence in China. According to the National Bureau of Statistics (NBS), urban built-up areas in China amounted to 12,856 sq km in 1990 and surged to 49,772 sq km by 2014, with an average annual growth rate of 5.56 per cent, while the urbanisation rate in the same period increased from 26.4 per cent to 54.8 per cent—an average annual growth rate of only 2.96 per cent—which means the growth rate of built-up areas is nearly two times that of urbanisation (see Table 23.1). This demonstrates that the speed of land urbanisation is much faster than that of population in China.

Table 23.1 China's urbanisation rate and amount of built-up area over time

	1990	2000	2010	2013	2014
Urbanisation rate (%)	26.4	36.2	50.0	53.7	54.8
Built-up area (sq km)	12,856	22,439	40,058	47,855	49,773

Source: NBS (2015c).

High pollution

According to the Ministry of Environmental Protection's 2015 *China Environmental State Bulletin*, among the first 74 cities implementing its new Ambient Air Quality Standards, the average number of days in which that standard was met in 2015 was about 260, with a standard-reaching rate of only 71.2 per cent. The average annual concentration of particulate matter (PM) 2.5 is 55 µg per cubic metre, which is 1.57 times that of China's secondary standard (35 µg per cu m). Among these 74 cities, only Zhoushan, Fuzhou, Xiamen, Shenzhen, Zhuhai, Jiangmen, Huizhou, Zhongshan, Haikou, Kunming and Lhasa fully met the air quality standards. In addition, according to China's surface water environment monitoring data, water with quality types I, II and III[1] accounted for 64.5 per cent of the total, while nearly 40 per cent did not meet the water quality standards in 2015.

Therefore, in the face of the highly carbonised and unsustainable traditional mode of urbanisation, new urbanisation—incorporating effective resource utilisation and environmental protection—is essential. Both academia and government departments have reached consensus on a new pattern of intensive, smart, low-carbon and green urbanisation. Premier Li Keqiang (2012) has said the new urbanisation should follow an intensive and low-carbon development mode, emphasising the efficient utilisation of natural resources and energy. Wei and Zhang (2011) and Gu (2013) hold that new urbanisation should take the road of green urbanisation and green governance.

New urbanisation with sustainable economic growth

At present, the environment of urbanisation development is undergoing profound changes in both China and globally, with traditional processes—promoted by traditional manufacturing industries—facing difficulties. Therefore, it is imperative to achieve industrial transformation and upgrading and take a new road of urbanisation with sustainable economic growth.

1 According to surface water environmental quality standards, water meeting quality types I, II and III can be used for drinking.

Traditionally, urban economic development has followed the investment and export-oriented model; however, the current development environment in China poses a severe challenge to the momentum of this model. The investment-oriented development model has made tremendous contributions to China's rapid economic development over the past few decades, but overreliance on investment for economic development is not sustainable. The RMB4 trillion rescue plan initiated in response to the Global Financial Crisis (GFC) in 2008 is a case in point. Government-led investment in infrastructure and real estate not only failed to solve the substantive problems in economic development, but also worsened structural contradictions and caused overproduction and other problems. In addition, the results of the sixth census (2010) of China indicate that the number of people over the age of 60 is 178 million—13.26 per cent of the total population and an increase of 2.93 percentage points compared with 2000. Moreover, under the influence of China's family planning policy, the proportion of the population born in the 1990s and 2000s is far below the current proportion of middle-aged and elderly people. The disappearance of the demographic dividend has already had an impact on China's export-oriented economy, which previously developed vigorously thanks to an unlimited supply of cheap labour. In addition, China's export-oriented economy, dominated by manufacturing industries, is at the lowest point of the 'smiling curve' and can obtain only extremely meagre profits in the global value chain. Therefore, with the rise of labour costs, the shortage of external demand caused by the GFC, the return of manufacturing industries to Europe and the United States and the shift of others to developing countries such as Vietnam and India, which have lower labour and land resource costs, the export-oriented development mode can no longer be regarded as a economic engine of China's future urbanisation.

A serious imbalance in industrial structure means this cannot be the core driver of urbanisation. To achieve the new urbanisation, industrial transformation and upgrading from traditional manufacturing to modern service industries must be realised. Li (2012) points out that the new urbanisation requires, in particular, the development of service industries. Currently, service industries in developed countries account for more than 70 per cent of total output value, which can absorb the maximum number of urban employees, and also helps to achieve the upgrading of the industrial structure. The impetus behind new urbanisation is not traditional investment and exports, but domestic 'green' consumption (Qiu 2009) and the synergistic development of urbanisation, industrialisation, informationalism and agricultural modernisation (Gu 2013).

New urbanisation with social justice and harmony

The traditional mode of urbanisation not only failed to realise common prosperity, but also caused social injustice and a widening of the gap between the rich and the poor. Therefore, pursuit of social justice and harmony has become an inevitable requirement of the new urbanisation, putting people at the core.

In 2014, the proportion of the rural population in China's total population was as high as 45 per cent, while total output from the agricultural sector was only 16 per cent of the national total, with a downward trend. At the same time, the urban population (including migrant workers from rural areas) represented only 55 per cent of the total population, but generated 84 per cent of national output, with a growing trend. That means 45 per cent of the population received only 16 per cent of total national income, while 55 per cent of the population received 84 per cent of total income (Figure 23.1), which indicates the paradox of socioeconomic development in China—that is, the coexistence of rising national income and rural poverty (Wen 2014).

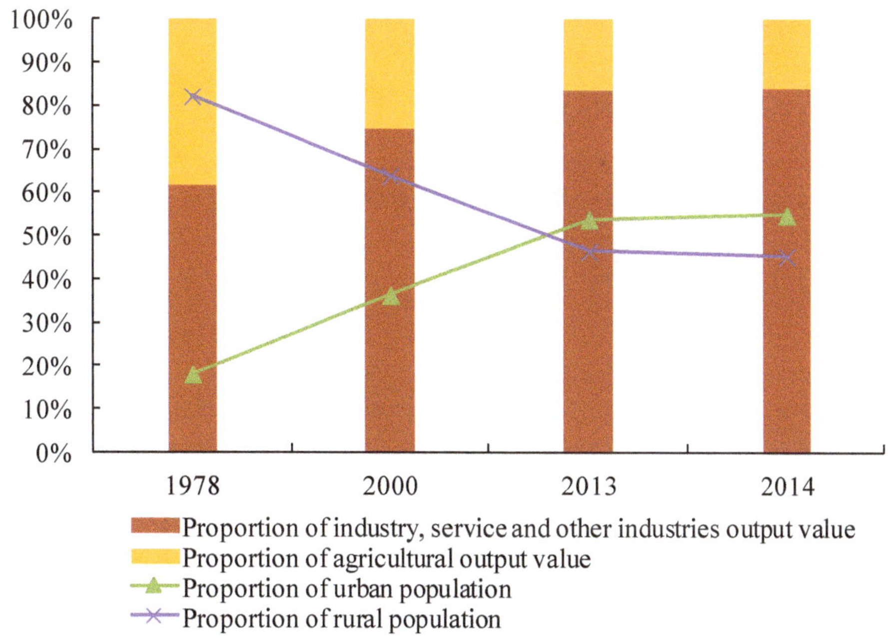

Figure 23.1 National income comparison between urban and rural populations

Source: NBS (2015c).

The obstruction caused by the *hukou* system is one important reason for this paradox (Wen 2014). Under the *hukou* system, large numbers of migrant workers cannot fully realise their citizenship in urban areas, nor can they enjoy basic public services in the city, including education, housing and medical care, which causes social problems for the children and elderly people left behind in rural areas. For example, in the Pearl River Delta, 20 million migrant workers were unemployed and without social security because of the GFC in 2008. In addition, the lack of integration of urban and rural land systems resulted in a lack of protection of farmers' property rights, and peasants whose land was expropriated found it difficult to receive fair compensation. Therefore, deepening people's urbanisation and pursuing social harmony and justice are essential requirements of the new urbanisation. This entails reform of the *hukou* and land systems from the institutional level.

New urbanisation with reasonable spatial structure

China's traditional mode of urbanisation was spatially unbalanced—for example, the urbanisation rate in the east of the country is much higher than in the central and western regions. According to data released by the NBS, in 2014, the urbanisation rate in eastern China was 61 per cent, while that in central China was 53 per cent and 49.7 per cent in the west. The regional differentiation of urbanisation levels is obvious, so it is imperative new urbanisation addresses this issue.

Mega-cities are agglomerated mainly in eastern China, which is also where urban diseases are mainly concentrated due to population expansion and relatively low level of city governance capacity. In central and western China, the development of mega-cities has been inadequate and the distribution of small and medium-sized cities and small towns is relatively loose. Due to the low levels of infrastructure and public services, socioeconomic development capacity is also hampered in central and western China. This spatial imbalance has led to large-scale regional population migration to the east and social problems associated with it, including for the children of migrants and elderly people left behind. Moreover, capital cities in all provinces have enjoyed rapid development due to favourable urban policies and resource levels, essentially creating a population–industrial agglomeration effect. However, the spillover effects of these cities on surrounding cities are weak. Therefore, further development of urbanisation should prevent the urban diseases and improve the city governance capacity. Metropolitan cluster development shall be adopted as the main strategy of promoting new urbanisation in order to construct polycentric metropolitan areas and to promote the transregional mobility of production factors. At the same time, development strategy should be implemented in light of local conditions and characteristics, embarking on a path of regional and urban–rural coordinated new urbanisation with reasonable spatial structure.

New urbanisation is inevitable in the era of globalisation and post-industrialisation. At present, all countries in the world experiencing the wave of globalisation have begun the transformation from traditional to post-industrialisation processes, including in urbanisation. As a national development strategy, China's urbanisation transformation has been concentrated in the development of new urbanisation. This, together with industrialisation, informationalism and agricultural modernisation, has created a path for synchronising the 'four modernisations' of sustainable development with Chinese characteristics. Among the four modernisations, urbanisation has special status, and accelerating that process is now a major task for China. After the eighteenth National Congress of the CPC explicitly proposed a road to new urbanisation with Chinese characteristics, the State Council promulgated its 'National New Urbanization Plan 2014–2020', which has positive strategic significance for the sustainable development of urbanisation (Hu and Pan 2014; Hu and Chen 2015). Since then, the thirteenth five-year plan has also put forward requirements for accelerating the pace of new urbanisation. The new urbanisation has therefore entered a new phase and its importance to China's future development is self-evident.

Defining new urbanisation

The concept of new urbanisation is rare in other countries. The most significant concept of urban renewal in the Western world is the theory of new urbanism, which emerged in the 1990s against the issue of urban sprawl, and which is considered the most influential global urban design trend of the past two decades. Although the theory of new urbanism has some value for the development of China's new urbanisation (Kong 2014), there are some essential differences with China in terms of the stage of medium-level development and rapid urbanisation and the definition of the concept of new urbanisation. The study of urbanisation in China has moved through conceptual stages—from urbanisation, to urbanisation with Chinese characteristics, to new urbanisation and to new urbanisation with Chinese characteristics—each stage of which is closely linked with national policies. Academics have been discussing the differences and connections between the concepts for a long time. This chapter focuses on new urbanisation, for which an accurate definition is a prerequisite for carrying out research. If there is no comprehensive and systematic understanding of new urbanisation, some aspects may be overemphasised while others are neglected in urbanisation practice , resulting in a situation in which some old problems are solved but many new ones arise (Hu 2013). Despite the name, new urbanisation is not a new concept, even though it does not yet have a unified definition. The basic idea is to explore a more quality-oriented approach to sustainable urbanisation, developing what is useful from traditional urbanisation and discarding what is not. The approach to sustainable urbanisation has become a heated topic, and the existing literature shows that different scholars hold diverging views (see Table 23.2).

Table 23.2 Definition of new urbanisation from selected literature

Scholars	Definitions
Hu (2005)	a) An idea of people-oriented and coordinated sustainable development; b) development of an intensive economy and a harmonious society as the goal; c) market mechanisms as the leading factor; d) large, medium and small cities have moderate scale, reasonable layout, coordinated structure, perfect network systems; e) interactive development with new industrialisation, informationalism and agricultural modernisation; f) support for industry, full employment opportunities, healthy ecological environment and urban–rural integration.
Wu et al. (2009)	New industrialisation and informationalism as driving forces to pursue an urbanisation path with urban–rural integration and coordinated development of population, economy, society, resources and the environment.
Qiu (2012)	From prioritising urban development to complementary urban–rural development, from high energy consumption to low energy consumption, from quantity of growth to quality improvement, from high environmental impact to low environmental impact, from extensive development to intensive development, from inequality to harmonious development.
Hu (2013)	Effective utilisation of natural resources, sustained economic growth, environmental protection, social fairness and harmony, rational spatial structure and smart cities; essentially a path of sustainable urbanisation.
Ni (2013)	a) Adhering to the principle of comprehensive, coordinated and sustainable development; b) population urbanisation as the core element; c) motivated by informationalism, agricultural industrialisation and new types of industrialisation; d) a model of intensified growth; e) government guidance and market mechanisms; f) sustainable development path to build an integrated urban–rural China.
Wei and Guan (2014)	Adhere to a path of people-centred, intensive intelligence, green and low carbon development, urban–rural integration and synchronisation of the four modernisations, with diversification, gradualism, intensiveness, harmony and sustainability.
Duan and Yin (2014)	Transformation from government-led to market-led; from exogenous urbanisation to endogenous urbanisation; from land urbanisation to population urbanisation; from an export and investment-driven economy to a consumption-driven economy; from one-dimensional economic goals to multidimensional goals of resource utilisation, environmental protection and social and economic development.
Li (2014)	People-oriented, low-carbon economy and new technology–led urbanisation.
Li et al. (2015)	Consideration of people as the core in overall planning, governance according to law and following a path of intensification and ecological protection to realise sustainable urbanisation.
Fang (2016)	Efficient and low-carbon, eco-friendly, economical and innovative, smart and safe, sustainable and healthy urbanisation.
Song and Jin (2016)	Urbanisation of lifestyles, employment patterns, public services, public space and social governance, and beautification of the living environment.

Source: Authors' selection from the relevant literature.

The literature review in Table 23.2 indicates that to draw a definition of new urbanisation, most scholars tend to start from a reflection on traditional urbanisation and compare the background, concept and goals of new and traditional urbanisation. The discussion has moved from abstract to concrete definitions. Although differences exist among scholars, some consensus has been reached on two aspects. The first is sustainable development, which is an inevitable choice for new urbanisation and the goal of all countries in the world. The second is people-centred urbanisation, which is an essential property of new urbanisation. The phenomenon of valuing materials more highly than people in urbanisation needs to be changed so that people's employment patterns, lifestyle, living environment and so on can be urbanised.

Traditionally, scholars understood the concept of sustainable development as the harmonious coexistence of humans and nature, embodied in the effective utilisation and protection of natural resources and the environment. In fact, sustainable development, in a broad sense, also includes sustainable organisational forms and institutional arrangements. Therefore, this chapter argues that new urbanisation is sustainable and people-centred urbanisation. This kind of sustainability manifests in the synergy between and balancing of the population, economy, natural resources and the environment, as well as sustainable institutional and planning arrangements. It entails not only the proper concentration of population and sustained economic growth, but also the efficient use of natural resources and environmental protection while demanding social fairness and harmony in institutional arrangements and rational spatial structure in urban planning.

Construction of an assessment indicator system for new urbanisation

After clarifying the definition of new urbanisation, it is necessary to discuss the empirical issues of it. There are normally two methods for measuring urbanisation. The first is the single-indicator method, using one indicator to measure the level of urbanisation. Relevant indicators include the proportions of the urban population and the nonagricultural population in overall population, the proportion of urban built-up areas in the country total, and so on. However, this method is prone to a one-sided pursuit of urban population growth or urban scale expansion. The other method of measurement is the composite indicators method, which measures the urbanisation level by building up an indicator system. However, traditional measurement indicators cannot cover all dimensions of new urbanisation. Against this background, we will establish a new indicator system to measure China's level of new urbanisation.

Literature review

Most research on the construction of a new urbanisation indicator system occurred after 2012. Scholars use various methods to construct indicator systems for different research areas and scales, such as urban agglomerations and provincial and prefecture-level cities (see Table 23.3). With the introduction of the concept of new urbanisation, more and more scholars are focusing on systematisation of urbanisation, and the research also shows a multidimensional trend.

Table 23.3 Study and measurement of new urbanisation indicator system by representative documents

Region	Scale	Scholars	Subject	Index
Nationwide	Province level	Yang (2013)	30 provinces	Five dimensions (economic, environmental, living, social, livelihood), 21 indicators
		Wang et al. (2015)	31 provinces	Four dimensions (economic, demographic, social, environmental), 23 indicators
Urban agglomeration	Prefecture level	Chang and Wang (2014)	3 provinces in Beijing–Tianjin–Hebei urban agglomeration	Five dimensions (public services, population, economy, social security, ecology), 21 indicators
		Yang et al. (2015)	8 cities in Shandong Peninsula urban agglomeration	Five dimensions (people-oriented, urban–rural planning, intensive and efficient, ecological, cultural) 100 indicators
Province	Prefecture level	Wang et al. (2013)	11 cities in Jiangxi province	Four dimensions (economy, population, infrastructure, environment), 15 indicators
		Wang et al. (2016)	11 cities in Hebei province	Four dimensions (economic, ecological, urban and rural areas, public services), 20 indicators
Prefecture-level city	Prefecture level	Guo et al. (2013)	Langfang	Five dimensions (population, living, economy, society, environment), 36 indicators
		Wang (2016)	Nanjing	Four dimensions (economic, social, population, spatial), 28 indicators
Province	County level	Xu and Zhong (2016)	18 counties in Hainan province	Seven dimensions (urbanisation level, public services, livelihood, facilities, environment, social economy, urban–rural coordination), 23 indicators
		Min et al. (2016)	District cities and 79 counties in Jiangxi Province	Six dimensions (population transfer, public services, economic development, urban construction, social management, urban–rural planning), 51 indicators

Source: Collected from relevant literature by the authors.

Several issues arise from consideration of the literature (Table 23.3). First, study of the basic theory is weak, and this lack of basic theoretical study—such as a definition of new urbanisation and the logical relationship between assessment and definition—is the root of the evaluation bias and insufficient applicability. Second, although some studies have defined the concept of new urbanisation, construction of an indicator system is limited in terms of the discussion level and empirical research. A one-sided pursuit of every aspect of the indicator system's construction may lead to a lack of internal logical connection among indicators. If such a system, lacking internal relations, is used for the assessment of new urbanisation, we may split the dimensions of urbanisation or risk conflict among the indicators, and fail to truly reflect the connotation of new urbanisation and cut off the relationship between normative and empirical research. Third, the existing literature rarely looks at the spatial patterns in new urbanisation in China; however, recognition of such patterns is a prerequisite for coordinated development. In view of the above problems, it is necessary to first clarify the theoretical issues and, further, based on a certain theoretical framework, guide the construction and application of a system of multidimensional assessment indicators.

Construction of the indicator system and explanations

The construction of the indicator system for new urbanisation in this chapter focuses mainly on multidimensional perspectives, aiming to overcome the limitations of the previously mentioned methods. Drawing on the existing relevant research, we construct a new urbanisation assessment indicators system with six dimensions—population, economy, natural resources, environment, social development and spatial aspects—which embody moderate population aggregation, sustained economic growth, efficient use of natural resources, environmental protection, social justice and harmony and reasonable spatial structure. Three representative indicators of each dimension are selected, and there are 18 specific indicators in total (see Table 23.4). The six dimensions are interrelated and work together to promote the development of new urbanisation. Among them, the proper concentration of population and sustained economic growth are the fundamental driving forces and the basis of and material guarantee for the coordinated development of all dimensions. The effective utilisation of natural resources and environmental protection are inevitable choices for sustained economic growth and structural transformation in the construction of new urbanisation in the new era in China. Social justice and harmony are at the core of realising people-oriented urbanisation. A rational spatial structure is an important task in coordinating regional and urban–rural development. Based on these considerations, a new urbanisation assessment indicator system with multidimensional perspectives will help to better grasp development goals at an integrated level and reflect the different characteristics and main problems of specific cities, which has important practical implications. In addition to the general principle of indicator selection—such as comprehensiveness, representativeness and data availability—it is worth noting that we use an extra 'outcome-oriented' principle to avoid double counting or the offset between positive and negative indicators. For example, with regard to the efficient use of natural resources, we will focus on how much benefit relevant investment has generated rather than on the investment itself; in terms of environmental protection, we will focus on what level of emissions achieves the standard instead of just the emissions level.

Table 23.4 Evaluation indicator system for China's new urbanisation

Target level	Level-two indicators	Level-three indicators	Indicator type	Indicator weight (%)
China's New Urbanisation Index (NUI)	Population dimension	Population density	Positive	5.6
		Urbanisation rate	Positive	5.6
		Proportion of temporary resident population to permanent resident population	Negative	5.6
	Economic dimension	GDP per capita	Positive	5.6
		Advancement index[1] of industrial structure	Positive	5.6
		GDP growth rate	Positive	5.6
	Natural resources dimension	Unit GDP water consumption	Negative	5.6
		Unit GDP land consumption	Negative	5.6
		Unit GDP electricity consumption	Negative	5.6
	Environmental dimension	Number of days that meet air quality standards	Positive	5.6
		Sewage treatment rate	Positive	5.6
		Domestic waste treatment rate	Positive	5.6
	Social dimension	Urban–rural income ratio[2]	Moderate	5.6
		Coverage rate of social security[3]	Positive	5.6
		Number of undergraduate universities per 10,000 college students[4]	Negative	5.6
	Spatial dimension	Road area per capita	Positive	5.6
		Rate of urban greenery coverage in built-up area	Positive	5.6
		Ratio of urban built-up area to total area	Positive	5.6

[1] Advancement index of industrial structure (written as W) is calculated as follows: first, according to the three industrial divisions, GDP will be divided into three parts, the proportion of each part's added value of GDP as a component of a space vector, thus a three-dimensional vector can be written as X0 = (x1,0, x2,0, x3,0). Then calculate the angles θ1, θ2 and θ3 between X0 and the vectors X1 = (1, 0, 0), X2 = (0, 1, 0) and X3 = (0, 0, 1), respectively, which are arranged from the lower industrial

level to the higher level. Where $\theta_j = \arccos\left(\frac{\sum_{i=1}^{3}(x_{i,j} \cdot x_{i,0})}{\sum_{i=1}^{3}(x^2_{i,j})^{1/2} \cdot \sum_{i=1}^{3}(x^2_{i,0})^{1/2}}\right)$, j = 1, 2, 3. Second, the formula for the value W is: $W = \sum_{k=1}^{3}\sum_{j=1}^{k}\theta_j$. The higher the value of W, the higher is the level of industrial structure (Fu 2010).

[2] The urban–rural income ratio is the ratio of the per capita disposable income of urban residents to that of rural residents.

[3] Social security coverage is the arithmetical average of pension insurance coverage, medical insurance coverage and unemployment insurance coverage.

[4] The ratio of the number of schools above undergraduate level per 10,000 undergraduate students.

Population dimension

Population concentration not only provides an important impetus to the process of urbanisation, but also reflects the results of urbanisation. It is therefore important in interpreting the level of urbanisation. In addition, population concentration integrates with many other important elements in the system of urbanisation, including the economy, society and the environment. In China's current stage of rapid urbanisation, many serious problems have been caused by the imbalance of various factors. It is imperative to explore a new path of urbanisation with moderate population concentration. With this in mind, two extra population indicators are selected while retaining the urbanisation rate: the obstacles posed by the *hukou* system and the carrying capacity of cities—that is, the share of the temporary resident population in the total resident population and urban population density, respectively. In a general sense, the population share of temporary residents reflects the mobility of the urban population and is also an indication of the attractiveness and vitality of a city. The reality of urbanisation in China at present, however, means the impeding effect of the *hukou* system on urbanisation is more evident, so we consider it a negative indicator.

Economic dimension

Sustained economic growth is the fundamental driver of new urbanisation. Based on the statistical indicators of existing economic sectors, three representative aspects are chosen: efficiency, structure and scale. Among them, GDP per capita represents economic performance and reflects the economic efficiency of production; the advancement index of industrial structure represents the economic structure. Industrial transformation and upgrading are the basis of sustainable development of the urban economy and the precondition for achieving new urbanisation, while the GDP growth rate characterises the economic scale and embodies economic growth. The three indicators are positive, confirming the sustainable development capacity of urban economy from a macro point of view.

Natural resources dimension

New urbanisation relies on the effective use of natural resources (Hu 2013), which is also a necessary requirement for sustainable development. In this dimension, to represent the three natural resources of water, land and energy utilisation efficiency, three negative indicators are chosen—unit GDP water consumption, unit GDP land consumption and unit GDP electricity consumption, respectively—to highlight the path of lower resource consumption for transformation to new urbanisation. The objective is to change the traditional urbanisation mode of high energy consumption. At the same time, it is consistent with the theory of new multidimensional urbanisation in developing new industrial system, such as low-carbon economy, recycling economy and green economy. Given the availability of data, this chapter replaces unit GDP energy consumption with unit GDP electricity consumption.

Environmental dimension

Environmental quality is an important criterion for measuring whether a city is liveable. Compared with traditional urbanisation, the new mode of urbanisation is reflected in the level of environmental protection and the sustainable development of the city, and is an important measure of whether or not humans and nature can coexist harmoniously. In terms of specific indicators, the sewage treatment rate, garbage disposal rate and number of days that meet air quality standards are selected as the indicators for water, garbage and air quality, respectively, which are related to the human living environment.

Social dimension

Social justice and harmony are at the core of realising people-centred new urbanisation. The theory of new urbanisation based on a multidimensional perspective holds that social justice and harmony mean coordination and protection of the public interest so that social fairness and justice can be effectively realised and maintained. The *hukou* system and public service provision are two important issues here. The relevant indicator for measuring the negative effects of the *hukou* system has been dealt with in the population dimension and will not be repeated here. In regard to public services, we select the social security coverage rate and the rate of undergraduate schools per 10,000 college students. The social security coverage rate is a composite index covering aspects of unemployment, health and pensions, and is an important measure of social welfare and an important factor in social stability. The rate of undergraduate universities per 10,000 college students embodies the problem of the fair distribution of educational resources, which is a hot issue in the current urbanisation process. The urban–rural income ratio characterises the differences in income between urban and rural areas, indicating the degree of social equity. The index is moderate in nature; some scholars think that a ratio of 1:1.2 is best (Wu et al. 2013)—and we agree.

Spatial dimension

Achieving a reasonable spatial structure is an important task in coordinating urban–rural and regional development and promoting new urbanisation. Theory and experience show that urban planning needs to avoid urban sprawl and other spatial issues, and that compactness in urban layout must be a basic feature of new urbanisation. To some extent, urban spatial structure is reflected in three main aspects: urban density, urban layout and urban morphology. At the same time, keeping the greenery rate as high as possible while building a compact city structurally is a challenging but necessary task. Based on the above criteria, three quantitative indicators are selected: per capita road area, greenery coverage rate and proportion of urban built-up area. Per capita road area and greenery coverage rate characterise the urban layout, in which the per capita road area represents traffic and commuter convenience in urban areas; and the greenery coverage rate reflects environmental liveability. In theory, there are reasonable standards for these measures, but for most cities in China, the current situation follows the idea that bigger is better (Wu et al. 2013). Urban morphology is closely related to the topography of the city; because of the lack of comparability of topographical features between cities, the proportion of urban built-up area in the total area is instead used to represent the urban scale. In addition, indicators of land use and population density are overlapped with urban density, so relevant indicators will not be selected again.

Research subject, method and data source

Subject

Based on the availability of data, this chapter takes as research objects 289 prefecture-level cities in China, excluding Taiwan Province, Sansha, Hong Kong and Macau.

Method

Data standardisation

Because the magnitude of each indicator is different and the different indicators are not directly comparable, they cannot be calculated directly. Therefore, it is necessary to standardise the raw data in data processing. This chapter uses the maximum difference standardisation method to conduct data standardisation, the formulas for which are as follows (Equations 23.1 and 23.2).

Equation 23.1

If the indicator is positive: $X_{ij} = \lfloor \max_j(x_{ij}) - x_{ij} \rfloor / \lfloor \max_j(x_{ij}) - \min_j(x_{ij}) \rfloor$

Equation 23.2

If the indicator is negative: $X_{ij} = \lfloor x_{ij} - \min_j(x_{ij}) \rfloor / \lfloor \max_j(x_{ij}) - \min_j(x_{ij}) \rfloor$

Although the urban–rural income ratio is a moderate indicator, its minimum value is 1.2, so it is suitable for the negative standardisation formula.

Index calculation

The general idea of index calculation is to weight each indicator and then sum to a weighted average. Common methods of weighting include the subjective weighting method (AHP, Delphi method), the objective weighting method (entropy method) and the comprehensive weighting method. Among them, a subjective weighting method, such as AHP, is an effective decision-making method combining quantitative and qualitative analysis, but this method has a lot of human interference. Although the objective weighting method has strong objectivity, it is easy to ignore the influence of data errors on the evaluation result, which will fail to reflect the reality of the complex evaluation object. The subjective and objective comprehensive weighting methods cannot completely eliminate the scientific failure of decision-making caused by the above drawbacks. More importantly, new urbanisation is sustainable urbanisation, which emphasises multidimensional synergy in the process of urbanisation. Therefore, to highlight the equal importance of each dimension, this chapter will calculate the index using the average weights method.

Data sources

The data collection year is 2014. The data are collected from the *China Urban Statistical Yearbook 2015* (NBS 2015e), and the missing values are supplemented by the *China Urban Construction Statistical Yearbook 2015* (NBS 2015d). The data for the proportion of temporary residents in the total resident population are taken from NBS (2015b); the urbanisation rate is from NBS (2015a) and the statistical communiqués of national economy and social development in 2014, the government work reports in 2015 and news portals of various provinces and cities. Given that the urbanisation rate in Shenzhen and Karamay is 100 per cent, the urban–rural income ratio cannot be calculated for these cities. For the data calculations to have mathematical meaning, such cities are treated at the optimal value—that is, the urban–rural income ratio is 1.2. The indicator for the number of days that meet air quality standards is from *China Environmental Statistical Yearbook* (NBS 2015b), *Statistical Yearbook of Provinces and Cities 2015* (NBS 2015f), *Statistical Bulletin of National Economic and Social Development* (NBS 2014) and the Ministry of Environmental Protection's data centre website;[2] the numbers of universities in different cities are from the Ministry of Education's website;[3] national-level data are from the *China Statistical Yearbook 2015* (NBS 2015c) and *China City Statistical Yearbook 2015* (NBS 2015a).

Results

Basic situation of China's new urbanisation

Through our calculations, we obtain the new urbanisation indexes (NUIs) for the country as a whole and for 289 cities above the prefecture level. We divide the country into three regions—east, central and west—and mark the NUIs of cities in various regions on the axes from largest to smallest (as shown in Figure 23.2). This indicates that the maximum and minimum NUIs in the east are larger than those in central and western China, and the maximum NUI in the central region is much the same as that in the west, but its minimum NUI is higher than that in the west, indicating that the new urbanisation level in the east is higher than that in the central and western regions, while that in central China is slightly higher than that in the west. China's new urbanisation level follows a stepwise decreasing pattern, from the east to the centre and then to the west. As a whole, this is in line with the regional differences in levels of socioeconomic development in China—that is, the more developed socioeconomic regions have higher NUIs. In addition, the difference between maximum and minimum NUIs is 27.93 percentage points in the east, which is more than that in the west (23.51 percentage points) and the centre (20.05 percentage points), indicating that central China has the smallest variation in the new urbanisation level. Although the new urbanisation level in eastern China is predominant as a whole, the differences among cities in this region

2 See datacenter.mep.gov.cn/websjzx/queryIndex.vm.

3 See www.moe.edu.cn.

are more pronounced than those in the central and western regions, raising even more serious problems for coordinated regional development. At the national level, China's NUI in 2014 was 47.75 per cent, which is 7.02 percentage points lower than the national urbanisation rate (54.77 per cent). This shows that the urbanisation rate overestimated China's new urbanisation level.

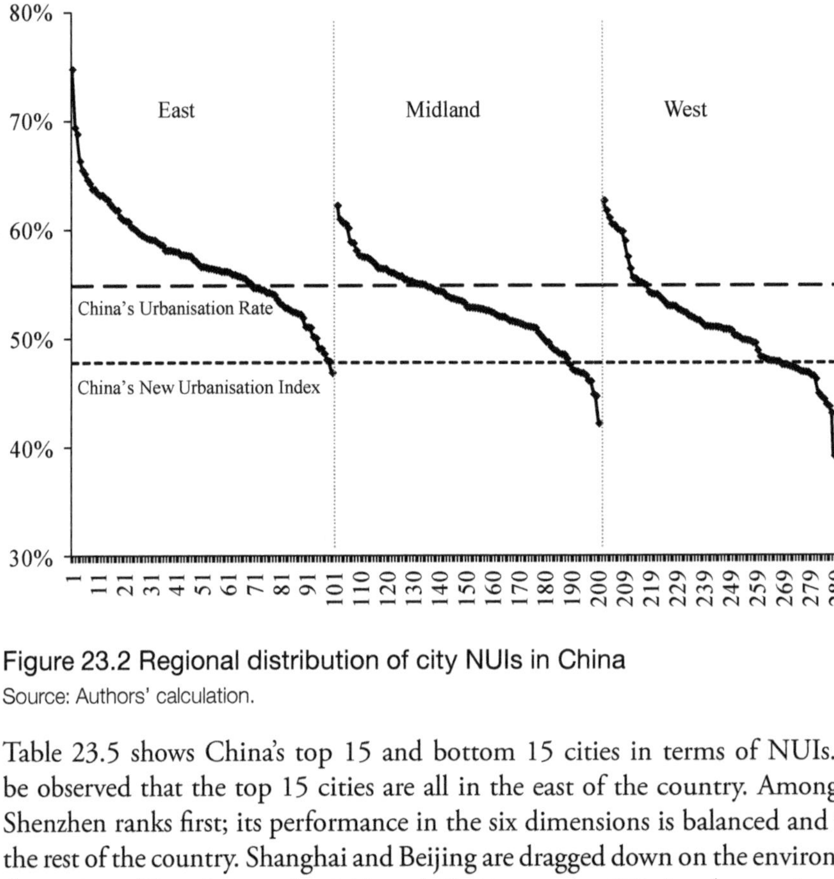

Figure 23.2 Regional distribution of city NUIs in China

Source: Authors' calculation.

Table 23.5 shows China's top 15 and bottom 15 cities in terms of NUIs. It can be observed that the top 15 cities are all in the east of the country. Among them, Shenzhen ranks first; its performance in the six dimensions is balanced and it leads the rest of the country. Shanghai and Beijing are dragged down on the environmental dimension (Shanghai ranks 144 and Beijing ranks 251 in the environmental dimension); they rank second and third, respectively, overall. With the exception of Shenzhen, although there are some differences in the rankings between the NUI and the urbanisation rate, the differences are relatively small; the bottom 15 cities are in central, western and north-eastern China. It is noteworthy that the ranking of NUIs is significantly different from that of urbanisation rates in Yichun and Hegang, due mainly to the poor level of sustainable economic development and inefficient use of resources in both cities. Water, electricity and land resource utilisation efficiencies are significantly lower than the national average, seriously restricting the development of new urbanisation.

Table 23.5 NUI rankings of the top 15 and bottom 15 Chinese cities

City	NUI		Urbanisation rate		Ranking difference[1]	City	NUI		Urbanisation rate		Ranking difference
	Value (%)	Rank	Value (%)	Rank			Value (%)	Rank	Value (%)	Rank	
Shenzhen	74.78	1	100.00	1	0	Zhongwei	46.58	275	32.74	265	–10
Shanghai	69.41	2	89.60	7	5	Baise	46.57	276	57.54	283	7
Beijing	68.84	3	86.35	12	9	Qingyang	46.24	277	31.55	284	7
Zhuhai	66.36	4	87.87	11	7	Xinzhou	46.13	278	44.45	209	–69
Shantou	65.53	5	69.85	46	41	Yuncheng	46.05	279	44.70	215	–64
Xiamen	65.18	6	88.80	9	3	Tianshui	44.92	280	33.91	279	–1
Dongguan	64.66	7	88.81	8	1	Ganzhou	44.86	281	33.14	223	–58
Nanjing	64.30	8	80.90	18	10	Yichun	44.69	282	43.99	15	–267
Tianjin	63.76	9	82.27	17	8	Haidong	44.62	283	35.35	282	–1
Wuxi	63.75	10	74.50	30	20	Chongzuo	44.38	284	84.00	274	–10
Zhoushan	63.38	11	66.30	62	51	Dingxi	43.93	285	28.77	287	2
Guangzhou	63.21	12	85.43	13	1	Lhasa	43.72	286	46.15	190	–96
Suzhou	63.20	13	74.00	31	18	Baiyin	43.10	287	44.39	216	–71
Zhongshan	62.96	14	88.07	10	–4	Hegang	42.19	288	76.59	25	–263
Weihai	62.81	15	61.32	82	67	Longnan	39.17	289	26.65	289	0

[1] The difference between ranking for the urbanisation rate and for the NUI.

Relationship between the NUI and the urbanisation rate

Traditionally, the urbanisation level is measured by the urbanisation rate—that is, the proportion of the urban population in the total population, which is equivalent to giving the indicator 100 per cent weight. It is clear that the traditional mode of urbanisation emphasises quantity of growth, while new urbanisation emphasises multidimensional synergistic development. Therefore, one of the purposes of constructing the new urbanisation indicator system is to weaken the weight of the urbanisation rate and increase the weights of indicators in other dimensions, achieving multidimensional and synergistic cooperation, which means that new urbanisation pays greater attention to the quality of development. Therefore, there is a big difference between the two modes in terms of quantity.

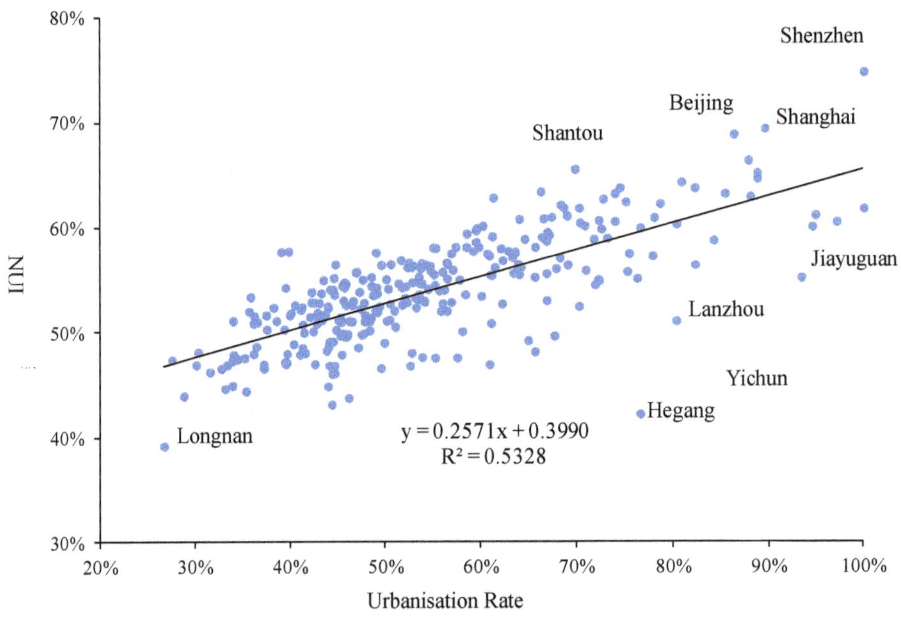

Figure 23.3 Relationship between NUI and urbanisation rate

Source: According to the authors' calculation.

Figure 23.3 depicts the linear relationship between the NUI and the urbanisation rate for cities in China. Intuitively, the slope of the line of fit is 0.2571. The statistical meaning can be expressed by saying that for every 1 per cent increase in the urbanisation rate, the NUI increases by only 0.2571 per cent, which is a significant mismatch. On the other hand, the fitting coefficient is only 53.28 per cent, which means that the linear relationship can explain only 53.28 per cent of the relationship between the two, indicating a positive correlation to a certain extent—that is, the higher the urbanisation rate, the higher is the NUI (for example, Shenzhen and

Shanghai); however, this is not always the case (for example, Yichun and Hegang). Therefore, new urbanisation is not simply a process of gathering the population in cities, but is more about the all-round development of cities, including the six dimensions of population, economy, resources, environment, society and space. The formulation of a new urbanisation plan also needs to change traditional thinking and shift from the single-dimensional perspective on the urbanisation rate to multidimensional perspectives.

Previously, it was believed that urbanisation is admittedly related to geographical, anthropological and sociological factors. However, economic factors determine the origin and development of cities in a much deeper level. Economic variables are the overriding factor (Bairoch 1991: 21).

There has been extensive debate in academic circles about the profound interaction between urbanisation and economic development. However, the related research is based more on the traditional measurement of urbanisation, providing relatively insufficient discussion of the relationship between new urbanisation and economic development. Because new urbanisation involves richer considerations of all dimensions of urban development compared with the traditional mode, the relationship between new urbanisation and economic development needs to be reconsidered.

Figure 23.4 depicts the quantitative relationship between the NUI, the urbanisation rate and economic development, in which GDP per capita characterises economic development. It can be observed that both the NUI and the urbanisation rate have a positive correlation with GDP per capita, which is consistent with the previous discussions. However, comparing Figures 23.4a and 23.4b, there is a certain difference between the two relationships. In the statistical sense, when GDP per capita increases by 1 unit, the NUI will increase by 0.013 percentage points and the urbanisation rate will increase by 0.038 percentage points. Therefore, the degree of correlation between GDP per capita and the urbanisation rate is three times that between GDP per capita and the NUI. Urbanisation has traditionally been heavily dependent on economic development and it proves Bairoch's (1991) assertion that economic variables are an overriding factor. Thus, economic development has become important in promoting the process of urbanisation; however, its role in this is far weaker than its role in promoting traditional urbanisation. The concept of new urbanisation weakens the influence of economic variables and emphasises multidimensional synergy, of which economic development is only one dimension.

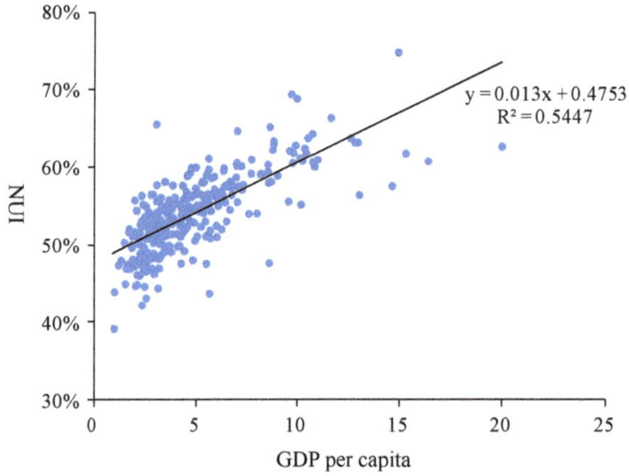

(a) NUI and GDP Per capita (10,000 yuan)

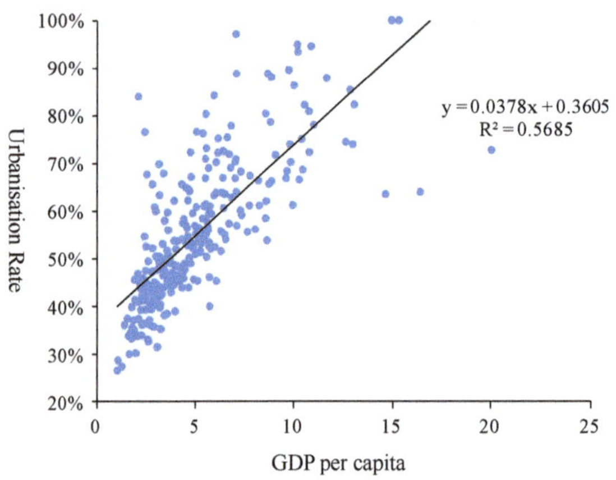

(b) Urbanisation Rate and GDP Per capita (10,000 yuan)

Figure 23.4 Relationships between new urbanisation, the urbanisation rate and economic development

Source: Authors' calculation.

Spatial distribution of China's new urbanisation

Spatial distribution comparison between the NUI and the urbanisation rate

To explore the spatial distribution pattern of China's new urbanisation, ArcGIS 10.0 software was used to make a spatial visualisation of the NUI and urbanisation rate rankings of cities above the prefecture level in China (see Figure 23.5). As can be seen from Figure 23.5a, the differences in NUI between regions and cities in China are significant. The top 15 cities for the NUI are all in the eastern coastal areas and are distributed mainly in three major economic circles—namely, the Beijing–Tianjin–Hebei, Yangtze River Delta and Pearl River Delta areas. The spatial distribution of the bottom 15 cities, however, is relatively scattered, but most are in north-eastern, central and western China.

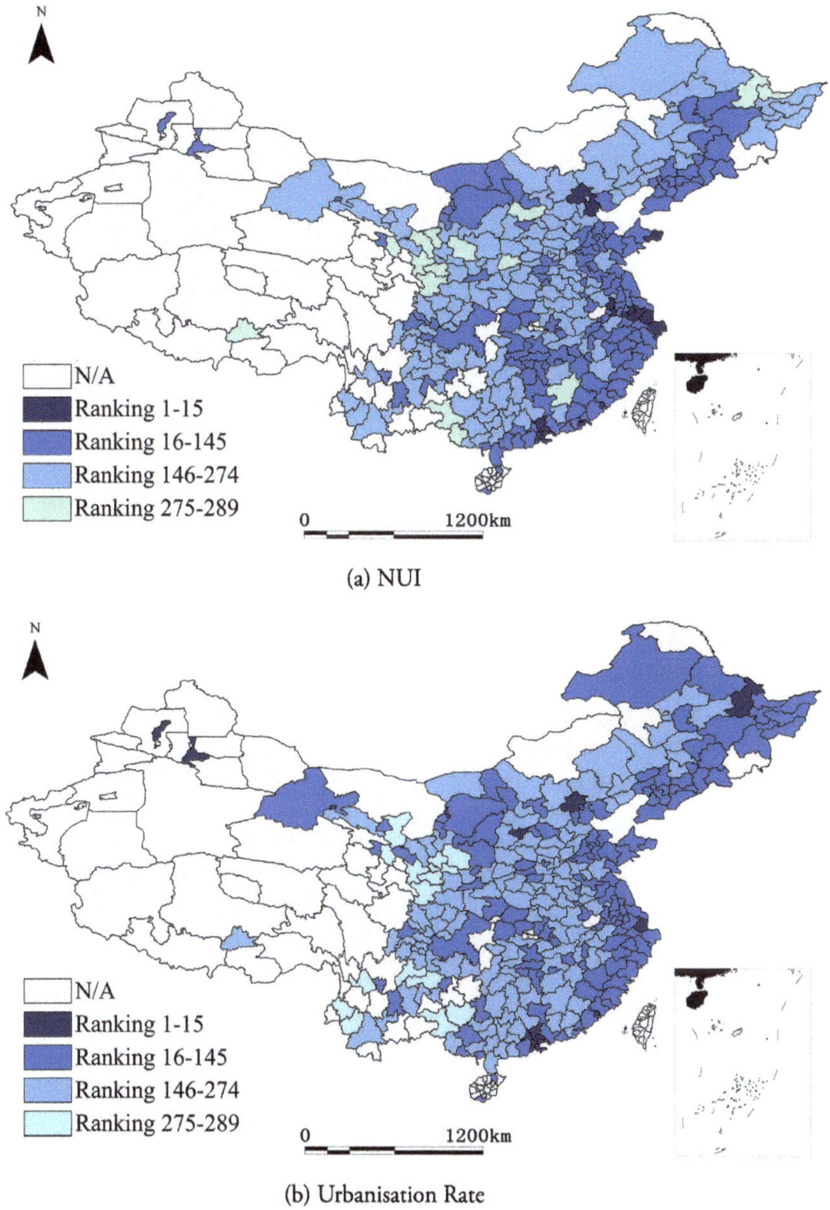

Figure 23.5 Spatial distributions of NUI and urbanisation rate rankings of cities above prefecture level in China

Source: Authors' calculation.

As for the spatial distribution of the urbanisation rate (Figure 23.5b), it is similar to the distribution of the NUI—that is, decreasing in a stepwise manner from the east to the centre then the west. The differences can be observed as well. First, the top 15 cities for the rate of urbanisation are more scattered than those for the NUI, and are distributed in the north-eastern region, the north-western region and China's three major economic circles. Second, the bottom 15 cities for the urbanisation rate are more concentrated, in the west of the country, compared with distribution for the NUI. In addition, the urbanisation rates of most cities in north-eastern China are higher than the NUIs. From the spatial distribution differences of the NUI and the urbanisation rate, we can also see that if new urbanisation is measured by the rate of urbanisation, there will be some overestimations or underestimations. This is in line with the previous discussion of the relationship between new urbanisation and the urbanisation rate.

With the exception of Shenzhen, Guangzhou and Longnan, mismatches between the NUI and urbanisation rate rankings of cities are universal, but the degree of this mismatch differs significantly. The number of cities that are overrated[4] is 127, accounting for 43.94 per cent of the total, and 159 cities are underrated, accounting for 55.02 per cent of the total. The mismatch degree is higher in cities in north-eastern China, where there is a concentration of cities whose rankings are overrated by more than 100 (ranking difference). Among them, Yichun has the largest degree of mismatch. Its NUI ranking is just 282, while its urbanisation rate rank is 15—a ranking gap of 267. The most underrated city is Maoming. Its NUI rank is 64, while its urbanisation rate rank is 260—a ranking gap of 196—due mainly to the fact the urbanisation rate indicator overlooks the city's performance in the dimensions of resource utilisation and environmental protection. Especially in the resource dimension, Maoming ranks significantly above the national average, in terms of water resources, electricity and land resource utilisation efficiencies.

As shown in Table 23.6, western China has the largest number of cities whose urbanisation rate overestimates their new urbanisation level, accounting for 16.61 per cent of the total number of cities and 37.8 per cent of the overestimated cities; the eastern region has the largest proportion of cities whose urbanisation rate underrates their new urbanisation level, accounting for 22.15 per cent of the total number of cities and 40.25 per cent of the total number of undervalued cities. This shows that using the urbanisation rate to measure the level of new urbanisation has, to an extent, dragged down the overall new urbanisation level in the east and pushed up that in the west.

4 The difference between ranking for the urbanisation rate and for the NUI refers to the value of the urbanisation ranking minus the ranking of the NUI. If the difference is positive, it means the urbanisation rate underrates the level of new urbanisation; if the difference is negative, it means the urbanisation rate overrates the level of new urbanisation.

As shown in Figure 23.6, the greater the ranking difference between the urbanisation rate and the NUI, the further the scattered points are from the 45° line. The area above the 45° line is the area in which the urbanisation rate underrates the level of new urbanisation, while below the 45° line is the area in which the urbanisation rate overrates the level of new urbanisation. We can see that cities such as Maoming and Zhanjiang belong to the group of cities that are seriously underrated, while Yichun and Hegang belong to the seriously overrated group.

Table 23.6 Regional distributions of NUI and urbanisation rate rankings of cities above prefecture level in China

Regions	Number of cities	Overrated		Underrated		No difference	
		Number of cities	Percentage of total number of cities (%)	Number of cities	Percentage of total number of cities (%)	Number of cities	Percentage of total number of cities (%)
Eastern	101	35	12.11	64	22.15	2	0.69
Central	100	44	15.22	56	19.38	0	0.00
Western	88	48	16.61	39	13.49	1	0.35
Nationwide	289	127	43.94	159	55.02	3	1.04

Source: Authors' calculation.

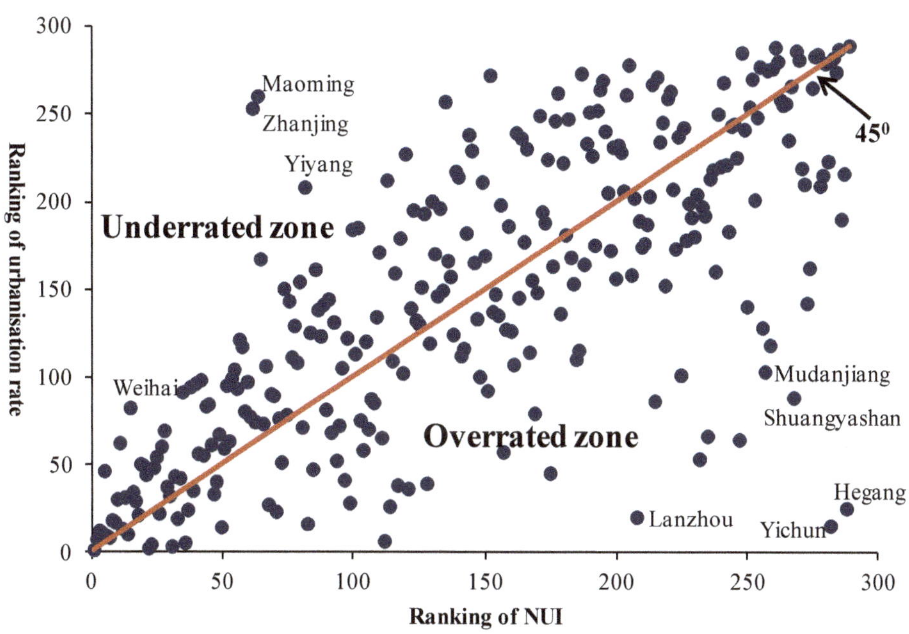

Figure 23.6 Ranking mismatches in the urbanisation rate and the NUI
Source: Authors' calculation.

China's new urbanisation dimensional spatial pattern

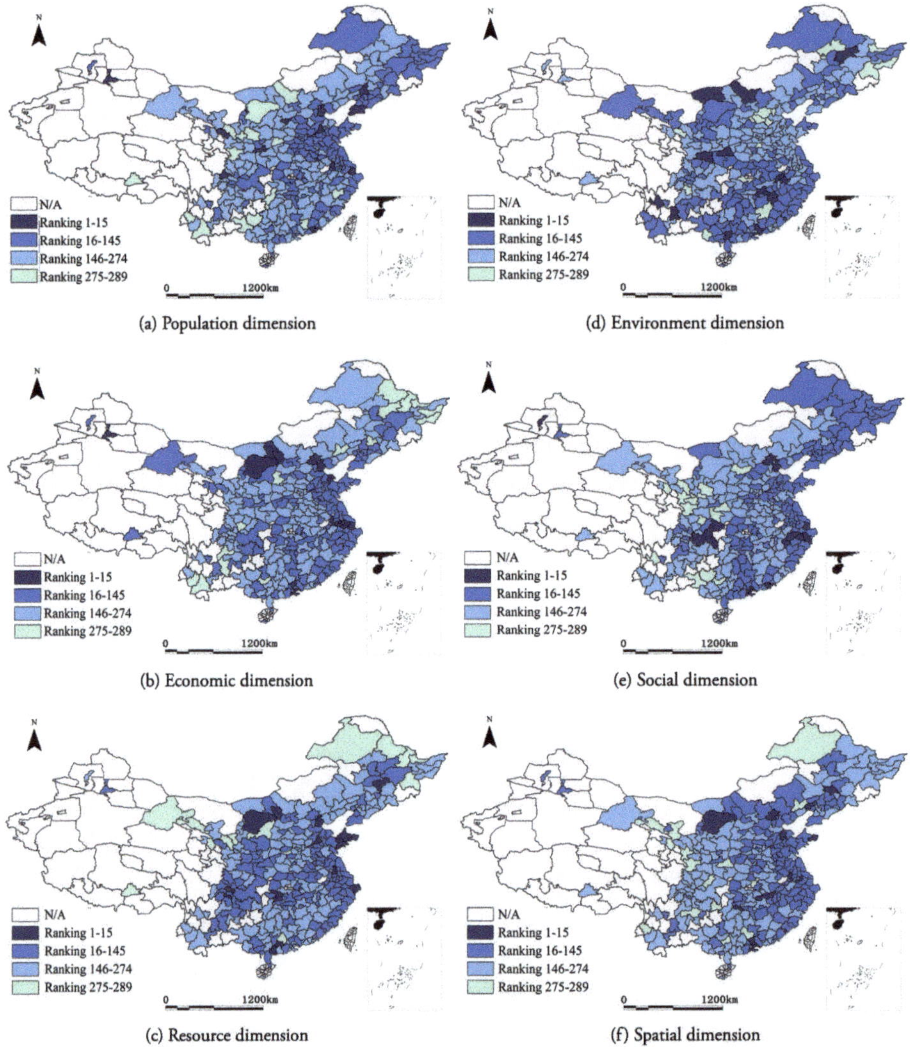

Figure 23.7 China's new urbanisation dimensional spatial pattern

Source: Authors' calculation.

Figure 23.7 depicts the dimensional spatial distributions of the levels of new urbanisation in China, including aspects of population, economy, resources, environment, society and space in cities above prefecture level. Several conclusions can be drawn. First, there is a high degree of similarity in the spatial distribution patterns of the population dimension and the urbanisation rate, indicating that population factors are the basis of both new and traditional modes of urbanisation. Second, there is a high degree of similarity in the spatial distribution pattern of the economy dimension and that of the NUI, which shows that although new urbanisation weakens the role of economic variables, sustained economic development remains a driving force and is also the basis of, and material guarantee for, codevelopment between various dimensions. Third, cities in the eastern coastal areas rank relatively high and cities in the north-east rank relatively low in terms of the resources dimension (most of the bottom 15 cities are in the north-east). Fourth, in the environmental dimension, the rankings of cities in northern China are generally low, especially in the Beijing–Tianjin–Hebei economic zone, which indicates that environmental pressures are relatively high there. For example, in Shijiazhuang, fewer than 100 days in a year meet air quality standards. Fifth, in the social dimension, spatial distribution follows a stepwise decreasing pattern from the east to central China and then to the west, which means the degree of social fairness and harmony is higher in developed areas than in less developed areas. Sixth, in terms of the spatial dimension, the eastern coastal cities rank higher than cities in the north-east, centre and west, indicating that the urban spatial structure in the east is more reasonable, while that in north-eastern, central and western cities needs to be improved. In addition, most of the bottom 15 ranked cities are in the north-east and west, indicating that there is a long way to go in building new urbanisation in these two regions. In north-eastern China, in particular, a sluggish economy makes this even harder. It is noteworthy that some cities in western China have a comparative advantage in the environmental dimension, so making good use of this—for example, by developing eco-tourism—could provide a breakthrough in realising catch-up development of new urbanisation in this region.

Concluding remarks

Traditionally, urbanisation has been promoted through high consumption and high pollution, leading to problems such as difficulties with economic transformation, social injustice and an unbalanced spatial structure. China's unsustainable traditional mode of urbanisation needs to urgently shift to a sustainable and people-centred mode. It was in this context that the idea of new urbanisation came into being. The problem of defining new urbanisation has long been discussed in academic communities, and the process has shifted from an abstract to a concrete definition. Based on an analysis of the literature, we find that scholars have reached a consensus on at least two aspects of this definition. The first is sustainable development; in the process of urbanisation, as well as adhering to the principle of achieving a harmonious coexistence between humans and nature, sustainable organisational forms and institutional arrangements are also needed. The second aspect is putting people at the centre of urbanisation. The previous method of situations that urbanise 'material' rather than human in the course of urbanisation must be change. Therefore, the new urbanisation not only entails the proper concentration of population and sustained economic growth, but also entails effective use of resources and calls for environment protection, while maintaining social fairness and harmony in institutional arrangements and rational spatial structure in urban planning. In order to explore the new urbanisation, its spatial pattern and its relationship with traditional urbanisation in China, this paper constructs a new indicator system of new urbanisation index. The empirical study shows that in 2014 China's NUI was 47.75 per cent, which is 7.02 percentage points lower than the national urbanisation rate (54.77 per cent), which indicate that the urbanisation rate overestimated the China's new urbanisation level. Therefore, if the new urbanisation level is measured using the urbanisation rate, there will be problems of overvaluation or undervaluation to varying degrees. Although economic factors are the main drivers of new urbanisation, their role is weaker than in traditional urbanisation—that is, the concept of new urbanisation weakens the influence of economic variables and stresses multidimensional coordination. In terms of spatial distribution, new urbanisation in China follows the regional distribution of the country's socioeconomic development, showing a stepwise decreasing spatial pattern from the east to the centre and then the west, which means that regions with higher socioeconomic development have higher NUIs.

A typical feature of traditional urbanisation is the simple pursuit of population concentration in urban areas, which is closely related to the traditional measurement of urbanisation (for example, the proportion of the urban population in total population or the proportion of urban built-up areas). This criterion has a direct impact on local governments' promotion of urbanisation, due to the one-sided emphasis on increasing the urban population and built-up areas, while ignoring aspects of resource utilisation, the environment, society and spatial structure, and eventually leading to unsustainable traditional urbanisation. The NUI developed in this chapter is a useful attempt to measure the rate of new urbanisation in the future. Compared with the urbanisation rate, the NUI emphasises that promotion of new urbanisation requires coordinated development in six dimensions, and any weak point in any dimension will drag down the new urbanisation level. Therefore, multidimensional new urbanisation requires a more accurate method for measuring urbanisation, and the establishment of a comprehensive and scientific assessment indicator system that will reflect the true level of new urbanisation.

The promotion of new urbanisation should adhere to practices of marketisation, intensification and ecological protection. First, urbanisation is a result of the logic of resource flows. The flow of resources such as people and capital is not based on the will of people, but is, rather, determined by market forces (Hu and Chen 2015). Therefore, new urbanisation must respect the power of the market, with proper government guidance. In reality, however, in China the government often controls urbanisation, which does not accord with the basic spirit of allowing the market to allocate resources. The regulation of urban administrative hierarchies is one such example. In the past, the development of heavy industry in north-eastern

China was strong and the effect of population agglomeration was remarkable. The state approved many prefecture-level cities in this region. Now, however, market forces have caused the flight of population and capital from this area, and some of the north-eastern cities cannot reach the standards of prefecture-level cities. In contrast, with the rapid development since China's period of reform and opening up, the economic improvement in some villages has resulted in a large population concentration and some have reached prefecture-level standards. All this is the result of market choices; however, further development of these cities and villages is subject to administrative regulation, and the market cannot lower or raise the administrative level of a city. Therefore, in the new urbanisation, we need to speed up reform of the administrative system and let the market determine the scale and speed of urbanisation.

Second, new urbanisation should focus on the efficient and intensive use of resources. Urban density is closely related to the intensive use of land resources, and plays an important role in urban development. The greater the urban density, the more developed will be the social division of labour, which is conducive to improvements in production efficiency. Increasing urban density can reduce information transaction costs and encourage the exchange of information and ideas, which can greatly benefit urban development (Zhou 2015). Therefore, it is necessary to change the 'sprawl' pattern of urbanisation in the future. Finally, the city is ultimately a typical complex ecosystem. Urbanisation is a process in which socioeconomic and environmental resource systems are constantly intertwined and coevolving. Cities are also the point of strongest interaction between socioeconomic and environmental resource systems. Therefore, we must look at urbanisation issues from a multidimensional perspective. If marketisation, intensification and ecological improvement are given enough attention, we can set the basic direction for new urbanisation. If, instead, we continue to promote traditional urbanisation, not only will the old problems remain, but also new problems may arise.

References

Bairoch, P. (1991), *Cities and Economic Development: From the dawn of history to the present*, Chicago: University of Chicago Press.

Chang, C. and Wang, Y. (2014), Indicator system construction and evaluation of new urbanisation in Beijing-Tianjin-Hebei metropolitan area, *Theory & Practice* 5: 115–17.

Duan, J. and Yin, Y. (2014), Interpretation of the connotation of new urbanization from a multidimensional perspective, *Journal of Suzhou University (Philosophy and Social Science Edition)* (5): 38–43.

Fang, C. (2016), *China's New Urbanization Development Report,* Beijing: Science China Press. doi.org/10.1007/978-3-662-49448-6.

Fu, L. (2010), An empirical research on industrial structure and economic growth, *Statistical Research* 27(8): 79–81.

Gu, S. (2013), Five transformations to realize China's urbanization, [in Chinese], The People's Congress of China, 10 June. Available from: www.npc.gov.cn/npc/zgrdzz/2013-07/10/content_1800614.htm.

Guo, Z., Sun, Y. and Zhang C. (2013), New urbanization level and compound index system in Langfang, *Journal of North China Institute of Aerospace Engineering* 23(4): 32–5.

Hu, B. (2013), 'Six-in-one': Road to new urbanization, [in Chinese], *Guangming Daily,* 28 June. Available from: epaper.gmw.cn/gmrb/html/2013-06/28/nw.D110000gmrb_20130628_1-11.htm?div=-1.

Hu, B. and Chen, C. (2015), New urbanization under globalization and the social implications in China, *Asia & the Pacific Policy Studies* (2): 34–43. doi.org/10.1002/app5.68.

Hu, B. and Pan, Q. (2014), China's new urbanization: Planning and improvement, *Journal of the Party School of the Central Committee of the CPC* 18(6): 89–93.

Hu, J. (2005), Study on the development of China's new urbanization, Doctoral dissertation, Southwest Agricultural University, Chongqing.

Kong, X. (2014), Valuable reference of new urbanism on the new pattern of urbanization in China, *Journal of Beihua University (Social Science)* 15(2): 30–5.

Li, K. (2012), Promoting urbanisation co-ordinately is the major strategic choice for realization of modernisation, [in Chinese], *Administration Reform* 11(4): 4–11.

Li, R., Zhao, Q. and Wang, W. (2015), Research on problems and countermeasures of urban villages reconstruction in the context of new urbanization, *Macroeconomics* (8): 41–7, 75.

Li, X. (2014), A comprehensive understanding of the connotation of new urbanization, [in Chinese], *People's Daily,* 18 December. Available from: theory.people.com.cn/n/2014/1218/c40531-26230279.html.

Lin, C. and Wang, Y. (2014), Construction and evaluation of new urbanization assessment indicator system in Beijing–Tianjin–Hebei metropolitan area, *Price: Theory & Practice* (5): 115–17.

Min, Z., Xu, W. and Li, Z. (2016), Construction and application of a new urbanization index system based on third party evaluation: Taking Jiangxi province as an example, *Urban Studies* 23(8): I0012–16.

Ministry of Environmental Protection (2015), *China Environmental State Bulletin*, Beijing: Ministry of Environmental Protection.

National Bureau of Statistics (NBS) (2014), *Statistical Bulletin of National Economic and Social Development 2014*, Beijing: China Statistics Press.

National Bureau of Statistics (NBS) (2015a), *China City Statistical Yearbook 2015*, Beijing: China Statistics Press.

National Bureau of Statistics (NBS) (2015b), *China Environmental Statistical Yearbook 2015*, Beijing: China Statistics Press.

National Bureau of Statistics (NBS) (2015c), *China Statistical Yearbook 2015*, Beijing: China Statistics Press.

National Bureau of Statistics (NBS) (2015d), *China Urban Construction Statistical Yearbook 2015*, Beijing: China Statistics Press.

National Bureau of Statistics (NBS) (2015e), *China Urban Statistical Yearbook 2015*, Beijing: China Statistics Press.

National Bureau of Statistics (NBS) (2015f), *Statistical Yearbook of Provinces and Cities 2015*, Beijing: China Statistics Press.

Ni, P. (2013), Basic model of new urbanization, specific path and promotion strategy, *Jianghai Academic Journal* 3(1): 87–94.

Qiu, B. (2009), Discrimination and analysis of urbanisation with Chinese characteristics: 'C mode'—Surpass the temptation of the 'A mode' and the muddiness of the 'B mode', *Urban Studies* (1): 1–7.

Qiu, B. (2012), New urbanization: From concept to action, *Administration Reform* (11): 11–18.

Song, L. and Jin, Y. (2016), Essential connotation of new urbanization, *Shandong Social Sciences* (4): 47–51.

Wang, B., Xie, F. and Huang, X. (2013), Construction of new urbanization evaluation index system: A case study of Jiangxi province, *Jiangxi Social Sciences* (8): 72–6.

Wang, D., Sheng, J. and Wang, H. (2016), Construction of new urbanization quality evaluation index system and empirical study: In Hebei province as an example, *Economy and Management* 30(5): 67–71.

Wang, J. (2016), Construction of new urbanization index system under the new normal: A case study of Nanjing, Jiangsu province, *Journal of Commercial Economics* (8): 146–8.

Wang, J., Yi, D. and Guo, L. (2015), Research on China's new urbanization index system construction and evaluation, *Modern Management Science* (6).

Wei, H. and Guan, X. (2014), The scientific connotation and strategic key points of new urbanization with Chinese characteristics, *Henan Social Sciences* 22(3): 17–26.

Wei, H. and Zhang, Y. (2011), Ideas and initiatives to comprehensively accelerate green transformation of urbanization in China, *Economic Review* (9): 15–19.

Wen, G. (2014), *My People Have No Land*, Hong Kong: Oriental Press.

Wu, D., Zhao, L. and Gao, W. (2013), Essential characteristics and evaluation of new-style urbanization, *Journal of Beihua University (Social Science)* 14(6): 33–7.

Wu, J., Wang, B. and Shen, L. (2009), Behavior of local government in the process of new urbanization in China, *Chinese Public Administration* (3): 88–91.

Xu, H. and Zhong, M. (2016), Construction and measurement of new-type urbanization index system in Hainan province, *Journal of Hebei University of Science and Technology (Social Science)* 16(1): 15–19.

Xu, L. and Cao, H. (2014), From measure to guidance: Galactic model of new-type urbanization and its evaluation system, *Journal of Public Administration* 11(1): 65–74.

Yang, H. (2013), Construction of quality evaluation index system of urbanization in China's new urbanization context, *Economic Research Guide* (20): 65–7.

Yang, Y., Wang, C., Zhang, L. and He, C. (2015), The establishment and application of the index system for quantitatively evaluating the status of new-type urbanization based on the national plan: A case of Shandong Peninsula urban agglomeration, *Economic Geography* 35(7): 51–8.

Zhou, Q. (2015), Next step of urbanization in China, *Chinese Rural Area Discovery* (4): 26–34.

24. China's 40 years of agricultural development and reform

Jikun Huang and Scott Rozelle

Since the founding of the People's Republic of China (PRC) more than seven decades ago, agriculture has experienced a roller-coaster development path (Lardy 1983). The first challenge began with the implementation of bold (but not always neat) land reform in which farmland and livestock were confiscated from landlords. The means of farm production were then distributed to villagers. The nation's planners then (mostly) successfully implemented the first 'five-year plan', in 1952–57. The next plan, however, during the Great Leap Forward, was more difficult. Growth slowed and China struggled to manage its land—and its people—through large communes. After experiencing the world's largest famine in the late 1950s and early 1960s, China's farm sector began to recover between 1962 and the mid-1960s. However, the political chaos of the Cultural Revolution spilled over into agriculture, which slowed that sector's growth and stymied rural development. This slowdown stretched through to the late 1970s.

So where did China's farming sector find itself in the late 1970s? Between 1952 and 1978, agricultural gross domestic product (GDP) grew at an average of 2 per cent annually. The average annual growth of per capita net income (inflation adjusted) in the countryside was even lower—only 1.75 per cent (NBS various years). Given that rural areas were mired in extreme poverty in the early 1950s, such anaemic growth meant the countryside was still impoverished when reformers took power in the late 1970s.

The past 40 years of development and reform have profoundly changed the landscape of China's agricultural and rural areas (Huang and Rozelle 2010). Despite limited natural resources, China has been able to meet its growing demand for food largely through its own agricultural production. Annual growth of real agricultural GDP averaged 4.5 per cent over the four decades. While the average annual population growth rate was only 1 per cent per annum, per capita GDP nearly quadrupled between 1978 and 2018 (NBS 2010, various years). China, with nearly 20 per cent of the world's population, but only 5 per cent of the world's fresh water and 8 per cent of its arable land, met 95 per cent of its own food demand in 2015 (Huang and Yang 2017).

China's agriculture has experienced rapid structural transformation during the past 40 years. Grain production dominated farm output in 1978, and in the late 1970s nearly the entire rural economy was engaged in on-farm employment. Agriculture has since diversified dramatically. The farm economy is now highly commercialised and tens of millions of farms produce high-value commodities. Where off-farm employment was once rare, today, a majority of rural household income is earned off-farm.

Growth in agriculture and rising off-farm employment have dramatically reduced rural poverty. The number of people in rural China in extreme poverty fell from 250 million in 1978 to less than 15 million in 2007 (NBS various years). The rural poverty rate fell from 32 per cent to less than 3 per cent. Even with a higher poverty threshold—RMB2,300 a day in 2010 prices, or slightly more than $2 a day in purchasing power parity (PPP) terms—rural poverty levels decreased from 166 million people (17.2 per cent) in 2010 to 30 million (3.1 per cent) in 2017 (NBS various years). China was the first developing country to meet the Millennium Development Goals target of reducing its population living in poverty by more than half, and accomplished this far ahead of the 2015 deadline. Today, the goal of China's government is the elimination of rural poverty by 2020.

While these achievements are impressive, the agricultural sector is facing great challenges. Food production has risen at the expense of the environment, creating tremendous challenges to achieving sustainable rural development (Zhang et al. 2013; Lu et al. 2015). Rising wages have increased the cost of food production and lowered China's agricultural competitiveness in global markets, while concerns about national food security are as high as ever (Huang 2013a; Han 2014). Despite steady growth in rural incomes, the rural–urban income gap remains high. In recent years, the government has sought to raise farmer incomes in part through a number of market and policy interventions (using its procurement system to support prices). While incomes did rise incrementally, the interventions created structural problems in agricultural commodity markets (Chen 2016; Huang and Yang 2017). In coming years, China's policymakers will have no option but to deal with issues of national food security, higher farmer incomes and sustainable agricultural development.

In 2017, China launched the multidimensional Rural Revitalisation Development Strategy, which will require China to harness lessons from its past development and policymaking. Reviewing the past 40 years will also provide lessons for the development of agriculture in other developing countries.

In the next section, we summarise 40 years of China's agricultural development. In section three, we discuss agricultural growth and the reform experience in the first three decades of China's reforms, while section four extends our analysis to today by focusing on the challenges of agricultural development and policy evolution since the early 2000s. The conclusion provides a discussion of policy implications.

Forty years of agricultural development

Agricultural growth

In the past four decades, agricultural output value in real terms has grown at an average rate of 5.4 per cent annually (Table 24.1), while annual growth of grain production was 2.1 per cent. China's cropping economy has steadily changed from a priority on grain to the production of higher-value cash crops and horticultural goods. The average annual growth rate for cotton reached 3.8 per cent, 5.3 per cent for sugarcane, 6.4 per cent for edible oils and 11.5 per cent for fruit over the 40 years. Livestock and aquaculture products have been growing even faster. Annual meat production rose by an average of 5.9 per cent and fish by 7.3 per cent per annum. Dairy increased most rapidly, at 9 per cent annually.

Table 24.1 Average annual growth rate of agriculture and national population in China, 1952–2016 (per cent)

	Pre-reform	Reform period[a]					
	1952–78	1978–84	1984–2000	2000–05	2005–10	2010–16	Average
Agricultural GDP	2.2	6.9	3.8	3.9	4.5	4.0	4.5
Agricultural gross output value	3.4	5.9	5.9	5.3	4.8	4.2	5.4
Grain	2.5	5.5	0.9	1.0	2.5	2.0	2.1
Cotton	4.0	17.9	–0.6	6.4	2.0	–1.7	3.8
Edible oil crops	1.4	17.6	6.4	0.9	1.5	2.0	6.4
Sugar crops	7.8	13.6	3.7	4.8	5.3	0.5	5.3
Fruits	4.0	8.5	12.5	26.2	5.8	4.8	11.5
Vegetables[b]	n.a.	4.6	8.3	3.1	1.5	2.2	5.2
Meat	n.a.	7.8	9.1	2.9	2.7	1.3	6.0
Pork, beef and mutton	4.4	11.4	7.5	2.9	2.4	1.0	5.9
Poultry	n.a.	n.a.	14.9	2.9	4.2	2.3	8.8
Dairy	n.a.	n.a.	8.2	25.6	5.7	–0.1	9.0
Fish	4.7	4.2	12.1	3.6	4.0	4.3	7.3
Population	2.0	1.4	1.2	0.6	0.5	0.5	1.0

n.a. data not available.

[a] Meat production data are available from 1979; poultry production data are available from 1985.

[b] Vegetables are measured in sown area; data are available from 1979. Notes: Except for vegetables, the growth rates of individual and groups of commodities are based on production data. Agricultural GDP and gross value refer to values in real terms.

Sources: Authors' estimations based on data from NBS (various years, 2010).

The average annual growth of real per capita gross agricultural output increased from 1.4 per cent during the period 1952–78 to 4.4 per cent during the period 1978–2016 (Table 24.1).

Changes in agricultural structure and rural employment

Both supply- and demand-side factors affected the trends in the transformation of farming. Overall economic growth, urbanisation and market development have fundamentally changed Chinese food consumption, and driven changes in the structure of agricultural production. Within the cropping sector, the share of area under nongrain cash crops increased from 20 per cent in 1978 to 32 per cent in 2016. Over the same period, the share of the noncrop sector (mainly livestock and fisheries) in total agricultural output value grew from 20 per cent to 47 per cent (NBS 2010, various years). These changes mainly reflect the gradual shift from staple food production towards more diverse, intensive and commercial agriculture.

Following the 1949 Communist revolution, the government focused on the increasing demand for grain to meet the consumption needs of its growing population. China used 89 per cent of its cultivated land for grain production in 1950. In 1980, more than 80 per cent of farmland was being used to produce grain (NBS 2010).

Agricultural diversification began its slow march in the early 1980s. The first step was the granting of greater autonomy over production decisions in 1978. While in the 1980s households had an obligation to produce and sell grain to the state procurement system, once they met their production quotas, they could produce other crops, livestock and fish. Governments allocated large sums for irrigation and new technologies.

It is easy to illustrate the consequences of these policies. In the early reform period (1977–84), grain production rose by 34 per cent (NBS 2010). As a result, farmers were able to allocate more land, water, labour and capital to cash crop production. This effort to diversify agriculture helped the rural population raise their earnings in the early reform years. During this stage, agriculture was fuelled by not only the emergence of higher-value cash crops, but also the rise of livestock production and sales. The share of area planted to cash crops (mainly vegetables, fruits, edible oils and cotton) increased from less than 20 per cent before 1980 to about one-third in the early 2000s. In the meantime, the share of cropping in total agricultural production decreased from 80 per cent in 1978 to 56 per cent in 2000. The share of agricultural output from livestock rose from less than 17 per cent in 1978 to more than 40 per cent after 2000 (NBS 2010).

There were many implications of this shift. Because the production of nongrain commodities and livestock is more labour intensive, the diversification of China's agricultural economy helped address the underemployment that had plagued rural China during the entire PRC period. Diversification led to an increase in the number of days farmers could work and this raised their income.

Since the 1990s, agriculture has steadily become more specialised and, in recent years, mechanisation has begun. Nonfarm employment has increased significantly. The rise in agricultural productivity and diversification and the booming growth of the national economy (in industry, construction and so on) have led to a fundamental shift in the rural economy. Since the early 1990s, there has been a strong rise in the movement of rural labour from agriculture to off-farm employment. Initially, this shift occurred mainly in rural areas when farmers gained employment in township and village enterprises (TVEs). This was an ideal stepping stone for what was to follow, because it allowed farmers to work part-time on the farm and part-time in the off-farm market (Rozelle et al. 1999).

As economic reforms expanded in the 1990s, the rise of urbanisation and China's move to promote labour-intensive manufacturing and construction provided an even stronger impetus to move off the farm. Farmers were working in rural and urban areas both as wage earners and in the self-employed business sector (Wang et al. 2011). With these new opportunities came an increase in the intensity of off-farm work (a rise in the number of months per year, days per month and hours per day), and such activities provided a huge boost to farmers' incomes.

In recent years, China's economic rise finally absorbed most of the available rural labour. Since the mid-2000s, off-farm wages have been rising and the rural economy has become even more specialised—with farmers specialising on-farm and large numbers of rural individuals specialising in nonfarm activities (Wang et al. 2017). These changes have, of course, affected the nature of farming. As more households began to work full-time off the farm, they also began to rent out their land (Gao et al. 2012). Those who stayed are the ones renting this land, which is behind a steady increase in farm size and increasing pressure to mechanise (Zhang et al. 2013; Huang and Ding 2016; Wang et al. 2016).

Major drivers of agricultural growth and reform experiences

Numerous studies have tried to examine the many factors contributing to China's agricultural growth. Our studies, which are consistent with many others, show that rural institutional innovation, technological change, market reform, trade liberalisation and investment in agriculture are among the major enabling factors of China's agricultural growth and transformation.

Institutional innovations

China's first rural reform, the household responsibility system (HRS), was implemented during the period 1978–84. This dismantled the people's communes and contracted cultivated land to individual households, mostly on the basis of the number of people and/or labourers in the household. Although the ownership of land remained collective, control and income rights belonged to individuals under the HRS. The first land contract term was 15 years. When this ended in the late 1990s, it was extended to 30 years for the second term. The government today is struggling with what to do when this contract period finishes.

The effects of the HRS on agricultural productivity, equitable distribution of land to farmers and rural poverty alleviation have been well documented. Most studies show the HRS accounted for 30–50 per cent of the total rise in agricultural output during the period 1978–84 (Fan 1991; Lin 1992; Huang and Rozelle 1996). Researchers also have revealed the empirical impacts that go beyond output. McMillan et al. (1989) demonstrate that the HRS raised total factor productivity (TFP), accounting for 90 per cent of its rise between 1978 and 1984. Jin et al. (2002) show that reform had a large effect on productivity, contributing to a rise in agricultural TFP. The significant positive impacts of the HRS on agricultural production and the equitable distribution of land were the major reasons for the massive reduction of rural poverty in the early 1980s. Rising agricultural productivity due to the HRS also facilitated China's transformation from grain-dominated to more diversified agriculture because farmers were able to shift their land and labour from grain to cash crops and livestock.

Over the past four decades, additional institutional changes targeted at raising agricultural productivity and facilitating rural transformation have been made. The major efforts in land use have been on stabilising the HRS in the late 1990s (Ji and Huang 2013) and developing institutional arrangements (such as township land rights transfers) to facilitate land consolidation since the mid-2000s (Huang and Ding 2016). Stabilising farmers' control and income from land contract rights is important because it provides incentives for farmers to invest in agriculture and land and stimulates land transfer among farmers, increasing farm size, which improves agricultural efficiency, productivity and incomes (Gao et al. 2012; Huang and Ji 2012; Jin and Deininger 2009). Huang and Ding (2016) show that one-third of the land contracted by households through the HRS was transferred among farmers.

Another, recent innovation in land institutions is *San-quan-fen-zhi*, which separates three rights: village collective landowner rights, individual household land contract rights and land operation rights. By separating a farmer's land operation rights from contract rights, the former can be transferred through the rental market while the original contracted farmers continue to hold the contract rights. It is hoped this reform can achieve equity of land distribution and efficient use of currently cultivated land through operation rights transfers.

Institutional reforms have also occurred in many other areas, including the gradual relaxation of the household registration system (*hukou*). Although *hukou* is still a binding policy in many areas, there has been progress, which has stimulated rural–urban migration and off-farm employment since the mid-2000s (Cai et al. 2007). Since the late 2000s, a number of institutional reforms and new laws have been piloted and implemented to promote professional farmer cooperatives and help farmers to commercialise their activities (Deng et al. 2010).

Despite the successful institutional reforms discussed above, there is still substantial room to improve the institutional environment governing land, labour and capital, and further reform of land institutions is needed to facilitate land consolidation. There is a need for stronger, more flexible and farmer-friendly financial institutions, and room to integrate China's rural and urban labour markets.

Technology changes

Over the past 40 years, China's agricultural research and development (R&D) and extension system has been reformed, contributing significantly to agricultural productivity growth.

There have been four stages of development and reform (Huang et al. 2009; Hu and Huang 2011). In the very early reform era, the number of agricultural research institutes increased from 597 in 1979 to 1,428 in 1985. During the same period, the total agricultural research staff grew from 22,000 to 102,000.

In the next phase, 1986–98, China tried to commercialise agricultural R&D (Rozelle et al. 1999). Because of fiscal shortages for research support and low staff salaries, policymakers encouraged institutes to engage in income-generating activities. During this time, the government changed its system of budget allocation from a planned system to one based on competitive funding initiatives (Jin et al. 2005). However, under the pressure of competition (and with commercialisation), the number of researchers decreased, from 102,000 in 1985 to 65,000 in 1996.

The third phase of research reform covered 1999 to 2006, and can be called the period of twin shifts: the transformation of the public R&D system and the rise of enterprise-based R&D. Initially, public research institutes were grouped into three functional types, each of which was provided with different levels of government funding. Public R&D institutes were fully funded by the government. The science and technology (S&T) service institutes were partially government funded. The technology development institutes were incorporated into the commercialisation efforts. This reform phase had two main goals: it attempted to form a high-quality (globally competitive) and efficient public agricultural R&D system and sought to encourage a technology-focused system of innovation led by the private sector. It should be noted, this reform faced huge resistance from most research institutes. And, while improvements in the publicly supported research institutes proceeded smoothly, the effort to shift technology development to the private sector was eventually phased out.

In the fourth phase, China is trying to develop a system to support innovation in agricultural technologies. This phase began in 2007 and is still in progress, and has seen funding for agricultural research increase significantly and public research institutes expand. The Technology Innovation System, with 50 subsystems for agricultural commodities, has been established, and the National Transgenic Modified Variety Development Special Program was initiated in 2008. By 2010, the number of public sector agricultural researchers in China had reached 96,300 (Huang et al. 2012).

Reform of the agricultural extension system has also evolved over time, moving through five stages:

1. The rapid development of extension institutions from 1978 to 1988. By the end of the 1980s, all townships had established agricultural technical extension stations, and the number of personnel reached 450,000.
2. The commercialisation and reallocation of the 'three management rights' (for personnel, finance and assets) of township extension stations from 1989 to 1993. Due to local fiscal shortages, the government allowed extension stations to conduct commercial activities to generate additional income. County governments shifted responsibility for extension stations to township-level governments. During this time, the number of extension personnel fell to 300,000.
3. From 1993 to 2000, county governments took back responsibility and invested heavily in the system. The number of personnel increased to more than 1 million by 2000.
4. There was yet another policy reversal in 2001–03. Responsibility was again shifted down to the township level. Because of fiscal constraints at this level, the number of extension agents fell to 849,000.

5. The final phase began in 2003, with county governments responsible for the extension system since that time, and more than 700,000 personnel employed. Funding comes from county governments with additional support from upper-level governments.

Despite experiencing a twisting path of reform in agricultural research and extension, China has developed a strong agricultural S&T innovation system. Its agricultural R&D system is the largest in the world in terms of staff and covers nearly every discipline in agriculture and related fields (Huang 2013b). China has also developed the largest public agricultural extension system in the world (Babu et al. 2015). While China's agricultural R&D was underfunded in the early and mid-1990s, investment has since increased significantly (Shi et al. 2008). We estimate that government expenditure on agricultural S&T reached more than RMB55 billion in 2015; agricultural R&D expenditure exceeded RMB26 billion in 2015. Over the past decade, an increasing number of enterprises have engaged in agricultural S&T activities (Hu and Huang 2011; Babu et al. 2015).

This investment has translated directly into productivity gains. Agricultural technological change is a primary source of agricultural productivity growth in the long run for all systems (including China's), and empirical research shows it has facilitated China's agricultural growth over the past several decades. China was one of the first developing countries to develop and extend 'green revolution' technology, in the 1960s (Stone 1988). Chinese scientists developed hybrid rice in the late 1970s. Technological changes in wheat, maize, cash crops and animal production have also been impressive since the 1990s (Jin et al. 2010). Empirical studies show the average annual growth rate of TFP in the grain sector increased about 3 per cent before the mid-2000s (Fan 1991; Fan and Zhang 2002; Jin et al. 2008). Rising grain productivity has enabled the country to gradually release its limited land and water resources for cash crop and livestock production. While the grain sector recorded high TFP growth, annual TFP growth rates for cash crops and livestock were even higher, exceeding 3.5 per cent in the period 1995–2005 (Jin et al. 2010). Since the mid-1990s, China's agricultural productivity growth has also relied on innovation from plant biotechnology. 'Bt cotton' is an example of one of the most successful uses of genetic modification technology in the developing world—a technological change that has benefited millions of farmers (Huang et al. 2002).

Despite these many successes, reform of the agricultural S&T system is unfinished. The current system for providing incentives for those engaged in agricultural S&T has not been used to full advantage (Huang 2013b). And there is a need for further reform to provide appropriate incentives to extension agents to attract more young professionals—something that is desperately needed to enhance the system's capabilities.

Market reform

China's institutional reforms began in rural areas, while market reforms were also launched in the farming sector, moving from rural to urban areas and from agriculture to industry and services. China did not abolish the planned economic system outright, but instead regarded the market as a supplement to the planned economy (Perkins 1994). Over the reform period, however, it gradually moved from the system of state purchases and sales to rely mostly on private markets.

China also adopted a gradual market reform approach in agriculture (Sicular 1988; Rozelle et al. 2000), which is thought to have facilitated the smooth transformation from the planned to a market economy. This gradual reform process is also thought to have helped to diversify China's agriculture during its transformation. Unlike transitional economies in Europe, China's leaders did not move to immediately dismantle the planned economy in favour of liberalised markets (Rozelle and Swinnen 2004). Liberalisation began only for nonstrategic products (such as vegetables and fruits), in the mid-1980s, gradually moving to animal products (fish and meat) and then to crops such as sugarcane, edible oils, cotton and grain—the products of strategic importance for China. Although grain market liberalisation was intermittent because of large fluctuations in grain production and prices in the 1980s and early 1990s, by the late 1990s, the government had all but phased out its direct market intervention (Huang et al. 2004; Huang and Rozelle 2006).

A caveat, of course, is that in recent years, the Chinese Government has sharply intervened in markets due to concerns over farmers' incomes and national grain security.

In the area of international trade, agricultural liberalisation was similarly slow to start, but proceeded steadily. The liberalisation of international trade started in the early 1990s with relaxation of trade restrictions and allowing nonstate actors access to agricultural commodity markets. After these initial moves, tariffs were steadily reduced (Huang et al. 2007). From the 1990s until China's accession to the World Trade Organization (WTO) in 2001, the average import tariff for all agricultural products was reduced from 42.2 per cent, in 1992, to 23.6 per cent in 1998 and 21 per cent in 2001. Tariff rates fell to 12 per cent in 2004, making China one of the most free agricultural trading nations in the world. China also made significant commitments and concessions in terms of domestic support and export subsidies (Anderson et al. 2004).

Accompanying and facilitating market reform were initiatives to aid farm commodity markets. Investment in roads and communications and policies to facilitate the free movement of goods across provincial and prefectural boundaries produced commodity markets that were among the most efficient in the world. By the early 2000s, almost all markets (92 per cent for rice, 98 per cent for soybean and 99 per cent for maize) moved together (Huang et al. 2004; Huang and Rozelle 2006). Because reform of agricultural products other than grain began relatively early, integrated national markets for these products were established earlier than for grain.

Market reforms have played an important role in agricultural growth, production structure and farmer incomes. Farmers have increased their allocative efficiency by basing their decisions on relative market prices (Huang and Rozelle 1996; de Brauw et al. 2004). The reforms also reduced the price of farm inputs and increased selling prices for agricultural commodities.

China's open-door policies in agriculture also saw it become increasingly integrated into international markets. By the mid-2000s, most agricultural commodity prices in China were almost equal to the price of imports at the border (Huang et al. 2009). Exports of labour-intensive products (such as horticulture and livestock) and imports of land and water-intensive commodities (soybeans, cotton, edible oils, sugar) have been rising. China's comparative trade advantage means the domestic farm economy has improved its resource allocation and agricultural production efficiency.

Investing in agriculture

Agricultural investment created the foundation for China's steady agricultural growth and rapid agricultural transformation. China is one of a few large countries to see substantial increases in agricultural investment in recent decades—the largest of which have been in water (irrigation and flood) control and land improvement. The area of irrigated agricultural land increased from 45 million hectares in 1978 to 67 million hectares in 2016 (NBS various years). Today, more than half of China's cultivated land is irrigated—a very high ratio by international standards. Investment in low- to mid-quality land has also helped to improve soil quality and raise agricultural production capacity.

Massive investment in rural roads and wholesale markets fostered market integration and linked hundreds of million of small farms with retailers and consumers. China has invested substantially in road infrastructure during the reform era. Highway mileage increased from 890,000 km in 1978 to 4.4 million km in 2013 (NBS various years). Today, nearly every village has access to a public paved road. Empirical evidence shows government spending on rural roads has very high impacts on agricultural transformation, off-farm employment and poverty reduction (Zhang et al. 2004).

Farmers have also significantly increased their own investments and use of inputs. In terms of fixed assets, farmer investments in irrigation (Wang et al. 2005) and agricultural machinery (Wang et al. 2016) have steadily risen over time. In terms of variable inputs, the use of chemical fertilisers and pesticides has increased dramatically since 1978. For example, total fertiliser inputs for China's farm sector increased from 8.84 million tonnes in 1978 to 59.84 million tonnes in 2016 (NBS various years), significantly raising crop yields.

Recent challenges, policy responses and reforms

This section focuses on the evolution of China's agricultural policies and draws heavily on the analysis in a recent paper by Huang and Yang (2017).

Emerging challenges

Achievements in the agricultural sector have been quite remarkable; however, it is clear that China's cropping, livestock and fisheries sectors are facing enormous new challenges. While average real income per capita in rural and urban areas has increased significantly in the past four decades, the urban–rural income gap remains wide. By 2003, the ratio of urban to rural incomes exceeded 3:1 (NBS 2010). Such levels of inequality can threaten social stability.

Ensuring national food security is also one of China's primary policy goals. Grain production reached a high in 1998 (of 512 million tonnes), but it fell to 431 million tonnes in 2003 (NBS 2010). At the same time, rising incomes have seen the demand for food—especially animal products—continue to rise. In fact, the dynamics between supply and demand hit a milestone in 2004, when for the first time, China shifted from being a net food exporter to a net food importer, and food imports have steadily increased. The cost of crop production in China has also risen—largely due to rapid wage growth in all economic sectors.

There are now concerns about the sustainability of China's agriculture. Research shows groundwater in northern China is being overdrawn and the water table is falling (MWR 2016). Soil degradation is being observed in many regions (Liu et al. 2013; Zhang et al. 2013; Lu et al. 2015) and excessive use of chemicals has caused serious pollution and soil degradation (Liu et al. 2013).

Responses to farm income and national food security challenges

In this subsection, we describe some of the government's responses to rising challenges.

Shifting from taxing to subsidising agriculture

In response to rising concerns about farmer income and food security, China has taken several major policy measures since 2004. As a demonstration of the government's commitment to 'three rural issues'—the agricultural sector, rural livelihoods and the future of farming communities—the Central Committee of the Communist Party of China (CPC) has, since 2004, issued a yearly 'No. 1 document' on the three rural issues.

The initial set of policies in 2004 included the abolition of taxes and fees and introduction of direct subsidy programs, the first of which were the direct grain subsidy, quality seed subsidy and machinery subsidy. After domestic prices of chemical fertilisers and other agricultural inputs rose in 2006, China's policymakers expanded the direct subsidy program to include an aggregate input subsidy.

The level of subsidies increased significantly as international prices surged in the late 2000s, especially during the Global Financial Crisis (GFC) of 2007–08. Almost all rural households with contract land received subsidies.

At their peak, the total amount of the four major subsidies reached RMB164.3 billion (US$26.1 billion), in 2012, or about 3.13 per cent of agricultural GDP. Additional recent farm subsidies include those for agricultural insurance, credit, land consolidation and soil conservation and improvement.

Despite this enormous investment, the subsidy program has had only moderate impact on farmers' incomes. In the late 2000s, China had more than 200 million rural households with land contracts. On a per farm household basis, even in 2012, the year with the highest level of subsidies, the average household received only RMB850 (US$130). The use of agricultural subsidies to raise farmer incomes is therefore meaningful mainly as a political statement demonstrating the government's commitment to the farming community.

Empirical studies found there was also only a limited impact from subsidies on production and therefore on national food security. Huang et al. (2011) found that subsidies were mostly being given to the land contractor (who often was not even farming), not the tiller, and that subsidies did not affect the level of inputs.

Initial policy response through market interventions

Beyond the use of subsidies to increase farmers' income and promote farm production, China's agricultural officials have also used price supports. The most important policy measure was the minimum procurement price initiative, which was launched for rice in 2004 and for wheat in 2006. There was also the temporary storage program (TSP) aimed at raising market prices, which was initiated for maize, soybean and rapeseed in 2008, cotton in 2011 and sugarcane in 2012.

While these price interventions did increase farmer incomes, they also generated a large price gap between China's domestic market and international commodity markets. During the GFC, China was able to prevent a significant rise in grain prices by drawing down stocks and applying trade controls (Yang et al. 2008). However, while global food prices fell sharply in late 2008, and have since fluctuated, after 2009, China continued to raise its domestic prices through the use of minimum prices and the TSP. As a consequence, significant price gaps between domestic and international markets increased after 2012. For example, by 2015, the wholesale price of maize was 40 per cent higher than the imported price; it reached 50 per cent in early 2016. Domestic wholesale prices of rice, wheat and cotton were also higher than international prices, by 30–50 per cent in 2015. Market intervention has also been shown to distort agricultural production, hurt livestock production and processing and ultimately led to a huge grain reserve in government storage facilities (Hejazi and Marchant 2017; Huang and Yang 2017).

Policy efforts to adjust the support system

Given the clearly unsustainable nature of the market intervention, China's leaders have changed farming sector policies. A review of the subsidy policy determined that the significant expenditure had produced only a moderate effect on farmer incomes and no increase in grain production.

In place of the subsidy and market intervention programs, several new policies have been implemented and the subsidy targets were changed. Officials gradually began to shift part of the budget from subsidising contractors to supporting more productivity-enhancing investments, such as land consolidation. In 2016, China merged all subsidies on grain, seed and aggregate inputs into a single general income support program.

China also has started to reduce the intensity of market interventions and phase out most price distorting policies. In 2013, the government lowered the minimum agricultural procurement price, before completely phasing out procurement programs for rapeseed, sugarcane and soybean. Procurement for maize (which had been the most distorting) was abolished in 2016. Currently, the target price policy is being implemented only for cotton in Xinjiang. And, while rice and wheat are still subject to the minimum price procurement program, procurement prices and grain levels have been reduced since 2015. The story of market intervention and reliberalisation supports the idea that market reforms were one of the major factors in the success of China's agricultural development and that China seems to be returning to a pro-market policy.

Responses to agricultural sustainability challenges

Recognising the resource constraints in its farming economy and the challenges for any country in meeting a strict set of sustainable development goals, the Chinese Government has made a strong commitment to agricultural investment. Since the mid-2000s, the Ministry of Agriculture has overseen significant public investment in land, water and technology, with the growth of agricultural investment exceeding the government's overall fiscal expenditure. Between 2004 and 2014, while the share of agriculture in GDP fell from 13 per cent to 9 per cent, its share in government expenditure rose from 8 per cent to 10 per cent (NBS various years). In 2011, China committed to investing about US$630 billion in water conservation during the period 2012–20. In addition to efforts to conserve water through better infrastructure, China is planning to establish a pricing mechanism that more appropriately reflects the cost of water to encourage water savings. Priority is also being given to raising the productivity of land and creating a system that protects and enhances the quality of farmland.

More significant is China's attempt to incorporate sustainable agriculture into the nation's overall development goals, including through: 1) substantially enhancing S&T innovation capacity and implementing the strategy to 'store food in technology' to boost agricultural productivity in the long run; 2) increasing investment in land and water infrastructure and implementing the 'storing food in land' production strategy to improve the quality of farmland and therefore agricultural production capacity in the long run; and 3) protecting the rural environment through reductions in fertiliser and pesticide use. These measures will undoubtedly play important roles in the sustainable development of Chinese agriculture in coming years.

Concluding remarks

China's agriculture has recorded remarkable achievements in the past four decades. Despite the increasing scarcity of water and arable land, China has largely been able to ensure its food security. Accompanying the rapid growth of agricultural output and incomes has been the significant change in the structure of agricultural production—from a sector based on staple grain production to one with a set of much more varied high-value commodities. There has also been a massive reduction in rural poverty.

We have argued that China's policymakers have generated this transformation through agricultural reform policies, which started in 1978 with the HRS, greatly improving farmers' production incentives and productivity. Other institutional changes involved giving farmers the freedom to rent land and allocate their labour in response to market signals, which were key parts of the reform package that improved agricultural productivity and facilitated the sector's transformation. Indeed, both domestic market reforms and international trade liberalisation improved the efficiency of resource allocation, stimulated agricultural structural change and helped millions of small farmers to sell their products.

The government has also overseen a number of direct investments. Agricultural S&T has become one of the primary sources of agricultural growth, and massive investment in rural infrastructure, particularly irrigation and roads, provided the foundation for agricultural productivity growth and successful liberalisation. Although there have been setbacks, in general, the government's efforts in institutional innovation, technological change, market reform and agricultural investment accelerated agricultural growth and transformation.

China's agriculture is, however, still facing many challenges. In response, a number of lessons can be learned from past successes and failures. In 2017, China initiated a national strategy on rural revitalisation. While this is an update of previous agricultural development programs, it has provided an even clearer pathway to agricultural transformation. It aims to establish an institutional framework and policy management to oversee the revitalisation of the rural sector by 2020. It commits China to largely modernise agriculture and the rural economy by 2035 and fully modernise by 2050.

The strategy also calls for higher-quality growth and stresses the importance of environmentally sustainable development.

Can this succeed? Of course, only the future will tell. However, we believe one thing is clear. If success is accomplished, it will be in no small part because for the past 40 years, there has been a series of innovative and bold reforms and large investments that have taken agriculture from where it was in 1978 to where it is today.

References

Anderson, K., Huang, J. and Ianchovichina, E. (2004), Will China's WTO accession worsen farm household income?, *China Economic Review* 15: 443–56. doi.org/10.1016/j.chieco.2004.06.007.

Babu, S. C., Huang, J., Venkatesh, P. and Zhang, Y. (2015), A comparative analysis of agricultural research and extension reforms in China and India, *China Agricultural Economic Review* 4: 541–72.

Cai, F., Du, Y. and Zhao, C. (2007), Regional labour market integration since China's WTO entry: Evidence from household-level data, in R. Garnaut and L. Song (eds), *China: Linking markets for growth*, Canberra: ANU E Press.

Chen, X. (2016), Three innovations in agricultural supply-side structural reform, *Rural Work Bulletin* (8): 34.

de Brauw, A., Huang, J. and Rozelle, S. (2004), The sequencing of reform policies in China's agricultural transition, *The Economics of Transition* 3: 427–65. doi.org/10.1111/j.0967-0750.2004.00188.x.

Deng, H., Huang, J., Xu, Z. and Rozelle, S. (2010), Policy support and emerging farmer professional cooperatives in rural China, *China Economic Review* 21: 495–507. doi.org/10.1016/j.chieco.2010.04.009.

Fan, S. (1991), Effects of technological change and institutional reform on production growth in Chinese agriculture, *American Journal of Agricultural Economics* 73: 266–75. doi.org/10.2307/1242711.

Fan, S. and Zhang, X. (2002), Production and productivity growth in Chinese agriculture: New national and regional measures, *Economic Development and Cultural Change* 50(4): 819–38. doi.org/10.1086/343136.

Gao, L., Huang, J. and Rozelle, S. (2012), Rental markets for cultivated land and agricultural investments in China, *Agricultural Economics* 43: 391–403. doi.org/10.1111/j.1574-0862.2012.00591.x.

Han, J. (2014), *China: Food security and agricultural going out, strategy research*, [in Chinese], Beijing: China Development Press.

Hejazi, M. and Marchant, M. A. (2017), China's evolving agricultural support policies, *Choice* 32: 1–7.

Hu, R. and Huang, J. (2011), The development and reform of agricultural research system: Policy evaluation and recommendations, *Science and Society* 3: 34–40.

Huang, J. (2013a), China's agricultural development in the new era: Opportunities, challenges, and strategies, [in Chinese], *Bulletin of Chinese Academy of Sciences* 3: 295–300.

Huang, J. (2013b), Deepening agricultural science and technology system reform and improving its innovation capacity, *Agricultural Economics and Management* 2: 5–8.

Huang, J. and Ding, J. (2016), Institutional innovation and policy support to facilitate small-scale farming transformation in China, *Agricultural Economics* 47: 309–17. doi.org/10.1111/agec.12309.

Huang, J. and Ji, X. (2012), The verification of the right to use farmland and farmers' long-term investment in farmland, *Management World* (9): 76–81.

Huang, J. and Rozelle, S. (1996), Technological change: The re-discovery of the engine of productivity growth in China's rice economy, *Journal of Development Economics* 49: 337–69. doi.org/10.1016/0304-3878(95)00065-8.

Huang, J. and Rozelle, S. (2006), The emergence of agricultural commodity markets in China, *China Economic Review* 17: 266–80. doi.org/10.1016/j.chieco.2006.04.008.

Huang, J. and Rozelle, S. (2010), Agricultural development, nutrition, and the policies behind China's success, *Asian Journal of Agriculture and Development* 7: 93–126.

Huang, J. and Rozelle, S. (2014), Agricultural R&D and extension, in S. Fan, R. Kanbur, S.-J. Wei and X. Zhang (eds), *The Oxford Companion to the Economics of China*, Oxford: Oxford University Press. doi.org/10.1093/acprof:oso/9780199678204.003.0051.

Huang, J. and Yang, G. (2017), Understanding recent challenges and new food policy in China, *Global Food Security* 12: 119–26. doi.org/10.1016/j.gfs.2016.10.002.

Huang, J., Hu, R., Cai, J. and Wang, X. (2012), Human research capacity in Chinese agbiotech, *Nature Biotechnology* 30(10): 1007. doi.org/10.1038/nbt.2386.

Huang, J., Liu, Y., Martin, W. and Rozelle, S. (2009), Changes in trade and domestic distortions affecting China's agriculture, *Food Policy* 34: 407–16. doi.org/10.1016/j.foodpol.2009.04.001.

Huang, J., Rozelle, S. and Chang, M. (2004), Tracking distortions in agriculture: China and its accession to the World Trade Organization, *The World Bank Economic Review* 1: 59–84. doi.org/10.1093/wber/lhh033.

Huang, J., Rozelle, S., Pray, C. and Wang, Q. (2002), Plant biotechnology in China, *Science* 25: 674–7. doi.org/10.1126/science.1067226.

Huang, J., Wang, X., Zhi, H., Huang, Z. and Rozelle, S. (2011), Subsidies and distortions in China's agriculture: Evidence from producer-level data, *Australian Journal of Agricultural and Resource Economics* 55: 53–71. doi.org/10.1111/j.1467-8489.2010.00527.x.

Huang, J., Yang, J., Xu, Z., Rozelle, S. and Li, N. (2007), Agricultural trade liberalization and poverty in China, *China Economic Review* 18: 244–65. doi.org/10.1016/j.chieco.2007.02.003.

Ji, X. and Huang, J. (2013), Evolution of farm land use rights during thirty years of reform in China: A comparative analysis of policy evolution and its implementation between 1978 and 2008, *Issues in Agricultural Economy* 5: 27–32.

Jin, S. and Deininger, K. (2009), Land rental markets in the process of rural structural transformation: Productivity and equity impacts from China, *Journal of Comparative Economics* 37(4): 629–46.

Jin, S., Huang, J., Hu, R. and Rozelle, S. (2002), The creation and spread of technology and total factor productivity in China's agriculture, *American Journal of Agricultural Economics* 84: 916–30. doi.org/10.1111/1467-8276.00043.

Jin, S., Ma, H., Huang, J., Hu, R. and Rozelle, S. (2010), Productivity, efficiency and technical change: measuring the performance of China's transforming agriculture, *Journal of Productivity Analysis* 33: 191–207.

Jin, S., Meng, E., Hu, R., Rozelle, S. and Huang, J. (2008), Contribution of wheat diversity to total factor productivity in China, *Journal of Agricultural and Resource Economics* 33(3): 449–72.

Jin, S., Rozelle, S., Alston, J. and Huang, J. (2005), Economies of scale and scope and the economic efficiency of China's agricultural research system, *International Economic Review* 46(3): 1033–57. doi.org/10.1111/j.1468-2354.2005.00356.x.

Lardy, N. R. (1983), *Agriculture in China's Modern Economic Development*, Cambridge: Cambridge University Press. doi.org/10.1017/CBO9780511528422.

Lin, J. (1992), Rural reforms and agricultural growth in China, *American Economic Review* 82: 34–51.

Liu, X., Zhang, Y., Han, W., Tang, A., Shen, J., Cui, Z., Vitousek, P., Erisman, J. W., Goulding, K., Christie, P., Fangmeier, A. and Zhang, F. (2013), Enhanced nitrogen deposition over China, *Nature* 494: 459–62. doi.org/10.1038/nature11917.

Lu, Y., Jenkins, A., Ferrier, R. C., Bailey, M., Gordon, I. J., Song, S., Huang, J., Jia, S., Zhang, F., Liu, X., Feng, Z. and Zhang, B. (2015), Addressing China's grand challenge of achieving food security while ensuring environmental sustainability, *Science Advances* 1: e1400039. doi.org/10.1126/sciadv.1400039.

McMillan, J., Walley, J. and Zhu, L. (1989), The impact of China's economic reforms on agricultural productivity growth, *Journal of Political Economy* 97: 781–807. doi.org/10.1086/261628.

Ministry of Water Resources (MWR) (2016), *Monthly Groundwater Dynamics*, May, Beijing: MWR.

National Bureau of Statistics (NBS) (various years), *China Statistical Yearbook*, Beijing: China Statistics Press.

National Bureau of Statistics (NBS) (2010), *China Compendium of Statistics 1949–2008*, Beijing: China Statistics Press.

Perkins, D. (1994), Completing China's move to the market, *Journal of Economic Perspectives* 8(2)(Spring): 23–46. doi.org/10.1257/jep.8.2.23.

Rozelle, S. and Swinnen, J. (2004), Success and failure of reform: Insights from the transition of agriculture, *Journal of Economic Literature* 42(3): 404–56. doi.org/10.1257/0022051041409048.

Rozelle, S., Li, G., Shen, M., Hughart, A. and Giles, J. (1999), Leaving China's farms: Survey results of new paths and remaining hurdles to rural migration, *China Quarterly* 158(June): 367–93. doi.org/10.1017/S0305741000005816.

Rozelle, S., Park, A., Huang, J. and Jin, H. (2000), Bureaucrat to entrepreneur: The changing role of the state in China's transitional commodity economy, *Economic Development and Cultural Change* 48(2): 227–52. doi.org/10.1086/452456.

Rozelle, S., Pray, C. E. and Huang, J. (1997), Agricultural research policy in China: Testing the limits of commercialization-led reform, *Comparative Economic Studies* 39(Summer): 37–71. doi.org/10.1057/ces.1997.8.

Shi, K., Hu, R., Huang, J., Li, S. and Xu, N. (2008), The funding and sources of funding in China's public agricultural research system and their variations among regions after the recent reform, *China Soft Science* 11: 79–84.

Sicular, T. (1988), Plan and market in China's agricultural commerce, *Journal of Political Economy* 96(2): 283–307. doi.org/10.1086/261537.

Stone, B. (1988), Developments in agricultural technology, *China Quarterly* 116: 767–822. doi.org/10.1017/S0305741000037954.

Wang, J., Huang, J. and Rozelle, S. (2005), Evolution of tubewell ownership and production in the North China Plain, *Australian Journal of Agricultural and Resource Economics* 49(June): 177–95. doi.org/10.1111/j.1467-8489.2005.00284.x.

Wang, X., Huang, J. and Rozelle, S. (2017), Off-farm employment and agricultural specialization in China, *China Economic Review* 42: 155–65. doi.org/10.1016/j.chieco.2016.09.004.

Wang, X., Huang, J., Zhang, L. and Rozelle, S. (2011), The rise of migration and the fall of self-employment in rural China's labor market, *China Economic Review* 4: 573–84. doi.org/10.1016/j.chieco.2011.07.005.

Wang, X., Yamauchi, F. and Huang, J. (2016), Rising wages, mechanization, and the substitution between capital and labor: Evidence from small scale farm system in China, *Agricultural Economics* 47: 309–17. doi.org/10.1111/agec.12231.

Yang, J., Huang, Z., Zhang, X. and Reardon, T. (2013), The rapid rise of cross-regional agricultural mechanization services in China, *American Journal of Agricultural Economics* 95(5): 1245–51. doi.org/10.1093/ajae/aat027.

Yang, J., Qiu, H., Huang, J. and Rozelle, S. (2008), Fighting global food price rises in the developing world: The response of China and its effect on domestic and world markets, *Agricultural Economics* 39: 453–64. doi.org/10.1111/j.1574-0862.2008.00351.x.

Zhang, F., Chen, X. and Vitousek, P. (2013), Chinese agriculture: An experiment for the world, *Nature* 497: 33–5. doi.org/10.1038/497033a.

Zhang, X., Fan, S., Zhang, L. and Huang, J. (2004), Local governance and public goods provision in rural China, *Journal of Public Economics* 88: 2857–71. doi.org/10.1016/j.jpubeco.2003.07.004.

Part IV: Energy and climate change

25. Energy price reform in China

ZhongXiang Zhang[1]

Before the 1978 economic reforms, China's economic management structure was modelled principally on that of the former Soviet Union, an essential feature of which was the adoption of a state-set pricing system. Under this system, the state-set prices of goods, including energy, reflect neither the production costs nor the influence of market forces. The structure of state-set prices was also irrational: the same types of goods were set at the same prices regardless of their quality, resulting in the underpricing and undersupply of goods of high quality. This system remained unchanged for a long period, and its inflexible and restrictive nature became increasingly apparent.

In 1984, the government required state-owned enterprises (SOEs) to sell up to a predetermined quota of goods at state-set prices, but they were allowed to sell any production above the quota at prices within a 20 per cent range above the state-set price. In February 1985, the 20 per cent limit was removed and prices for surplus could be negotiated freely between buyers and sellers (Wu and Zhao 1987). At that point, the dual pricing system was formally instituted—introducing, among other things, economic efficiency in the use of resources—and was generally considered a positive, cautious step towards full market pricing.[2] According to a survey of 17 provincial markets in March 1989, SOEs still received part of their allocation for energy inputs—particularly crude oil and electricity—at the state-set prices, which were much lower than market prices, four years after the introduction of the dual pricing system (Zhang 1998).

Confronted with energy shortages and insufficient investment in energy conservation, China had been reforming its energy prices as part of sweeping price reforms initiated in 1993. The pace and scale of the energy pricing reform differ across energy types. This chapter discusses the evolution of price reforms for coal, petroleum products, natural gas, electricity and renewable energy, providing some analysis of these energy price reforms and suggesting a few areas where further reform would allow the market to play a decisive role in resource allocation.

1 This chapter builds on Zhang (2014), and was financially supported by the National Natural Science Foundation of China (grant nos 71690243 and 71373055). The views expressed here are those of the author, who bears sole responsibility for any errors and omissions that may remain.

2 See Wu and Zhao (1987) and Singh (1992) for general discussion of the pros and cons of the dual-pricing system, and Albouy (1991) for its impact on coal.

Coal prices

Coal dominates China's energy mix. Its price has been set at different rates since 1993, according to its use. Under the two-track system for coal prices, the price for non-utility use (so-called market coal) was determined by the market, whereas the price of coal for utility use (so-called power coal) was based on a 'guidance price' set by the National Development and Reform Commission (NDRC)—often at rates lower than prevailing market rates. Coal producers are required to sell to large power producers at the controlled prices for utility coal (IEA 2009). However, as the share of coal going to utility use increased and coal prices rose while power tariffs remained fixed, electricity generators found it increasingly difficult to obtain coal and cover the cost of generation (Rosen and Houser 2007). In 2004, the NDRC abolished its guidance price for power coal and set price bands for negotiations between coal producers and electricity generators. The NDRC widened those bands in 2005; in 2006, it scrapped them altogether (Williams and Kahrl 2008).

With electricity tariffs remaining controlled and flat, many electricity generators were unable to absorb the ensuing fuel cost increases and suffered huge losses. Responding to electricity generators' concerns, the NDRC in May 2005 proposed a coal–electricity price 'co-movement' mechanism through which electricity tariffs would be raised if coal prices rose by 5 per cent or more in no less than six months and electricity generators would be allowed to pass up to 70 per cent of increased fuel costs on to grid companies, and grid companies could pass those costs on to consumers. However, because of fears of inflation, the co-movement policy was not implemented even when the conditions were met, and power tariffs continue to remain flat while coal prices rise (Williams and Kahrl 2008; Fisher-Vanden 2009; Li 2009). This increased the pressure on electricity generators and led to lobbying efforts to receive higher tariffs.

In December 2012, the State Council announced it would abolish the two-track system for coal prices. The price of coal for utility use, as for that of coal for non-utility use, would be determined by the market. Moreover, it revised the coal–electricity price co-movement mechanism so that electricity tariffs would be adjusted if fluctuations in coal prices went beyond 5 per cent or more in 12 months, and electricity generators would be allowed to pass up to 90 per cent of increased fuel costs on to grid companies, instead of the existing 70 per cent threshold (State Council 2012).

To implement the co-movement mechanism in a more open and transparent manner, the NDRC (2015) further specified the details of its operation in December 2015. Since the beginning of 2016, within a one-year cycle, electricity tariffs will be adjusted if utility coal prices increase by RMB30–150 per tonne relative to the 2014 average reference prices for utility coal. The more frequent the fluctuations in coal prices, the lower are co-movement coefficients. When coal prices rise less than RMB30 per tonne, generators have to absorb the total fuel cost increase;the co-movement mechanism is also not triggered if coal prices rise more than RMB150 per tonne.

It should be noted that this co-movement mechanism is not an automatic trigger, and it may not be implemented even if the conditions are met. Indeed, the average increases in coal prices in the whole of 2017 and into the beginning of 2018 fell within the specified range, but the co-movement was not implemented. This could be because implementing the mechanism by raising power tariffs would hurt the profitability of downstream power users in the current, less favourable global economic environment.

Petroleum product prices

Domestic crude oil prices have tracked international prices since 1998, but this has not been the case with petroleum products. While China has raised its producer prices of gasoline and diesel several times, domestic oil refiners have still been feeling the pinch because crude oil prices have been linked directly to international prices and thus have been allowed to rise, while prices for refined oil products have not. To address this disconnect, the government has implemented, since May 2009, a pricing mechanism whereby domestic petroleum product prices are adjusted upward if the moving average of international crude oil prices—based on the composite Brent, Dubai and Cinta crude oil prices—rose by more than 4 per cent within 22 consecutive working days. However, this cycle of price adjustments has triggered widespread complaints, as it often failed to reflect fluctuations in the international market.

In March 2013, the NDRC launched a market-oriented petroleum product pricing mechanism to better reflect refiners' costs and adapt to fluctuations in global crude oil prices in a more timely manner. This automatic pricing mechanism shortens the adjustment period to 10 working days and removes the 4 per cent threshold. The composition of the basket of crudes to which oil prices are linked is also adjusted (Liu 2012; Zhu 2013).

In January 2016, the NDRC further specified that no price adjustments would be made if international crude oil prices fell below US$40 a barrel. Confronted with high costs of domestic production, this floor price is said to maintain domestic production close to current levels, in response to China's stagnating domestic oil production and a growing hunger for foreign oil (Zhang 2016).

Natural gas prices

The natural gas price has long been set below producers' production costs and does not reflect the relationship between supply and demand or the prices for alternative fuels. This has not only led to Chinese domestic gas producers' being reluctant to increase investments in production, but also constrained the imports of more costly natural gas from overseas. In June 2010, China increased the domestic producer price of natural gas by 25 per cent (Wan 2010). In December 2011, China carried out a pilot reform of the natural gas pricing mechanism in Guangdong province and the Guangxi Zhuang Autonomous Region. This reform replaced the long-used cost-plus pricing method with the 'netback market value pricing' approach. Under this mechanism, pricing benchmarks are selected and pegged to prices of alternative fuels formed by market forces to establish a price linkage mechanism between natural gas and its alternatives (NDRC 2011).

Since July 2013, the pilot scheme trialled in Guangdong and Guangxi has been implemented nationwide for all volumes above the 2012 gas consumption level. At the same time, natural gas prices were raised for nonresidential users based on a two-tiered approach. Under this reform, the NDRC sets caps on citygate gas prices for different provinces, instead of setting the ex-factory prices for domestic onshore and imported piped gas, while consumers and suppliers are allowed to negotiate their specific prices as long as they do not exceed the price ceilings. Moreover, a lower price is set for the 2012 consumption volume, with citygate prices capped. A higher price is set for any volumes above the 2012 consumption level. This price is pegged to 85 per cent of the basket price of alternative fuels such as fuel oil and liquefied petroleum gas using a 60 per cent and 40 per cent weight, respectively. The government intended to steadily raise the lower-tier prices so both price bands converged by 2015 (NDRC 2013b). Given the declining costs of alternative fuels, natural gas prices for nonresidential users were lowered in November 2015 and again in September 2017 (NDRC 2015, 2017b, 2017c).

Given that residential natural gas prices have been capped at levels much lower than those for nonresidential users, provinces such as Jiangsu, Henan and Hunan implemented tiered tariffs for household use of natural gas. The NDRC (2014) mandated in March 2014 that this pricing mechanism would be expanded to the whole country before the end of 2015. The pricing mechanism set three price bands associated with three tiers of consumption, with the first covering 80 per cent of the average monthly consumption volumes for household users, and the second the next 15 per cent. The third tier would cover any consumption above 95 per cent of the monthly household average. Consumption at the second and third tiers is charged accordingly at 120 per cent and 150 per cent of the first-tier price, respectively (NDRC 2014). Based on this guidance and taking its own circumstances into account, each province determines the consumption volume for each tier.

In the meantime, China has gradually allowed the market to determine the prices for a variety of gases. Since 2013, the prices for shale gas, coalbed methane and coal gas have been completely liberalised. Liberalisation continued with LNG prices, in September 2014; with prices for all other direct users, except gas used for fertilisers, in April 2015; prices for gas storage facilities, in October 2016; and prices for natural gas for fertilisers, in November 2016. Fujian province has piloted citygate gas prices since November 2016. Since September 2017, the prices for all volumes traded at the Shanghai and Chongqing gas exchange centres are set by the market (NDRC 2013c, 2015, 2017b).

As a result of these reforms, prices for more than 80 per cent of natural gas consumption for nonresidential use are determined by the market, of which more than 50 per cent is entirely set by the market and about 30 per cent is set by the flexible mechanism of reference prices supplemented with allowable fluctuation ranges (NDRC 2017c; Zhu 2017). Despite significant progress, more work needs to be done to formulate a fully market-oriented price. For specific prices, reforms involve introducing differential pricing policies to reflect seasonal price disparities, off-peak price disparities, interruptive gas prices and gas storage prices. More fundamentally, further progress in natural gas pricing reforms requires the deepening reform of the whole natural gas industry chain by opening the natural gas upstream and downstream markets and regulating the midstream pipeline transport market, as market-oriented natural gas prices can only be formed based on a competitive natural gas industry structure. The NDRC has been laying the foundation for third-party access to pipeline networks by reforming the network transportation price mechanism under the principle of allowable costs plus reasonable profits. In August 2017, the NDRC (2017a) released the verified pipeline network transportation costs for 13 natural gas long-distance pipeline transport enterprises under the common method, principle and standards. On average, the verified pipeline network transportation costs of these enterprises have been cut by 15 per cent, reducing a burden of RMB10 billion on downstream enterprises (Zhu 2017). The National Energy Administration needs to develop a third-party access policy so that parties as well as owners are able to access the pipeline network, formulating specific procedures and regulations for pipeline network access and establishing a platform for pipeline network information disclosure. Moreover, various types of investors should be encouraged to participate in the construction of pipeline networks, liquefied natural gas (LNG) terminals, gas storage facilities and other related facilities. By ownership unbundling, setting up an independent system operator and building an independent transmission operator, China could gradually separate natural gas pipeline transport and production and marketing, eventually leading to the independence of the pipeline network (Dong et al. 2017).

Electricity tariffs

The electricity industry in China was nationalised when the Communist Party assumed power in 1949, and has been in a process of reform since the 1980s (Ngan 2010; Zeng et al. 2016). In 2002, the State Council (2002) issued unbundling reform to separate power plants from power grids. Dismantling the vertically integrated power system into independent companies was the first attempt to establish a market-oriented mechanism, and it has since influenced China's power management mechanism. While China's unbundling reform has achieved a degree of success in the generation sector (Xie et al. 2012), electricity tariffs have remained under the control of the central government since the split-up of the State Power Corporation and the separation of electricity generation from its transmission and distribution in 2002. While electricity tariffs were raised a few times under the coal–electricity price co-movement mechanism, they remain flat and regulated. This not only reduces the effectiveness of moves to address the daunting challenges in cutting emissions and strengthening industrial upgrading, but also complicates the implementation of pilot carbon trading schemes in the Chinese power sector. Carbon trading creates a new impetus for power pricing reforms to allow the pass-through of carbon costs in the electricity sector.

China launched a new round of power industry reform in March 2015 (CCCPC and State Council 2015), in which pricing mechanism reform features prominently. Grids will not make profits by charging the gap between the on-grid price and the electricity price for users. Instead, they are supposed to earn their income by charging a transmission and distribution fee, which is determined by the NDRC. The scheme, piloted in Yunnan province, encourages large power users to negotiate directly with generators. Generators then sell power to the grid at transaction prices, which are negotiated by generators and users. As a result, the combination of the transaction price, transmission and distribution fee and government funds forms the price of electricity for industrial and commercial users, who account for more than 80 per cent of national power usage. The volume of power transacted and traded on the market increased from 10 per cent of total electricity sales in 2015 to 23 per cent in 2016 (Zhu 2017). The government aims to further increase this proportion. Meanwhile, tariffs for residential and agricultural power use continue to be regulated by the government (CCCPC and State Council 2015).

In the course of this comprehensive and complex power pricing reform, the government has offered power price premiums for desulfurisation and denitrification, and has charged differentiated, tiered power tariffs with the aim of conserving electricity and protecting the environment (NDRC 2013a, 2013c; NDRC and MIIT 2013).

Power price premium for desulfurisation and denitrification

With the burning of coal responsible for 90 per cent of China's total sulfur dioxide emissions, and coal-fired power generation accounting for half of the national total, the Chinese Government mandated that new coal-fired units must be equipped with a flue-gas desulfurisation (FGD) facility and plants built after 1997 must have begun to retrofit an FGD facility before 2010. During the twelfth five-year-plan period, electricity generators were required to install flue-gas denitrification as well. All coal-fired plants across the country with unit capacity of 300 megawatts (MW) or more and those in the eastern region and provincial capitals with unit capacity of 200 MW were required to install denitrification facilities.

While electricity tariffs remain controlled and flat, the government has offered a premium for all new coal-fired units since 2004. Given that China's sulfur dioxide emissions in 2005 were supposed to stay at the 2000 level but were in fact 5 per cent above that level, in 2007, the government decided to extend the premium to electricity generated by existing coal-fired power plants (that is, those built before 2004) with FGD facilities installed to encourage the installation and operation of FGD facilities at large coal-fired power plants (NDRC and SEPA 2007). The premium was equivalent to the average estimated cost of operating the technology. Other policies favourable to FGD-equipped power plants have been implemented—for example, giving them priority in grid connection and allowing them to operate longer than plants that do not install FGD capacity. Some provincial governments provide even more favourable policies, leading to priority dispatching of power from units with FGD in Shandong and Shanxi provinces. With the declining capital cost of FGD, newly installed desulfurisation capacity in 2006 was greater than the combined total over the previous 10 years, accounting for 30 per cent of total installed thermal (mostly coal-fired) capacity. By 2011, the portion of coal-fired units with FGD rose to 90 per cent of the total installed thermal capacity—from just 13.5 per cent in 2005 (Sina Net 2009; CEC and EDF 2012). As a result, China met its 2010 target of a 10 per cent cut in sulfur dioxide emissions one year ahead of schedule. The Harvard China Project estimates that China's sulfur dioxide reduction policy in the eleventh five-year-plan period resulted in negative economic costs and enormous benefits to human health—between 12,000 and 74,000 premature deaths avoided in 2010 (Nielsen and Ho 2013).

In November 2011, the government also offered a premium for electricity generated by power plants with FGD in 14 provinces or equivalent. At the beginning of 2013, the price premium was extended to all coal-fired power plants equipped with denitrification facilities (NDRC 2013a), and was increased to RMB0.01 per kilowatt hour (kWh) in September 2013 (NDRC 2013c).

Differentiated power tariffs

The NDRC (2006) ordered provincial governments to implement differentiated tariffs that charge more for companies classified as 'eliminated' or 'restrained' types in eight energy-guzzling industries, including cement, aluminium, iron and steel and ferroalloy from 1 October 2006. While provinces such as Shanxi charged differentiated tariffs even higher than the level required by the central government (Zhang et al. 2011), other provinces and regions have been offering preferential power tariffs to struggling local energy-intensive industries. The NDRC and five central ministries and agencies jointly ordered utilities to stop offering preferential power tariffs to energy-intensive industries by June 2010 and instead charge the punitive differentiated tariffs. Those utilities that failed to implement the differentiated tariffs were to pay a fine five times that of the differentiated tariffs multiplied by the volume of electricity sold (Zhu 2010).

Tiered power tariffs

With China's residential electricity demand set to increase as income grows and the price of residential electricity remaining below actual costs, the NDRC implemented three-tier tariffs for household electricity use in July 2012. The effectiveness of the new tariff mechanism depends on the price and income elasticities of residential electricity demand among income groups. However, very little information exists regarding these parameters in China. Based on the monthly microlevel data of Beijing urban households from 2002 to 2009, Jin and Zhang (2013) estimate these two parameters with both the almost-ideal demand system and the linear double-logarithmic model specifications. Their estimated price elasticity is close to unity and increases as income grows. This suggests that it might be effective to use pricing policies for demand-side management to adjust the electricity consumption of high-income groups. On the other hand, given that the estimated income elasticity is low, supporting policies are needed for low-income groups severely hit by increasing tariffs. In this regard, the authors suggest that either directly subsidising low-income families or rationally setting the price levels of different tariff blocks can help improve the distributional effects of tariff reform.

From the beginning of 2014, the NDRC expanded the three-tiered electricity pricing approach to the aluminium sector to phase out outdated production capacity and promote more rapid industrial restructuring (Gao 2013; NDRC and MIIT 2013). A similar tiered pricing policy applies to other industries, such as cement, to force upgrades in the drive for sustainable and healthy development.

Renewable power tariffs

From a long-term perspective, widespread use of renewable energy is a real solution for energy supply problems. Increasing the share of renewable energy in the total primary energy supply not only enhances energy security, but also is good for the environment and conducive to good health. China has set targets for alternative energy sources to meet 15 per cent of its energy requirements by 2020 and the share of non–fossil fuel use to be 20 per cent by 2030.

The Chinese Government initially supported solar energy through 'golden sun' investment subsidies (Zhang 2011, 2013). After years of simply taking advantage of overseas orders to drive down the cost of manufacturing solar panels, feed-in tariffs for solar power were enacted in July 2011 to create China's own solar power market. Wind power had benefited from bidding-based tariffs since 2003 (Zhang 2010, 2011, 2013). With total installed capacity of 5.9 gigawatts (GW) at the end of 2007, China had already surpassed its goal to achieve 5 GW by 2010, and met its 2020 target of 30 GW of wind power 10 years ahead of schedule. With both power demand and installed wind power capacity increasing faster than planned, and further deterioration of the environment, combined with the fact the country is facing great pressure both inside and outside international climate negotiations to be more ambitious in combating global climate change, China has raised its wind power target to 200 GW of wind power capacity in operation by 2020. This revised target is 170 GW more than the 30 GW target set in September 2007, and three times the United Kingdom's entire current power capacity.

In August 2009, the supportive policy for wind power was replaced with feed-in tariffs. Under this policy, four wind energy areas were designated based on the quality of their wind energy resources and the conditions they provided for project engineering and construction (NDRC 2009). On-grid tariffs were set accordingly as benchmarks for wind power projects. The levels were comparable with the tariffs the NDRC had approved in the previous several years in most regions, and were substantially higher than those set through bidding. By letting investors know the expected rate of return on their projects by announcing on-grid tariffs upfront, the Chinese Government aims to encourage the development of high-quality wind energy resources. In the meantime, this system will encourage wind power plants to reduce the costs of investment and operation and increase their economic efficiency, thus promoting the healthy development of the wider wind industry in China (Zhang 2010, 2011, 2013).

Under China's Renewable Energy Law, registered power generators are granted access to grids, which are required to purchase the full amount of renewable energy generated. Over the past 10 years, the cost of wind power projects has been declining (IRENA 2018) but on-grid tariff benchmarks in each zone remained unchanged until 2015. This induces wind power developers to focus only on production costs and not demand, and thus has led to a huge surplus in installed capacity—in particular, in northern and western China, where there are richer wind resources and where the installed capacity is concentrated, but which are far from the load centres. Consequently, a large amount of generated wind power has to be curtailed due to limited local demand or grid system stability constraints (Xia and Song 2017). China now aims to increase its total installed wind power capacity to 200 GW by 2020 and implement a green dispatch system to favour renewable power generation in the electricity grid. In this context, China needs to significantly improve its power grids and coordinate the development of wind power with the planning and construction of grids, including smart grids. New transmission lines should be constructed at the same time as wind power farms are built. Given the significantly scaled-up wind power capacity planned for 2020, China should now place more emphasis on companies ensuring the actual flow of power to the grid than on meeting capacity (Zhang 2010, 2011, 2014). Taking all these issues together, policies for feed-in tariffs and guaranteed purchases of renewable power need to be adapted to the new situation and alternative policies explored to solve the curtailment problem and to encourage wind power developers to choose locations close to the load centre.

Conclusions

China has determined to assign the market a decisive role in allocating resources. To that end, getting energy prices right is crucial. Since 1984, China has been making great efforts towards reforming energy prices, and has made great achievements. However, such reforms are far from complete. While under the current pricing mechanism for petroleum products prices fluctuate along with global crude oil prices, they decouple from the domestic market. Future reform of the petroleum product pricing mechanism should take domestic factors into account so that prices can better reflect the relationship between domestic supply and demand. From a long-term perspective, however, a complete marketisation of petroleum product prices will depend on the extent to which the central government is able to break the monopoly power of the three national oil corporations over oil imports, exploration, production and pipeline networks.

While the price for more than 80 per cent of China's natural gas consumption by nonresidential users is determined by the market, more work needs to be done to formulate a fully market-oriented price. Fundamentally, further progress requires deepening reform of the whole natural gas industry chain under a guiding principle of opening the upstream and downstream markets and regulating the midstream pipeline transport market. In this context, reforming the network transportation price mechanism and laying the foundation for third-party access to the pipeline network are crucial. The NDRC is moving in the right direction, verifying the transportation costs of long-distance natural gas pipeline enterprises under the common method, principle and standards. It needs to develop a third-party access policy so that parties as well as owners are able to access the pipeline network. China could gradually separate natural gas pipeline transport and production and marketing, eventually leading to the independence of the pipeline network.

While China has been reforming its electricity industry structure since 2002, the two main grid corporations—the State Grid and China Southern Power Grid—undertake the transmission, distribution and sale of electricity. As the only designated buyers of electricity from generators and distributors and sellers of electricity, they hold a monopoly in their respective areas. This monopoly power and the lack of competition in the electricity market have often attracted criticism. In my view, however, to establish a competitive power market, splitting the grid is not necessary, but separating the sale of electricity from grid transmission and distribution is a must. Only then can electricity sales be opened up and electricity-selling companies independent of grids set up in each region. This has been the key goal of a round of power industry reform China has undertaken since March 2015. Grids will not make profits by charging the gap between the on-grid price and the electricity price for users. Instead, grids will earn their income by charging a transmission and distribution fee determined by the NDRC. However, this could raise a variety of thorny issues, one of which is dispatching power when selling prices differ but the grid's source of income has already been set. Another could be how to lower power tariffs. This requires either power generators or grids giving up some profits in the value chain, given that power generators have low profit margins and the grids' source of income is based on the verified transmission and distribution fee and allowable profits. For renewable power, the policies of a feed-in tariff and guaranteed renewable power purchases help the widespread use of renewable power. These favourable policies must be adapted to the new situation of a surplus and mismatch between generation locations and the load centre, and alternative policies must be explored to solve the problem of curtailment and to encourage wind power developers to choose locations close to the load centre, in addition to increasing the grid transmission capacity and transporting electricity from western and northern China to the south-east by building more ultra-high-voltage transmission lines.

For coal, whether the revised coal–electricity price co-movement mechanism will be able to address potential conflicts between coal producers and power generators remains to be seen. This is because a one-year cycle of adjustment is long and the reference prices for utility coal remain stable relative to the rapid pace of China's overall reform and changing market conditions. Moreover, although the two-track system for coal prices has been abolished, it is still very difficult to establish a nationwide coal market as railway freight capacity has not been liberalised. This means that if rail wagons are not included in any liberalisation, purchased coal cannot reach the load centres. Thus, future reform has to be undertaken considering the entire coal value chain, targeting reform at those parts that need to be liberalised but which are, to a large extent, still controlled by the government. However, even if such reform is undertaken, coal prices will not fully reflect the cost of production because of officially controlled costs and the distorted prices of other production factors. Coal prices also do not include negative externalities. Clearly, the imposition of market-based environmental instruments can internalise externality costs in market prices. Indeed, implementing carbon trading not only creates a new impetus for power pricing reforms to allow the pass-through of carbon costs in the electricity sector, but can also help internalise externality costs in market prices.

References

Albouy, Y. (1991), *Coal pricing in China: Issues and reform strategy*, World Bank Discussion Paper No. 138, Washington, DC: The World Bank.

Central Committee of the Communist Party of China (CCCPC) and State Council (2015), Relative policies on further deepening the reform of the power industry, [in Chinese], *Zhongfa* (9)(15 March). Available from: www.ne21.com/news/show-64828.html.

China Electricity Council (CEC) and Environmental Defense Fund (EDF) (2012), *Studies on Pollution Cutting in China's Power Industry*, Beijing: CEC and EDF.

Dong, X. C., Pi, G. L., Ma, Z. W. and Dong, C. (2017), The reform of the natural gas industry in the PR of China, Renewable and Sustainable Energy Reviews 73: 582–93. doi.org/10.1016/j.rser.2017.01.157.

Fisher-Vanden, K. (2009), Energy in China: Understanding past trends and future directions, *International Review of Environmental and Resource Economics* 3(3): 217–44. doi.org/10.1561/101.00000026.

Gao, M., Wang, Z., Wu, Q. and Yang, Y. (2013), Natural gas pricing mechanism reform and its impacts on future energy options in China, *Energy and Environment* 24(7–8): 1209–28. doi.org/10.1260/0958-305X.24.7-8.1209.

Gao, S. Y. (2013), NDRC to implement tiered power prices for aluminium smelters, the production costs expected to increase, [in Chinese], *Caixin Net*, 23 December. Available from: industry.caijing.com.cn/2013-12-23/113726942.html.

Harvard China Project (2014), The comprehensive costs and benefits of NOx controls in China, Draft prepared by Harvard University for Energy Foundation, 3 June.

International Energy Agency (IEA) (2009), *Cleaner Coal in China*, Paris: IEA.

International Renewable Energy Agency (IRENA) (2018), *Renewable Power Generation Costs in 2017*, Abu Dhabi: IRENA.

Jin, Y. and Zhang, S. (2013), Elasticity estimates of urban resident demand for electricity: A case study in Beijing, *Energy and Environment* 24(7): 1229–48. doi.org/10.1260/0958-305X.24.7-8.1229.

Li, C. (2013), Enhancing the fight against air pollution raises the costs of large coal users, abatement costs of coal-fired plants expected to increase by yuan 200 billion, *Securities Daily*, 7 November.

Li, Q. (2009), Renewed call for raising electricity tariffs, [in Chinese], *Caijing Magazine* (20)(28 September). Available from: magazine.caijing.com.cn/2009-09-26/110265506_1.html.

Liu, C. (2012), Lack of transparency over parameters to set domestic prices of gasoline and diesel triggered suspension, [in Chinese], *Time Weekly*, 29 March. Available from: news.sina.com.cn/c/sd/2012-03-29/151024195106.shtml.

National Development and Reform Commission (NDRC) (2006), *Suggestions for improving the policy on differentiated tariffs*, [in Chinese], September, Beijing: NDRC. Available from: www.gov.cn/zwgk/2006-09/22/content_396258.htm.

National Development and Reform Commission (NDRC) (2009), *A circular on improving on-grid feed-in tariffs for wind power*, [in Chinese], 22 July, Beijing: NDRC.

National Development and Reform Commission (NDRC) (2011), *A circular on pilot reform of the natural gas pricing mechanism in Guangdong province and Guangxi Zhuang Autonomous Region*, [in Chinese], NDRC Price No. 3033, 26 December, Beijing: NDRC.

National Development and Reform Commission (NDRC) (2013a), *NDRC expanded the pilot scope of the price premium for coal-fired power plants equipped with denitrification facility*, [in Chinese], 9 January, Beijing: NDRC. Available from: www.gov.cn/gzdt/2013-01/09/content_2308249.htm.

National Development and Reform Commission (NDRC) (2013b), *A circular on setting the natural gas price*, [in Chinese], NDRC Price No. 1246, 28 June, Beijing: NDRC. Available from: zfxxgk.ndrc.gov.cn/PublicItemView.aspx?ItemID={3a41d88a-bf29-47d7-b25d-189c6a64e274}.

National Development and Reform Commission (NDRC) (2013c), *Further improvement of the policy on renewable energy and environmental-related electricity pricing*, [in Chinese], 30 August, Beijing: NDRC.

National Development and Reform Commission (NDRC) (2014), *Guidance policies on tier tariffs for residential use of natural gas*, [in Chinese], NDRC Price No. 467, 20 March, Beijing: NDRC. Available from: www.ndrc.gov.cn/zcfb/zcfbtz/201403/t20140321_603692.html.

National Development and Reform Commission (NDRC) (2015), *A circular on specifics on the coal–electricity price co-movement mechanism*, [in Chinese], NDRC Price No. 3169, 31 December, Beijing: NDRC. Available from: jgs.ndrc.gov.cn/zcfg/201512/t20151231_770446.html.

National Development and Reform Commission (NDRC) (2017a), *A circular on the verified pipeline network cross-province transportation costs*, [in Chinese], NDRC Price No. 1581, 29 August, Beijing: NDRC. Available from: www.ndrc.gov.cn/zcfb/gfxwj/201708/t20170830_859306.html.

National Development and Reform Commission (NDRC) (2017b), *A circular on citygate natural gas prices for nonresidential users*, [in Chinese], NDRC Price No. 1582, 29 August, Beijing: NDRC. Available from: www.ndrc.gov.cn/zcfb/gfxwj/201708/t20170830_859307.html.

National Development and Reform Commission (NDRC) (2017c), *Natural Gas Price Reform in China Since the 18th Central Committee of the Communist Party of China*, [in Chinese], October, Beijing: NDRC. Available from: www.ndrc.gov.cn/xwzx/xwfb/201710/t20171021_864325.html.

National Development and Reform Commission (NDRC) and Ministry of Industry and Information Technology (MIIT) (2013), *A circular on levering aluminium smelters with tiered power prices*, [in Chinese], NDRC Price No. 2530, 13 December, Beijing: NDRC.

National Development and Reform Commission (NDRC) and State Environmental Protection Agency of China (SEPA) (2007), *Administrative Measures for Power Price Premium for FGD by Coal-fired Power Plants and the Operation of FGD Facility*, [in Chinese], 11 June, Beijing: NDRC.

Ngan, H. W. (2010), Electricity regulation and electricity market reforms in China, *Energy Policy* 38(5): 2142–8. doi.org/10.1016/j.enpol.2009.06.044.

Nielsen, C. and Ho, M. (eds) (2013), *Clearer Skies over China: Reconciling air quality, climate and economic goals*, Cambridge, MA: MIT Press. doi.org/10.7551/mitpress/9780262019880.001.0001.

Rosen, D. H. and Houser, T. (2007), *China Energy: A guide for the perplexed*, Washington, DC: Peterson Institute for International Economics.

Sina Net (2009), SO_2 cutting goal expected to come ahead of schedule, [in Chinese], *Sina Net*, 7 July. Available from: finance.sina.com.cn/roll/20090707/04346447872.shtml.

Singh, I. (1992), *China: Industrial policies for an economy in transition*, World Bank Discussion Paper No. 143, Washington, DC: The World Bank.

State Council (2002), *The electric power institutional reform*, The General Office No. 5, 10 February, Beijing: State Council.

State Council (2012), *The guidance policies on deepening the reform of the utility coal market*, [in Chinese], The General Office No. 57, 20 December, Beijing: State Council. Available from: www.gov.cn/zwgk/2012-12/25/content_2298187.htm.

Wan, X. (2010), Reform of natural gas price broke ground: A one-time 25% hike, [in Chinese], *Daily Economic News*, 1 June. Available from: finance.sina.com.cn/roll/20100601/03408034884.shtml.

Williams, J. H. and Kahrl, F. (2008), Electricity reform and sustainable development in China, *Environmental Research Letters* 3(4): 1–14. doi.org/10.1088/1748-9326/3/4/044009.

Wu, J. and Zhao, R. (1987), The dual pricing system in China's industry, *Journal of Comparative Economics* 11(3): 309–18. doi.org/10.1016/0147-5967(87)90057-6.

Xia, F. and Song, F. (2017), The uneven development of wind power in China: Determinants and the role of supporting policies, *Energy Economics* 67: 278–86. doi.org/10.1016/j.eneco.2017.08.008.

Xie, B. C., Fan, Y. and Qu, Q. Q. (2012), Does generation form influence environmental efficiency performance? An analysis of China's power system, *Applied Energy* 96: 261–71. doi.org/10.1016/j.apenergy.2011.11.011.

Xu, Y., Williams, R. H. and Socolow, R. H. (2009), China's rapid deployment of SO_2 scrubbers, *Energy & Environmental Science* 2(5): 459–65. doi.org/10.1039/b901357c.

Zeng, M., Yang, Y. Q., Wang, L. H. and Sun, J. H. (2016), The power industry reform in China 2015: Policies, evaluations and solutions, *Renewable and Sustainable Energy* 57: 94–110. doi.org/10.1016/j.rser.2015.12.203.

Zhang, D., Aunan, K., Seip, H. M. and Vennemo, H. (2011), The energy intensity target in China's 11th five-year plan period: Local implementation and achievements in Shanxi province, *Energy Policy* 39(7): 4115–24. doi.org/10.1016/j.enpol.2011.03.085.

Zhang, Z. X. (1998), *The Economics of Energy Policy in China: Implications for global climate change*, New Horizons in Environmental Economics Series, Cheltenham, UK: Edward Elgar.

Zhang, Z. X. (2010), China in the transition to a low-carbon economy, *Energy Policy* 38: 6638–53. doi.org/10.1016/j.enpol.2010.06.034.

Zhang, Z. X. (2011), *Energy and Environmental Policy in China: Towards a low-carbon economy*, New Horizons in Environmental Economics Series, Cheltenham, UK: Edward Elgar. doi.org/10.4337/9780857938169.

Zhang, Z. X. (2013), An analysis of China's energy demand and supply policy framework, *Wiley Interdisciplinary Reviews: Energy and Environment* 2(4): 422–40.

Zhang, Z. X. (2014), Energy prices, subsidies and resource tax reform in China, *Asia and the Pacific Policy Studies* 1(3): 439–54. doi.org/10.1002/app5.46.

Zhang, Z. X. (2016), How to deal with 'China's energy threat theory': State-owned energy corporations' overseas acquisitions and investment and associated financial support, *Frontiers* (November): 49–62.

Zhu, J.H. (2010), Six ministries and agencies claim those utilities that fail to implement the differentiated tariffs will face a penalty five times the revenues received. *People Net*, 22 May. Available at: finance.sina.com.cn/chanjing/cyxw/20100522/07037984663.shtml.

Zhu, J. H. (2013), The adjustment period of oil prices shortened to ten working days, with the four percent threshold scrapped, *People Net-People's Daily*, 27 March.

Zhu, X. H. (2017), Moving from market-oriented reform towards fine regulation: The changing energy price policy in China, Paper presented at Second Symposium on Energy, Environmental and Industrial Economics, Tianjin University, China, 11 November.

26. The evolution and transformation of China's climate change response strategy: From preventing 'black swan' events to reducing 'grey rhino' risks

Jiahua Pan

China has long known the havoc extreme weather events can wreak on its people and society. After the founding of the People's Republic of China (PRC), infrastructure construction on a massive scale—especially in the area of water conservation projects—greatly improved the country's ability to deal with natural disasters. The increased flow of ideas into China from the outside world since the start of its reform and opening-up has improved understanding of global climate change, and has helped to raise public awareness about 'black swan' events—that is, events that are as difficult to predict as they may be socially and economically devastating. As China continues apace on its course towards industrialisation, global climate change, of which surface temperature rise has been the primary symptom, not only threatens the climate security of the world as a whole, but has also become a source of serious 'grey rhino' risks—that is, obvious dangers that are nonetheless overlooked, potentially jeopardising the prospect of sustainable development in China. China's climate change response strategy has evolved, starting with an exclusive emphasis on defensive measures that were passive and reactionary and transforming into one with a greater focus on tackling the challenges head-on with proactive measures. This strategic transition has also helped advance the construction of an ecological civilisation. It is incumbent on China, given its international obligations to help achieve global ecological security, to work together with other signatories to meet the targets set out in the Paris agreement. Just as importantly, this is also what needs to be done to realise a harmonious coexistence between humanity and nature.

Deepening understanding and broadening the scope of action

When China's policy of reform and opening-up was first adopted towards the end of the 1970s, climate change was exclusively a topic of scientific study. It was subsequently included among the environmental and development issues on which China engaged with international politics, marking the beginning of the country's involvement in the international effort to respond to climate change. As reform and opening-up unfolded and China's economy grew, strategic deliberation on the issue also deepened. Thinking shifted from the realisation that climate abnormality was attributable to climate change in the 1980s, to becoming alert to 'black swan' extreme weather events that merit special preventive measures in the 1990s, and then to arriving at a fuller understanding of what climate change really means—finally becoming what China is now: an active player in the global campaign to tackle the problem. At the same time, the country went through a similar process in regard to action plans and their execution. In the early 1990s, China primarily saw itself as a country that was morally a follower or an observer of such efforts. By the late 1990s, however, the country had established itself as an active player among developing countries both committed to and capable of proactively pushing for the protection of their development rights and greater climate justice. By 2010, China had, with its notable achievements in transformative development, become a world leader in efforts to safeguard the ecological security of planet Earth, respond to climate change and, in particular, to meet the challenges posed by 'grey rhino' risks. For analytical purposes, we divide the history of China's thinking and action on climate change into five stages: disaster prevention, involvement in scientific study, defending emission rights, coordinating development and taking a leadership role.

Stage one: 1978–89

Climate disaster prevention was the theme of the first stage of China's response to climate change, which started in 1978 and lasted until 1989, when climate change was perceived as extreme weather events. During this period, responding to climate change was not yet officially on the government's policy agenda. Once the policy of reform and opening-up was adopted, economic growth took centre-stage in all policy deliberation and formulation and became the country's top priority. Even though concepts such as the greenhouse effect, global warming and climate change were beginning to appear in the Chinese media, they did not garner serious attention from the public and so were never regarded as a development issue. While the release of *Our Common Future* (also known as the Brundtland Report) by the World Commission on Environment and Development (WCED 1987) did help raise awareness inside China about issues of ecological destruction and environmental pollution, climate change was largely seen as a problem of climate abnormalities causing extreme weather events. In addition to a limited number of articles providing a general introduction to the topic (for example, Zhang and Liu 2013), at that time Chinese research on 'climate change' was limited mostly to studies of the impact of meteorological disasters and discussions of policy responses (Xu 1990). Policies related to this issue in the five-year plan for national economic and social development called for improvements in forecasts for calamitous weather and earthquakes, and work to reduce damage caused by natural disasters.[1] Almost no mention was made of either mitigation of or adaptation to climate change.

Stage two: 1990–97

The second phase in China's involvement in international action on climate change was from 1990 to 1997. The government's climate change response policies during this period mostly revolved around engaging in and keeping up with actions taken by the rest of the international community. In response to the release of a scientific evaluation report prepared by the Intergovernmental Panel on Climate Change (IPCC) on the science behind, impact of and countermeasures for climate change, the Intergovernmental Negotiating Committee was established in 1990 under the auspices of the United Nations. The committee's mandate was to oversee and coordinate negotiations among governments over climate change–related international agreements and treaties. To participate in this process, the Chinese Government set up the National Climate Change Coordination Task Force in 1990, under the State Council's Committee on Environmental Protection. There are two reasons we consider this a notable period in China's participation in scientific research: 1) the Chinese task force was headed by Song Jian, a state councillor primarily responsible for science, technology and environmental protection; and 2) the office for the task force was set up inside the China Meteorological Administration (CMA) (Zou 2008). The CMA, as the body charged with executing China's participation in the IPCC, organised a team of Chinese researchers to compile a scientific evaluation report on climate change (IPCC 1990). That work began in 1988 and was completed by 1990. In 1990, then premier Li Peng, representing the Chinese Government, signed the UN Framework Convention on Climate Change (UNFCCC). State councillor Song, State Scientific and Technological Commission (now Ministry of Science and Technology) deputy commissioner Deng Nan, CMA chief Zou Jingming and China Environmental Protection Administration (now Ministry of Environmental Protection) chief Qu Geping were on hand at the signing ceremony.[2]

1 In both the ninth five-year plan, released in 1990, and the tenth five-year plan, the only climate-related provision dealt with the prevention of weather disasters.

2 Despite their membership of the coordinating team, agencies in charge of environmental protection did not play a leadership role in China's involvement in international efforts on climate change. China's involvement was due largely to the fact that the signing ceremony for the UN Framework Convention on Climate Change took place at the UN Conference on Environment and Development (UNCED), also known as the Earth Summit, in Rio de Janeiro in 1992, which China attended.

Stage three: 1998–2006

The third phase of China's international involvement in efforts to tackle climate change began in 1998 and lasted until 2006. The Chinese Government in this period focused mostly on asserting and defending the country's rights to development and, as such, attached relatively less importance to domestic actions than it might have. With the conclusion of negotiations over the Kyoto Protocol[3] in 1997, the Chinese Government came to the realisation that climate change was not simply a scientific and environmental issue, and was also a development issue. This led to the establishment in 1998 of the National Climate Change Response Policy Coordination Task Force, with Zeng Peiyan, then chair of the National Planning Committee, appointed as its head. The office of the task force was also moved from the CMA to the National Planning Committee, a central government body in charge of macroeconomic development planning and management. In 2003, chair of the National Development and Reform Commission (NDRC), Ma Kai, became the head of the task force. The Kyoto Protocol, acceptance of which by many signatories was grudging at best and resentful at worse, took effect in 2005. Instead of succumbing to mounting pressure from many developed countries to act aggressively to reduce its greenhouse gas emissions, China stood its ground on its status as a developing country and its right to pursue economic development. The government maintained, however, that China was committed to the principle of common but differentiated responsibilities as reflected in the Kyoto Protocol and was prepared to take action—albeit with financial support from developed countries—to reduce emissions and adapt to climate change. China's active involvement in the implementation of the Clean Development Mechanism[4] set out in the Kyoto Protocol is testament to that commitment.

Stage four: 2007–13

The next stage, covering the period 2007–13, was defined by a strategic emphasis on coordinated development. In 2007, the Chinese Government began to shift the focus of its climate change policies towards coordinating domestic action and international engagement. In particular, action plans would be introduced and executed domestically, while on the international front, China's resolve to reduce emissions would be affirmed while the country worked to wean itself off dependency

3 The Berlin mandate adopted at the 1995 UN climate conference in Berlin marked the onset of a negotiation process that culminated in the Kyoto Protocol in 1997, which called on developed countries to reduce their own greenhouse gas emissions and provide developing countries with the funding and technologies needed to pursue low-carbon development. However, opposition from a small number of countries, including the United States, caused an eight-year delay in the protocol's implementation, which did not begin until 2005, amid lingering resistance.

4 The Clean Development Mechanism is the twelfth clause in the Kyoto Protocol. It requires developed countries to help developing countries reduce their emissions by providing financial and technological support, and allows the emissions reductions attributable to such support to count towards the developed country's total emissions reduction achieved.

on financial support from developed countries. Due in large part to the development and increased strategic significance of the issue of climate change, the government decided in 2007 to elevate the standing of the climate change leadership group by granting it more powers and greater authority. In addition, a department dedicated to climate change response–related matters was established under the NDRC. In June of that year, the State Council decided to set up a leadership group to oversee climate change responses, energy conservation and emissions reduction. The Chinese premier was to be the group's head, with the chair of the NDRC as its chief of staff. Negotiations at the Bali climate change conference in 2007 produced, among other things, agreements regarding the second commitment period for the Kyoto Protocol and long-term actions for developing and developed countries. In the same year, the State Council officially released the 'National Plan on Responding to Climate Change', which had been jointly drafted by a number of government agencies, including the NDRC (State Council 2007). Prior to the 2009 UN climate conference in Copenhagen, while continuing to maintain the country's status as a developing country, the Chinese Government was anything but a foot-dragger on concrete climate action. It submitted its emissions reduction target for the year 2020, which was based on its 2005 emissions level, and made clear its decision not to seek financial assistance from developed countries. The twelfth five-year plan for economic and social development (2011–15) contained an entire chapter on responding to climate change—a first in the history of the five-year plans.

Stage five: 2014 – present

The year 2014 marked a strategic turning point in China's policy response to climate change. Proactivity replaced passivity, taking the lead replaced following others, domestic actions were ramped up and playing a leadership role on the international stage became an important objective. At the Asia-Pacific Economic Cooperation (APEC) senior officials informal meeting in 2014, leaders of the United States and China issued a joint statement (Office of the Press Secretary 2014),[5] setting out agreements that had been reached on core issues in the Paris climate accord and committing their respective countries to emissions reduction goals. In September 2015, the leaders of the two countries issued another joint statement[6] reaffirming their determination to work together to push the Paris climate change talks towards a successful outcome.

5 In the statement, the leaders of the two countries announced their respective national action plans for responding to climate change in the years beyond 2020, in recognition of the fact that such actions must form an integral part of any concerted effort to achieve low-carbon transformation of the economy and to keep temperature rise below 2°C. The US target is to reduce its aggregrate emissions to 26–28 per cent below its 2005 level by 2025 and to make good faith efforts towards achieving the higher end of that range. For its part, China intends to reach peak carbon dioxide emissions by 2030—possibly earlier—and to increase to about 20 per cent the share of non–fossil fuel energy in its total primary energy consumption. Both sides agreed to continue to pursue these objectives and to intensify efforts over time.

6 Chinese President Xi Jinping met with then US president Barack Obama in Washington, DC, on 25 September 2015. The two sides announced their respective plans to deepen cooperation in fighting climate change.

On 3 September 2016, Chinese President Xi Jinping and US president Barack Obama submitted their legal instruments for formal approval of the Paris agreement to then UN Secretary-General Ban Ki-moon at the G20 summit in Hangzhou, China. China's thirteenth five-year plan also contained calls for more aggressive actions to respond to climate change. In his report to the nineteenth National Congress of the Communist Party of China (CPC), President Xi made it clear that, for China, modernisation meant modernisation of the harmonious coexistence of nature and human beings. It was incumbent on China, President Xi averred, to take the lead in international cooperation on climate change responses and to engage in, contribute to and lead efforts to build a global ecological civilisation (Xi 2017: 71).

Since it was first introduced to the issues of climate change and responses to it, the Chinese Government's understanding has deepened, and it has continued to ramp up efforts to tackle the problem. Policy priority shifted gradually from shaky disaster forecasting to engaging in scientific and technological research, to asserting and defending the country's rights to pursue economic development, to coordinating action on the domestic and international fronts and, finally, to the situation today—working to fulfil China's domestic responsibilities as well as meeting its international obligations.

Internal drivers of development transformation

Some of the causal factors behind this shift in policy orientation and prioritisation were related directly to the country's domestic situation. At the top of the list were changes over time in carbon dioxide emissions from the burning of fossil fuels. Second, the dynamic evolution of the mutual impacts of economic development and environmental amenity indicated the need to augment the country's climate change response capabilities. Third, China's rapid economic expansion had already come up against physical–spatial constraints. In the face of problems related to climate change—which are essentially global in scope—China must, in addition to doing what is in the best interests of the Chinese people, contribute its fair share towards international efforts to achieve global climate security.

Emissions trajectory and associated sense of responsibility

Before the start of its reform and opening-up, China ranked much lower than developed countries in terms of both aggregate and per capita greenhouse gas emissions, even though some other low-income countries such as India and those in Africa were ranked even lower (Figures 26.1a and 26.1b). The country's aggregate emissions accounted for 6 per cent of the global total, while China was one-fourth of the global average in terms of per capita emissions. The reform and opening-up ushered in an era of brisk economic growth, which also led to significant increases in the country's carbon dioxide emissions. Even so, China reached only one-half of the global average in terms of per capita emissions by 1989.

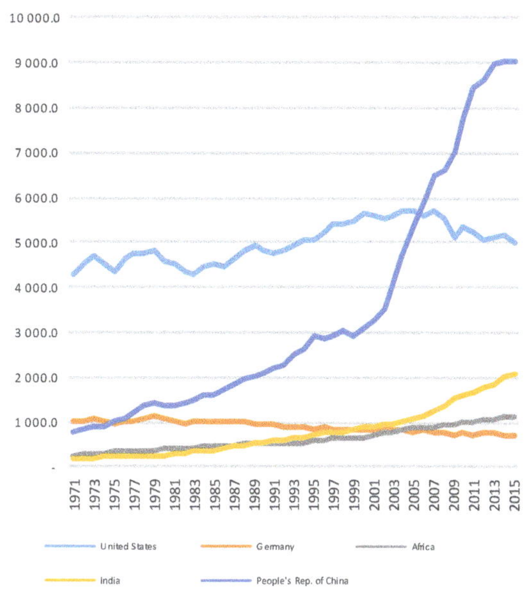

Figure 26.1(a) Changes in aggregate carbon dioxide emissions in selected countries and regions, 1971–2015 (1 million metric tonnes)

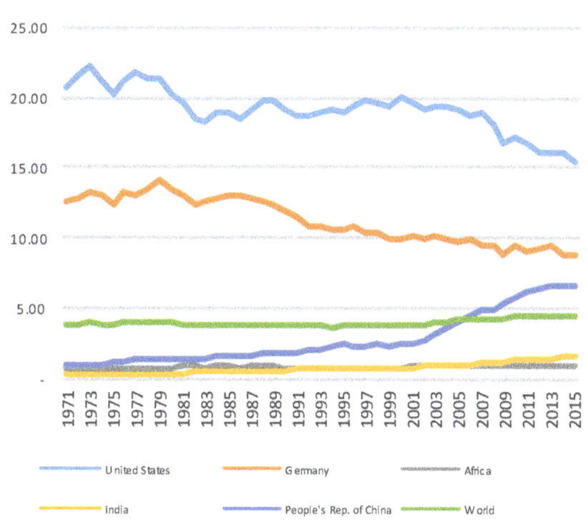

Figure 26.1(b) Changes in per capita carbon dioxide emissions in selected countries and regions, 1971–2015 (metric tonnes)

Source: IEA (2017).

By 1998, that percentage had grown to two-thirds. Both aggregate and per capita emissions levels rose sharply after 1998 and, by 2006, in terms of aggregate emissions, China became number one in the world and, at the per capita level, it surpassed the global average. By 2013, China was emitting more carbon dioxide than the United States and the European Union combined, and exceeded the EU average in per capita terms. China was initially something of an onlooker while it was trying to better understand the issue of climate change and, by 1998, it used its voice to draw attention to the issues of climate justice and development rights (Pan 2002a, 2002b). By 2006, China had become the 'world's factory' as a result of shifts in international trade patterns; it had high emissions on the production side, but still low emissions on the consumption side (Pan et al. 2008). By 2013, in comparison with not just other developing countries but also some developed countries, China was already among the largest carbon emitters in the world. Scientific research and evaluation have shown carbon dioxide emissions are the chief contributor to climate change, so, as China's carbon emissions followed an upward trajectory, so, too, did its sense of responsibility and obligation to act.

Strong growth and greater economic prowess

Prior to its reform and opening-up, China's gross domestic product (GDP) was just 5 per cent of that of the United States, and represented just 1.5 per cent of global GDP. After just 10 years of rapid economic growth under the new reform policies, in 1989, the volume of the Chinese economy had reached 10 per cent of that of the United States, and accounted for more than 2 per cent of the global total. These numbers grew to 16 per cent and 4 per cent, respectively, by 1997, and to more than 25 per cent and 6.6 per cent, respectively, by 2006. When the era known as the economic 'new normal' started in 2013, the Chinese economy was half the size of the United States', and accounted for 10.85 per cent of the aggregate size of the global economy. China has been the world's second-largest economy since 2010 and has maintained a medium to high rate of economic growth since 2014. By 2017, China's contribution to the global economy was about 15 per cent (World Bank 2017). However, at less than 80 per cent of the global average, per capita income in China is still far lower than in developed countries, although it is higher by a considerable margin than many low-income countries. According to classification criteria used by the World Bank and the International Monetary Fund, China is now ranked among the world's upper–middle-income countries. After the launch of China's 'Belt and Road Initiative' (BRI), outbound investment grew at a phenomenal rate. All of this has helped to greatly strengthen the country's capacity to respond to climate change, both domestically and at the international level.

Pressure from the growing need to protect and preserve nature and the environment

China is an ecologically fragile country. The Chinese people have lived since time immemorial with the constant threat to their survival and quality of life posed by natural disasters, primarily in the form of catastrophic weather events. Although China sent an official delegation to the UN Conference on the Human Environment in Stockholm in 1972 and this was followed by the establishment of the Office of Environmental Protection under the State Council, before the launch of its reform and opening-up, and possibly until as late as 1989, ecological deterioration was the main environmental problem the country faced. After the Framework Convention on Climate Change was signed at the UN Conference on Environment and Development (UNCED) in Rio de Janeiro in 1992, the Chinese Government became one of the first countries in the world to introduce a national plan for promoting sustainable development (State Council 1994). However, this did not immediately make the environment a top priority, as it came in last among the three areas of focus for sustainable development, after population and resources. In 1998, what had been the Environmental Protection Administration—a body under and not a part of the State Council, and not even a ministerial-level governmental agency—was upgraded to become a 'state administration', rendering it institutionally on a par with all other ministries.[7] It would be another 10 years, however, before the organisation was officially named the Ministry of Environmental Protection and became a constitutive organ inside the State Council, in 2008. The focus of the organisation's work evolved over the decades. Before 1998, its chief tasks related to setting national standards for various environmental indicators, but no cap was placed on the aggregate level of allowable pollutants. In 2008, a cap on aggregate pollution was introduced that made allowances for historical accumulations. It was not until 2013 that quality control for the various environmental media started. The focus of air pollution abatement efforts shifted from sulfur dioxide to nitrogen oxide and to particulate matter (PM) 2.5—all of which are attributable to the burning of fossil fuel. Reducing emissions of carbon dioxide from fossil fuel combustion would, therefore, help manage air quality. In addition, the continuing worsening trend of water quality in China is related to climate change–induced changes to the country's hydrological landscape. A retreating snowline and melting glaciers caused

7 In 1988, the Chinese Bureau of Environmental Protection, which was an agency under the former Ministry of Urban and Rural Construction and Environmental Protection, was separated from that ministry and placed under the direct administration of the State Council. In 1993, the administrative ranking of this organisation was upgraded to subministry, one level below ministry. In 1998, with the approval of the first plenum of the ninth National Congress of the CPC, and in accordance with pertinent provisions in the State Council's organisational reform plan, the organisation was further upgraded to ministerial level, and renamed the State Administration for Environmental Protection. In 2008, with the approval of the first plenum of the eleventh National Congress and in accordance with State Council provisions, the Ministry of Environmental Protection was established (State Council 2008).

by temperature rises are expected to lead to a 20 per cent increase in total lake surface area on the Qinghai–Tibet Plateau (Ding 2017). Even under the assumption of a 1.5°C temperature rise, an estimated one-third of glaciers across Asia are expected to disappear (Kraaijenbrink et al. 2017), effectively depriving the Yangtze, Yellow, Mekong and Yarlung Tsangpo rivers of their source water. This means that responding to climate change is something China does not because others have asked it to, but because it is something it wants to do (Xi 2014).

Spatial constraints on physical expansion

China has a vast territory and large population, and it takes a prodigious amount of high-energy and resource-intensive production and consumption to improve the country's infrastructure and its people's living standards. This entails rapid growth and places enormous demands on sources of energy and other raw materials as the process of industrialisation and urbanisation continues.

However, the accumulation of material wealth and increases in consumption are bound to hit a 'ceiling' sooner or later (Pan 2015). Once the construction of regional infrastructure such as railways, highways and airports reaches saturation point, basic material needs such as those for housing, transportation and food have been adequately met and population growth begins to taper off, pressure on the national economy to continue to expand physically will also begin to ease, before dissipating altogether.

We can see this by looking at the production of steel and iron to meet the needs of infrastructure and housing construction (NBS various years). China's production of raw steel was 61,000 tonnes in 1950, 23.74 million tonnes in 1977, 61.59 million tonnes in 1989, 100 million tonnes in 1996, 423 million tonnes in 2006, 779 million tonnes in 2013 and 823 million tonnes in 2014. The number dropped slightly in 2016, to 808 million tonnes (NBS 2017). In 2016, 2.06 billion mobile phones and 290 million computers were produced in China. According to data from the National Bureau of Statistics (NBS), by 2016 the average living area for each Chinese was 40.8 sq m—36.6 sq m for urban residents and 45.8 sq m for rural residents (NBS Office of Household Survey 2017). By the end of 2017, there were 310 million motor vehicles in China, including 217 million cars. The fact that overcapacity exists in areas such as iron and steel, coal and building construction indicates that the national economy is on the verge of reaching the upper limits of its physical expansion. The beginning of the 'new normal' era in 2013 was in fact a sign of the constraints imposed by the 'ceiling'—a constraint that forced the transition from focusing exclusively on quantitative growth to paying equal attention to qualitative improvement. This also suggests that, regardless of whether the need to limit greenhouse gas emissions places constraints on growth, the amount of room available for further physical expansion of the national economy has been diminishing and is on course to become negative.

Future outlook

So far, the evolution of China's climate change policy response has largely reflected the changing world order and international conditions. Further policy changes in the future will be driven increasingly by China's commitment to helping other countries work together on issues that affect all of humanity.

Grasping the international economic and political landscape

The international economic and political landscape of the twenty-first century is markedly different from that of the twentieth century. It behoves China to continue to make whatever necessary adjustments to its climate change response strategies and policies befit the changes taking place in the world at large.

The opposition between a global West and a global East that defined the world order in the Cold War era was displaced in the 1990s by the division of the world into a global North and a global South, during which the G7 called the shots when it came to the world order and the direction of development. Since the beginning of the twenty-first century, the North–South bifurcation has itself been replaced with a tripartite division into developed countries, emerging economies and developing countries (Pan and Chen 2016). The G7 has also been replaced with the more inclusive G20, comprising emerging economies in addition to the G7 countries.

As far as future needs, technologies and the demographic outlook are concerned (UN 2017), this tripartite division covers five distinct types of economies. Developed countries can be further divided into two groups: the 'super saturated' and the 'technologically expansionary'. The former includes EU countries and Japan, which have already maxed out their allowable development space and have begun to see zero or even negative population growth; while the latter, represented by the United States and Australia, are still growing in population size, have ample room within their own territories for further growth and development and have enormous innovative capacity.

Among the emerging economies, we can identify three subtypes. China is representative of the subtype characterised by a population size that is about to peak and set to shrink in the long term, that has medium to high incomes and is on the verge of maxing out the available physical space for further development within its national borders. We might call this subtype 'near-saturated'. Then there is the subtype of which India is representative, which might be called 'consumption expansionary'. These countries are growing at a relatively brisk rate in terms of population size, although that growth is expected to plateau in the long run; they have low to medium incomes and plenty of physical space within their borders to accommodate further growth in the national economy. Finally, there is what we might call the 'population expansionary' category, which includes low-income high population–growth countries with large areas within their territories that are as yet undeveloped and which are vulnerable to the impacts of climate change (see Figure 26.2).

As for greenhouse gas emissions, EU countries and Japan will see negative growth, the United States will see its emissions decline despite its growing population largely thanks to technological advances, while China will differ little from other developed countries as far as this issue is concerned. Emissions levels in India are expected to experience strong growth until 2050. As for Africa, even assuming minimal increases in per capita emissions, the prospect of a continent-wide population of 4 billion and the vast amounts of energy and resources needed to meet their basic needs may prove to be the most challenging obstacle to the world meeting the emissions targets set in the Paris agreement. Against this backdrop, an appropriate choice for China would be to help defend and strengthen the Paris agreement, including its emissions reduction targets and the verification mechanism specified therein, and to play a leadership role in international efforts to achieve zero emissions after 2050.

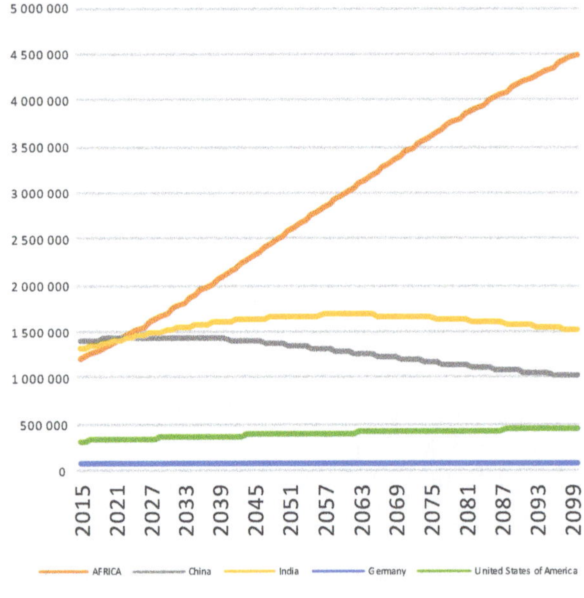

Figure 26.2 Future demographic trends (1,000 people, medium fertility rate)
Source: UN (2017).

A world leader in low-carbon development and transformation

China will speed up its low-carbon development and transformation. According to data released by the International Renewable Energy Agency (IRENA 2017), in terms of both the growth rate and the aggregate scale of generation capacity for renewable energy, China surpasses not just other developing countries, but also—and by a significant margin—some developed countries. In 2007, China contributed 15 per cent of total global generation capacity for renewable energy, while the US contribution stood at only 11 per cent (Table 26.1). By 2016, China's contribution had risen to 27 per cent, while the US share stayed at 11 per cent. Over the period 2006–17, the world's total renewable energy generation capacity grew by 100 per cent—higher than the growth rate in the United States. By contrast, the growth rate for China was 270 per cent, which does not even taken into account growth in China's solar and bioenergy sectors. Finally, China is number one in the world in terms of both the growth rate and the existing stock of electric vehicles.

Table 26.1 Generating capacity for renewable energy in selected economies (megawatts)

	2007	%	2016	%	2016/2007 (%)
World	990,968	1.00	2,007,658	1.00	1.03
Africa	22,938	0.02	38,285	0.02	0.67
China	148,543	0.15	545,916	0.27	2.68
India	41,867	0.04	90,748	0.05	1.17
Germany	35,602	0.04	104,704	0.05	1.94
United States	107,917	0.11	214,776	0.11	0.99

Source: IRENA (2017).

Risk management and disaster prevention in a warming world

According to IPCC scientific evaluation reports, global temperature rise will continue unabated. Like 'grey rhinos', the climate change risks are huge, although incremental and gradual. Faced with the prospect of a retreating snowline on the Qinghai–Tibet Plateau, rapidly melting glaciers and a sharp reduction in the amount of source water for some of the country's major rivers, the Chinese Government would be wise to engage in long-term thinking when it comes to issues such as the spatial distribution of industry and the layout of cities. Sea level will most likely continue to rise—and by a significant amount—constituting another potential threat. For the Yangtze River Delta, Pearl River Delta and Bohai Bay areas, in particular—which together make up the most economically vital and population-dense region in China—the risks are serious and clear. Planting trees can help augment the land's capacity for carbon sequestration and draining lakes to restore farmland could help boost the country's resilience and mitigate its vulnerability. Rapidly growing low-income countries are also potential source countries for climate refugees—yet another looming global-scale challenge.

China's proposal for climate governance

The construction of an ecological civilisation that is unfolding in China has facilitated the world's transition to a path of sustainable development. During the negotiations leading up to the signing of the Paris agreement and since it came into effect, China has, together with the United States, made significant contributions to moving the process forward. To meet the targets set in the Paris agreement, the world must work together and seek to secure benefits for all.

China, for its part, should play a leading role wherever and whenever it can, including sharing with other countries its own ideas about solutions to the problems of global climate security. Now and in the future, whatever the world order may be, China must take its international obligations seriously and behave accordingly. In fact, what China has done in the area of emissions reduction and developing renewable resources is powerful testament of how it already holds itself to these high standards. Of course, China's actions will not be enough on their own, nor can China provide low-income developing countries with the funds they need to deal with climate change.

President Xi has announced the Chinese Government's goal of realising nationwide modernisation by 2035 (Xi 2017: 71). By that time, the Chinese economy will conceivably exceed that of the United States in aggregate size, but will still be less than one-third the US level in per capita terms.[8] China's leadership role in the world in dealing with global climate change cannot consist of it directly providing others with the things they need. Nor is teaching others how to procure the things they need the solution. If people do not change the way they think, there is little chance the right actions will be taken voluntarily.

China's solution should essentially follow a Chinese path towards the construction of an ecological civilisation. This requires China to show others the way, so all parties will be willing to take appropriate actions, coordinate their efforts and work together to build a shared future for humanity and to realise the harmonious coexistence of humanity and nature.

8 According to data made available by the World Economic Information Network (2017), in 2017, US GDP was US$19.36 trillion—1.58 times China's GDP of US$12.24 trillion. Per capita GDP in the United States was US$59,500—6.92 times that of China, which was US$8,600. This means that, by 2035, while a doubling of China's per capita GDP and zero growth in the US figure would result in China surpassing the United States in terms of the aggregate size of the economy, in per capita terms, China will still be less than one-third the US figure.

Conclusion and discussion

Ever since China first became internationally involved in efforts to address climate change, the country's strategies and concrete actions have undergone profound changes, reflecting not only the industrialisation and urbanisation processes domestically, but also the evolving international economic and geopolitical situation. In broad outline, we can trace these changes to two decades before the beginning of reform and opening-up, when the primary concern in China was grappling with weather-related disasters and catching up with scientific understanding of global climate change. Back then, China was at best a follower on the international stage, with relatively limited engagement. Given the situation at the time in terms of the aggregate and per capita size of the Chinese economy, aggregate and per capita carbon emissions, the country's capacity for mitigation and adaptation, its own understanding of the issue and what was expected of it by others in the world, the country's main policy focus was reducing the damage caused by natural disasters to ensure steady development of the national economy. In other words, the emphasis was on preventing 'black swan' events.

Now that China has overtaken the United States in aggregate emissions and the European Union in per capita emissions, the impact of climate change on the country is becoming increasingly pronounced—as are the adverse impacts of environmental pollution and ecological degradation on economic development and people's welfare. Data on water shortages, melting glaciers and sea level rise, among other things, point towards the emergence of 'grey rhinos'—something to which policymakers must pay close attention.

Meanwhile, an economically much more powerful China is also far more capable and effective than it has ever been in dealing with extreme weather events. Given the enormous size of the Chinese territory, marked regional disparity in economic development levels and the devastating impact natural disasters have historically had on the society and the economy, it is all but inevitable that Chinese people are particularly cognisant of and sensitive to the risks associated with 'black swan' weather disasters. With the two-track negotiations leading to the Bali climate road map and the appointment of the Chinese premier as head of the leadership group overseeing the country's climate change response policies and actions, the exclusive focus on events that are difficult to predict and socially and economically devastating has been replaced with a more balanced approach that also includes heightened awareness of and improved preparedness for 'hidden in plain sight' dangers that tend to be overlooked or dismissed.

As the second decade of the twenty-first century opened, China embarked on a new leg of its journey towards greater prosperity for all—the economic 'new normal'—and the construction of socialism with Chinese characteristics has also turned a new page. The international community has hightened expectations of what China can and will do, and China has met those expectations by taking on greater responsibilities as a key global player. China no longer just follows; it now also tries to lead. The 'inaction' approach adopted by developed countries represented by the United States, the rapid industrialisation and urbanisation of South Asian countries with growing populations and the enormous potential emissions and climate risks faced by developing countries in Africa all constitute sources of 'grey rhino' risks that could trigger calamitous weather disasters that may, in some cases, turn into catastrophes.

China has seen surface temperature and sea level rises higher than the world average. The glaciers that have always supplied source water for China's major rivers are melting away. Moreover, its vulnerable coastal region is also the most developed and economically vital in the country. Pushing forward the construction of an ecological civilisation in China and meeting head-on the challenges posed by grey rhino risks are of paramount importance to China's rejuvenation and its future prospects for sustainable development. What was a national strategy of responding to climate change has evolved into a 'Chinese solution' to the challenges of grey rhino climate risks—a solution that places equal weight on strengthening domestic actions and taking a leading role on the international stage.

References

Ding, Y. (ed.) (2017), The impact of cryospheric changes on lakes, in *Cold Region Hydrology*, Beijing: Beijing Science Press.

Intergovernmental Panel on Climate Change (IPCC) (1990), *Climate change: The IPCC response strategies*, IPCC First Assessment Report, Geneva: IPCC. Available from: www.ipcc.ch/publications_and_data/publications_ipcc_first_assessment_1990_wg3.shtml.

International Energy Agency (IEA) (2017), *CO2 Emissions from Fossil Fuel Combustion 2017 Highlights*, Paris: IEA.

International Renewable Energy Agency (IRENA) (2017), *Renewable Energy Statistics 2017*, Abu Dhabi: IRENA.

Kraaijenbrink, P. D. A., Bierkens, M. F. P., Lutz, A. F. and Immerzeel, W. W. (2017), Impact of a global temperature rise of 1.5 degrees Celsius on Asia's glaciers, [Letter], *Nature* 549(14 September): 257–60. Available from: www.nature.com/nature/journal/v549/n7671/full/nature23878.html?foxtrotcallback=true. doi.org/10.1038/nature23878.

National Bureau of Statistics (NBS) (various years), *China Statistical Yearbook*, Beijing: China Statistics Press.

National Bureau of Statistics (NBS) (2017), *2016 National Economic and Social Development Statistical Bulletin*, Beijing: China Statistics Press.

National Bureau of Statistics (NBS) Office of Household Survey (2017), *Continuing brisk growth of people's income and increase in standard of living: A report on achievements in economic and social development since the 18th CPC National Congress (part VII)*, 6 July, Beijing: NBS Office of Household Survey.

Office of the Press Secretary (2014), US–China joint announcement on climate change, 12 November, Beijing, Washington, DC: Office of the Press Secretary.

Pan, J. (2002a), *A conceptual framework for analysis of human development potentials and demand for greenhouse gas emissions*, Global Change and Economic Development Working Paper 2002-10, Beijing: Chinese Academy of Social Sciences.

Pan, J. (2002b), Human development rights and developing countries' basic emissions needs, *Chinese Social Sciences Today* (6).

Pan, J. (2015), *Ecological Construction and Environmental Protection in China*, Beijing: China Social Sciences Press.

Pan, J. and Chen, Z. (2016), *A Transformative Agenda: Sustainable development goals for 2030*, Beijing: Social Sciences Academic Press.

Pan, J., Phillips, J. and Ying, C. (2008), China's balance of emissions embodied in trade: Approaches to measurement and allocating international responsibility, *Oxford Review of Economic Policy* 24(2): 354–76. doi.org/10.1093/oxrep/grn016.

State Council (1994), *China's Agenda 21: White paper on China's population, environment and development in the 21st century*, 25 March, Beijing: State Council.

State Council (2007), *Notice on the release of the PRC national plan on climate change response*, State Council Document No. [2007]17, Beijing: State Council.

State Council (2008), *11th Five Year Plan for National Economic and Social Development of the People's Republic of China*, State Council Document No. [2008]11, Beijing: State Council.

United Nations (UN) (2017), *World Population Prospects: The 2017 revision*, DVD edn, New York: Population Division, Department of Economic and Social Affairs.

World Bank (2017), Open data, Washington, DC: The World Bank. Available from: data.worldbank.org/.

World Commission on Environment and Development (WCED) (1987), *Our Common Future*, Oxford: Oxford University Press.

World Economic Information Network (2017), 2017 world GDP ranking (nominal gross domestic product world ranking), [in Chinese], *World Economy*. Available from: www.8pu.com/gdp/ranking_2017.html.

Xi, J. (2014), Xi Jinping meets with US Secretary of State Kerry, *Xinhuanet.com*, 14 February. Available from: news.xinhuanet.com/politics/2014-02/14/c_119341954.htm.

Xi, J. (2017), Secure a decisive victory in building a moderately prosperous society in all respects and strive for the great success of socialism with Chinese characteristics for a new era, Speech to nineteenth National Congress of the Communist Party of China, Beijing.

Xu, G. (1990), The impact of climate change on Xinjiang's agriculture in the 1990s: Evaluation and policy responses, *Meteorological Study of Desert and Oasis* (6): 2–5.

Zhang, Z. and Liu, Y. (2013), A meta-quantitative analysis of studies in China on climate change, *Modern Intelligence* 7(33): 125–9.

Zou, J. (2008), National climate change response leadership group, *World Environment* (2): 93.

Part V: Trade, investment and global integration

27. China and the global trading system: Then and now

Peter Drysdale and Samuel Hardwick[1]

The achievement

Openness to international trade and investment has been integral to Chinese economic transformation over the past four decades. Within that relatively short time, China has profoundly changed the way it engages with the rest of the world. The development of domestic markets—a key element of Chinese reform—has been significantly enhanced by integration into international markets via trade, investment flows, technology transfers, people-to-people exchanges and the spread of knowledge.

China's reforms coincided with an era of increasing globalisation, which was characterised by a more open global trading environment resulting from significant reduction in tariffs and other forms of trade protection. In the postwar period, these reforms were driven by various rounds of multilateral trade negotiations under the auspices of the General Agreement on Tariffs and Trade (GATT) and, later, the World Trade Organization (WTO). After the late 1980s, unilateral liberalisation in the Western Pacific region gathered pace under regional cooperation arrangements such as the Asia-Pacific Economic Cooperation (APEC) forum.

The new era was marked by two key factors: rapid adjustment in the structure of world trade in response to more open cross-border flows of goods, capital, people and technology; and rapid reductions in transaction costs because of substantial improvements in transport, communication and information technologies. International markets presented China with opportunities greater than those available during Japan's and South Korea's periods of extraordinary growth (Brandt and Rawski 2008: 13). China's seizing of these opportunities has enhanced global interdependence to a degree the world has never seen before.

China's integration into the global economy brought one-fifth of the world's population into the international economic system, increasing market potential and integration to an unprecedented level. The increased scale and depth of international specialisation propelled by enlarged global markets offered new opportunities to

1 We are most grateful to Nishanth Pathy for his excellent and expeditious editorial and substantial input into the final form of this chapter, and to Shiro Armstrong for his wise suggestions in the crafting of its argument. Any remaining errors are, of course, our responsibility alone.

boost world production, trade and consumption, with the potential for increasing the welfare of all countries involved (Golley and Song 2011). It promised an era of unsurpassed global economic growth and prosperity—a 'golden age' of world economic growth.

The promise of the golden age is now under a shadow. The era of globalisation is challenged, in part because of the shifts in the global economy and global power that China's trade and economic success delivered to the world; in part, because of deep structural problems and their mismanagement in other countries. The dimensions of the challenge, and what course might be open to deal with it, we turn to at the end of the chapter.

Multilateralism and China's trade story in perspective

A global framework promoting open trade and investment enabled China's integration into the world economy. A central element was the rules-based GATT and then WTO trading system. While much of China's early economic engagement with the world was concentrated in the Asia-Pacific region, it was China's accession to the WTO, the commitments it made in the process leading up to that and its acceptance of the global rules that underpinned its international economic integration.

Although China had taken important steps towards liberalisation and regional engagement in the reform of its economy and trading system prior to 2001—notably through the establishment and spread of special economic zones (SEZs) and successive rounds of trade liberalisation—WTO accession was a watershed moment in China's trade and economic reform. Joining the WTO drove a suite of domestic reforms, lifted investor confidence in China at home and abroad and precipitated rapid growth in China's contribution to world trade. Now, 17 years on, amid pressing new developments that are shaking global economic governance, China and its partners have a major joint stake in securing those interests in a healthy, WTO-led global trading system.

There were many twists and turns along the 15-year road towards WTO accession. APEC, a regional initiative with global objectives, offered a critical pathway. The 1995 APEC summit in Osaka provided the platform for China to announce a massive unilateral trade liberalisation—the largest ever undertaken by a single country in the postwar period—as down payment on the way to WTO accession.

China's economic reform became increasingly linked to trade liberalisation. In the mid-1980s, China embarked on opening up procurements of strategic raw materials such as iron ore from international markets through large-scale purchases from Australia. These were necessary as inputs into developing modern industrial capacity. This initiative has profoundly changed China's participation in the international economy. China also saw common cause with the interests of developing economies in dismantling export controls over trade in textiles and other labour-intensive exports. Through Asian economic cooperation, particularly through APEC, China embraced a globalist, multilateral approach to international integration. Like other regional players, China was favoured by an open approach to integration under the multilateral trading system in fostering trade expansion (EABER and CCIEE 2016: 40).

The protocols of Chinese accession to the WTO were more demanding than those placed on other developing economies and even those of established developed country members (namely in respect of limitations on the application of export controls) (Branstetter and Lardy 2008: 655). China's commitment to the protocols of accession to the WTO entailed large-scale national economic reform. Markets in manufacturing and commodities across the country became increasingly open and competitive. This process saw deeper integration of the national economy and accelerated the integration of the Chinese economy into international markets. The effect of reforms and integration was not simply a more efficient allocation of resources through the closer alignment of domestic with international prices—that had largely been achieved in the half-decade or so before accession. The substantive impact of the regime change was WTO members' and China's new confidence in undertaking trade with one another—trade that rose dramatically in the years immediately after accession in 2001 (Armstrong 2012).

The global system, underpinned by the GATT/WTO and multilateral financial institutions, was never static. It has evolved, for example, in managing international trade rules, through the GATT to the WTO with its stronger dispute settlement mechanisms. New economic and political risks and challenges required the adaptation and evolution of these institutions and their supplementation with others. The global financial crisis (GFC) saw the emergence of the G20 as a forum for national leaders. China's rise as a source of international capital later saw its commitment to the Asian Infrastructure Investment Bank (AIIB) and the Belt and Road Initiative (BRI). But there remain many areas of international commerce, such as foreign direct investment (FDI), not covered by the comprehensive multilateral regime, such as that which governs trade. Rapid shifts in the structure of the global economy and the digital revolution are now creating enormous pressure to strengthen and adapt international trade institutions to deal with these new pressures.

An increasingly important dimension of world trade, for which the rules are still being written, is the free and secure movement of digital data across borders. The growth of the digital economy means that domestic data regulations, including data localisation and internet filtering, have the potential to present significant obstacles to free trade (Meltzer 2017). Yet the treatment of data regulation in the global trade architecture remains underdeveloped. A stronger framework for addressing these issues (and others in the cybersecurity domain) will be necessary for the next phase in writing the rules of the global economy. As a major economy, China will have to play a substantive part in this.

Another question is the use of trade-restrictive measures in political disputes. There are legitimate applications of trade sanctions under international law, such as the trade sanctions imposed on North Korea (which, in any case, is not a signatory to the WTO) under UN resolutions.[2] But there are also instances in which China and other countries have deployed commercial restrictions in political retaliation against trading partners, such as in the case of China's retaliation to South Korea's Terminal High Altitude Area Defense (THAAD) announcement in March 2017. These cases highlight areas where international rules are inadequate or underdeveloped, or where norms and expectations are seen as malleable. How to manage these political risks around hard-letter rules is now an active object of interest in the working of the global economic system.

Healthy, rules-based and inclusive global institutions have been and continue to be central to the prosperity of China and its economic partners. The region's long-term economic and political stability and security will depend in significant part on how resilient global institutions are to the pressures put on them by shocks and structural changes in the global economy, and how those institutions adapt to these changes—in particular, to the rise of China and other emerging economies.

Liberalisation and reform

In 1980, two years into China's reform and opening, the Chinese economy accounted for 2 per cent of global gross domestic product (GDP). Today, it is the world's largest economy in purchasing power parity (PPP) terms and the second largest—at 15 per cent of global GDP—as measured at current exchange rates in US dollars. Much of the near double-digit growth between 1980 and 2016[3] stemmed from the more efficient allocation of resources that came with the transition from a planned to a mixed market economy. A major driver, however, particularly after 2001, was export growth (Yao 2013: 45).

Rapid industrialisation and waves of rural–urban migration gave China its comparative advantage in labour-intensive manufacturing industries (Yao 2013: 51). The move to freer trade, facilitated by participation in regional and global arrangements, unlocked this potential and enabled China to become the world's leading exporter of manufactured goods—a position it has retained each year since

2 The latest of which is Resolution 2375, restricting crude oil imports.

3 Authors' calculations based on data from the World Bank (2018).

2008 (WTO Secretariat 2018). China's share of world manufacturing exports expanded most rapidly in the period following WTO accession, from 5 per cent in 2001 to 17 per cent in 2016 (Figure 27.1).

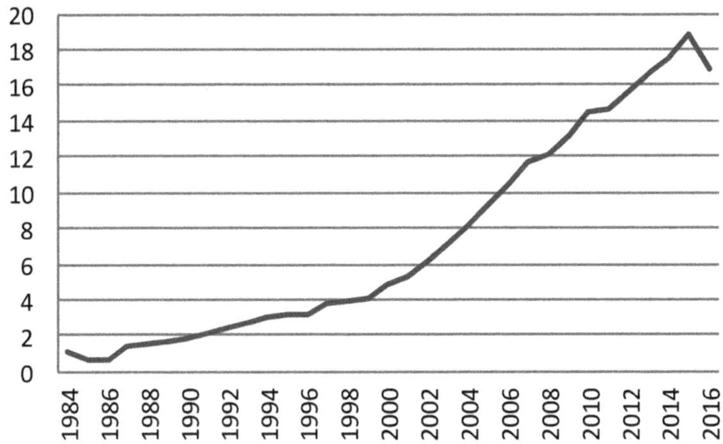

Figure 27.1 China's share of world manufacturing exports, 1984–2016 (per cent)
Source: Authors' calculations based on data from the World Bank (2018).

Massive migration from rural to urban China supplied the labour force needed to fuel industrialisation. Without the internationalisation of China's economy, there would have been no way for China's industrial sector to absorb the large number of rural migrant workers. A key element of China's integration into the global economy therefore has been the absorption of a large proportion of rural migrant workers into its booming export sector. This allowed a process of unprecedented urbanisation to take place, increasing the urban population by about 300 million over the past 30 years. This urbanisation contributed to gains in Chinese productivity, rapid economic growth and increasing shares of world production and trade (Song 2013: 25).

This pattern of development enabled China to capitalise on its underlying comparative advantage, although what constitutes China's comparative advantage has itself changed dynamically over time. At the beginning of the reform period, exports were predominantly agricultural products and primary goods such as coal and oil. During the first two decades of reform, the share of labour-intensive products such as textiles rose. In the first decade of the twenty-first century, exports of capital-intensive products such as steel, machinery, electronics and automobiles were on the rise. In the future, China is more likely to produce and export technology-intensive products such as equipment, software and green technology (Song 2013: 25–6).

China has been one of the biggest beneficiaries of globalisation over the past 30 years, gaining enormously from engaging in international production, trade, capital flow, technological transfer and people-to-people interactions. This was especially true after China entered the WTO in 2001. China's average tariff rate was reduced further, from 14.1 per cent in 2001 to 3.7 per cent in 2010. During this 10-year period, China's total exports and imports increased by 5.9 and 5.7 times, respectively, and its total GDP more than doubled. In 2016, China's total imports amounted to US$1.6 trillion, accounting for 11 per cent of world imports.[4]

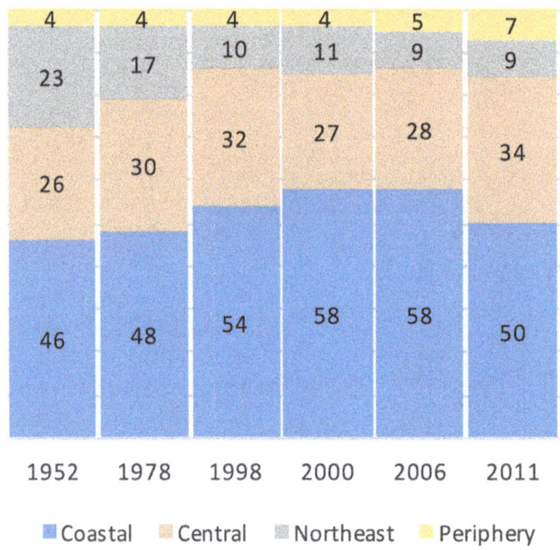

Figure 27.2 Regional distribution of industrial value added, 1952–2011 (per cent)

Notes: Regional categorisations are based on Lemoine et al. (2015). 'Coastal' includes Fujian, Guangdong, Hainan, Hebei, Jiangsu, Shandong, Zhejiang, Beijing, Shanghai and Tianjin. 'Central' refers to Anhui, Chongqing, Gansu, Guizhou, Henan, Hubei, Hunan, Jiangxi, Qinghai, Shaanxi, Shanxi, Sichuan, Yunnan and Chongqing. 'North-east' includes Liaoning, Jilin and Heilongjiang. 'Periphery' includes Guangxi, Inner Mongolia, Ningxia, Tibet and Xinjiang. Lemoine et al. (2015: 60) find that China has entered a 'new phase in its growth trajectory' since the mid-2000s, marked by the rebalancing of economic growth and industrial output away from the coast.

Sources: Compiled from Lemoine et al. (2015: 45) and data from the National Bureau of Statistics of China (NBS various years).

For China, economic openness also functioned as a catalyst to domestic institutional and policy reform. Embarking on the long road towards accession to the GATT, and later the WTO, meant eventual and fundamental change to China's basic institutional and policy settings. As Chinese policymakers struggled with building the domestic market economy in the first two decades of the reform period, the years after WTO accession served to entrench them nationally (Gewirtz 2017: 265–6). Adhering to WTO principles not only made China's trading regime more transparent, reliable

4 Export and import data are from World Integrated Trade Solution (WITS 2018). Weighted average tariff and GDP data are from the World Bank (2018).

and efficient. More importantly, in complying with WTO requirements, Chinese institutions—economic, legal, social and political—have also become more aligned with international practice. These institutional changes contributed to the Chinese economy's remarkable performance post-WTO accession through their impact across the whole economy. This is seen most readily in the growing share of manufacturing and national output outside the SEZs and preferenced coastal zones after 2001 (see Figure 27.2).

China joining the WTO was a strategic and economic milestone, but it was not a turning point in the direction of reform and trade liberalisation. China had already undertaken gradual unilateral steps to liberalise its international trade in the 1980s. This push ramped up in the lead-up to accession (Branstetter and Lardy 2008: 634–5).

China first requested to rejoin the GATT in 1986 (Liang 2002: 685).[5] The path to joining the WTO was marked by multiple rounds of concessions and more than one dead end. Negotiations collapsed after the Tiananmen Square incident in 1989 and hit another major stalemate in 1994.[6] After making substantial additional commitments—including on tariffs, intellectual property rights and service sector access—China signed bilateral WTO accession agreements with the United States in November 1999, and with the European Union in 2000.

After opening up to international trade, China's access to the US market was initially circumscribed under the Jackson–Vanik provisions of the *Trade Act of 1974* under which the US president had power to deny 'permanent normal trade relations' to states that impeded the right or opportunity of its citizens to emigrate and had not signed a bilateral commercial agreement with the United States. The Jackson–Vanik provisions required the issue of a yearly presidential waiver to allow China's access to the US market until its signing of the bilateral treaty of accession to the WTO (Pregelj 2005: 10). Removal of the huge uncertainties around the Jackson–Vanik waiver was a significant boost to confidence in trade with the United States, which in the first two decades of China's opening up had been underrepresented in Chinese markets.

5 Australia not only encouraged China's entry into large-scale international resource procurements at this time, it also became a principal source of technical assistance and advice on the long path to WTO accession (EABER and CCIEE 2016: 40, 185–6).

6 China aimed to join the GATT by the end of 1994, as a founding member of the WTO. After China made substantial concessions throughout that year, the United States requested that China join GATT as a developed country and presented a new set of reform guidelines. These guidelines proved politically untenable for China, and negotiations entered a stalemate in late 1994. Informal talks between China and GATT parties restarted in mid-1995, with more talks scheduled for October. The October talks were postponed at the request of the United States, but rescheduled following then president Jiang Zemin's liberalisation announcement at the November APEC summit in Osaka. See Liang (2002: 698, 703, 707).

Regional path to WTO accession and global integration

From 1991, APEC was the primary international forum facilitating China's liberalisation. With Beijing formally espousing open regionalism in 1995, APEC provided China with a platform to communicate its reform goals, demonstrate credibility ahead of WTO accession and make large-scale voluntary commitments to unilateral liberalisation in the context of APEC's individual action plans.

China's unilateral trade reforms in the 1990s, like its participation in APEC, cannot be viewed independently of its broader strategic goal of WTO accession. At that time, China's approach to its existing international agreements was an indication that its entry to the WTO would represent an assurance of credibility and commitment to the steps it had already taken (Drysdale 2000: 19). In April 1999, then premier Zhu Rongji made clear the role of WTO accession in his broader national reform strategy, declaring at a press conference in the United States:

> If China wants to join the WTO … then China must play by the rules of the game. China cannot do that without making concessions … such concessions might bring about a very huge impact on China's national impact on some state-owned enterprises, and also on China's market.
>
> But … we will be able to stand such impact. And the competition arising from such impact will also promote a more rapid and more healthy development of China's national economy. (Office of the Press Secretary 1999)

When Zhu made these comments, China was nearing the end of a decade of transformative reform and liberalisation. It had abolished export subsidies and then lowered tariffs on 43 commodities in 1991. Further tariff cuts occurred in 1992, 1993, 1996 and 1997, with China's weighted average tariff rate falling from 32 per cent to less than 16 per cent over these years (World Bank 2018).

There were also breakthroughs in the liberalisation of services, which was then China's most protected sector. In 1992, the first foreign insurance firm opened for business, in Shanghai and Guangzhou, and, in 1995, Morgan Stanley and the China Construction Bank formed China's first joint-venture investment bank (Zhang 2000: 8). The number of domestic firms given international trading rights expanded from 800 in 1985 to 12,000 a decade later, and to 35,000 by 2001 (Branstetter and Lardy 2008: 635).

The 1990s saw major reform of import quotas and licensing, alongside broader shifts in the nature of government intervention in firms' activities. 'Mandatory plans' setting export quotas and rules around the use of foreign exchange were replaced with 'guidance plans', in which intervention was conducted primarily through taxes, credit and exchange rate policy (Zhang 2000: 7). In the late 1980s, at their peak, quotas and licences covered nearly half of all Chinese imports; that had dropped to around 18 per cent by the end of 1992 (Branstetter and Lardy 2008: 635).

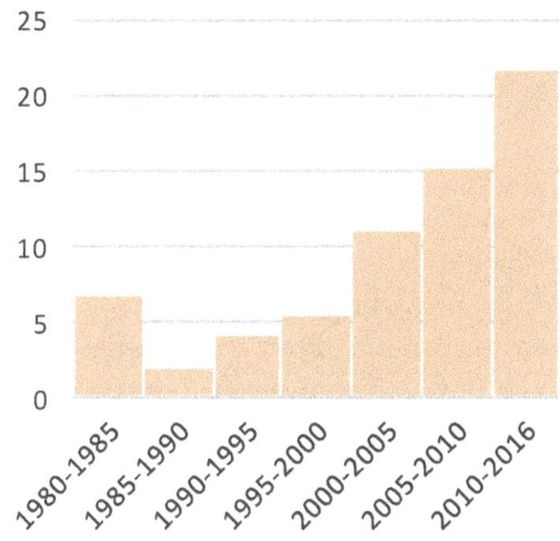

Figure 27.3 China's share of world trade growth, 1980–2016 (per cent)

Note: Trade here equals imports plus exports.

Source: Authors' calculations based on data from WTO Secretariat (2018).

APEC's role was important in making this liberalisation possible, and in shaping China's path to the WTO. Its flexibility and emphasis on concerted unilateral action made it the ideal vehicle for China—a developing country then in the relatively early stages of transition from a planned to a market economy—to articulate its reform ambitions on the regional stage, where its international interests were largely concentrated. APEC provided a platform for China to demonstrate its willingness and political capacity to undergo economic reform and pursue greater integration with the global economy. In 1995, at the Osaka APEC meeting, then Chinese president Jiang Zemin declared a 30 per cent tariff cut on 4,000 import items—an effective reduction of China's average tariff rate from 36 per cent to 23 per cent in one fell swoop (Zhang 2000: 11–12).

APEC's system of individual action plans (IAPs) and collective action plans (CAPs)—annual reports that documented countries' free trade and investment policies and goals—provided transparent, externally reviewed guidelines for China's trade reforms in the years after Osaka. China's 1996 IAP, for example, set goals of cutting average tariff rates to 15 per cent by 2000, 10 per cent by 2010 (both of which were achieved) and 5 per cent by 2020 (which has been achieved already) (Zhang 2000: 11).[7]

An essential part of China's 1990s APEC strategy was gathering regional support for its WTO accession. Australia from the very beginning encouraged China's application to join the WTO and provided ongoing technical assistance along the way. Through demonstrating its commitment to its East Asian and Pacific

7 Weighted average tariff data from the World Bank (2018).

neighbours on a range of issues, China's participation in APEC consolidated its support in the region. And, as with joining the WTO, China's APEC commitments provided impetus for domestic reform through drawing on external pressure (Yang and Huang 2000: 91).

China and other Asian economies became integral parts of supply chains that drove economic integration and growth in East Asia and globally. Through these supply chains, emerging economies in East Asia joined the globalisation process and embraced the rules of an open trade and investment regime. Fears in South-East Asia of competition from China were proven to be unfounded given the opportunities that opened up from joining expanded production networks centred on China. APEC played an important role in leading this process through concerted unilateral liberalisation, including China's massive liberalisation before its accession to the WTO (Garnaut 2012: 22). APEC also laid the groundwork for the information technology agreement that liberalised trade in electronic products and was critical to building Asian supply chains. These were the foundations for comprehensive Asian and trans-Pacific economic integration and multilateral cooperation.

Impact on trade and investment

For China, WTO membership ushered in a period of unprecedented trade growth (Figure 27.3). The rise of global production networks meant important opportunities for China's export and processing trade growth and major rewards for China's greater integration with the global economy—something then premier Zhu Rongji and China's head negotiator, Long Yongtu, understood well throughout the accession process. In 2000, Long wrote:

> planned economies have never been part of economic globalisation. China's economy must become a market economy in order to become part of the global economic system, as well as the economic globalisation process. (Quoted in Branstetter and Lardy 2008: 650)

There has arguably been no country for which WTO accession has involved deeper economic, institutional, legal and political change and reform than China (Halverson 2004: 322). China made more substantial reform commitments in joining the organisation than had previously been required of any new member. Although classified as a developing country (despite deep objections from the United States), China agreed to a range of concessions from which developing countries were typically exempt (Garnaut and Huang 2000: 27).

As part of its accession arrangement, China committed to lower its average industrial tariff rate to 8.9 per cent, to remove all licence requirements and import quotas on manufactured goods before 2005 and (with a small number of exceptions) to abolish the 'designated trading' system (whereby the central government permitted selected domestic companies to trade certain commodities internationally). China agreed to cut the average statutory tariff rate for agricultural goods from 21 per cent to 15 per cent, meeting developed country protocols (Branstetter and Lardy 2008: 650–3). The accession agreement also involved substantial opening in services—particularly in distribution, telecommunications, education, banking and financial services. By 2004, it had phased out all geographic and ownership restrictions on retail and wholesale activities (Branstetter and Lardy 2008: 657).

The 2017 Office of the US Trade Representative (USTR) report on WTO compliance acknowledged China's compliance with its WTO commitments on trading rights, its timely abolition of quotas and the designated trading system and its progress on tariff cuts (Office of the USTR 2018: 33–8).

The reforms that accompanied WTO accession significantly improved China's FDI regime in terms of national treatment and transparency. China's FDI policies since 2001 have placed greater emphasis on consistency and conformity with international rules (Chen 2011: 85). WTO membership meant the introduction of an independent judicial review and, for multinationals in China, a dispute resolution mechanism with the opportunity for appeal (Armstrong 2009: 116). Membership also put external pressure on competition and industrial policy reform, as well as intellectual property rights and enforcement (Chen 2011: 85), although this remains an area of real dispute with the United States, Europe and Japan. In the five years following accession, Chinese inbound FDI flows grew at an annual average of 22 per cent (compared with 4 per cent in the five years prior)[8] and China became significantly more open to foreign investment than most countries at a similar level of development and many of its Asian neighbours, including those that were much more developed.

The impact of WTO membership on investor confidence and Chinese policy credibility—though harder to measure—is central to understanding the calculus of participation in the global rules-based system. WTO accession mitigated information asymmetry and unpredictability, which signalled (in the case of Japanese firms) China's arrival as a 'real market'—despite historically being seen as a risky investment environment (Armstrong 2009: 118).

Reform-minded Chinese policymakers used WTO membership to overcome domestic political resistance to reform and reform fatigue. International engagement became an engine of domestic development and reform (Armstrong 2009: 113).

> The belief that the WTO is a 'public good' has taken hold in China, and membership in the WTO is a driving force for market reforms. WTO entry transformed how the global multilateral trading system is viewed, not only by sceptics in the government but, more importantly, in the public mindset. (Wang 2011)

8 Authors' calculations based on data from the World Bank (2018).

Preferential trade and the new regionalism

China's powerful trade and economic growth accelerated the rise of East Asian economies as a major centre of global economic integration. But towards the end of the 1990s, on the cusp of China's accession to the WTO, the Asian Financial Crisis saw an undermining of confidence in global solutions and in Washington's commitment to them. These were the circumstances that spawned the establishment of the Association of Southeast Asian Nations Plus Three (ASEAN+3) arrangements and the emergence of a new regionalism in East Asia. This was not only a consequence of Asia's complex response to Washington's handling of the Asian Financial Crisis; there was also a more general loss of faith in global arrangements such as the International Monetary Fund (IMF) and in the capacity of APEC to deal with the problems of the time. There had been intensification of preferential trading initiatives elsewhere in the world—with the negotiation of the North American Free Trade Agreement (NAFTA) and the extension of Europe's preferential arrangements—that cut across the principles of open regionalism on which APEC had been built. All these developments seemed to justify heading off in a new direction with ASEAN+3 and the negotiation of preferential trading arrangements in East Asia (Drysdale and Terada 2007; Drysdale and Armstrong 2015: 180–1).[9]

What emerged in East Asia and across the Pacific was the proliferation of a set of preferential bilateral trade arrangements—Asian countries have signed more than 110 since 2001—ordered around the power and leverage of the larger economies. Although ASEAN was a target for several of these arrangements, the different character of the ASEAN-plus bilateral free-trade areas still reflected the interests of the larger partners. Japan was at the centre of this shift in international economic diplomacy, but China's agreement with ASEAN was among one of the first major successes in East Asian bilateral trade diplomacy (Drysdale and Armstrong 2015: 182–3).

Bilateral trade agreements had little impact on trade gains; the liberalisation benefits were extremely limited and their rules-of-origin provisions flew in the face of trade that was increasingly intermediated through production networks across many countries in the region and beyond. Bilateral trade agreements were pursued as diplomatic trophies more than for the contribution they might make to economic welfare through trade reform (Drysdale and Armstrong 2015: 184). Importantly, Asia's trade is multilaterally oriented across the region and globally, so the structure of Asian trading interests recommended much more broadly based regional or multilateral trading arrangements—hence the attraction to 'megaregional' agreements that were outward-looking and sought to embrace a global liberalisation

9 The China–ASEAN framework agreement was signed in November 2002 and an FTA came into force in 2010. A China–New Zealand FTA was signed in 2008, and a China–Australia FTA was initiated in 2005 and signed in 2014.

agenda. Reform and opening had been undertaken in a global context and had been underpinned by the global trading system. Asian interests are still best managed in that context (Armstrong and Pangestu 2018: 31).

The launch of negotiations on the Trans-Pacific Partnership (TPP) (in APEC's backyard, led by the United States) and, later, on the Regional Comprehensive Economic Partnership (RCEP) (under the umbrella of ASEAN) dominated thinking about regional integration over the past half-decade. RCEP, unlike the TPP, involved all of Asia's major economies. Both agreements were designed in part to leverage value out of the plethora of bilateral free trade agreements (FTAs) negotiated over the preceding 15 years. The TPP was explicitly a key element in the Obama administration's 'pivot to Asia'. Having not been invited to participate in the TPP, China remained open to TPP membership and framed its participation in RCEP in the broader context of the idea of the Free Trade Area of Asia and the Pacific (FTAAP) through APEC (APEC 2014). Although the many bilateral FTAs already signed brought no significant trade or domestic reform in the region, the difficulties in concluding the Doha Round of negotiations produced a hiatus in multilateral trade reform and shifted emphasis to these megaregional trade initiatives.

Today, with US President Donald Trump's withdrawal from the TPP and his assault on multilateral trade arrangements, there is deep uncertainty about strategies to protect Asia's interests in the global trade regime. China's response to these new circumstances will be crucial. China's integration into the international economy was engineered under the umbrella of multilateral liberalisation, as earlier was Japan's and that of the rest of Asia. China remains, as President Xi Jinping made clear at the World Economic Forum in Davos in 2017 and the Boao Forum for Asia in April 2018, a major stakeholder in the established international trading system (Xi 2017; Bloomberg News 2018).

The breakdown of Doha Round negotiations gave impetus to region-wide arrangements such as the TPP and RCEP as instruments of regional reform and liberalisation. Since the election of President Trump, they have also become important weapons in the armoury for defending against the assault on the international trading system.

The United States withdrew from the TPP on President Trump's third day in office. It remains highly unlikely there will be a serious US effort to rejoin the TPP in the medium term. Despite its smaller size and geopolitical importance, the renamed Comprehensive and Progressive Agreement for Trans-Pacific Partnership (CPTPP), signed in March 2018 and still to be ratified by most signatories, declared the willingness of Asian and Pacific leaders to hold the line against rising US protectionism. It may also yet give momentum to the completion of RCEP negotiations, which involve seven of the 11 CPTPP members, plus China and India (Armstrong 2018).

The CPTPP freezes certain US-led intellectual property provisions in the TPP, including patent term extension obligations, which makes the agreement more attractive for regional developing countries to join. China's entry, however, is a distant prospect, as each CPTPP signatory has veto power over new entrants, even if they meet requirements.

RCEP—ASEAN's response to the TPP—is the most significant proposal for trade liberalisation on the table today in Asia or, for that matter, anywhere in the world. It matters because of its size and scope and because it involves the negotiation not only of binding liberalisation, but also of economic cooperation goals. Since China, India, Indonesia and other developing countries in Asia will have trouble joining the TPP in the foreseeable future, an ambitious and high-quality RCEP can help promote integration across the Asia-Pacific region. If RCEP governments are to maximise the value of economic integration and freer trade, they will need to go beyond negotiating a single-undertaking trade deal along TPP lines (Drysdale 2016). Leveraging ASEAN centrality, RCEP will be crucial for deepening this economic interdependence, moving the region closer to a single market and production base and thus underpinning future political and security cooperation in the region (Drysdale 2017: 78). RCEP's strengths—its size and its economic and political diversity—are also its major challenges. Yet in the context of a declining US presence in Asia, greater economic interdependence and cooperation between smaller regional players will be more important for outcomes in the Asia-Pacific, both economically and politically.

The 16-country RCEP offers an opportunity:

> to salve the sometimes fractious political relations among the Asian powers. Just as the TPP provided cover for Japan to do a deal with the United States, RCEP provides cover for improved Chinese–Japanese and Chinese–Indian economic relations where political sensitivities might make negotiating bilateral deals too difficult. (Armstrong 2017)

Habituating China and other rising economies in a rules-based system in this way would further regional economic integration and also be an important Asian contribution to keeping the global trading system open. This would reinforce geopolitical stability in the Western Pacific while making a bold commitment to global openness (Armstrong 2017).

Globalisation and connectivity

Connectivity is increasingly seen as a major factor in realising the potential from economic integration. An important dimension of improving connectivity and development outcomes is infrastructure investment.

The BRI, which encompasses the multilateral AIIB, is a major new Chinese strategy for achieving sustainable development through strengthening connectivity with partner countries and realising mutually beneficial economic relations. It is an overarching strategy of enormous scale and ambition for deepening China's integration into the international economy. Its aims are many—including securing increased openness through improved connectivity and achieving inclusiveness based on mutual interest and benefit—but they are, importantly, directed to expanding global frontiers of growth through sustainable development. It offers a framework for deepening international economic cooperation through a platform of open regionalism that promotes economic integration through improving five types of links: policy, infrastructure, trade and investment, financial exchanges and people-to-people exchanges (EAF 2017).

The BRI's core objectives relate to building infrastructural capacities to promote economic integration through improved connectivity, avoiding adverse impacts from development projects and creating wealth for future generations—not just one-off growth in incomes for some in the present generation.

With a high priority put on consultation and cooperation, the BRI can be seen as an important opportunity for diversifying and strengthening China's bilateral, regional and global cooperation in a multitude of institutional settings and arrangements that promote both economic and political security.

There are two main risks. The first relates to China's own policy in developing the BRI. Although the initiative is defined as inclusive and is designed to create mutual benefit, this goal will not be easy to achieve and will require a huge effort in international economic diplomacy and in building the capacities with which to engage. The porous policy institutions and environment of developing partners make this a particularly challenging task. The second, interdependent risk relates to the policies that other countries adopt towards China and the extent to which the principles of engagement take multilateral interests into account. Exclusively bilateral engagement will reduce partner options and limit the potential gains for growth and development (EAF 2017).

It is too soon to judge the impact of the BRI in these dimensions, but what is clear (and inevitable) in such an undertaking is that improvement on all these fronts is needed. The pattern of investment in energy projects, for example, has not been notably supportive of green growth, the environmental impact of some projects is subject to question and there are some 'white elephant' projects that waste resources for future generations. Resolving the policy inconsistencies and dilemmas that will help to avoid these less favourable outcomes is a major interest and priority. Success critically depends on the terms of engagement between China and its partners.

The Belt and Road Forum in May 2017 was innovative and strategic in its invitation to national partners and international and regional organisations to join in getting the terms of engagement right (EAF 2017). Among the principles that are important to getting better outcomes on BRI objectives are: appeal to multilateral frameworks in financing and setting the standards of project development where possible; appeal to global and regional best practice in bilateral cooperation efforts; engagement with international consortia in project development and delivery; giving priority to sorting out objectives and goals with partners and socialising them carefully; and the patient alignment of interests and goals with those partners. This requires deep institutional infrastructure for cooperation and intensification of people-to-people exchanges, which will take some time.

The success or failure of the BRI—not only for China's economic diplomacy, but also for outcomes in the global economic regime—will depend on whether countries such as Australia, Japan and the European powers make the choice to join in multilateral engagement. The alternative is a world of transactional bilateral deals that threaten to corrode the openness of the global economic regime—a regime already at serious risk (EAF 2017).

Trade and political clout

The story of the globalisation of the Chinese economy is essentially about China signing on to the global rules-based trade regime through accession to the WTO and committing to large-scale domestic market reforms in compliance with those rules. This strategic choice delivered massive gains through trade to both China and its partners in the global economy. The realisation of huge gains from trade was not without large adjustment costs, in both China and its global trading partners, but the net gains from China's trade and growth, as noted above, have been enormous. They are reflected in the palpable lift in the welfare of the Chinese people, the impact on global incomes and the expanded consumption possibilities around the globe delivered by low-cost Chinese products.

There are two additional elements, however, that qualify this largely good news story and are important to how the next chapters of the Chinese trade story might unfold. Both have to do with the completeness of the rules-based system—first, in respect of how it constrains behaviour in the international markets it presently covers, and second, in respect of what issues in trade and commerce are still not covered within a multilateral framework. Any system of rules or norms is challenged intrinsically by the nature of its observance and by evolving circumstances that demand its extension in various ways. The trade regime is specially challenged in both these ways, partly but not only because of the level of pressure put on it by China's success.

The first issue to consider is China's observance of the extant rules. In a number of ways, the trade rules that have applied to China are stricter than those that apply to other WTO members. The protocols of China's accession to the WTO bound it to remove all taxes and surcharges, in principle, from its export goods, including raw materials. Only in the most exceptional circumstances is China allowed under WTO rules to limit exports—for example, through regulatory restrictions or export duties. This was the basis for action undertaken by the United States, Japan and the European Union against China for restricting exports of 'rare earth elements' in 2012 (Drysdale 2013). The protocols of China's accession to the WTO also subjected it to 'nonmarket economy' treatment under antidumping rules, and gave other members greater latitude in penalising Chinese imports on the grounds they are being dumped.

The rare earths case is perhaps the most frequently cited example of China using trade restrictions to exercise political clout inconsistently with the rules. Other examples include a freeze on Norwegian salmon imports after human rights activist Liu Xiaobo was awarded the Nobel Peace Prize and the economic measures imposed on South Korea following its announcement of installation of the THAAD missile defence system against North Korea.

In September 2010, a Chinese trawler and a Japanese coast guard vessel collided in the East China Sea. The Chinese captain was arrested and temporarily detained. Amid the tensions that followed, it was widely reported that China had stopped exporting certain rare earth metals (which are used in smartphone and other high-tech production) to Japan (King and Armstrong 2013). The United States, Japan and the European Union requested consultation with China, formally opening three WTO dispute cases, in March 2012. While it is doubtful these restrictions were in fact used as an instrument of political coercion, as was commonly assumed (King and Armstrong 2013), when the panel found that China's export duties and quotas on the rare earths were in violation of its WTO commitments, China removed the measures, and full implementation of the panel's recommendations was recognised, despite an attempt at appeal from the United States, in May 2015 (WTO 2015).

China's observance of the trade rules in the rare earths case represents substantial vindication of the effectiveness of and protections provided by the international trade regime.[10] As observed elsewhere, a dispute of this kind in the prewar period (when such a regime was absent) is likely to have resulted in serious political conflict (Armstrong 2009: 158–61).

10 Previous cases reveal that these rules on export trade have not applied universally. One striking example is the US embargo on soybean exports in 1973, at a time when Japan obtained about 92 per cent of its annual consumption of soybeans (a major staple) from the United States (see NYT 1973). The experience encouraged Australia to enter a treaty with Japan—its biggest food and raw materials market at the time—stipulating explicitly that it would not apply export restrictions to these commodities. In so doing, Australia sought to close the gap in assurances on export restrictions in the global system that the soybean case had opened (Drysdale 2013).

In the South Korean THAAD case, despite Seoul's assurances that the THAAD system would 'not be used against a third party' such as China and despite then South Korean deputy prime minister Yoo Il-ho's prediction that, as a WTO member, 'China may find it difficult to take punitive economic measures on political issues', China took a number of economic measures aimed at putting pressure on Seoul (Lee 2017).[11]

The measures used against South Korea—like those used against Norway and the Philippines in other cases—were carefully crafted through the use of domestic regulations and controls so as not to offend against the letter of international trade law. While China's economic heft may have been used to exert political influence over partners, such action (however carefully crafted) is likely to diminish China's credibility in shaping and participating in the global economic institutions that have enabled its rise. In the South Korean case:

> [I]t [was] in Beijing's interests for Seoul to reverse its THAAD decision; it [was] also in Beijing's interests for the rules and institutions of the international trading system, broadly, to hold together. (Lim and Ferguson 2017)

South Korea did not initiate a formal WTO dispute over the measures prompted by the installation of THAAD, but it did raise the matter with the WTO Council for Trade in Services to share the issue with 'multilateral parties'. A Chinese Commerce Ministry spokesperson responded that '[o]nly trade that complies with WTO rules can be considered fair trade' (Kong 2017).

These cases draw attention to areas in which the WTO-based system needs to be strengthened through its extension to cover related regulatory issues. With all its strengths, the system is imperfect and incomplete. The measures against South Korean products and firms were largely regulatory, often based on safety regulations or censorship, and hence difficult to formally dispute through the present WTO framework. They are issues for future negotiation.

A more important aspect of the question of using trade leverage for political clout around the rules relates to how observing the letter but not also the spirit of trade law may act to compromise trust in China's observance of the rules. Despite the

11 The measures targeted South Korea's entertainment, tourism and retail sectors. Between August 2016 and March 2017, several South Korean television programs were banned in China. Online South Korean video games were denied regulatory approval and concerts featuring popular South Korean performers were cancelled. Citing safety issues, regulators banned the sale of certain South Korean consumer products, including air purifiers and cosmetics. Applications by Korean airlines for new charter flights were denied, and the Chinese National Tourism Administration told agencies to reduce the sale of tour packages to South Korea. A South Korean 'hypermarket' conglomerate, Lotte, had transferred land (a golf course) to the government for THAAD's development. Within months, regulators had closed 87 of 112 Chinese Lotte stores—all for alleged safety violations—costing the conglomerate an estimated US$2.2 billion. Beijing denied the THAAD issue and the economic measures were connected. Nonetheless, the measures contributed to heightened perceptions of Chinese political risk. See Meick and Salidjanova (2017: 7) and Lee (2017).

large presence of state-owned entities and its one-party political system, China's attempts to uphold, and its observance of, international trade rules have generally been positive features of its participation in the system and have been favourably viewed internationally. In China, the WTO is arguably one of the most widely recognised and respected international organisations (Wang 2011). A narrative that plausibly connects developments in China's political system to lessened confidence in the reliability of its stake in the rules-based trading system would be damaging both to China and to the global system.

The pressures and priorities today

Two issues of significance in the conduct of international commerce today that are not yet systematically comprehended within multilateral trade rules or other multilateral institutions are foreign investment and cyber trade—international transactions and business made possible by the revolution in information technology. The foreign investment issue has been around for some time, and foreign investment has played a major role in China's economic modernisation. Its role has been larger in terms of its contribution to trade and income growth than in more advanced economies such as Japan or South Korea. The information technology revolution is a new phenomenon, the applications of which were in their infancy when China acceded to the WTO. A third area where the multilateral rules need to be extended is in services trade, where current General Agreement on Trade in Services (GATS) rules provide only partial coverage. Plurilateral initiatives such as the Trade in Services Agreement are under negotiation, and bilateral and regional agreements attempt to liberalise and protect the delivery of services behind the border, but they are an area where WTO coverage needs extension.

Foreign investment

East Asia's integration into the global economy has been closely linked to the role of foreign investment in the growth of efficient production networks and production chains across the region. Foreign investment has also been a major source of the international diffusion of technology and knowhow. China's early openness to foreign investment, initially through SEZs, saw it rapidly become the major centre of global manufacturing growth. In the early decades of China's opening, foreign-invested firms were the major source of Chinese trade and output growth. While Chinese foreign investment policy restricted foreign ownership shares in most activities that serviced the domestic market (commonly to 50 per cent or less in joint ventures with local enterprises), investment was welcomed as a source of international knowhow and technology and an agent of export growth. China was more open to foreign investment than most countries at a similar stage of economic development. It soon became the largest emerging market destination for foreign investment and, in 2016, the third-largest destination in the world (UNCTAD 2017: 12).

Meanwhile, the growth of China's industrial and investment capacity recommended opening up to investment abroad in search of resources, new international markets and technology as well as lower cost bases for production abroad as wage and other costs rose in China. In less than two decades, China has become the second-largest source of direct investment internationally, after the United States (UNCTAD 2017: xi).

Today, China is a major object of policy interest both as a destination for foreign investment and as a new investor in markets around the world. Obstacles to investment in China and their impact on the structure of competition between Chinese and US or European firms have become major issues in economic diplomacy. At the same time, anxieties about the rapid surge in and the special character of Chinese investment, with its preponderance of state-owned enterprises in many areas, have triggered more restrictive approaches to Chinese investment in a number of jurisdictions. As direct investment flows into and out of China have become more important, the lack of a global investment regime is emerging as a significant gap in the multilateral architecture.

In the absence of a multilateral investment regime, countries will have to suffice with a mix of both unilateral policies (mostly on the initiative of host countries) and bilateral arrangements under investment treaties and economic agreements that have varying provisions and protections. There is no bilateral investment treaty between China and the United States; a treaty has been under negotiation but so far there has been little progress.

This is currently an issue of huge importance. The Trump administration has launched a trade war against China ostensibly because of China's unfair treatment of American investors. Foreign investment ownership restrictions, it argues, force American and other foreign firms to surrender technologies to Chinese competitors. Trump's argument has some merit, although the measures China has used to build technological capabilities through investment policy have been part of the policy approach to promoting industrial development across all the 'catch-up' countries (including Japan). Negotiating this issue does not recommend or necessitate tearing down the rules-based global trading system to achieve a more satisfactory investment regime.

The interest in articulating a set of common multilateral principles for foreign investment—for both facilitating pre-establishment foreign investment (before it enters a country) and the national treatment of post-establishment foreign investment—is thus a high priority (EABER and CCIEE 2016: 229). The WTO investment facilitation initiative in 2017 offers a possible route forward multilaterally. But, realistically, the urgency of resolving these issues is likely to see bilateral settlements (between China and the United States) dominate outcomes if broader regional interests cannot productively be brought to bear on them.

Cyber trade and next generation trade rules

The huge growth of international transactions and business made possible by the revolution in information technology has taken place since the establishment of the WTO in 1995. When the Uruguay Round was negotiated (1986–94), the digital landscape and its effects on international commerce were in their infancy. More recent bilateral and regional agreements, such as the United States–Korea Free Trade Agreement (KORUS FTA) and the TPP, have begun to grapple with data issues, but the WTO has no explicit framework outside of norms such as transparency and nondiscrimination covering the big issues that the digital revolution presents for international policymakers.

The negotiation of the rules for cyber trade is now among the most important questions that confront the international trade regime. This is a new issue not yet systematically comprehended within the multilateral trade rules or other multilateral institutions. It requires the resolution of enormously complex technical and political issues among the major players such as China, the United States and Europe, but every country has a stake in this debate. Thus, it is far better that the resolution be multilaterally based (within the WTO or a related framework), but that is likely only if one or more of the key players, such as China, resolutely insists on a multilateral approach.

The regulation of international digital trade raises highly contested economic and political questions. There are strongly divergent policy approaches that reflect differences over the protection of established leaders in the business, alternative approaches to development, approaches to social and political control and the protection of security interests (Kennedy 2018). An open multilateral approach would provide the most credible framework through which countries can open formal disputes or defend their data regulation policies as they relate to international trade.

Existing trade agreements have tended to be vague on data regulation, although they represent valuable steps in developing international norms around the free flow of data. In 2011, the KORUS FTA became the first treaty with a binding commitment on data regulation, specifying that firms must 'endeavour to refrain from imposing or maintaining unnecessary barrier[s] to electronic information flows across borders', although this is subject to a binding exceptions provision (Meltzer 2013: 17; Office of the USTR 2010). Under the TPP and its replacement, the CPTPP, parties can bring disputes against data localisation measures, although there are sectoral exceptions for government and financial services (Selby 2017: 218).

Another regional framework has been proposed by the European Commission, which suggests abolishing localisation laws for nonpersonal data as part of the EU Digital Single Market strategy (EC 2017).

Data localisation—the requirement that firms physically locate their servers within the country in which the data were generated—is an area of interest for trade and cybersecurity policymakers alike. Given the role of data flows in global production chains, as well as the growth of e-commerce and trade in data collection and analysis services, these laws create trade costs. Countries with less developed internet service industries, including China, have been more likely to introduce data localisation laws (Selby 2017: 232). The challenge will be to minimise the impact of these regulatory regimes on trade costs while remaining sensitive to different parties' capabilities and legitimate policy interests about data security.

China is the major focus of angst over internet filtering, including for the purposes of censorship, which has been acknowledged as a trade barrier by the United States since 2016 (Allen-Abrahamian et al. 2016). In recent years, debate ramped up over whether the United States should address the Chinese Government's internet filtering through the WTO. The Chinese Government's block list includes the US giants Google, Facebook, Twitter and YouTube—often to the benefit of domestic firms such as the Chinese search engine Baidu (Barfield 2016). Calls for a US WTO challenge against China often hark back to a 2005 dispute, which interpreted bans on foreign service providers as a 'zero quota' and hence in violation of the GATS. The likely counter from China would be to invoke a 'public order' exception and claim that reversing the ban would present a threat 'to one of the fundamental interests of society' (Wu 2006: 283–4; WTO 1995). Despite USTR reports identifying China's internet filtering as a trade barrier, a challenge over the issue has not yet been mounted at a high level, and the result is difficult to predict. China will be the key in transitioning towards a comprehensive multilateral framework for regulating cyber trade.

Larger countries or groups of countries will set protection standards, but these may inhibit data flows. The European Union introduced the General Data Protection Regulation in May 2018, which regulates how EU citizens' data are used, including by companies based outside the European Union that offer goods or services for European customers (EC 2018a, 2018b). How this will affect global data flows is not yet clear, but multilateral rulemaking would avoid potential complications.

What is clear is that global rules on internet filtering are not sufficiently developed to deal with the growing economic implications of data regulation, filtering and censorship; and that China's future participation in a regime that deals with these issues will clearly be contingent on it securing a stake in the institutions that underpin the regime. If left unresolved, this issue will further corrode confidence in the broader global trade regime.

Age of uncertainty

Today the global trading system has entered an age of uncertainty: the multilateral rules-based trade regime is under assault and the liberal economic order that has underpinned trade growth and global prosperity is under threat from its chief architect, the United States. No response to this uncertainty is more important than China's.

Some people think the difficulties in international economic policy we face today all arose with the election of US President Donald Trump. That is an oversimplification of the matter. These difficulties are a consequence of significant shocks to economic and trade systems through the GFC as well as long-term structural changes in the global economy that have been shaking the system for some time.

These changes include the emergence of China and its accommodation in the global system. In North America itself, there are long-term structural problems that are the origin of the maldistribution of gains from international trade on which Trump built his political claim to the presidency. Trump and many of his followers blame China for these American woes, but most are structural problems of the United States' own making and their solution is in American hands alone. They require deep institutional and policy shifts and a different approach to social as well as international trade policy.

The notion that the United States has not reaped huge benefits and gains from international trade is false; US national income growth has been boosted massively by the gains from trade. But the distribution of the gains from trade is poorly served by domestic institutions (health, education, adjustment policies) and by policies that have seen real household incomes remain stagnant for decades. This will not change quickly, and certainly not in a presidential term; it will take a generation to fix.

Trump has declared trade war to right the wrongs he says the United States has been done by its trading partners, notably China. He blames them for US trade deficits. That, of course, is not the case. US trade deficits are a product of the United States spending more than it earns and covering the extra spending by importing capital in some form or other. There are issues to be negotiated with the rules of international trade and commerce, but they have little to do with righting international trade imbalances.

Trump's trade war is yet to be engaged, but if it is merely a negotiating tactic designed to shift the system forward, it is a costly and risky one. His talk of trade war has spooked financial markets. His fuelling of spending through tax cuts and delayed-action trade war will add to US imports through lifting US spending and front-loaded purchases from abroad. More importantly, his flouting of WTO trade rules and misidentification of trade restrictions as the cause of US trade deficits blow the credibility of US trade policy leadership, making it easier for other countries to tear down the system (EAF 2018).

China's importance in the global economy is second only to the United States. Its response to US action on trade will be crucial.

'The mood in Washington has shifted from engaging with China to hedging against it', Yang Yao (2018) argues. Yao identifies technological competition as the underlying issue that now confronts the China–United States relationship. The major justification for Trump's ill-advised declaration of trade war is Chinese 'theft' of US intellectual property and 'forced technology transfer'.

> Punitive tariffs are just the warm up for a coming marathon in technological competition. In the years ahead, it is highly likely that the Trump administration will tighten up its control on Chinese companies' merger and acquisition activities in the United States. (Yao 2018)

Measures to transfer technology through investment policy have been part of policy to promote industrial development across all the 'catch-up' countries, such as Japan and South Korea, as well as China. Historically, of course, the United States played the same game (Morris 2012). State-led industrial policies have also been used to promote technological advancement. The additional dimension in China's case is the alleged state-mandated theft. All of that certainly needs to be negotiated and now needs to change. But none of this recommends tearing down the global trading system. The priority should rather be on investment facilitation, an investment agreement that deals with these issues and building a multilateral-based international digital economy regime.

As for China's response:

> [I]t is imperative for policymakers to recognise the change of attitude in Washington and form a new strategy to deal with the United States … The right long-term response is to continue China's reform and opening policy, which has been critical to China's 40 years of high growth. (Yao 2018)

For the rest of the world, wait-and-see strategies are no longer viable. This is a time that requires strategic response, particularly from partners in Asia. China cannot frame the right response alone.

Asia has more at stake in the global system than any other part of the world; its economies depend on the open rules-based system not only for their economic prosperity, but also for their political security. The appeal to the rules-based system is a critical dimension of protecting economic security and of political security more broadly. Asian countries need to stand firm in the face of the threat to the global trade regime. The dynamic of Asian growth depends on remaining committed to the trade reform agenda and encouraging entrenchment and deepening—including by China, the South-East Asian economies and India—of the open rules-based international trading system (EAF 2018).

References

Allen-Abrahamian, B., Shirk, S., Parker, E. and de Jonquières, G. (2016), Should internet censorship be considered a trade issue?, *ChinaFile*, 12 April. Available from: www.chinafile.com/conversation/should-internet-censorship-be-considered-trade-issue.

Armstrong, S. (2009), The Japan–China economic relationship: Distance, institutions and politics, PhD thesis, The Australian National University, Canberra.

Armstrong, S. (2012), The politics of Japan–China trade and the role of the world trade system, *The World Economy* 35(9): 1102–20. doi.org/10.1111/j.1467-9701.2012.01473.x.

Armstrong, S. (2017), A new deal in Asia, *Foreign Affairs*, 17 March. Available from: www.foreignaffairs.com/articles/asia/2017-03-17/new-deal-asia.

Armstrong, S. (2018), The new Trans-Pacific Partnership hunkers down against Trump, *East Asia Forum*, 4 March. Available from: www.eastasiaforum.org/2018/03/04/the-new-trans-pacific-partnership-hunkers-down-against-trump/.

Armstrong, S. and Pangestu, M. (2018), Asian economic integration: The state of play, in S. Armstrong and T. Westland (eds), *Asian Economic Integration in an Era of Global Uncertainty*, Canberra: ANU Press. doi.org/10.22459/AEIEGU.01.2018.

Asia-Pacific Economic Cooperation (APEC) (2014), Annex A: The Beijing roadmap for APEC's contribution to the realization of the FTAAP, in *2014 Leaders' Declaration*, Singapore: APEC Secretariat. Available from: www.apec.org/Meeting-Papers/Leaders-Declarations/2014/2014_aelm/2014_aelm_annexa.aspx.

Barfield, C. (2016), A WTO challenge to China's internet censorship is long overdue, *East Asia Forum*, 26 May. Available from: www.eastasiaforum.org/2016/05/26/a-wto-challenge-to-chinas-internet-censorship-is-long-overdue/.

Bloomberg News (2018), China's Xi pledges greater openness amid Trump trade dispute, *Bloomberg News*, 10 April. Available from: www.bloomberg.com/news/articles/2018-04-09/xi-set-for-landmark-economic-speech-as-trump-trade-fight-simmers.

Brandt, L. and Rawski, T. G. (2008), China's great economic transformation, in L. Brandt and T. G. Rawski (eds), *China's Great Economic Transformation*, Cambridge: Cambridge University Press.

Branstetter, L. and Lardy, N. (2008), China's embrace of globalization, in L. Brandt and T. G. Rawski (eds), *China's Great Economic Transformation*, Cambridge: Cambridge University Press. doi.org/10.1017/CBO9780511754234.017.

Chen, C. (2011), The development of China's FDI laws and policies after WTO accession, in J. Golley and L. Song (eds), *Rising China: Global challenges and opportunities*, Canberra: ANU E Press.

Drysdale, P. (2000), Open regionalism, APEC and China's international trade strategies, in P. Drysdale, Y. Zhang and L. Song (eds), *APEC and Liberalisation of the Chinese Economy*, Canberra: Asia Pacific Press.

Drysdale, P. (2013), China and the norms of trade, *East Asia Forum*, 19 August. Available from: www.eastasiaforum.org/2013/08/19/china-and-the-norms-of-trade/.

Drysdale, P. (2016), The regional trade deal with China and India that's twice the size of TPP, *The Australian Financial Review*, 26 April. Available from: www.afr.com/opinion/the-regional-trade-deal-with-china-and-india-thats-twice-the-size-of-tpp-20160426-goeyzj.

Drysdale, P. (2017), ASEAN: The experiment in open regionalism that succeeded, in R. Sta. Maria, S. Urata and P. S. Intal, jr (eds), *The ASEAN Economic Community Into 2025 and Beyond*, Jakarta: Economic Research Institute for ASEAN and East Asia. Available from: eria.org/5.1.ASEAN_50_Vol_5_Drysdale.pdf.

Drysdale, P. and Armstrong, S. (2015), Foreign economic policy strategies and economic performance, in Y. Funabashi and B. Kushner (eds), *Examining Japan's Lost Decades*, London: Routledge.

Drysdale, P. and Terada, T. (eds) (2007), *Asia-Pacific Economic Cooperation: Critical perspectives on the world economy*, London: Routledge.

East Asia Forum (EAF) (2017), How to respond to China's Belt and Road Initiative, *East Asia Forum*, 15 May. Available from: www.eastasiaforum.org/2017/05/15/how-to-respond-to-chinas-belt-and-road-initiative/.

East Asia Forum (EAF) (2018), China–US trade face-off, *East Asia Forum*, 16 April. Available from: www.eastasiaforum.org/2018/04/16/china-us-trade-face-off/.

East Asian Bureau of Economic Research (EABER) and China Center for International Economic Exchanges (CCIEE) (2016), *Partnership for Change: Australia–China joint economic report*, Canberra: ANU Press.

European Commission (EC) (2017), Free flow of non-personal data, Brussels: EC. Available from: ec.europa.eu/digital-single-market/en/free-flow-non-personal-data.

European Commission (EC) (2018a), What does the General Data Protection Regulation (GDPR) govern?, Brussels: EC. Available from: ec.europa.eu/info/law/law-topic/data-protection/reform/what-does-general-data-protection-regulation-gdpr-govern_en.

European Commission (EC) (2018b), Who does the data protection law apply to?, Brussels: EC. Available from: ec.europa.eu/info/law/law-topic/data-protection/reform/rules-business-and-organisations/application-regulation/who-does-data-protection-law-apply_en.

Garnaut, R. (2012), Indonesia in the new world balance, in A. Reid (ed.), *Indonesia Rising: The repositioning of Asia's third giant*, Singapore: Institute of Southeast Asian Studies. doi.org/10.1355/9789814380416-008.

Garnaut, R. and Huang, Y. (2000), China and the future of the international trading system, in P. Drysdale and L. Song (eds), *China's Entry to the WTO: Strategic issues and quantitative assessments*, London: Routledge. doi.org/10.4324/9780203398227_chapter_2.

Gewirtz, J. (2017), *Unlikely Partners: Chinese reformers, Western economists, and the making of global China*, Cambridge, MA: Harvard University Press. doi.org/10.4159/9780674973459.

Golley, J. and Song, L. (2011), China's rise in a changing world, in J. Golley and L. Song (eds), *Rising China: Global challenges and opportunities*, Canberra: ANU E Press.

Halverson, K. (2004), China's WTO accession: Economic, legal, and political implications, *Boston College International and Comparative Law Review* 27(2): 319–70.

Kennedy, A. (2018), How Trump is losing the high-tech fight with China, *East Asia Forum*, 27 May. Available from: www.eastasiaforum.org/2018/05/27/how-trump-is-losing-the-high-tech-fight-with-china/.

King, A. and Armstrong, S. (2013), Did China really ban rare earth metals exports to Japan?, *East Asia Forum*, 18 August. Available from: www.eastasiaforum.org/2013/08/18/did-china-really-ban-rare-earth-metals-exports-to-japan/.

Kong, K. (2017), South Korea lobbies China at WTO over missile shield trade spat, *Bloomberg*, 20 March. Available from: www.bloomberg.com/news/articles/2017-03-20/south-korea-lobbies-china-at-wto-over-missile-shield-trade-spat.

Lee, J. (2017), Back to normal? The end of the THAAD dispute between China and South Korea, *China Brief* 17(15). Available from: jamestown.org/program/back-normal-end-thaad-dispute-china-south-korea/.

Lemoine, F., Poncet, S. and Unal, D. (2015), Spatial rebalancing and industrial convergence in China, *China Economic Review* 34: 39–63. doi.org/10.1016/j.chieco.2015.03.007.

Liang, W. (2002), China's WTO negotiation process and its implications, *Journal of Contemporary China* 11(33): 683–719. doi.org/10.1080/1067056022000008878.

Lim, D. J. and Ferguson, V. (2017), Costs of Chinese boycotts cut both ways, *East Asia Forum*, 5 April. Available from: www.eastasiaforum.org/2017/04/05/costs-of-chinese-boycotts-cut-both-ways/.

Meick, E. and Salidjanova, N. (2017), *China's response to US–South Korean Missile Defense System deployment and its implications*, Report for the US–China Economic and Security Review Commission, Washington, DC: US Congress.

Meltzer, J. P. (2013), *The internet, cross-border data flows and international trade*, Issues in Technology Innovation Report, 25 February, Washington, DC: Center for Technology Innovation at The Brookings Institution. Available from: www.brookings.edu/wp-content/uploads/2016/06/internet-data-and-trade-meltzer.pdf.

Meltzer, J. P. (2017), Global digital trade 1: Market opportunities and key foreign trade restrictions, *Testimony*, 12 April, Washington, DC: The Brookings Institution. Available from: www.brookings.edu/testimonies/global-digital-trade-1-market-opportunities-and-key-foreign-trade-restrictions/.

Morris, C. (2012), We were pirates, too, *Foreign Policy*, 6 December. Available from: www.foreignpolicy.com/2012/12/06/we-were-pirates-too/.

National Bureau of Statistics of China (NBS) (various years), *China Statistical Yearbook*. Available from: www.stats.gov.cn/english/statisticaldata/annualdata/.

The New York Times (NYT) (1973), Japanese upset by US soybean curbs, *The New York Times*, 7 July. Available from: www.nytimes.com/1973/07/07/archives/japanese-upset-by-us-soybean-curbs-u-s-ban-on-soybean-exports-is.html.

Office of the Press Secretary (1999), Joint press conference with President Clinton and Premier Zhu Rongji of the People's Republic of China, 8 April, Presidential Hall, Washington, DC. Available from: clintonwhitehouse4.archives.gov/textonly/WH/New/html/19990408-1109.html.

Office of the United States Trade Representative (USTR) (2010), *Free Trade Agreement between the United States of America and the Republic of Korea*, Washington, DC: Office of the USTR. Available from: ustr.gov/trade-agreements/free-trade-agreements/korus-fta/final-text.

Office of the United States Trade Representative (USTR) (2018), *2017 Report to Congress on China's WTO Compliance*, Washington, DC: Office of the USTR.

Pregelj, V. N. (2005), *The Jackson–Vanik amendment: A survey*, CRS Report for Congress, Washington, DC: Congressional Research Service, The Library of Congress.

Selby, J. (2017), Data localization laws: Trade barriers or legitimate responses to cybersecurity risks, or both?, *International Journal of Law and Information Technology* 25: 213–32. doi.org/10.1093/ijlit/eax010Selby.

Song, L. (2013), China's rapid growth and development: A historical and international context, in Y. Huang and M. Yu (eds), *China's New Role in the World Economy*, London: Routledge.

United Nations Conference on Trade and Development (UNCTAD) (2017), *World Investment Report 2017: Investment and the digital economy*, Geneva: UNCTAD. Available from: unctad.org/en/PublicationsLibrary/wir2017_en.pdf.

Wang, Y. (2011), China's development since WTO accession, *East Asia Forum*, 6 October. Available from: www.eastasiaforum.org/2011/10/06/chinas-development-since-wto-accension/.

World Bank (2009), *China—From poor areas to poor people: China's evolving poverty reduction agenda—an assessment of poverty and inequality*, Poverty Assessment No. 47349, Washington, DC: The World Bank. Available from: documents.worldbank.org/curated/en/816851468219918783/China-From-poor-areas-to-poor-people-Chinas-evolving-poverty-reduction-agenda-an-assessment-of-poverty-and-inequality.

World Bank (2018), World Bank Open Data. Available from: data.worldbank.org/.

World Integrated Trade Solution (WITS) (2018), China trade statistics. Available from: wits.worldbank.org/CountryProfile/en/CHN.

World Trade Organization (WTO) (1995), General Agreement on Trade in Services: Article XIV Note 5, in *Uruguay Round Agreement*, Geneva: WTO. Available from: www.wto.org/english/docs_e/legal_e/26-gats_01_e.htm#fnt-5.

World Trade Organization (WTO) (2015), *China: Measures related to the exportation of rare earths, tungsten and molybdenum*, Dispute Settlement No. 431, Geneva: WTO. Available from: www.wto.org/english/tratop_e/dispu_e/cases_e/ds431_e.htm.

World Trade Organization Secretariat (WTO Secretariat) (2018), Time series on international trade. Available from: stat.wto.org/StatisticalProgram/WSDBStatProgramHome.aspx?Language=E.

Wu, T. (2006), The world trade law of censorship and internet filtering, *Chicago Journal of International Law* 7(1): 263–87.

Xi, J. (2017), Jointly shoulder responsibility of our times, promote global growth, Keynote speech, 2017 World Economic Forum, 17 January, Davos, Switzerland. Available from: www.china.org.cn/node_7247529/content_40569136.htm.

Yang, Y. and Huang, Y. (2000), How important is APEC to China?, in P. Drysdale, Y. Zhang and L. Song (eds), *APEC and Liberalisation of the Chinese Economy*, Canberra: Asia Pacific Press.

Yao, Y. (2013), Double transition and China's export-led growth, in Y. Huang and M. Yu (eds), *China's New Role in the World Economy*, London: Routledge.

Yao, Y. (2018), Another messy falling out in China–US relations, *East Asia Forum*, 15 April. Available from: www.eastasiaforum.org/2018/04/15/another-messy-falling-out-in-china-us-relations/.

Zhang, Y. (2000), Liberalisation of the Chinese economy: APEC, WTO and tariff reductions, in P. Drysdale, Y. Zhang and L. Song (eds), *APEC and Liberalisation of the Chinese Economy*, Canberra: Asia Pacific Press.

28. China's foreign trade: Reform, performance and contribution to economic growth

Kunwang Li and Wei Jiang

Over the past four decades, China has successfully transformed from a nearly closed state into a fully integrated international economy and has become an active participant in global markets. In particular, since China's accession to the World Trade Organization (WTO), its foreign trade has achieved rapid growth and transformation. Integration into international production networks and global value chains has seen China evolve into a global manufacturing and trade centre, contributing to its rapid economic growth.

This chapter briefly reviews China's foreign trade policy transformation since 1978, and then examines the performance of China's trade and its impact on economic growth.

The reform of China's foreign trade system: Historical survey

Prior to adopting the open-door policy in 1978, China pursued an inward-looking development strategy, which utilised import-substitution industrialisation. This led to a development pattern common in developing countries in the 1950s. China's policy was extremely restrictive towards foreign economic relations. Imports only made up for shortages in domestic production of essential raw materials and capital goods. Exports were only a means to provide foreign exchange for imports. As a result, China failed to make full use of foreign trade to accelerate economic development.

In December 1978, foreign trade reform was launched as an integral part of economic reform. China has since developed from an autarchic, inward-looking state into one of the major players in the international market. Moreover, China's approach to trade reform has been consistent with its overall approach to the transformation of the economy: gradual changes, dualistic in nature, with parallel pricing, a focus on administrative decentralisation and retention of ultimate control at the centre. Looking back, trade reform and liberalisation fall into three distinct episodes: the administrative decentralisation of trade planning to lower levels of government, together with increased exports through improvements in economic incentives, from 1978 to 1991; the first real moves towards trade liberalisation, from 1992 to 2000; and comprehensive liberalisation and rapid integration with global trade since accession to the WTO in 2001.

The initial stage (1978–91)

Reforms in the first period included administrative decentralisation of trade planning, foreign exchange retention, the foreign trade contract responsibility system, adoption of a more realistic exchange rate and other measures that reduced the bias against exports. The fundamental objective of these reforms was to raise the role of exports in China's economic development.

One of the first steps was to decentralise the authority to engage in foreign trade. To arouse the enthusiasm of localities and industrial departments towards exports, the central government gave them greater powers of export administration. The national foreign trade corporations (FTCs) lost their monopolistic powers and their provincial branches were allowed to become independent financial and operational bodies. Each province was permitted to create its own trade agencies and corporations to engage in direct trading of its products. In July 1979, regulations for foreign investment were promulgated and foreign-funded enterprises were given authority to import raw materials and capital goods for their production. These enterprises were also authorised to export their own products directly. A number of special economic zones, 29 provinces, autonomous regions and municipalities, and the cities of Guangzhou, Dalian, Wuhan, Xian, Shenyang, Harbin, Chongqing, Qingdao and Hainan Island were also permitted to open up ports to engage in foreign trade.

As a result, the number of export trade companies increased from 12 in 1978 to about 1,200 in 1986, reaching a peak of 5,075 in 1988. This initially generated competition for export supply, and created the preconditions for later liberalisation. However, the state still controlled trade through various administrative devices.

There was also a reduction in the scope of foreign trade planning and the introduction of a two-tier system for the management and administration of foreign trade. Exclusive mandatory and advisory planning was replaced with combined mandatory and advisory planning. The export plan covered 100 per cent of exports in 1978; this fell to 45 per cent in 1988 and 15 per cent by the end of 1991. Imports covered by the plan similarly fell to about 15 per cent of the total in 1992 (Lardy 1992; World Bank 1993). From 1985 to 1989, reform reduced administrative controls and gradually removed the government from trade management. For example, import licences were introduced to replace direct planning controls on trade.

China also introduced several measures to promote exports, including the dual exchange rate, the foreign trade contract responsibility system and export rebates.

China's trade regime in the early 1990s could be described as a 'protected export promotion system' (Koves and Marer 1991). It simultaneously sought to promote exports via incentives, while offering significant domestic protection. This system had played an important role in South Korea's export-led strategy. China's import regime has remained highly protective. In 1992, China's unweighted average nominal tariff rate was 43.1 per cent, which was relatively high by international standards—the third highest among large developing countries, after India and Pakistan.

The second stage (1992–2000)

China signed a memorandum of understanding with the United States in October 1991, giving commitments to reduce quantitative import restrictions and tariffs.

On 1 January 1992, import tariffs were reduced on 225 products, from an average rate of 45 per cent to 30 per cent. In addition, China abolished import surcharges of between 20 and 80 per cent on 14 products, in April 1992. In December of that year, it lowered tariffs by an average of 7.3 per cent on an additional 3,371 items. Effective on 1 January 1994, China reduced tariffs on 2,818 items by an average of 8.8 per cent. Tariffs on more than 200 agricultural and industrial items were reduced by an average of 50 per cent, with none less than 35 per cent.

Then president Jiang Zemin announced at the Asia-Pacific Economic Cooperation (APEC) summit in Osaka in November 1995 that China would adopt a new round of tariff reduction in 1996, lowering the unweighted average tariff on 4,000 items, from 35.9 per cent to about 23 per cent.

By 1992, there were 1,247 items covered by import licensing, import quotas and other measures, accounting for 17.5 per cent of the total. Of these, about 12 per cent of imports were covered by import licensing and 5.7 per cent by other quantitative forms of control. Since 1992, China has taken some important steps to gradually reduce its nontariff barriers. In its 1992 agreement with the United States, China pledged to eliminate 90 per cent of its nontariff barriers over time, reducing the number of quantitative restrictions (QRs) from 1,247 to 240 by the year 2000. In January 1993, it was officially announced that all import substitution lists would be abolished.

The third stage: Post-WTO accession

China's accession to the WTO in December 2001 was a milestone in the history of its reform and opening up. It marked recognition by the international community of China's market-oriented reform and the extension of international standards and rules in the Chinese market.

After joining the WTO, China has implemented its commitments in various ways.

Regulations and laws

A large number of laws and administrative regulations on trade have been reviewed and amended to remove inconsistencies with those of the WTO on national treatment. The foreign trade approval system for trade operations licensing has been abolished. All enterprises in China have rights to trade, except those covering a small number of products in which state monopolies remain: grain, cotton and other agricultural products, coal, metal minerals, crude oil and refined oil. These reforms and policy adjustments have significantly improved the transparency of the economic and trade laws, regulations and policies.

Tariffs

Tariff rates for all taxable items have been reduced. The average tariff rate for most favoured nations (MFNs) dropped from 15.6 per cent in 2001 to 9.7 per cent in 2005, and from 14.3 per cent to 8.9 per cent for manufactured goods. Tariff rates for automobiles and spare parts and textiles and clothing were reduced by almost half, while those for agricultural products fell from 23.2 per cent to 14.6 per cent. There is not much difference between the applied and bound tariff rates, making tariffs more predictable. In January 2005, the tariff rates for all information and technology products were reduced to zero from the pre–WTO accession level of 13.3 per cent under the Information Technology Agreement.

Nontariff barriers

After WTO accession, China began to phase out import licences and quotas and specific bidding requirements, all of which had been removed by 1 January 2005. Import licensing procedures have been simplified and transparency improved. New import licensing systems have been implemented since September 2005, and tariff quotas have been retained for only some agricultural products and chemical fertilisers.

Trade-related investment measures

For consistency with the Agreement on Trade-Related Investment Measures (TRIM), trade and foreign exchange balances, local content and export performance requirements in foreign capital laws and regulations have been cancelled.

Trade-related intellectual property rights

For consistency with the WTO Agreement on Trade-Related Aspects of Intellectual Property Rights (TRIPS), China's copyright, trademark and patent laws were amended in 2001 to ensure national and MFN treatment for foreigners was consistent with the TRIPS agreement. Minimum law enforcement standards for the protection of intellectual property rights were set up.

Trade in services

China has undertaken a much broader commitment to the opening of service industries to WTO members than is the norm for developing countries. It has opened more than 100 of the 160-plus sectors and nine of the 12 main categories in the General Agreement on Trade in Services (GATS) list. China has made even greater changes in some industries with immense commercial significance, such as banking, securities, insurance, telecommunications, retail and distribution and professional services. By 2006, China had lifted local content, business scope and share proportion restrictions. For example, China has abolished the requirements relating to local content, export performance, technology transfer and research and development for those sectors in which it had made liberalisation commitments.

Since 2006, the liberalisation of import trade has been continued, but, in general, little progress has been made. The average implementation tariff rate has not been significantly reduced (Table 28.1).

Table 28.1 China's tariff structure, 2015

Products	Number of lines	Average (%)
Live animals and products	488	11.5
Vegetable products	511	14.1
Fats and oils	56	12.6
Prepared food, beverages and tobacco	306	17.4
Mineral products	201	3.0
Chemicals and products thereof	1,289	6.4
Plastics, rubber and articles thereof	274	9.2
Raw hides and skins, leather and its products	106	12.0
Wood and wood articles	208	4.4
Wood pulp, paper and paperboard	162	5.2
Textiles and textile articles	1,141	11.4
Footwear, headgear and so on	71	17.9
Articles of stone, plaster and cement	197	12.8
Precious stones and metals, pearls	90	10.0
Base metals and articles thereof	770	7.0
Machinery, electrical equipment and so on	1,512	7.9
Transport equipment	351	13.1
Precision equipment	335	9.4
Arms and ammunition	21	13.0
Works of art, etc	10	8.0
Miscellaneous manufactured articles	186	10.7
Total	8,285	9.5

Note: Calculations are based on MFN applied tariffs at the Harmonised System eight-digit tariff line level.
Source: WTO Secretariat (2016).

Trade disputes and friction between China and its main trading partners have become increasingly serious with the rapid growth of China's exports and since the collapse of global trade during the Global Financial Crisis (GFC) in 2008. Since 1995, more and more antidumping measures have been initiated against Chinese goods. By the end of 2016, China had been the subject of 866 antidumping measures—the highest number in the world. India has initiated the most antidumping measures against China, followed by the United States and the European Union (Figure 28.1).

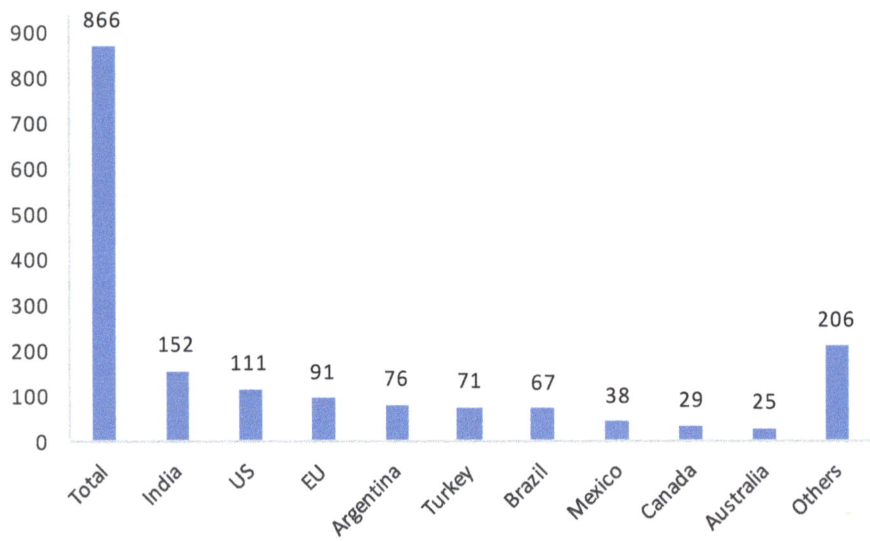

Figure 28.1 Number of antidumping measures against China by trading partners, 1995–2016

Source: WTO (2018).

There are still some challenges for further reform of China's trade regime.

Liberalisation is still required for audiovisual products, books and other products, and for distribution of these products, as well as pharmaceuticals, crude oil and refined oil. Liberalisation is also required of direct selling and the participation of nonstate enterprises in some areas of state monopoly trading.

There are still various barriers to entry and commercial restrictions in service sectors such as banking, securities, insurance, telecommunications, transportation, postal and couriers. These include discriminatory minimum capital requirements, application restrictions for establishing branches, requirements for economic testing and mandatory joint venture requirements; the nationalisation component is also still on the high side. The entry threshold for private and foreign-funded enterprises is still high.

For intellectual property rights, civil procedures and relief need to be improved. Light administrative penalties and high thresholds for criminal proceedings do not deter piracy and infringements. Law enforcement needs to be strengthened. Cooperation between executive departments is weak and there is still local protectionism and administrative corruption. The outcome is weak protection of online intellectual property products.

In government procurement, laws and regulations retain priority to state-owned enterprises (SOEs) and discriminate against foreign suppliers.

In industrial policy, SOEs receive various central and local government financial subsidies, other special subsidies, preferential and policy loans and investment and tax subsidies. These discriminate against imported goods and foreign enterprises. China's notification of subsidies to the WTO is not timely, accurate or comprehensive. Industrial policies for some sectors (such as automobiles and steel) constitute trade and investment barriers. The concept of 'national economic security' is blurred when antitrust law is used to implement industrial policies, and the treatment of administrative monopolies and SOEs is not clear.

In summary, the reform of China's trade system promoted domestic economic reform and accelerated growth in the role of markets. China's trade policy has been increasingly neutral and liberal. These changes have contributed to rapid trade expansion and economic growth in China.

The performance of China's trade

China's foreign trade has experienced 40 years of rapid development. The total value of imports and exports increased from US$206 billion in 1978 to US$4.1 trillion in 2017. Exports increased from US$10 billion to US$2.2 trillion, while imports increased from US$11 billion to US$1.8 trillion. From 1978 to 2017, the average annual growth rate of China's total foreign trade, at 14.1 per cent, was far higher than the global average. From China's accession to the WTO in 2001 to the GFC in 2008, China's value of trade increased annually. Since the slowdown in world trade growth, the growth rate of Chinese exports has also rapidly declined.

China's global ranking in the scale of foreign trade has risen from 32 in 1978 to number one. Figure 28.2 shows the evolution of the shares of total exports for China, the United States, Germany and Japan in the period 1995–2015. The proportion of

China's exports in global trade increased from less than 2 per cent in 1978 to about 13 per cent in 2015. China's share in global exports has fallen over the past two years, but, at 12 per cent, remains larger than any other country.

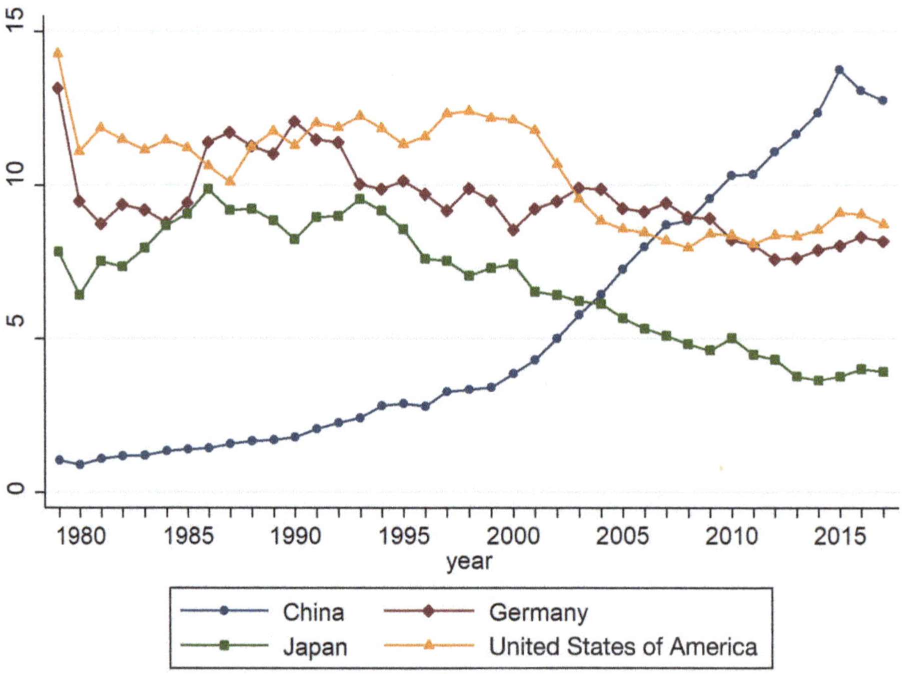

Figure 28.2 The evolution of China's share of world trade (per cent)
Source: Calculated from UN Comtrade database (comtrade.un.org).

In the past 40 years, great changes have taken place in the structure of China's trade. The leading exports changed from resource-based products to light textile products, and then gradually to mechanical and electrical products and then to high-tech products. The proportion of manufacturing products has increased from less than 50 per cent in the initial period of reform and opening-up to more than 90 per cent. Table 28.2 decomposes all manufacturing products into four categories—low technology, medium technology, high technology and others—for China and the world. The share of low-tech exports has always been above the world average, but declined rapidly after China's WTO accession. On the other hand, since accession, the proportion of high-tech products has risen sharply—to far above the world average.

The rapid transformation of China's export structure is closely related to the country's processing trade. Since the early 1990s, with the encouragement of the opening up of processing trade and the massive entry of foreign-invested enterprises, processing trade and the proportion of imports and exports have increased rapidly. In 1981, the total import and export value of processing trade was only US$2.5 billion, as 5.7 per cent of the total Chinese import and export value. By 2007, the total value of imports and exports in processing trade reached US$986 billion (US$618 billion for exports and US$368 billion for imports, respectively). Electrical products made a large contribution to these figures.

Table 28.2 Structural change of exports by technology: China and the world (per cent)

		1985	1990	1995	2000	2005	2010	2016
Low-tech	China	17.0	40.2	46.4	41.2	15.9	29.3	30.9
	World	14.1	16.6	16.7	14.7	9.7	13.0	14.5
Medium-tech	China	4.9	20.8	18.9	19.6	23.0	24.0	24.5
	World	32.4	33.5	32.6	29.6	26.8	27.6	29.7
High-tech	China	2.1	5.3	13.0	22.4	41.0	34.9	32.6
	World	13.3	15.6	19.6	23.0	18.6	19.6	21.3
Others	China	76.1	31.6	21.1	16.1	19.9	11.4	11.3
	World	37.5	31.1	27.3	27.6	44.6	33.9	27.7

Source: Calculated from UN Comtrade database.

To better guide the transformation and upgrading of processing trade, in September 2006, the Ministry of Finance, the National Development and Reform Commission (NDRC), the Ministry of Commerce and other government agencies jointly issued the 'Regulations on Adjusting the Tax Refund Rates for Certain Products and Adding the Catalogue of Prohibited Products for Processing Trade'. This introduced significant changes and, with the reform of China's exchange rate system and the GFC, contributed to a decline in the share of China's processing trade in total trade (Figure 28.3).

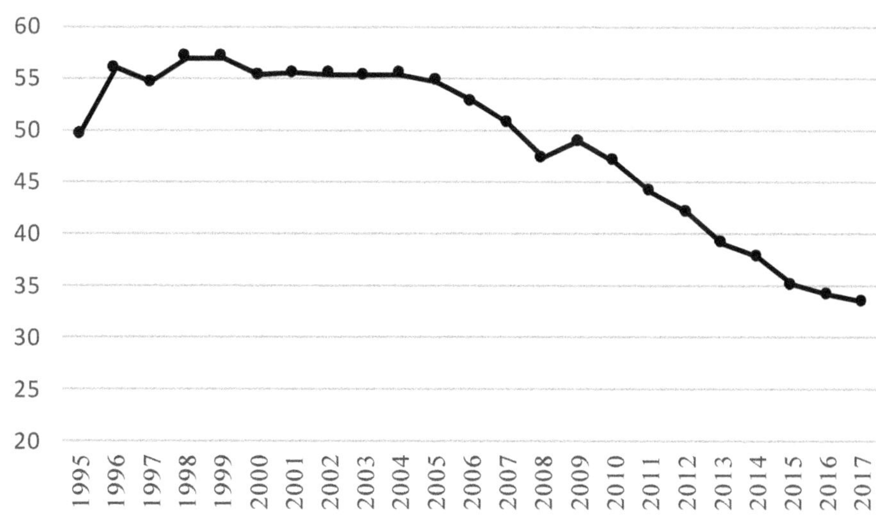

Figure 28.3 The share of processing trade in China's exports (per cent)

Sources: NBS (various years [a], [b]).

There were great imbalances in the development of China's foreign trade in the early stages of reform and opening up, especially between the eastern, central and western regions of the country. The eastern region has always been at the centre of China's foreign trade development, and this advantage continues to deepen (Figure 28.4). After the GFC in 2008, the central and western regions' shares in total trade increased, while the eastern region's share declined. On the whole, however, although the shares of exports in the central and western regions have risen rapidly, the eastern region remains the core of China's foreign trade development.

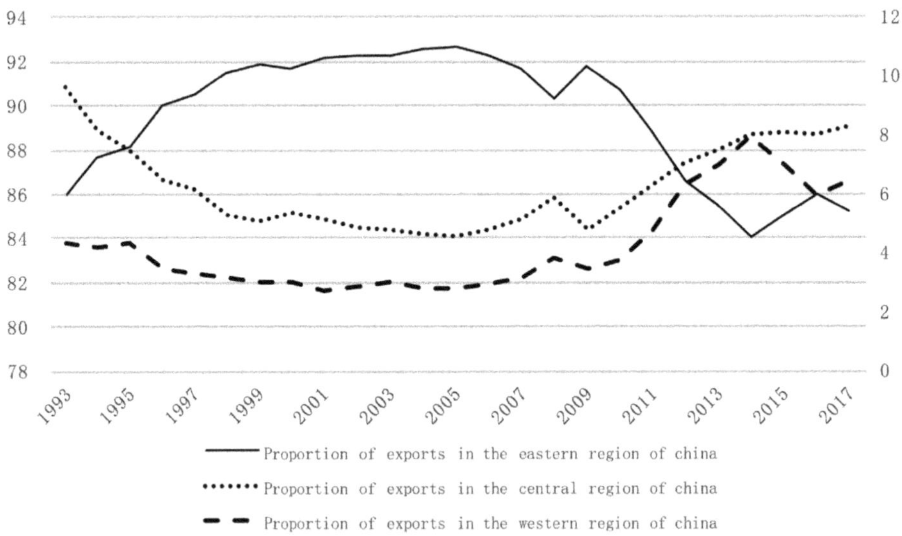

Figure 28.4 The evolution of China's exports by region (per cent)

Note: The vertical axis on the left indicates the eastern region's share in exports, while the vertical axis on the right indicates the shares of the central and western regions.

Sources: NBS (various years [a], [b]).

China has gradually changed from having a narrow geographic focus for its trade into a global trading power. China once used Hong Kong heavily as a transit port, but increasingly smaller proportions of Chinese exports now go through that city (Figures 28.5a and 28.5b). The US share in China's total exports has risen sharply, while Japan's has experienced a sharp decline. After the reform and opening-up, China's export destinations became more diverse.

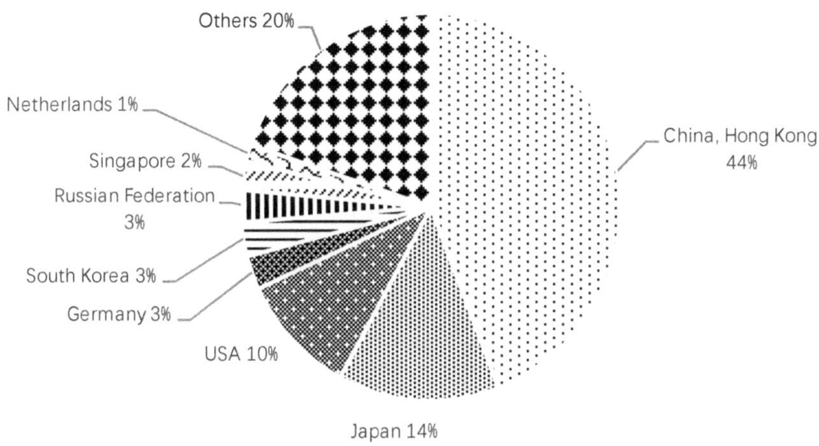

Figure 28.5a Market distribution of destinations for Chinese exports, 1995

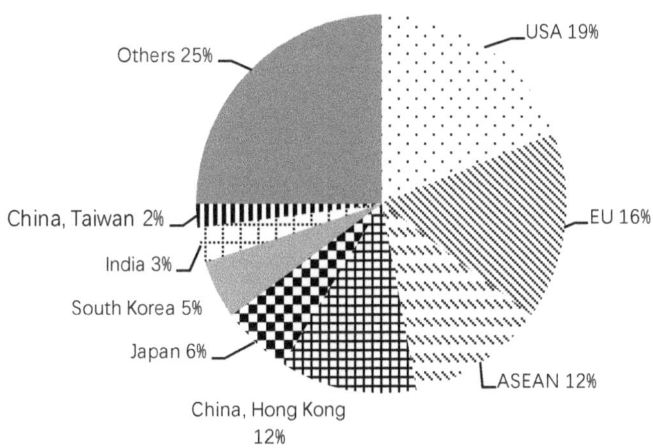

Figure 28.5b Market distribution of destinations for Chinese exports, 2017

Sources: NBS (various years [a], [b]).

With China's accession to the WTO, the ownership structure of enterprises participating in foreign trade has undergone major changes. Before 1998, SOEs dominated China's export growth. After 1998, however, as China gradually began to reform the right to engage in foreign trade, private enterprises have become the most important for China's export growth (Figures 28.6a and 28.6b).

During the reform period, foreign-funded enterprises have been an increasingly important part of China's export growth, and their share in total trade rose from 31 per cent to 43 per cent—slightly lower than the export contribution of Chinese private firms.

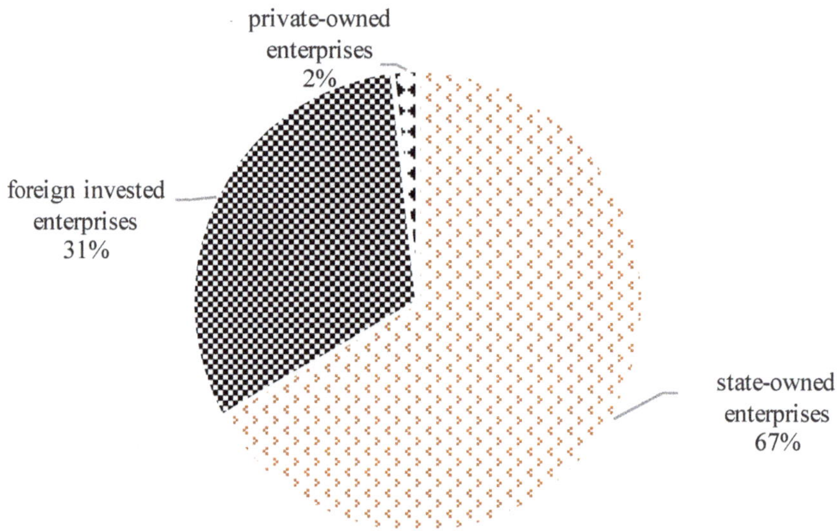

Figure 28.6a Ownership structure of China's exports, 1995

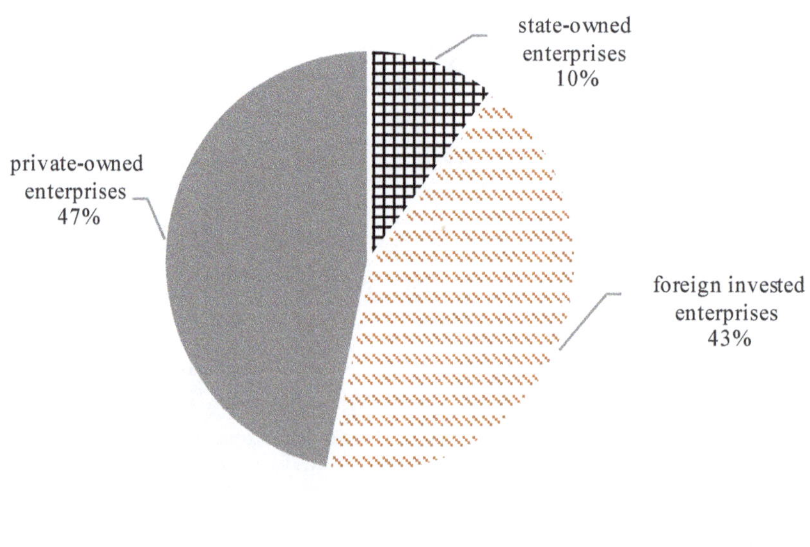

Figure 28.6b Ownership structure of China's exports, 2017

Sources: NBS (various years [a], [b]).

The dominant feature of China's rapid export growth has been the use of abundant and relatively cheap labour as a source of comparative advantage. This had to change—and there are signs now that Chinese exports have been caught in a low-quality trap. Figure 28.7 uses the relative unit value method to differentiate high-quality and low-quality export goods. Specifically, the unit value of export product *i* is calculated at the product level, and the ratio of the two, $\gamma_i = UV_i / \overline{UV}_i$, is then calculated by taking the value of the global average export unit, $\overline{UV}_i$ (the trade-weighted geometric mean of the value of export units of all of that country's products), as a reference. According to the size of γ_i, the quality of export products is divided into two categories: 1) if $\gamma_i > 1$, the export quality of the country's product *i* is relatively high—higher than the world average—and is classified as a high-end product; 2) if $\gamma_i < 1$, the export quality of the country's product *i* is lower than the global average and is classified as a low-end product. Figure 28.7 shows the performance of Chinese exports in high and low-end markets. Most of China's exports are of low-quality goods to the global market, and the disproportionate presence of low-end products became increasingly obvious after China's accession to the WTO.

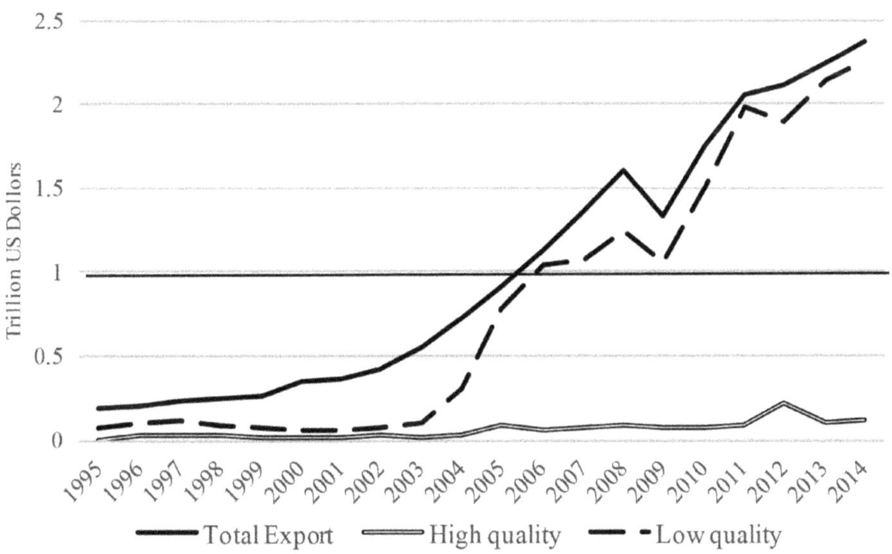

Figure 28.7 Evolution of relative prices and quality of export products in China

Source: Calculated from BACI database (www.cepii.fr/CEPII/en/bdd_modele/presentation.asp?id=1).

Impacts of trade on China's economic growth: Firm-level evaluation

Exports have several effects on economic growth. First, according to the traditional theory of comparative advantage, international trade will improve the allocation of resources in different industries through specialised production and inter-industry resource allocation, so as to raise per capita income. Second, Melitz (2003) has highlighted a new trade gain through intra-industry reallocation across firms. These reallocations towards more efficient firms mean trade may generate aggregate productivity gains.

In the initial period of reform and opening, the development of international trade prompted China to exploit its comparative advantages in labour-intensive products such as textiles and clothing, significantly changing China's industrial and trade structure and greatly improving its inter-industry resource allocation. With the development of its processing trade, China rapidly gained a dominant position in the labour-intensive phase of the global production division of labour and secured a huge market share in processing trade, which is dominated by mechanical and electrical products.

The rapid rise of export companies—especially private companies—has improved the efficiency of resource allocation among domestic enterprises. With the continuous opening up of investment and trade management rights, China has created a more competitive market economy. High-efficiency export companies have gradually taken a leading role in the market and squeezed out a large number of inefficient companies, thereby improving the dynamic efficiency of the market.

Exports increase productivity through selection and learning effects. To test the impact of exports on economic growth, we use the Chinese Industrial Enterprise Database for 1998–2007.[1] The econometric model is introduced as follows (Equation 28.1).

Equation 28.1

$$\ln\left(\frac{Vadd_{it}}{Vadd_{i,t-1}}\right) = \alpha + \beta Export_{it} + \gamma_i + \gamma_t + \mu_{it}$$

1 There are two reasons we adopt this database: first, the firm-level data that can be used to calculate productivity are limited to this period; second, this period coincides with China's accession to the WTO. China's trade system has since undergone profound changes and trade liberalisation has also advanced rapidly, making it appropriate to examine the impact of trade on economic growth based on the database for this period.

In Equation 28.1, $Vadd_{it}$ is the added value of enterprise *i* in year *t*, and *Export* is the export variable of the enterprise. This is a dummy variable: if this company exports, it takes a value of 1; otherwise, it is set at 0. To avoid missing important explanatory variables, the fixed effects at the firm level and the year level are added into the econometric model.

Table 28.3 shows the dummy variables of export enterprises are significantly positive at the 1 per cent level. The growth rate of value added for export enterprises is significantly higher than that for non-export enterprises. The average value-added growth rate of export enterprises is higher than that of non-export enterprises, by 5.3 per cent.

Table 28.3 The effect of exports on economic growth

	(1)	(2)
Export dummy	0.053***	0.054***
	(0.004)	(0.004)
Firm fixed effect	Yes	Yes
Year fixed effect	No	Yes
R^2	0.021	0.084
Observations	1,422,946	1,422,946

*** denote significant at 1 per cent level

Note: Standard errors are in parentheses.

Exports are an important driver of China's economic growth, but does growth come from the increase in factor inputs or the increase in productivity? Here we decompose the sources of China's economic growth. Following the Solow growth model, we decompose the growth of China's manufacturing output into factor and productivity growth.

We use the China Industrial Enterprise Database for 1998–2007 to estimate firm level TFP following Olley and Pakes (1996) method. This method can resolve issues with the omitted variable and sample selection bias. The exact form of the estimate is as follows (Equation 28.2).

Equation 28.2

$$Y_{it} = \beta_0 + \beta_L L_{it} + \beta_K K_{it} + \eta_{it} + \varepsilon_{it}$$

In Equation 28.2, *Y*, *L* and *K* represent the value added of an enterprise, the number of employees and the capital stock, respectively. We apply a price deflator to added value. We adopted the perpetual inventory method and the investment price deflator to estimate the enterprise's capital stock. In Equation 28.2, η_{it} represents a productivity shock that was observed by business decision-makers without the productivity impact observed by researchers; ε_{it} is a productivity shock that was not observed by corporate policymakers or researchers.

Table 28.4 sets out the contribution of factor accumulation and productivity growth to economic growth, and indicates that productivity growth contributed 96.7 per cent in 2002—up from a low of 27.2 per cent in 1999. The increase in productivity has always been the most powerful driving force of China's economic growth.

Table 28.4 The contribution of factor accumulation and TFP growth to economic growth (per cent)

Year	Value-added growth	TFP		Inputs	
		Growth	Contribution	Growth	Contribution
1999	12.7	4.7	37.2	8.0	62.8
2000	15.7	11.7	74.5	4.0	25.5
2001	12.2	10.0	82.1	2.2	17.9
2002	18.3	17.7	96.7	0.6	3.3
2003	26.6	14.8	55.6	11.8	44.4
2004	29.4	20.6	70.3	8.7	29.7
2005	25.2	20.2	80.2	5.0	19.8
2006	24.8	19.7	79.3	5.1	20.7
2007	24.2	10.7	44.4	13.4	55.6

Productivity is a key driver of China's economic growth, and the export level is the most important determinant of productivity growth. This section will further clarify the contribution of exports to China's productivity growth.

This chapter divides all enterprises into export and non-export enterprises. In Table 28.5, we present the results of calculations of the average productivity level of both export and non-export enterprises in different years, and of a T-test for the productivity differences between exporters and non-exporters. Table 28.5 shows that the productivity level of China's non-export enterprises was 1.401 in 1998 and for export enterprises, it was 1.992. The higher productivity of export enterprises is significant at the 1 per cent level. The significance is similar through the period 1998–2007. The average productivity level of export enterprises is significantly higher than that of non-export enterprises.

In Table 28.6, we decompose the contribution of export and non-export enterprises to the weighted average productivity of Chinese manufacturing enterprises. The decomposition results in Table 28.5 show that through 1998–2007, the average contribution of Chinese exporters to TFP reached 48–58 per cent. The decomposition results in Table 28.5 show that the contribution of export enterprises to the TFP growth rate reached 62 per cent, and export enterprises are also the most important source of China's productivity growth.

Table 28.5 TFP difference between non-exporters and exporters

Year	Non-exporters	Exporters	Difference
1998	1.401	1.992	–0.591***
1999	1.484	2.063	–0.579***
2000	1.635	2.210	–0.575***
2001	1.808	2.291	–0.483***
2002	1.956	2.393	–0.437***
2003	2.172	2.554	–0.382***
2004	2.381	2.633	–0.252***
2005	2.523	2.784	–0.261***
2006	2.676	2.886	–0.211***
2007	2.850	2.965	–0.115***

*** denote significant at 1 per cent level

Notes: Standard errors are in parentheses.

Table 28.6 Contribution to TFP of non-exporters and exporters

Year	Contribution to TFP				Contribution to TFP growth			
	Non-exporters		Exporters		Non-exporters		Exporters	
1998	1.090	(45.0)	1.330	(55.0)	0.102	(50.0)	0.102	(50.0)
1999	1.132	(45.6)	1.352	(54.4)	0.106	(52.0)	0.098	(48.0)
2000	1.154	(44.1)	1.466	(55.9)	0.079	(48.9)	0.082	(51.1)
2001	1.216	(44.9)	1.494	(55.1)	0.104	(44.9)	0.128	(55.1)
2002	1.261	(44.3)	1.583	(55.7)	0.103	(45.6)	0.123	(54.4)
2003	1.313	(44.2)	1.659	(55.8)	0.077	(37.9)	0.125	(62.1)
2004	1.326	(42.4)	1.801	(57.6)	0.136	(48.0)	0.148	(52.0)
2005	1.424	(45.0)	1.742	(55.0)	0.122	(55.8)	0.096	(44.2)
2006	1.458	(46.2)	1.699	(53.8)	0.117	(59.5)	0.079	(40.5)
2007	1.627	(51.4)	1.538	(48.6)	0.102	(50.0)	0.102	(50.1)

Notes: The figures in parentheses are the percentage of contribution.

Conclusion

Trade liberalisation and the reform of its economic system have created a solid institutional foundation for the rapid development of China's foreign trade. These changes have also brought China's foreign trade to the fore by improving the efficiency of resource allocation and contributing to dynamic efficiency.

China's foreign trade development faces challenges. First, the pace of economic reform has shown signs of slowing since the eighteenth National Congress, and trade liberalisation needs to be deepened. The main obstacles to this are political pressure and pressure from interest groups, especially large SOEs. Second, the external market environment continues to deteriorate, with increasing trade friction between China and its major trading partners and emerging markets. Third, export-led growth has reached its limit. A new model of development with greater emphasis on a balance between internal and external demand is required.

References

Amit, M. and Freund, C. (2010), The anatomy of China's export growth, in R. C. Feenstra and S.-J. Wei (eds), *China's Growing Role in World Trade*, Chicago: University of Chicago Press.

Jarreau, J. and Poncet, S. (2011), Export sophistication and economic growth: Evidence from China, *Journal of Development Economics* 97(2): 281–92. doi.org/10.1016/j.jdeveco.2011.04.001.

Koves, A. and Marer, P. (1991), *Foreign Economic Liberalization: Transformation in socialist and market economies*, Boulder, CO: Westview Press.

Lardy, N. R. (1992), Chinese Foreign Trade, *The China Quarterly* (131): 691–720.

Li, K. and Song, L. (2011), The technological content of China's exports and the need for quality upgrading, in J. Golley and L. Song (eds), *Rising China: Global challenges and opportunities*, Canberra: ANU E Press.

Li, K. and Wang, X. (2009), China's foreign trade: Trends and issues after WTO accession, in C. Chen (ed.), *China's Integration with the Global Economy*, Cheltenham, UK: Edward Elgar. doi.org/10.4337/9781848449091.00007.

Lin, J. Y. and Li, Y. (2003), Export and economic growth in China: A demand-oriented analysis, [in Chinese], *China Economic Quarterly* (3): 779–94.

Melitz, M. J. (2003), The impact of trade on intra-industry reallocations and aggregate industry productivity, *Econometrica* 71(6): 1695–725. doi.org/10.1111/1468-0262.00467.

National Bureau of Statistics (NBS) (various years [a]), *China Foreign Economic Statistical Yearbook*, Beijing: China Statistics Press.

National Bureau of Statistics (NBS) (various years [b]), *China Trade and External Economic Statistical Yearbook*, Beijing: China Statistics Press.

Olley, G. and Pakes, A. (1996), The dynamics of productivity in the telecommunications equipment industry, *Econometrica* 6: 1263–97. doi.org/10.2307/2171831.

Song, L. (1996), Institutional change, trade composition, and export supply potential in China, in M. Guitian and R. Mundell (eds), *Inflation and Growth in China*, Washington, DC: International Monetary Fund.

Wang, X., Li, K., Xie, S. and Hou, J. (2013), How is US trade policy towards China determined?, *China Economic Review* 27: 25–36. doi.org/10.1016/j.chieco.2013.07.008.

World Bank (1993), *China Trade Policy*, Report No.11568-CHA, Washington, DC: World Bank.

World Trade Organization (WTO) (2018), *Trade Topics: Anti-dumping*, Washington, DC: WTO. Available from: www.wto.org/english/tratop_e/adp_e/adp_e.htm.

World Trade Organization (WTO) Secretariat (2016), *Trade Policy Review: China*, 12 October, Washington, DC: WTO.

Yu, M. (2015), Processing trade, tariff reductions and firm productivity: Evidence from Chinese firms, *Economic Journal* 125(585): 943–88. doi.org/10.1111/ecoj.12127.

29. The liberalisation of FDI policies and the impacts of FDI on China's economic development

Chunlai Chen

Foreign direct investment (FDI) has been one of the most significant features of China's economic reform and opening up to the outside world. By the end of 2016, China had attracted a total of US$1.35 trillion in FDI stock (UNCTAD various issues), making it the largest FDI recipient in the developing world. The large volumes of FDI inflows have contributed greatly to China's economy in terms of capital formation, employment creation, export expansion and technology transfer, and have exerted significant impacts on its economic growth and structural changes.

This chapter provides a brief review of the liberalisation and development of China's FDI policies since late 1978, discusses the main characteristics of FDI in China, examines the main impacts of FDI on China's economy and provides some policy suggestions for China to further attract and benefit from FDI.

The background of China's opening up to FDI

The shift in China's policies towards attracting FDI reflects important political changes.[1] In 1975, when Deng Xiaoping emerged from political obscurity, he commissioned the drafting of a series of documents outlining the 'four modernisations'—the modernisation of agriculture, industry, science and technology, and national defence—which were raised at the fourth National People's Congress in January of that year. The authors of these documents, and particularly Deng Xiaoping, believed the achievement of these modernisations and other such initiatives would be crucial to China's economic development. However, these efforts were fiercely attacked by radicals as 'capitalist' and, eventually, Deng was removed from all party and government posts.

It is no surprise that Deng Xiaoping reintroduced these ideas immediately after his return to power in 1978, and China's economic reforms were launched later that year. The ideas Deng had proposed in 1975—to introduce and acquire advanced technology and management methods from foreign countries—were developed

1 For a detailed discussion of the political implications of China's foreign trade and FDI reforms, see Shirk (1994).

further to allow inward FDI into China's domestic economy. Drawing on the experience of other developing economies in attracting and utilising FDI, the Chinese leadership recognised that FDI was an effective way to acquire advanced technology and equipment from foreign countries quickly and with minimal cost. FDI was also a means of better utilising China's resources in the absence of domestic capital, and of providing valuable experience of modern economic management skills. It is clear the Chinese leadership was politically sincere in its desire to attract FDI, even though such investment also risked bringing capitalist influence into China.

The political endorsement of inward FDI in the late 1970s was rationalised by the necessity of achieving a recovery from the economic disruption caused by the Cultural Revolution. The search for foreign capital seemed to be inevitable. A package deal that provides technology, management skills and access to international markets, as well as capital, was naturally the best choice for China's decision-makers. The fundamental shift in Communist Party thinking from 'class struggle' towards 'socialist economic construction' and, even more significantly, the urgent demand for economic development greatly facilitated the initial changes to China's FDI policy. As a result, at the second session of the fifth National People's Congress in July 1979, the Law on Joint Ventures Using Chinese and Foreign Investment was passed, granting FDI legal status in China.

The liberalisation of China's FDI policies and FDI inflows into China

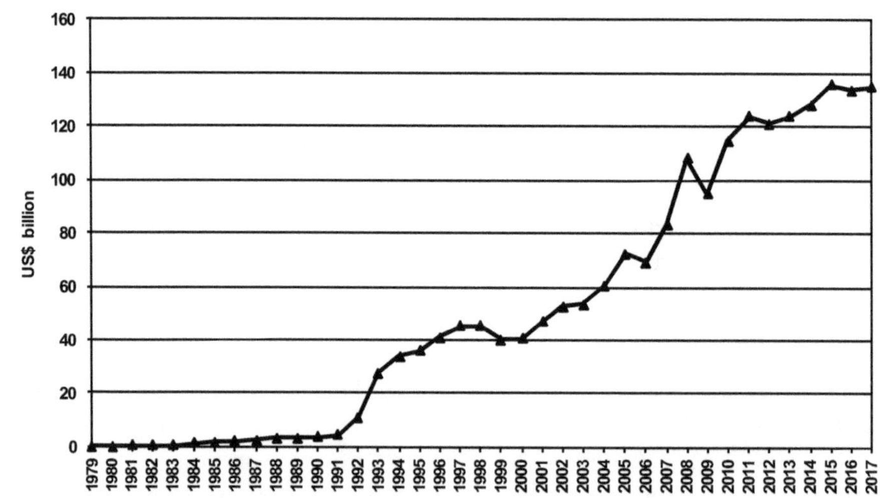

Figure 29.1 FDI inflows into China, 1979–2017 (current US$)

Sources: UNCTAD (various issues).

Figure 29.1 shows the growth of FDI inflows into China from 1979 to 2017 in three phases: 1979–91, 1992–2001 and 2002–17. In each phase, FDI inflows are closely related to the liberalisation and development of China's legal framework and FDI policies.

The first phase, 1979–91

Following the adoption of the 'open-door policy' in late 1978 and the release of the Equity Joint Venture Law in 1979, China established four special economic zones (SEZs)—Shenzhen, Zhuhai, Xiamen and Shantou—in Guangdong and Fujian provinces in 1980. During the period 1984–91, the Chinese Government made significant efforts to liberalise FDI policies and attract FDI inflows. This included opening more areas to FDI, such as Hainan Island and 14 coastal cities across 10 provinces in 1984; opening the Yangtze River Delta, the Pearl River Delta and the Min Nan Delta in 1985; and opening the Shanghai Pudong New Development Zone and then the entire coastal area to FDI in 1988 (Liu et al. 1993). To encourage FDI inflows, the Chinese Government offered special tax incentives to foreign investors, which are reflected in the Equity Joint Venture Income Tax Law, the Foreign Enterprise Income Tax Law and the Industrial and Commercial Tax Provisions.

The government also introduced a series of laws and regulations to encourage FDI inflows (Wei 1994; Chen 2011), including the Regulations for the Implementation of the Law on Chinese-Foreign Equity Joint Ventures in 1983, the Law on Enterprises Operated Exclusively with Foreign Capital and the Provisions of the State Council on the Encouragement of Foreign Investment in 1986 and the Law on Chinese–Foreign Contractual Joint Ventures in 1988.

The uneven regional implementation of the open strategy for FDI—from the SEZs to coastal cities and then to the entire coastal area—has enabled the coastal region to gain more benefits than others. Consequently, the gaps in economic development and income level between the coastal region and the inland areas have enlarged since the late 1980s. There have been benefits for the inland economies, but the process of diffusion from the coast to the inland has been slow. The outflow of skilled workers, technical personnel and capital from inland areas to the coastal region has been increasing (Chen 2017). In response, in the 1990s, the Chinese Government gradually moved the implementation of its FDI policies to create a more level playing field throughout the country.

In the first phase of opening to the world, because the Chinese Government was very prudent in introducing FDI into its domestic economy, foreign investors were cautious about investing in China. During the period 1979–91, FDI inflows into China averaged US$1.8 billion annually.

The second phase, 1992–2001

The second phase of FDI began in 1992, following Deng Xiaoping's tour of China's southern coastal, economically open areas and SEZs. Deng's tour set the scene for China's move away from the formerly uneven regional implementation to a nationwide application of open policies for FDI. The Chinese Government implemented a series of new policies and regulations that would encourage FDI inflows. These included gradually shifting the application of preferential FDI policies from regional to local and national industrial development priorities, and opening 52 cities to foreign investors. The preferential policies granted to the 14 coastal cities were applied to these new cities, and more than 15 border cities and counties in the south-west, north-west, north and north-east of China were declared open-border cities. Some services industries—such as aviation, telecommunications, banking and retail trade—were opened to FDI participation in a limited and experimental fashion. To further develop foreign trade and processing industries in coastal areas, more duty-free zones were to be established. In addition, the government allowed foreign businesspeople—those with an intention to set up FDI firms at a later stage and land developers—to buy land use rights for the building of infrastructure facilities, including residential, commercial, industrial and recreational real estate (Wei 1994). To boost economic growth and, therefore, to reduce the economic development gap between coastal, central and western regions, the Chinese Government launched the Western Development Strategy in 1998, which covered 12 provinces, municipalities and autonomous regions.

In the 1990s, the Chinese Government further liberalised its FDI regime. In 1990, the Amendments to the Equity Joint Venture Law and the Wholly Foreign-owned Enterprise Implementing Rules were adopted. New regulations adopted after 1991 included the Foreign Investment Enterprise and Foreign Enterprise Income Tax Law, the Copyright Law, the Software Protection Regulations, the Patent Law Amendments, the Trademark Law, the Regulatory Provisions of Foreign Banks, the Securities Exchange Law, the Banking Law, the Foreign Exchange Control Regulations, the Company Law, the Interim Provisions Concerning Some Issues on the Establishment of Companies Limited by Shares with Foreign Investment, the Interim Provisions on Guiding Foreign Investment Direction and the Catalogue for the Guidance of Foreign Investment Industries.

In the second phase, China established a more consistent and systematic FDI regulatory framework. The results were astounding. In 1992, inflows of FDI into China reached US$11 billion, doubling the figure for 1991. In 1993, inflows doubled again, reaching US$27.5 billion. The high growth of FDI inflows continued from 1994 to 1997; however, they slowed after 1997 and declined in 1999 and 2000, mainly because of the East Asian Financial Crisis, which substantially weakened the outward investment abilities of East and South-East Asian economies, which had been important investors in China.

The third phase, 2002–17

The third phase began in 2002 after China's entry to the World Trade Organization (WTO) the previous year. In anticipation of China's entry to the WTO, the Chinese Government amended the Wholly Foreign-owned Enterprise Law and the Contractual Joint Venture Law in 2000 and the Equity Joint Venture Law in 2001. After entry, China issued a series of regulations to fulfil its commitments to the WTO. In 2005, the new Company Law was issued, simplifying company establishment requirements and expanding the rights of shareholders. In 2003, it issued the Interim Provisions on Mergers and Acquisitions of Domestic Enterprises by Foreign Investors and, after a three-year trial, the Regulations for Merger with and Acquisition of Domestic Enterprises by Foreign Investors were issued, in October 2006. These regulations established new rules for foreign investors acquiring interests in China's domestic companies, in line with international practice.

After more than 10 years of debate and drafting, China enacted its first Anti-Monopoly Law in 2007. The Anti-Monopoly Law itself does not distinguish between foreign and domestic businesses. However, until July 2009, foreign investors were also subject to pre-merger notification and competition review under the provisions on mergers and acquisitions (M&As). To ensure the M&A provisions agreed with the Anti-Monopoly Law and the State Council's provisions on Thresholds for Declaration of Concentrations of Undertakings, the government revised the M&A provisions in July 2009. Foreign buyers were then subject to only one competition notification and review requirement, under the Anti-Monopoly Law.

In March 2007, Chinese lawmakers passed the Enterprise Income Tax Law, unifying the tax rates for foreign and domestic enterprises. The new tax rate for both domestic and foreign enterprises was 25 per cent. The law took effect on 1 January 2008 and unified the tax rates for domestic firms and FDI. Many tax incentives and tax holidays for foreign investors in the old code were changed or eliminated.

In February 2002, China issued the Provisions on Guiding the Orientation of Foreign Investment, which classified FDI into 'encouraged', 'permitted', 'restricted' and 'prohibited' categories. The provisions encourage both a greater geographic dispersion of FDI inflows within China and greater FDI inflows into the targeted economic sectors and industries. To guide FDI into the targeted industries in accordance with China's economic and industrial development strategy, the government amended its Catalogue for the Guidance of Foreign Investment Industries in 2004, 2007, 2011, 2015 and 2017. The latest version, the 2017 catalogue, which took effect on 28 July, introduced a national negative list, specifying the industries in which FDI is restricted or prohibited. Industries falling under the 'restricted' category are subject to controls such as shareholding limits, and must receive prior approval from the Ministry of Commerce. Industries in the prohibited category are completely closed to FDI. The 2017 catalogue shows the Chinese market is continuing to open to foreign investors, with an overall trend of liberalisation. These changes demonstrate that China is serious about upgrading its industrial structure through utilising foreign capital to achieve sound economic development.

Two characteristics of regulatory change in the 2000s distinguish it from the 1980s and the 1990s. First, emphasis has been placed on the creation and development of a more consistent and systematic regulatory framework. Second, greater efforts have been made to conform to international FDI requirements.

In the third phase, after a period of falling FDI inflows, China's WTO accession was followed by a lift in such flows. FDI inflows increased from US$46.9 billion in 2001 to US$108.3 billion in 2008. However, the Global Financial Crisis saw inflows into China decline to US$95 billion in 2009, before recovering to US$114.7 billion in 2010 and US$135 billion in 2017.

The characteristics of FDI in China

The sources of FDI in China

Table 29.1 presents the top 15 investors in China to the end of 2014. Hong Kong (China) holds the dominant position, followed by British Virgin Islands, Japan, the United States, Singapore, Taiwan (China), South Korea, Cayman Islands, Germany, Samoa, the United Kingdom, Netherlands, France, Mauritius and Macau (China). Together, the top 15 investors accounted for 87.5 per cent of total FDI inflows into China at the end of 2014.

Table 29.1 The top 15 FDI investors in China by the end of 2014

	End 2014	
	(US$ billion)	(%)
Hong Kong (China)	746.9	46.5
British Virgin Islands	141.8	8.8
Japan	98.6	6.1
United States	75.4	4.7
Singapore	72.3	4.5
Taiwan (China)	61.2	3.8
Korea	59.9	3.7
Cayman Islands	28.7	1.8
Germany	23.9	1.5
Samoa	23.4	1.5

	End 2014	
	(US$ billion)	(%)
United Kingdom	19.2	1.2
Netherlands	14.7	0.9
France	13.6	0.9
Mauritius	13.0	0.8
Macau (China)	11.9	0.7
Others	200.8	12.5
Total	1,605.3	100.0

Source: MOC (2015).

FDI in China was dominated by developing economies, accounting for 68.7 per cent of the total (Figure 29.2). A large share was held by tax haven economies, accounting for 13.1 per cent of the total.

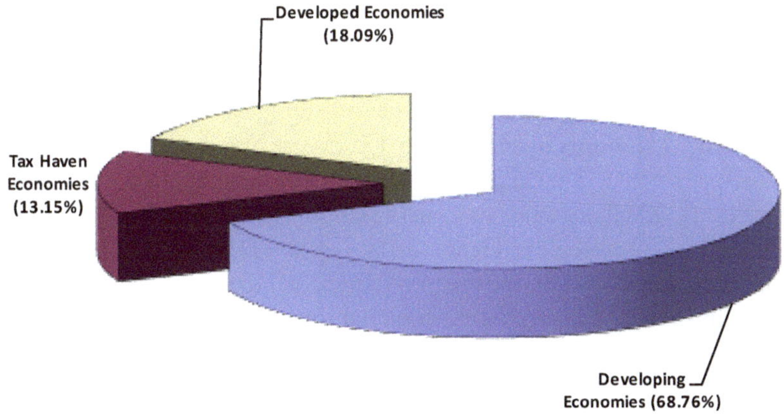

Figure 29.2 Sources of FDI in China by the end of 2014
Source: MOC (2015).

The regional distribution of FDI in China

FDI inflows have been concentrated overwhelmingly in the eastern region of China (Figure 29.3); however, inflows here have been slowing since 2012, alongside large increases in the central and western regions. Annual FDI inflows into the central region have reached more than US$10 billion since 2009 and annual FDI inflows into the western region reached more than US$10 billion in 2013 and 2014.

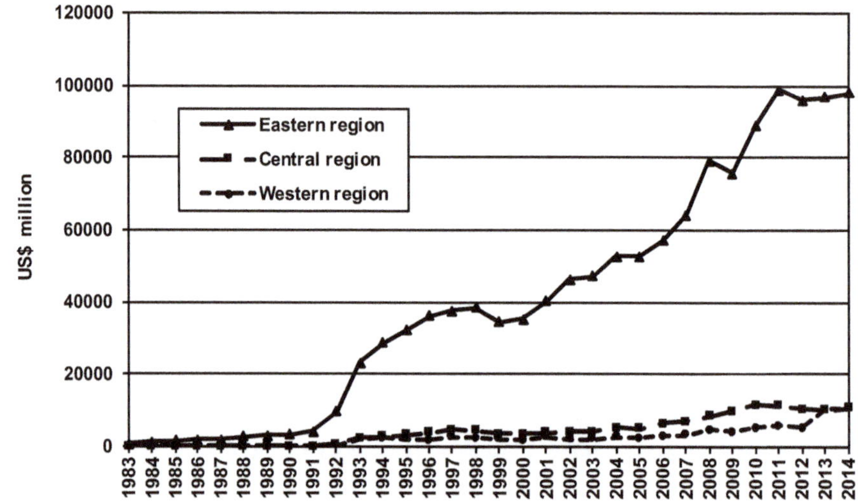

Figure 29.3 FDI inflows into China by region, 1983–2014 (current US$)

Sources: Data for 1983–2005 are from NBS (various issues); data for 2006–14 are from MOC (various issues).

From 1983 to 2014, Guangdong (14.6 per cent) and Jiangsu (14.5 per cent) were the recipients of the largest amounts of FDI among China's eastern provinces, followed by Liaoning (8.7 per cent), Shanghai (7.1 per cent), Shandong (6.5 per cent), Fujian (5.9 per cent), Zhejiang (5.9 per cent), Tianjin (5.3 per cent) and Beijing (3.7 per cent). In the central region, Henan is the largest FDI recipient, attracting 3.3 per cent of the national total. In the western region, Sichuan attracted the largest amount of FDI inflows (2.7 per cent of the national total).

Overall, as Figure 29.4 shows, by the end of 2014, FDI in China was overwhelmingly concentrated in the eastern region, accounting for 85.2 per cent of the total.

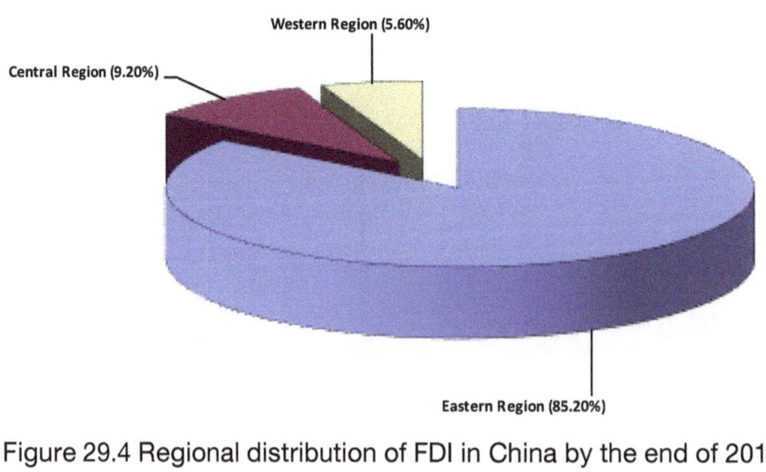

Figure 29.4 Regional distribution of FDI in China by the end of 2014

Sources: Data for 1983–2005 complied from NBS (various issues); and for 2006–14, from MOC (various issues).

Sectoral distribution of FDI in China

FDI overwhelmingly flowed into the manufacturing sector before 2009 (Figure 29.5). However, since 2010, FDI inflows into the manufacturing sector have slowed, and declined after 2012. By contrast, FDI inflows into the services sector started to increase rapidly and surpassed inflows into the manufacturing sector in 2010. In 2014, FDI inflows into the manufacturing sector totalled US$39.9 billion, while those for the services sector reached US$77.5 billion—nearly double the amount into manufacturing.

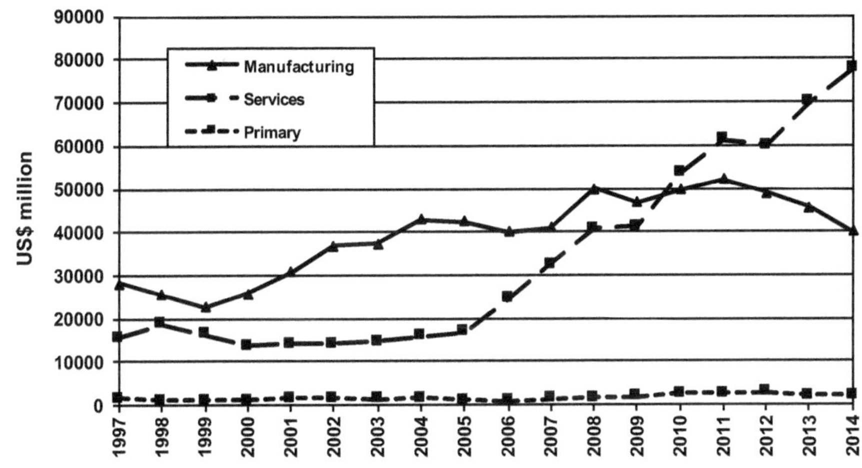

Figure 29.5 FDI inflows into China by sector, 1997–2014 (current US$)

Sources: NBS (various issues).

By the end of 2014, as shown in Figure 29.6, the manufacturing sector attracted 52.7 per cent, the services sector attracted 44.9 per cent, while the primary sector attracted only 2.3 per cent of total FDI inflows into China during the period 1997–2014.[2]

Overall, FDI in China is characterised by the dominance of investors from developing economies, a heavy concentration of FDI in the coastal region and flows going overwhelmingly into the manufacturing sector before 2009, but increasingly into the services sector since 2010.

2 Data for FDI inflows into sectors are not available before 1997.

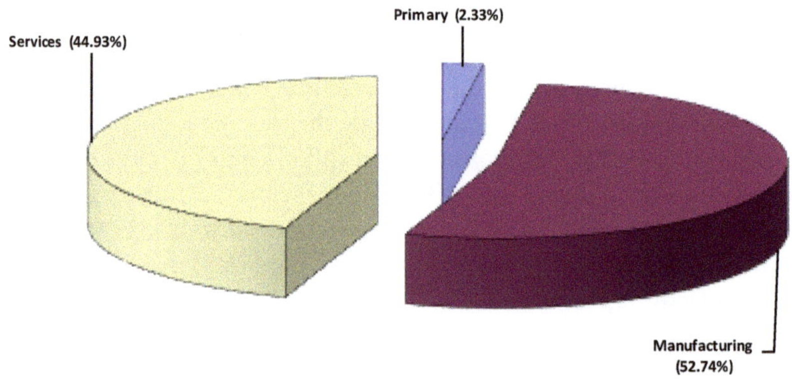

Figure 29.6 Sectoral distribution of FDI in China by the end of 2014

Sources: Compiled from NBS (various issues).

The impacts of FDI on China's economic development

According to Dunning's 'ownership advantage, location advantage and internalisation advantage' (OLI) framework (Dunning 1993), FDI brings with it a package of capital, technology, production know-how, modern management and marketing skills, information, competition and other firm-specific intangible assets. Therefore, it is expected that FDI will contribute to the host country's economic development through capital formation, employment creation, technology transfers and knowledge spillovers. During the past four decades, China has attracted large amounts of FDI inflows, totalling US$1.35 trillion at the end of 2016. This section discusses how FDI has impacted China's economic development in terms of economic growth and productivity spillovers, export promotion, income distribution and urbanisation.

Economic growth and productivity spillovers

The increase in labour and capital inputs and advances in technology are sources of economic growth, to which FDI contributes through employment creation, capital formation, technology transfers and knowledge spillovers. FDI differs from domestic investment in three important aspects. First, FDI accelerates the speed of adoption of general-purpose technologies[3] in host countries, each of which is capable of raising the aggregate productivity of labour and capital. Second, FDI is imbued with

3 General-purpose technologies are technological inventions that affect the entire global economic system. Some recent examples include the computer, the internet and the mobile phone.

new technologies and other intangible proprietary assets otherwise unavailable in the host country. Such technologies can shift the host country's production frontier to a new level. Third, FDI may generate positive knowledge spillovers to boost the host country's economic growth. FDI can improve the productivity and efficiency of local firms through knowledge spillovers such as learning by doing or learning by watching (demonstration effects), research and development (R&D), human resource movement, training, vertical industrial linkages, technical assistance and exposure to fierce competition.

How has FDI contributed to China's economic growth? FDI can promote China's economic growth through four channels. First, FDI inflows increase demand for labour and create employment. FDI firms hired 29.6 million workers, or 7.5 per cent of China's total urban employment, in 2014. The increase in employment contributes to an increase in total output, thus promoting economic growth. Second, FDI inflows increase China's fixed capital formation. By the end of 2016, China had attracted US$1.35 trillion in FDI stock, which has contributed to the country's fixed capital formation and, therefore, boosted its economic growth. Third, FDI is a leading source of technology transfer and human capital augmentation in developing countries (Dunning 1993). FDI is therefore expected to accelerate China's economic growth through technological progress. Fourth, through knowledge spillovers, FDI is expected to increase the productivity and efficiency of domestic Chinese firms.

The impact of FDI on China's economic growth has been studied extensively, finding that FDI has played a positive role. For example, Chen et al. (1995) find that FDI has been positively associated with economic growth and an increase in total fixed investment in China. Dees (1998) finds evidence supporting the view that FDI affects China's growth through the diffusion of knowledge and ideas. Tang et al. (2008) find that FDI complements rather than crowding out domestic investment. FDI has not only assisted in overcoming a shortage of capital, it has also stimulated economic growth through complementing domestic investment in China. Whalley and Xin (2010) find that China's foreign-invested enterprises may have contributed more than 40 per cent of China's economic growth in 2003 and 2004 and, without this inward FDI, China's overall GDP growth rate could have been about 3.4 percentage points lower. Chen (2011) finds that FDI contributes to China's economic growth both directly through increasing capital input and indirectly through positive knowledge spillovers. During the period 1986–2005, of the 11.77 per cent average growth rate of China's real GDP, 1.4 percentage points came from direct and indirect contributions of FDI, which constituted 12.43 per cent of the total growth rate in that period.

Some empirical studies find that the economic and technological conditions of a recipient economy influence the extent to which FDI contributes to growth. For example, Buckley et al. (2002) find that the growth-promoting effects of FDI are more evident in the more developed provinces than in those that are less developed, and that the full benefits of FDI are realised when competition in local markets is at its strongest. Yao and Wei (2007) find that FDI has positive and significant impacts on China's economic growth; however, the positive impact is greater in the eastern than in the central and western regions. Tuan et al. (2009) find that while FDI exerted spillover effects and affected the total factor productivity (TFP) growth of the recipients, major technology and knowledge-related factors—including the R&D and human capital of recipients—also played critical roles. Chen (2017) finds that FDI has contributed to China's economic growth directly through capital augmentation and technological progress and indirectly through knowledge spillovers to the local economy. That study also finds the contribution of FDI is influenced by local economic and technological conditions. FDI exerts a stronger impact on economic growth through capital augmentation and technological progress in the developed coastal provinces than in the less-developed inland provinces. While FDI has a positive and significant impact on economic growth through knowledge spillovers in the developed coastal provinces, such positive spillovers from FDI are absent in the less-developed inland provinces.

Empirical studies have also found evidence that FDI has generated positive productivity spillovers to China's domestic firms. For example, Xu and Sheng (2012) find that FDI has positive spillover effects on domestic firms' productivity in the same industry within the same region. Chen (2011) finds that FDI has significant positive spillover effects on the productivity of Chinese domestic firms within the same industry in the manufacturing sector. However, the study finds that FDI does not have significant spillover effects on domestic firms' productivity through backward and forward industrial linkages. This is mainly because of FDI firms' heavy engagement in processing trade, which breaks down the industry linkages between FDI and domestic firms. These suggest that host countries could enlarge the positive spillover effects of FDI and thereby foster domestic firm productivity by strengthening industrial linkages between domestic and FDI firms.

Export promotion

FDI has played a significant role in China's export expansion. Figure 29.7 presents the export performance of FDI firms from 1986 to 2014. FDI firms' exports rose from US$600 million in 1986 to US$791 billion in 2008 and to US$1 trillion in 2014. As a result, the importance of FDI firms to China's exports increased from only 1.9 per cent in 1986 to 45.9 per cent in 2014, and FDI firms have rapidly become a major exporting group.

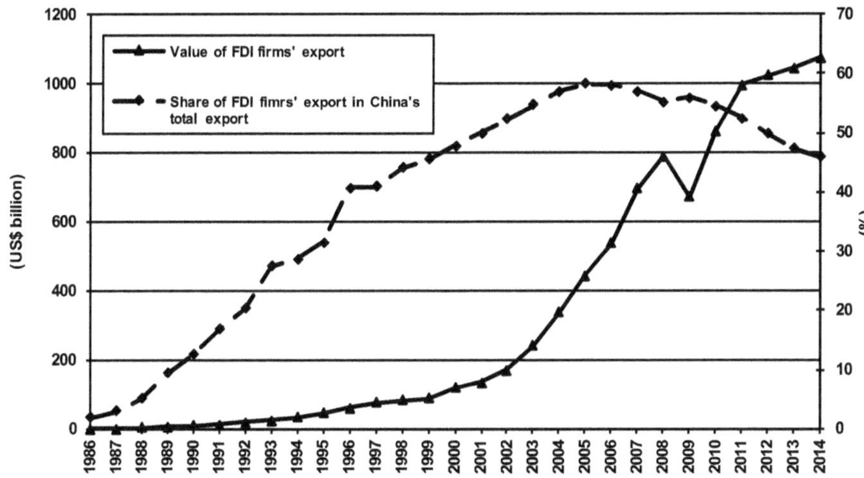

Figure 29.7 Export performance of FDI firms, 1986–2014 (current US$)

Source: MOC (2015).

One significant feature of FDI in promoting China's international trade is its heavy engagement in processing trade,[4] especially in the coastal region. As Table 29.2 shows, during the period 2002–12, FDI firms' processing trade accounted for more than 80 per cent of China's total processing trade and more than 60 per cent of FDI firms' total trade. In particular, FDI firms' processing exports accounted for more than 70 per cent of their total exports.

Table 29.2 The performance of FDI firms' processing trade, 2002–12

Year	FDI firms' processing trade as a percentage of China's total processing trade	FDI firms' processing trade as a percentage of FDI firms' total trade	FDI firms' processing exports as a percentage of FDI firms' total exports
2002	75.7	69.3	79.2
2003	79.6	68.2	79.2
2004	81.9	67.9	78.7
2005	83.7	69.5	78.0
2006	84.9	68.1	76.5
2007	84.3	66.1	74.9
2008	84.5	63.1	72.4

4 Processing trade activities include 'processing or assembling with imported materials' and 'processing or assembling with supplied materials'. For the former, processing firms import—free of customs duty—materials and components that are used to produce finished goods and export them to international markets. In the case of processing or assembling with supplied materials, the processing firms process or assemble duty-free materials and components supplied by foreign firms and export finished products. They are paid a fee for the processing or assembling activities. The foreign firms control both the supply of the materials and all the international marketing of the processed or assembled products.

Year	FDI firms' processing trade as a percentage of China's total processing trade	FDI firms' processing trade as a percentage of FDI firms' total trade	FDI firms' processing exports as a percentage of FDI firms' total exports
2009	84.1	62.8	73.4
2010	83.9	60.7	72.0
2011	83.1	58.3	70.3
2012	81.7	58.0	69.9

Sources: Calculated from MOC (various issues; 2015).

Empirical studies have found strong evidence that FDI promotes Chinese exports and that the relationship between FDI inflows and bilateral trade is complementary (for example, Lardy 1995; Chen 1999; Hu and Ma 1999; Liu et al. 2001; Li 2003).

However, are there impacts from FDI on the exports of China's domestic firms? Theoretically, FDI firms can generate export spillovers to domestic firms through three main channels. First, FDI firms can reduce the export costs of domestic firms through knowledge spillovers, thus encouraging domestic firms to increase exports (for example, Aitken et al. 1997; Greenaway et al. 2004). Second, FDI firms can generate positive technology spillovers to domestic firms to increase their productivity, which may improve their competitiveness and increase their exports (for example, Barrios et al. 2003; Javorcik 2004). Third, FDI firms can strengthen domestic industrial linkages through supplying and purchasing intermediate inputs, which not only will increase the productivity of domestic firms in the upstream and downstream industries, but also will promote their involvement in international production specialisation, thus enhancing domestic firms' ability to export (for example, Javorcik 2004; Kneller and Pisu 2007).

Empirical studies have found strong evidence that FDI has positive spillover effects on the export decisions and performance of Chinese domestic firms (for example, Zheng et al. 2004; Ma 2006, Buck et al. 2007; Cheung 2010; Sun 2012). However, such effects vary across regions and among different types of firms. For example, Sun (2009) finds that FDI has stronger spillover effects on domestic exports in the coastal region than in inland regions. Chen (2011) finds that FDI firms have a positive impact on the export propensity of domestic firms in the same industry through demonstration effects, and this is generated mainly by high-exporting FDI firms. The study also finds some evidence that FDI firms—in particular, high-exporting FDI firms—have positive export spillover effects on domestic firms in downstream industries through forward industrial linkage, meaning domestic firms can access good-quality and cheap intermediate inputs from upstream FDI firms. Such firms can therefore reduce their production costs, improve competitiveness and increase exports. However, the study does not find significant evidence that FDI firms—particularly high-exporting ones—generate export spillover effects to domestic firms through backward industrial linkage. One explanation is that FDI firms in China are highly engaged in processing trade and therefore generate no significant backward spillover effects to domestic firms. Chen et al. (2013) find that FDI firms have generated positive export spillover effects on Chinese domestic firms' export decisions, export–sales ratio and export value. However, these effects are most likely to be observed in domestic enterprises that are not state-owned.

Income distribution

For the past 40 years, China has achieved remarkable results in increasing per capita income and improving the living standards of the Chinese people, which has been attributed to rapid economic growth. Despite this, income inequality in China has actually worsened. Based on the government's official calculations, the Gini coefficient reached 0.49 in 2008, before falling to 0.46 in 2015 (China Economy Net 2016). Has FDI contributed to increasing or reducing income inequality in China? It is expected that FDI will affect the host country's income distribution through its contribution to economic growth, changing resource endowments and its impacts on employment and wage structures. Theoretically, according to the Kuznets inverted-U curve hypothesis (Kuznets 1955), income inequality increases in the early stage of development, but declines once a certain stage of development is reached. Empirical evidence shows that FDI contributes to developing countries' economic growth and development (for example, Dunning 1993; Caves 1996). As a result, although FDI may initially increase income inequality, its benefits will eventually spread throughout the whole economy and it could in the long run facilitate more even income distribution in developing countries through its development effects (Tsai 1995; Chen 2017). Furthermore, FDI brings capital into capital-scarce developing countries, which not only increases their productive capital stock, but also changes their capital–labour ratio (Dunning 1993). As a result, FDI inflows should reduce the relative returns on capital of labour and, therefore, reduce income inequality in capital-scarce developing countries (Lin et al. 2013). In addition, FDI creates employment, which is especially important in developing countries with a large amount of surplus labour. According to the conventional Heckscher–Ohlin model and the Stolper–Samuelson theorem (Krugman and Obstfeld 1991), if a developing country is relatively well-endowed with unskilled labour, to take advantage of the relatively abundant factors of production, FDI should be concentrated in activities that use that unskilled labour more intensively (Lee and Vivarelli 2006; Ucal et al. 2014). As a result, FDI should lead to an increase in the demand for unskilled labour, which not only increases the incomes of previously unemployed labourers, but also drives up the wages of unskilled workers relative to those of skilled workers. Consequently, income inequality will decline as FDI increases. Therefore, through economic growth and development, capital formation and employment creation, FDI tends to reduce income inequality in developing countries.

However, some empirical studies have found that FDI has contributed to the widening of income inequality between the inland and coastal regions in China (for example, Zhang and Zhang 2003; Fu 2004). Wan et al. (2007) find that the effects of FDI contribute to a positive and substantial share of regional inequality and the share rises over time.

In contrast, Jalil (2012) finds that income inequality rises with the increase of economic openness (measured by the openness of FDI and trade) and then starts to fall once that openness reaches a critical point. Chen (2016) finds that FDI has directly contributed to reducing urban–rural income inequality through employment creation for rural unskilled labour, knowledge spillovers from labour movement and economic development of the local economy, which contribute to increasing rural household incomes. Chen (2017) finds that the impact of FDI on urban–rural income inequality is not linear. Overall, empirical studies reveal that while FDI in China has contributed to a widening of the income gap between the coastal and inland regions, it has also contributed to a reduction in income inequality, especially urban–rural income inequality, as FDI continues to increase.

Urbanisation

Urbanisation is the shift of population from rural to urban areas and the gradual increase in the proportion of people living in urban areas. People are motivated to leave the primary sector to work in the secondary and tertiary sectors and migrate from rural areas to urban areas because of push factors from the countryside and pull factors from the city. On the one hand, during the process of economic development and the expansion of industrialisation and urbanisation, the traditional agricultural sector will decline and many farmers will lose their land, which will produce a large surplus of rural labourers, who will be pushed into cities to look for jobs. On the other hand, the expansion of modern manufacturing and services sectors in cities will provide a lot of employment opportunities and higher incomes, which will pull surplus rural labour into urban areas.

How has FDI impacted China's urbanisation rate? By the end of 2016, China had attracted US$1.35 trillion in FDI stock, of which 97 per cent was in the secondary and tertiary sectors. FDI has therefore played a significant role in China's economic development and structural change and has greatly enhanced both the push and pull forces for urbanisation.

The share of the value of the primary sector in GDP declined from 27.9 per cent in 1978 to 9.2 per cent in 2014, while the share of the value of the secondary and tertiary sectors increased from 72.1 per cent to 90.8 per cent in the same period. Despite the decline of the primary sector, however, China's agricultural productivity has grown rapidly since the start of reforms in 1978. The large volumes of FDI inflows have led to more efficient resource allocation, rapid dissemination of new agricultural technologies (including improved seed varieties and animal breeds) and the widespread application of agricultural mechanisation. These have laid a broad foundation for improved agricultural productivity (Wang et al. 2013; Zhang and Wan 2015). The decline of the share of the primary sector in the national economy and the increase in agricultural productivity have produced large numbers of surplus rural labourers, many of whom have been pushed to migrate to urban areas to look for new employment opportunities.

Second, FDI inflows have led to large-scale land acquisition in China (Li et al. 2016), in which governments acquire rural land to lease to urban businesses, especially to FDI firms. In China, land acquisition has been a common practice for local governments to boost economic growth. While the pace of industrialisation and urbanisation accelerates due to the effects of FDI inflows, Chinese officials estimate that approximately 2 million rural residents lose their land each year (Nelson 2012). Once an agreement is reached between local governments and rural collectives, farmers receive compensation and are moved to newly built resettlement housing in urban or peri-urban areas, becoming in effect formal urban residents (Li et al. 2016).

In terms of the pull factors, while FDI has predominately flowed into the secondary and tertiary sectors, it has led to the rapid development of labour-intensive and export-oriented manufacturing sectors. This has created huge employment opportunities and has absorbed most of the surplus rural labour in urban areas. As a result, FDI firms have hired large numbers of rural migrants. For example, in the manufacturing sector, FDI firms hired more than 26 million workers, accounting for one-third of China's manufacturing labour force in 2008 (Chen 2011); and in the national economy, FDI firms hired 29.6 million workers or 7.5 per cent of China's total urban employment in 2014 (NBS various issues). Therefore, the increasing labour demand in urban areas due to FDI inflows will continue to pull surplus rural labour to the cities.

Second, FDI firms in China tend to pay their employees higher wages than do domestic firms. In the manufacturing sector, on average, the wages paid by FDI firms are more than two times higher than those of domestic firms (Chen 2011). This not only increases the average wage in the manufacturing sector, but also can produce positive spillover effects on the wages of domestic firms when they compete in the labour market. In addition, FDI may also increase overall income levels in urban areas. Both factors will encourage surplus rural labour to move to cities to seek new jobs and higher incomes.

Empirical studies using national, regional and provincial-level data find that FDI has made a significant contribution to urbanisation in China. However, this positive impact is greater in coastal than in inland provinces (for example, Shi and Hamnett 2002; Zhang 2002; Chubarov and Brooker 2013). A number of studies using city-level data for all prefecture cities in China find similarly positive impacts. These impacts, however, vary from region to region, with a positive impact in coastal cities, but no significant impact in inland cities (Wu and Chen 2016). In addition, FDI in the coastal region has a negative interregional impact on urbanisation in inland cities (Chen and Wu 2017). This is related to the massive migration of labour from inland rural areas to coastal urban areas because of the large volume of FDI inflows there, which impedes the process of inland urbanisation.

Conclusion

During the past four decades, China's change of attitude from restricting to passively attracting and then to actively seeking inward FDI has been fully reflected in the evolution of its FDI policies, laws and regulations. In all policy relating to FDI, the Chinese Government has been taking a positive but gradual approach to reform. In general, this process has proved relatively successful, which has been reflected in the quality of the evolving foreign investment environment and the rapid growth of FDI inflows into China.

Although China has achieved substantial progress in its FDI policy liberalisation, its current FDI policy can be further improved, particularly in respect to transparency, market access and the protection of intellectual property rights. With respect to the principle of transparency, China maintains a complex application process for FDI approval, which could be simplified and made more transparent through further policy liberalisation.

In terms of market access, although the 2017 catalogue signals an attempt to build a friendlier investment environment for foreign investors in China, it does not remove as many restrictions as those investors had hoped. The European Union Chamber of Commerce in China (2017), for example, said the catalogue falls short of expectations, and they would like to see it removed entirely in favour of a shorter and more simplified negative list. The protection of intellectual property rights has long been an issue in China. The weak enforcement of such protection not only has a negative impact on foreign investors' decisions to bring technology into the country, but also could have negative impacts on China's industrial upgrading and the diffusion of knowledge spillovers from FDI to the domestic economy (Chen 2011). Although there have been some improvements, especially since China's accession to the WTO, it is still very important for China to further strengthen intellectual property rights protection.

The uneven regional distribution of FDI, which is concentrated in the coastal region, has greatly contributed to the economic growth of coastal provinces. However, empirical studies reveal that this has had negative impacts on inland provinces in terms of economic growth, urban–rural income inequality and urbanisation rates (for example, Fu 2004; Chen 2015, 2017). China should therefore design policies to help improve economic and technological conditions in inland regions, as well as the overall investment environment, to attract greater FDI inflows. The launch of the Western Development Strategy in 1998 was an important step in the right direction and the implementation of the One Belt and One Road initiative since 2013 will further improve the investment environment in the inland regions. At the same time, these regions should maximise their advantages of cheap labour and land to attract FDI and domestic firms from the coastal region and abroad, to promote economic growth and development. Finally, China should encourage and enhance knowledge spillovers from FDI to its economy. The Chinese Government should encourage contact, information exchange, production and technological cooperation, joint R&D activities, industrial linkages as well as competition between FDI firms and domestic firms in general and between coastal FDI firms and inland firms in particular, to accelerate the diffusion of positive knowledge spillovers from FDI to China's economy.

References

Aitken, B., Hanson, H. and Harrison, A. (1997), Spillovers, foreign direct investment, and export behaviour, *Journal of International Economics* 43(1): 103–32. doi.org/10.1016/S0022-1996(96)01464-X.

Barrios, S., Gorg, H. and Strobl, E. (2003), Explaining firms' export behaviour: R&D, spillovers and the destination market, *Oxford Bulletin of Economics and Statistics* 65(4): 475–96. doi.org/10.1111/1468-0084.t01-1-00058.

Buck, T., Liu, X., Wei, Y. and Liu, X. (2007), The trade development path and export spillovers in China: A missing link?, *Management International Review* 47(5): 683–706. doi.org/10.1007/s11575-007-0040-2.

Buckley, P., Clegg, J., Wang, C. and Cross, A. (2002), FDI, regional differences and economic growth: Panel data evidence from China, *Transnational Corporations* 2(1): 1–28.

Caves, R. (1996), *Multinational Enterprise and Economic Analysis*, 2nd edn, Cambridge: Cambridge University Press.

Chen, C. (1999), The impact of FDI and trade, in Y. Wu (ed.), *Foreign Direct Investment and Economic Growth in China*, Cheltenham, UK: Edward Elgar.

Chen, C. (2011), *Foreign Direct Investment in China: Location determinants, investor differences and economic impacts*, Cheltenham, UK: Edward Elgar. doi.org/10.4337/9781781001141.

Chen, C. (2015), Do inland provinces benefit from coastal foreign direct investment in China?, *China & World Economy* 23(3): 22–41. doi.org/10.1111/cwe.12112.

Chen, C. (2016), The impact of foreign direct investment on urban–rural income inequality: Evidence from China, *China Agricultural Economic Review* 8(3): 480–97. doi.org/10.1108/CAER-09-2015-0124.

Chen, C. (2017), *Foreign Direct Investment and the Chinese Economy: A critical assessment*, Cheltenham, UK: Edward Elgar. doi.org/10.4337/9781785369735.

Chen, C. and Wu, Y. (2017), Interregional impact of foreign direct investment on China's inland urbanisation, *Singapore Economic Review* 63(1): 1–21.

Chen, C., Chang, L. and Zhang, Y. (1995), The role of foreign direct investment in China's post-1978 economic development, *World Development* 23(4): 691–703. doi.org/10.1016/0305-750X(94)00143-M.

Chen, C., Sheng, Y. and Findlay, C. (2013), Export spillovers of FDI on domestic firms, *Review of International Economics* 21(5): 841–56. doi.org/10.1111/roie.12074.

Cheung, K. (2010), Spillover effects of FDI via exports on innovation performance of China's high-technology industries, *Journal of Contemporary China* 19(65): 541–57. doi.org/10.1080/10670561003666152.

China Economy Net (2016), China's Gini coefficient is 0.462 in 2015: The lowest in 12 years, [in Chinese], *China Economy Net*, 19 January. Available from: www.ce.cn/xwzx/gnsz/gdxw/201601/19/t20160119_8372526.shtml.

Chubarov, I. and Brooker, D. (2013), Multiple pathways to global city formation: A functional approach and review of recent evidence in China, *Cities* 35(8): 181–9. doi.org/10.1016/j.cities.2013.05.008.

Dees, S. (1998), Foreign direct investment in China: Determinants and effects, *Economics of Planning* 31(2): 175–94. doi.org/10.1023/A:1003576930461.

Dunning, J. (1993), *Multinational Enterprises and the Global Economy*, Wokingham, UK: Addison-Wesley.

European Union Chamber of Commerce in China (2017), Revised foreign investment catalogue falls short of expectations, Press release, 5 July, Beijing: European Union Chamber of Commerce in China. Available from: www.europeanchamber.com.cn/en/press-releases/2568/revised_foreign_investment_catalogue_falls_short_of_expectations.

Fu, X. (2004), Limited linkages from growth engines and regional disparities in China, *Journal of Comparative Economics* 32(1): 148–64. doi.org/10.1016/j.jce.2003.10.004.

Greenaway, D., Sousa, N. and Wakelin, K. (2004), Do domestic firms learn to export from multinationals?, *European Journal of Political Economy* 20(4): 1027–43. doi.org/10.1016/j.ejpoleco.2003.12.006.

Hu, X. and Ma, Y. (1999), International intra-industry trade of China, *Review of World Economics* 135(1): 82–101. doi.org/10.1007/BF02708160.

Jalil, A. (2012), Modelling income inequality and openness in the framework of Kuznets curve: New evidence from China, *Economic Modelling* 29(2): 309–15. doi.org/10.1016/j.econmod.2011.10.012.

Javorcik, B. (2004), Does foreign direct investment increase the productivity of domestic firms? In search of spillovers through backward linkages, *The American Economic Review* 94(3): 605–27. doi.org/10.1257/0002828041464605.

Kneller, R. and Pisu, M. (2007), Industrial linkages and export spillovers from FDI, *The World Economy* 30(1): 105–34. doi.org/10.1111/j.1467-9701.2007.00874.x.

Krugman, P. and Obstfeld, M. (1991), *International Economics: Theory and policy*, 2nd edn, New York: Harper Collins.

Kuznets, S. (1955), Economic growth and income inequality, *American Economic Review* 45(1): 1–28.

Lardy, N. (1995), The role of foreign trade and investment in China's economic transformation, *The China Quarterly* 144: 1065–82. doi.org/10.1017/S0305741000004732.

Lee, E. and Vivarelli, M. (2006), *The social impact of globalization in the developing countries*, IZA Discussion Paper No. 1925, Bonn: Institute of Labor Economics. Available from: ftp.iza.org/dp1925.pdf.

Li, B., Chen, C. and Hu, B. (2016), Governing urbanization and the new urbanization plan in China, *Environment and Urbanization* 28(2): 515–34. doi.org/10.1177/0956247816647345.

Li, Y. (2003), The impact of FDI on trade: Evidence from China's bilateral trade, *Journal of the Academy of Business and Economics* 2(2): 1–11.

Lin, S., Kim, D. and Wu, Y. (2013), Foreign direct investment and income inequality: Human capital matters, *Journal of Regional Science* 53(5): 874–96. doi.org/10.1111/jors.12077.

Liu, X., He, C., Lu, Z., Fan, B. and Zhou, J. (eds) (1993), *Guide to China's Foreign Economic and Trade Policies*, Beijing: Economic Management Press.

Liu, X., Wang, C. and Wei, Y. (2001), Causal links between FDI and trade in China, *China Economic Review* 12(2–3): 190–202.

Ma, A. (2006), Export spillovers to Chinese firms: Evidence from provincial data, *Journal of Chinese Economic and Business Studies* 4(2): 127–49. doi.org/10.1080/14765280600736908.

Ministry of Commerce (MOC) (various issues), *Foreign Investment Report*, Beijing: Ministry of Commerce of China.

Ministry of Commerce (MOC) (2015), *Statistics on FDI in China, 2015*, Beijing: Ministry of Commerce of China.

National Bureau of Statistics (NBS) (various issues), *China Statistical Yearbook*, Beijing: China Statistics Press.

Nelson, C. (2012), Land reform effects in China, *China Business Review: The Magazine of the US–China Business Council*, 1 October. Available from: www.chinabusinessreview.com/land-reform-efforts-in-china/.

Shi, Y. and Hamnett, C. (2002), The potential and prospect for global cities in China: In the context of the world system, *Geoforum* 33(1): 121–35. doi.org/10.1016/S0016-7185(01)00026-4.

Shirk, S. (1994), *How China Opened its Door: The political success of the PRC's foreign trade and investment reforms*, Washington, DC: The Brookings Institution.

Sun, S. (2009), How does FDI affect domestic firms' exports? Industrial evidence, *World Economy* 32(8): 1203–22. doi.org/10.1111/j.1467-9701.2009.01175.x.

Sun, S. (2012), The role of FDI in domestic exporting: Evidence from China, *Journal of Asian Economics* 23(4): 434–41. doi.org/10.1016/j.asieco.2012.03.004.

Tang, S., Selvanathan, E. and Selvanathan, S. (2008), Foreign direct investment, domestic investment and economic growth in China: A time series analysis, *World Economy* 31(10): 1292–309. doi.org/10.1111/j.1467-9701.2008.01129.x.

Tsai, P. (1995), Foreign direct investment and income inequality: Further evidence, *World Development* 23(3): 469–83. doi.org/10.1016/0305-750X(95)00136-Z.

Tuan, C., Ng, L. and Zhao, B. (2009), China's post-economic reform growth: The role of FDI and productivity progress, *Journal of Asian Economics* 20(3): 280–93. doi.org/10.1016/j.asieco.2009.02.010.

Ucal, M., Bilgin, M. and Haug, A. (2014), *Income inequality and FDI: Evidence with Turkish data*, MPRA Paper No. 61104, Munich: Munich Personal RePEc Archive. Available from: mpra.ub.uni-muenchen.de/61104/.

United Nations Conference on Trade and Development (UNCTAD) (various issues), *World Investment Report*, New York and Geneva: United Nations Publications.

Wan, G., Lu, M. and Chen, Z. (2007), Globalization and regional income inequality: Empirical evidence from within China, *Review of Income and Wealth* 53(1): 35–59. doi.org/10.1111/j.1475-4991.2007.00217.x.

Wang, S., Tuan, F., Gale, F., Somwaru, A. and Hansen, J. (2013), China's regional agricultural productivity growth in 1985–2007: A multilateral comparison, *Agricultural Economics* 44(2): 241–51. doi.org/10.1111/agec.12008.

Wei, J. (1994), *Chinese Foreign Investment Laws and Policies: Evolution and transformation*, Westport, CT: Quorum Books.

Whalley, J. and Xin, X. (2010), China's FDI and non-FDI economies and the sustainability of future high Chinese growth, *China Economic Review* 21(1): 123–35. doi.org/10.1016/j.chieco.2009.11.004.

Wu, Y. and Chen, C. (2016), The impact of foreign direct investment on urbanization in China, *Journal of the Asia Pacific Economy* 21(3): 339–56. doi.org/10.1080/13547860.2016.1176641.

Xu, X. and Sheng, Y. (2012), Are FDI spillovers regional? Firm-level evidence from China, *Journal of Asian Economics* 23(3): 244–58. doi.org/10.1016/j.asieco.2010.11.009.

Yao, S. and Wei, K. (2007), Economic growth in the presence of FDI: The perspective of newly industrializing economies, *Journal of Comparative Economics* 35(1): 211–34. doi.org/10.1016/j.jce.2006.10.007.

Zhang, K. (2002), What explains China's rising urbanization in the reform era?, *Urban Studies* 39(12): 2301–15. doi.org/10.1080/0042098022000033881.

Zhang, X. and Zhang, K. (2003), How does globalization affect regional inequality within a developing country? Evidence from China, *Journal of Development Studies* 39(4): 47–67. doi.org/10.1080/713869425.

Zhang, Y. and Wan, G. (2015), International trade and urbanization in developing countries: Evidence from Asia, *Social Sciences in China* 36(2): 186–204. doi.org/10.1080/02529203.2015.1029679.

Zheng, P., Siler, P. and Giorgioni, G. (2004), FDI and the export performance of Chinese indigenous firms: A regional approach, *Journal of Chinese Economic and Business Studies* 2(1): 55–71. doi.org/10.1080/1476528031000l631381.

30. Outward direct investment: Restricted, relaxed and regulated stages of development

Bijun Wang and Kailin Gao

Introduction

China's four decades of economic reform have been aimed at liberalising markets, upgrading the industrial structure, enhancing enterprises' competitiveness and integrating China into the global economy. China's foray into outward direct investment (ODI) took shape gradually. In 2016, China became the world's second-largest outward investor after the United States, with $196.2 billion of ODI flows.[1]

This chapter analyses the development of China's ODI activities and regulations over the past 40 years, and divides the evolution of its ODI policies into three stages, each of which was defined by a distinct approach: the 'restricted' stage (1978–99), the 'relaxed' stage (2000–16) and the 'regulated' stage (2016 onwards).

Before 2000, capital shortages prompted China to restrict capital outflows and to invite capital inflows. By the end of 1990, China's ODI stock was only $4.5 billion, accounting for 0.2 per cent of the global total. In 1991, the Opinions on Strengthening the Management of Overseas Investment Projects submitted by the State Planning Commission[2] to the State Council said that China did not possess the conditions to pursue large-scale outward investment. This document became the most influential source of policy guidance over the next decade, setting 'restriction' as the main tone of China's ODI policy (Li 2008). Meanwhile, due to fears of overseas speculation and the loss of state assets, the government did not relax the approval procedures for investing abroad.

In the 1990s, China was gradually transformed from a planned to a socialist market economy. Following its accession to the World Trade Organization (WTO) in 2001, China set out on a new journey of liberalisation and its overseas investment began to take off. 'Going out' was one of the key strategies in China's Tenth Five-Year Plan (2001–05), to enhance the international competiveness of Chinese enterprises

1 All dollar amounts in this chapter are US$.

2 The State Planning Commission, founded in 1952, was the predecessor to the National Development and Reform Commission (NDRC). It was renamed the State Development Planning Commission (SDPC) in 1998. After merging with the State Council Office for Restructuring the Economic System (SCORES) and part of the State Economic and Trade Commission (SETC) in 2003, the SDPC was restructured into the NDRC.

(Zhang 2011). To support the implementation of this strategy, there was a shift in ODI regulations from a requirement for examination and approval to simply approval in 2004.

The relaxed policy drove the growth of China's ODI flows, while the Global Financial Crisis (GFC) opened doors to Chinese investors after 2008 (see Figure 30.1). In response to the growing enthusiasm for overseas investment, the Ministry of Commerce (MOFCOM), in 2009, and the National Development and Reform Commission (NDRC), in 2011, further decentralised their approval authority. The system managing China's ODI stepped into its 'registration-based and approval-supplemented' stage in 2014, greatly facilitating the 'going out' of Chinese enterprises.

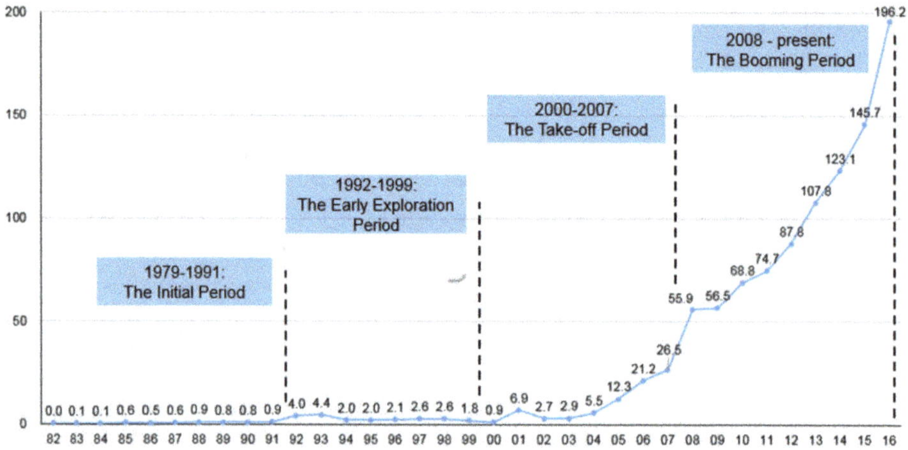

Figure 30.1 Development stages of China's ODI flows ($ billion)

Sources: ODI flow data for 1982–2001 from the UNCTAD Statistics (unctadstat.unctad.org/EN/); and for 2002–16, from NDRC (2017a).

However, large-scale and imbalanced ODI activities in 2016 caused Chinese policymakers to strengthen regulations. After a series of interim measures, Chinese nonfinancial ODI dropped by 29.4 per cent in 2017. The growth in overseas investment revealed weaknesses in legal compliance, social responsibility, investment decisions and debt structure. Aware of these risks, the NDRC issued ODI regulations at the end of 2017, aiming to strengthen supervision. Rather than reflecting a lack of support for investors, this move indicates the Chinese Government's intention to improve investment quality and efficiency and to support eligible enterprises in going global.

Section two discusses the 'restricted' stage of ODI, from 1978 to 1999; section three summarises the 'relaxed' stage, from 2000 to 2016; section four introduces the 'regulated' stage, from 2016 onwards; while section five concludes.

Restricted stage, 1978–99

Before 2000, capital shortages prompted China to invite capital inflows and restrict capital outflows. To invest overseas, Chinese enterprises had to apply for approval on a case-by-case basis, which led directly to a very small amount of overseas investment. From 1982 to 1999,[3] China's average annual ODI flow was only $1.5 billion. By the end of 1999, China's ODI stock was $27 billion, representing 0.4 per cent of the global total, ranking China number 23 in the world.

For the very few Chinese ODI activities in this 'restricted' stage, a key motivation was facilitating trade and improving access to foreign resources. From 1979 to 1993, 61 per cent of Chinese ODI flowed to Hong Kong and Macau, establishing window and trading companies. The second-largest destination was North America (15 per cent), followed by Oceania (8 per cent), Asia-Pacific excluding Hong Kong and Macau (5 per cent), Central and Eastern Europe (5 per cent) and Africa, Latin America and Western Europe (2 per cent each) (UNCTAD 1995). Until 1994, 60 per cent of Chinese ODI flowed to trade-related services, followed by approximately 25 per cent in natural resources and 15 per cent in manufacturing (Cai 1999).

The initial period, 1979–91

Before 1991, few laws or regulations were directed at ODI.[4] Only state-owned enterprises (SOEs) were allowed to invest overseas and approval on a case-by-case basis was required regardless of the investment amount. Chinese outward investors at that time were companies developed to conduct foreign trade and a small number of companies engaged in primary processing industries (NDRC 2017a). From 1982 to 1991, China's annual average ODI flow was only $537 million, with the stock accumulating to $5.4 billion.

There were two reasons for the small scale. Stringent foreign exchange controls constrained enterprises. With small volumes of exports and scarce foreign currency, China restricted foreign exchange to purchases of urgently needed materials, equipment and technologies from overseas. Enterprises were required to apply to the State Council for special approval for foreign exchange used in overseas investment. This arduous procedure dampened firms' ODI activities.

3 Data on China's ODI flows are available after 1982 from the United Nations Conference on Trade and Development (UNCTAD) Statistics (unctadstat.unctad.org/EN/).

4 Regulations issued before 1991 include, but are not limited to, the Provisional Regulations Governing the Control and the Approval Procedure for Opening Non-Trade Enterprises Overseas (July 1985) and Regulations Governing the Approval for Setting Up Trade-Related Enterprises Overseas (July 1988). Both were issued by MOFCOM. See Appendix for the major ODI regulations in China from 1978 to 2017.

On the other hand, China was still a centrally planned economy during this period and enterprises were not motivated to invest overseas. At that time, SOEs were the mainstay of the national economy, the raw materials needed for production were centrally organised and their products sold well. Facing little market pressure, Chinese enterprises were not incentivised to invest abroad. During this period, the private economy was still in its infancy and conditions for globalisation were insufficient.

The early exploration period, 1992–99

In the 1990s, persistent trade surpluses and high foreign direct investment (FDI) inflows helped China accumulate foreign exchange. Its foreign reserve holdings increased from $21.7 billion in 1991 to $154.7 billion in 1999. Meanwhile, China gradually transformed from a planned to a socialist market economy, and the market increasingly became an important channel of resource allocation.

Faced with increasingly fierce competition, companies needed both to obtain cheaper and more reliable supplies of raw materials and to open up international markets for larger sales. Outward investment therefore became important. The average ODI flow from 1992 to 1999 was $2.7 billion (0.8 per cent of the global average), compared with only $537 million from 1982 to 1991 (0.4 per cent). China's ODI development in the 1990s was strong in assembly and processing as well as energy and resources.

Despite the stringent restrictions imposed in 1991, Deng Xiaoping's southern tour in 1992 injected confidence into China's overseas investment activities. China's ODI flow jumped from $931 million in 1991 to $4 billion in 1992 and $4.4 billion in 1993. In 1994, China unified the dual-track exchange rate system and the one-time depreciation of about 50 per cent[5] led directly to a 55 per cent reduction in China's ODI flow, from $4.4 billion in 1993 to $2 billion in 1994.

ODI policy was further tightened in the wake of the East Asian Financial Crisis from 1997. China's ODI flow stagnated at just above $2.5 billion in 1997 and 1998, and the number of ODI projects approved dramatically declined.

5 In 1994, China unified its dual exchange rate system by aligning official and swap centre rates, officially devaluing the yuan to the swap centre rate of 8.7 to the dollar, which was much weaker than the official rate of 5.8 to the dollar.

The relaxed stage, 2000–16

With its WTO accession in 2001, China embarked on a new journey of liberalisation. From 2000 to 2016, China continued to relax its ODI regulations, assuming an increasingly prominent position in global overseas investment. From 2002 to 2016,[6] China's ODI flow registered a 35.8 per cent average annual growth rate, and its global ranking (share) increased from 26 (0.5 per cent) to second (13.5 per cent). China's ODI flows exceeded FDI inflows from 2014 to 2016.[7]

Simplify approval procedures, delegate approval authority and increase approval efficiency

The 'going out' strategy proposed in the early 2000s supported a shift from restriction to relaxation and then encouragement of ODI. Meanwhile, free trade agreements, double taxation avoidance agreements and bilateral investment treaties with many countries improved conditions for Chinese enterprises investing abroad.

Although the going out strategy was proposed in 2000, the rules for its implementation were not introduced until 2004. In July of that year, the State Council issued its Decision on Reforming the Investment Systems, declaring a shift in ODI regulations from a requirement for examination and approval to simply approval. ODI projects without government investment were to seek approval or registration, depending on the sector and the value of the investment.

The main approval departments are the NDRC (for ODI projects) and MOFCOM (for ODI enterprises). The State Administration of Foreign Exchange (SAFE) is responsible for managing foreign exchange. The Ministry of Finance (MOF), the State-owned Assets Supervision and Administration Commission of the State Council (SASAC) and the Ministry of Industry and Information Technology (MIIT) are responsible for managing state assets, with the People's Bank of China (PBC), the China Banking Regulatory Commission (CBRC) and the China Insurance Regulatory Commission (CIRC) managing the overseas investments of financial institutions.

In October 2004, the NDRC and MOFCOM promulgated detailed policies to simplify ODI approval procedures, delegate approval authority and increase the efficiency of approvals. Since enterprises would be responsible for their gains and losses, project proposals and feasibility reports were no longer required. The NDRC's approval threshold was raised from the original $1 million to $30–200 million for

6 Data on China's ODI flows from NDRC (2017a) are available from 2002.

7 This refers to FDI actually utilised in China. The data come from the National Bureau of Statistics (NBS) National Data (data.stats.gov.cn/english/easyquery.htm?cn=C01).

resource development projects and $10–50 million for other projects.[8] Resource development projects under $30 million and non–resource development projects under $10 million implemented by central state–owned enterprises (central SOEs) had to be registered with the NDRC. If local enterprises[9] implemented such projects, approval was required from the provincial development and reform commissions. The NDRC was required to give a result within 20 working days (with an extension of up to 10 working days), down from the original 60 working days. The response time in each procedure was also strictly specified, aiming to avoid delays in domestic approval procedures that would hamper overseas investment.

These policy changes contributed to the growth of China's ODI flow, which almost doubled from $2.9 billion in 2003 to $5.5 billion in 2004 and $12.3 billion in 2005.

Most ODI projects only require registration

In the aftermath of the GFC in 2008, numerous enterprises from developed countries were faced with a shortage of funds, shrinking markets and operational difficulties. Their market value shrivelled, opening doors to Chinese enterprises. While global FDI inflows fell by 14 per cent in 2008 (UNCTAD 2009), China's ODI flow more than doubled, to $55.9 billion, in 2008.

In response to the growth in overseas investment, MOFCOM, in 2009, and the NDRC, in 2011, further decentralised their approval authority.[10] MOFCOM was to approve only projects with investment over $100 million, and was required to make its decisions within three working days. The NDRC's approval threshold was further increased, from the previous $30–200 million for resource development projects and $10–50 million for other projects, to more than $300 million for resource development projects and more than $100 million for other projects.[11] MOFCOM introduced three other measures to facilitate ODI. First, MOFCOM or local commercial departments no longer needed to seek advice from China's embassies and consulates except for investments exceeding $100 million, some special ODI

8 Resource development projects with an investment of over $200 million and projects using more than $50 million in foreign exchange should seek approval from the State Council.

9 Enterprises other than central SOEs are referred to as local enterprises, which include, but are not limited to, SOEs owned by provincial, city-level and county-level governments, privately owned enterprises and foreign enterprises.

10 In 2009, MOFCOM published revised Administrative Measures for Overseas Investment. In 2011, the NDRC released its Notice on Decentralization and Approval of Overseas Investment Projects.

11 According to the Notice on Decentralization and Approval of Overseas Investment Projects released by NDRC in 2011, special projects, regardless of the investment amount, should first be reviewed by the provincial DRCs or central SOEs, and then approved by the NDRC. Otherwise, they should be approved first by the NDRC and then by the State Council. These special projects include investments in a country with no diplomatic relations with China, countries under international sanctions and those afflicted by war and turmoil, as well as investments in sensitive industries including telecommunications, cross-border water utilisation, large-scale land development, electricity networks and news media.

projects[12] or investments in energy and resources sectors. Second, the environmental and safety status of host economies as well as the destination distribution of Chinese ODI would be excluded from the scope of review. Third, the reinvestment of Chinese overseas enterprises need only be registered with MOFCOM within one month of completing legal formalities.

In 2014, the release by the NDRC of the Measures for the Administration of Approval and Registration of Overseas Investment Projects (Order No. 9) and MOFCOM's revised Administrative Measures for Overseas Investment (Order No. 3) shifted Chinese ODI to a 'registration-based and approval-supplemented' system.

Under this system, only projects involving sensitive industries or countries or with Chinese investment of over $1 billion needed to obtain official approval. Other projects needed only to submit relevant materials and file a record directly with their provincial DRC, instead of submitting to the county, city and provincial levels. The provincial DRCs then submitted an opinion on the project and a report to the NDRC for registration.

Order No. 9 created a relaxed institutional environment for established Chinese overseas enterprises. If they wanted to reinvest abroad, they were exempt from the approval and registration procedures, and the response time was guaranteed. For general projects in line with the state's ODI policies, the NDRC must issue a confirmation letter within seven working days of receiving the project information report.

At present, registration is the primary regulatory process for Chinese ODI projects. From the release of Order No. 3 on 9 September 2014 to 8 September 2016, MOFCOM and local commercial authorities processed 21,157 ODI cases. Of these, only 0.5 per cent went through the approval process, while 99.5 per cent went through the more convenient registration system. This has greatly facilitated the process of 'going out' for Chinese enterprises.

China becomes the world's second-largest ODI nation

These policies lifted China's levels of ODI more than threefold within nine years, and China became the world's second-largest source of ODI flows in 2016.

By the end of 2016, China's ODI stock amounted to $1.36 trillion, covering 190 countries and presenting the following four characteristics (see Table 30.1).

12 According to the revised Administrative Measures for Overseas Investment published by MOFCOM in 2009, the special projects include investments in specific countries or regions, investments related to multinational or regional interests and the establishment of a company overseas for special purposes (the list of specific countries or regions was determined by MOFCOM with the Ministry of Foreign Affairs and other relevant departments).

China's ODI stock was concentrated largely in Asia (67 per cent), followed by Latin America (15.3 per cent), Europe (6.4 per cent), North America (5.6 per cent), Africa (2.9 per cent) and Oceania (2.8 per cent). In Asia, the major investment destinations were Hong Kong (China) (57.5 per cent) and Association of Southeast Asian Nations (ASEAN) members (5.3 per cent). And among the ASEAN countries, Singapore (2.5 per cent) and Indonesia (0.7 per cent) attracted the most investment.

Tax havens remained important destinations. Among these, Cayman Islands (7.7 per cent) and the British Virgins Islands (6.5 per cent) ranked second and third, respectively, in absorbing China's ODI stock. In these regions, investment often takes the form of entities controlled by Chinese enterprises or platforms moving capital across borders without actual production facilities.

Developing economies continued to draw the lion's share of China's ODI stock (85.9 per cent), compared with 14.1 per cent for developed economies. Specifically, Hong Kong (China) and ASEAN members accounted for 67 per cent and 6.1 per cent, respectively, of China's ODI stock in developing and transitional economies, while the European Union and the United States accounted for 36.5 per cent and 31.7 per cent, respectively, in developed economies.

China's stock of ODI in the nations included in the One Belt and One Road scheme reached $129.4 billion in 2016, representing 9.5 per cent of the total. The major recipients were Singapore, Russia, Indonesia, Laos, Kazakhstan and Vietnam.

Table 30.1 Top 10 destinations for China's ODI stock, 2003 and 2016

Rank	2016			2003		
	Destination	Stock ($ billion)	Share (%)	Destination	Stock ($ billion)	Share (%)
1	Hong Kong (China)	780.8	57.5	Hong Kong (China)	24.6	74.2
2	Cayman Islands	104.2	7.7	Cayman Islands	3.7	11.1
3	British Virgin Islands	88.8	6.5	British Virgin Islands	0.6	1.6
4	United States	60.6	4.4	United States	0.5	1.5
5	Singapore	33.5	2.5	Macau (China)	0.5	1.3
6	Australia	33.4	2.5	Australia	0.4	1.3
7	Netherlands	20.6	1.5	Korea	0.2	0.7
8	United Kingdom	17.6	1.3	Singapore	0.2	0.5
9	Russia	13.0	1.0	Thailand	0.2	0.5
10	Canada	12.7	0.9	Zambia	0.1	0.4
Total		1,165.2	85.8		31.0	93.1

Sources: MOFCOM et al. (various issues).

Comparing 2016 with 2003, three changes have taken place in terms of regional distribution:

1. Chinese enterprises invested in more diverse destinations in 2016 than in 2003.
2. The shares of Hong Kong and Macau in China's ODI have dropped significantly. More and more Chinese enterprises are capable of investing directly in overseas destinations without the need to use Hong Kong or Macau as investment platforms.
3. Developed countries accounted for a growing share of China's ODI stock, rising from 7.4 per cent in 2009 to 14.1 per cent in 2016.[13] Particularly noticeable was the United States, whose share increased by 2.9 percentage points. The Netherlands and Canada significantly increased their rankings, to seventh and tenth, respectively, in 2016.[14]

Table 30.2 Sectoral distribution of China's ODI stock, 2006 and 2016

Sector	2016		2006	
	Stock ($ billion)	Share (%)	Stock ($ billion)	Share (%)
Leasing and business services	474.0	34.9	19.5	21.5
Financial intermediation	177.3	13.1	15.6	17.2
Wholesale and retail trades	169.2	12.5	13.0	14.3
Mining	152.4	11.2	18.0	19.8
Manufacturing	108.1	8.0	7.5	8.3
Information transmission, computer services and software	64.8	4.8	1.5	1.6
Real estate	46.1	3.4	2.0	2.2
Transport, storage and postal services	41.4	3.1	7.6	8.4
Construction	32.4	2.4	1.6	1.7
Production and supply of electricity, gas and water	22.8	1.7	–	–
Scientific research, technical services	19.72	1.5	1.12	1.2
Services to households and other services	16.9	1.2	1.2	1.3
Agriculture, forestry, animal husbandry and fisheries	14.9	1.1	0.8	0.9
Culture, sports and entertainment	7.9	0.6	–	–

13 The *Statistical Bulletin of China's Outward Foreign Direct Investment* began to calculate the share of China's ODI stock in developed countries in 2009.

14 The shares of China's ODI stock in the Netherlands and Canada are not available from MOFCOM et al. (various issues), as they released only the top 20 destinations.

Sector	2016		2006	
	Stock ($ billion)	Share (%)	Stock ($ billion)	Share (%)
Hotels and catering services	4.2	0.3	–	–
Management of water conservancy, environmental public facilities	3.6	0.3	0.9	1.0
Health, social security and social welfare	0.9	0.1	–	–
Education	0.7	0.1	–	–
Other	–	–	0.5	0.6

– not available

Note: Among the sectors covered, 'Leasing and business services' in 2016 was headed 'Business services' in 2003. The data for 2016 referred to the 'Scientific research, technical services' sector, but to 'Technical services and geologic prospecting' in 2003. Moreover, the 2003 *Statistical Bulletin of China's Outward Foreign Direct Investment* included the sector 'Other', while the 2016 bulletin did not.

Sources: MOFCOM et al. (various issues).

The share of resources declined while that of technology increased between 2006 and 2016[15] (see Table 30.2). The mining sector experienced the largest decline, which reflects the diminishing importance of resource-intensive industries in Chinese development and the slump in international commodity markets. Leasing and business services, information transmission, computer services and software all rose. The proportion in scientific research and technical services also expanded. More and more Chinese enterprises are looking to invest in overseas high-tech industries, to enhance their competitiveness and climb up the value chain.

Local enterprises are developing rapidly, and surpassed the investment levels of central SOEs for three years after 2014, becoming the main force for China's nonfinancial overseas investment. From 2003 to 2016, the share of local enterprises in China's nonfinancial ODI flows increased from 26.6 per cent to 83 per cent. However, the assets of central SOEs still constitute the main body of China's assets abroad, responsible for more than half, but their share dropped from 91.1 per cent in 2003 to 55.6 per cent in 2016 (Figure 30.2).

15 The 2003 *Statistical Bulletin of China's Outward Foreign Direct Investment* included only 11 sectors, compared with 14 in 2006 and 18 in 2016. To better illustrate changes in various sectors, we compare sectoral distribution between 2006 and 2016, rather than 2003 and 2016.

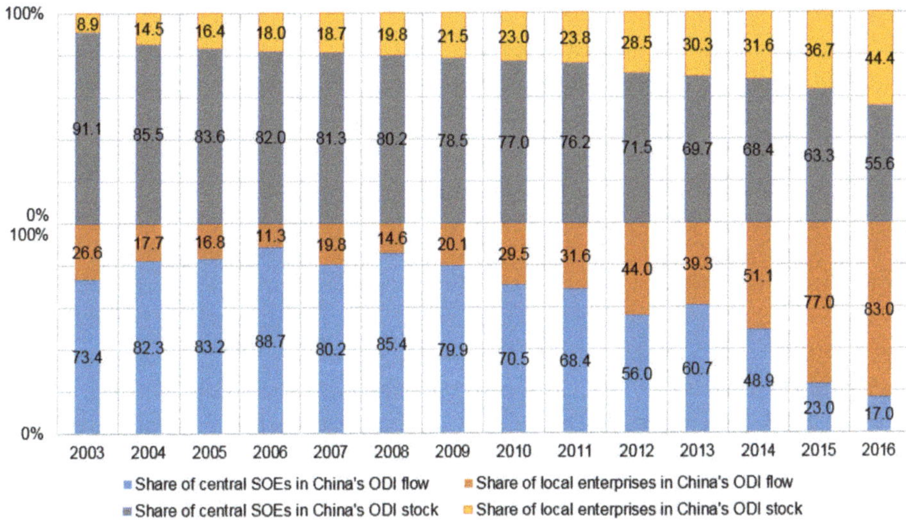

Figure 30.2 Shares of central SOEs and local enterprises in China's ODI flows and stock, 2003–16

Sources: MOFCOM et al. (various issues).

The regulated stage, 2016 onwards

The year 2016 was a turning point in China's ODI policies, which moved from a relaxed to a regulated setting. In 2016, global ODI dropped by 2 per cent, but China's ODI soared by 34.7 per cent, with its nonfinancial ODI developing even faster, by 49.3 per cent. Some industries have shown an unusually strong pattern: ODI flows in the hotels and catering industry increased by 124.8 per cent, followed by 121.4 per cent in culture, sports and entertainment industries and 95.8 per cent in real estate.[16]

Irrational ODI and potential risks alert Chinese policymakers

A weakening renminbi and China's rapidly shrinking foreign reserves worried the Chinese Government. From the end of 2016, Chinese policymakers began to strengthen the authenticity examination of overseas investments, paying close attention to ODI in real estate, hotels, cinemas, entertainment and sports clubs,

16 From 2008 to 2016, China's ODI flow registered an average growth rate of 27.8 per cent. However, over the same period, the three sectors—namely, hotels and catering services; culture, sports and entertainment; and real estate—grew at an alarming average annual rate of 111.4 per cent, 187.6 per cent and 54.1 per cent, respectively, which was well above the average growth of China's ODI flows. Data comes from the NBS National Data (data.stats.gov.cn/english/easyquery.htm?cn=C01).

which were regarded as 'irrational' due to their weak linkages to either the real economy or the firms' main businesses. In August 2017, the NDRC issued a guideline jointly with relevant departments, classifying ODI into 'encouraged', 'restricted' and 'prohibited' categories.[17] After a series of interim measures, Chinese nonfinancial ODI flows dropped by 29.4 per cent in 2017, with no new ODI projects in real estate, sports and entertainment.

Apart from 'irrational' outward investment, massive overseas investment has also posed three major challenges to China. First, some enterprises have low awareness of legal compliance and a weak sense of social responsibility, which has damaged the reputation of Chinese enterprises and products as well as China's image internationally. With China's capital going overseas, Chinese companies have begun to influence local communities in ODI destinations. However, some enterprises only value commercial efficiency and have poor awareness of production safety, and little concern for the safety of employees. Some enterprises use money to motivate excessive overtime, increase work intensity and extend working hours; they sometimes ignore local laws, hire workers without contracts or dismiss employees arbitrarily, causing frequent labour disputes. Some Chinese overseas companies rely on unconventional low-cost strategies, sacrificing product quality for low prices. Some pay insufficient attention to local environmental protection and do not strictly honour their contracts. Widely exposed misbehaviour of this nature has adversely affected the reputation of Chinese enterprises and products.

Second, large-scale Chinese ODI can adversely affect the country's balance of payments and exchange rate stability. Poor investment decisions and risk management often lead to financial losses, reducing the investment returns flowing back to China. Some enterprises illegally acquire foreign exchange, transfer assets abroad and engage in money laundering. Capital flight disguised in ODI activities has taken various forms.

Third, decision-making mistakes and high levels of debt have caused major economic losses for some ODI projects and may negatively affect Chinese domestic financial stability. Chinese enterprises are still newcomers to the international investment arena, lacking investment experience and having poor access to information. Most enterprises have not established subsidiaries and branches abroad, while some have set up only simple offices. This has limited enterprises' ability to establish long-term and stable relations with governments, nongovernmental organisations and communities in host countries. Poor decision-making and risk-taking can cause severe losses. Meanwhile, many Chinese enterprises rely mainly on large-

17 In August 2017, the NDRC, MOFCOM, the PBC and the Ministry of Foreign Affairs jointly issued the Guidance on Further Directing and Regulating the Direction of Overseas Investments, classifying China's ODI into 'encouraged', 'restricted' and 'prohibited' categories. The 'restricted' category includes real estate, hotels, cinemas, the entertainment industry and sport clubs.

scale borrowings to fund their overseas investment. High levels of debt impose serious financial pressures, increasing the probability of capital chain ruptures and aggravating China's financial risks.

Long-term institution building under way

Aware of these risks, the NDRC issued two important regulations at the end of 2017. The first was the Code of Conduct for Overseas Investment by Private Enterprises, issued on 18 December. It obliges private companies to improve their internal management, observe legal requirements at home and abroad, fulfil their social responsibilities, protect the environment and strengthen overseas risk management. The equivalent code of conduct for SOEs is being drafted. The second is the Administrative Measures for Overseas Investments by Enterprises (Order No. 11), issued on 26 December, which came into force on 1 March 2018 and replaces Order No. 9, issued in August 2014.

Order No. 11 includes three main policy changes to regulate overseas investment:

> It expands the transactions covered. In contrast with Order No. 9, Order No. 11 expressly covers overseas investment by foreign entities controlled by Chinese enterprises and citizens. It determines that to make a sensitive investment using a controlled foreign entity, the investor needs to seek approval from the NDRC.[18] To make a non-sensitive investment over $300 million using a controlled foreign entity, the investor needs to submit a report to the NDRC. No approval or registration is required. To make a non-sensitive investment below $300 million using a controlled entity, no approval, registration, or reporting is required.
>
> Order No. 11 contains regulatory mechanisms to improve collaborative supervision—including online monitoring, interviews, written inquiries and random verification—and project monitoring, including the introduction of project completion reports, significant adverse event reports and inquiries into important issues.
>
> Order No. 11 also improves disciplinary measures and proposes establishing a record of violations. It clarifies punishments for misconduct and violations including malicious partition, false declarations, unfair competition, illegal financing, failure to report when necessary, improperly obtaining approval or registration documents, implementing projects without approval and anything that threatens or harms the national interest or security. Meanwhile, an enterprise's violations record will be published on national credit information–sharing platforms to facilitate joint punishment with other relevant departments.

18 According to Order No. 11, sensitive projects include projects in sensitive countries or regions, and projects in sensitive industries. Sensitive countries or regions include those with no diplomatic relations with China, those afflicted by war and turmoil, those under international sanctions and other sensitive countries or regions. Sensitive industries include development, production and maintenance of weaponry, cross-border water utilisation, news media and other industries constrained under relevant Chinese laws, regulations and policies.

The recent policy changes do not signal diminished support for Chinese ODI. Order No. 11 adopts several approaches to facilitate overseas investment—for example, it eliminates the information report system and a confirmation letter from the NDRC is no longer required. It also allows local enterprises to file directly with the NDRC for approval and eliminates provincial-level review.

Challenges ahead and sharing opportunities

Despite rapid development, China's ODI faces both domestic and international pressures. Domestically, Chinese enterprises must confront value-chain upgrading, environmental sustainability and rising labour costs. There are many low-end products with excess inventories, while high-end sectors are heavily dependent on imports. Investors have difficulty adjusting to increasingly eco-friendly policies. Companies engaged in extensive resource-grabbing modes of production face an urgent need to transform and upgrade. Compared with other developing countries, China's advantage in low labour costs has gradually weakened. With China facing an ageing population, growing demand for labour in an expanding economy and the strengthening of demands for workers' rights, labour becomes more and more expensive.

Internationally, challenges include industrial restructuring, evolving international rules and new trends in investment regulations. The world is riding a new wave of industrial restructuring. The GFC has damaged the real economy in developed countries. Adjustments have been made through bankruptcy, mergers and acquisitions (M&A) and reorganisation. The increasing labour force in developing countries engaged in global production and the transformation of some emerging economies has forced the reindustrialisation of developed countries. At the same time, the development of new industries may bring about a new global industrial revolution. Production of shale gas in the United States and falling renewable energy costs in China and many other countries have triggered an energy revolution.

Western countries are establishing a comprehensive system of rules in trade, investment and services. Changes in the trade rules centre on three major negotiations: the 'east line' of the Trans-Pacific Partnership (TPP),[19] the 'west line' of the Transatlantic Trade and Investment Partnership (TTIP) and the 'middle line' of the international Trade in Services Agreement (TISA). One theme of these agreements is bolstering investment liberalisation, expanding the regulatory power and policy space of host governments, attaching greater importance to environmental and labour standards, reinforcing SOE regulations and promoting competition.

19 US President Donald Trump signed an executive order withdrawing the United States from the proposed Trans-Pacific Partnership trade deal in January 2017.

Despite the risks, challenges and difficulties ahead, the positive effects of China's overseas investment have been widely confirmed. These effects include improving firm productivity, expanding domestic employment, increasing domestic exports, improving export quality and accelerating the upgrading of trade structure. However, these positive effects are not inevitable. They are closely related to the capabilities of enterprises, the types of investment and the industries and host countries for that investment. Enterprises need to have a certain degree of absorptive capacity to manage all kinds of strategic assets acquired through ODI. To improve such capacity, enterprises will have to continuously accumulate human capital and increase R&D investment.

ODI is also an important channel by which China contributes to the world (Wang et al. 2014; Wang and Li 2017). On the one hand, overseas Chinese enterprises have contributed greatly to taxation and employment in host countries. In 2016, taxes paid by overseas Chinese enterprises totalled nearly $30 billion. At the end of that year, the total number of employees in Chinese ODI firms was 2.87 million, of which 1.43 million (46.9 per cent) were foreign employees. Job creation in Africa was even more significant. Chinese firms created 38,417 jobs in Africa in 2016—the most of any country, and more than three times the number of jobs created by US firms (Ernst & Young 2017). On the other hand, large volumes of China's ODI went into infrastructure, enhancing connectivity and promoting economic growth in developing countries. With more eligible enterprises going global under the supervision of the Chinese Government, greater contributions from technology transfer and industrial upgrading to the host economies are expected.

Concluding remarks

China is now the significant player in the international investment arena; however, ODI can be a double-edged sword. At present, the negative impacts of China's ODI are reflected mainly at the micro-enterprise level, including frequent investment mistakes, huge investment losses, difficulties in integration after M&A and failures to assimilate into host countries. At a national level, capital flight has taken place under the cover of outward investment. Firms' misconduct abroad has not gravely damaged China's international image, because there are mainly sporadic cases.

There is no evidence that China's ODI leads to a reduction in domestic employment or the hollowing-out of domestic industries. This is a result of the current features of China's overseas investment. Chinese enterprises focus mainly on seeking markets or strategic assets, and it is uncommon to shift marginal industries abroad with the purpose of reducing costs and raising efficiency. This is because cost advantages still exist in China: facing rising domestic production costs, many Chinese companies relocate their manufacturing facilities to China's vast inland areas rather than to the uncertainty of foreign countries. In addition, ODI currently is not accompanied by large-scale capital flight, and has not negatively affected the balance of payments and exchange rate stability. This is assisted by the fact that China's capital account has not been fully liberalised.

However, as China's domestic production costs increase and economic restructuring continues, it will be necessary to guard against the negative impacts of large-scale outward investment and to prevent any future problems. While strengthening supervision, Chinese policymakers also need to respect the main goals of enterprises and the major role of the market.

References

Cai, K. G. (1999), Outward foreign direct investment: A novel dimension of China's integration into the regional and global economy, *China Quarterly* 160: 856–80. doi.org/10.1017/S0305741000001363.

Ernst & Young (2017), *EY's Attractiveness Program Africa: Connectivity redefined*, London: Ernst & Young.

Li, B. (2008), China's foreign investment policy formulation and prospects, [in Chinese], *Foreign Trade and Economic Practices* (4): 4–6.

Ministry of Commerce (MOFCOM) (2004), Provisions on the Examination and Approval of Investment to Run Enterprises Abroad, [in Chinese]. Available from: www.mofcom.gov.cn/article/b/bf/200410/20041000288142.shtml.

Ministry of Commerce (MOFCOM) (2009), Administrative Measures for Overseas Investment, [in Chinese]. Available from: www.mofcom.gov.cn/article/b/g/200904/20090406184759.shtml.

Ministry of Commerce (MOFCOM) (2014), Administrative Measures for Overseas Investment, [in Chinese]. Available from: www.mofcom.gov.cn/article/b/c/201409/20140900723361.shtml.

Ministry of Commerce, National Bureau of Statistics and State Administration of Foreign Exchange (various issues), *Statistical Bulletin of China's Outward Foreign Direct Investment*, Beijing: China Statistics Press.

National Development and Reform Commission (NDRC) (2011), Notice on Decentralization and Approval of Overseas Investment Projects, [in Chinese]. Available from: www.ndrc.gov.cn/zcfb/zcfbtz/201103/t20110318_399946.html.

National Development and Reform Commission (NDRC) (2014), Measures for the Administration of Approval and Record-filing of Overseas Investment Projects, [in Chinese]. Available from: www.ndrc.gov.cn/zcfb/zcfbl/201404/t20140410_606600.html.

National Development and Reform Commission (NDRC) (2017a), *Report on China's Overseas Investment*, Beijing: Chinese People's Publishing House.

National Development and Reform Commission (NDRC) (2017b), Administrative Measures for Overseas Investments by Enterprises, [in Chinese]. Available from: www.ndrc.gov.cn/zcfb/zcfbl/201712/t20171226_871560.html.

National Development and Reform Commission (NDRC) (2017c), Code of Conduct for the Overseas Investment by Private Enterprises, [in Chinese]. Available from: www.ndrc.gov.cn/gzdt/201712/t20171218_870751.html.

State Council (1991), The Opinions on Strengthening the Management of Overseas Investment Project, [in Chinese]. Available from: www.szpb.gov.cn/xxgk/zcfggfxwj/zcfg01/200809/t20080910_38457.htm.

State Council (2004), Decision on Reforming the Investment System, [in Chinese]. Available from: www.fdi.gov.cn/CorpSvc/Temp/T3/Product.aspx?idInfo=10000491&idCorp=1800000121&iproject=23&record=66325.

United Nations Conference on Trade and Development (UNCTAD) (1995), *World Investment Report 1995: Transnational corporations and competitiveness*, New York: United Nations Publications.

United Nations Conference on Trade and Development (UNCTAD) (2009), *World Investment Report: Transnational corporations, agricultural production and development*, New York: United Nations Publications.

United Nations Conference on Trade and Development (UNCTAD) (2017), *World Investment Report: Investment and the digital economy*, New York: United Nations Publications.

Voss, H., Buckley, P. J., & Cross, A. R. (2008), Thirty years of Chinese outward foreign direct investment. Paper presented at the 19th CEA (UK) Conference: China's Three Decades of Economic Reform (1978–2008), University of Cambridge, UK, 1–2 April.

Wang, B. and Li, X. (2017), From world factory to world investor: The new way of China integrating into the world, *China Economic Journal* 10(2): 175–93. doi.org/10.1080/17538963.2017.1320047.

Wang, B., Mao, R. and Gou, Q. (2014), Overseas impacts of China's outward direct investment, *Asian Economic Policy Review* 9(2): 227–49. doi.org/10.1111/aepr.12065.

Zhang, Y. (2011), Accelerating the implementation of the 'going out' strategy, [in Chinese], *China's Economy and Trade* (8): 4–13.

Appendix

Table 30.A1 The Major ODI Regulations in China: 1978–2017

Issued	Enunciator	Regulation
1985 July	MOFCOM	Provisional Regulations Governing the Control and the Approval Procedure for Opening Non-Trade Enterprises Overseas
1988 July	MOFCOM	Regulations Governing the Approval of Setting Up of Trade-Related Enterprises Overseas
1991 March	State Council	Opinions on Strengthening the Management of Overseas Investment Project
2004 July	State Council	Decision on Reforming the Investment System
2004 Oct	MOFCOM	Provisions on the Examination and Approval of Investment to Run Enterprises Abroad
2004 Oct	NDRC	Interim Administrative Measures for Approving Investment Projects Overseas
2009 March	MOFCOM	Administrative Measures for Overseas Investment
2011 Feb	NDRC	Notice on Decentralization and Approval of Overseas Investment Projects
2014 April	NDRC	Measures for the Administration of Approval and Registration of Overseas Investment Projects
2014 September	MOFCOM	Administrative Measures for Overseas Investment
2017 December	NDRC	Code of Conduct for the Overseas Investment by Private Enterprises
2017 December	NDRC	Administrative Measures for Overseas Investments by Enterprises

Sources: Voss et al. (2008), State Council (1991, 2004), MOFCOM (2004, 2009, 2014), NDRC (2004, 2011, 2014, 2017b, 2017c).

31. A US perspective on China's external economic disputes in the past 40 years and in the coming 40 years

Wing Thye Woo[1]

There are many US perspectives on China. For the purposes of this chapter, the relevant distinction is between the United States–first perspective on China and the internationalist US perspective.[2] In this chapter, we employ the internationalist US perspective.

This clarification is important because recent discussions about US–Sino economic interaction have been increasingly conflated with issues of US–Sino competition for global influence. This conflation between economic competition and geostrategic positioning is occurring globally, resulting in the increasing weaponisation of global economic transactions—for example, China banned the export of rare earth elements to Japan in 2010,[3] the United States banned the export of high technology to the Chinese company ZTE in 2018 and Western Europe is enforcing trade sanctions on Russia.

The analysis of economic interaction is normally predicated on finding a win–win outcome based on the principle of 'willing buyer–willing seller' operationalised through profit maximisation. The analysis of geostrategic contests, on the other hand, is usually predicated on a zero-sum outcome. The increasing conflation of these two analyses is what has motivated us to title this chapter 'A US perspective on China's external economic disputes', rather than 'An economic perspective of China's external disputes'.

The distinction between the United States–first perspective and the internationalist US perspective is as follows: the former not only puts US interests above the interests of other communities, it also strives to maintain US supremacy in the management of world affairs. Blackwill and Tellis (2015: 4) offer a good example of the United States–first perspective on China:

1 The subject of this chapter deserves a book-length treatment to do it justice, but I am adhering to an 8,000-word limit to be less boring. I thank Jeremy Lim, Yu Miaojie and Gao Kailin for their help with data, and am most grateful to Ligang Song, Elizabeth Buchanan, Xiaolan Fu and Jan Borrie for their advice and patience.

2 We chose the more awkward term 'United States–first' over 'America-first' because a United States–first proponent may not be a Trump acolyte.

3 King and Armstrong (2013) have raised doubts about the existence of the 2010 ban on rare earth exports.

> Because the American effort to 'integrate' China into the liberal international order has now generated new threats to U.S. primacy in Asia—and could result in a consequential challenge to American power globally—Washington needs a new grand strategy toward China that centers on balancing the rise of Chinese power rather than continuing to assist its ascendancy … [There must be] the clear recognition that preserving U.S. primacy in the global system ought to remain the central objective of U.S. grand strategy in the twenty-first century.

The internationalist US perspective on China also puts primacy on US interests, but it recognises that long-run US interests are usually better served when the United States is working in partnership with the rest of the world to solve common problems such as climate change and financial contagion. The internationalist US perspective recognises and accepts the legitimate concerns of China regarding its national security and economic prosperity, but it will mobilise its allies to counter unreasonable Chinese actions to impose its will on others. The internationalist US perspective on China does not consider being number one in the global system a primary policy objective.[4]

China's external economic disputes

China's journey of external economic engagement has been marked by many disputes, and it is safe to predict that its future course will generate new ones. This chapter hopes to help reduce the intensity and frequency of future international economic disputes, in two ways.

The first is to draw lessons for how to better manage disputes by reviewing two protracted and bitter external economic disputes of the past 40 years: 1) the dispute over China's exchange rate policy and its chronically large trade surplus; and 2) the dispute over China's industrial policy.

The second way we hope to attenuate future disputes is to offer some suggestions on how external economic management should be conducted in the next 40 years as China actively expands its international economic connectivity programs—for example, the Regional Comprehensive Economic Partnership (RCEP) and internationalisation of the renminbi. The initiative from China's agenda for improving international economic connectivity on which we have chosen to focus is the Belt and Road Initiative (BRI).

4 Patriotism is definitely not a distinguishing characteristic of these two perspectives; only weak-minded scoundrels would introduce this term into the discussion of US–Sino economic engagement. (It was Samuel Johnson who said 'Patriotism is the last refuge of a scoundrel'. See: www.samueljohnson.com/refuge.html.)

The BRI is representative of China's readiness to take on the role of a responsible stakeholder that Robert Zoellick (2005) had challenged China to undertake. But as China takes on this new role, the existing major powers have shown themselves to be uncomfortable with China's greater influence in the international arena. For example, some pundits have claimed that the true objective of China's infrastructure loan program is to lure poor economies into taking on more loans than they can service and then pressuring these indebted countries to support China's geostrategic interests (Bloomberg News 2018; Hodge 2018; Malinao 2018). This conspiratorial theory of debt-trap diplomacy heightens competition among the big powers and leads to international disputes. China clearly has its work cut out in the next 40 years to show that such suspicions about the BRI are unjustified.

Summarising some of this chapter's key conclusions, we find with regard to the occasional highly dramatic dispute over China's exchange rate and trade imbalance that they have frequently been marked by analytical confusion over the meaning of the term 'equilibrium exchange rate'. Second, China's trade imbalance reflects the economic conditions both in China and abroad, and the efficient and fair solution of the problem usually requires policy changes not only in China, but also in other major countries—notably, the United States. Our third conclusion is that the dispute over exchange rate alignment has served as a diversion from 1) addressing the underlying structural factors causing the trade imbalance, and 2) improving the inadequacy of US job transition programs that has exacerbated US unhappiness with the trade imbalance.

In terms of industrial policy disputes, the first conclusion is that the issue of forced technology transfers is largely a dispute about a large economy using its market power to benefit itself at the expense of its trade partners. The second conclusion is that this use of market power will normally be only temporary because of the almost inevitable retaliation by other large countries, which is why we do not see the imposition of optimum tariffs by large importers. The third conclusion is that the notion of national security commonly adopted in the debate over US trade policy is overly broad and short-sighted and, unless these two aspects are corrected in US understanding of national security, the economic dynamism of the United States will be damaged and US national security weakened in the long run.

In terms of the BRI, the first conclusion is that, as the number of BRI projects grows, and as the number of partner countries increases, the number of economic disputes involving China will grow. Second, China should ensure that BRI projects in each country are economically beneficial to the general population of that country and not politically biased just towards the government in power at the time. Unlike in China, in most countries, governments come and go relatively frequently. The third conclusion is that China must develop a good understanding of the economic problems and sociopolitical contradictions in recipient countries to be able to pre-empt or settle economic disputes. Fourth, disputes in general will arise when China starts displaying the overbearing, arrogant attitude that often guided the actions of big powers (such as the United States and Russia) in the past. Fifth, economic disputes are a systemic feature of the present uncoordinated multi-polar world.

The dispute over China's chronic trade surpluses and exchange rate policy

Figure 31.1 uses gross domestic product (GDP) to normalise the trade imbalance to provide a better measure of its impact on the economy. China's trade account surplus has been more than 2 per cent of GDP since 1996; it averaged more than 5 per cent in the period 2005–08 and reached 8.6 per cent in 2007. The relevant point is that China's trade surpluses in the past 20 years (1997–2016) have been not only persistent, but also large enough—3.8 per cent of GDP on average—to create much discontent in many developed countries, and particularly in the United States, about the displacement of labour by imports from China.

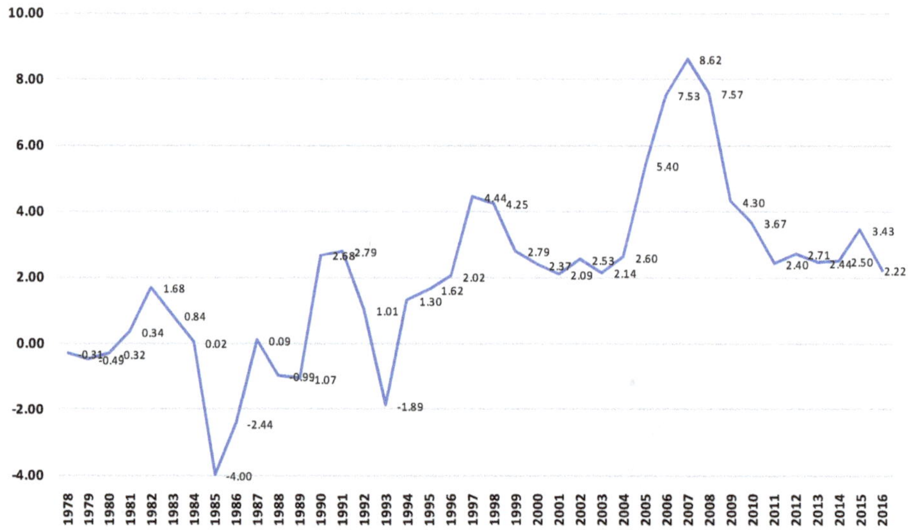

Figure 31.1 China current account balance (percentage of GDP)

Source: All China Data Center (chinadataonline.org).

Figure 31.2 shows the overall US trade account balance and the bilateral United States–China trade account balance over the period 1992–2017.[5] The overall US trade account deficit enlarged rapidly, from 1.52 per cent of GDP in 1992 to a peak of 6.04 per cent in 2006. The overall US trade account deficit settled at about 4 per cent of GDP for the period 2013–17. The fact that the United States post–Global Financial Crisis (GFC) continues to borrow a large amount annually from overseas suggests the overspending and undersaving in its economy are structural and not cyclical in nature. The outstanding practitioner of these twin traits is the Government of the United States, whose military expenditure continues to soar and whose taxes are cut to pay off the plutocrats who finance elections.

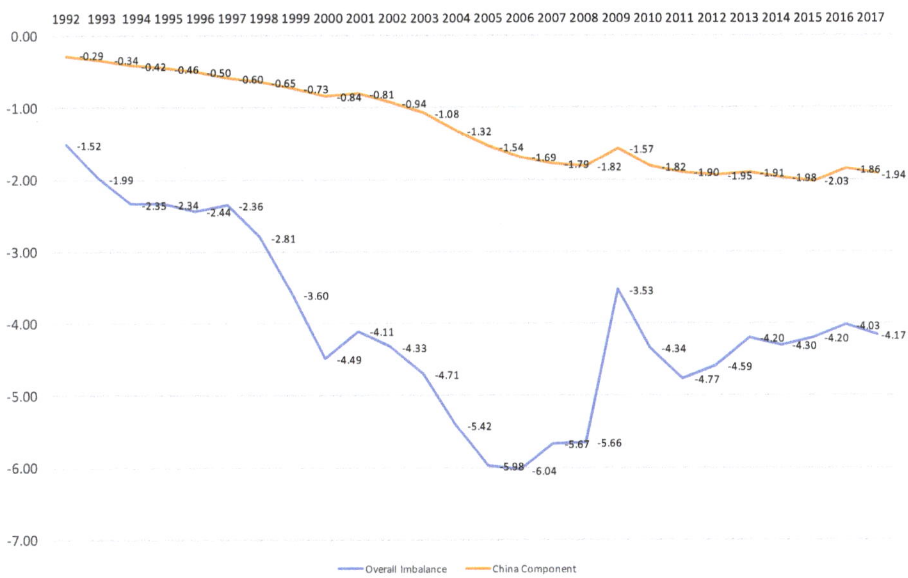

Figure 31.2 US trade balance in goods (percentage of GDP)

Source: US Census Bureau for trade data, US Government (2013, 2018) for GDP data.

Given the significant shrinkage of the overall US trade deficit after 2006, and the expansion of the bilateral US–Sino trade deficit after 2006, the latter now accounts for a much larger part of the former. The bilateral trade deficit grew from about 17 per cent of the overall US trade deficit in 1993–94 to 46 per cent in 2016–17. It is no wonder, then, that the policy community and general public in the United States have now been persuaded to regard Chinese imports as the major cause of the country's de-industrialisation.

5 This is the trade imbalance in the trade of goods.

Much of the unhappiness among members of the US Congress and the public originates from the perception that China has cheated the international community in its management of external economic engagement. Specifically, many analysts have accused China of a mercantilist policy of keeping its currency, the renminbi, undervalued vis-à-vis the US dollar—that is, keeping the renminbi–US dollar exchange rate cheaper than the value of the equilibrium exchange rate.

What is the correct level for the exchange rate?

The economics profession defines the equilibrium market price of an item as the price that equates the supply with the demand for that item—that is, the equilibrium exchange rate is the market-clearing exchange rate in the absence of central bank intervention. So, even though the renminbi has appreciated substantially against the US dollar since China's system of multiple exchange rates was ended in 1994, the fact that the foreign exchange reserves of the People's Bank of China (PBC) have increased greatly over this period is *prima facie* evidence that the PBC has been preventing the renminbi from strengthening to its equilibrium (market-clearing) value.

While it is intellectually fulfilling to show conclusively that the renminbi is truly undervalued, the important information needed for policymaking is the degree of undervaluation. A renminbi undervaluation of 20 per cent will merit a policy response from the US Government, but an undervaluation of less than 8 per cent might not be worth reacting to.

There are two commonly used methods to compute the equilibrium exchange rate.

The first assumes values for the price elasticity of exports and imports, and then works back from the actual value of the exchange rate to the exchange rate that is consistent with a current account (CA) balance, which is equal in size but opposite in sign to a given capital account (KA) balance (for example, Goldstein 2006). The capriciousness of the size and the sign of this exogenously-set KA balance is obvious. Should the KA balance not be set according to the national objectives, economic conditions and the settings of the other policy instruments? We call the Goldstein-imputed exchange rate the 'equilibrium exchange rate under exogenous KA'.

The second popular way to calculate the equilibrium exchange rate is the purchasing power parity (PPP) approach, which posits 'that in the long run exchange rates should move towards the rate that would equalise the prices of an identical basket of goods and services … in any two countries' (The Economist 2018).

This view inspired *The Economist* magazine to construct a PPP exchange rate based on the prices of McDonald's Big Mac hamburgers sold in different countries. In January 2018, with the actual exchange rate at RMB6.43 per US$1, it cost RMB20.4 to buy a Big Mac in China and US$5.28 in the United States. So, is it meaningful to say that the Chinese exchange rate was undervalued by almost 40 per cent in January 2018?

The answer is no, because the prices of the hamburgers included nontradable inputs and the prices of nontradables were lower in China than in the United States. In general, the prices of nontradables are lower in developing countries than in developed countries because labour costs are lower in the former. With economic development, the prices of nontradables in the developing country will rise to bring its price ratio of nontradables to tradables in line with that in the developed country, and the equilibrium exchange rate will then equal the PPP exchange rate.

The fact that the PBC has been accumulating foreign reserves in almost every period means the renminbi is undervalued according to the 'market-clearing' definition. However, what would happen if China were to go further in its marketisation of foreign exchange transactions by opening its KA—that is, removing its capital controls? Diversification of asset portfolios by private Chinese agents would surely result in a great outflow of funds, possibly causing the renminbi to depreciate from its present value of RMB6.4 per US$1 to, say, RMB6.8 per US$1.

The reality is that China will inevitably open its KA, especially since it wishes to internationalise the renminbi to promote its use by non-Chinese residents. One could therefore reasonably argue that the correct equilibrium exchange rate to use is the 'equilibrium exchange rate under open KA'. The analytical importance for the debate on China's exchange rate is that the equilibrium exchange rate under open KA is weaker than the equilibrium exchange rate under exogenous K (i.e. the Goldstein-style imputed exchange rate) and the PPP exchange rate.

The correct way to think about exchange rate management is to analyse the issue within the context of overall macroeconomic management and not just its impact on the balance of payments. The general point is that because the balance of payments is only one of the main outcomes of concern and because the exchange rate is only one of the ways to affect the balance of payments, it is seldom optimal to concentrate exclusively on one policy target and then employ only one policy tool to achieve that single target.

Understanding the evolution of China's current account balance

There are quite a number of China-centric explanations[6] for China's chronic trade surplus, and we will discuss the two that seem the most credible:

1. the dysfunctional financial market theory, which attributes the imbalance to the inability of China's largely unreformed financial system to intermediate all savings into investment
2. the aggressive industrial policy theory, which attributes the trade imbalance to China's promotion of exports and suppression of imports.

The dysfunctional financial market theory focuses on the aggregate-level accounting identity that the overall CA balance is determined by the fiscal position of the government and the savings and investment decisions of state-controlled enterprises (SCEs).[7] For the past decade, the Chinese fiscal position has been a small deficit, so it is not the cause of the swelling CA surpluses in the 2000s. The CA surplus exists because the sum of savings in SCEs and the private sector exceeds the sum of their investment expenditure, and it has expanded steadily because the nongovernment savings rate has been rising faster than the growth of nongovernment investment.

Why has China's financial system failed to translate savings into investment? This was not always the situation. Before 1994, the voracious absorption of bank loans by SCEs to invest recklessly kept the CA usually negative and the creation of nonperforming loans (NPLs) high. When the government implemented stricter controls on state-owned banks (SOBs) from 1994 onwards (for example, removing top bank officials if their bank loaned more than its credit quota or allowed the NPL ratio to increase too rapidly), the banks slowed the growth of loans to SCEs. This created an excess of savings because the SOB-dominated financial sector did not then rechannel the released savings (which were also increasing) to finance investment in the private sector.

This failure in financial intermediation by the SOBs is quite understandable. First, the legal status of private enterprises was, until recently, lower than that of state enterprises; and second, there was no reliable way to assess the balance sheets of

6 'China-centric' because they ignore the obvious fact that the current account balance is also determined by foreign, and notably US, economic conditions.

7 The SCE category covers companies that are classified as state-owned enterprises (SOEs), joint ventures and joint-stock companies, which are controlled by third parties (e.g. legal persons) who are answerable to the state. To understand how the principal–agent problem in SCEs has shaped China's macroeconomic performance, see Woo (2006; 2017).

private enterprises, which were naturally eager to escape taxation. The upshot was that the residual excess savings leaked abroad in the form of the CA surplus. Inadequate financial intermediation has made developing China a capital exporting country!

This perverse phenomenon in China is not new. Until the mid-1980s, Taiwan experienced this problem when all its banks were state-owned and operated under a civil service regulation that required each loan officer to repay any bad loan that they approved. The result was a massive failure in financial intermediation that caused Taiwan's CA surplus to be 21 per cent of GDP in 1986. The reason China has not been producing the gargantuan CA surpluses seen in Taiwan in the mid-1980s is the still large amount of SCE investments.

The important point is that savings behaviour is not independent of the sophistication of the financial system (Liu and Woo 1994). An advanced financial system will have a variety of financial institutions to enable pooling of risks by providing medical, pension and unemployment insurance and to transform savings into education, housing and other types of investment loans to the private sector. *Ceteris paribus*, the more sophisticated a financial system, the lower will be the savings rate.

The second credible theory for China's chronic trade surplus is the aggressive industrial policy, which views China's anomalous trade imbalance as the unintentional outcome of, first, the overriding economic and political priority in China to create jobs for its underemployed (surplus) labour force; and second, widespread belief in the efficacy of infant industry protection—ambiguously labelled the 'promotion of indigenous innovation'—in accelerating China's movement up the value-added ladder. The resulting mix of export promotion and import suppression measures accelerated the simultaneous growth of export firms (which increased exports) and import competing firms (which decreased imports), and hence kept the trade balance in surplus.[8]

There is now adequate evidence, however, that a large component of China's industrial policy has actually reduced China's welfare in addition to enlarging its trade surplus, especially in the period 2008–17. Woo (2017) points out that the Chinese Government's practice of bailing out lossmaking SCEs caused the SCEs to overinvest, resulting in huge excess capacity in heavy industries and crowding out of the private sector. The former outcome led many SCEs to dump their products in foreign markets, which worsened China's trade imbalance. The return on equity (ROE) for SCEs dropped from 15.6 per cent in 2007 to 7 per cent in 2017.[9]

8 The explanation that the undervalued renminbi is responsible for China's trade imbalance is in fact an instance of the aggressive industry policy theory. The subsidy–tariff combination is equivalent to the undervaluation of a currency (see Woo 2004).

9 ROE data are from Cho and Kawase (2018). Also see Tan et al. (2016) for a discussion of China's zombie firms.

Clearly, lowering the tension in trade disputes with the United States would require that:

- China accelerates the development of its financial sector if the dysfunctional financial market theory is correct
- China reduces export incentives and import barriers—especially from rent-seeking industries with low rates of ROE if the aggressive industrial policy theory is correct.

Regardless of which theory is right, both actions should be undertaken because both enhance China's economic welfare, with one also lowering the probability of a trade war with the United States.

As to how the United States should react to China's subsidy-cum-tariff industrial policy, we begin by making two points. The first is that World Trade Organization (WTO) rules allow developing countries to engage in some protectionist measures to nurture their industrialisation. The second point is that China's industrial policies have only accelerated an economic development process that has been unfolding since 1978. The final outcome of low value-added industries in the United States being displaced by Chinese imports is inevitable because the United States is a capital-rich country and China is a labour-rich country.

The US policy package to deal with the closure of these low value-added firms due to Chinese exports should contain three elements in common with its policies to deal with the closure of low-tech firms due to technological change:

1. a US unemployment insurance scheme that incentivises acceptance of low-wage jobs—for example, a negative income tax system
2. widely accessible US job retraining programs that are effective
3. science, technology, engineering and mathematics (STEM) programs in US high schools and universities that are high quality and attractive to the average student.

It is a sad failure of US socioeconomic management that only highly flawed versions of these three programs are in operation, and that little effort has been made to improve them.

There is one big difference between the policy package to address job losses from increased imports and that addressing job losses from new technology. The difference is that tariffs can be imposed on imports, but injunctions cannot be put on technological progress. There is, therefore, a good case for a temporary tariff when the government needs time to start (or expand) an unemployment insurance scheme and a job retraining program for displaced workers.

So far, we have identified an array of structural factors and macroeconomic policies behind the US and Chinese trade imbalances—for example, dysfunctional financial markets in China and large government budget deficits in the United States. Instead of insisting on renminbi appreciation as the primary method for reducing US unhappiness with trade deficits, it would be more efficient to:

- directly address the specific reasons behind the trade imbalance in each country
- strengthen the above three job transition programs to deal with the loss of low-skilled jobs in the United States.

The competition for high-technology industries

One proven, powerful way to increase economic prosperity is to increase productivity; and the proven way to increase productivity is innovation—technological, institutional and product innovation. It has therefore been standard practice for a growth-oriented government to strengthen the country's indigenous capacity to innovate and to accelerate the acquisition of innovations from abroad. These two activities are usually not independent of each other. The knowledge of how someone abroad has solved a problem could enable a local scientist to come up with an improvement to the original innovation. The more developed a country, the more likely it is that these two activities will interact synergistically.

The Chinese Government has been working diligently to transition China's economy to innovation-based growth, and it has achieved substantial progress on this front (see Fu 2015; Fu et al. 2016). China's latest plan for industrial upgrading is the 'Made in China 2025' (MC-25) initiative unveiled in 2015. MC-25 aims to establish China as a 'manufacturing powerhouse' with global dominance in new high-tech areas such as artificial intelligence, robotics, advanced microchips, new energy vehicles, aviation and space travel, autonomous driving systems, solar cells, machine tools, biopharmaceuticals, medical devices, telecommunication devices and electronic sensors. The first step in China's planned journey to global leadership in high technology is the achievement by 2025 of self-sufficiency in the materials and parts used in such high-tech products. Self-sufficiency is defined as local content making up 70 per cent of the product.

The ambitious range of high-tech products in MC-25 and its intended clustering of most parts of the production chain within China have sent tremors through the high-tech business community and governments in the rest of the world. Because there was a perception that China had previously used industrial policy instruments that were not WTO sanctioned to reach its present technological level, many US observers saw MC-25 as a Chinese Government–led drive to break 'international rules to build cutting-edge industries of the future' (Bradsher and Rappeport 2018).

Peter Navarro, a policy advisor to US President Donald Trump, recently summed up his view of what China has been doing as follows:

> In textbook economics, trade is a win–win … [but] America's trade with China is as far from that model as the Earth is from Mars … Why is the textbook model failing? The answer is … [China's] state-directed investments, nonmarket economy, and disregard for the rule of law.
>
> The problem's taproot is Chinese intellectual-property theft and the forced transfer of foreign technology as a condition of accessing China's market … [which allowed] Chinese companies to move rapidly up the innovation curve at much lower cost than their foreign competitors, which must recoup the cost of research and development through higher prices. (Navarro 2018)

The view that is rapidly gaining influence is that the real dispute in US–Sino economic interaction is not the size of China's trade imbalance, but China's intellectual piracy. As David Joy, Chief Market Strategist for Ameriprise Financial, has said, forced technology transfer is 'actually the biggest issue, more even than currency valuation. Being forced to give up technology for access to [the] market is essentially blackmail' (Joy, quoted by Isidore 2012).

And Chuck Schumer, the minority leader in the US House of Representatives, has criticised the perennial focus of US administrations on the bilateral US–Sino trade deficit as asinine:

> China's trade negotiators must be laughing themselves all the way back to Beijing … They're playing us for fools—temporary purchase of some goods, while China continues to steal our family jewels, the things that have made America great: the intellectual property, the know-how in the highest end industries. It makes no sense. (Bennett and Bender 2018)

US dissatisfaction with Chinese trade has now expanded from unhappiness over the loss of US jobs due to exchange rate manipulation by China to include discontent over the loss of future high-paying jobs in high-tech industries because of forced technology transfer to China.

We organise our evaluation of the recent round of charges of unfair trade practices against China by discussing the four main instruments of China's industrial policy identified by its critics:[10]

1. import restrictions (for example, tariffs, quotas)
2. production subsidies (for example, export subsidies, low-interest loans, cheap land, preferential tax rates)

10 The use of an undervalued exchange rate as an industrial policy tool has already been discussed adequately in the previous sections of this chapter.

3. forced transfer of technology (for example, industrial espionage, demanding the surrender of production technology in exchange for market access, imposing local content requirements)
4. 'cradle-snatching' of new technology (for example, purchasing technology licences, funding start-ups in Silicon Valley, setting up research and development centres in technologically advanced countries).

Import restrictions and production subsidies

Because learning-by-doing is an irrefutable phenomenon, it is often used to justify the use of import restrictions to induce the establishment of a targeted new industry. Such examples abound in China: China's ban on Google created Baidu, its ban on Twitter created Weibo, its ban on WhatsApp created WeChat, its ban on PayPal created Taobao and its ban on eBay created Alibaba. While these bans are bad for those US companies, they could have increased consumer surplus worldwide because it is now commonly acknowledged that the services provided by WeChat and Alibaba are at least as good as those of WhatsApp and Amazon.

The establishment of the targeted new industry can also be induced by production subsidies. In some cases, the learning experience occurs effectively only when the production level is above a certain critical minimum. When this minimum is larger than the size of the domestic market, production subsidies could be employed to expand production beyond the minimum by exporting the surplus output.

As noted earlier, WTO rules allow developing economies to use tariffs and subsidies to nurture some types of new industries, especially technologically advanced industries. It is usually only in cases where subsidies are used to expand production beyond domestic demand, resulting in significant exports, that the impacted country has a convincing complaint about the exporting country's violation of WTO protocol.

However, because many observers regard China as unusually successful in raising its infant industries into globally competitive industries, President Trump has demanded reciprocity in US–Sino trade—that is, a Chinese firm can receive tariff protection (or a production subsidy) only if its US competitor is similarly protected by the US Government. China has emphasised its developing country status (its per capita income being less than one-third of US per capita income) and rejected President Trump's demand for reciprocity in trade.

After 40 years of rapid economic development, China's continued use of WTO-sanctioned incentives to promote infant industries is no longer viewed sympathetically in the advanced countries. Former director-general of the WTO Pascal Lamy has pointed out that China is now not only the second largest economy in the world, but also the biggest producer of a wide range of products (such as cement and desktop computers) and concluded that it is dishonest for China to pretend that it is similar to India, Senegal or Botswana. He believes China still has to do more to 'ensure a level playing field between Chinese producers and foreign producers, whether they produce inside China or outside of China' (cited in Bradsher and Rappeport 2018).

Our discussion of China's use of import restrictions and production subsidies must not create the impression that they have been very beneficial for China's economic growth. This is because the present pervasive excess industrial capacity and the incongruous twin phenomena of inland ghost cities and coastal real estate bubbles are also products of China's production subsidy system. China's inability to enforce hard budget constraints on SCEs is now threatening the financial sector with an explosion of NPLs, and undermining overall total factor productivity growth through the crowding out of the private sector. It is therefore wrong to offer a glowing assessment of China's system of import restrictions and production subsidies as being good for China despite its successful nurturing of manufacturing powerhouses such as Hai Er and cutting-edge technology firms such as Huawei.

Forced transfer of technology

A foreign firm that wishes to sell its products in China is sometimes told that its market access is conditional on setting up production facilities in China in the form of a joint venture with a major government-linked company (which could become a future competitor in markets outside China). If it were Singapore instead of China that presented this choice to the foreign firm, the foreign firm could well decide to forgo the small Singapore market. But because the Chinese market is very large and because other competing foreign firms are also seeking access to China's market with similar technology, a foreign firm will be more willing to trade its production technology for monopoly access to China's market.

The outcome of the above practice by China is the equivalent of getting a lower price for the foreign product in the long term, which is very similar to the bulk discount that big buyers are able to extract from their suppliers, and very similar to the 'optimum tariff' that a large importer is wont to impose on its trade partner. In essence, the buyer in both cases is using their market power to extract a lower price for the product.

As the principle of 'willing buyer–willing seller' holds in the two examples above, it may seem a strange use of language to call this voluntary transaction a 'forced transfer of technology'. This language is justified only if the real picture of the use of such market power is akin to a schoolyard setting in which a big boy is demanding a bite of a small boy's sandwich. The universal schoolyard parlance to describe the big boy is 'a bully'.

Is the exercise of market power always an act of bullying? Frankly, we are not sure. But for those who are sure that it is, Martin Feldstein (2018) is correct in describing the willing buyer–willing seller defence of this Chinese method of acquiring technology as 'disingenuous'.

US firms have long complained quietly but bitterly to US Government officials about China's use of its market power to pay an effectively lower price for goods. As mandated technology transfer contravenes WTO rules on market access, the US Government could have helped these US firms out earlier by either filing a formal complaint to the WTO or confronting China with an ultimatum to stop the use of its market power or face retaliatory action such as a US ban on exports of high-tech inputs to China.

The readiness of the injured party to retaliate is most likely the reason we do not see newspaper reports on the use of optimum tariffs by large countries. The expectation of retaliation is what keeps acts of economic aggression such as optimum tariffs in check.

It is therefore a puzzle that it is only now that the US Government is willing to take action against China's economically aggressive act of forced technology transfers. The answer to this puzzle is complicated because it involves several factors coming together to create the critical mass of political pressure to spur the government into action.

The past reluctance to act could have been influenced by factors such as:

- the absence of a coordination mechanism among competing foreign firms to collectively reject China's demands and collectively request their governments to file WTO complaints
- the perception by the US Government that the technology involved is not frontier technology that is critical for overall US competitiveness or national security
- bureaucratic inertia and incompetence
- the importance of China as an ally in international affairs
- possible liberal guilt about China's poverty and previous Western transgressions against China.

The recent turnaround in US policy on mandated technology transfers is likely due to a combination of developments:

- the technology that China is now demanding is truly frontier technology that is necessary for the development of the next generation of high value-added products
- the recognition that China is turning out to be more of a strategic competitor than a potential strategic partner
- the sense that China should not be treated like a developing economy because it has, after all, become the biggest aid donor to Africa and many parts of Asia.

Given the inevitability of retaliatory action by the advanced economies, led by the United States, and the fact the exercise of market power is instinctively regarded as bullying behaviour, China should stop using its market power to exact technology transfers to avoid a trade war with the United States and its allies. This new behaviour is the same as the non-imposition of optimum tariffs by large countries. A new phase in China's use of industrial policy tools has arrived.

Cradle-snatching of new technology

The Committee on Foreign Investment in the United States (CFIUS) is an interagency body that reviews transactions that would give control of a US firm or technology to a foreign entity and rejects those that would hurt US national security. The truth is that CFIUS faces extreme difficulties in doing its job well, and this point is brought home most glaringly when one considers the following two cases.

> **Case 1:** CFIUS will approve transactions for which the product/technology has no military applications and reject transactions for which the product/technology has military applications. However, most products and technologies can be weaponised. A terrorist can drive a car into the crowd leaving a rock concert. A KGB agent could place advertisements for vodka on a website she bought or she could post fake news to help get Donald Trump elected for a second term.
>
> **Case 2:** The level of a country's national security depends on the quality of its weapons. The richer the country, the higher is the quality of weapons that it can afford. Since economic power is the basis of national security, should CFIUS ever approve the sale of any productivity-enhancing technology to Russian firms?

In short, if CFIUS is to take its job description literally, 'CFIUS really should be managing all global trade'.[11]

The MC-25 program states explicitly that it will seek to buy the next generation of high-technology products—for example, by buying promising start-ups. There is, therefore, great fear in the United States and other advanced countries that the next generation of high technology could be appropriated by Chinese firms, possibly even through unfair means. Laskai (2018) reported:

> Circumstantial evidence confirms this suspicion … Take the example of Fujian Grand Chips, a purportedly private Chinese company that attempted to acquire German machine maker Aixtron in 2016. Shortly before it staged a public takeover of Aixtron, another Fujian-based company San'an Optoelectronics canceled a critical order from Aixtron on dubious grounds, sending its stock tumbling and presenting Fujian Grand Chips with an opportunity to swoop in. Both Fujian Grand Chips and San'an Optoelectronics shared a common investor: an important national

11 Observation by Paul Rosenzweig, former CFIUS staff member, cited in Bennett and Bender (2018).

> semiconductor fund controlled by Beijing. The acquisition was stymied by an 11th-hour intervention by government officials but demonstrated how Beijing can drive investing abroad, often in a highly coordinated manner.

Given the possible conspiratorial nature of the actions of the two Chinese firms in the preceding example, one could be misled to conclude that there is paranoia in Washington, DC, today when one reads:

> Senate Majority Whip, John Comity (R-Texas) regularly warns his colleagues that China is using private-sector investments to pilfer American technology. China has 'weaponized' its investments in America 'in order to vacuum up U.S. industrial capabilities from American companies … [The goal is] to turn our own technology and know-how against us in an effort to erase our national security advantage'. (Bennett and Bender 2018)

Since Comity's use of the word 'pilfer' means to 'steal', it is befuddling when one reads that Peter Navarro (2018) sees the opposite outcome from China's purchases:

> [China has been] targeting American companies based on strategic and military goals rather than pure economic considerations … [and hence has been] often willing to pay distortive prices, far above what the free market would dictate.

This clash in perceptions of whether the Chinese are paying enough for American technology is not because there is no consistency in paranoia, but because Comity and Navarro's definition of national security is too broad—and too short-sighted.

Their definition is too broad because it automatically equates an increase in Chinese economic competitiveness with a decrease in US national security. Since Comity and Navarro do not want the United States to do anything to strengthen its economic competitors, they would restrain the technology-rich United States from selling technology-intensive goods to foreigners when economic theory shows that this has mutually beneficial outcomes.

The Comity and Navarro definition of national security is also short-sighted because US economic dynamism is reinforced when it faces foreign competition. The immediate short-term outcome in economic competition is a zero-sum game, but the long-run outcome is a win–win situation. This is the virtue of a modern private market system that works in concert with the provision of public goods by the government and with vigorous research in the basic sciences conducted by universities (which are competing against each for glory and funding).

The Comity and Navarro conception of national security is also based on the false notion that Chinese investors (and perhaps Chinese bureaucrats) are much smarter than the Japanese investors who flooded into the United States in the late 1980s and early 1990s, buying assets such as the Rockefeller Center in 1989—activity that frequently ended in tears. Furthermore, their perception of the threat from Chinese investment does not take into account the fact that most start-ups fail and that

Chinese investors cannot afford to buy all the start-ups that bubble up in Silicon Valley, Silicon Forest, Silicon Alley and along Route 128—not to mention other technological centres outside the United States.

Probable future external economic disputes with China

A new international economic normal is asserting itself with the emergence of China and India as economic powerhouses alongside North America, Europe, Japan and Russia. This new international normal will be consolidated further as other large developing countries, such as Brazil, Indonesia and Nigeria, begin growing faster. The toppling of US hegemony by the emergence of a multipolar world has greatly heighted US concern about its national security.

President Trump's present trade wars on multiple fronts reflect both this heightened concern about national security and the hesitation of the United States in continuing to promote economic globalisation. Our prediction is that the settlement of the present US–Sino trade dispute will inevitably be followed by new disputes breaking out over other trade issues until the leaders of the different spheres of influence can agree to deepen multilateral free trade. Economic disputes are a systemic feature of an uncoordinated multipolar political order.

The new regional economic institutions that China is helping to establish—such as the Asian Infrastructure Investment Bank (AIIB) and the RCEP—and the global economic connectivity it is trying to enhance through programs such as the BRI and the Shanghai Cooperation Council could strengthen economic globalisation and enrich the countries in its neighbourhood. However, as the number of BRI projects grows and the number of partner countries increases, the number of economic disputes in which China will be involved will climb.

There are many reasons for this outcome besides the fact that the increased interaction creates more occasions for disagreement. The government in a partner country might find it politically expedient to divert public attention away from its own internal policy failures using the alleged outrageous acts of a foreign bully. Or China might want to unite competing political factions within its borders by highlighting how it is being taken advantage of by some partner countries.

As China strengthens its leadership status in Asian affairs, it must develop adequate understanding of the economic problems and sociopolitical contradictions in other Asian countries so as to settle disputes with them. When China acquires this understanding of its neighbours, it will be able to appreciate the political earthquakes developing beneath the seemingly quiescent surface in some of these countries, and be prepared to prevent economic disputes occurring.

For example, close identification with the foreign government of the day, when that government is highly disliked by its own people, paves the way to economic disputes when there is a change of government in that country. This necessitates that China:

1. keeps the various relationships it has with each country on separate tracks: government-to-government relations, business-to-business relations and people-to-people relations
2. ensures that BRI projects benefit the general population in the host country and are not politically biased towards the government of the day.

The present state of China–Malaysia relations is an illustration of some of the points made above. China seemed unaware that the relationship between the Malaysian Government and its people was very different from that in China; and that although the Malaysian Barisan Nasional[12] coalition had been in power for almost as long as the Communist Party of China, it actually had feet of clay.

The origin of today's China–Malaysia economic dispute lies in China's purchase of several overpriced power stations from the Malaysian sovereign wealth fund, 1-MDB, which had been bankrupted by embezzlement.[13] This asset sale allowed 1-MDB to meet the debt servicing that was coming due. About the same time, the Malaysian Government of prime minister Najib Razak awarded major contracts for two rail projects to Chinese construction companies: the high-speed rail (HSR) connecting Kuala Lumpur and Singapore and the railway linking the east and west coasts of peninsular Malaysia, the East Coast Railway Link. Both projects are part of the BRI.

When Najib Razak was voted out of office on 9 May 2018 (much to the surprise of the Chinese Embassy in Kuala Lumpur), the new government led by Mahathir Mohamad discovered it had inherited a much larger debt than that declared on the public record. One of the megaprojects the new government cancelled to contain the debt level was the Kuala Lumpur–Singapore HSR project.

The Chinese newspaper *Global Times* then published an article stressing the sanctity of signed contracts, reminding Malaysia of the huge financial penalty of cancelling the HSR project and warning that China had lots of profitable investment options elsewhere besides Malaysia (Hu 2018). While this was not an official article of the Chinese Government, most Malaysian analysts interpreted it as the opening shot of an economic dispute. This dispute has not escalated, but only because the new Malaysian Government has wisely decided not to respond.

12 The Barisan Nasional (National Front) is a large coalition centred on the three race-based political parties that formed the Alliance Party in 1957.

13 US Department of Justice (2017) is a court filing on 1MDB.

Another major determinant of the frequency and intensity of future economic conflict between China and other countries is the attitude that is likely to guide China's actions. Disputes of all kinds will become more frequent when China starts making the same mistakes made by other world powers in the past. Economic exploitation, interference in internal affairs and arrogance are the seeds of economic and political disputes between countries.

Conclusions

The increasing conflation of economic analysis and national security considerations in the discussion of US–Sino economic engagement highlights the importance of the work of CFIUS. It needs to be immediately given a new operational mandate and the resources to conduct systematic examination of the relevant transactions occurring through multiple avenues—for example, bankruptcy courts and venture capital firms. The new mandate to CFIUS must not be broad in scope. There should be a defined list of technologies it will cover and this list should be updated every 18 months.

Finally, we want to register our opposition to the many recommendations to ban collaborative research with Chinese scientists (see Swanson and Bradsher 2018). This type of recommendation is akin to 'driving a bulldozer towards a rose garden' (Bennett and Bender 2018).

References

Bennett, C. and Bender, B. (2018), How China acquires 'the crown jewels' of US technology, *South China Morning Post*, 22 May. Available from: www.scmp.com/print/news/china/diplomacy-defence/article/2147288/how-china-acquires-crown-jewels-us-technology.

Blackwill, R. D. and Tellis, A. (2015), *Revising US Grand Strategy Toward China*, New York: Council for Foreign Relations.

Bloomberg News (2018), Chinese port project could land Myanmar in debt trap, *The Straits Times*, 13 May. Available from: www.straitstimes.com/asia/se-asia/chinese-port-project-could-land-myanmar-in-debt-trap.

Bradsher, K. and Rappeport, A. (2018), The trade issue that most divides US and China isn't tariffs, *The New York Times*, 26 March. Available from: www.nytimes.com/2018/03/26/business/china-us-trade.html.

Cho, Y. and Kawase, K. (2018), How China's state-backed companies fell behind, *Nikkei Asian Review*, 23 May. Available from: asia.nikkei.com/Spotlight/Cover-Story/How-China-s-state-backed-companies-fell-behind.

The Economist (2018), The Big Mac index: Global exchange rates, to go, *The Economist*, 17 January. Available from: www.economist.com/content/big-mac-index.

Feldstein, M. (2018), The next step for Chinese economic policy, *Project Syndicate*, 23 April. Available from: www.project-syndicate.org/commentary/china-wto-mandatory-technology-transfer-by-martin-feldstein-2018-04.

Fu, X. (2015), *China's Path to Innovation*, Cambridge: Cambridge University Press. doi.org/10.1017/CBO9781107110953.

Fu, X., Woo, W. T. and Hou, J. (2016), Technological innovation policy in China: The lessons, and the necessary changes ahead, *Economic Change and Restructuring* 49(2–3): 139–57.

Goldstein, M. (2006), Renminbi controversies, *Cato Journal* 26(2) (Spring/Summer).

Hodge, A. (2018), China's debt-trap diplomacy snares our Asian neighbours, *The Weekend Australian*, 13 January. Available from: www.theaustralian.com.au/news/world/chinas-debttrap-diplomacy-snares-our-asian-neighbours/news-story/7c6b04ac4e473f96d9ff3b7ec5abe102.

Hu, W. (2018), Ditching Chinese-built high-speed rail project will carry high costs for Malaysia, *Global Times*, 31 May. Available from: www.globaltimes.cn/content/1105043.shtml.

Isidore, C. (2012), US vs China: The trade battles, *CNN Money*, 13 March. Available from: money.cnn.com/2012/03/13/news/international/china-trade/index.htm.

King, A. and Armstrong, S. (2013), Did China really ban rare earth metals exports to Japan?, *East Asia Forum*, 18 August. Available from: www.eastasiaforum.org/2013/08/18/did-china-really-ban-rare-earth-metals-exports-to-japan/.

Laskai, L. (2018), Why does everyone hate Made in China 2025? Blog post, Council on Foreign Relations, 28 March. Available from: www.cfr.org/blog/why-does-everyone-hate-made-china-2025.

Liu, L.-Y. and Woo, W. T. (1994), Saving behavior under imperfect financial markets and the current account consequences, *Economic Journal* 104(424): 512–27. doi.org/10.2307/2234628.

Malinao, A. L. (2018), China's debt-trap diplomacy: Inquirer columnist, *The Straits Times*, 25 January. Available from: www.straitstimes.com/asia/se-asia/chinas-debt-trap-diplomacy-inquirer-columnist.

Navarro, P. (2018), China's faux comparative advantage, *Wall Street Journal*, 15 April. Available from: www.wsj.com/articles/chinas-faux-comparative-advantage-1523817868.

Swanson, A. and Bradsher, K. (2018), White House considers restricting Chinese researchers over espionage fears, *The New York Times*, 30 April. Available from: www.nytimes.com/2018/04/30/us/politics/trump-china-researchers-espionage.html.

Tan, Y., Huang, Y. and Woo, W. T. (2016), Zombie firms and the crowding-out of private investment in China, *Asian Economic Papers* 15(3): 32–55. doi.org/10.1162/ASEP_a_00474.

US Census Bureau (n.d.-a), Foreign trade: Trade in goods with China. Available from: www.census.gov/foreign-trade/balance/c5700.html.

US Census Bureau (n.d.-b), Business and industry: Time series/trend charts. Available from: www.census.gov/econ/currentdata/?program=FTD.

US Department of Justice (2017), United States District Court for the Central District of California. United States of America vs Certain rights to and interests in the Viceroy Hotel Group No. CV 17-4438, 15 June. Available from: www.justice.gov/opa/press-release/file/973671/download.

US Government (2013), *Economic report of the president*, Washington, DC: US Government Publishing Office. Available from: www.gpo.gov/fdsys/pkg/ERP-2013/pdf/ERP-2013.pdf.

US Government (2018), *Economic report of the president*, Washington, DC: US Government Publishing Office. Available from: www.gpo.gov/fdsys/pkg/ERP-2018/pdf/ERP-2018.pdf.

Woo, W. T. (2004), Serious inadequacies of the Washington consensus: Misunderstanding the poor by the brightest, in J. J. Teunissen and A. Akkerman (eds), *Diversity in Development: Reconsidering the Washington Consensus*, The Hague: Forum on Debt and Development.

Woo, W. T. (2006), The structural nature of internal and external imbalances in China, *Journal of Chinese Economic and Business Studies* 4(1): 1–20. doi.org/10.1080/14765280600551208.

Woo, W. T. (2017), China's soft budget constraint on the demand side undermines its supply-side structural reforms, *China Economic Review*. doi.org/10.1016/j.chieco.2017.09.010.

Zoellick, R. B. (2005), Whither China: From membership to responsibility?, Remarks to National Committee on US–China Relations, New York City, 21 September. Available from: 2001-2009.state.gov/s/d/former/zoellick/rem/53682.htm.

Index